Sterling Silver
Flatware

Value & Identification Guide

Mark F. Moran

Published by

An F&W Publications Company

700 East State Street • Iola, WI 54990-0001
715-445-2214 • 888-457-2873
www.krause.com

Our toll-free number to place an order or obtain a free catalog is 800-258-0929.

Edited by Mary Sieber
Designed by Wendy Wendt

Library of Congress Catalog Number: 2002113158
ISBN: 0-87349-608-6

Printed in the United States of America

Contents

Introduction

The Event of Dining

It may be difficult to imagine a time when a meal was an event rather than just a time to consume food. Those of us who pull a knife, fork, or spoon out of a drawer don't stop to wonder if we have the right instrument for salad, fish, berries, cold meat, pastry, chipped beef, or sardines.

The book you are holding is an introduction and guide for collectors who treasure the time when the event of dining meant a dizzying array of sterling silver flatware. Here you will find hundreds of patterns by large silver manufacturers and independent craftsmen. Though dominated by American makers, we have also included information on English and continental designs.

We have also provided a handy icon reference to tell at a glance the function of a piece of flatware: Is it a baby fork or a grill fork? A gumbo soup spoon or a cream soup spoon? A luncheon knife or a dinner knife? These icons will be a quick reference tool.

Getting Started

Trying to find a match for a specific silver pattern is just the first step. Let's say you don't know the exact name of your pattern, but it has a rose motif. There are more than 50 silver patterns in this book that have "rose" in the title. Once you track down the matching pattern, the details begin to emerge: flared tines, crimped bowls, beveled blades, gold wash, handle length and style, bolsters, piercings, scallops, stainless or silver-plate parts, youth or infant use…it's all here.

Each pattern is identified by the name, maker, and year of introduction: Chased Romantique by Alvin Silver, 1933. Of course, some patterns have been in production for more than 100 years, but the vast majority of listings are for pieces made close to the time of introduction. This book covers patterns that were made primarily from the early 19th century to the 1960s, and unless otherwise noted, all pieces are presumed to be in mint or near-mint condition.

We have also included prices for monogrammed pieces, which can be 15 to 25 percent less than those without monograms.

The majority of listings can be thought of as a "last name first" format: We begin with the basic form and add details. For instance:

"Butter spreader, hollow handle, modern, stainless, 6 1/4 in." Translated:

The hollow-handled butter spreader has a modern-style stainless blade (as opposed to a blunt or french-style variation) and is 6 1/4 inches long overall.

In addition to these basic listings, we have selected hundreds of the harder-to-find examples and provided detailed images with longer descriptions. Finally, we have an extensive list of patterns sold in sets, sometimes numbering more than 100 pieces.

The Prices

Using the resources of nationally recognized dealers, we have gathered a comprehensive range of prices, but the most important thing to remember is the word "range." Price guides may get you into the ballpark, but they won't teach you how to play the game. The price of a specific silver piece or set of pieces depends on the dealer's investment, and that includes the time involved in acquiring the item, the research that went into it, travel, etc.

A dealer with a shop may buy an item from a customer who walks in off the street, and set his or her price accordingly. Another dealer may travel hundreds of miles to attend a show, buy a similar piece, and factor the added expense into the ticket price.

There are still regional differences to consider, despite the pervasive influence of the Internet. The work of the great silversmiths of Baltimore or Boston will still be found in greater numbers and variety in the Northeast, and the demands of regional collectors also help establish price. But someone scouting a shop in Arizona or Louisiana or Oregon may be able to find a "sleeper"—a piece from one part of the country that is undervalued in another.

Also affecting price is rarity and use: An infant feeding spoon is a lot harder to track down than a simple teaspoon. So be sure to compare details and function when trying to determine value.

The most important thing to remember is that a price guide is just one tool in the collector's quest. Attending auctions, antique shows, and estate sales, surfing the 'Net, talking to dealers and other collectors, making mistakes and learning from them—these are all part of the hunt.

Introduction

Pattern Poll

In a random survey of American silver dealers, we asked for a top-10 list of the most popular flatware patterns. Here are some of the responses we received:

"I find that Reed & Barton's Francis I is seen as about the most desirable in general and seems to fetch the highest price. Then anything Gorham is desirable in America. Overseas, this is not the case. I travel quite a lot and find that overseas, in England and the English ex-colonies, the Kings pattern and then the Queens pattern are highly sought after. It seems that like everything else, desirability is a reflection of the nationality of the subject."

Acanthus by Georg Jensen

"Definitely, Georg Jensen heads the list of silver flatware in demand and prices. I find it amazing what people are prepared to pay for it."

"[My top sellers, though] not in any particular order, Fairfax, Chantilly, Repoussé, Francis I, Grande Baroque, Prelude, Strasbourg, maybe Buttercup or Joan of Arc, and lately a few people have been looking for Lily by Whiting."

"Chantilly, Repoussé, Francis I, Prelude, Old Master, French Provincial—all in no particular order. Of course, popularity varies from region to region, and the South seems particularly fond of the dressier, more ornate patterns."

"Yes to Jensen (as a top pick), but we do not get a lot of his items in, (and) when we do, they do not last …."

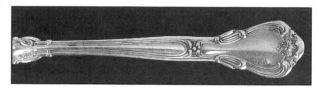

Chantilly by Gorham

"I would say the following patterns are the most actively requested by people at our shop: Chantilly, Strasbourg, Fairfax, Buttercup, and Versailles by Gorham; Lily and Louis XV by Whiting; Royal Danish and Prelude by International; Francis I by Reed & Barton; Grande Baroque, Les Cinq Fleurs and Violet by Wallace; Repoussé and Old Maryland Engraved by Kirk; Rose by Stieff; Audubon by Tiffany; King Richard, Old Master, and Old Colonial by Towle; Bridal Rose by Alvin; William & Mary by Lunt; Damask Rose by Oneida; and Baltimore Rose by Schofield."

Fakes and Reproductions

Dealers we surveyed are divided on how many fakes and reproductions are in existence. As with any collecting area, it's best to stick with a reputable source, someone who will stand behind their merchandise. Dealers get fooled too, and most are quick to remedy the situation, if only to get bad merchandise off the market. Here are some dealers' thoughts on the subject:

"It's not really a matter of 'reproductions' with sterling. Many very old patterns are still made (Chantilly by Gorham was introduced in 1895 and is still one of the top five patterns; Repoussé by Kirk has been around since the 1840s). What you have to look out for is the poor quality of new sterling, relative to the old. The finishes are different, and the hand-chasing is nonexistent on new pieces. I doubt there is anyone alive who still knows how to do that kind of work .... If you put new next to old (in many cases) there is a very obvious difference in the workmanship, and it is invariably the new that suffers by comparison. Old sterling is usually less expensive than the new, too—with some exceptions, based on complexity, beauty, scarcity, and so on."

• • •

"Cast serving pieces in Whiting's Lily and Les Six Fleurs by Reed & Barton do keep appearing on the market. My guess is they are being made in Mexico. The pieces do not have the Whiting or the Reed & Barton hallmarks. They have only 'sterling' printed on the back, and the back shank has tiny bead marks left from casting. An original piece has the hallmark of the manufacturer and the word 'sterling,' and has a clean look on the shank."

• • •

"Some ... dealers are making up pieces, and in many cases are not telling the public. They are making cheese scoops from tablespoons, horse radish scoops from dessert spoons, baby pushers from teaspoons, and the market is loaded with asparagus servers made using dinner knife handles .... Plain serving tablespoons are pierced to produce the slotted tablespoons. Ice cream forks are made from teaspoons, especially in the early patterns, and so are the ice cream spoons. The only way one can tell a difference is via knowledge, knowing the original form of the bowl in the pattern.

"Another thing that is done: the removal of monograms and not disclosing it. Depending upon the patterns, the silver can be purchased very cheap, monograms removed, and then sold at the prices of silver without monograms."

"With most flatware patterns I do not think there is much to worry about. It is certainly possible to reproduce flatware, but in most cases the cost would be much greater than (that of) the same piece found in the second-hand market. Most of the reproductions I have seen have been of popular, heavy floral turn-of-the-century patterns in rather badly cast serving pieces (although occasionally a quite good example may be seen).

"A second problem might be fabricating an interesting bowl or tines and adding that to an original handle. The biggest reproduction job I recall seeing was a large set of 12 settings of Gorham Raphael (1874); they had soup spoons, bouillon spoons, butter spreaders, and cold meat forks made to go with it, c.1950-1975. The front side was very well done but the back side was left plain as opposed to the original intricate design."

Repairs, Replacements and Wear

Some silver sellers offer repair services (untwisting tines, smoothing bowls) and can even make up replacements for damaged pieces, or remove old monograms. Others offer special polishing services that can maintain the silver's patina without stripping away years of mellow luster.

The issue of judging and grading wear to silver is a bit more subjective.

Said one dealer: "To the best of my knowledge there is no system similar to that employed by numismatists. A general rule is that if the highest point of decoration is still visible, but has slight wear, the piece is acceptable.

"For example, if the helmet's visor on a piece of Medallion flatware has a bit of loss but can still be plainly seen, it's okay. Or if the face on a piece of Gorham Versailles has slight wear to the nose but is still clearly visible, the piece is acceptable."

Sterling Matching Service in Topsfield, Massachusetts, offers these tips on cleaning old silver:

1. Use the least abrasive silver polish, preferably Twinkle Silver Polish or 3M's Tarni-Shield. Twinkle can be found in most grocery stores.

2. Do not use chemical dips they contain acid and may damage stainless steel blades.

3. Use a very small amount of polish, applying with cotton balls or cellulose sponge. Proceed over surfaces, turning the item to polish new places, not going over and over on the same place, as the tarnish you are removing can scratch.

4. *Do not* place silverware in the dishwasher. Detergents are too harsh and may damage the silver. Drying with heat may melt the cement that holds the blades in the handles, causing loose blades. Continued washing in the dishwasher removes the oxidation (the black part) that enhances the design.

5. Hand-wash flatware immediately after use to eliminate pitting of the silver by salt in the food. Knife blades become pitted and cannot be repaired, but must be replaced.

Other recommended silver cleaners include Goddard's Long Shine Silver Polish and Silver Wash, and Wright's Anti-Tarnish Silver Polish and Silver Cream.

Decorative Styles In British Silver

Rococo

The rococo style is now generally regarded as one of France's most original and delightful contributions to the arts, so it is hard to believe the antagonism it provoked in contemporary critics.

By the early 1720s the first hint of rococo could be seen in England, and it was a complete change from anything that had gone before. The smiths adopted the style with great enthusiasm as the decoration was so fantastical compared to the plain elegant style that preceded it. The change was mainly one of emphasis in decoration rather than in form. The swirling movement of water is one of the main elements of the rococo, along with masks and naturalistic floral displays. The shell was a common motif—its frilly fluted edges and crusty surface texture perfectly suited the aim of rococo ornamentation.

By the 1760s the style had lost its sculptural quality and the work was in danger of becoming quite crude.

Neoclassical

The waning interest in rococo meant that the neoclassical style became very popular in the second half of the 18th century, and classical decoration based on ancient Greece and Rome came into fashion. At this time no wealthy young Englishman's education was complete without spending at least a year on a tour of the continent.

The archeological excavations of Pompeii and Herculaneum in the 1750s made the ancient world very immediate, also revealing a wealth of domestic styles that greatly influenced all aspects of contemporary fashion. Swags, urns, wreaths, rams' heads, Greek key borders, and drop-ring handles were in frequent use in silver, although often large areas were left unadorned so that the reflective surfaces emphasized the elegance of the shapes and the grace of the proportions. Smiths were quick to realize that the classic fluted stone column made an ideal shaft for a candlestick, and despite small variations on the theme, this style remains popular today. Subtle but significant changes in the 1790s meant that the neoclassical style gave way to plainer decoration as the century reached its close.

Regency

Strictly speaking, this style lasted from 1811 to 1820 when the affairs of the country were in the hands of Prince Regent (later George IV). Not only did he become patron of many silversmiths of the time, but also his keen interest in antique styles helped to develop the designs of domestic silverware.

The term "regency" is often used to include pieces from the late 1790s to 1830s. It describes pieces that are often similar to the earlier neoclassical style yet are inclined to be pompous and heavy, often characterized by applied gadroon (rope-twist) borders, with added shells and floral motifs. Sometimes Egyptian motifs are apparent, reflecting the interest of these ancient styles and excessive details.

Victorian

There was more silverware made in the 19th century than ever before or after. The middle class had a newfound wealth and the British Empire was at its height. The Industrial Revolution was transforming the old craft trades, and innovations by plate manufacturers meant great competition for the traditional silversmiths making items by hand.

The 18th century passion for antiquarianism continued into the early Victorian era, stimulating a revival of several historic styles that all flourished simultaneously. Naturalism was added to the rococo, gothic, neoclassical, etc., styles that were popular and could be seen in abundance at the great exhibitions. Towards the end of the century the Arts & Crafts movement came about as a reaction against the stylized and mass-produced articles now typical of the period.

Naturalistic

At the beginning of the 1800s, experimental work from London influenced the world. The use of nature in neoclassical decoration now lost its symmetry and formality; natural forms were not only used as decoration but also took over the whole structure. This is a predominant feature especially between 1825-1850. At the Great Exhibition of 1851, naturalism ran riot through the English Section. Botanical interest was very high at this time, and developments in travel introduced exotic plants and flowers. This was also the time when landscape gardens were very popular for pleasure and social functions, and this enthusiasm is reflected in the ornamentation of silver.

Gothic

This style can be characterized by a boldness of form and echoes of medieval architecture, such as spires, pointed arches and cast figures. It enjoyed a limited vogue and was mostly confined to ecclesiastical silver, although it was used in moderation on domestic pieces.

Arts & Crafts

The Arts & Crafts movement came into being with the founding of the Art Workers Guild in 1884, followed by the Arts & Crafts exhibition society four years later. It was not only an aesthetic movement but also a social one, expressing the widespread dissatisfaction with the quality of mass-produced items.

An admiration for folk art and for the old guilds of medieval craftsmen was also apparent. Large silver manufacturing companies realized that a precious metal and mass production did not really work well together, so they turned to artists and designers for guidance.

The principle beliefs of the Arts & Crafts movement was that items should always be what they seemed—no jugs disguised as castle turrets, etc. These beliefs meant the decoration should enhance the piece, not conceal it, and that silver should never be made to do something out of character. The hand-hammered finish is one of the main characteristics of this style. The smiths encouraged the inequalities of surfaces, and as a result the pieces catch the eye in a way that the precision and symmetry of machine-made objects do not.

Arts & Crafts ideas were started by John Ruskin and given expression by William Morris. The movement also influenced workers such as Charles Robert Ashbee, who believed that good design and craftsmanship could not come out of mechanical and industrial organizations. This could be said about silversmithing, as the use of machinery was by no means essential. He put his ideas into practice in 1887 when he founded the School and Guild of Handicraft, and his shapes were kept as simple as possible.

Aesthetic

The aesthetic style is characterized by oriental-style engraving and applied decoration, often incorporating bamboo, birds of paradise, cranes, butterflies, and stylized fan-work. It was at its height during the 1860s through the 1880s, but became overelaborate and was left behind by major interest in the cleaner lines of the Arts & Crafts movement.

Art Nouveau

This style was first introduced to England circa 1890, and was a product of the Arts & Crafts movement started by William Morris, et al, and the pre-Raphaelites. It was a revolt against the mass-produced wares of the Victorian era and was adapted to silverware, showing free-flowing lines, often asymmetrical, with intertwining floral patterns, insects, and female faces depicting a great influence from Japanese art. The one main characteristic seen in most art nouveau pieces is a long line with a quick curve at the end. This has been said to be reflective of the social mood of the time. Eventually it was its own extravagance that led to its demise.

Art Deco

A style that became popular in the late 1920s and early 1930s, art deco was a movement against the naturalistic feel of the art nouveau designs. Art deco drew together various elements: structured floral motifs, stylized curves, geometric shapes and abstract patterns. These ideas run simultaneously with the cubist movement in fine art, and similarities of the bold graphic shapes are obvious.

Modernism

In the 1950s there came about a complete change in style. Postwar Britain had a renewed interest in form with the emphasis on sleek modern shapes. Form did not necessarily have to follow function, and form was the most important factor.

The early 1960s saw the Modernist ideal of pure line and form together with unadorned surfaces that challenge the traditional equation of high style. The admiration for handmade items did not blind the new generation of craftsmen against the potentials of mass production. Their aim was to balance mechanization and hand finish so that silver was again being put to its best use, as a metal for items of luxury and decoration.

Courtesy of Bryan Douglas Antique Silver, London

Resources

Here are some excellent resources for both the beginning and advanced collector of sterling silver flatware.

Replacements, Ltd.
1089 Knox Rd.
P.O. Box 26029, Dept. W7
Greensboro, NC 27420
(800) REPLACE (737-5223)
or (336) 697-3000
Fax: (336) 697-3100
TDD (800) 270-3708 (Hearing Impaired)
http://www.replacements.com
E-mail: inquire@replacements.com

Antique Cupboard Inc.
1936 MacArthur Rd.
Waukesha, WI 53188
(800) 637-4583
http://www.antiquecupboard.com
E-mail: info@antiquecupboard.com

Bruce Cherner Antique Silver
Boston Antique Co-op II
119 Charles St.
Boston, MA 02114
(978) 635-8089
Mailing address:
P.O. Box 2975
Acton, MA 01720
http://www.cyberattic.com/~cherner/index.html
E-mail: Bacherner@aol.com

Imperial Half Bushel
831 N. Howard St.
Baltimore, MD 21201
(410) 462-1192
http://www.imperialhalfbushel.com/index.html
E-mail: ihb@imperialhalfbushel.com

Brenda Ginsberg Art & Antiques
20166 Back Nine Dr.
Boca Raton, FL 33498
(561) 883-6082
http://www.brendaginsberg.com
E-mail: antiques@brendaginsberg.com

Renee Mann
RM Services
4505 Harding Rd., #133

Nashville, TN 37205
(800) 851-2055
http://www.rmsterling.com
E-mail: info@rmsterling.com

SilverAgent
3212 West End Ave., Ste. 203
Nashville, TN 37203
(615) 467-0860
Fax: (615) 467-0857
http://www.silveragent.com
E-mail: info@silveragent.com

The Antique Guild
113 N. Fairfax St.
Alexandria, VA 22314
(800) 518-7322
(703) 836-1048
Fax: (703) 836-1253
http://www.theantiqueguild.net
E-mail: zendog@theantiqueguild.net

Louisville Antique Mall
900 Goss Ave.
Louisville, KY 40217
http://www.louisvilleantiquemall.com
E-mail: lam@tias.com

Sterling Matching Services
P.O. Box 46
Topsfield, MA 01983-1614
(978) 887-2610
Fax: (978) 561-1172
http://www.sterlingmatching.com
E-mail: dorothy@sterlingmatching.com

Bryan Douglas Antique Silver
12 & 14 London Silver Vaults
Chancery Ln.
London WC2A 1QS
England
(020) 7405-8862
Telephone & Fax: (020) 7242-7073
http://www.bryandouglas.co.uk
E-mail: sales@bryandouglas.co.uk

Silver Magazine
P.O. Box 9690
Rancho Santa Fe, CA 92067-4690
(858) 756-1054
Fax: (858) 756-9928
http://www.silvermag.com
E-mail: silver@silvermag.com

Words of Thanks

This book would not have been possible without the good wishes and assistance of many people, including:

Phil Dreis of Antique Cupboard Inc. of Waukesha, Wisconsin

Bryan Douglas of Bryan Douglas Antique Silver in London

Dorothy of Sterling Matching Services, a former high school French teacher whose silver passion "mushroomed into a burning desire to develop a sterling silver matching service" that has been going for almost 30 years. (And she still goes by her first name only.)

Renee Mann of RM Services

Brenda Ginsberg of Brenda Ginsberg Art & Antiques

Bruce Cherner of Bruce Cherner Antique Silver

Richard and Kae Townsend of the Iridescent House in Rochester, Minnesota

Silver Companies & Patterns

Alvin Silver

Apollo, 1900
Avila, 1969
Bridal Bouquet, 1932
Bridal Rose, 1903
Chapel Bells, 1939
Chased Romantique, 1933
Chateau Rose, 1940
Chippendale-Old, 1900
Della Robbia, 1922
Eternal Rose, 1963
Fleur de Lis, 1907
Florence Nightingale, 1919
Florentine, 1900
Francis I, 1910
French Scroll, 1953
Gainsborough, 1930
Hamilton, 1910
Hampton, 1910/1912
Majestic, 1900
Maryland, 1910
Melrose, 1910
Miss Alvin, 1931
Morning Glory, 1909
Orange Blossom-Old, 1905
Orange Blossom-New, 1920
Pirouette, 1961
Prince Eugene, 1950
Raleigh, 1900
Raphael, 1902
Richmond, 1929
Romantique, 1933
Rosecrest, 1955
Southern Charm, 1947
Spring Bud, 1956
Vivaldi, 1966
William Penn, 1907

Amston Silver

Athene, 1913
Champlain, 1915
Ecstasy, 1951

Birks Silver

Chantilly
George II-Plain, 1914
Louis XV, 1914
Old English-Plain

Concord Silver

Concord, 1930

Dominick & Haff

Century, 1900
Charles II, 1894
Chippendale, 1885
Contempora, 1930
King, 1880
La Salle, 1928
Labors of Cupid, 1900
Marie Antoinette, 1917
Mazarin, 1892
New King, 1898
No. 10, 1896
Old English Antique, 1880
Pointed Antique, 1895
Queen Anne-Plain, 1910
Renaissance, 1894
Rococo, 1888
Victoria, 1901
Virginia, 1912

Durgin Silver

Bead, 1893
Chatham, 1915
Chatham, Hammered, 1915
Chrysanthemum, 1893
Colfax, 1922
Cromwell, 1893
Dauphin, 1897
English Rose, 1955
Essex, 1911
Fairfax, 1910
Fairfax No. 1-Engraved, 1910
Hunt Club, 1930
Iris, 1900
Lenox, 1912
Louis XV, 1891
Madame Royale, 1897

Marechal Niel, 1896
New Standish, 1905
New Vintage, 1904
Orange Blossom, 1898
Sheaf Of Wheat, 1887
Victorian/Sheraton, 1910/1918
Watteau, 1891

Easterling Silver

American Classic, 1944
Helene, 1955
Horizon, 1944
Rose Spray, 1955
Rosemary, 1944
Southern Grandeur, 1944

Fine Arts Silver

Crown Princess, 1949
Processional, 1947
Romance Of The Stars, 1959
Romance Rose, 1960
Southern Colonial, 1945
Tranquility, 1947

Frank Smith

American Chippendale, 1905
Chippendale-Old, 1917
Countess, 1928
Federal Cotillion, 1901
Fiddle Shell/Alden, 1914
Fiddle Thread, 1902
George VI, 1912
Lion, 1905
Newport Shell, 1910
Pilgrim, 1909
Woodlily, 1945

Frank Whiting Silver

Adams, 1944
Athene/Crescendo, 1890
Botticelli, 1949
Georgian Shell, 1948
Lily/Floral, 1910
Neapolitan/Kings Court, 1895
Princess Ingrid, 1945
Rose Of Sharon, 1954
Talisman Rose, 1948
Troubadour, 1950/1932
Victoria/Florence, 1905

Georg Jensen-Denmark

Acanthus, 1917
Acorn, 1915
Beaded, 1916
Bernadotte, 1939
Blossom, 1919
Cactus, 1930
Caravelle, 1957
Continental, 1908
Cypress, 1954
Old Danish, 1947
Parallel, 1931
Pyramid, 1927
Scroll, 1927

Gorham Silver

Adam, 1907
Albemarle, 1894/1912
Alencon Lace, 1965
Andante, 1963
Aspen, 1963
Baronial-Old, 1898
Bead, 1893
Birds Nest, 1865
Blithe Spirit, 1959
Buckingham, 1910
Buttercup, 1899
Cambridge, 1899
Camellia, 1942
Celeste, 1956
Chantilly, 1895
Chapel Rose, 1963
Chelsea Manor, 1966
Chesterfield, 1908
Chrysanthemum, 1885
Cinderella, 1925
Classique, 1961
Clermont, 1915
Cluny, 1880/1883
Colfax, 1922
Colonial, 1885
Corinthian, 1872
Cottage, 1861
Covington, 1914
Cromwell, 1900
Decor, 1953
Dolly Madison, 1929
Edgeworth, 1922
English Gadroon, 1939
Epic, 1941

Esprit, 1963
Etruscan, 1913
Etruscan-Engraved, 1913
Fairfax, 1910
Firelight, 1959
Fleury, 1909
Florentine/Florenz, 1901
Fontainebleau, 1880
Gold Tip, 1952
Golden Wheat, 1952
Gorham-Plain, 1933
Gossamer, 1965
Governor's Lady, 1937
Grecian
Greenbrier, 1938
Henry II, 1900
Hispana/Sovereign, 1968
Hunt Club, 1930
Imperial Chrysanthemum, 1894
Jefferson, 1907
King Edward, 1936
King George, 1894
Kings II, 1885
Kings III, 1885
Lady Washington
La Scala, 1964
Lancaster, 1897
Lansdowne, 1917
Lily, 1870
Lily of the Valley, 1950
Louis XIV, 1870
Louis XV, 1891
Luxembourg, 1893
Lyric, 1940
Madam Jumel, 1908
Marguerite, 1901
Marie Antoinette, 1890
Medallion, 1864
Medici-Old, 1880
Melrose, 1948
Melrose, 1908
Mothers-New, 1926
Mothers-Old, 1875
Mythologique, 1894
New Tipt, 1871
Newcastle, 1895
Nocturne, 1938
Norfolk/Villa Norfolk, 1904
Old Colony-New, 1926
Old English Tipt, 1870

Old French, 1905
Old London-Plain, 1916
Old Masters, 1885
Olive, 1865
Paris, 1900
Perspective, 1959
Piper, 1882
Plymouth, 1911
Poppy, 1902
Portsmouth, 1918
Princess Patricia, 1926
Providence, 1920
Raphael, 1875
Roanoke, 1913
Rondo, 1951
Rose Marie, 1933
Rose Tiara, 1963
Royal Oak, 1904
Sea Rose, 1958
Secret Garden, 1959
Shamrock V, 1931
Sovereign-Old, 1941
Spotswood, 1912
St. Cloud, 1885
St. Dunstan-Chased, 1917
Stardust, 1957
Strasbourg, 1897
Theme, 1954
Threaded Antique, 1855
Trilogy, 1969
Tuileries, 1906
Versailles, 1888
Violet, 1890
Virginiana, 1904/1905
White Paisley, 1966
Willow, 1954
Wreath, 1911
Zodiac

Hallmark Silver

Ballad, 1942
Ribbon Rose, 1942

International Silver

1810, 1930
Abbottsford, 1907
Angelique, 1959
Avalon, 1900
Berkeley, 1915
Blossom Time, 1950

Brandon, 1913
Breton Rose, 1954
Bridal Veil, 1950
Brocade, 1950
Cloeta, 1904
Colonial Shell, 1941
Continental, 1934
Courtship, 1936
Dawn Rose, 1969
Deerfield/Beacon Hill, 1913
Devonshire, 1914
Du Barry, 1968
Edgewood, 1909
Elegance, 1934
Elsinore, 1931
Empress, 1932
Enchanted Rose, 1954
Enchantress, 1937
Fontaine, 1924
Frontenac, 1903
Gadroon, 1933
Georgian Maid, 1923
Governor Bradford, 1913
Grande Regency, 1969
Irene, 1902
Joan of Arc, 1940
La Rochelle, 1909
Lady Betty, 1920
Lambeth Manor, 1952
Mademoiselle, 1964
Maintenon, 1933
Margaret-New, 1912
Margaret-Old, 1907
Masterpiece, 1963
May Melody, 1952
Mille Fleurs, 1904
Minuet, 1925
Moonbeam, 1948
Moonglow, 1938
Napoleon, 1910
Norse, 1937
Northern Lights, 1946
Old Charleston, 1951
Orleans, 1936
Pansy, 1909
Pantheon, 1920
Pine Spray, 1957
Pine Tree, 1927
Prelude, 1939
Primrose, 1936

Queen's Lace, 1949
Radiant Rose, 1938
Revere, 1898
Rhapsody-New, 1957
Rhapsody-Old, 1931
Richelieu, 1935
Riviera, 1936
Rosalind-New, 1921
Rose Ballet, 1962
Royal Danish, 1939
Royal Rose, 1938
Sculptured Beauty, 1957
Serenity, 1940
Shirley, 1910
Silver Iris, 1955
Silver Melody, 1955
Silver Rhythm, 1953
Sonja, 1937
Southern Treasure, 1953
Splendor, 1939
Spring Bouquet, 1940
Spring Glory, 1942
Springtime, 1935
Stardust, 1937
Stratford, 1902
Swan Lake, 1960
Theseum, 1922
Torchlight, 1954
Trianon, 1921
Trousseau, 1934
Valencia, 1965
Vision, 1961
Warwick, 1898
Wedding Bells, 1948
Wedgwood, 1924
Wesley, 1912
Westminster, 1915
Whitehall-New, 1938
Wild Rose-New, 1948
Wild Rose-Old/Rosalind, 1908
Windermere, 1939

Jenkins & Jenkins

Repoussé

Kirk Stieff Silver

Betsy Patterson-Engraved, 1932
Betsy Patterson-Plain, 1932
Calvert, 1927
Carrollton, 1961

Cheryl, 1962
Chrysanthemum, 1904
Clinton, 1925
Corsage, 1935
Cynthia-Plain, 1957
Diamond Star, 1958
Fiddle
Fiddle Thread
Florentine, 1962
Forget-Me-Not, 1910
Golden Winslow, 1850
Homewood, 1938
King, 1825
Kingsley, 1959
Lady Claire-Hand Engraved, 1925
Mayflower, 1846
Old Maryland-Engraved, 1936
Old Maryland-Plain, 1850
Personna, 1959
Primrose, 1933
Princess-Hand Chased, 1915
Puritan, 1922
Quadrille, 1950
Repoussé, 1924
Repoussé, 1828
Repoussé, 1896 - 925/100 Back
  Stamp
Rose, 1937
Rose Motif, 1954
Royal Dynasty, 1966
Severn, 1940
Signet-Plain, 1958
Silver Surf, 1956
Stieff Rose, 1892
Wadefield, 1850
Williamsburg Queen Anne, 1940
Winslow, 1850

Knowles

Angelo
Trianon

Lunt Silver

Alexandra, 1961
American Directoire, 1931
American Victorian, 1941
Belle Meade, 1967
Carillon, 1957
Charles II, 1934
Chased Classic, 1936

Chateau/Chateau Thierry, 1919
Chatelaine, 1894
Colonial Manor, 1940
Colonial Theme, 1964
Contrast, 1956, Black Nylon Handle
Coronet, 1932
Counterpoint, 1969
Delacourt, 1966
Early American-Engraved, 1926
Early American-Plain, 1926
Early Colonial, 1930
Eloquence, 1953
English Shell, 1937
Festival, 1936
Floral Lace, 1967
Granado, 1929
Jefferson
Lace Point, 1965
Madrigal, 1962
Mary II, 1923
Memory Lane, 1949
Mignonette, 1960
Modern Classic, 1934
Modern Victorian, 1941
Monticello, 1908
Mount Vernon, 1905
Nellie Custis, 1915
Pendant Of Fruit, 1939
Raindrop, 1959
Rapallo, 1968
Regency, 1935
Rondelay, 1963
Rose Elegance, 1958
Spring Serenade, 1957
Starfire, 1955
Summer Song, 1954
Sweetheart Rose, 1951
William & Mary, 1921

Manchester Silver

Amaryllis, 1951
American Beauty, 1935
Beacon, 1936
Copenhagen, 1936
Duke of Windsor, 1937
Fleetwood, 1910
Gadroonette, 1938
Leonore, 1939
Manchester, 1932

Mary Warren, 1910/1932
Park Avenue, 1931
Polly Lawton, 1935
Silver Stream, 1934
Southern Rose, 1933
Valenciennes, 1938

National Silver

Intermezzo, 1940
Margaret Rose, 1938
Narcissus, 1936
Overture, 1936
Princess Elizabeth, 1942

Northumbria Silver

Normandy Rose, Date Unknown

Old Newbury Silver

Crafters
Moulton, 1800
Oak Leaf, 1939
Old Newbury, 1800

Oneida/Heirloom Silver

Afterglow, 1956
Belle Rose, 1963
Bountiful, 1967
Damask Rose, 1946
Dover, 1968
Du Maurier, 1967
Engagement, 1952
First Frost, 1965
Flower Lane, 1957
Grandeur, 1960
Heiress, 1942
King Cedric, 1949
Lasting Spring, 1949
Mansion House, 1948 Bright Finish
Martinique, 1967
Mediterranea, 1967
Melbourne, 1952
Reigning Beauty, 1953
Rubaiyat, 1969
Satin Beauty, 1966
Sentimental, 1960
Silver Rose, 1956
Stanton Hall, 1951
Twilight, 1942
Virginian, 1942
Vivant, 1961
Will O'Wisp, 1968
Young Love, 1958

Reed & Barton Silver

Amaryllis, 1901
Autumn Leaves, 1957
Burgundy, 1949
Cameo, 1959
Cellini, 1967
Cellini-Engraved, 1967
Chambord, 1909
Classic Fashion, 1926
Classic Rose, 1954
Clovelly, 1912
Columbia, 1912
Da Vinci, 1967
Dancing Flowers, 1950
Devon, 1911
Diadem, 1967
Diamond, 1958
Dimension, 1961
Dorothy Quincy, 1912
Elegante/L'Elegante, 1940/1900
English Provincial, 1965
Florentine Lace, 1951
Fragrance, 1941
Francis I, 1907, Eagle/R/Lion Stamp
Francis I, "Patent Pending" Stamp
Francis I, "Reed & Barton" Stamp
Francis I-Sterling And Gold, 1907
French Antique, 1901
French Renaissance, 1941
Georgian Rose, 1941
Grande Renaissance, 1967
Guildhall, 1941
Hampton Court, 1964
Hawthorne, 1934
Hepplewhite-Chased, 1907
Hepplewhite-Engraved, 1907
Hepplewhite-Plain, 1907
Heritage, 1924
Intaglio, 1905
Jubilee, 1936
Kings, 1890
La Marquise, 1895
La Parisienne, 1902
La Perle, 1902
La Reine, 1893
Lark, 1960
Les Cinq Fleurs, 1900
Les Six Fleurs, 1901
Love Disarmed, 1899

Majestic, 1894
Marlborough, 1906
Petite Fleur, 1961
Pointed Antique, 1895
Pointed Antique-Hammered, 1895
Renaissance Scroll, 1969
Romaine/Monique, 1933
Rose Cascade, 1957
Savannah, 1962
Silver Sculpture, 1954
Silver Wheat, 1952
Spanish Baroque, 1965
Star, 1960
Tapestry, 1964
Tara, 1955
Trajan, 1892

Richard Dimes Co.

Debutante, 1918

Royal Crest Silver

Castle Rose, 1942
Promise, 1948
Wild Flower, 1942

Schofield Co.

Baltimore Rose-Decor, 1905
Baltimore Rose-Plain, 1905
Elizabeth Tudor Hammered, 1907
Josephine, 1899
Lorraine, 1896

State House Silver

Formality, 1942
Inaugural, 1942
Stately, 1948

Tiffany & Co.

Atlantis, 1899
Audubon, 1871
Bamboo, 1961
Beekman, 1956
Broom Corn, 1890
Castilian, 1929
Century, 1937
Chrysanthemum, 1880
Clinton, 1912
Colonial, 1895
English King, 1870
English King, 1885
Faneuil, 1910

Feather Edge, 1901
Flemish, 1911
Hamilton, 1938
Hampton, 1934
Japanese, 1871
King William/Antique, 1870
Marquise, 1902
Palm, 1871
Palmette, 1947
Persian, 1872
Provence, 1961
Queen Anne, 1870
Rat Tail, 1958
Renaissance, 1905
Richelieu, 1892
Salem, 1956
San Lorenzo, 1916
Saratoga, 1870
Shell & Thread, 1905
St. Dunstan, 1909
St. James, 1898
Tiffany, 1869
Vine/Fruits & Flowers, 1892
Wave Edge, 1884
Windham, 1923
Winthrop, 1909

Towle

Aristocrat, 1934
Awakening, 1958
Benjamin Franklin, 1904
Candlelight, 1934
Canterbury, 1893
Cascade, 1933
Charlemagne, 1963
Chased Diana, 1928
Chippendale, 1937
Colonial Thread, 1950
Contessina, 1965
Contour, 1950
Country Manor, 1966
Craftsman, 1932
Debussy, 1959
D'Orleans, 1923
Dorothy Manners, 1919
Drury Lane, 1939
El Grandee, 1964
Esplanade, 1952
Federal Cotillion, 1901
Fiddle Thread, 1902

Fontana, 1957
French Colonial, 1940
French Provincial, 1948
Georgian, 1898
King Richard, 1932
Lady Constance, 1922
Lady Diana, 1928
Lady Mary, 1917
Lafayette, 1905
Laureate, 1968
Legato, 1962
Louis XIV, 1924
Madeira, 1948
Marie Louise, 1939
Mary Chilton, 1912
Meadow Song, 1967
Newport Shell, 1910
Novantique, 1969
Old Brocade, 1932
Old Colonial, 1895
Old English, 1892
Old Lace, 1939
Old Master, 1942
Old Mirror, 1940
Old Newbury/Newbury, 1900
Paul Revere, 1906
Peachtree Manor, 1956
Petit Point, 1957
Pomona, 1887
R.S.V.P., 1965
Rambler Rose, 1937
Rose Solitaire, 1954
Royal Windsor, 1935
Scroll & Bead, 1940
Sculptured Rose, 1961
Seville, 1926
Silver Flutes, 1941
Silver Plumes, 1939
Silver Spray, 1956
Southwind, 1952
Spanish Provincial, 1967
Symphony, 1931
Vespera, 1961
Virginia Carvel, 1919
Virginia Lee, 1920

Tuttle Silver

Beauvoir, 1967
Colonial Fiddle, 1925
Feather Edge, 1938

Hannah Hull, 1927
Lamerie, 1936
Onslow, 1931

Unger Brothers Silver

Cupid Sunbeam, 1904
Cupid's Nosegay, 1904
Douvaine, 1890

Wallace Silver

America, 1915
Carnation, 1909
Carthage, 1917
Corinthian, 1911
Dauphine, 1916
Dawn Mist, 1963
Debutante, 1960
Discovery, 1957
Eton, 1903
Evening Mist, 1963
Feliciana, 1969
Figured Shell, 1874
Georgian Colonial, 1932
Grand Colonial, 1942
Grande Baroque, 1941
Hampton, 1904
Irian, 1902
Juliet, 1924
King Christian, 1940
Kings, 1903
La Reine, 1921
Lamerie, 1936
Larkspur, 1939
Lotus, 1935
Louvre, 1893
Lucerne, 1896
Madison, 1913
Meadow Rose, 1907
Melanie, 1959
Michele, 1968
Monterey, 1922
My Love, 1958
Nile, 1908
Normandie, 1933
Orange Blossom, 1923
Orchid Elegance, 1956
Penrose, 1962
Peony, 1906
Princess Anne, 1926
Princess Mary, 1922

Puritan, 1909
Putnam, 1912
Renaissance, 1925
Rheims, 1919
Rhythm, 1929
Romance of the Sea, 1950
Rose, 1898/1888
Rose Point, 1934
Royal Rose, 1962
Royal Satin, 1965
Saxon, 1910
Shenandoah, 1966
Silver Swirl, 1955
Sir Christopher, 1936
Spanish Lace, 1964
Sterling Rose, 1955
Stradivari, 1937
Violet, 1904
Waltz of Spring, 1952
Washington, 1911
Waverly, 1890
Windsor Rose, 1940
Windsor/Victoria, 1957
Wishing Star, 1954

Watson Silver

Colonial Fiddle, 1925
Foxhall, 1942
George II, 1937
George II Rex, 1936, Hand Chased
John Alden, 1911
Juliana, 1938
Lamerie, 1936
Lily, 1902
Lotus, 1935
Martha Washington, 1912
Meadow Rose, 1907
Mount Vernon, 1907
Navarre, 1908
Orchid
Wentworth, 1913
Windsor Rose, 1940

Weidlich Sterling

Ancestry, 1940
Lady Sterling, 1925
Virginia Sterling, 1929

Westmorland Silver

Enchanting Orchid, 1950
George & Martha Washington, 1940
John & Priscilla, 1940
Lady Hilton, 1940
Milburn Rose, 1940

Whiting Division-Silver

Adam, 1907
Alhambra, 1880
Antique Lily-Engraved, 1882
Arabesque, 1875
Armor, 1875
Bead, 1880
Berry, 1880
Colonial Engraved
Duke of York, 1900
Egyptian, 1875
Heraldic, 1880
Hyperion, 1888
Imperial Queen, 1893
Japanese, 1874
King Albert, 1919
King Edward, 1901
Lady Baltimore, 1910
Lily, 1902
Lily of the Valley, 1885
Louis XV, 1891
Madam Jumel, 1908
Madam Morris, 1909
Mandarin, 1918
Old King, 1890
Pompadour, 1898
Radiant, 1895
Stratford, 1910
Violet, 1905

Wood & Hughes

Byzantine
Fiddle
Gadroon, 1860
Louis XV, 1880

Other American Makers

English/Continental/Asian/Other

Silverware Profiles

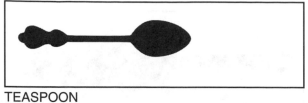

TEASPOON

PLACE SPOON

CREAM SOUP SPOON

BOUILLON SPOON

GUMBO SPOON

FRUIT SPOON

FIVE O'CLOCK TEASPOON

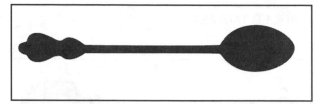

ICED TEA SPOON

DEMITASSE SPOON

INFANT FEEDING SPOON

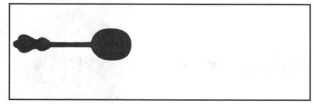

BABY SPOON

Silverware Profiles

PIERCED TABLESPOON

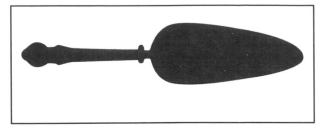

PIE & CAKE SERVER

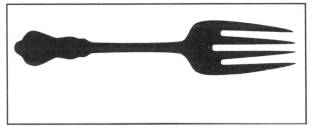

CASSEROLE SPOON

PIE SERVER

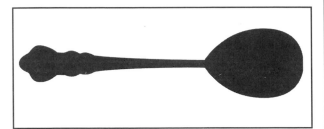

COLD MEAT FORK

CHEESE SERVING KNIFE

TOMATO SERVER

Silverware Profiles

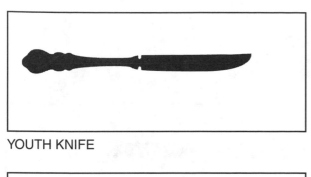

YOUTH KNIFE

DESSERT FORK

LUNCHEON FORK

ICE CREAM FORK

DINNER FORK

OYSTER/COCKTAIL FORK

GRILL FORK - LONG HANDLE

PICKLE FORK

SALAD FORK

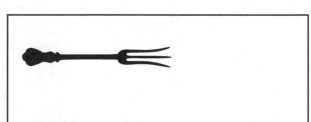

LEMON FORK

Silverware Profiles

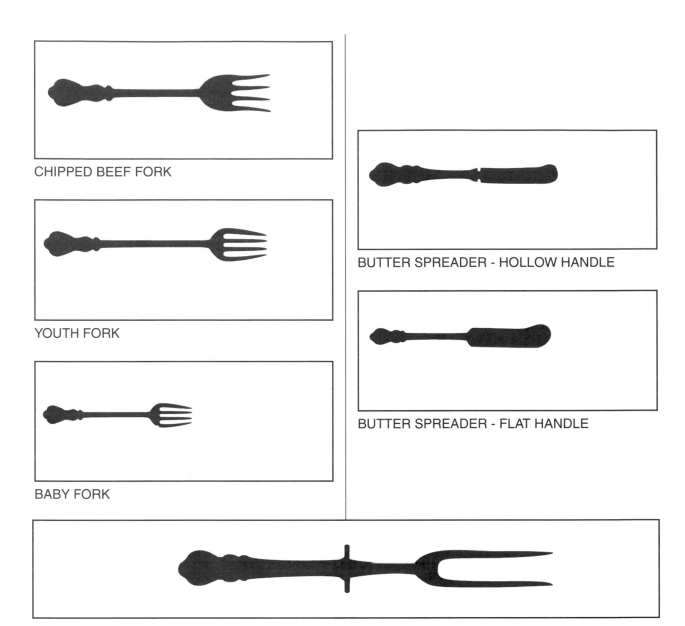

CHIPPED BEEF FORK

YOUTH FORK

BABY FORK

BUTTER SPREADER - HOLLOW HANDLE

BUTTER SPREADER - FLAT HANDLE

CARVING FORK

Silverware Profiles

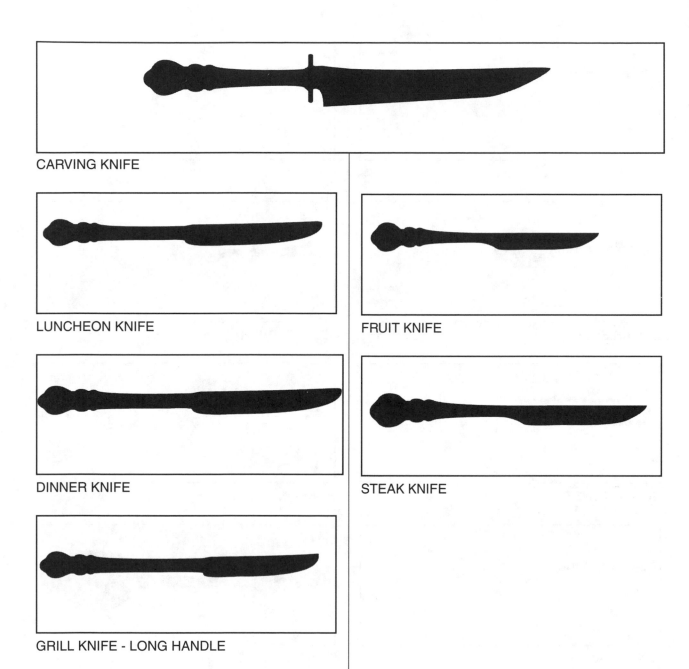

CARVING KNIFE

LUNCHEON KNIFE

FRUIT KNIFE

DINNER KNIFE

STEAK KNIFE

GRILL KNIFE - LONG HANDLE

Silverware Profiles

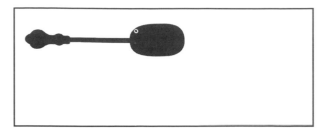

SUGAR SPOON

CREAM LADLE

SUGAR SHELL

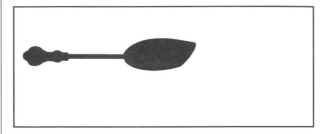

JELLY SERVER

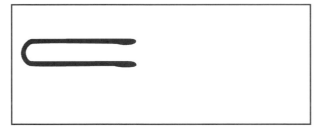

SUGAR TONGS

BONBON SPOON

GRAVY LADLE

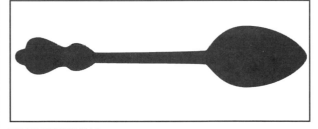

TABLESPOON

How to Set Your Table

On the right side of the plate, place the entree knife with the blade facing in toward the plate. To the right of the knife place the teaspoon. To the right of the teaspoon, place the soup spoon (either with a round or oval bowl).

To the left of the plate, place the entree fork and then the salad fork. If a bread plate is used, place it either to the left of the forks or slightly above them. Place the bread and butter knife either on the bread plate or above the plate with the blade facing toward the dinner plate. Glasses go above the knives with the water glass closest to the plate. Wine glasses go to the right of the water glass. The napkin may go on the plate or be placed to the left of the forks. The teacup and saucer (if used) go to the right of the soup spoon.

Dinner size knives are between 9 1/2 to 10 inches long. Forks are between 7 1/2 to 8 inches long. The luncheon size knife is approximately 9 inches long. The forks are approximately 7 inches long.

In the 1950s, a third size was made by some companies, called the place size. It has a knife that is usually about 9 1/4 inches long. The handle is usually longer than the handles on either the luncheon knife or dinner fork. The fork is usually 7 1/4 inches long.

All three sizes are still being made. Luncheon size settings, place size settings, or dinner size settings may be used for the same occasions.

A "continental size" found in some European countries, which is even larger than the dinner size, is being made in a few patterns.

The basic serving pieces are a table serving spoon, pierced (slotted) table serving spoon, meat serving fork, master butter server, and sugar spoon, plus a gravy ladle and, if required, a pie/cake server.

Alvin

ALVIN CORP.

Alvin Manufacturing Co. was founded in 1886 in Irvington, New Jersey. It became Alvin Silver Co. in 1919. The Gorham Co. bought most of the firm's assets in 1928 and changed the name to Alvin Corp. Company marks include an ornate capital A flanked by a winged dragon; they also produced a line called Lullaby Sterling.

Apollo by Alvin Silver, 1900

Butter spreader, flat handle, 5 3/4 in.. . . . . $16
Butter-master, flat handle, 6 5/8 in. $30
Fork, 6 3/4 in.. . . . . $30
Fork, 7 1/8 in.. . . . . $42
Fork-cocktail, 5 1/2 in. $25
Fork-cold meat/serving small, solid,
    6 3/8 in. $60
Fork-pastry, bar, pierced, 6 in. $40
Fork-strawberry, 4 3/4 in. $30
Knife-fruit, plate blade, individual,
    6 1/8 in. $28
Knife-old french/hollow, 9 3/4 in. $40
Ladle-gravy/solid, 6 1/4 in. $63
Spoon-dessert/oval soup, 7 in. $40
Spoon-fruit, 5 3/4 in. $30
Spoon-iced tea, 7 5/8 in. $40
Spoon-soup/round bowl, gumbo,
    6 7/8 in. $35
Spoon-sugar spoon, 5 5/8 in. $32
Spoon-teaspoon, (five o'clock),
    5 1/8 in. $15
Spoon-teaspoon, 5 3/4 in. $20
Tablespoon, (serving spoon),
    8 1/2 in. $55
Tablespoon, (serving spoon), pierced,
    8 1/2 in. $60

The following pieces have monograms:
Butter spreader, flat handle,
    5 3/4 in. $12
Butter-master, flat handle,
    6 5/8 in. $24
Fork, 7 1/2 in.. . . . . $30

Fork, 7 1/8 in.. . . . . $30
Fork-cocktail, 5 1/2 in. $21
Fork-pastry, 6 in. $25
Knife-old french, hollow, 8 7/8 in. $24
Spoon-fruit, 5 3/4 in.. $24
Spoon-soup/round bowl, bouillon,
    5 1/4 in. $20
Spoon-soup/round bowl, gumbo,
    6 7/8 in. $29
Spoon-sugar spoon, 5 5/8 in. $24
Spoon-teaspoon, 5 3/4 in. $16
Tablespoon, (serving spoon),
    8 1/2 in. $40

Avila by Alvin, 1969

Butter spreader, hollow handle, modern,
    stainless, 6 7/8 in. $28
Butter-master, hollow handle,
    7 3/8 in. $35
Fork, 7 1/2 in. $40
Fork-cocktail, 5 3/4 in. $32
Fork-cold meat/serving, medium, solid,
    8 5/8 in. $90
Fork-salad, individual, bar pierce,
    6 7/8 in. $44
Knife-modern, hollow handle, 9 in. $34
Spoon-dessert/oval soup, 6 7/8 in.. . . . . $45
Spoon-iced tea, 7 3/4 in. $40
Spoon-sugar, 6 1/8 in. $40
Spoon-teaspoon, 6 in. $22
Tablespoon, (serving spoon),
    8 3/4 in. $85

Bridal Bouquet by Alvin, 1932

Butter spreader, flat handle, 5 3/4 in.. . . . . $20
Butter spreader, hollow handle, modern, stainless,
    6 1/4 in. $26
Butter spreader, hollow handle, paddle stainless,
    no stamp, 6 in. $26
Butter-master, flat handle, 7 in. $33
Carving set, two piece, small-stainless
    blade, steak $150
Fork, 7 1/4 in.. . . . . $36

Fork, 7 7/8 in.. . . . . $45
Fork-carving, large-stainless prongs, roast,
    10 3/4 in. $75
Fork-cocktail, 5 3/8 in. $26
Fork-cold meat/serving, small, solid,
    7 1/2 in. $90
Fork-ice cream no indent,
    5 1/2 in. $36
Fork-salad, individual, 6 1/2 in. $40
Knife-carving, small, stainless blade, steak, no
    stamp, 10 1/4 in. $75
Knife-fruit, stainless blade, individual,
    7 in. $36
Knife-modern, hollow handle,
    9 in. $40
Knife-modern, hollow handle, no stamp,
    9 in. $40
Knife-new french, hollow handle,
    9 5/8 in. $50
Knife-new french, hollow handle,
    8 7/8 in. $40
Knife-new french, hollow handle, no stamp,
    8 7/8 in. $40
Knife-sharpener/steel, small, steak,
    13 3/8 in. $75
Ladle-cream, solid piece,
    5 1/4 in. $45
Ladle-gravy, solid piece,
    5 7/8 in. $80
Napkin clip, (made for five o'clock) $25
Salad set, 2 pieces, plastic bowl,
    11 1/2 in. $90
Server-jelly, 6 1/4 in. $34
Server-pastry, stainless bowl,
    9 in. $75
Server-pie, stainless blade,
    9 3/4 in. $75
Spoon-casserole, smooth bowl, solid,
    8 7/8 in. $110
Spoon-demitasse, 4 1/4 in. $25
Spoon-fruit, 5 7/8 in. $33
Spoon-iced tea, 7 1/2 in. $30
Spoon-preserve, 7 3/8 in. $80
Spoon-soup, round bowl, cream,
    6 1/4 in. $38
Spoon-sugar, 5 7/8 in. $30
Spoon-teaspoon, (five o'clock),
    5 3/4 in. $22
Spoon-teaspoon, 6 in. $22
Tablespoon, (serving spoon),
    8 5/8 in. $80
Tongs-sugar, 4 in. $55

Bridal Rose by Alvin, 1903

Fork, 6 3/4 in. $90
Fork, 7 1/2 in. $150
Fork-cocktail, 5 5/8 in. $70
Fork-salad/pastry, individual, bar pierce,
    6 in. $170
Knife-blunt, hollow handle, plate blade,
    9 in. $140
Knife-old french, hollow handle, plate blade,
    9 in. $140
Ladle-gravy, solid piece, 6 5/8 in. $280
Spoon-demitasse, gold wash, 4 1/8 in. $50
Spoon-fruit, 5 3/4 in.. $70
Spoon-olive, short-pierced bowl,
    5 7/8 in. $160
Spoon-soup, round bowl, bouillon, 5 in. $80
Spoon-soup, round bowl, gumbo,
    6 7/8 in. $130
Spoon-sugar, 6 in. $100
Spoon-teaspoon, (five o'clock),
    5 1/4 in. $30
Tablespoon, (serving spoon),
    8 3/8 in. $150
Tablespoon, (serving spoon), pierced,
    8 3/8 in. $170
Tongs-sugar, 3 7/8 in.. . . . . $140
Tongs-sugar, 4 5/8 in.. . . . . $140

Alvin Bridal Rose infant feeding spoon. Excellent condition, monogrammed "Theodora," 3 1/2 in. $75.

Alvin

Chapel Bells by Alvin, 1939

Baby cup sterling handle, made w/spoon $80
Butter spreader, hollow handle, modern, stainless,
    6 1/4 in. $28
Butter spreader, flat handle, 5 3/4 in.. . . . . $10
Butter-master, flat handle, 7 in. $30
Carving set, two piece, large stainless blade,
    roast $140
Fork, 7 1/4 in.. . . . . $18
Fork, 8 in.. . . . . $25
Fork-baby, 4 1/8 in. $40
Fork-cocktail, 5 3/8 in. $24
Fork-cold meat/serving, small, solid,
    7 3/8 in. $70
Fork-pickle/olive-short handle, 5 3/4 in.. . . . . . $34
Fork-salad, individual, 6 1/2 in. $20
Knife-modern, hollow handle,
    8 7/8 in. $28
Knife-modern, hollow handle,
    9 1/2 in. $45
Knife-new french, hollow handle,
    8 7/8 in. $30
Knife-new french, hollow handle,
    9 1/2 in. $45
Ladle-cream, solid piece, 5 1/4 in.. . . . . $50
Ladle-gravy, solid piece, 5 3/4 in.. . . . . $60
Ladle-gravy, solid piece, 6 1/8 in.. . . . . $60
Napkin clip (made for cream soup) $20
Server-pie, stainless blade, 10 in. $60
Server-tomato, solid piece, 7 3/4 in. $96
Spoon-baby, straight handle,
    4 1/8 in. $40
Spoon-demitasse, 4 1/4 in. $20
Spoon-dessert/oval soup, 6 7/8 in. $46
Spoon-fruit, 5 7/8 in. $36
Spoon-iced tea, 7 1/2 in. $27
Spoon-soup, round bowl, bouillon,
    5 1/2 in. $40
Spoon-soup, round bowl, cream, 6 1/4 in.. . . . $17
Spoon-soup, round bowl, gumbo, 6 7/8 in. . . . $38
Spoon-sugar, 6 in.. . . . . $20
Spoon-teaspoon, (five o'clock), 5 1/2 in. $16
Spoon-teaspoon, 6 in.. . . . . $14
Tablespoon, (serving spoon), pierced,
    8 1/2 in. $80
Tablespoon, (serving spoon), 8 1/2 in.. . . . . . . $50
Tongs-sugar, 4 in. $60

Chased Romantique by Alvin, 1933

Butter spreader, flat handle, 5 5/8 in.. . . . . $12
Butter-master, flat handle, 7 1/8 in. $30
Carving set, two piece, small, stainless
    blade, steak $120
Fork, 7 1/4 in.. . . . . $15
Fork, 7 7/8 in.. . . . . $24
Fork-carving, small, stainless prongs,
    steak, 8 5/8 in. $60
Fork-ice cream, 5 5/8 in. $30
Fork-salad, individual, clover pierced,
    6 1/2 in. $20
Knife-carving, small, stainless blade, steak,
    9 7/8 in. $60
Knife-modern, hollow handle, 9 in.. . . . . $34
Knife-new french, hollow handle,
    8 7/8 in. $34
Knife-new french, hollow handle,
    9 5/8 in. $35
Ladle-cream, solid piece, 5 3/8 in.. . . . . $45
Ladle-gravy, solid piece, 5 7/8 in.. . . . . $70
Napkin clip (made for teaspoons) $16
Spoon-fruit, 5 7/8 in.. . . . . $40
Spoon-iced tea, 7 1/2 in. $20
Spoon-soup, round bowl, bouillon,
    5 1/2 in. $28
Spoon-soup, round bowl, cream,
    6 1/4 in. $18
Spoon-soup, round bowl, gumbo,
    6 7/8 in. $40
Spoon-sugar, 6 1/8 in. $18
Spoon-teaspoon, (five o'clock), 5 5/8 in. $10
Spoon-teaspoon, 6 in.. . . . . $12
Tablespoon, (serving spoon), 8 1/2 in.. . . . . . . $70
Tablespoon, (serving spoon), pierced,
    8 1/2 in. $80

Chateau Rose by Alvin, 1940

Butter spreader, hollow handle, stainless,
    6 1/8 in. $30
Butter spreader, flat handle, 5 3/4 in.. . . . . $15

Butter-master, flat handle, 7 1/8 in. $35
Butter-master, hollow handle, 6 3/4 in. $35
Fork, 7 1/4 in.. . . . . $30
Fork, 7 7/8 ind $18
Tablespoon, (serving spoon), 8 1/2 in.. . . . . . $80

Chippendale-Old by Alvin, 1900

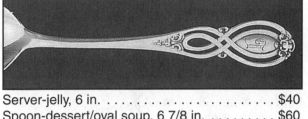

Server-jelly, 6 in. $40
Spoon-dessert/oval soup, 6 7/8 in. $60
Spoon-olive/short-pierced bowl,
    6 1/8 in.. . . . . $100
Spoon-teaspoon, 5 7/8 in.. . . . . $30

Della Robbia by Alvin, 1922

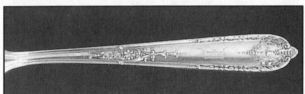

Butter spreader, hollow handle, stainless,
    6 in. $30
Butter spreader, flat handle, 5 3/4 in.. . . . . . . $20
Butter-master, flat handle, 7 1/8 in. $38
Fork, 7 1/8 in.. . . . . $22
Fork, 7 5/8 in.. . . . . $30
Fork-carving, small, stainless prongs, steak,
    8 3/8 in. $60
Fork-cocktail, 5 3/4 in. $30
Fork-cold meat/serving, small, solid,
    7 5/8 in. $85
Fork-ice cream, 3 tines, 5 5/8 in.. . . . . $45
Fork-ice cream, 4 tines, 5 3/4 in.. . . . . $50
Fork-ice cream, pierced, 5 5/8 in. $45
Fork-salad, individual, 6 3/8 in. $40
Knife-carving, small, stainless blade, steak,
    10 1/8 in.. . . . . $60
Knife-new french, hollow handle,
    8 7/8 in.. . . . . $32
Knife-old french, hollow handle,
    9 7/8 in.. . . . . $45
Ladle-cream, solid piece, 5 1/2 in.. . . . . $50
Server-pie, stainless blade, 10 in. $70
Spoon-casserole, smooth bowl, solid,
    9 1/4 in.. . . . . $110

Spoon-demitasse, 4 1/8 in. $20
Spoon-fruit, 5 3/4 in.. . . . . $38
Spoon-iced tea, 8 in. $30
Spoon-soup, round bowl, bouillon,
    5 1/4 in. $34
Spoon-soup, round bowl, cream,
    6 1/4 in. $50
Spoon-soup, round bowl, gumbo,
    7 1/4 in. $40
Spoon-sugar, 6 in. $34
Spoon-teaspoon, 5 7/8 in. $12
Tablespoon, (serving spoon),
    8 5/8 in. $80
Tablespoon, (serving spoon), pierced,
    8 5/8 in. $100

Eternal Rose by Alvin, 1963

Fork, 7 1/4 in.. . . . . $50
Fork-cocktail, 5 7/8 in. $28
Fork-salad, individual, 6 5/8 in. $43
Knife-modern, hollow handle, 9 in.. . . . . $35
Spoon-dessert/oval soup, oval bowl,
    6 5/8 in. $50
Spoon-iced tea, 7 1/8 in. $38
Spoon-sugar, 6 in. $36
Tablespoon, (serving spoon),
    8 1/2 in. $90

Fleur de Lis by Alvin, 1907

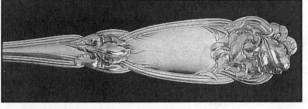

Fork, 6 3/4 in.. . . . . $46
Fork-pastry, bar, 6 in. $65
Spoon-casserole, smooth bowl, solid,
    7 3/8 in. $120
Spoon-demitasse, 3 3/4 in. $27
Spoon-fruit, 5 1/2 in.. . . . . $40
Spoon-soup, round bowl, bouillon,
    5 3/8 in. $50
Spoon-soup, round bowl, gumbo,
    7 in. $65
Spoon-sugar, 5 7/8 in. $48
Spoon-teaspoon, (five o'clock), 5 1/4 in. $26
Spoon-teaspoon, 5 7/8 in. $34
Tablespoon, (serving spoon), 8 1/4 in.. . . . . . $80

Florence Nightingale by Alvin, 1919

Butter spreader, flat handle, 5 5/8 in......... $24
Fork, 7 1/4 in.......................... $34
Fork, 7 3/4 in.......................... $50
Fork-cocktail, 5 1/2 in................... $30
Fork-cold meat/serving, small, solid,
    7 1/4 in............................ $65
Ladle-gravy, solid piece, 7 5/8 in.......... $80
Server-jelly, 5 1/2 in.................... $30
Spoon-demitasse, 4 1/8 in................ $20
Spoon-five o'clock/youth, 5 1/4 in......... $16
Spoon-fruit, 5 3/4 in.................... $34
Spoon-iced tea, 7 3/4 in................. $34
Spoon-sugar, 5 5/8 in................... $35
Spoon-teaspoon, (five o'clock),
    5 1/2 in............................ $15
Spoon-teaspoon, 5 3/4 in................. $20
Tablespoon, (serving spoon),
    8 1/2 in............................ $65
Tablespoon, (serving spoon), pierced
    8 1/2 in............................ $80

Florentine by Alvin, 1900

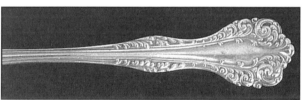

Butter spreader, flat handle, 6 in........... $30
Fork, 6 3/4 in.......................... $48
Fork, 7 1/2 in.......................... $70
Fork-cocktail, 5 3/8 in.................. $30
Fork-cold meat/serving, small, solid,
    7 in............................... $100
Fork-pie, 3 tines, 6 3/8 in.............. $50
Fork-youth, 6 in........................ $50
Ladle-gravy, solid piece, 5 5/8 in......... $100
Server-fish, solid, large, 9 1/2 in.......... $250
Spoon-casserole, smooth bowl, solid,
    8 1/2 in............................ $120
Spoon-demitasse, 4 1/8 in................ $28
Spoon-dessert/oval soup, 6 7/8 in. $60
Spoon-fruit, 5 3/4 in.................... $40
Spoon-soup, round bowl, gumbo,
    6 7/8 in............................ $60
Spoon-teaspoon, (five o'clock),
    5 in............................... $25
Spoon-teaspoon, 5 3/4 in................. $32
Tongs-sugar, 4 in. $65

Francis I by Alvin, 1910

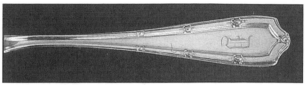

Butter spreader, flat handle, 6 in........... $18
Butter-master, flat handle, 6 7/8 in. $32
Fork, 6 3/4 in.......................... $24
Fork, 7 1/2 in.......................... $40
Fork-cocktail, 5 1/2 in.................. $16
Fork-cold meat/serving, small, solid,
    7 1/8 in............................ $70
Fork-ice cream, 5 1/4 in. $34
Fork-pastry, 6 bar $30.
Knife-new french, hollow handle, 8 7/8 in. $24
Knife-new french, hollow handle, 9 5/8 in. $40
Knife-old french, hollow handle, 8 7/8 in...... $24
Knife-old french, hollow handle, 9 3/4 in...... $40
Spoon-demitasse, 4 1/8 in. $17
Spoon-dessert/oval soup, 7 in.............. $40
Spoon-fruit, 5 7/8 in..................... $27
Spoon-soup, round bowl, bouillon, 5 in....... $22
Spoon-soup, round bowl, gumbo, 6 7/8 in..... $40
Spoon-teaspoon, (five o'clock), 5 1/4 in. $15
Spoon-teaspoon, 5 5/8 in. $15
Tablespoon, (serving spoon), 8 1/2 in........ $55

French Scroll by Alvin, 1953

Butter spreader, hollow handle, modern, stainless,
    6 1/4 in............................ $24
Butter-master, flat handle, 7 in. $34
Butter-master, hollow handle, 6 3/4 in........ $35
Carving set, 2 pieces, large, stainless
    blade, roast $160
Fork, 7 1/4 in.......................... $35
Fork, 8 in............................. $40
Fork-cold meat/serving, small, solid,
    7 3/8 in............................ $90
Fork-salad, individual, 6 1/2 in. $40
Knife-modern, hollow handle, 8 7/8 in........ $32
Knife-modern, hollow handle, 9 5/8 in........ $44
Knife-steak, individual, 8 3/4 in............ $50
Ladle-gravy, solid piece, 6 1/8 in........... $80
Napkin clip (made for teaspoons) $28

Spoon-fruit, 5 7/8 in. $36
Spoon-iced tea, 7 1/2 in. $36
Spoon-soup, round bowl, cream,
   6 3/8 in. $36
Spoon-sugar, 6 in. $36
Spoon-teaspoon, 5 7/8 in. $22
Tablespoon, (serving spoon), pierced,
   8 3/8 in. $100
Tablespoon, (serving spoon), 8 3/8 in. $80

Gainsborough by Alvin, 1930

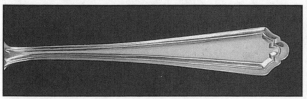

Butter spreader, flat handle, 5 5/8 in. $15
Butter-master, flat handle, 6 7/8 in. $30
Fork, 7 1/8 in. $30
Fork, 7 7/8 in. $44
Fork-cocktail, 5 3/8 in. $22
Fork-salad, individual, 6 1/2 in. $28
Knife-new french, hollow handle,
   8 1/2 in. $30
Knife-new french, hollow handle,
   9 1/2 in. $40
Ladle-gravy, solid piece, 6 7/8 in. $70
Spoon-demitasse, 4 1/4 in. $20
Spoon-dessert/oval soup, 7 in. $36
Spoon-fruit, 5 7/8 in. $30
Spoon-iced tea, 7 1/2 in. $34
Spoon-soup, round bowl, bouillon, 5 1/8 in. . . . $30
Spoon-soup, round bowl, cream, 6 1/4 in. $32
Spoon-soup, round bowl, gumbo, 6 7/8 in. . . . $35
Spoon-sugar, 6 in. $30
Spoon-teaspoon, (five o'clock), 5 3/4 in. $15
Spoon-teaspoon, 6 in. $17
Tablespoon, (serving spoon), 8 5/8 in. $60

Hamilton by Alvin, 1910

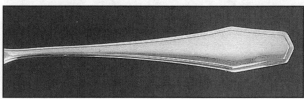

Butter spreader, flat handle, 5 7/8 in. $15
Butter-master, flat handle, 6 7/8 in. $30
Fork, 6 3/4 in. $17
Fork, 7 1/2 in. $34

Fork-baby, 4 in. $28
Fork-cocktail, 5 1/2 in. $12
Fork-lemon, 5 3/8 in. $17
Fork-pickle/olive, short handle, 1 1/4 in. tine,
   6 in. $17
Fork-salad, individual, 4 tine bar, 6 in. $33
Knife-fruit, silver plate blade, individual,
   6 1/4 in. $26
Knife-new french, hollow handle, 8 3/4 in. $20
Knife-new french, hollow handle, 9 3/4 in. $35
Knife-old french, hollow handle, 9 in. $20
Ladle-cream, solid piece, 5 3/4 in. $30
Ladle-gravy, solid piece, 7 3/8 in. $60
Spoon-demitasse, 4 1/8 in. $15
Spoon-fruit, 5 3/4 in. $17
Spoon-iced tea, 7 3/4 in. $28
Spoon-preserve 7 1/4 in. $38
Spoon-soup, round bowl, bouillon,
   4 7/8 in. $20
Spoon-soup, round bowl, gumbo,
   6 7/8 in. $30
Spoon-sugar, 6 in. $30
Spoon-teaspoon, (five o'clock), 3 3/4 in. handle,
   5 5/8 in. $12
Spoon-teaspoon, 5 7/8 in. $13
Spoon-youth, 3 1/2 in. handle, 5 1/4 in. $16
Tablespoon, (serving spoon), 8 3/8 in. $50
Tongs-sugar, 2 7/8 in. $45

Hampton by Alvin, 1910/1912

Butter spreader, flat handle, 5 5/8 in. $23
Fork, 7 1/4 in. $28
Fork, 7 3/4 in. $45
Fork-cocktail, 5 3/8 in. $26
Fork-pickle/olive, short handle, 5 5/8 in. $26
Fork-salad, individual, 6 in. $33
Knife-old french, hollow handle, 9 in. $25
Ladle-cream, solid piece, 5 1/4 in. $36
Ladle-gravy, solid piece, 7 1/2 in. $80
Spoon-demitasse, 4 in. $18
Spoon-dessert/oval soup, 7 1/8 in. $34
Spoon-soup, round bowl bouillon, 5 in. $20
Spoon-soup, round bowl, gumbo, 7 in. $35
Spoon-sugar, 5 7/8 in. $30
Spoon-teaspoon, (five o'clock), 5 1/2 in. $15
Spoon-teaspoon, 5 3/4 in. $16
Tablespoon, (serving spoon), 8 1/2 in. $60

Alvin

Majestic by Alvin, 1900

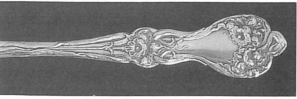

Fork, 6 3/4 in.. . . . . $47
Fork-cold meat/serving, small, solid,
   7 1/4 in.. . . . . $120
Fork-pastry, bar pierce, 5 7/8 in. $120
Knife-blunt, hollow handle, 8 1/4 in.. . . . . . . $50
Knife-old french, hollow handle, 8 3/4 in.. . . . $50
Ladle-cream, solid piece, 5 3/4 in.. . . . . $100
Spoon-demitasse, 4 1/8 in. $28
Spoon-dessert/oval soup, 7 in. $60
Spoon-fruit, 5 1/4 in. $44
Spoon-fruit, 5 3/4 in. $44
Spoon-ice cream, 5 1/4 in.. . . . . $50
Spoon-soup, round bowl, bouillon, 4 7/8 in.. . . $43
Spoon-soup, round bowl, gumbo, 6 7/8 in. . . . $60
Spoon-sugar shell, 6 1/8 in.. . . . . $45
Spoon-teaspoon, (five o'clock), 5 1/8 in. $25
Spoon-teaspoon, 5 3/4 in. $30
Tablespoon, (serving spoon), 8 1/8 in.. . . . . . $90

Maryland by Alvin, 1910

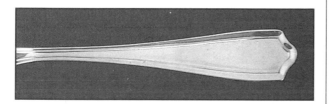

Butter spreader, flat handle, 6 in.. . . . . $20
Butter-master, flat handle, 6 7/8 in. $28
Fork, 6 7/8 in.. . . . . $33
Fork, 7 1/2 in.. . . . . $46
Fork-carving, small, stainless prongs, steak,
   8 3/4 in. $44
Fork-cocktail, 5 1/2 in. $23
Fork-cold meat/serving, medium, solid,
   8 3/8 in. $70
Fork-cold meat/serving, small, solid,
   7 1/8 in. $60
Fork-ice cream, 5 3/8 in. $35
Fork-pastry, bar, 6 in. $30
Fork-pie, 3 tines, 6 in.. . . . . $30
Knife-new french, hollow handle,
   8 3/4 in. $26
Knife-new french, hollow handle,
   9 3/4 in. $37
Knife-old french, hollow handle,
   9 3/4 in. $37
Knife-old french, hollow handle, 9 in.. . . . . . . $27
Ladle-gravy, solid piece, 7 3/8 in.. . . . . $70
Sardine-tined fork/serving, solid,
   5 7/8 in. $60
Server-jelly, 5 1/2 in.. . . . . $27
Server-tomato, solid piece, 7 5/8 in.. . . . . $80
Spoon-bon-bon, 4 1/4 in. $30
Spoon-chocolate, short handle, 4 in. $20
Spoon-demitasse, 4 1/8 in. $14
Spoon-five o'clock/youth, 5 1/4 in. $15
Spoon-iced tea, 7 7/8 in. $28
Spoon-olive, short pierced bowl, 5 7/8 in. $70
Spoon-salad serving, solid piece,
   9 1/4 in. $80
Spoon-soup, round bowl, bouillon, 5 in.. . . . . . $24
Spoon-sugar, 5 7/8 in. $24

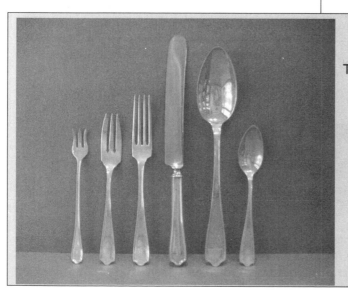

Thirty-eight pieces Alvin Maryland
   (c.1910): 6 tablespoons, 6 luncheon
   knives, 6 luncheon forks, 6 salad
   forks, 6 teaspoons, 6 cocktail forks,
   1 sugar spoon, and 1 butter knife.
   Monogram "M." $500.

Spoon-teaspoon, (five o'clock), no rim bowl,
5 1/2 in. $14
Spoon-teaspoon, 5 3/4 in. $18
Tablespoon, (serving spoon), pierced,
8 3/8 in. $60
Tablespoon, (serving spoon), 8 3/8 in. $50

Melrose by Alvin, 1910

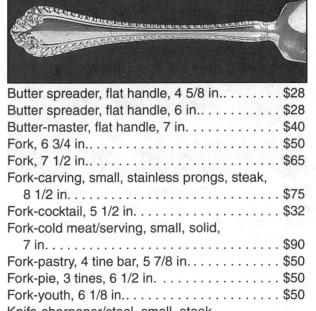

Butter spreader, flat handle, 4 5/8 in. $28
Butter spreader, flat handle, 6 in. $28
Butter-master, flat handle, 7 in. $40
Fork, 6 3/4 in. $50
Fork, 7 1/2 in. $65
Fork-carving, small, stainless prongs, steak,
8 1/2 in. $75
Fork-cocktail, 5 1/2 in. $32
Fork-cold meat/serving, small, solid,
7 in. $90
Fork-pastry, 4 tine bar, 5 7/8 in. $50
Fork-pie, 3 tines, 6 1/2 in. $50
Fork-youth, 6 1/8 in. $50
Knife-sharpener/steel, small, steak,
9 3/8 in. $75
Ladle-gravy, solid piece, 6 3/4 in. $90
Pick-nut, 4 5/8 in. $60
Server-fish, solid small, 9 1/2 in. $94
Server-tomato, solid piece, 7 1/2 in. $100
Spoon-bon-bon, 4 1/2 in. $48
Spoon-bon-bon, 5 5/8 in. $48
Spoon-bon-bon, 5 in. $48
Spoon-casserole/shell, solid,
8 3/8 in. $130
Spoon-demitasse, 4 in. $24
Spoon-dessert/oval soup, 7 in. $40
Spoon-jelly, large, 7 in. $70
Spoon-olive, short pierced bowl,
6 1/8 in. $100
Spoon-soup, round bowl, bouillon,
4 1/8 in. $40
Spoon-soup, round bowl, bouillon,
4 3/4 in. $40
Spoon-soup, round bowl, gumbo,
6 7/8 in. $50
Spoon-sugar shell, 5 3/4 in. $45
Spoon-teaspoon, (five o'clock), 5 in. $28

Spoon-teaspoon, 5 3/4 in. $26
Tablespoon, (serving spoon), 8 in. $90

Miss Alvin by Alvin, 1931

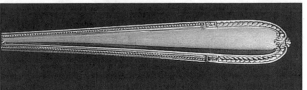

Butter spreader, flat handle, 5 5/8 in. $23
Butter-master, flat handle, 7 in. $34
Fork, 7 1/8 in. $34
Fork, 7 7/8 in. $45
Fork-cocktail, 5 1/2 in. $18
Fork-pickle/olive, short handle,
5 7/8 in. $30
Fork-salad, individual, 6 1/2 in. $30
Knife-new french, hollow handle,
8 3/4 in. $33
Ladle-cream, solid piece, 5 1/8 in. $50
Ladle-gravy, solid piece, 6 3/8 in. $75
Server-jelly, 6 1/4 in. $30
Server-pie, stainless blade, 9 3/8 in. $60
Spoon-dessert/oval soup, 7 1/8 in. $33
Spoon-fruit, 5 7/8 in. $30
Spoon-iced tea, 7 1/2 in. $34
Spoon-soup, round bowl, bouillon,
5 1/2 in. $30
Spoon-soup, round bowl, cream,
6 1/4 in. $30
Spoon-sugar, 6 1/8 in. $36
Spoon-teaspoon, 6 in. $16
Tablespoon, (serving spoon),
8 5/8 in. $65
Tongs-sugar, 4 5/8 in. $60

Morning Glory by Alvin, 1909

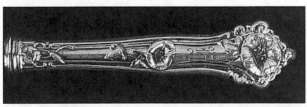

Fork, 6 3/4 in. $70
Fork, 7 1/2 in. $80
Fork-youth, 6 in. $80
Spoon-demitasse, 4 in. $30
Spoon-dessert/oval soup, 7 1/8 in. $90
Spoon-fruit, 5 3/4 in. $70
Spoon-teaspoon, 5 3/4 in. $50

Orange Blossom-Old by Alvin, 1905

Fork, 6 7/8 in.. . . . . $80
Spoon-five o'clock/youth, 5 1/4 in.. . . . . $40
Spoon-soup, round bowl, bouillon,
    4 7/8 in.. . . . . $60
Spoon-soup, round bowl, gumbo,
    6 7/8 in.. . . . . $120
Spoon-teaspoon, no design, 5 7/8 in. $45
Tablespoon, (serving spoon), 8 1/2 in.. . . . . . $160

Orange Blossom-New by Alvin, 1920

Butter spreader, flat handle, 5 5/8 in.. . . . . . . $27
Fork, 7 1/2 in.. . . . . $50
Fork, 7 in.. . . . . $45
Fork-cocktail, 5 1/2 in. $28
Knife-new french, hollow handle, 8 3/4 in.. . . . $34
Knife-old french, hollow handle, 8 3/4 in.. . . . . $34
Server-pie, silver plate blade, 9 3/4 in. $70
Spoon-dessert/oval soup, 7 1/4 in. $50
Spoon-sugar, 6 in.. . . . . $40
Spoon-teaspoon, 5 3/4 in. $22
Tablespoon, (serving spoon), 8 1/2 in.. . . . . . . $80

Pirouette by Alvin, 1961

Fork, 7 1/2 in.. . . . . $40
Fork-cold meat/serving, small, solid,
    7 3/8 in.. . . . . $100
Fork-salad, individual, 6 1/2 in. $45
Knife-modern, hollow handle, 9 1/4 in. $36
Ladle-gravy, solid piece, 6 1/4 in.. . . . . $100
Spoon-dessert/oval soup, 7 in. $45
Spoon-sugar, 6 in.. . . . . $38
Spoon-teaspoon, 6 in.. . . . . $26
Tablespoon, (serving spoon), 8 1/2 in.. . . . . . . $90

Prince Eugene by Alvin, 1950

Butter spreader, hollow handle, stainless,
    6 in.. . . . . $30
Butter spreader, flat handle, 5 3/4 in.. . . . . . . $28
Butter-master, flat handle, 7 1/8 in. $42
Fork, 7 1/4 in.. . . . . $32
Fork, 7 7/8 in.. . . . . $40
Fork-salad, individual, 6 3/4 in. $45
Knife-modern, hollow handle, 9 1/2 in.. . . . . . . $50
Knife-modern, hollow handle, 9 in.. . . . . $36
Spoon-sugar, 6 in. $40
Spoon-teaspoon, 5 7/8 in. $24
Tablespoon, (serving spoon), 8 5/8 in.. . . . . . $100

Raleigh by Alvin, 1900

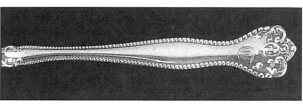

Butter spreader, flat handle, paddle blade,
    5 3/8 in. $25
Butter spreader, flat handle, paddle blade,
    6 1/8 in. $25
Butter spreader, flat handle, point blade,
    5 3/8 in. $25
Carving set, 2 pieces, large, stainless blade,
    roast. $140
Fork, 6 3/4 in.. . . . . $28
Fork, 7 1/2 in.. . . . . $55
Fork-chipped beef, small, 6 1/8 in.. . . . . $66
Fork-cocktail, 5 3/8 in. $22
Fork-cocktail, gold wash, 5 3/8 in. $22
Fork-cold meat/serving, medium, solid,
    8 5/8 in. $90
Fork-cold meat/serving, small, solid,
    7 1/2 in. $75
Fork-ice cream, crimp bowl, 4 7/8 in.. . . . . . . $48
Fork-ice cream, scallop bowl, 4 7/8 in.. . . . . . $48
Fork-lemon, 4 3/4 in. $30
Knife-orange, silver plate blade, 7 1/8 in.. . . . . $45
Knife-pie, solid, large, 8 7/8 in.. . . . . $130
Ladle-gravy, solid piece, 6 7/8 in.. . . . . $90
Spoon-casserole, smooth bowl, solid,
    8 3/4 in. $100
Spoon-chocolate, short handle, large, gold wash,
    4 3/4 in. $28
Spoon-demitasse, 4 1/4 in. $24
Spoon-dessert/oval soup, 7 in.. . . . . $40
Spoon-fruit, 6 in.. . . . . $35
Spoon-fruit, gold wash, 6 in.. . . . . $35
Spoon-ice, 8 3/8 in. $140

Spoon-salad serving, solid piece 9 1/8 in.... $104
Spoon-salt/master, 3 3/4 in............... $24
Spoon-soup, round bowl, bouillon,
   4 7/8 in............................. $30
Spoon-soup, round bowl, gumbo, 7 in...... $37
Spoon-sugar, 5 1/4 in.................... $36
Spoon-sugar, 6 in....................... $36
Spoon-teaspoon, (five o'clock), 5 1/8 in..... $20
Spoon-teaspoon, 6 in.................... $20
Tablespoon, (serving spoon), 8 3/8 in........ $75
Tablespoon, (serving spoon), pierced,
   8 3/8 in............................. $90
Tongs-sugar, 3 3/4 in. $55

Raphael by Alvin, 1902

Fork-cold meat/serving, large, solid, bar pierce,
   9 1/4 in...........................$1,000
Spoon-sugar, 6 in...................... $150

Richmond by Alvin, 1929

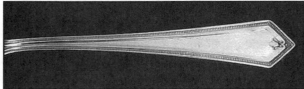

Butter-master, flat handle, 6 7/8 in. $36
Fork, 7 5/8 in........................... $40
Fork, 7 in.............................. $35
Fork-cocktail, 5 1/2 in. $20
Fork-cold meat/serving, small, solid,
   7 1/4 in............................. $80
Fork-pie, 3 tines, 5 7/8 in. $44
Fork-salad, individual, 6 in. $35
Knife-new french, hollow handle, 9 5/8 in..... $40
Ladle-gravy, solid piece, 7 1/4 in.......... $70
Napkin clip (made for teaspoons) $20
Server-pie, silver plate blade, 10 in. $58
Server-pie, stainless blade, 9 1/2 in......... $58
Spoon-bon-bon, 6 1/8 in................. $40
Spoon-demitasse, 4 in. $18
Spoon-dessert/oval soup, 7 1/4 in. $44
Spoon-fruit, 5 3/4 in.................... $30
Spoon-iced tea, 7 3/4 in. $32
Spoon-soup, round bowl, bouillon, 5 in........ $22

Spoon-soup, round bowl, gumbo,
   7 1/4 in.............................. $40
Spoon-sugar, 5 7/8 in. $40
Spoon-teaspoon, (five o'clock),
   5 1/2 in.............................. $14
Spoon-teaspoon, 5 3/4 in. $15
Tablespoon, (serving spoon), 8 3/8 in........ $70

Romantique by Alvin, 1933

Butter spreader, flat handle, 5 1/2 in......... $12
Fork, 7 1/4 in........................... $20
Fork, 8 in.............................. $34
Fork-cocktail, 5 1/2 in. $26
Fork-grille (viand), 7 5/8 in. $34
Fork-salad, individual, heart slot, 6 5/8 in..... $20
Knife-carving, small, stainless blade/steak,
   10 in. $50
Knife-modern, hollow handle, 8 5/8 in........ $30
Knife-modern, hollow handle, 9 5/8 in........ $40
Knife-modern, hollow handle, 9 in.......... $30
Knife-new french, hollow handle,
   9 5/8 in............................. $38
Knife-new french, hollow handle, no stamp,
   9 5/8 in............................. $38
Ladle-gravy, solid piece, 6 in.............. $86
Spoon-demitasse, 4 3/8 in. $20
Spoon-dessert/oval soup, 6 7/8 in........... $36
Spoon-fruit, 5 7/8 in..................... $32
Spoon-iced tea, 7 1/2 in. $30
Spoon-soup, round bowl, bouillon,
   5 1/2 in.............................. $26
Spoon-soup, round bowl, cream,
   6 1/4 in.............................. $18
Spoon-soup, round bowl, gumbo,
   6 7/8 in.............................. $36
Spoon-sugar, 6 in. $30
Spoon-teaspoon, (five o'clock), 5 5/8 in. $17
Spoon-teaspoon, 6 in..................... $15
Tablespoon, (serving spoon), 8 1/2 in........ $56

Rosecrest by Alvin, 1955

Butter spreader, hollow handle, modern, stainless,
6 1/4 in. $18
Butter spreader, flat handle, 5 3/4 in.. . . . . $18
Butter-master, flat handle, 7 in. $36
Carving set, two piece, large, stainless blade,
roast $140
Fork, 7 3/8 in.. . . . . $30
Fork, 8 1/8 in.. . . . . $40
Fork-cold meat/serving, small, solid,
7 1/2 in. $70
Fork-pickle/olive, short handle,
5 3/4 in. $26
Fork-salad serving, solid piece, 9 in. $104
Fork-salad, individual, 6 5/8 in. $34
Knife-ham slicer, stainless blade,
14 3/8 in. $80
Knife-modern, hollow handle, 8 7/8 in. $30
Knife-modern, hollow handle, 9 5/8 in. $40
Knife-sharpener/steel, small, steak,
14 1/2 in. $55
Ladle-gravy, solid piece, 6 in.. . . . . $80
Server-cheese, stainless blade,
6 3/4 in. $48
Server-pie, stainless blade, 10 1/8 in. $65
Spoon-dessert/oval soup, 6 7/8 in. $36
Spoon-iced tea, 7 5/8 in. $34
Spoon-salad serving, solid piece, 9 in. $104
Spoon-soup, round bowl, cream,
6 3/8 in. $24
Spoon-sugar, 6 1/8 in. $32
Spoon-teaspoon, 6 in. $17
Tablespoon, (serving spoon), 8 1/2 in.. . . . . . . $65
Tablespoon, (serving spoon), pierced,
8 1/2 in. $80

Southern Charm by Alvin, 1947

Butter spreader, hollow handle, modern, stainless,
6 1/4 in. $20
Butter spreader, flat handle,
5 3/4 in. $15
Butter-master, flat handle, 7 in. $30
Fork, 7 1/4 in.. . . . . $32
Fork, 8 in.. . . . . $36
Fork-baby, 4 1/4 in. $40
Fork-cocktail, 5 5/8 in. $20
Fork-pickle/olive, short handle, 5 3/4 in. $32

Fork-salad, individual, 6 1/2 in. $30
Fork-youth, 6 1/8 in. $45
Knife-new french, hollow handle,
9 5/8 in. $35
Ladle-gravy, solid piece, 5 7/8 in. $80
Napkin clip (made for teaspoons) $22
Spoon-demitasse, 4 1/4 in. $20
Spoon-dessert/oval soup, 6 7/8 in.. . . . . $46
Spoon-soup, round bowl, cream,
6 1/4 in. $20
Spoon-sugar, 6 in. $30
Spoon-teaspoon, 6 in. $17
Tablespoon, (serving spoon), 8 3/8 in.. . . . . . . $60

Spring Bud by Alvin, 1956

Butter spreader, hollow handle, modern, stainless,
6 1/4 in. $20
Fork, 7 1/4 in.. . . . . $34
Fork, 8 in.. . . . . $45
Fork-cold meat/serving, small, solid,
7 1/2 in. $70
Fork-salad, individual, 6 5/8 in. $30
Knife-modern, hollow handle,
8 7/8 in. $30
Knife-modern, hollow handle,
9 1/2 in. $48
Ladle-gravy, solid piece, 5 5/8 in.. . . . . $70
Server-pie, stainless blade, 10 in. $55
Spoon-iced tea, 7 5/8 in. $30
Spoon-soup, round bowl, cream,
6 3/8 in. $30
Spoon-sugar, 6 in. $30
Spoon-teaspoon, 5 7/8 in. $22
Tablespoon, (serving spoon), 8 1/2 in.. . . . . . . $60

Vivaldi by Alvin, 1966

Fork, 7 1/2 in.. . . . . $44
Spoon-dessert/oval soup, 6 7/8 in.. . . . . $70
Spoon-sugar, 6 in. $50
Spoon-teaspoon, 6 in. $34

William Penn by Alvin, 1907

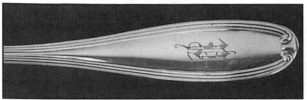

Butter spreader, flat handle, 6 in.. . . . . $22
Fork, 6 3/4 in.. . . . . $45
Fork, 7 1/2 in.. . . . . $64
Fork, 7 1/8 in.. . . . . $45
Fork-cocktail, 5 1/2 in. $28
Fork-cold meat/serving, small, solid,
  7 1/8 in.. . . . . $70

Ladle-cream, solid piece, 5 3/8 in. $46
Spoon-demitasse, 4 5/8 in. $22
Spoon-dessert/oval soup, 7 in.. . . . . $36
Spoon-dressing, large, solid, with button,
  12 7/8 in. $180
Spoon-fruit, 5 3/4 in.. . . . . $36
Spoon-soup, round bowl, bouillon,
  5 3/8 in. $30
Spoon-soup, round bowl, gumbo, 7 in.. . . . . . . $40
Spoon-sugar, 5 7/8 in. $36
Spoon-teaspoon, (five o'clock),
  5 1/2 in. $20
Spoon-youth, 5 1/8 in. $33
Tablespoon, (serving spoon),
  8 1/4 in. $60

Alvin

Amston Silver

AMSTON SILVER CO. INC.

Based in Meriden, Connecticut, Amston Silver Co. Inc. went out of business in the 1960s, and its patterns were acquired by Crown Silver Co.

Athene by Amston, 1913

Butter spreader, flat handle, 5 7/8 in.. . . . . $24
Fork, 7 1/8 in.. . . . . $33
Fork-salad serving, solid piece, 9 3/8 in.. . . . $140
Fork-salad, individual, 6 1/2 in. $43
Knife-fillet, 8 5/8 in. $45
Ladle-cream, solid piece, 5 7/8 in.. . . . . $45
Sardine fork, serving, solid, large, 5 tines,
    8 1/8 in.. . . . . $80
Spoon-iced tea, 8 1/4 in. $30
Spoon-soup, round bowl, cream, 6 1/4 in.. . . . $36
Spoon-teaspoon, 5 7/8 in.. . . . . $25

Champlain by Amston, 1915

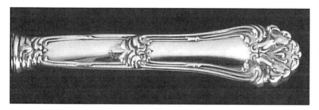

Butter spreader, flat handle, 5 7/8 in.. . . . . . . $26
Butter-master, flat handle, 7 in. $38
Carving set, 3 pieces, large, stainless blade,
    roast $230
Fork, 7 1/2 in.. . . . . $55
Fork, 7 in.. . . . . $35
Fork-cocktail, 6 in. $28

Fork-cold meat/serving, large, solid, 9 in. $85
Fork-salad, individual, 6 1/2 in. $45
Knife-modern, hollow handle, 8 7/8 in.. . . . . . . $40
Knife-modern, hollow handle, no stamp,
    8 7/8 in. $40
Knife-new french, hollow handle, no stamp,
    8 7/8 in. $40
Ladle-gravy, solid piece, 6 in.. . . . . $70
Poultry shears, 11 1/2 in.. . . . . $180
Salad set, 2 pieces, solid $220
Server-jelly, 6 1/4 in.. . . . . $38
Server-pie/stainless blade, 10 1/4 in.. . . . . $75
Spoon-casserole, smooth, solid, 8 3/4 in. . . . $110
Spoon-demitasse, 4 1/4 in. $22
Spoon-dessert/oval soup, 7 in.. . . . . $40
Spoon-iced tea, 8 3/8 in. $35
Spoon-soup, round bowl, gumbo, 6 1/4 in.. . . . $40
Spoon-teaspoon, 6 in. $20
Tablespoon, (serving spoon), 8 1/4 in.. . . . . . . $90

Ecstasy by Amston, 1951

Butter spreader, hollow handle, solid
    paddle, 6 in.. . . . . $30
Butter-master, flat handle, 6 7/8 in. $32
Fork, 7 3/4 in.. . . . . $50
Fork, 7 in.. . . . . $34
Fork-cold meat/serving, small, solid,
    7 3/4 in. $80
Fork-salad, individual, 6 3/8 in. $47
Knife-modern, hollow handle, 9 5/8 in.. . . . . . . $40
Knife-modern, hollow handle, 9 in.. . . . . $34
Spoon-demitasse, 4 1/8 in. $28
Spoon-place/oval soup, oval bowl,
    5 3/4 in. $50
Spoon-teaspoon, 5 7/8 in. $24
Tablespoon, (serving spoon), 8 1/2 in.. . . . . . . $80

BIRKS

Henry Birks & Co. was established in Montreal, Quebec, in 1879, and became Henry Birks & Sons in 1893. It acquired Gorham Co. of Canada Ltd. in 1907. The company used date letters as early as 1898, and later adopted hallmarks, which covered the years 1904 to 1962.

Chantilly by Birks

Butter spreader, flat handle, 6 1/8 in.. . . . . . . $26
Butter-master, flat handle, 6 3/8 in. $36
Fork, 7 5/8 in.. . . . . $65
Fork, 7 in.. . . . . $50
Fork-baby, 4 1/4 in. $40
Fork-cocktail, 5 3/4 in. $30
Fork-cold meat/serving, small, solid,
 7 1/8 in.. . . . . $70
Fork-lemon, 4 3/8 in. $34
Fork-pickle/olive, short handle, 6 in. $30
Fork-salad, individual, 6 1/4 in. $50
Fork-youth, 6 in.. . . . . $48
Knife-modern, hollow handle, 9 1/2 in. $50
Knife-new french, hollow handle,
 8 5/8 in.. . . . . $40
Knife-new french, hollow handle,
 9 7/8 in.. . . . . $55
Knife-youth, 7 1/4 in. $44
Ladle-gravy, solid piece, 5 7/8 in.. . . . . $80
Opener-bottle, stainless bowl, 6 in. $40
Server-cheese, stainless blade, 6 5/8 in.. . . . $48
Server-pie, stainless blade, 9 1/8 in. $80
Spoon-baby, straight handle, 4 1/4 in.. . . . . . $40
Spoon-demitasse, 4 1/4 in. $24
Spoon-dessert/oval soup, 7 in. $50
Spoon-fruit, 5 5/8 in. $50
Spoon-soup, round bowl, cream,
 5 7/8 in.. . . . . $55
Spoon-soup, round bowl, gumbo,
 6 1/2 in.. . . . . $55
Spoon-sugar, 5 1/2 in. $40
Spoon-teaspoon, (five o'clock), 5 1/8 in. $22
Spoon-teaspoon, 5 7/8 in. $26
Tablespoon, (serving spoon), 8 1/2 in.. . . . . . $90

George II-Plain by Birks, 1914

Butter spreader, flat handle, 6 3/8 in.. . . . . . . $22
Fork, 7 1/4 in.. . . . . $57
Fork-salad, individual, 6 1/4 in. $50

Knife-modern, pistol, 8 3/4 in. $36
Knife-modern, pistol, 9 3/4 in. $40
Spoon-demitasse, 4 1/8 in. $21
Spoon-fruit, 6 in.. . . . . $48
Spoon-soup, round bowl, cream,
 6 1/8 in. $45
Spoon-teaspoon, (five o'clock), 5 3/8 in. $28

Forty-one pieces Birks Lamerie: 8 luncheon knives, 8 luncheon forks, 8 salad forks, 8 large teaspoons, 6 coffee spoons, 1 sauce ladle, 1 butter knife, and 1 sugar spoon. No monogram. Twenty-five pieces made 1937, the rest 1945. Knife 9 in. with stainless steel french blade, luncheon fork 7 1/8 in. $1,000

Louis XV by Birks, 1914

Butter spreader, hollow handle, stainless
 paddle, 6 3/4 in. $34
Butter spreader, flat handle, 5 1/8 in.. . . . . . . $42
Butter spreader, flat handle, 6 in. $42
Butter-master, flat handle, 6 1/2 in. $44
Fork, 6 7/8 in.. . . . . $48
Fork, 7 1/2 in.. . . . . $70
Fork-cocktail, 5 3/4 in. $48
Fork-cold meat/serving, small, solid,
 7 1/8 in. $100
Fork-fish, silver plate tines, hollow handle,
 individual, 7 1/8 in.. . . . . $60
Fork-ice cream, 5 in. $75
Fork-pastry, 5 7/8 bar $65

Louis XV by Birks, 1914

Fork-pickle/olive, short handle, no notch,
2 tines, 6 in. $44

Fork-pickle/olive, short handle, notch,
2 tines, 6 in. $44

Fork-salad, individual, 6 in. $60

Knife-breakfast, stainless blade,
7 1/8 in. $50

Knife-carving, large, stainless blade,
roast, 14 1/4 in. $110

Knife-fish, silver plate blade, individual,
8 1/4 In. $60

Knife-fish, solid, individual, 7 1/4 in. $60

Knife-modern, hollow handle, 8 5/8 in. $50

Knife-modern, hollow handle, 9 1/2 in. $60

Knife-new french, hollow handle,
8 5/8 in. $50

Knife-old french, hollow handle, 8 7/8 in. $50

Knife-youth, 7 1/8 in. $55

Ladle-cream, solid piece, 6 in. $70

Nutcracker, solid, 6 1/2 in. $100

Pick-butter, 2 tines, 5 5/8 in. $60

Server/knife, fish, stainless blade, 10 in. $100

Server-pie, stainless blade, 10 1/8 in. $80

Spoon-casserole, smooth, solid,
gold wash, 7 5/8 in. $140

Spoon-demitasse, 4 in. $22

Spoon-dessert/oval soup, 7 1/8 in. $70

Spoon-place/oval soup, 6 3/4 in. $70

Spoon-salad serving/wooden bowl,
10 1/8 in. $60

Spoon-soup, round bowl, bouillon,
4 7/8 in. $50

Spoon-soup, round bowl, bouillon,
5 1/8 in. $50

Spoon-soup, round bowl, cream,
5 3/4 in. $60

Spoon-soup, round bowl, gumbo,
6 7/8 in. $80

Spoon-sugar, 5 1/2 in. $55

Spoon-sugar, 6 in. $55

Spoon-teaspoon, (five o'clock), 5 1/4 in. $18

Spoon-teaspoon, 5 3/4 in. $30

Tablespoon, (serving spoon), 8 1/2 in. $80

Tongs-sugar, 4 1/8 in. $65

Old English-Plain by Birks

Fork, tipped end, 7 3/4 in. $60

Fork-salad, individual, 5 7/8 in. $45

Spoon-teaspoon, 5 5/8 in. $30

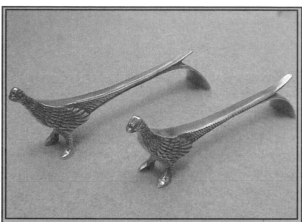

Peacock knife rests. 3 1/4 in. long; 1 1/4 in. high; good condition; marked "BIRKS STERLING." $175/pair

CONCORD SILVER CO.

Concord Silver Co. began in 1925 in Concord, New Hampshire. It went into bankruptcy and was reorganized as Concord Silversmiths Ltd. in 1939. Silver production was halted in 1942. Crown Silver Co. later purchased Concord's dies.

Concord by Concord, 1930

Butter spreader, flat handle, 5 5/8 in.........$23
Butter-master, flat handle, 7 in..............$38
Carving set, two piece, large stainless
    blade, roast $140
Fork, 7 1/4 in.............................$45
Fork, 7 7/8 in.............................$60
Fork-baby, 4 1/2 in.......................$40
Fork-cocktail, 5 7/8 in....................$30
Fork-cold meat/serving, medium, solid,
    8 3/8 in................................$85
Fork-ice cream, 5 3/4 in...................$46
Fork-lemon, 3 flared tines, 4 1/2 in..........$32

Fork-pickle/olive, short handle, 6 1/8 in....... $30
Fork-salad, individual, 6 1/4 in. $40
Knife-new french, hollow handle,
    8 5/8 in. $35
Knife-new french, hollow handle,
    9 3/4 in. $45
Knife-new french, hollow handle, 9 in. $35
Ladle-gravy, solid piece, 5 7/8 in............ $85
Server-cheese, stainless blade, 6 5/8 in..... $48
Server-jelly, 6 1/2 in. $35
Server-pie, stainless blade, 10 1/8 in........ $60
Spoon-bon-bon, 4 7/8 in. $44
Spoon-demitasse, 4 3/8 in................. $20
Spoon-dessert/oval soup, 7 1/4 in. $50
Spoon-iced tea, 7 5/8 in................... $40
Spoon-soup, round bowl, bouillon,
    5 3/8 in. $36
Spoon-soup, round bowl, cream,
    6 3/8 in. $45
Spoon-soup, round bowl, gumbo, 7 in........ $50
Spoon-sugar, 6 1/8 in..................... $40
Spoon-teaspoon, 5 7/8 in.................. $23
Tablespoon, (serving spoon), 8 3/4 in. $85

DOMINICK & HAFF

Dominick & Haff began in New York in 1872, and earned a reputation as an innovative designer of silver wares. The firm's success led it to acquire the assets of other manufacturers, including the dies of Adams & Shaw in 1880. The company was sold to Reed & Barton in 1928.

Century by Dominick & Haff, 1900

Butter spreader, flat handle, 5 5/8 in.. . . . . $34
Fork, 7 3/4 in.. . . . . $80
Fork, 7 in.. . . . . $45
Fork-cocktail, gold wash, 5 3/8 in.. . . . . $30
Fork-cold meat/serving, small, solid,
   7 1/2 in.. . . . . $90
Fork-salad, individual, 6 in. $70
Knife-old french, hollow handle,
   8 5/8 in. $50
Knife-old french, hollow handle,
   9 3/4 in. $60
Ladle-gravy, solid piece, 6 1/4 in.. . . . . $94
Spoon-bon-bon, 4 3/4 in.. . . . . $50
Spoon-demitasse, gold wash, 4 1/4 in. $28
Spoon-dessert/oval soup, 7 in. $50
Spoon-fruit, 5 5/8 in. $36
Spoon-iced tea, 7 3/8 in. $50
Spoon-place/oval soup, 6 3/8 in.. . . . . $56
Spoon-salt/master, 3 1/2 in.. . . . . $28
Spoon-soup, round bowl, cream,
   5 1/4 in.. . . . . $60
Spoon-soup, round bowl, gumbo, 7 in. $60
Spoon-sugar, 6 1/8 in.. . . . . $48
Spoon-teaspoon, (five o'clock),
   5 5/8 in.. . . . . $28
Spoon-teaspoon, 5 7/8 in. $36
Tablespoon, (serving spoon), 8 3/8 in.. . . . . . $90
Tongs-sugar, 4 in. $70

Charles II by Dominick & Haff, 1894

Fork, 6 7/8 in.. . . . . $60
Spoon-chocolate, short handle, 5 in.. . . . . . . $40
Spoon-demitasse, 4 1/4 in. $26

Spoon-dessert/oval soup, 7 in.. . . . . $60
Spoon-soup, round bowl, gumbo, 7 in.. . . . . . $70
Spoon-teaspoon, (five o'clock), 5 5/8 in. $28

Chippendale by Dominick & Haff, 1885

Fork-youth, 6 3/8 in.. . . . . $48
Knife-youth, 7 1/8 in. $40

Contempora by Dominick & Haff, 1930

Butter-master, flat handle, 7 1/2 in. $45
Fork, 7 1/4 in.. . . . . $45
Fork-cold meat/serving, large, solid,
   9 1/8 in. $90
Fork-salad, individual, bar, 6 1/4 in.. . . . . $46
Knife-new french, hollow handle,
   9 3/4 in. $50
Knife-new french, hollow handle, stainless
   blade, 8 5/8 in. $35
Ladle-gravy, solid piece, 6 1/2 in.. . . . . $90
Spoon-soup, round bowl, gumbo,
   6 7/8 in. $55
Spoon-sugar, 6 1/8 in. $44
Spoon-teaspoon, 6 in. $24
Tablespoon, (serving spoon), 8 5/8 in.. . . . . . $80

King by Dominick & Haff, 1880

Fork, 7 5/8 in.. . . . . $80
Fork-cocktail, 5 1/4 in. $40
Fork-fish, solid, individual, 7 1/4 in. $60
Knife-new french, hollow handle,
   8 3/4 in. $70
Knife-old french, hollow handle, silver
   plate blade, 8 1/2 in.. . . . . $70
Spoon-soup, round bowl, cream, 6 in. $60

Spoon-soup, round bowl, gumbo, 7 in. $70
Spoon-teaspoon, 6 in. $40
Tablespoon, (serving spoon), 8 1/2 in. $80

The following pieces have monograms:
Fork, 6 7/8 in. $36
Fork, 7 5/8 in. $50
Knife-new french, hollow handle, 8 3/4 in. $60
Spoon-demitasse, 4 1/4 in. $21
Spoon-dessert/oval soup, 7 in. $40
Spoon-soup, round bowl, bouillon,
    5 1/4 in. $40
Spoon-soup, round bowl, gumbo, 7 in. $50
Spoon-teaspoon, 6 in. $24
Tablespoon, (serving spoon), 8 1/2 in. $70
Tablespoon, (serving spoon), pierced,
    8 1/2 in. $80

La Salle by Dominick & Haff, 1928

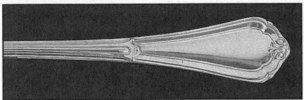

Butter spreader, flat handle, 5 7/8 in. $22
Butter-master, flat handle, 7 5/8 in. $43
Carving set, two piece, small, stainless
    blade, steak. $120
Fork, 7 1/4 in. $34
Fork, 7 7/8 in. $44
Fork-baby, 4 1/8 in. $40
Fork-cocktail, 3 tines, 5 5/8 in. $20
Fork-cold meat/serving, medium, solid,
    8 3/4 in. $80
Fork-cold meat/serving, small, solid,
    7 7/8 in. $70
Fork-dessert, no bar, 6 1/4 in. $50
Fork-salad, individual, bar, 6 1/4 in. $43
Knife-carving, large, stainless blade, roast,
    11 3/8 in. $70
Knife-new french, hollow handle,
    9 3/4 in. $45
Knife-new french, hollow handle, bolster,
    8 7/8 in. $30
Knife-new french, hollow handle, bolster,
    9 3/4 in. $45
Ladle-cream, solid piece, 5 1/2 in. $48
Ladle-gravy, solid piece, 6 3/4 in. $90
Server-jelly, 6 3/4 in. $34
Spoon-casserole, smooth, solid,
    8 3/4 in. $110

Spoon-dessert/oval soup, 7 1/8 in. $44
Spoon-iced tea, 7 1/2 in. $32
Spoon-soup, round bowl, bouillon, 5 in. $25
Spoon-soup, round bowl, cream, 6 1/4 in. $50
Spoon-sugar, 6 1/4 in. $38
Spoon-teaspoon, 6 in. $22
Tablespoon, (serving spoon), 8 3/8 in. $70

Labors of Cupid by Dominick & Haff, 1900

(The following pieces are newer examples of this
    pattern.)
Butter-master, hollow handle, 6 7/8 in. $90
Fork, 7 7/8 in. $130
Fork, 7 in. $120
Fork-cold meat/serving, large, solid, 4 tines,
    9 3/8 in. $300
Fork-salad, individual, bar, 6 1/8 in. $100
Knife-new french, hollow handle, 8 3/4 in. $70
Knife-new french, hollow handle, 9 5/8 in. . . . $100
Ladle-cream, solid piece, 5 3/8 in. $180
Ladle-gravy, solid piece, 6 1/8 in. $160
Salad set, 2 pieces, solid $600
Server-asparagus, hollow handle, silver
    plate hood, 9 1/2 in. $80
Server-pie, stainless blade, 9 3/8 in. $80
Spoon-dessert/oval soup, 7 in. $130
Spoon-sugar shell, 6 in. $150
Spoon-teaspoon, 6 1/8 in. $60
Tablespoon, (serving spoon), 8 5/8 in. $180
Tablespoon, (serving spoon), pierced,
    8 5/8 in. $180

Marie Antoinette by Dominick & Haff, 1917

Butter spreader, flat handle, 5 3/4 in. $27
Fork, 7 1/8 in. $45
Fork, 7 3/4 in. $55

Dominick & Haff

Fork-dessert, bar, pierce, 6 1/8 in.......... $50
Fork-lemon, 4 7/8 in..................... $35
Fork-salad, individual, heart slot,
    6 1/8 in............................ $56
Fork-salad, individual, point slot,
    6 1/4 in............................ $56
Knife-old french, hollow handle, silver plate
    blade, 9 in.......................... $40
Server-cheese, silver plate blade,
    6 1/8 in............................ $70
Spoon-dessert/oval soup, 7 1/8 in. $55
Spoon-fruit, 5 3/4 in.................... $44
Spoon-iced tea, 7 5/8 in................. $34
Spoon-soup, round bowl, bouillon,
    5 3/8 in............................ $50
Spoon-soup, round bowl, gumbo, 7 in. $65
Spoon-sugar, 1 3/4 in. bowl, 5 5/8 in. $40
Spoon-sugar, 2 in. bowl, 6 in. $40
Spoon-teaspoon, (five o'clock),
    5 3/4 in............................ $18
Spoon-teaspoon, 6 in.................... $28

The following pieces have monograms:
Butter spreader, flat handle, 5 3/4 in......... $21
Butter-master, flat handle, 7 3/8 in. $33
Carving set, 3 piece, large stainless
    blade, roast $170
Fork, 7 1/8 in........................... $34
Fork, 7 3/4 in........................... $42
Fork-baby, 4 3/8 in. $32
Fork-dessert, 6 1/8 in................... $38
Fork-ice cream, 5 5/8 in................. $38
Fork-lemon, 4 7/8 in.................... $27
Fork-salad, individual, 6 1/8 in. $42
Knife-blunt, hollow handle, 9 3/4 in......... $38
Ladle-cream, solid piece, 4 7/8 in.......... $40
Server-cheese, silver plate blade,
    6 1/8 in............................ $57
Server-jelly, 6 1/4 in. $29
Server-pie, silver plate blade, 10 1/4 in. $57
Spoon-casserole, pierced, solid, 9 1/4 in. ... $100
Spoon-demitasse, 4 1/4 in. $19
Spoon-dessert/oval soup, 7 1/8 in. $42
Spoon-fruit, 5 3/4 in. $33
Spoon-iced tea, 7 5/8 in. $27
Spoon-olive, short, pierced bowl, 7 1/2 in. $75
Spoon-salt/master, 3 1/4 in................ $21
Spoon-soup, round bowl, bouillon, 5 3/8 in.... $38
Spoon-soup, round bowl, gumbo, 7 in. $53
Spoon-sugar, 6 in....................... $34
Spoon-teaspoon, 6 in.................... $23
Tablespoon, (serving spoon), 8 3/8 in........ $70
Tongs-sugar, 4 1/8 in. $53

Mazarin by Dominick & Haff, 1892

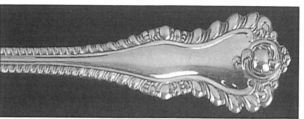

Butter spreader-hollow handle, silver plate
    blade, 6 1/8 in...................... $42
Fork, 7 in.............................. $50
Fork-strawberry, 5 in..................... $40
Ladle-gravy, solid piece, 6 1/8 in........... $120
Spoon-bon-bon, 4 3/4 in.................. $40
Spoon-fruit, 1 7/8 in. bowl, 5 1/2 in. $38
Spoon-fruit, 2 in. bowl, 5 3/4 in.......... $38
Spoon-fruit, gold wash, 5 1/2 in............ $38
Spoon-fruit, gold wash, 5 3/4 in............ $38
Spoon-iced tea, 7 1/2 in. $90
Spoon-preserve, gold wash, 7 5/8 in........ $70
Spoon-soup, round bowl, gumbo, 6 7/8 in.... $70
Spoon-sugar, gold wash, 5 5/8 in. $45
Spoon-teaspoon, (five o'clock), 5 3/4 in. $22
Spoon-youth, 5 1/4 in. $50
Tablespoon, (serving spoon), 5 1/2 in.
    handle, 8 1/2 in..................... $70
Tablespoon, (serving spoon), 5 1/8 in.
    handle, 8 in........................ $70

The following pieces have monograms:
Fork, 7 in.............................. $36
Fork-salad, individual, 6 1/4 in. $80
Fork-strawberry, 5 in..................... $28
Spoon-demitasse, 4 1/4 in. $23
Spoon-dessert/oval soup, 7 1/8 in.......... $45
Spoon-soup, round bowl, gumbo, 6 7/8 in..... $50
Spoon-teaspoon, 6 in. $22
Spoon-youth, 5 1/4 in. $36
Tablespoon, (serving spoon), 8 1/2 in........ $53
Tablespoon, (serving spoon), 8 in........... $53

New King by Dominick & Haff, 1898

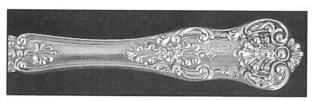

Knife-old french, hollow handle, silver plate
    blade, 8 1/2 in...................... $70
Spoon-dessert/oval soup, 7 in.............. $80

Spoon-soup, round bowl, cream, 3 3/4 in.
   handle, 5 1/4 in.. . . . . $80

The following pieces have monograms:
Fork, 6 7/8 in.. . . . . $50
Knife-old french, hollow handle, 9 3/4 in.. . . . . $70
Spoon-demitasse, 4 1/4 in. $32
Spoon-soup, round bowl, bouillon, 4 3/4 in.. . . $60
Spoon-soup, round bowl, cream, 5 1/4 in.. . . . . $72
Spoon-soup, round bowl, gumbo, 7 in. $70
Tablespoon, (serving spoon), 8 3/8 in.. . . . . . . $90

No. 10 by Dominick & Haff, 1896

Fork, 6 7/8 in.. . . . . $50
Fork, 7 3/4 in.. . . . . $70
Fork-cocktail, 5 3/8 in.. . . . . $30
Fork-cold meat/serving, medium, solid,
   8 1/2 in.. . . . . $100
Fork-ice cream, 5 1/4 in. $60
Knife-old french, hollow handle, 8 1/2 in.. . . . . $60
Ladle-cream, solid piece, 5 1/8 in.. . . . . $53
Ladle-gravy, solid piece, 6 in.. . . . . $90
Server-fish, solid, large, 11 1/4 in.. . . . . $400
Spoon-bon-bon, 4 3/4 in.. . . . . $45
Spoon-egg, gold wash, 4 3/8 in. $48
Spoon-soup, round bowl, gumbo, 7 in. $70
Spoon-sugar, 6 1/8 in.. . . . . $48
Spoon-teaspoon, 6 in.. . . . . $26

The following pieces have monograms:
Fork, 6 7/8 in.. . . . . $38
Fork, 7 3/4 in.. . . . . $53
Fork-youth, 6 1/4 in.. . . . . $38
Knife-blunt, hollow handle, 8 1/2 in.. . . . . $45
Knife-old french, hollow handle, 10 in.. . . . . . . $60
Knife-youth, 7 1/8 in. $32
Spoon-chocolate, short handle, large,
   4 1/4 in.. . . . . $36
Spoon-demitasse, 4 1/4 in. $21
Spoon-dessert/oval soup, 7 in. $45
Spoon-five o'clock/youth, 5 1/4 in.. . . . . $18
Spoon-soup, round bowl, gumbo, 7 in. $53
Spoon-sugar, 6 1/8 in.. . . . . $36
Spoon-teaspoon, (five o'clock), 5 5/8 in. $21
Spoon-teaspoon, 6 in.. . . . . $20
Tablespoon, (serving spoon), 8 3/8 in.. . . . . . . $70

Old English Antique by Dominick & Haff, 1880

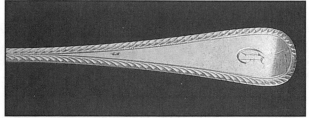

Butter spreader, flat handle, 5 7/8 in.. . . . . . . $30
Butter-master, flat handle, 7 3/8 in. $46
Fork, 7 1/8 in.. . . . . $45
Fork, 7 7/8 in.. . . . . $60
Fork-cocktail, no bevel, 5 1/4 in.. . . . . $28
Fork-cold meat/serving, medium, solid,
   8 7/8 in. $85
Fork-cold meat/serving, small, solid,
   7 3/4 in. $80
Fork-cold meat/serving, small, solid, no
   bevel, 7 1/8 in. $80
Fork-dessert, bar, 6 1/8 in.. . . . . $50
Fork-ice cream, 5 3/8 in. $50
Fork-pickle/olive, short handle, 5 3/8 in.. . . . . . $30
Fork-salad, individual, no bar, 6 1/8 in. $55
Ladle-gravy, solid piece, 6 1/2 in.. . . . . $85
Server-jelly, 6 3/8 in.. . . . . $30
Spoon-demitasse, 4 1/2 in. $24
Spoon-dessert/oval soup, 7 in.. . . . . $50
Spoon-iced tea, 7 3/8 in. $34
Spoon-salad serving, solid piece, 8 in. $100
Spoon-soup, round bowl, bouillon, 3 1/8 in.
   handle, 4 3/4 in.. $44
Spoon-soup, round bowl, bouillon, 3 3/4 in.
   handle, 5 1/4 in.. $44
Spoon-soup, round bowl, cream, 6 in. $50
Spoon-sugar shell, 6 1/4 in.. . . . . $40
Spoon-teaspoon, 6 1/8 in. $30
Tablespoon, (serving spoon), 8 3/8 in.. . . . . . . $80

Pointed Antique by Dominick & Haff, 1895

Butter spreader, flat handle, 5 7/8 in.. . . . . . . $20
Butter-master, flat handle, 7 3/8 in. $30
Fork, 7 1/4 in.. . . . . $24
Fork, 8 in.. . . . . $50
Fork-baby, 4 1/4 in.. $35
Fork-carving, small, stainless prongs/steak,
   8 7/8 in. $60
Fork-cold meat/serving, medium, solid, 8 in. . . $50

Fork-dessert, bar pierce, 6 3/8 in. $38
Fork-fish, solid, individual, no slot, 6 1/4 in. . . . $70
Fork-ice cream, 5 5/8 in. $40
Fork-lemon, 1 3/4 in. tines, 5 1/8 in. $23
Fork-pickle/olive, short handle, 1 3/8 in. tines,
    5 1/2 in. $26
Fork-salad, individual, heart slot, 6 3/8 in. $33
Fork-youth, 6 1/2 in. $60
Knife-crumb/crumber, large, 12 1/2 in. $360
Knife-new french, hollow handle, stainless
    blade, 8 3/4 in. $35
Knife-new french, hollow handle, stainless
    blade, 9 5/8 in. $50
Knife-old french, hollow handle, silver plate
    blade, 8 1/2 in. $35
Knife-old french, hollow handle, stainless
    blade, 8 1/2 in. $35
Knife-old french, hollow handle, stainless
    blade, 9 5/8 in. $50
Knife-orange, silver plate blade, 7 1/2 in. $45
Knife-orange, silver plate blade, 7 in. $45
Ladle-cream, solid piece, 1 5/8 in. wide bowl,
    4 5/8 in. $43
Ladle-cream, solid piece, 2 in. wide bowl,
    5 1/4 in. $43
Ladle-gravy, solid piece, 6 5/8 in. $70
Server-jelly, tip bowl, 6 3/8 in. $30
Server-pie and cake, stainless blade,
    10 1/2 in. $70
Spoon-baby, straight handle, 4 1/4 in. $35
Spoon-bon-bon, no pierce, 5 1/8 in. $32
Spoon-demitasse, 3 1/8 in. handle,
    4 5/8 in. $18
Spoon-fruit, no rib bowl, 5 3/8 in. $40
Spoon-fruit, rib bowl, 6 in. $40
Spoon-iced tea, 7 3/4 in. $30
Spoon-infant feeding, 5 1/2 in. $40
Spoon-soup, round bowl, bouillon, 3 1/4 in.
    handle, 4 3/4 in. $26
Spoon-soup, round bowl, bouillon, 3 7/8 in.
    handle, 5 3/8 in. $26
Spoon-soup, round bowl, cream, 6 1/8 in. $32
Spoon-soup, round bowl, gumbo, 7 1/8 in. . . . $40
Spoon-sugar shell, 5 1/2 in. $25
Spoon-sugar shell, 6 1/2 in. $25
Spoon-teaspoon, (five o'clock), 5 5/8 in. $20
Spoon-teaspoon, 6 1/8 in. $14
Spoon-youth, 5 1/2 in. $20
Tablespoon, (serving spoon), 8 1/2 in. $50
Tablespoon, (serving spoon), pierced,
    8 1/2 in. $70
Tongs-sugar, 5 1/8 in. $50

Queen Anne-Plain by Dominick & Haff, 1910

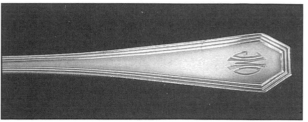

Butter spreader, flat handle, 2 3/4 in. blade,
    5 5/8 in. $27
Butter spreader, flat handle, 3 in. blade,
    5 7/8 in. $27
Carving set, 2 pieces, small, stainless blade,
    steak $130
Fork, 6 7/8 in. $33
Fork, 7 5/8 in. $50
Fork-cocktail, 5 1/2 in. $22
Fork-cold meat/serving, small, solid,
    7 1/2 in. $80
Fork-dessert, no bar, 5 3/4 in. $44
Fork-fish, solid, individual, no bevel, 7 in. $70
Fork-ice cream, pierce, 5 1/2 in. $46
Fork-pickle/olive, short handle, 3 tines,
    5 5/8 in. $32
Fork-salad, individual, bar, 6 1/4 in. $43
Fork-strawberry, 5 in. $40
Fork-youth, 6 3/8 in. $48
Knife-blunt, hollow handle, 8 1/2 in. $34
Knife-fruit, silver plate blade, individual,
    6 3/8 in. $35
Knife-fruit, stainless blade, individual,
    6 3/8 in. $35
Knife-new french, hollow handle, bolster,
    9 5/8 in. $50
Knife-old french, hollow handle, silver
    plate blade, 9 3/4 in. $50
Knife-old french, hollow handle, stainless
    blade, 8 1/4 in. $34
Knife-old french, hollow handle, stainless
    blade, 9 3/4 in. $50
Knife-orange, silver plate blade, 7 in. $40
Knife-sharpener/steel, small, steak,
    10 3/4 in. $65
Ladle-gravy, solid piece, 6 1/8 in. $90
Sardine fork, serving, solid, 6 tines, 6 in. $85
Server-cheese, stainless blade, 6 1/8 in. $46
Server-jelly, 6 1/4 in. $35
Spoon-bon-bon, 4 3/4 in. $45
Spoon-demitasse, 4 3/8 in. $20
Spoon-dessert/oval soup, 7 1/8 in. $50

Spoon-fruit, 5 1/2 in. $38
Spoon-ice cream, rim bowl, 5 1/2 in. $45
Spoon-iced tea, 7 1/2 in. $38
Spoon-olive, short, pierced bowl, 5 7/8 in. . . . $90
Spoon-soup, round bowl, bouillon, 3 5/8 in.
   handle, 5 1/4 in. $28
Spoon-soup, round bowl, bouillon, 3 in.
   handle, 4 5/8 in. $28
Spoon-soup, round bowl, cream, 5 7/8 in. . . . $45
Spoon-soup, round bowl, gumbo, 6 7/8 in. . . . $48
Spoon-sugar, rim bowl, 6 in. $34
Spoon-teaspoon, (five o'clock), 5 5/8 in. . . . $18
Spoon-teaspoon, 5 7/8 in. $22
Tablespoon, (serving spoon), 8 1/4 in. $80
Tongs-sugar, claw tip, 3 1/4 in. $60
Tongs-sugar, claw tip, 4 1/2 in. $60

Renaissance by Dominick & Haff, 1894

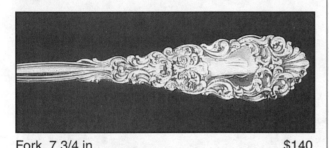

Fork, 7 3/4 in. $140
Spoon-demitasse, 4 1/4 in. $70

The following pieces have monograms:
Fork, 7 3/4 in. $120
Fork, 7 in. $80
Ladle-cream, solid piece, 5 1/8 in. $140
Spoon-casserole, solid, oversize, 9 in. $500
Spoon-claret, solid piece, 14 1/2 in. $400
Spoon-cracker, 7 3/8 in. $540
Spoon-jam, 7 1/4 in. $130
Spoon-teaspoon, (five o'clock), 5 5/8 in. $50
Spoon-teaspoon, 6 in. $65

Rococo by Dominick & Haff, 1888

Butter spreader, flat handle, 5 1/4 in. $80
X Fork, 6 7/8 in. $45
Fork, 7 1/2 in. $80

Knife-fruit, solid, individual, 6 1/2 in. $80
Spoon-bon-bon, 4 3/8 in. $55
Spoon-demitasse, 4 1/4 in. $30
Spoon-dessert/oval soup, 7 1/8 in. $60
Spoon-teaspoon, 6 in. $28

The following pieces have monograms:
Spoon-dessert/oval soup, 7 1/8 in. $45
Spoon-teaspoon, 6 in. $23
Tongs-sugar, 3 1/4 in. $63

Victoria by Dominick & Haff, 1901

Spoon-soup, round bowl, bouillon, 4 7/8 in. . . . $60
Tablespoon, (serving spoon), 8 3/8 in. $110

The following pieces have monograms:
Fork, 7 3/4 in. $60
Fork, 7 in. $45
Knife-blunt, hollow handle, 8 1/2 in. $55
Knife-old french, hollow handle, 9 3/4 in. $60

Virginia by Dominick & Haff, 1912

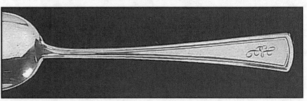

Butter spreader, flat handle, 5 5/8 in. $25
Fork, 7 1/8 in. $40
Fork, 7 3/4 in. $50
Fork-dessert, bar, 6 1/8 in. $45
Fork-pickle/olive, short handle, 5 5/8 in. $32
Fork-salad, individual, heart slot, 6 1/8 in. . . . $46
Knife-blunt, hollow handle, silver plate blade,
   9 5/8 in. $45
Knife-old french, hollow handle, stainless
   blade, 9 5/8 in. $45
Ladle-gravy, solid piece, 4 5/8 in. handle,
   6 1/4 in. $90
Server-jelly, 6 1/8 in. $34
Spoon-baby, straight handle, 4 1/4 in. $35
Spoon-bon-bon, pierced, 4 7/8 in. $46
Spoon-dessert/oval soup, 7 1/8 in. $50
Spoon-iced tea, 7 1/2 in. $37
Spoon-olive, short, pierced bowl, 5 7/8 in. . . . $80
Spoon-soup, round bowl, bouillon, 5 1/4 in. . . . $36
Spoon-soup, round bowl, gumbo, 7 in. $50
Spoon-sugar, 5 7/8 in. $45
Spoon-teaspoon, 5 3/4 in. $24
Tablespoon, (serving spoon), 8 3/8 in. $80

Dominick & Haff

Dominick & Haff floral acid etched fried egg server. The elongated oval blade is pierced; fine overall condition; 8 1/8 in.; monogrammed "MEL" (reverse) in conjoined script. $350

Dominick & Haff floral acid etched fish set. Excellent condition; monogrammed "MEL" in conjoined script (reverse); length of slice: 10 3/8 in. $775

Three-piece Dominick & Haff youth set, "pro patria." Each piece is embossed with the United States seal, and the motto "pro patria." Excellent condition, no monogram, length of spoon: 4 1/4 in. $185

DURGIN

William B. Durgin started his company in Concord, New Hampshire in 1853, and it grew to become one of the largest flatware and hollowware manufacturers in the United States. Gorham Co. purchased the firm in 1905, and production was moved to Providence, Rhode Island in 1931.

Bead by Durgin, 1893

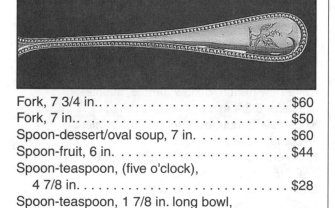

Fork, 7 3/4 in.. . . . . $60
Fork, 7 in.. . . . . $50
Spoon-dessert/oval soup, 7 in. $60
Spoon-fruit, 6 in. $44
Spoon-teaspoon, (five o'clock),
    4 7/8 in.. . . . . $28
Spoon-teaspoon, 1 7/8 in. long bowl,
    5 3/4 in.. . . . . $26
Spoon-teaspoon, 2 1/4 in. long bowl,
    6 1/8 in.. . . . . $26
Tablespoon, (serving spoon), 8 1/4 in.. . . . . . . $75

Chatham by Durgin, 1915

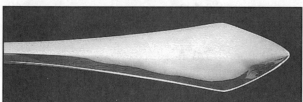

Butter spreader, flat handle, 2 3/4 in. handle,
    5 1/4 in.. . . . . $18
Butter spreader, flat handle, 3 in. handle,
    5 5/8 in.. . . . . $18
Fork, 7 1/4 in.. . . . . $45
Fork, 7 7/8 in.. . . . . $50
Fork-baby, 4 1/4 in. $36
Fork-cocktail, 5 5/8 in. $28
Fork-cold meat/serving, small, solid,
    7 1/2 in.. . . . . $60
Fork-ice cream, 5 1/2 in. $38
Fork-pickle/olive, long handle,
    7 1/2 in. $45

Fork-salad, individual, 4 tines,
    6 1/8 in. $30
Fork-youth, 6 1/4 in.. $38
Knife-old french, hollow handle, bolster,
    8 3/4 in. $33
Knife-old french, hollow handle, bolster,
    9 3/4 in. $45
Ladle-cream, solid piece, 5 1/4 in. $40
Ladle-gravy, solid piece, 6 in.. . . . . $70
Sardine fork, serving, solid, 5 tines,
    6 in. $80
Server-cheese, silver plate blade,
    6 3/8 in. $55
Server-jelly, 6 1/8 in.. $30
Server-pie and cake, stainless blade,
    10 in. $55
Server-pie, silver plate blade,
    10 1/8 in. $55
Server-pie, silver plate blade,
    9 5/8 in. $55
Spoon-demitasse, 4 1/4 in. $18
Spoon-fruit, 5 3/4 in.. $33
Spoon-iced tea, 7 1/2 in. $34
Spoon-soup, round bowl, bouillon,
    5 3/8 in. $28
Spoon-soup, round bowl, gumbo,
    7 in. $40
Spoon-sugar, 6 in. $40
Spoon-teaspoon, (five o'clock),
    5 5/8 in. $17
Spoon-teaspoon, 5 7/8 in. $24
Tablespoon, (serving spoon),
    8 5/8 in. $60
Tongs-sugar, 3 5/8 in.. . . . . $55

Chatham, Hammered by Durgin, 1915

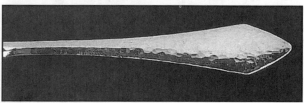

Butter spreader, flat handle, 5 1/4 in. $30
Butter-master, flat handle, 6 7/8 in. $40
Carving set, 2 pieces, small, stainless blade,
    steak $150
Fork, 7 1/4 in.. . . . . $50
Fork, 8 in.. . . . . $70
Fork-cocktail, 5 1/2 in. $34
Fork-cold meat/serving, small, solid,
    7 1/2 in. $90

Fork-ice cream, 5 1/2 in. $55
Fork-lemon, 5 in. $34
Fork-pickle/olive, long handle,
   7 5/8 in. $50
Fork-pie, 3 tines, bar, 6 in. $55
Fork-salad, individual, 6 1/8 in. $50
Ladle-cream, solid piece, 5 1/4 in. $50
Ladle-gravy, solid piece, 6 3/8 in. $90
Server-jelly, 6 1/4 in. $36
Server-tomato, solid piece, 8 1/8 in. $100
Spoon-casserole, smooth, solid,
   8 3/4 in. $100
Spoon-demitasse, 4 1/4 in. $24
Spoon-dessert/oval soup, 7 1/4 in. $55
Spoon-soup, round bowl, bouillon,
   5 3/8 in. $55
Spoon-soup, round bowl, cream,
   6 1/4 in. $50
Spoon-soup, round bowl, gumbo, 7 in. $55
Spoon-sugar, 5 7/8 in. $44
Spoon-teaspoon, 5 7/8 in. $30
Tablespoon, (serving spoon),
   8 5/8 in. $90
Tongs-sugar, 4 5/8 in. $60

Chrysanthemum by Durgin, 1893

Fork-cocktail, gold wash, 5 1/2 in. $80
Fork-youth, 6 1/2 in. $100
Spoon-demitasse, 4 1/4 in. $70
The following pieces have monograms:
Fork, 7 1/2 in. $120
Fork-cocktail, 5 1/2 in. $75
Spoon-teaspoon, 5 3/4 in. $75
Spoon-casserole, smooth, solid,
   8 7/8 in. $480

> Antique American silver youth knife, fork, and
>   spoon in the Chrysanthemum pattern (1893);
>   made by the Wm. B. Durgin Co. of Concord,
>   New Hampshire, and retailed by James R.
>   Armiger of Baltimore, Maryland. Monogram
>   "HWM." Original green cloth gift box. Knife
>   7 3/4 in., fork 6 in., spoon 5 3/4 in. $280

Colfax by Durgin, 1922

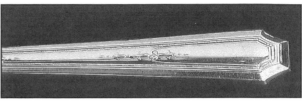

Butter spreader, flat handle, 5 1/2 in. $30
Fork, 7 1/4 in. $40
Fork, 7 7/8 in. $60
Fork-cold meat/serving, medium, solid,
   8 3/4 in. $100
Fork-lemon, 5 in. $35
Fork-pickle/olive, short handle, 5 5/8 in. $35
Fork-salad, individual, 6 1/4 in. $45
Knife-fruit, stainless blade/individual,
   6 7/8 in. $40
Knife-new french, hollow handle, stainless
   blade, 8 3/4 in. $35
Knife-new french, hollow handle, stainless
   blade, 9 5/8 in. $47
Knife-old french, hollow handle, bolster,
   9 1/8 in. $35
Ladle-cream, solid piece, 5 in. $50
Ladle-gravy, solid piece, 6 in. $100
Server-cheese, silver plate blade,
   6 1/2 in. $65
Server-jelly, 6 1/4 in. $35
Server-pie, silver plate blade, 9 1/2 in. $70
Spoon-bon-bon, 4 7/8 in. $44
Spoon-dessert/oval soup, 7 1/8 in. $70
Spoon-fruit, 5 7/8 in. $40
Spoon-relish, 6 1/4 in. $40
Spoon-soup, round bowl, bouillon,
   5 1/4 in. $30
Spoon-sugar, 5 7/8 in. $40
Spoon-teaspoon, (five o'clock), 5 5/8 in. $18
Spoon-teaspoon, 5 7/8 in. $24
Tablespoon, (serving spoon), 8 1/2 in. $70
Tongs-sugar, 3 5/8 in. $60

The following pieces have monograms:
Butter spreader, flat handle, 5 1/2 in. $25
Butter-master, flat handle, 6 7/8 in. $40
Carving set, two piece, small-stainless
   blade, steak $120
Fork, 7 1/4 in. $30
Fork, 7 7/8 in. $50
Fork-carving, small, stainless prongs,
   steak, 9 in. $60
Fork-chipped beef/medium, 8 3/4 in. $90
Fork-cocktail, 5 5/8 in. $20

Fork-cold meat/serving, medium, solid,
8 3/4 in. $85
Fork-cold meat/serving, small, solid,
7 1/2 in. $75
Fork-ice cream, 5 1/2 in. $42
Fork-lemon, 5 in. $32
Fork-pickle/olive, short handle, 5 5/8 in. $32
Fork-pickle/olive, short handle, 6 1/8 in. $32
Fork-salad, individual, 6 1/4 in. $38
Knife-new french, hollow handle,
8 3/4 in. $30
Knife-new french, hollow handle,
9 5/8 in. $40
Knife-old french, hollow handle,
9 7/8 in. $40
Knife-old french, hollow handle, bolster,
8 5/8 in. $30
Knife-old french, hollow handle, bolster,
9 5/8 in. $40
Ladle-cream, solid piece, 5 in. $48
Ladle-gravy, solid piece, 6 in. $80
Server-jelly, 6 1/4 in. $32
Server-tomato, solid piece, 6 5/8 in. $95
Spoon-bon-bon, 4 7/8 in. $42
Spoon-demitasse, 4 1/8 in. $20
Spoon-dessert/oval soup, 7 1/8 in. $55
Spoon-five o'clock/youth, 5 in. $20
Spoon-fruit, 5 7/8 in. $35
Spoon-iced tea, 7 1/2 in. $35
Spoon-relish, 6 1/4 in. $38
Spoon-soup, round bowl, bouillon,
5 1/4 in. $25
Spoon-soup, round bowl, gumbo,
6 7/8 in. $45
Spoon-sugar, 5 7/8 in. $35
Spoon-teaspoon, (five o'clock), 5 5/8 in. $15
Spoon-teaspoon, 5 7/8 in. $20
Tablespoon, (serving spoon), 8 1/2 in. $60
Tongs-sugar, 4 1/2 in. $50

Cromwell by Durgin, 1893

Fork, 7 in. $40
Fork-cocktail, 5 5/8 in. $40
Spoon-demitasse, gold wash, 4 1/8 in. $28
Spoon-dessert/oval soup, 7 in. $60
Spoon-fruit, 6 in. $40

Spoon-soup, round bowl, bouillon,
5 5/8 in. $44
Spoon-soup, round bowl, cream,
5 7/8 in. $50
Spoon-sugar, 5 7/8 in. $45
Tablespoon, (serving spoon), 8 1/4 in. $85
Tongs-sugar, 5 3/4 in. $80

The following pieces have monograms:
Fork, 7 5/8 in. $53
Fork-cocktail, 5 5/8 in. $27
Spoon-demitasse, 4 1/8 in. $20
Spoon-dessert/oval soup, 7 in. $45
Spoon-fruit, 6 in. $30
Spoon-soup, round bowl, gumbo,
6 7/8 in. $45
Spoon-teaspoon, (five o'clock), 5 3/8 in. $21
Spoon-teaspoon, 5 7/8 in. $26
Tablespoon, (serving spoon), 8 1/4 in. $66

Dauphin by Durgin, 1897

English Rose by Durgin, 1955

Fork, 7 in. $50
Fork-cocktail, 5 3/8 in. $34
Fork-cold meat/serving, medium, solid,
8 1/2 in. $100
Fork-salad, individual, 6 1/4 in. $55
Knife-modern, hollow handle, 9 in. $50
Ladle-gravy, solid piece, 6 in. $100
Spoon-dessert/oval soup, 7 in. $40
Spoon-iced tea, 7 5/8 in. $50
Spoon-sugar, 5 7/8 in. $48
Spoon-teaspoon, 5 7/8 in. $32
Tablespoon, (serving spoon), 8 1/2 in. $90

Essex by Durgin, 1911

Fork, round bowl, 7 1/4 in. $50

Fork-cold meat/serving, small, solid,
    7 1/2 in. $90
Knife-old french, hollow handle, bolster,
    9 3/4 in. $50
Spoon-bon-bon, 4 7/8 in. $48
Spoon-egg, 5 1/2 in. $48
Spoon-fruit, 6 in. $40
Spoon-soup, round bowl, gumbo, 7 in. $60
Tablespoon, (serving spoon), 8 1/2 in. $90

Fairfax by Durgin, 1910

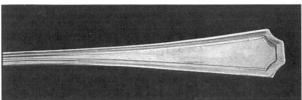

Butter-master, flat handle, 6 7/8 in. $34
Fork, 7 1/4 in. $28
Fork-baby, 4 1/4 in. $36
Fork-carving, small, stainless prongs, steak,
    8 5/8 in. $50
Fork-carving, small, stainless prongs,
    stcak, 9 in. $50
Fork-cocktail, 3 tines, 5 1/2 in. $24
Fork-cold meat/serving, small, solid,
    7 1/2 in. $70
Fork-lemon, 5 in. $25
Knife-old french, hollow handle, silver plate
    blade, 8 5/8 in. $30
Knife-old french, hollow handle, stainless
    blade,
    8 5/8 in. $30
Ladle-cream, solid piece, 1 7/8 in. bowl,
    5 1/8 in. $40
Ladle-gravy, solid piece, 6 3/8 in. $80
Server-cheese, silver plate blade,
    6 1/2 in. $47
Server-jelly, 6 1/4 in. $36
Server-pie, silver plate blade, 10 1/8 in. $60
Spoon-baby, straight handle, 3 5/8 in. $36
Spoon-bon-bon, 4 7/8 in. $40
Spoon-dessert/oval soup, 7 1/8 in. $50
Spoon-soup, round bowl, bouillon, 3 5/8 in.
    handle, 5 3/8 in. $25
Spoon-soup, round bowl, gumbo, 6 7/8 in. . . . $46
Spoon-sugar, 5 7/8 in. $30
Spoon-teaspoon, (five o'clock), 5 in. $20
Spoon-teaspoon, 5 3/4 in. $20
Tablespoon, (serving spoon), tear bowl,
    8 1/8 in. $60
Tongs-sugar, 3 1/2 in. $50

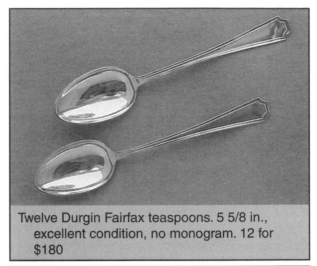

Twelve Durgin Fairfax teaspoons. 5 5/8 in., excellent condition, no monogram. 12 for $180

Forty pieces Durgin Fairfax (1910): 8 each luncheon knives, luncheon forks, salad forks, teaspoons, and large soup spoons. All monogram "EFR" except one "B." Knife 8 5/8 in. with stainless steel blunt blade, luncheon fork 7 1/8 in., soup spoon 6 3/4 in. One knife monogram scratched. $700

Fairfax No. 4-Engraved by Durgin, 1910

Fork-salad, individual, 6 1/8 in. $38
Spoon-soup, round bowl, bouillon,
    5 1/4 in. $30

Spoon-soup, round bowl, gumbo,
6 7/8 in. $70
Spoon-teaspoon, (five o'clock),
5 5/8 in. $21
Tablespoon, (serving spoon),
8 1/2 in. $70

Hunt Club by Durgin, 1930

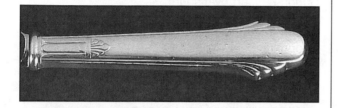

Iris by Durgin, 1900

Ladle-gravy, solid piece, 7 5/8 in. $650

Lenox by Durgin, 1912

Butter spreader, flat handle, 2 3/4 in. handle,
5 1/4 in. $30
Butter-master, flat handle, 6 7/8 in. $44
Fork, 7 1/4 in. $50
Fork, 8 in. $60
Fork-carving, small, stainless prongs, steak,
9 in. $75
Fork-cocktail, 5 5/8 in. $30
Fork-cocktail, gold wash, 5 5/8 in. $30
Fork-cold meat/serving, small, solid,
7 1/2 in. $90
Fork-salad, individual, 6 1/8 in. $50
Knife-old french, hollow handle, bolster,
8 5/8 in. $40
Knife-old french, hollow handle, bolster,
9 3/4 in. $50
Ladle-gravy, solid piece, 6 in. $90
Spoon-bon-bon, 4 7/8 in. $46

Spoon-demitasse, 4 1/4 in. $24
Spoon-dessert/oval soup,
7 1/8 in. $50
Spoon-iced tea, 7 1/2 in. $40
Spoon-olive, long handle, 8 in. $160
Spoon-serving, solid, tear bowl,
8 5/8 in. $110
Spoon-soup, round bowl, bouillon,
5 1/4 in. $46
Spoon-sugar, 6 in. $46
Spoon-sugar, gold wash, 6 in. $46
Spoon-teaspoon, (five o'clock),
5 5/8 in. $26
Spoon-teaspoon, 5 7/8 in. $30
Tablespoon, (serving spoon),
8 5/8 in. $90

Louis XV by Durgin, 1891

Fork, 7 5/8 in. $70
Fork-oyster, short handle, 5 3/4 in. $60
Fork-pickle/olive, long handle,
7 in. $70
Fork-salad, individual, 6 1/4 in. $110
Spoon-demitasse, 4 1/4 in. $40
Spoon-dessert/oval soup, 7 1/8 in. $70
Spoon-fruit, 5 3/4 in. $44
Spoon-teaspoon, (five o'clock),
5 in. $28
Spoon-teaspoon, 5 3/4 in. $28

Madame Royale by Durgin, 1897

Aunt Etta Anderson

2 K
2 F
2 Tsp
2 Salad

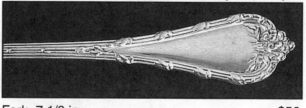

Fork, 7 1/8 in. $56
Spoon-demitasse, 4 1/4 in. $30
Spoon-dessert/oval soup,
7 1/8 in. $60
Spoon-soup, round bowl, gumbo,
7 in. $65
Tablespoon, (serving spoon),
8 1/4 in. $90

yes

The following pieces have monograms:
Butter spreader, flat handle, 5 3/8 in......... $23
Fork, 7 1/8 in.............................. $44
Spoon-teaspoon, (five o'clock),
    5 3/8 in.............................. $21
Spoon-teaspoon, 5 7/8 in................ $24

Marechal Niel by Durgin, 1896

Fork, 7 1/8 in............................ $70
Tablespoon, (serving spoon), 8 3/8 in....... $100

The following pieces have monograms:
Knife-blunt, hollow handle, 8 5/8 in......... $70
Spoon-teaspoon, 5 7/8 in................ $40

Durgin New Queens asparagus server. 9 1/4 in., fine condition, monogrammed "MW" (script, front). $350

New Standish by Durgin, 1905

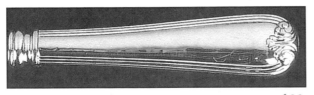

Fork-cocktail, 5 1/2 in.................... $30

Fork-ice cream, 5 5/8 in................. $50
Fork-youth, 6 1/8 in..................... $45
Spoon-fruit, 5 3/4 in.................... $38
Ladle-cream, solid piece, 5 in.............. $46
Ladle-gravy, solid piece,
    6 7/8 in.......................... $90
Spoon-demitasse, 4 1/4 in. $22
Spoon-demitasse, gold wash,
    4 1/4 in........................... $22
Spoon-dessert/oval soup,
    7 1/8 in........................... $40
Spoon-fruit, gold wash, 5 3/4 in.......... $38
Spoon-iced tea, 7 5/8 in. $40
Spoon-jam, 6 in......................... $35
Spoon-soup, round bowl, bouillon,
    5 1/4 in........................... $36
Spoon-soup, round bowl, cream,
    5 1/2 in........................... $50
Spoon-soup, round bowl, gumbo,
    6 7/8 in........................... $50
Spoon-teaspoon, (five o'clock),
    5 5/8 in........................... $22
Tablespoon, (serving spoon),
    8 1/2 in........................... $80
Tongs-sugar, 3 1/2 in.................... $66

The following pieces have monograms:
Butter spreader, flat handle, 5 1/4 in........ $20
Fork, 7 1/8 in........................... $37
Fork, 7 3/4 in........................... $43
Fork-carving, large, stainless prongs, roast,
    11 in.............................. $53
Fork-cocktail, 5 1/2 in. $23
Fork-strawberry, 4 7/8 in................ $30
Ladle-gravy, solid piece, 6 7/8 in............ $70
Sardine fork, serving, solid, 6 in. $70
Spoon-fruit, 5 3/4 in.................... $30
Spoon-jam, 7 in......................... $27
Spoon-soup, round bowl, cream,
    5 1/2 in........................... $38
Spoon-soup, round bowl, gumbo,
    6 7/8 in........................... $40
Spoon-soup, round bowl, gumbo,
    7 1/8 in........................... $40
Spoon-teaspoon, 5 3/4 in. $23
Tongs-sugar, 3 1/2 in.................... $50

New Vintage by Durgin, 1904

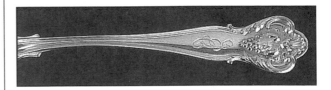

The following pieces have monograms:

Fork, 7 in.. . . . . $53
Spoon-fruit, 5 3/4 in. $36
Spoon-place/oval soup,
   6 1/8 in. $50
Spoon-soup, round bowl, bouillon,
   5 1/4 in. $48
Spoon-teaspoon, (five o'clock),
   5 5/8 in. $23
Spoon-teaspoon, 5 7/8 in. $30
Tablespoon, (serving spoon),
   8 3/8 in. $86

Orange Blossom by Durgin, 1898

Fork-salad, individual, 6 in. $100
Spoon-fruit, 5 1/2 in. $70
Spoon-ice cream, 5 3/8 in.. . . . . $90
Spoon-soup, round bowl, bouillon,
   5 3/8 in. $80
Spoon-teaspoon, 5 1/2 in. $60

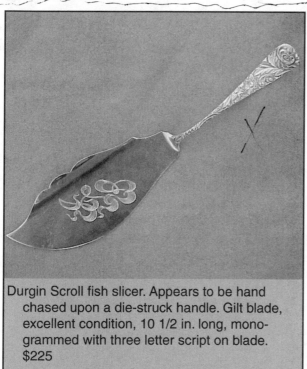

Durgin Scroll fish slicer. Appears to be hand chased upon a die-struck handle. Gilt blade, excellent condition, 10 1/2 in. long, monogrammed with three letter script on blade. $225

Sheaf of Wheat by Durgin, 1887

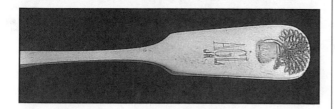

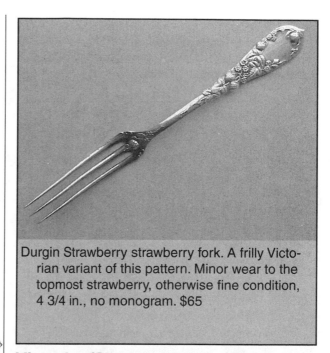

Durgin Strawberry strawberry fork. A frilly Victorian variant of this pattern. Minor wear to the topmost strawberry, otherwise fine condition, 4 3/4 in., no monogram. $65

Victorian/Sheraton by Durgin, 1910/1918

Butter spreader, flat handle, 2 5/8 in. handle,
   5 1/4 in. $24
Butter spreader, flat handle, 2 7/8 in. handle,
   5 5/8 in. $24
Butter-master, flat handle, 6 7/8 in. $44
Fork, 7 1/4 in.. . . . . $36
Fork, 8 in.. . . . . $60
Fork-cocktail, 5 1/2 in. $30
Fork-cold meat/serving, small, solid,
   7 1/2 in. $90
Fork-ice cream, 5 3/4 in. $60
Knife-old french, hollow handle, 9 3/4 in. $50
Knife-old french, hollow handle, bolster,
   8 5/8 in. $40
Knife-youth, 7 5/8 in. $40
Spoon-demitasse, 4 1/4 in. $26
Spoon-dessert/oval soup, 7 1/4 in.. . . . . $55
Spoon-five o'clock/youth, 5 1/8 in. $20
Spoon-fruit, 5 7/8 in.. . . . . $36
Spoon-soup, round bowl, bouillon,
   5 1/2 in. $48
Spoon-soup, round bowl, gumbo,
   6 7/8 in. $65

Durgin

Spoon-teaspoon, 5 3/4 in. $30
Tablespoon, (serving spoon), 8 3/8 in.. . . . . . . $90

Watteau by Durgin, 1891

Butter spreader, flat handle, 5 1/4 in.. . . . . . . $36
Fork, 7 1/8 in.. . . . . $48
Fork, 7 5/8 in.. . . . . $90
Fork-youth, 6 1/8 in.. . . . . $50
Spoon-bon-bon, 5 1/2 in.. . . . . $50

Spoon-teaspoon, (five o'clock), 5 1/4 in. $22
Spoon-teaspoon, 5 7/8 in. $28
Spoon-youth, 5 in. $45
Tablespoon, (serving spoon), pierced,
    8 3/8 in. $100
Tablespoon, (serving spoon), 8 3/8 in.. . . . . . . $90

The following pieces have monograms:
Fork, 7 1/8 in.. . . . . $38
Pick-butter, 2 tines, 5 5/8 in.. . . . . $48
Spoon-dessert/oval soup, 7 in.. . . . . $45
Spoon-soup, round bowl, bouillon,
    5 5/8 in. $38
Spoon-soup, round bowl, gumbo, 7 in.. . . . . . . $53
Spoon-teaspoon, (five o'clock), 5 1/4 in. $17
Spoon-teaspoon, 5 7/8 in. $21
Tablespoon, (serving spoon), 8 3/8 in.. . . . . . . $70

EASTERLING CO.

Easterling Co. began in Chicago in 1944. Sterling assets were sold to the Westerling Co. in 1974, with Gorham producing the patterns.

American Classic by Easterling, 1944

Butter spreader, hollow handle, modern,
    stainless, 6 7/8 in. $26
Butter spreader, flat handle, 5 3/4 in. $26
Butter-master, flat handle, 7 in. $15
Carving set, two piece, small, stainless
    blade, steak $80
Fork, 7 1/4 in. $20
Fork-carving, small, stainless prongs,
    steak, 8 1/2 in. $40
Fork-cocktail, 5 5/8 in. $24
Fork-cold meat/serving, medium, solid,
    8 in. $45
Fork-salad, individual, 6 5/8 in. $30
Knife-modern, hollow handle, 8 7/8 in. $30
Knife-new french, hollow handle, 8 7/8 in. $30
Ladle-cream, solid piece, 5 1/8 in. $40
Ladle-gravy, solid piece, 6 1/2 in. $30
Napkin clip (made for sugar spoons) $25
Napkin clip (made for teaspoons),
    1 3/8 in. $20
Server-jelly, 6 1/4 in. $30
Server-tomato, solid piece, 8 1/8 in. $80
Spoon-dessert/oval soup, 7 1/8 in. $37
Spoon-iced tea, 7 1/2 in. $30
Spoon-soup, round bowl, cream, 6 3/8 in. $28
Spoon-sugar, 6 in. $14
Spoon-teaspoon, 6 in. $12
Tablespoon, (serving spoon), 8 1/2 in. $60

Helene by Easterling, 1955

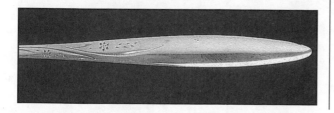

Butter spreader, hollow handle, modern,
    stainless, 6 3/4 in. $20
Butter-master, flat handle, 7 in. $18
Carving set, 2 pieces, small, stainless blade,
    steak $100
Fork, 7 1/4 in. $30
Fork-salad, individual, 6 5/8 in. $24
Knife-carving, small, stainless blade, steak,
    10 1/4 in. $50
Knife-modern, hollow handle, 8 7/8 in. $20
Ladle-gravy, solid piece, 6 3/8 in. $70
Spoon-iced tea, 7 1/2 in. $30
Spoon-sugar, 6 1/8 in. $18
Spoon-teaspoon, 5 7/8 in. $15

Horizon by Easterling, 1944

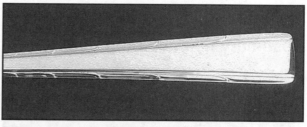

Butter-master, flat handle, 7 in. $14
Fork, 7 3/8 in. $17
Fork-carving, small, stainless prongs,
    steak, 8 1/2 in. $40
Fork-cocktail, 5 3/4 in. $20
Fork-cold meat/serving, medium, solid,
    8 1/8 in. $50
Fork-salad, individual, 6 5/8 in. $23
Knife-carving, small, stainless blade, steak,
    10 1/4 in. $40
Knife-modern, hollow handle, 8 3/4 in. $24
Knife-new french, hollow handle,
    8 3/4 in. $24
Ladle-gravy, solid piece, 6 3/8 in. $40
Napkin clip (made for teaspoons),
    2 1/8 in. $20
Server-jelly, 6 1/8 in. $25
Server-pie and cake, stainless blade
    replaced, 10 1/4 in. $45
Server-tomato, solid piece, 8 1/8 in. $65
Spoon-demitasse, 4 3/8 in. $17
Spoon-dessert/oval soup, 7 1/8 in. $36
Spoon-soup, round bowl, cream,
    6 3/8 in. $30
Spoon-sugar, 6 in. $14
Spoon-teaspoon, 6 in. $12
Tablespoon, (serving spoon),
    8 1/2 in. $50

Easterling

Rose Spray by Easterling, 1955

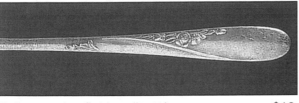

Butter-master, flat handle, 7 in. $18
Fork, 7 1/4 in.. . . . . $28
Fork-cocktail, 5 5/8 in. $24
Fork-salad, individual, 6 5/8 in. $30
Ladle-gravy, solid piece, 6 3/8 in.. . . . . $55
Spoon-iced tea, 7 5/8 in. $30
Spoon-soup, round bowl, cream,
    6 3/8 in. $34
Spoon-sugar, 6 in. $26
Spoon-teaspoon, 6 in. $11

Rosemary by Easterling, 1944

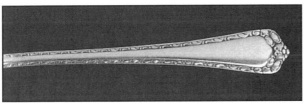

Butter spreader, flat handle, 5 3/4 in. $20
Butter-master, flat handle, 7 in. $15
Carving set, 2 pieces, small, stainless blade,
    steak $90
Fork, 7 3/8 in.. . . . . $23
Fork-carving, small, stainless prongs,
    steak $44
Fork-cocktail, 5 5/8 in. $20
Fork-cold meat/serving, medium, solid,
    8 1/8 in. $45
Fork-salad, individual, 6 5/8 in. $26

Knife-carving, small, stainless blade, steak,
    10 1/8 in. $44
Knife-new french, hollow handle,
    8 7/8 in. $28
Ladle-gravy, solid piece, 6 3/8 in. $45
Server-tomato, solid piece, 8 1/8 in. $60
Spoon-iced tea, 7 1/2 in. $24
Spoon-soup, round bowl, cream,
    6 3/8 in. $25
Spoon-sugar, 6 in. $15
Spoon-teaspoon, 6 in. $12
Tablespoon, (serving spoon), 8 1/2 in. $45
Tablespoon, (serving spoon), pierced,
    8 1/2 in. $60

Southern Grandeur by Easterling, 1944

Butter spreader, flat handle, 5 3/4 in. $24
Butter-master, flat handle, 7 in. $20
Carving set, 2 pieces, small, stainless
    blade, steak $90
Fork, 7 1/4 in.. . . . . $24
Fork-salad, individual, 6 3/4 in. $40
Knife-new french, hollow handle, 8 7/8 in. $28
Ladle-gravy, solid piece, 6 1/2 in. $50
Salad set, 2 pieces, wooden bowl $70
Server-tomato, solid piece, 8 1/8 in. $80
Spoon-demitasse, 4 1/4 in. $22
Spoon-iced tea, 7 5/8 in. $35
Spoon-soup, round bowl, cream, 6 3/8 in. $40
Spoon-sugar, 6 in. $16
Spoon-teaspoon, 6 in. $14

FINE ARTS STERLING CO.

Fine Arts Sterling Silver Co. was established in 1944 in Philadelphia, Pennsylvania, selling patterns made by International Silver Co., and was moved to Morgantown, Pennsylvania in 1972. After moving to Jenkintown, Pennsylvania in 1977, Fine Arts went out of business in 1979.

Crown Princess by Fine Arts, 1949

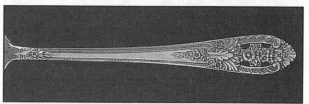

Butter spreader, hollow handle, stainless paddle, 6 1/4 in........................ $30
Butter spreader, flat handle, 5 7/8 in......... $28
Butter-master, flat handle, 7 1/4 in.......... $34
Carving set, 2 pieces, large, stainless blade, roast $160
Fork, 7 1/4 in................................ $38
Fork-cocktail, 5 5/8 in. $30
Fork-cold meat/serving, large, solid, 9 1/8 in................................. $75
Fork-ice cream, 5 7/8 in. $50
Fork-salad, individual, 6 1/2 in. $43
Knife-modern, hollow handle, 9 1/4 in. $40
Knife-steak, individual, 8 5/8 in.............. $50
Ladle-gravy, solid piece, 6 1/4 in............. $80
Ladle-gravy, solid piece, 6 7/8 in............. $80
Napkin clip (made for five o'clock) $22
Salad set, 2 pieces, wooden bowl $90
Server-jelly, 5 1/8 in. $34
Server-pie, stainless blade, 10 1/4 in. $55
Spoon-demitasse, 4 1/8 in. $28
Spoon-dessert/oval soup, 6 7/8 in. $42
Spoon-iced tea, 7 3/8 in. $40
Spoon-salad serving, wooden bowl, 11 in. $45
Spoon-soup, round bowl, cream, 6 5/8 in................................... $36
Spoon-sugar, 5 7/8 in. $38
Spoon-teaspoon, (five o'clock), 5 3/8 in. $15
Spoon-teaspoon, 6 in. $16
Tablespoon, (serving spoon), 8 1/2 in........ $70
Tablespoon, (serving spoon), pierced, 3 tines, 8 1/2 in................................ $90

Processional by Fine Arts, 1947

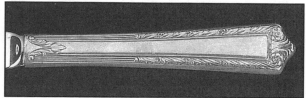

Butter spreader, hollow handle, stainless paddle, 6 1/4 in........................ $26
Butter spreader, flat handle, 5 3/4 in......... $20
Butter-master, flat handle, 7 1/4 in. $35
Carving set, two piece, small, stainless blade, steak $130
Fork, 7 1/4 in................................ $23
Fork-cocktail, 5 5/8 in. $28
Fork-cold meat/serving, large, solid, 9 1/8 in................................. $80
Fork-ice cream, 5 3/4 in. $38
Fork-lemon, 4 3/4 in. $34
Fork-salad, individual, 6 1/2 in. $40
Knife-modern, hollow handle, 9 1/4 in....... $30
Ladle-cream, solid piece, 4 1/8 in. $38
Ladle-gravy, solid piece, 6 1/2 in............. $75
Server-jelly, 6 5/8 in........................ $28
Server-pie, stainless blade, 10 3/8 in. $70
Server-tomato, solid piece, 8 in............. $90
Spoon-demitasse, 4 1/4 in. $28
Spoon-dessert/oval soup, 6 7/8 in........... $46
Spoon-iced tea, 7 3/8 in. $34
Spoon-soup, round bowl, cream, 6 1/2 in. $20
Spoon-sugar, 6 in. $20
Spoon-teaspoon, (five o'clock), 5 3/8 in. $16
Spoon-teaspoon, 6 in. $13
Tablespoon, (serving spoon), 8 1/2 in........ $48

Romance of the Stars by Fine Arts, 1959

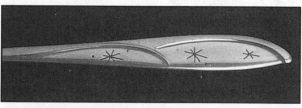

Butter spreader, hollow handle, modern, stainless paddle, 6 3/8 in............... $15
Butter-master, flat handle, 7 1/4 in. $25
Fork, 7 1/4 in................................ $32
Fork-cocktail, 5 5/8 in. $24
Fork-cold meat/serving, large, solid, 9 1/8 in................................. $80

Fine Arts Sterling

Fork-salad, individual, 6 5/8 in. $25
Knife-modern, hollow handle, 9 1/4 in. $22
Ladle-gravy, solid piece, 6 1/8 in. $70
Server-pie, stainless blade, 10 5/8 in. $50
Spoon-casserole, smooth, solid, 9 1/4 in. . . . $70
Spoon-dessert/oval soup, 6 5/8 in. $28
Spoon-iced tea, 7 1/2 in. $30
Spoon-teaspoon, 6 in. $18
Tablespoon, (serving spoon), 8 1/2 in. $55

Romance Rose by Fine Arts, 1960

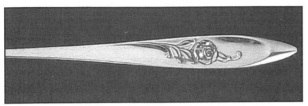

Butter spreader, hollow handle, modern,
 stainless paddle, 6 1/2 in. $20
Fork, 7 1/2 in. $37
Fork-cold meat/serving, medium, solid,
 8 1/4 in. $70
Fork-salad, individual, 6 5/8 in. $30
Knife-modern, hollow handle, 9 1/8 in. $24
Ladle-gravy, solid piece, 6 1/4 in. $70
Spoon-dessert/oval soup, 7 1/8 in. $34
Spoon-sugar, 6 1/4 in. $36
Spoon-teaspoon, 6 1/4 in. $20

Southern Colonial by Fine Arts, 1945

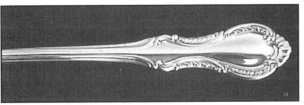

Butter spreader, hollow handle, stainless
 paddle, 6 1/8 in. $26
Butter spreader, flat handle, 5 3/4 in. $23
Butter-master, flat handle, 7 in. $34
Fork, 7 3/8 in. $30
Fork-cold meat/serving, medium, solid,
 8 7/8 in. $90
Fork-salad, individual, 6 1/2 in. $38
Knife-modern, hollow handle, 9 1/4 in. $36
Ladle-gravy, solid piece, 6 1/2 in. $80
Napkin clip (made for teaspoons) $22
Spoon-demitasse, 4 1/8 in. $24
Spoon-iced tea, 7 3/8 in. $36
Spoon-soup, round bowl, cream, 6 1/2 in. . . . $26

Spoon-sugar, 6 in. $30
Spoon-teaspoon, (five o'clock), 5 3/8 in. $20
Spoon-teaspoon, 5 7/8 in. $18
Tablespoon, (serving spoon), 8 1/4 in. $70
Tablespoon, (serving spoon), pierced,
 8 1/4 in. $90

Tranquility by Fine Arts, 1947

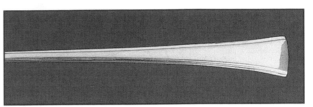

Butter spreader, hollow handle, stainless
 paddle, 6 1/4 in. $20
Butter spreader, flat handle, 5 3/4 in. $13
Butter-master, flat handle, 7 1/4 in. $27
Carving set, two piece, small, stainless
 blade, steak $110
Fork, 7 1/4 in. $20
Fork-carving, large, stainless prongs,
 roast, 11 in. $60
Fork-carving, small, stainless prongs,
 steak, 8 7/8 in. $55
Fork-cocktail, 5 5/8 in. $17
Fork-cold meat/serving, large, solid,
 9 1/8 in. $80
Fork-ice cream, 5 1/2 in. $34
Fork-lemon, 4 3/4 in. $28
Fork-salad, individual, 6 1/2 in. $26
Knife-bar, hollow handle, 8 1/8 in. $36
Knife-carving, large, stainless blade,
 roast, 13 in. $60
Ladle-cream, solid piece, 4 1/4 in. $40
Ladle-gravy, solid piece, 6 5/8 in. $60
Napkin clip (made for teaspoons) $16
Server-jelly, 5 in. $25
Server-jelly, 6 1/2 in. $25
Server-pie, stainless blade, 10 1/4 in. $55
Server-tomato, solid piece, 8 1/8 in. $70
Spoon-bon-bon, 4 3/4 in. $34
Spoon-demitasse, 4 1/8 in. $20
Spoon-dessert/oval soup, 6 7/8 in. $35
Spoon-iced tea, 7 3/8 in. $24
Spoon-soup, round bowl, cream, 6 1/2 in. . . . $16
Spoon-sugar, 5 7/8 in. $25
Spoon-teaspoon, 6 in. $12
Tablespoon, (serving spoon), pierced,
 8 1/2 in. $70
Tablespoon, (serving spoon), 8 1/2 in. $48

FRANK W. SMITH SILVER CO.

Frank W. Smith Silver Co. Inc. began in 1886 in Gardner, Massachusetts. The firm was sold in 1917 and ceased silver manufacturing in 1930. Company marks include a lion on a crescent moon entwined with the letter S, an S in a circle flanked by conical shapes, and an S surrounded by double scrolls. A subsidiary of Reed & Barton bought the silver assets in 1958, and the flatware manufacturing was moved to North Attleboro, Massachusetts.

American Chippendale by Frank Smith, 1905

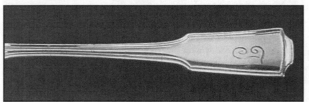

Butter-master, flat handle, 7 1/8 in.	$36
Fork, 7 1/2 in.	$70
Fork, 7 in.	$38
Fork-chipped beef, small, 6 1/4 in.	$90
Fork-cocktail, 3 tines, 5 3/8 in.	$43
Fork-cold meat/serving, small, solid, 7 1/2 in.	$80
Fork-dessert, no bevel, 6 in.	$60
Fork-lemon, 4 3/4 in.	$60
Fork-salad, individual, 6 in.	$44
Knife-modern, hollow handle, 8 1/4 in.	$45
Knife-old french, hollow handle, silver plate blade, 8 5/8 in.	$45
Knife-old french, hollow handle, stainless blade, 9 5/8 in.	$50
Ladle-gravy, solid piece, scallop bowl, 6 3/8 in.	$60
Ladle-gravy, solid piece, smooth bowl, 6 3/8 in.	$60
Spoon-demitasse, 4 1/2 in.	$26
Spoon-dessert/oval soup, 7 in.	$50
Spoon-five o'clock/youth, 3 3/8 in. handle, 5 1/4 in.	$24
Spoon-fruit, 5 1/2 in.	$45
Spoon-iced tea, 7 1/2 in.	$36
Spoon-soup, round bowl, cream, 6 in.	$45
Spoon-soup, round bowl, gumbo, 7 in.	$70
Spoon-sugar, rim bowl, 5 3/4 in.	$40

Spoon-teaspoon, (five o'clock), 3 3/4 in. long handle, 5 5/8 in.	
Spoon-teaspoon, 4 in. long handle, 5 7/8 in.	$35
Tablespoon, (serving spoon), 8 in.	$60
Tablespoon, (serving spoon), pierced, 8 in.	$80

Chippendale-Old by Frank Smith, 1917

Fork, 7 1/2 in.	$57
Fork-salad, individual, no bevel, 6 1/4 in.	$50
Spoon-bon-bon, 4 3/4 in.	$48
Spoon-dessert/oval soup, 7 in.	$42
Spoon-teaspoon, 5 3/4 in.	$26

The following pieces have monograms:

Butter spreader, flat handle, 5 5/8 in.	$18
Butter-master, flat handle, 7 in.	$33
Fork, 6 7/8 in.	$30

Countess by Frank Smith, 1928

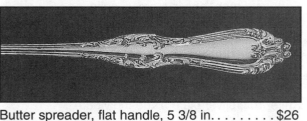

Butter spreader, flat handle, 5 3/8 in.	$26
Butter-master, flat handle, 7 in.	$40
Fork, 7 1/2 in.	$60
Fork, 7 1/8 in.	$40
Fork-cold meat/serving, small, solid, 7 1/2 in.	$90
Fork-salad, individual, 6 1/8 in.	$50
Fork-youth, 6 in.	$50
Knife-new french, hollow handle, stainless blade, 8 3/4 in.	$40
Knife-new french, hollow handle, stainless blade, 9 5/8 in.	$50
Ladle-cream, solid piece, 5 1/2 in.	$50
Ladle-gravy, solid piece, 5 1/2 in.	$90
Spoon-iced tea, 7 1/4 in.	$36
Spoon-soup, round bowl, bouillon, 3 5/8 in. handle, 5 3/8 in.	$40
Spoon-soup, round bowl, cream, 3 7/8 in. handle, 5 5/8 in.	$36
Spoon-sugar, 5 5/8 in.	$46
Spoon-teaspoon, (five o'clock), 5 3/8 in.	$20
Spoon-teaspoon, 5 3/4 in.	$28
Tablespoon, (serving spoon), 8 in.	$60

Federal Cotillion by Frank Smith, 1901

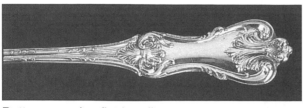

Butter spreader, flat handle,
5 5/8 in. $28
Butter-master, flat handle, 7 in. $48
Carving set, two piece, large, stainless blade,
roast $180
Carving set, two piece, small, stainless
blade, steak. $100
Fork, 7 1/4 in.. . . . . $46
Fork, 7 5/8 in.. . . . . $70
Fork-carving, large, stainless prongs, roast,
10 3/4 in. $90
Fork-carving, small, stainless prongs, steak,
8 3/4 in. $50
Fork-cocktail, 5 1/2 in. $40
Fork-cold meat/serving, small, solid, no
bevel, 7 5/8 ln. $90
Fork-dessert, 5 3/4 in. $60
Fork-salad, individual, 6 1/4 in. $45
Knife-carving, small, stainless blade, steak,
10 1/4 in. $50
Knife-fruit, silver plate blade-individual,
6 1/2 in. $45
Knife-modern, hollow handle, 4 in. long
handle, 9 1/2 in.. . . . . $50
Knife-new french, hollow handle,
8 3/8 in. $46
Knife-new french, hollow handle,
9 1/4 in. $46
Knife-new french, hollow handle,
9 5/8 in. $50
Knife-new french, hollow handle, bolster,
8 3/4 in. $46
Knife-sharpener/steel, small, steak $85
Ladle-gravy, solid piece, 7 in.. . . . . $90
Napkin clip (made for teaspoons) $36
Spoon-demitasse, 4 3/8 in. $24
Spoon-dessert/oval soup, 7 in. $50
Spoon-fruit, 5 3/4 in. $46
Spoon-fruit, 5 5/8 in. $45
Spoon-iced tea, 5 1/2 in. long handle,
7 3/8 in. $48
Spoon-parfait, solid piece, 6 in. handle,
8 in. $50

Spoon-soup, round bowl, bouillon,
5 1/4 in. $46
Spoon-soup, round bowl, cream,
3 7/8 in. handle, 5 5/8 in. $48
Spoon-soup, round bowl, cream, 4 1/8 in.
handle, 5 7/8 in. $48
Spoon-soup, round bowl, gumbo,
6 7/8 in. $70
Spoon-teaspoon, (five o'clock),
5 1/2 in. $30
Spoon-teaspoon, 5 3/4 in. $30
Tablespoon, (serving spoon), 8 1/8 in. $80

Fiddle Shell/Alden by Frank Smith, 1914

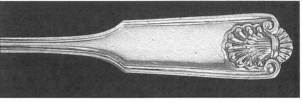

Butter-master, flat handle, 7 1/8 in. $40
Fork, 7 1/2 in. $70
Fork, 7 1/4 in. $50
Fork-cocktail, 5 5/8 in. $38
Fork-cold meat/serving, small, solid,
7 1/2 in. $90
Fork-ice cream, 5 1/2 in. $40
Fork-salad, individual, indented,
6 5/8 in. $45
Fork-salad, individual, no indent,
6 5/8 in. $45
Fork-snail, 2 tines bar, 6 in. $50
Fork-strawberry, square bowl, 5 in. $30
Knife-new french, hollow handle, bolster,
no stamp, 8 3/4 in. $40
Knife-steak, individual, 8 in. $50
Ladle-gravy, solid piece, 6 1/4 in. $80
Spoon-demitasse, 4 1/4 in. $25
Spoon-dessert/oval soup, 7 in.. . . . . $50
Spoon-fruit, 5 3/4 in.. $44
Spoon-iced tea, 7 3/8 in. $40
Spoon-soup, round bowl, cream,
6 1/4 in. $40
Spoon-soup, round bowl, gumbo, no design,
6 7/8 in. $60
Spoon-sugar, indent bowl, 5 3/4 in. $40
Spoon-sugar, no indent, 5 3/4 in.. . . . . $40
Spoon-teaspoon, 5 3/4 in. $40
Tablespoon, (serving spoon),
8 1/2 in. $90
Tablespoon, (serving spoon), pierced,
8 1/4 in. $90

Fiddle Thread by Frank Smith, 1902

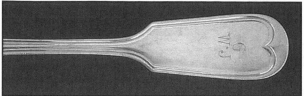

Butter spreader, hollow handle, paddle stainless,
6 in. $40
Carving set, two piece, small, stainless blade,
steak $100
Cleaver-cheese, stainless blade, 6 7/8 in..... $45
Fork, 7 1/2 in............................ $80
Fork, 7 1/8 in............................ $60
Fork-cold meat/serving, small, solid,
7 1/2 in. $90
Fork-salad, individual, 6 in. $45
Fork-strawberry, 5 1/8 in................. $30
Knife-new french, hollow handle, stainless
blade, 8 3/4 in........................ $46
Knife-new french, hollow handle, stainless
blade, 8 3/8 in........................ $46
Ladle-gravy, solid piece, 6 1/4 in.......... $100
Spoon-casserole, smooth, solid,
7 3/4 in. $130
Spoon-demitasse, 4 3/8 in. $28
Spoon-dessert/oval soup, 7 1/8 in. $50
Spoon-iced tea, 7 1/4 in. $45
Spoon-sugar, indent side, 5 3/4 in. $40
Spoon-sugar, no indent, 5 3/4 in........... $40
Spoon-teaspoon, 3 3/4 in. handle,
5 3/4 in. $40
Spoon-teaspoon, 4 in. handle, 6 in......... $40
Tablespoon, (serving spoon), 8 1/8 in....... $90
Tablespoon, (serving spoon), pierced,
8 1/8 in. $90

George VI by Frank Smith, 1912

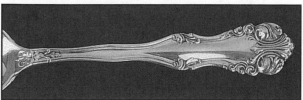

Fork, 7 in................................ $45
Knife-blunt, hollow handle, 8 3/4 in......... $34
Knife-modern, hollow handle, 8 3/8 in. $34
Spoon-soup, round bowl, bouillon, 5 3/4 in.... $50
Spoon-teaspoon, 5 3/4 in................. $30
Tablespoon, (serving spoon), 8 1/4 in....... $80

The following piece has a monogram:
Spoon-teaspoon, (five o'clock), 5 3/8 in. $15

Lion by Frank Smith, 1905

Tablespoon, (serving spoon), 8 1/2 in....... $150

Newport Shell by Frank Smith, 1910

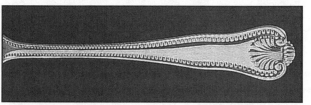

Butter spreader, flat handle, 5 3/8 in........ $38
Carving set, two piece, small, stainless blade,
steak $100
Fork, 7 1/8 in............................ $40
Fork-carving, small, stainless prongs, steak,
9 1/8 in. $50
Fork-cold meat/serving, medium, solid,
8 1/4 in. $90
Fork-ice cream, 5 1/2 in. $65
Fork-lettuce serving large, 9 in. $105
Fork-lettuce serving large, gold wash,
9 in. $105
Fork-salad, individual, 6 in. $54
Knife-carving, small stainless blade, steak,
10 3/8 in. $50
Ladle-gravy, solid piece, 7 in............... $90
Ladle-soup, solid piece, 10 in. $310
Server-pie and cake, stainless blade,
10 1/4 in. $50
Spoon-demitasse, 4 1/2 in. $28
Spoon-demitasse, 4 in. $28
Spoon-iced tea, 7 3/8 in. $38
Spoon-soup, round bowl, bouillon,
5 1/2 in. $36
Spoon-soup, round bowl, cream, 5 5/8 in..... $40
Spoon-teaspoon, (five o'clock), 5 1/2 in. $22
Spoon-teaspoon, 5 3/4 in. $27
Tablespoon, (serving spoon), 8 1/2 in....... $85
Tablespoon, (serving spoon), pierced,
8 1/2 in. $95
Tongs-sugar, 4 1/2 in..................... $70

Pilgrim by Frank Smith, 1909

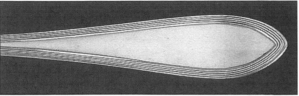

Fork-ice cream, 5 1/2 in. $55
Ladle-soup, solid piece, 12 1/2 in. $350
Spoon-demitasse, 4 1/2 in. $26
Spoon-teaspoon, (five o'clock),
    5 5/8 in. $28
The following pieces have monograms:
Butter spreader, flat handle,
    5 3/4 in. $23
Fork, 6 7/8 in. $44
Fork-cocktail, 5 1/2 in. $27
Fork-salad, individual, 6 1/8 in. $45
Knife-blunt, hollow handle, 9 3/4 in. $45
Ladle-cream, solid piece, 5 1/8 in. $40
Spoon-demitasse, 4 1/2 in. $20
Spoon-dessert/oval soup, 7 in. $42
Spoon-egg, 4 5/8 in. $36
Spoon-fruit, 5 3/4 in. $33
Spoon-soup, round bowl, bouillon,
    5 5/8 in. $42
Spoon-soup, round bowl, gumbo, 7 in. $53
Spoon-teaspoon, 6 in. $24
Tablespoon, (serving spoon),
    8 1/2 in. $70

Woodlily by Frank Smith, 1945

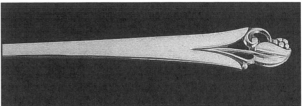

Butter spreader, hollow handle, solid paddle,
    6 1/4 in. $34
Butter spreader, flat handle, 6 1/4 in. $25
Fork, 4 tines, 7 3/8 in. $47
Fork, 4 tines, 8 in. $70
Fork-cocktail, 3 tines, 5 3/4 in. $30
Fork-ice cream, 3 tines, 6 3/8 in. $60
Fork-salad serving, solid piece,
    9 1/8 in. $130
Fork-salad, individual, 3 tines, 6 7/8 in. $50
Knife-modern, hollow handle, no notch,
    8 7/8 in. $50
Knife-new french, hollow handle, beveled
    blade, 9 1/8 in. $50
Spoon-demitasse, 4 1/4 in. $34
Spoon-dessert/oval soup, 7 3/8 in. $64
Spoon-soup, round bowl, bouillon,
    5 3/4 in. $58
Spoon-soup, round bowl, cream, 6 1/2 in. $48
Spoon-sugar, egg bowl, 6 1/2 in. $47
Spoon-teaspoon, 6 1/2 in. $20
Tablespoon, (serving spoon), 8 1/8 in. $100

FRANK M. WHITING CO.

Frank M. Whiting Co. began making silverware in North Attleboro, Massachusetts in 1878, when it was know as Holbrook, Whiting & Albee. The company became a part of Ellmore Silver Co. in about 1940, and that firm went out of business around 1960. Crown Silver Co. of New York later acquired the Whiting dies. The company mark of a griffon and a shield with a W was used up to 1896, and later a W in a circle flanked by stylized leaves.

Adams by Frank Whiting, 1944

Carving set, two piece, small, stainless blade,
  steak $100
Cutter-cheese, wired, 8 1/4 in.. .... $55
Fork, 7 1/4 in.. .... $40
Fork, 8 in.. .... $46
Fork-baby, 4 1/4 in. $33
Fork-lemon, 4 3/4 in. $24
Fork-salad, individual, indented bowl,
  6 1/8 in. $40
Fork-salad, individual, no indent,
  6 3/8 in. $40
Knife-bar, hollow handle, 8 3/4 in. $34
Knife-new french, hollow handle, 9 5/8 in..... $40
Ladle-cream, solid piece, 5 in.. .... $34
Salad set, 2 pieces, wooden bowl $70
Server-cheese, stainless blade, 5 7/8 in...... $40
Spoon-baby, straight handle, 4 1/2 in........ $33
Spoon-soup, round bowl, bouillon,
  5 3/8 in. $28
Spoon-soup, round bowl, cream, 6 in........ $30
Spoon-teaspoon, (five o'clock), 5 3/8 in. $18

Athene/Crescendo by Frank Whiting, 1890

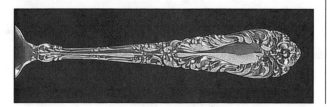

Fork, 7 1/8 in. $44
Fork-breakfast, 6 3/4 in. $50
Fork-salad, individual, 6 1/2 in. $50
Knife-carving, small, stainless blade, steak,
  10 3/8 in. $75
Knife-fillet, 8 5/8 in.. .... $53
Knife-modern, hollow handle,
  9 3/4 in. $80
Knife-new french, hollow handle,
  9 5/8 in. $80
Knife-steak, individual, 8 3/4 in. $50
Spoon-iced tea, 8 1/4 in. $40
Spoon-sugar, 5 5/8 in. $50
Spoon-teaspoon, 5 7/8 in. $27

Botticelli by Frank Whiting, 1949

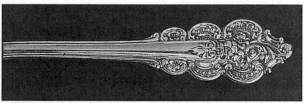

Carving set, 2 pieces, small, stainless blade,
  steak $170

Georgian Shell by Frank Whiting, 1948

Butter spreader, flat handle,
  5 5/8 in. $17
Butter-master, flat handle, 7 in. $50
Carving set, 2 pieces, small, stainless blade,
  steak $120
Fork, 7 1/4 in. $43
Fork, 8 in.. .... $60
Fork-carving, large, stainless prongs, roast,
  11 1/2 in. $80
Fork-carving, small, stainless prongs, steak,
  9 1/8 in. $60
Fork-cocktail, 5 5/8 in. $35
Fork-pickle/olive, short handle, 3 tines bar,
  5 5/8 in. $40
Fork-salad serving, wooden prongs,
  10 1/2 in. $50
Fork-salad, individual, 6 1/4 in. $45

Knife-carving, small, stainless blade, stieak,
  10 1/2 in. $60
Knife-fillet, 8 5/8 in. $60
Knife-new french, hollow handle,
  9 3/8 in. $37
Knife-steak, individual, 9 1/8 in.. . . . . $60
Ladle-gravy, solid piece, 6 3/8 in.. . . . . $110
Sardine fork, serving, solid, 5 tines,
  7 3/8 in. $90
Server-cheese, stainless blade,
  6 1/2 in. $55
Spoon-dessert/oval soup, 7 1/4 in. $60
Spoon-fruit, 5 7/8 in. $45
Spoon-iced tea, 7 1/2 in. $38
Spoon-soup, round bowl, cream,
  6 1/4 in. $36
Spoon-soup, round bowl, gumbo,
  7 in. $60
Spoon-sugar, 6 in. $50
Spoon-teaspoon, 5 7/8 in. $28

Lily/Floral by Frank Whiting, 1910

Butter spreader, flat handle, 5 3/4 in.. . . . . . . $20
Carving set, 2 pieces, large, stainless blade,
  roast $200
Carving set, 2 piece, small, stainless blade,
  steak $140
Fork, 7 in.. . . . . $40
Fork-carving, large, stainless prongs, roast,
  11 1/4 in. $100
Fork-carving, small, stainless prongs, steak,
  9 1/2 in. $70
Fork-salad serving, solid piece, 8 7/8 in.. . . . $240
Fork-salad, individual, 6 1/2 in. $50
Knife-carving, large, stainless blade, roast,
  13 1/2 in. $100
Knife-carving, small, stainless blade, steak,
  10 1/2 in. $70
Knife-new french, hollow handle, 3 3/4 in. handle,
  9 in. $40
Knife-new french, hollow handle, 4 in. handle,
  9 in. $40
Knife-steak, individual, 9 3/8 in.. . . . . $50
Spoon-soup, round bowl, cream,
  6 1/8 in. $40
Spoon-teaspoon, 6 in. $22

Neapolitan/Kings Court by Frank Whiting, 1895

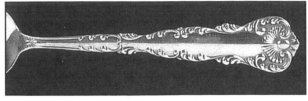

Butter spreader, flat handle, 5 3/4 in.. . . . . . . $18
Butter-master, flat handle, 7 in. $32
Carving set, 2 pieces large, stainless blade,
  roast. $150
Carving set, 2 pieces, small, stainless blade,
  steak $120
Fork, 6 3/4 in. $38
Fork, 7 1/8 in. $38
Fork-cocktail, 6 in. $32
Fork-dessert, 6 . . . . $45
Fork-salad, individual, 6 5/8 in. $48
Fork-youth, 5 7/8 in.. . . . . $50
Knife-breakfast, silver plate blade,
  8 1/4 in. $37
Knife-new french, hollow handle, 9 in. $40
Knife-old french, hollow handle, 9 1/2 in.. . . . . $60
Ladle-cream, solid piece, 5 1/2 in. $50
Ladle-gravy, solid piece, 6 1/4 in.. . . . . $95
Ladle-soup, solid piece, 11 3/8 in. $260
Sardine fork, serving, solid, 8 1/4 in. $90
Spoon-demitasse, 4 1/2 in. $34
Spoon-dessert/oval soup 7 1/8 in. $45
Spoon-fruit, 5 7/8 in.. . . . . $50
Spoon-iced tea, 8 1/8 in. $35
Spoon-soup, round bowl, cream, 6 in. $35
Spoon-soup, round bowl, cream, 6 3/8 in. $35
Spoon-soup, round bowl, gumbo,
  6 3/4 in. $48
Spoon-sugar, 6 in. $38
Spoon-teaspoon, (five o'clock), 5 3/8 in. $16
Spoon-teaspoon, 6 in. $18
Tablespoon, (serving spoon), 8 1/8 in.. . . . . . . $65
Tongs-sugar, 3 1/2 in.. . . . . $48

Princess Ingrid by Frank Whiting, 1945

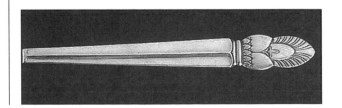

Butter spreader, hollow handle, solid paddle,
6 1/8 in. $28
Fork, 7 1/8 in. $45
Fork, 7 3/4 in. $80
Fork-carving, large, stainless prongs, roast,
10 7/8 in. $60
Fork-carving, large, stainless prongs, roast,
11 5/8 in. $60
Fork-carving, small, stainless prongs, steak,
9 3/8 in. $50
Fork-carving, small, stainless prongs, steak,
9 in. $50
Fork-cocktail, 5 5/8 in. $30
Fork-salad, individual, 6 1/4 in. $60
Knife-carving, large, stainless blade, roast,
13 1/2 in. $60
Knife-modern, hollow handle, 9 3/4 in. $70
Knife-modern, hollow handle, 9 in. $40
Poultry shears, 11 1/2 in. $150
Server-pie, stainless blade, 10 in. $60
Server-pie, stainless blade, 9 1/2 in. $60
Spoon-demitasse, 4 1/4 in. $22
Spoon-iced tea, 7 3/8 in. $36
Spoon-soup, round bowl, cream,
6 1/4 in. $40
Spoon-sugar, 6 1/8 in. $40
Spoon-teaspoon, 6 1/8 in. $30
Tablespoon, (serving spoon), 8 5/8 in. $90

Rose of Sharon by Frank Whiting, 1954

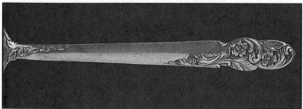

Butter spreader, hollow handle, paddle solid,
6 in. $40
Fork, 7 1/8 in. $48
Fork, 7 3/4 in. $60
Fork-cold meat/serving, large, solid,
9 1/8 in. $110
Fork-salad, individual, 6 1/2 in. $60
Knife-modern, hollow handle, 9 3/4 in. $43
Knife-modern, hollow handle, 9 in. $40
Spoon-iced tea, 7 3/8 in. $45
Spoon-soup, round bowl, cream,
6 3/8 in. $46
Spoon-teaspoon, 5 7/8 in. $30

Talisman Rose by Frank Whiting, 1948

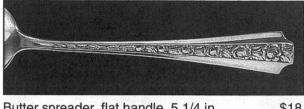

Butter spreader, flat handle, 5 1/4 in. $18
Butter spreader, flat handle, 5 3/4 in. $18
Butter-master, flat handle, 6 7/8 in. $32
Carving set, 2 pieces, large, stainless blade,
roast. $140
Fork, 7 1/8 in. $30
Fork, 7 7/8 in. $50
Fork-cocktail, 5 5/8 in. $20
Fork-cold meat/serving, medium, solid,
7 7/8 in. $90
Fork-ice cream, 5 5/8 in. $40
Fork-lemon, 3 tines bar, 5 5/8 in. $24
Fork-salad, individual, 6 1/8 in. $45
Fork-youth, 6 in. $40
Knife-modern, hollow handle, 8 3/4 in. $33
Knife-new french, hollow handle, 8 3/4 in. $33
Knife-new french, hollow handle, 9 5/8 in. $46
Knife-sharpener/steel, steak, 14 in. $60
Knife-youth, 7 1/2 in. $40
Ladle-cream, solid piece, 5 1/4 in. $45
Ladle-gravy, solid piece, 6 1/8 in. $60
Spoon-dessert/oval soup, 7 1/8 in. $40
Spoon-iced tea, 7 1/2 in. $34
Spoon-soup, round bowl, bouillon, 5 1/2 in. . . . $32
Spoon-soup, round bowl, cream, 6 3/8 in. $30
Spoon-soup, round bowl, gumbo, 6 7/8 in. $40
Spoon-sugar, 6 in. $40
Spoon-teaspoon, 5 3/4 in. $18
Tablespoon, (serving spoon), 8 1/2 in. $70

Troubadour by Frank Whiting, 1932/1950

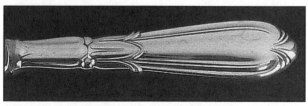

Butter spreader, flat handle, 5 5/8 in. $24
Butter-master, flat handle, 7 in. $38
Carving set, 2 pieces, large, stainless blade,
roast. $120

Troubadour by Frank Whiting, 1932/1950

Carving set, 2 pieces, small, stainless blade,
steak $100
Fork, 7 1/4 in.. . . . . $34
Fork, 7 7/8 in.. . . . . $48
Fork-carving, small, stainless prongs, steak,
9 3/8 in. $50
Fork-cocktail, 5 3/4 in. $26
Fork-cold meat/serving, medium, solid,
8 1/2 in. $84
Fork-pickle/olive, short handle, 6 1/4 in. $30
Fork-salad, individual, 6 3/8 in. $34
Knife-carving, large, stainless blade, roast,
14 1/8 in. $60
Knife-carving, small, stainless blade, steak,
10 3/4 in. $50
Knife-carving, small, stainless blade, steak,
10 in. $50
Knife-modern, hollow handle, 5 1/4 in. blade,
8 3/4 in. $30
Knife-new french, hollow handle, 8 3/4 in. $30
Knife-sharpener/steel, steak, 12 3/8 in. $50
Knife-sharpener/steel, steak, 13 1/2 in. $50
Ladle-gravy, solid piece, 6 in.. . . . . $80
Spoon-dessert/oval soup, 7 1/4 in. $40
Spoon-fruit, 6 in. $32
Spoon-iced tea, 7 5/8 in. $38
Spoon-salt, individual, 2 1/4 in. $16
Spoon-soup, round bowl, bouillon, 5 3/8 in.. . . $28
Spoon-soup, round bowl, cream, 6 1/2 in.. . . . $32
Spoon-soup, round bowl, gumbo, 7 in. $40
Spoon-sugar, 6 in.. . . . . $40

Spoon-teaspoon, 6 in. $20
Tablespoon, (serving spoon), 8 5/8 in. $70

Victoria/Florence by Frank Whiting, 1905

Butter spreader, flat handle, 5 3/4 in. $24
Carving set, 2 pieces, small, stainless blade,
steak $100
Fork, 6 7/8 in.. . . . . $34
Fork-cocktail, 6 in. $32
Fork-salad, individual, 6 3/8 in. $48
Knife-carving, small, stainless blade, steak,
10 1/2 in. $50
Ladle-gravy, solid piece, 6 in.. . . . . $90
Spoon-demitasse, 4 1/4 in. $28
Spoon-dessert/oval soup, 6 7/8 in.. . . . . $50
Spoon-iced tea, 8 1/4 in. $36
Spoon-soup, round bowl, bouillon,
5 3/4 in. $34
Spoon-soup, round bowl, cream, 6 1/4 in. $35
Spoon-soup, round bowl, gumbo,
6 3/4 in. $58
Spoon-teaspoon, tear bowl, 6 1/8 in. $24
Tablespoon, (serving spoon), 8 in.. . . . . $85

GEORG JENSEN

Georg Jensen's silver business opened in Copenhagen, Denmark, in 1904 and became one of the leading producers of silverware in the world. The mark on sterling is a wreath topped by a crown and the words Georg Jensen Inc. An American company, Georg Jensen Inc. USA started in New York in 1941 and ceased production about nine years later.

Acanthus by Georg Jensen-Denmark, 1917

Butter spreader, hollow handle, paddle solid,
  6 in. $100
Carving set, 3 pieces, large stainless blade,
  roast, ... $800
Fork, 6 5/8 in. $100
Fork, 7 1/8 in. $110
Fork-cocktail, 5 5/8 in. $80
Fork-cold meat/server, large, 2 tines,
  8 1/8 in. $220
Fork-cold meat/server, small, 2 tines,
  6 1/4 in. $80
Fork-fish/serving, solid, large, 10 in. $600
Fork-fish, solid, individual, 3 tines, 6 5/8 in. . . $80
Fork-lemon, 4 3/4 in. $70
Fork-pastry, 4 tines, 5 7/8 in. $75
Fork-pastry, 3 tines, 5 5/8 in. $75
Fork-pickle/olive, short handle, 6 1/4 in. $90
Fork-salad, individual, 6 3/4 in. $120
Fork-serving, solid, medium, 8 7/8 in. $380
Fork-serving, solid, small, 8 1/8 in. $280
Knife-cake, large, stainless blade,
  10 1/2 in. $180
Knife-carving, small, stainless blade, steak,
  10 1/2 in. $280
Knife-dinner, long handle, modern, no serrate,
  9 in. $120
Knife-fruit, stainless blade, individual,
  6 3/4 in. $78
Knife-modern, hollow handle, 3 3/8 in. handle,
  7 7/8 in. $98
Knife-modern, hollow handle, 3 5/8 in. handle,
  9 in. $120

Ladle-cream, solid piece, 6 3/8 in. $250
Ladle-gravy, solid piece, 7 3/8 in. $500
Opener-bottle, stainless bowl, 4 5/8 in. $100
Server-cake, solid piece, large, 8 7/8 in. $400
Server-tomato, horn blade, 8 1/8 in. $200
Server-tomato, small, solid piece,
  6 7/8 in. $500
Serving set, solid, medium, ... $700
Spoon-demitasse, 3 3/4 in. $50
Spoon-fish, serving, solid, 10 7/8 in. $800
Spoon-fruit, slender, 6 in. $100
Spoon-fruit, triangular, 6 in. $100
Spoon-iced tea, 7 1/4 in. $80
Spoon-jam, 6 in. $100
Spoon-mustard, stainless bowl, ... $80
Spoon-pie, chased, 9 1/4 in. $700
Spoon-salt, individual, 2 1/2 in. $48
Spoon-serving, solid, large, 9 3/8 in. $500
Spoon-serving, solid, small, egg bowl,
  8 1/8 in. $240
Spoon-soup, round bowl, bouillon,
  5 3/4 in. $90
Spoon-sugar, 4 1/4 in. $90
Spoon-teaspoon, 5 1/8 in. $90
Spoon-teaspoon, 5 3/4 in. $90
Spoon-teaspoon, large-youth, 6 1/8 in. $90
Tablespoon, (serving spoon), tear bowl,
  8 1/8 in. $250
Tongs-sugar, 4 1/4 in. $190

Acorn by Georg Jensen-Denmark, 1915

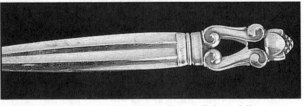

Butter spreader, hollow handle, solid paddle,
  5 7/8 in. $90
Butter spreader, hollow handle, stainless paddle,
  6 1/4 in. $98
Carving set, two piece, large stainless blade,
  roast, ... $800
Fish-fork/salad, solid, individual/small,
  6 1/2 in. $95
Food pusher, 3 3/4 in. $140
Fork, 4 7/8 in. handle, 7 1/2 in. $150
Fork-carving, large, stainless prongs, roast,
  10 3/4 in. $400
Fork-cold meat/server, small, 2 tines,
  6 5/8 in. $140

Georg Jensen

Fork-date, 2 tines, 4 5/8 in. $80
Fork-European, 5 7/8 in. handle, 7 in. $180
Fork-oyster, short handle, 3 flared tines,
    5 3/4 in. $100
Fork-salad/serving, stainless prongs, 8 in. . . . $150
Fork-youth, 5 5/8 in. $90
Knife-bar, hollow handle, 8 3/8 in. $100
Knife-cake, large, stainless blade,
    10 5/8 in. $160
Knife-carving, large, stainless blade, roast,
    12 1/2 in. $400
Knife-cheese, stainless blade, 7 7/8 in. $120
Knife-dinner, 4 3/4 in. handle, modern,
    9 in. $160
Knife-dinner, 5 in. handle, modern, no notch,
    9 1/8 in. $160
Knife-fruit, stainless blade, individual,
    6 3/4 in. $90
Knife-luncheon, 4 1/2 in. handle, modern,
    8 in. $140
Knife-modern, hollow 3 1/2 in. handle,
    8 in. $120
Knife-modern, hollow 3 7/8 in. handle,
    9 1/8 in. $140
Knife-modern, European, hollow 4 in. handle,
    9 3/4 in. $150
Knife-youth, solid piece, 7 in. $150
Ladle-cream, solid piece, 6 1/4 in. $180
Ladle-gravy, solid piece, 8 in. $450
Nut pick-set of six, ... $500
Plane-cheese, stainless plane, 8 1/4 in. $130
Salad set, 2 pieces, stainless bowl, ... $300
Scoop-cheese, solid piece, 7 in. $170
Serving set, solid, large, hollow handle,
    8 5/8 in. $900
Serving set, solid, small, 8 in. $600
Spoon-demitasse, 3 7/8 in. $80
Spoon-dessert/oval soup, tear bowl,
    6 3/4 in. $160
Spoon-fruit, triangular, 5 7/8 in. $130
Spoon-iced tea, 7 3/8 in. $130
Spoon-jam, 5 7/8 in. $100
Spoon-place/oval soup, 7 5/8 in. $180
Spoon-serving, solid, small, egg bowl,
    8 in. $300
Spoon-soup/bouillon, oval bowl,
    5 7/8 in. $100
Spoon-soup, round bowl, cream,
    6 3/8 in. $140
Spoon-sugar, 4 1/8 in. $100
Spoon-teaspoon, (five o'clock), 4 3/8 in. $50
Spoon-teaspoon, 5 3/4 in. $90
Spoon-teaspoon, large, youth, 6 1/8 in. $75
Spoon-teaspoon, small, youth, 5 1/8 in. $80

Sugar shovel, 4 1/4 in. $100
Tablespoon, (serving spoon), tear bowl,
    8 in. $240

Beaded by Georg Jensen-Denmark, 1916

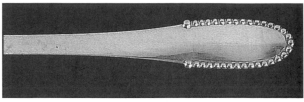

Butter spreader, flat handle, 5 3/4 in. $140
Fork, 4 tines, 6 7/8 in. $150
Fork, 7 1/8 in. $160
Fork-fish, solid, individual, 3 tines,
    6 3/4 in. $150
Knife-modern, hollow handle, 8 7/8 in. $160
Spoon-demitasse, 3 7/8 in. $70
Spoon-place/oval soup, 7 1/4 in. $160
Spoon-serving, solid, small, 8 in. $400
Spoon-teaspoon, large, youth, 5 7/8 in. $100

Bernadotte by Georg Jensen-Denmark, 1939

Butter spreader, hollow handle, paddle solid,
    6 in. $120
Butter spreader, hollow handle, paddle stainless,
    6 in. $120
Fork, 7 5/8 in. $110
Fork-cold meat/serving, medium, 2 tines,
    8 1/4 in. $220
Fork-fish, solid, individual, 3 tines,
    6 3/4 in. $100
Fork-serving, solid, small, 8 1/4 in. $300
Knife-dinner, long handle, modern,
    8 5/8 in. $120
Knife-fish, solid, individual, 7 3/4 in. $120
Knife-luncheon, long handle, modern,
    7 3/4 in. $100
Knife-modern, hollow handle, 8 3/4 in. $110
Serving set, solid, small, 8 1/4 in. $600
Spoon-dessert/oval soup, 7 1/4 in. $110
Spoon-fruit, 6 in. $110

Spoon-iced tea, 7 1/4 in. $160
Spoon-jam, 5 7/8 in. $110
Spoon-place/oval soup, 7 3/4 in. $120
Spoon-serving, solid, small, 8 1/4 in. $300
Spoon-soup, round bowl, cream,
   6 3/8 in. $120
Spoon-teaspoon, (five o'clock),
   4 1/4 in. $100
Spoon-teaspoon, large, youth, 6 3/8 in. $110
Tongs-sugar, 4 1/4 in. $300

Blossom by
Georg Jensen-Denmark, 1919

Fork, 4 tines, 7 1/2 in. $550
Knife-modern, hollow handle, 9 in. $550
Spoon-teaspoon, large, youth, 6 in. $300
Tongs-sugar, 3 3/4 in. $350

Cactus by Georg Jensen-Denmark, 1930

Butter spreader, hollow handle, solid paddle,
   6 1/8 in. $150
Carving set, 2 pieces, large, stainless blade,
   roast, ... $750
Fork, 6 1/2 in. $140
Fork, 7 1/4 in. $160
Fork-compote, medium, 6 5/8 in. $280
Fork-European, 7 3/4 in. $170
Fork-salad, individual, 6 1/4 in. $150
Knife-fruit, stainless blade, individual,
   6 7/8 in. $130
Knife-modern, hollow 3 1/2 in. handle,
   8 in. $140
Knife-modern, hollow 3 5/8 in. handle,
   9 in. $170
Ladle-gravy, solid piece, 7 3/8 in. $470
Poultry shears. 10 in. $500
Spoon-demitasse, 3 1/2 in. $80
Spoon-serving, solid, small, 8 in. $300
Spoon-soup, round bowl, bouillon, round bowl,
   5 3/8 in. $120
Spoon-teaspoon, 4 7/8 in. $120
Spoon-teaspoon, 5 3/8 in. $120
Spoon-teaspoon, large, youth,
   5 7/8 in. $120

Caravelle by
Georg Jensen-Denmark, 1957

Butter spreader, flat handle, 6 1/8 in. $115
Fork, 6 3/4 in. $100
Fork, 7 1/2 in. $120
Fork-cold meat/serving, large, 4 tines,
   9 1/8 in. $270
Fork-fish, solid, individual, 6 1/2 in. $120
Fork-fruit, solid, individual, 5 7/8 in. $100
Fork-pastry, 5 5/8 in. $98
Knife-fruit, stainless blade, individual,
   6 3/4 in. $80
Knife-modern, hollow handle, 7 5/8 in. $110
Knife-modern, hollow handle, 8 3/4 in. $140
Server-cake, solid piece, 10 3/8 in. $440
Spoon-demitasse, 4 1/8 in. $70
Spoon-dessert/oval soup, 6 3/4 in. $120
Spoon-place/oval soup, 7 5/8 in. $140
Spoon-serving, solid, medium, 8 5/8 in. $340
Spoon-teaspoon, large, youth, 5 3/4 in. $90

Continental by
Georg Jensen-Denmark, 1908

Carving set, 2 pieces, small, stainless blade,
   steak, ... $460
Fork, 1 3/4 in. tines, 7 1/4 in. $140
Knife-luncheon, long handle, modern, 4 1/2 in.
   handle, hammered finish, 8 1/4 in. $110
Spoon-demitasse, hammered finish,
   3 3/4 in. $60

Cypress by
Georg Jensen-Denmark, 1954

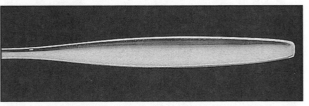

Butter spreader, flat handle, 6 1/4 in. $55
Fork, 7 1/2 in. $65
Fork, no bevel tines, 6 3/4 in. $64
Fork-cocktail, 5 5/8 in. $70

Georg Jensen

Fork-cold meat/serving, medium, 2 tines,
8 1/4 in. $100
Fork-cold meat/serving, small, 2 tines,
6 3/4 in. $80
Fork-lemon, 4 1/2 in. $46
Fork-pastry, 5 7/8 in. $65
Fork-salad, individual, 2 bevel tines,
6 3/4 in. $70
Knife-dinner, long handle, modern, 9 in. $75
Knife-fruit, stainless blade, individual,
6 3/4 in. $60
Ladle-gravy, solid piece, 8 1/8 in. $190
Opener-bottle, stainless bowl, 5 1/2 in. $110
Salad set, 2 pieces, stainless bowl, 9 in. . . . $240
Server-pie, solid, small, 8 3/4 in. $200
Serving set, solid, large, 9 7/8 in. $680
Serving set, solid, small, 8 1/2 in. $350
Spoon-dessert/oval soup, 7 in. $75
Spoon-fruit, 6 1/8 in. $75
Spoon-iced tea, 7 3/8 in. $60
Spoon-mocha, 3 1/2 in. $40
Spoon-place/oval soup, 7 7/8 in. $80
Spoon-serving, solid, large, 9 7/8 in. $340
Spoon-serving, solid, small, 8 1/2 in. $180
Spoon-soup, round bowl, cream,
5 3/4 in. $75
Spoon-soup, round bowl, gumbo, 7 in. $85
Spoon-sugar, 4 3/8 in. $90
Spoon-teaspoon, (five o'clock), 4 1/2 in. $40
Spoon-teaspoon, 5 1/8 in. $45
Spoon-teaspoon, large, youth, 6 in. $46

Old Danish by
Georg Jensen-Denmark, 1947

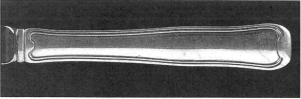

Knife-dinner, long handle, modern,
8 7/8 in. $90
Spoon-dessert/oval soup, 7 1/4 in. $120
Spoon-place/oval soup, 6 3/4 in. $120
Spoon-teaspoon, youth, 6 in. $80

Parallel by Georg Jensen-Denmark,
1931

Fork, 7 1/8 in. $170
Fork-fish, solid, individual, 6 3/8 in. $110
Fork-salad, individual, 6 1/4 in. $200
Knife-dinner, long handle, modern,
8 3/8 in. $170
Knife-modern, hollow handle, 3 5/8 in. handle,
9 in. $170
Spoon-place/oval soup, 7 1/2 in. $200
Spoon-soup, round bowl, cream,
6 3/8 in. $120
Spoon-teaspoon, 5 5/8 in. $120

Pyramid by
Georg Jensen-Denmark, 1927

Spoon-place/oval soup, 7 3/4 in. $140

Scroll by Georg Jensen-Denmark,
1927

Butter spreader, hollow handle, solid paddle,
5 3/4 in. $160
Fork, 7 1/8 in. $200
Fork-fish, solid, individual, 3 tines,
6 3/8 in. $160
Fork-pastry, 5 5/8 in. $160
Knife-fruit, stainless blade, individual,
6 1/2 in. $160
Knife-modern, hollow handle,
7 5/8 in. $200
Knife-modern, hollow handle, 8 7/8 in. $200
Knife-youth, 6 1/2 in. $140
Server-pie, solid, small, 8 1/8 in. $700
Spoon-dessert/oval soup, 6 5/8 in. $280
Spoon-iced tea, 7 1/8 in. $170
Spoon-soup, round bowl, bouillon,
5 1/4 in. $160

GORHAM

The company that became the Gorham Corp. was founded about 1817 by Jabez Gorham in Providence, Rhode Island, and became the Gorham Manufacturing Co. in 1863.

Jabez Gorham started making silver in 1831 in a shop on Steeple Street in Providence. Born to a family of eight, he was apprenticed to New England silversmith Nehemiah Dodge. Dodge was one of the founders of the silver and jewelry crafts industry in 18th century New England.

After his seven-year apprenticeship with Dodge, Jabez formed his own business. He created the "French filigree" chain, as well as a wide selection of handcrafted pieces. The firm began producing "coin silver" spoons (made from melted coins).

Jabez's son, John, took total control of the company when Jabez retired. By 1875, there were more than 400 employees, and in 1890 Gorham moved to a new site in Providence. An office building designed in 1905 by architect Stanford White was located on Fifth Avenue in New York City.

The company's trademark—lion/anchor/G—was first used in the mid-1800s; later pieces are marked "Gorham Sterling." After the turn of the century, Gorham began acquiring other silver firms, include Whiting, Durgin, Kerr, Mt. Vernon, and Alvin.

Adam by Gorham, 1907

Fish-fork/salad, solid, individual, large,
    6 1/4 in. $58
Fork, 7 1/8 in. $27
Fork, 7 7/8 in. $40
Fork-cold meat/serving, small, solid,
    7 3/8 in. $80
Fork-salad, individual, 7 3/8 in. $80
Knife-new french, hollow handle,
    9 5/8 in. $46
Spoon-soup, round bowl, bouillon,
    5 1/8 in. $24
Spoon-soup, round bowl, cream,
    6 1/4 in. $30

Spoon-teaspoon, 6 1/8 in. $16
Spoon-teaspoon, 6 1/8 in. $22

Albemarle by Gorham, 1894/1912

Butter spreader, flat handle, 5 5/8 in. $26
Fork, 7 5/8 in. $60
Fork, 7 in. $45
Knife-old french, hollow handle,
    8 1/2 in. $35
Spoon-demitasse, 4 1/4 in. $24
Spoon-dessert/oval soup, 7 1/8 in. $50
Spoon-soup, round bowl, bouillon, 5 in. $30
Spoon-soup, round bowl, gumbo,
    6 7/8 in. $46
Spoon-sugar, 5 7/8 in. $44
Spoon-teaspoon, 5 3/4 in. $18

The following pieces have monograms:
Butter spreader, flat handle, 5 5/8 in. $20
Fork, 7 in. $36
Spoon-dessert/oval soup, 7 1/8 in. $38
Spoon-teaspoon, (five o'clock),
    5 3/8 in. $18
Spoon-teaspoon, 5 3/4 in. $14

Alencon Lace by Gorham, 1965

Butter-master, hollow handle, 6 3/4 in. $47
Carving set, 2 pieces, small, stainless blade,
    steak $140
Fork, 7 1/2 in. $60
Fork-carving, small, stainless prongs, steak,
    9 1/2 in. $70
Fork-cocktail, 5 3/4 in. $48
Fork-salad, individual, 6 3/4 in. $60
Knife-carving, small, stainless blade, steak,
    12 in. $70
Knife-modern, hollow handle, 9 1/4 in. $45
Ladle-gravy, solid piece, 7 1/8 in. $130
Ladle-punch, stainless bowl, 13 7/8 in. $140

Gorham

Server-lasagna, stainless blade,
  11 7/8 in. $80
Server-pasta, stainless bowl, 11 in. $80
Server-pie and cake, stainless blade,
  10 1/2 in. $80
Spoon-dessert/oval soup, 6 7/8 in............$60
Spoon-iced tea, 7 5/8 in. $60
Spoon-sugar shell, 6 3/8 in.................$50

Andante by Gorham, 1963

Butter spreader, hollow handle, modern, stainless
  paddle, 6 1/2 in.........................$33
Fork, 7 1/8 in..............................$44
Fork-salad, individual, 6 3/4 in. $55
Knife-modern, hollow handle,
  9 in......................................$40
Spoon-dessert/oval soup,
  6 1/2 in...................................$60
Spoon-iced tea, 7 1/4 in. $40
Spoon-sugar, 5 7/8 in.......................$40
Spoon-teaspoon, 6 in........................$25
Tablespoon, (serving spoon),
  8 1/2 in.................................$110
Tablespoon, (serving spoon), pierced,
  8 1/2 in.................................$120

Eighteen pieces Gorham Antique (c.1875): 6 dessert spoons, 6 dessert forks, and 6 teaspoons. Monogram "H." Together with the 6 original mother-of-pearl handled dessert knives by the Connecticut Plate Co. Knife 7 3/4 in. with silver plated steel blunt blade, dessert spoon 7 1/2 in., fork 6 3/4 in long. $450

Aspen by Gorham, 1963

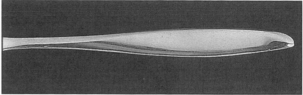

Butter spreader, hollow handle, modern, stainless
  paddle, 6 7/8 in..........................$20
Butter-master, hollow handle, 7 3/8 in........$34
Fork, 7 1/8 in. $30
Fork-cocktail, 5 3/4 in. $28
Fork-ice cream, 5 1/2 in.....................$38
Fork-salad, individual, 6 5/8 in. $33
Knife-modern, hollow handle, 8 3/4 in........$30
Spoon-dessert/oval soup, 6 5/8 in. $36
Spoon-sugar, 6 in. $34
Spoon-teaspoon, 6 in........................$22

Baronial-Old by Gorham, 1898

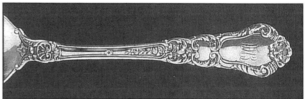

Carving set, 2 pieces, large, stainless blade,
  roast...................................$200
Fork, 7 in..................................$46
Fork-cocktail, pierced bowl, 5 3/4 in..........$30
Fork-ice cream, gold wash, 4 3/4 in..........$70
Knife-blunt, hollow handle, 9 3/4 in..........$70
Knife-fruit, silver plate blade, individual,
  6 7/8 in.................................$38
Knife-new french, hollow handle,
  8 1/2 in.................................$50
Knife-sharpener/steel, small, steak,
  14 in. $100
Server-macaroni, 10 1/4 in. $400
Spoon-dessert/oval soup, 7 in...............$80
Spoon-soup, round bowl, bouillon, 5 in. $45
Tablespoon, (serving spoon), 8 5/8 in. $90

The following pieces have monograms:
Butter spreader, flat handle, 5 7/8 in. $25
Fork, 7 in..................................$36
Fork-carving, large, stainless prongs,
  roast, 11 in.............................$80
Fork-olive, 5 3/4 in.........................$30
Knife-blunt, hollow handle,
  8 1/2 in.................................$40

Knife-fish, serving, solid, large, 12 in. $300
Knife-new french, hollow handle, 8 1/2 in......$40
Knife-new french, hollow handle, 9 3/4 in......$55
Knife-old french, hollow handle, 8 5/8 in.......$40
Spoon-dessert/oval soup, 7 in. $58
Spoon-ice cream, 5 1/8 in....................$50
Spoon-soup, round bowl, bouillon, 5 in........$36
Tablespoon, (serving spoon), 8 5/8 in.........$75

Bead by Gorham, 1893

Butter-master, flat handle, 7 1/8 in............$44
Fork, 7 3/4 in...............................$70
Knife-new french, hollow handle,
    9 1/2 in.................................$60
Knife-old french, hollow handle, 9 1/2 in.......$60
Spoon-dessert/oval soup, 7 1/8 in............$60
Spoon-teaspoon, 5 7/8 in. $30

Birds Nest by Gorham, 1865

Blithe Spirit by Gorham, 1959

Butter spreader, hollow handle, modern, stainless
    paddle, 6 3/4 in..........................$15
Butter-master, hollow handle, 7 1/8 in..........$30
Fork, 7 3/8 in...............................$36
Fork-cold meat/serving, medium, solid,
    8 7/8 in.................................$70
Fork-lemon, 4 3/4 in........................$24
Fork-pickle/olive, short handle,
    5 7/8 in.................................$24
Fork-salad, individual, 6 3/4 in. $32
Knife-modern, hollow handle, 9 1/4 in.........$28
Ladle-cream, solid piece, 5 1/8 in. $40
Server-pie and cake, stainless blade,
    10 3/4 in. $57
Spoon-dessert/oval soup, 6 7/8 in............$35
Spoon-iced tea, 7 1/2 in. $28
Spoon-sugar, 6 1/8 in.......................$28

Spoon-teaspoon, 6 in......................$17
Tablespoon, (serving spoon), 8 5/8 in. $60
Tablespoon, (serving spoon), pierced,
    8 5/8 in.................................$70

Buckingham by Gorham, 1910

Butter spreader, hollow handle, modern, stainless,
    6 1/4 in.................................$27
Fork, 7 1/2 in. $58
Fork, 7 in..................................$44
Fork-cocktail, 5 3/8 in......................$25
Fork-pastry, bar, pierce, 6 1/4 in............$48
Knife-modern, hollow handle, 8 3/4 in........$35
Knife-new french, hollow handle, 9 1/2 in. $50
Knife-old french, hollow handle, 9 3/4 in. $50
Ladle-gravy, solid, 7 5/8 in.................$90
Salad set, 2 pieces, solid piece, 9 in. $220
Server-pie and cake, stainless blade
    replaced, 10 1/4 in. $70
Spoon-demitasse, 4 3/8 in..................$20
Spoon-demitasse, gold wash, 4 3/8 in.......$20
Spoon-fruit, 5 3/4 in. $35
Spoon-soup, round bowl, bouillon,
    5 1/4 in.................................$40
Spoon-soup, round bowl, cream, 5 7/8 in. $50
Spoon-soup, round bowl, gumbo, 6 5/8 in.....$50
Tablespoon, (serving spoon), 8 1/2 in. $90
Tongs-sugar, 4 1/4 in. $66

Buttercup by Gorham, 1899

Gorham's Buttercup was first introduced in 1899.
    Pieces made prior to approximately 1950 will
    have the "lion/anchor/G" back stamp. Pieces
    marked with "Gorham Sterling" were produced
    after 1950.

Baby set, 2 pieces $60
Butter spreader, hollow handle, modern, stainless
    paddle, 6 1/4 in..........................$38

Gorham

Butter-master, hollow handle, 6 3/4 in.........$36
Carving set, 2 pieces, small, stainless blade,
    steak.....................................$120
Fork, (place size), 5 in. handle, 7 1/2 in. $44
Fork, 7 in..$38
Fork-baby, 4 3/8 in. $30
Fork-carving, small, stainless prongs, steak,
    9 5/8 in....................................$50
Fork-cocktail, 5 1/2 in........................$30
Fork-cold meat/serving, medium, solid,
    8 1/8 in....................................$80
Fork-fish, stainless tines, hollow handle,
    individual, 8 in. $54
Fork-ice cream, 5 1/4 in......................$44
Fork-lemon, 4 3/8 in...........................$34
Fork-salad (place size), 6 3/4 in.............$36
Fork-salad serving, stainless prongs,
    11 1/4 in. $45
Fork-strawberry, 4 3/4 in. $40
Knife-carving, small, stainless blade, steak,
    12 1/8 in. $50
Knife-cheese, stainless blade, 7 in. $50
Knife-fish, stainless blade, individual,
    8 5/8 in....................................$54
Knife-modern, hollow (place size), 4 1/4 in.
    handle, 9 1/8 in...........................$33
Knife-modern, hollow handle, 3 5/8 in. handle,
    8 3/4 in....................................$36
Knife-modern, hollow handle, 4 in. handle,
    9 5/8 in....................................$48
Knife-new french, hollow handle,
    8 3/4 in....................................$36
Knife-new french, hollow handle, 9 5/8 in......$48
Knife-steak, individual, no bevel, 9 1/4 in......$44
Knife-wedding cake, stainless blade,
    12 1/2 in. $45
Ladle-cream, solid piece, 5 1/4 in. $50
Ladle-gravy, solid piece, 6 1/8 in. $85
Ladle-punch, stainless bowl, 13 5/8 in. $70
Ladle-soup, stainless bowl, 11 3/4 in. $70
Napkin clip (made for teaspoons)............$26
Salad set, 2 pieces, solid piece.............$280
Salad set, 2 pieces, stainless bowl...........$90
Scoop-ice, silver plate bowl, 9 1/8 in..........$50
Server-asparagus, hollow handle, silver plate
    hood, 9 3/4 in. $60
Server-lasagna, stainless blade, 12 in. $45
Server-pastry, stainless bowl, 9 3/8 in. $48
Server-pie and cake, stainless blade,
    10 5/8 in. $50
Server-pie, stainless blade, 10 1/4 in. $50
Spoon-baby, straight handle, 4 1/2 in.........$30
Spoon-casserole, smooth, stainless bowl,
    10 3/4 in. $45
Spoon-fruit, 5 5/8 in..........................$45
Spoon-iced tea, 7 1/2 in. $42
Spoon-infant feeding, 5 3/4 in...............$38
Spoon-oval soup (place size), 6 3/4 in. $46
Spoon-salad serving, solid piece, 9 in. $140

Spoon-salad serving, stainless bowl,
    11 1/4 in...................................$45
Spoon-soup, round bowl, cream, 6 1/4 in. $44
Spoon-sugar, 6 in. $44
Spoon-teaspoon, 5 3/4 in....................$22
Tablespoon, (serving spoon), 8 3/8 in. $80
Tongs-asparagus, solid piece, 8 3/4 in. $300

Cambridge by Gorham, 1899

Butter spreader, hollow handle, modern, stainless,
    6 1/4 in....................................$34
Butter spreader, flat handle, 5 7/8 in. $30
Fork, 7 3/4 in. $48
Fork, 7 in...................................$32
Fork-cocktail, 5 3/8 in......................$24
Fork-cocktail, gold wash, 5 3/8 in............$24
Fork-pickle/olive, long handle, 8 1/4 in........$60
Fork-pickle/olive, short handle, 3 tines,
    5 3/4 in....................................$40
Ladle-gravy, solid piece, gold wash, 7 in......$95
Spoon-demitasse, 4 1/8 in...................$24
Spoon-demitasse, gold wash, 4 1/8 in........$24
Spoon-dessert/oval soup, 7 in...............$46
Spoon-fruit, 5 3/4 in. $40
Spoon-iced tea, 7 1/2 in....................$60
Spoon-olive, long handle, gold wash,
    8 1/2 in....................................$160
Spoon-soup, round bowl, bouillon, 5 in. $35
Spoon-soup, round bowl, cream, 5 7/8 in. $60
Spoon-soup, round bowl, gumbo, 6 7/8 in..... $50
Spoon-teaspoon, (five o'clock), 5 3/8 in....... $17
Tablespoon, (serving spoon), 8 1/2 in. $70
Tongs-sugar, 4 in...........................$50

The following pieces have monograms:
Butter spreader, flat handle, 5 7/8 in. $23
Fork, 7 3/4 in. $38
Fork, 7 in...................................$25
Fork-cocktail, 5 3/8 in......................$18
Fork-lettuce, serving, large, 9 1/4 in.........$100
Fork-pie, 5 3/4 in. $40
Fork-salad, individual, 5 7/8 in. $50
Fork-youth, 6 in. $36
Knife-blunt, hollow handle, 8 1/2 in...........$32
Knife-blunt, hollow handle, 9 3/4 in...........$45
Ladle-gravy, solid piece, 7 in.................$80
Spoon-demitasse, 4 1/8 in...................$18

Spoon-dessert/oval soup, 7 in. $35
Spoon-fruit, 5 3/4 in. $30
Spoon-iced tea, 7 1/2 in. $45
Spoon-soup, round bowl, bouillon, 5 in. $27
Spoon-soup, round bowl, gumbo, 6 7/8 in. $38
Spoon-teaspoon, (five o'clock), 5 3/8 in. $13
Spoon-teaspoon, 5 3/4 in. $15
Tablespoon, (serving spoon), 8 1/2 in. $50
Tablespoon, (serving spoon), pierced,
    8 1/2 in. $70

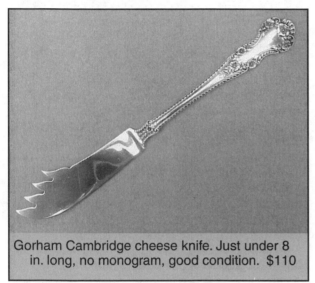

Gorham Cambridge cheese knife. Just under 8
in. long, no monogram, good condition. $110

Camellia by Gorham, 1942

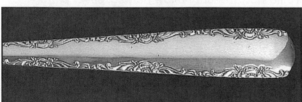

Butter spreader, hollow handle, modern, stainless,
    6 1/4 in. $22
Butter spreader, hollow handle, stainless paddle,
    6 1/8 in. $22
Butter spreader, flat handle, 5 3/4 in. $15
Butter-master, flat handle, 7 1/8 in. $35
Butter-master, hollow handle, 6 5/8 in. $35
Carving set, 2 pieces, large, stainless blade,
    roast $130
Carving set, 2 pieces, small, stainless blade,
    steak $96
Fork, 5 1/8 in. handle, 7 7/8 in. $46
Fork, 7 1/4 in. $22
Fork-cocktail, 5 5/8 in. $26
Fork-cold meat/serving, medium, solid,
    8 1/8 in. $90
Fork-lemon, 4 1/2 in. $32

Fork-pickle/olive, short handle, 2 tines,
    5 7/8 in. $32
Fork-salad, individual, 4 1/4 in. handle,
    6 1/2 in. $32
Knife-carving, small, stainless blade, steak,
    10 3/8 in. $48
Knife-cheese, stainless blade, 7 in. $40
Knife-modern, hollow 4 1/4 in. handle,
    9 5/8 in. $42
Knife-modern, hollow 4 in. handle,
    8 7/8 in. $36
Knife-new french, hollow, 4 in. handle,
    8 7/8 in. $36
Ladle-cream, solid piece, 5 1/4 in. $40
Ladle-gravy, solid piece, 6 1/2 in. $70
Napkin clip (made for teaspoons) $20
Server-jelly, 6 1/8 in. $32
Server-pastry, stainless bowl, 9 5/8 in. $50
Server-pie and cake, stainless blade,
    10 5/8 in. $48
Server-pie, stainless blade, 10 1/8 in. $50
Spoon-bon-bon, 4 3/4 in. $36
Spoon-demitasse, 4 1/4 in. $24
Spoon-dessert/oval soup, 6 7/8 in. $56
Spoon-iced tea, 7 1/2 in. $38
Spoon-oval soup (place size), 6 3/4 in. $50
Spoon-soup, round bowl, cream, 6 1/4 in. $33
Spoon-soup, round bowl, bouillon,
    5 1/2 in. $34
Spoon-sugar, 6 1/8 in. $28
Spoon-teaspoon, 5 7/8 in. $16
Tablespoon, (serving spoon), 8 1/2 in. $70
Tongs-sugar, 4 in. $56

Celeste by Gorham, 1956

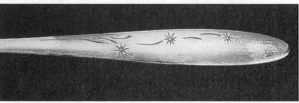

Butter spreader, hollow handle, modern, stainless
    paddle, 6 1/2 in. $12
Butter-master, hollow handle, 7 in. $23
Carving set, 2 pieces, small, stainless blade,
    steak $120
Fork, 7 5/8 in. $30
Fork-baby, 4 1/2 in. $38
Fork-cocktail, 5 3/4 in. $22
Fork-cold meat/serving, medium, solid,
    8 5/8 in. $70
Fork-ice cream, 5 5/8 in. $36
Fork-lemon, 4 in. $18
Fork-pickle/olive, short handle, 5 7/8 in. $20

Fork-salad, individual, 7 in. $30
Knife-carving, small, stainless blade, steak,
  10 3/4 in. $60
Knife-cheese, stainless blade, 7 1/2 in. $36
Knife-cheese, stainless blade, 7 in. $36
Knife-modern, hollow handle, 9 3/8 in.........$22
Ladle-cream, solid piece, 5 1/4 in. $40
Ladle-gravy, solid piece, 6 3/4 in. $70
Napkin clip (made for sugar) $25
Server-cheese, stainless blade, 7 in..........$35
Server-jelly, 6 1/4 in........................$28
Server-pastry, stainless bowl, 10 in...........$50
Server-pie and cake, stainless blade,
  10 3/4 in. $50
Server-pie, solid piece, 9 7/8 in. $110
Spoon-baby, straight handle, 4 3/8 in. $38
Spoon-bon-bon, 4 1/4 in. $30
Spoon-chocolate, short handle,
  5 5/8 in...................................$23
Spoon-dessert/oval soup, 7 1/8 in............$34
Spoon-iced tea, 7 1/2 in. $40
Spoon-sugar, 6 1/4 in........................$18
Spoon-teaspoon, 6 in........................$15
Tablespoon, (serving spoon), 8 5/8 in.........$60

Chantilly by Gorham, 1895

Gorham's Chantilly was first introduced in 1895.
  Pieces made prior to approximately 1950 will
  have a "lion/anchor/G" back stamp. Pieces
  marked with "Gorham Sterling" were produced
  after 1950.

Butter spreader, hollow handle, stainless paddle,
  no notch, 6 in. $30
Butter spreader, flat handle, 5 7/8 in..........$28
Butter-master, flat handle, 6 3/4 in...........$40
Butter-master, flat handle, 7 3/4 in...........$40
Butter-master, hollow handle, notch,
  6 5/8 in..................................$42
Carving set, 2 pieces, small, stainless blade,
  steak...................................$130
Fish-fork/salad, solid, individual, small,
  5 3/4 in..................................$50
Fish-fork/salad, solid, individual, small, gold
  wash, 5 3/4 in............................$50
Fork, 2 in. tines, 7 1/2 in. $60
Fork, 7 in..................................$28
Fork-baby, 4 1/2 in. $45

Fork-carving, large, stainless prongs, roast,
  11 1/4 in.................................$80
Fork-carving, small, stainless prongs, steak,
  8 1/2 in. $64
Fork-cocktail, 5 1/2 in. $30
Fork-cold meat/serving, small, solid,
  6 3/8 in..................................$90
Fork-cold meat/serving, medium, solid,
  8 1/2 in.................................$100
Fork-cold meat/serving, medium, solid,
  8 in. $100
Fork-ice cream, no pierce, 5 1/2 in...........$50
Fork-lettuce serving, large, 9 3/8 in. $90
Fork-salad serving, solid, 8 3/4 in...........$130
Fork-salad serving, solid, gold wash,
  8 3/4 in.................................$130
Fork-salad, individual, 6 3/8 in. $50
Fork-serving, solid, 4 tines, 8 1/2 in..........$90
Fork-youth, 6 in. $42
Knife-blunt, hollow handle, silver plate blade,
  8 1/2 in..................................$40
Knife-blunt, hollow handle, silver plate blade,
  9 3/4 in..................................$50
Knife-carving, small, stainless blade, steak,
  10 1/2 in.................................$64
Knife-fruit, silver plate blade, individual,
  6 7/8 in..................................$45
Knife-fruit, stainless blade, individual,
  7 in. $50
Knife-modern, hollow handle, stainless blade,
  9 5/8 in..................................$50
Knife-new french, hollow handle, silver plate
  blade, 8 7/8 in...........................$40
Knife-new french, hollow handle, stainless
  blade, 8 7/8 in...........................$40
Knife-new french, hollow handle, stainless
  blade, 8 in. $40
Knife-new french, hollow handle, stainless
  blade, 9 5/8 in...........................$50
Knife-old french, hollow handle, silver plate
  blade, 8 5/8 in...........................$40
Knife-old french, hollow handle, silver plate
  blade, 9 5/8 in...........................$50
Ladle-gravy, solid piece, 6 3/4 in............$100
Ladle-punch, solid piece, gold wash,
  14 in. $1,000
Napkin clip (made for teaspoons) $28
Server-cheese, silver plate blade, 6 in........$70
Server-jelly, 6 1/8 in. $40
Server-pastry, stainless bowl, 9 7/8 in........$45
Server-tomato, solid piece, 7 1/2 in. $120
Spoon-baby, straight handle, no emboss,
  4 1/2 in..................................$45
Spoon-casserole, smooth, solid, 8 3/4 in. ...$160
Spoon-demitasse, 4 1/8 in..................$30
Spoon-dressing, large, solid, 12 1/2 in. $280

Spoon-iced tea, 7 1/2 in. $34
Spoon-lettuce, 9 1/2 in. $90
Spoon-olive, long handle, 8 1/2 in. $100
Spoon-soup, round bowl, bouillon, 5 in........$35
Spoon-soup, round bowl, cream, 6 1/4 in......$43
Spoon-soup, round bowl, gumbo, 6 5/8 in. $60
Spoon-sugar shell, 6 in. $42
Spoon-teaspoon, (five o'clock), 5 1/2 in. $24
Spoon-teaspoon, 5 3/4 in. $22
Tablespoon, (serving spoon), 8 1/2 in.........$75
Tongs-sugar, 4 1/4 in. $60

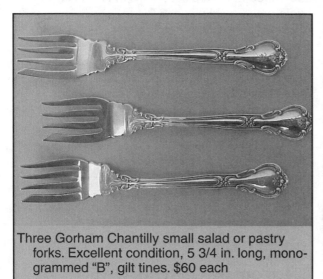

Three Gorham Chantilly small salad or pastry forks. Excellent condition, 5 3/4 in. long, monogrammed "B", gilt tines. $60 each

Chapel Rose by Gorham, 1963

Fork, 7 1/8 in. $25
Fork-salad, individual, 6 1/2 in. $24
Knife-modern, hollow handle, 8 7/8 in........$20
Spoon-teaspoon, 6 in. $14

Chelsea Manor by Gorham, 1966

Butter-master, hollow handle, 7 in............$32
Fork, 7 1/2 in. $48

Fork-salad, individual, 6 3/4 in. $40
Knife-modern, hollow handle, 9 1/8 in........ $33
Spoon-dessert/oval soup, 6 7/8 in. $50
Spoon-sugar, 6 in. $25
Spoon-teaspoon, 6 in. $25
Tablespoon, (serving spoon), 8 5/8 in. $70

Chesterfield by Gorham, 1908

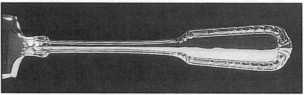

Butter spreader, flat handle, 6 in............ $30
Fork, 7 5/8 in. $50
Fork, 7 in. $45
Fork-cocktail, 5 5/8 in. $30
Fork, fish/salad, solid, individual, 2 wide
　　tines, 5 7/8 in. $50
Fork-ice cream, 5 1/2 in. $50
Fork-salad, individual, 6 3/4 in. $50
Knife-fish, solid, individual, no indent,
　　7 7/8 in. $55
Knife-old french, hollow handle, 8 3/4 in. $40
Knife-old french, hollow handle, 9 3/4 in. $50
Knife-orange, silver plate blade, 6 7/8 in...... $40
Spoon-dessert/oval soup, 7 1/8 in. $60
Spoon-fruit, 5 3/4 in. $35
Spoon-soup, round bowl, cream, 6 5/8 in. $60
Spoon-sugar, 5 7/8 in. $48
Spoon-teaspoon, (five o'clock), 5 1/2 in...... $18
Spoon-teaspoon, 5 7/8 in. $30
Tablespoon, (serving spoon), 8 3/8 in. $70
Tongs-sugar, 5 in. $70

Chrysanthemum by Gorham, 1885

Fork-youth, 6 in. $60
Spoon-demitasse, 4 1/8 in. $30
Spoon-jelly/large, 7 1/4 in. $90
Spoon-teaspoon, (five o'clock), 5 3/4 in...... $24
Spoon-teaspoon, 6 in. $34
Tablespoon, (serving spoon), 8 3/8 in. $100
The following pieces have monograms:
Ladle-gravy, solid piece, 7 1/4 in............ $75

Spoon-demitasse, 4 in......................$20
Spoon-teaspoon, 6 in.......................$24
Tablespoon, (serving spoon), 8 3/8 in.........$70

Cinderella by Gorham, 1925

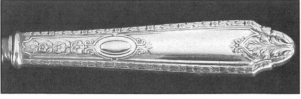

Butter spreader, flat handle, 5 1/2 in..........$22
Butter-master, flat handle, 6 3/4 in............$34
Carving set, 2 pieces, small, stainless blade,
    steak....................................$120
Fork, 7 1/4 in.............................$40
Fork, 7 3/4 in.............................$45
Fork-carving, small, stainless prongs, steak,
    9 in....................................$60
Fork-cocktail, 5 3/8 in......................$30
Fork-cold meat/serving, small, solid, 7 in......$80
Fork-salad, individual, 6 1/4 in...............$40
Knife-carving, small, stainless blade, steak,
    10 in...................................$60
Knife-new french, hollow handle,
    9 1/2 in.................................$47
Knife-old french, hollow handle, 8 1/2 in.......$35
Knife-old french, hollow handle, 9 1/2 in.......$47
Ladle-gravy, solid piece, gold wash,
    6 3/4 in.................................$80
Server-pie, silver plate blade, 10 in...........$70
Spoon-demitasse, 4 1/8 in. $20
Spoon-soup, round bowl, bouillon,
    5 1/4 in.................................$35
Spoon-sugar, 6 in..........................$35
Spoon-teaspoon, (five o'clock),
    5 3/8 in.................................$16
Spoon-teaspoon, 3 3/4 in. handle,
    5 3/4 in.................................$20
Tablespoon, (serving spoon), 8 3/8 in.........$70
Tablespoon, (serving spoon), pierced,
    8 3/8 in.................................$80

Classique by Gorham, 1961

Butter-master, hollow handle, 7 in. $24
Carving set, 2 pieces, large, stainless blade,
    roast.................................. $150
Fork, 7 3/8 in. $38
Fork-cold meat, serving, medium, solid,
    8 3/4 in................................. $65
Fork-pickle/olive, short handle, 6 in. $25
Fork-salad serving, solid piece, 8 3/4 in. $100
Fork-salad, individual, 6 3/4 in. $40
Knife-modern, hollow handle, 9 in. $28
Ladle-cream, solid piece, 5 1/8 in............ $40
Ladle-gravy, solid piece, 6 3/4 in............. $70
Napkin clip, (made for teaspoons)........... $24
Salad set, 2 pieces, wooden bowl,
    11 1/8 in................................ $80
Server-jelly, 6 3/8 in. $34
Server-pie and cake, stainless blade,
    11 in................................... $46
Server-pie and cake, stainless blade replaced,
    11 in................................... $56
Spoon-bon-bon, 4 5/8 in. $35
Spoon-sugar, 6 in. $28
Spoon-teaspoon, 6 in....................... $20
Tablespoon, (serving spoon), 8 5/8 in. $70
Tablespoon, (serving spoon), pierced,
    8 5/8 in................................. $70

Clermont by Gorham, 1915

Butter spreader, flat handle, 5 1/2 in. $24
Butter-master, flat handle, 6 7/8 in........... $38
Carving set, 2 pieces, small, stainless blade,
    steak $100
Fork, 7 1/8 in. $48
Fork, 7 5/8 in. $60
Fork-cocktail, 5 3/8 in. $30
Fork-cold meat, serving, small, solid,
    7 1/4 in................................. $76
Fork-cold meat, serving, medium, solid,
    8 7/8 in................................. $80
Fork-pastry, 4 tines bar, 6 1/4 in............. $35
Knife-old french, hollow handle, 8 5/8 in. $34
Knife-old french, hollow handle, 9 5/8 in. $45
Ladle-cream, solid piece, 5 1/4 in............ $46
Ladle-gravy, solid piece, 6 1/8 in............. $80
Server-jelly, 6 1/4 in. $30
Spoon-iced tea, 8 1/8 in.................... $60

Spoon-soup, round bowl, bouillon,
5 3/8 in. $30
Spoon-sugar, 5 7/8 in. $40
Spoon-teaspoon, (five o'clock), 5 3/8 in. $15
Spoon-teaspoon, 5 3/4 in. $20
Tablespoon, (serving spoon), 8 1/2 in. $70
Tablespoon, (serving spoon), pierced,
8 1/2 in. $80
Tongs-sugar, 4 1/4 in. $60

Cluny by Gorham, 1880/1883

Fork-dessert/luncheon, solid piece,
6 3/4 in. $100
Spoon-teaspoon, 6 in. $60
Tablespoon, (serving spoon), 8 1/4 in. $160

Colfax by Gorham, 1922

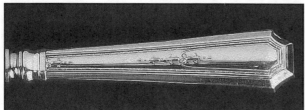

Fork, 7 1/4 in. $40
Fork, 7 3/4 in. $60
Knife-new french, hollow handle, 8 5/8 in. $30
Ladle-gravy, solid piece, 6 in. $100
Scoop-ice, silver plate bowl, 8 3/4 in. $60
Server-asparagus, hollow handle, silver
plate hood, 9 5/8 in. $60
Spoon-demitasse, gold wash, 4 1/8 in. $24
Spoon-dessert/oval soup, 7 1/8 in. $50
Spoon-soup, round bowl, cream, 5 7/8 in. $40
Spoon-teaspoon, 5 5/8 in. $26

The following pieces have monograms:
Butter spreader, flat handle, 5 1/2 in. $18
Fork, 7 1/4 in. $30
Fork, 7 3/4 in. $45
Fork-pickle/olive, short handle, 6 in. $20
Knife-new french, hollow handle, 8 5/8 in. $23
Knife-old french, hollow handle, 8 5/8 in. $23
Server-cheese, stainless blade, 6 5/8 in. $30
Server-pie, stainless blade, 9 3/8 in. $42

Spoon-demitasse, 4 1/8 in. $15
Spoon-soup, round bowl, cream, 5 7/8 in. $27
Spoon-teaspoon, (five o'clock), 5 5/8 in. $15
Spoon-teaspoon, 5 5/8 in. $18

Colonial by Gorham, 1885

Fork, 6 3/4 in. $35
Fork, 7 1/2 in. $50
Fork-cocktail, 5 5/8 in. $30
Knife-crumb/crumber, large, 12 3/8 in. $350
Ladle-soup, solid piece, 12 3/8 in. $400
Spoon-demitasse, gold wash, 4 1/4 in. $20
Spoon-place/oval soup, 6 3/4 in. $40
Spoon-teaspoon, 5 3/4 in. $25
Tablespoon, (serving spoon), 8 1/4 in. $70
Tongs-sugar, 5 1/4 in. $60

Corinthian by Gorham, 1872

Fork, 7 3/4 in. $75
Spoon-teaspoon, (five o'clock), gold wash,
4 7/8 in. $30
Spoon-teaspoon, 6 in. $50

Cottage by Gorham, 1861

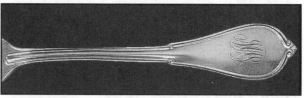

Fork, 6 7/8 in. $50
Fork, 7 3/4 in. $70
Spoon-dessert/oval soup, 7 in. $60
Spoon-teaspoon, 5 7/8 in. $30
Tablespoon, (serving spoon), 8 3/8 in. $80

The following piece has a monogram:
Fork, 6 7/8 in. $38

Gorham

Covington by Gorham, 1914

Fork, 7 3/4 in.............................$50
Fork, 7 in...............................$40
Fork-cocktail, 5 3/8 in....................$30
Fork-salad, individual, 6 1/2 in.............$34
Knife-fruit, silver plate blade, individual,
　6 7/8 in..................................$38
Knife-old french, hollow handle, 8 1/2 in......$33
Knife-old french, hollow handle, 9 1/2 in......$44
Ladle-cream, solid piece, 5 3/8 in. $45
Spoon-soup, round bowl, bouillon, 5 1/4 in. ...$28
Spoon-soup, round bowl, gumbo, 6 7/8 in. $40
Tablespoon, (serving spoon), 8 5/8 in.........$70

Cromwell by Gorham, 1900

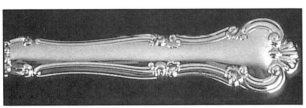

Carving set, 2 pieces, large, stainless blade,
　roast $150
Fork, 7 1/8 in.............................$46
Fork, 7 5/8 in.............................$70
Fork-cocktail, 5 5/8 in.....................$30
Fork-ice cream, gold wash, 5 1/2 in. $48
Fork-youth, 6 in...........................$50
Knife-crumb/crumber, large, 12 1/8 in........$440
Knife-new french, hollow handle, 8 1/2 in......$40
Knife-orange, silver plate blade, 7 3/8 in......$45
Spoon-dessert/oval soup, 7 1/8 in...........$50
Spoon-fruit, 5 3/4 in. $40
Spoon-soup, round bowl, gumbo, 6 7/8 in. $70
Spoon-teaspoon, 5 7/8 in. $30

Decor by Gorham, 1953

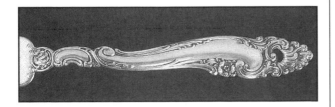

Butter spreader, hollow handle, modern, stainless
　paddle, 6 1/4 in........................$36
Butter-master, hollow handle, 6 7/8 in........$70
Fork, 7 1/4 in. $45
Fork, 7 3/4 in. $100
Fork-cocktail, 5 3/4 in. $46
Fork-cold meat/serving, medium, solid,
　8 1/8 in.................................$160
Fork-salad, individual, 3 tines, 6 1/2 in. $65
Knife-modern, hollow handle, 9 in. $42
Ladle-gravy, solid piece, 6 1/4 in............$150
Server-cheese, stainless blade, 6 3/4 in......$80
Server-pie and cake, stainless blade,
　10 3/4 in................................$130
Spoon-demitasse, 4 3/8 in..................$40
Spoon-iced tea, 7 5/8 in...................$65
Spoon-soup, round bowl, cream, 6 1/2 in. $56
Spoon-teaspoon, 6 in......................$25
Tablespoon, (serving spoon), 8 1/2 in. $140
Tablespoon, (serving spoon), pierced,
　8 1/2 in.................................$140

Dolly Madison by Gorham, 1929

Butter spreader, flat handle, 5 5/8 in. $20
Butter-master, flat handle, 7 in. $40
Fork, 7 in.................................$32
Fork-cocktail, 5 1/2 in. $26
Fork-cold meat/serving, medium, solid,
　8 in. $80
Fork-ice cream, 5 1/2 in. $40
Knife-carving, small, stainless blade, steak,
　10 1/8 in................................$64
Knife-new french, pistol, 9 3/4 in............$48
Knife-new french, pistol, bolster, 8 1/2 in......$35
Knife-old french, hollow handle, 8 5/8 in. $35
Knife-sharpener/steel, small, steak,
　10 1/2 in................................$65
Ladle-cream, solid piece, 5 1/8 in............$40
Ladle-gravy, solid piece, 6 3/4 in............$85
Server-cucumber, large, 6 1/2 in............$75
Server-tomato, solid piece, 7 3/4 in. $90
Spoon-casserole, smooth, solid, 8 in........$100
Spoon-demitasse, 4 1/4 in..................$16
Spoon-soup, round bowl, bouillon,
　5 1/2 in.................................$28
Spoon-soup, round bowl, cream, 6 1/4 in. $50
Spoon-sugar, 6 in. $40

Spoon-teaspoon, (five o'clock), 5 5/8 in. $20
Spoon-teaspoon, 6 in. $20
Tablespoon, (serving spoon), 8 1/2 in. $75
Tongs-sugar, 4 3/4 in. $48

Edgeworth by Gorham, 1922

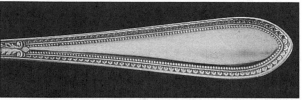

Butter spreader, flat handle, 5 1/2 in. $30
Fork, 7 1/8 in. $28
Fork, 8 in. $50
Fork-carving, small, stainless prongs, steak,
 9 in. $60
Fork-cocktail, 5 1/2 in. $26
Fork-ice cream, 5 3/8 in. $50
Fork-salad, individual, 6 1/2 in. $34
Knife-new french, hollow handle, stainless
 blade, 8 5/8 in. $33
Knife-old french, hollow handle, stainless
 blade, 9 1/8 in. $33
Pick-nut, 6 in. $52
Server-tomato, solid piece, 7 3/4 in. $90
Spoon-bon-bon, 5 in. $45
Spoon-casserole, smooth, solid,
 8 3/4 In. $100
Spoon-demitasse, 4 3/8 in. $23
Spoon-demitasse, gold wash, 4 3/8 in. $23
Spoon-dessert/oval soup, 7 1/8 in. $50
Spoon-fruit, 5 3/4 in. $26
Spoon-fruit, gold wash, 5 3/4 in. $26
Spoon-iced tea, 8 in. $30
Spoon-salad serving, solid piece,
 9 1/8 in. $100
Spoon-soup, round bowl, bouillon,
 5 1/4 in. $22
Spoon-soup, round bowl, cream, 6 1/4 in. $38
Spoon-teaspoon, (five o'clock), 5 5/8 in. $20
Spoon-teaspoon, 5 7/8 in. $25
Tablespoon, (serving spoon), 8 5/8 in. $80
Tongs-sugar, 4 1/4 in. $55

English Gadroon by Gorham, 1939

Butter spreader, hollow handle, modern, stainless
 paddle, 6 1/4 in. $28
Butter spreader, flat handle, 5 3/4 in. $22
Butter-master, flat handle, 7 in. $50
Butter-master, hollow handle, 6 3/4 in. $50
Carving set, 2 pieces, small, stainless blade,
 steak $120
Fork, 2 1/4 in. tines, 7 5/8 in. $60
Fork, 7 1/8 in. $36
Fork-carving, large, stainless prongs, roast,
 9 3/4 in. $70
Fork-cocktail, 5 3/8 in. $26
Fork-cold meat, serving, medium, solid,
 8 in. $100
Fork-salad serving, stainless prongs, 3 tines,
 11 1/4 in. $50
Fork-salad, individual, 6 1/4 in. $45
Knife-carving, large, stainless blade, roast,
 12 in. $70
Knife-modern, hollow handle, 8 7/8 in. $40
Knife-modern, hollow handle, 9 5/8 in. $50
Knife-new french, hollow handle, 8 7/8 in. $40
Ladle-gravy, solid piece, 6 1/4 in. $90
Ladle-punch, stainless bowl, 14 1/8 in. $140
Ladle-soup, stainless bowl, 11 3/4 in. $140
Napkin clip (made for teaspoons) $30
Server-lasagna, stainless blade,
 11 7/8 in. $60
Server-pasta, stainless bowl, 11 in. $60
Server-pie and cake, stainless blade,
 10 3/4 in. $60
Server-pie, stainless blade, 10 1/4 in. $70
Spoon-demitasse, 4 1/4 in. $28
Spoon-dessert/oval soup, 6 7/8 in. $60
Spoon-iced tea, 7 1/2 in. $40
Spoon-oval soup (place size), 2 3/8 in. bowl,
 7 in. $60
Spoon-soup, round bowl, cream,
 6 1/4 in. $50
Spoon-sugar shell, 6 1/4 in. $40
Spoon-teaspoon, 5 7/8 in. $23
Tablespoon, (serving spoon), 8 1/2 in. $85

Epic by Gorham, 1941

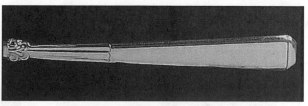

Butter spreader, hollow handle, stainless paddle,
 6 in. $32

Epic by Gorham, 1941

Butter spreader, flat handle, 5 5/8 in..........$30
Fork-cold meat/serving, small, solid,
    7 3/4 in..................................$90
Fork-salad, individual, 6 1/2 in...............$45
Knife-new french, hollow handle,
    9 7/8 in..................................$50
Ladle-gravy, solid piece, 6 5/8 in. $95
Server-jelly, 6 1/4 in.........................$38
Server-pie, stainless blade, 10 1/8 in. $70
Spoon-soup, round bowl, cream,
    6 3/8 in..................................$48
Spoon-soup, round bowl, gumbo,
    6 7/8 in..................................$58
Spoon-sugar, 6 in.............................$48
Spoon-teaspoon, 6 in..........................$30
Tablespoon, (serving spoon), 8 1/2 in.........$90
Tablespoon, (serving spoon), pierced,
    8 1/2 in.................................$100

Esprit by Gorham, 1963

Butter spreader, hollow handle, modern, stainless
    paddle, 7 in.............................$30
Butter-master, hollow handle, 7 1/4 in........$33
Fork, 7 3/8 in................................$46
Fork-cold meat/serving, medium, solid,
    8 3/4 in..................................$95
Fork-pickle/olive, short handle, 6 in..........$30
Fork-salad, individual, 6 3/4 in...............$50
Knife-modern, hollow handle, 9 in............$34
Ladle-gravy, solid piece, 7 in................$85
Server-jelly, 6 3/8 in. $40
Spoon-bon-bon, pierced, 4 5/8 in. $38
Spoon-bon-bon, triangular, 6 in..............$38
Spoon-sugar, egg bowl, 6 1/4 in. $33
Spoon-teaspoon, 6 in.........................$28
Tablespoon, (serving spoon), 8 5/8 in.........$75
Tablespoon, (serving spoon), pierced,
    8 3/4 in.................................$100

Etruscan by Gorham, 1913

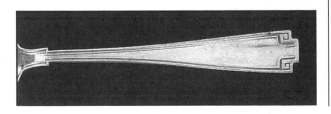

Butter spreader, hollow handle, modern, stainless
    paddle, 6 1/4 in.........................$34
Butter spreader, flat handle, 5 3/4 in. $24
Butter-master, flat handle, 3 1/2 in. handle,
    7 in. $44
Carving set, 2 pieces, small, stainless blade,
    steak $120
Fork, 7 5/8 in. $60
Fork, 7 in...................................$32
Fork-carving, small, stainless prongs, steak,
    8 1/2 in.................................$60
Fork-carving, small, stainless prongs, steak,
    8 3/4 in.................................$60
Fork-carving, small, stainless prongs, steak,
    9 1/4 in.................................$60
Fork-cocktail, bevel tines, 5 3/8 in. $26
Fork-cocktail, no bevel, 5 3/8 in. $26
Fork-cold meat/serving, small, solid,
    6 1/4 in................................$110
Fork-pastry, bar, pierced, 6 in. $50
Fork-salad serving, stainless prongs,
    11 in. $60
Fork-salad, individual, diamond slot,
    6 1/4 in.................................$54
Knife-carving, small, stainless blade, steak,
    11 3/4 in................................$60
Knife-carving, small, stainless blade, steak,
    9 7/8 in.................................$60
Knife-modern, hollow handle, stainless blade,
    9 5/8 in. $54
Knife-old french, hollow handle, silver plate
    blade, 8 1/2 in..........................$40
Knife-old french, hollow handle, stainless
    blade, 8 1/2 in..........................$40
Knife-old french, hollow handle, stainless
    blade, 9 3/4 in..........................$50
Ladle-cream, solid piece, 5 1/8 in............$50
Ladle-cream, solid piece, 5 7/8 in............$50
Ladle-gravy, solid piece, 7 in...............$120
Ladle-punch, stainless bowl,
    13 5/8 in...............................$120
Ladle-soup, stainless bowl, 11 1/8 in........$120
Napkin clip (made for teaspoons) $22
Server-jelly, 5 1/2 in. $30
Server-lasagna, stainless blade,
    11 1/2 in................................$60
Server-pasta, stainless bowl, 11 in...........$60
Server-pie and cake, stainless blade,
    10 3/8 in................................$60
Server-pie, silver plate blade, 10 in. $60
Server-pie, stainless blade, 9 1/4 in..........$60
Spoon-casserole, smooth, stainless bowl,
    10 3/4 in................................$60
Spoon-demitasse, gold wash, 4 1/4 in........$25

Spoon-dessert/oval soup, 7 in. $70
Spoon-iced tea, 7 1/2 in. $44
Spoon-olive, short, pierced bowl,
    5 3/4 in. $80
Spoon-soup, round bowl, bouillon,
    5 1/4 in. $30
Spoon-soup, round bowl, cream,
    6 1/4 in. $60
Spoon-soup, round bowl, gumbo,
    6 5/8 in. $50
Spoon-sugar, square bowl, 5 7/8 in. $36
Spoon-teaspoon, (five o'clock), 5 3/8 in. $15
Spoon-teaspoon, 5 3/4 in. $16
Tablespoon, (serving spoon), 8 3/8 in. $80
Tongs-sugar, 4 1/4 in. $60

Etruscan-Engraved by Gorham, 1913

Butter spreader, flat handle, 5 3/4 in. $22
Fork, 7 1/2 in. $45
Fork, 7 in. $40
Knife-old french, hollow handle, 8 1/2 in. $33
Spoon-soup, round bowl, bouillon,
    5 3/8 in. $30
Spoon-sugar, 5 3/4 in. $40
Spoon-teaspoon, (five o'clock), 5 1/2 in. $20
Spoon-teaspoon, 5 3/4 in. $20

Fairfax by Gorham, 1910

Baby set, 2 pieces. $76
Butter spreader, hollow handle, modern,
    stainless paddle, 6 1/8 in. $32
Butter-master, hollow handle, 6 3/4 in. $40
Carving set, 2 pieces, small, stainless blade,
    steak. $110
Fork, (place size), 4 7/8 in. handle,
    7 1/2 in. $55
Fork, 7 1/4 in. $42
Fork-carving, small, stainless prongs, steak,
    8 3/4 in. $55
Fork-cocktail, 5 5/8 in. $34
Fork-cold meat/serving, medium, solid,
    straight tines, 8 5/8 in. $100
Fork-ice cream, 5 1/2 in. $55
Fork-pastry, bar, 6 in. $50

Fork-pickle/olive, short handle, 2 tines,
    5 7/8 in. $36
Fork-salad (place size), 4 1/2 in. handle,
    6 1/2 in. $45
Fork-salad serving, solid piece, flared tines,
    8 5/8 in. $150
Fork-salad serving, stainless prongs,
    11 1/4 in. $45
Fork-salad, individual, 4 in. handle,
    6 1/4 in. $44
Fork-strawberry, 4 3/4 in. $40
Knife-carving, small, stainless blade, steak,
    9 7/8 in. $55
Knife-modern, hollow handle, stainless blade,
    8 7/8 in. $36
Knife-modern, hollow handle, stainless blade,
    9 3/4 in. $50
Knife-new french, hollow handle, silver plate
    blade, 8 3/4 in. $35
Knife-new french, hollow handle, stainless
    blade, 9 5/8 in. $50
Knife-old french, hollow handle, silver plate
    blade, 8 7/8 in. $35
Knife-old french, hollow handle, silver plate
    blade, 9 5/8 in. $50
Knife-old french, hollow handle, silver plate
    blade, 9 1/4 in. $35
Knife-old french, hollow handle, stainless
    blade, 8 5/8 in. $35
Knife-old french, hollow handle, stainless
    blade, 8 7/8 in. $35
Knife-sharpener/steel, small, steak,
    13 1/2 in. $60
Knife-steak, individual, 9 1/4 in. $54
Knife-wedding cake, stainless blade,
    12 1/4 in. $48
Ladle-cream, solid piece, 5 1/4 in. $54
Ladle-gravy, solid piece, 6 1/8 in. $100
Ladle-punch, stainless bowl, 13 3/4 in. $80
Ladle-soup, stainless bowl, 11 in. $70
Napkin clip (made for teaspoons) $35
Scoop-ice, silver plate bowl, 8 7/8 in. $60
Server-asparagus, hollow handle, silver
    plate hood, 9 5/8 in. $55
Server-cheese, stainless blade,
    6 1/2 in. $50
Server-lasagna, stainless blade,
    11 7/8 in. $45
Server-pasta, stainless bowl, 11 1/8 in. $45
Server-pie and cake, stainless blade,
    10 1/2 in. $60
Server-pie, stainless blade, 10 in. $56

Server-tomato, solid piece, 8 3/8 in..........$120
Spoon-bon-bon, 4 7/8 in....................$50
Spoon-casserole, smooth stainless bowl,
    10 7/8 in. $50
Spoon-demitasse, 4 1/4 in. $26
Spoon-demitasse, 4 1/8 in. $26
Spoon-dessert/oval soup, 7 1/8 in...........$60
Spoon-fruit, pointed bowl, 5 7/8 in...........$50
Spoon-iced tea, 7 3/8 in. $48
Spoon-infant feeding, 5 5/8 in...............$40
Spoon-oval soup (place size), 6 3/4 in. $50
Spoon-salad serving, solid piece, egg bowl,
    8 5/8 in...................................$150
Spoon-salad serving, wooden bowl,
    10 7/8 in. $45
Spoon-salt, individual, 2 5/8 in...............$12
Spoon-sugar, 5 7/8 in.......................$40
Spoon-teaspoon, 5 3/4 in. $23
Tablespoon, (serving spoon), tear bowl,
    8 1/2 in..................................$85

Firelight by Gorham, 1959

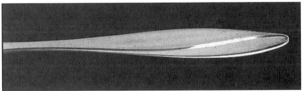

Butter spreader, hollow handle, modern, stainless
    paddle, 6 3/4 in..........................$24
Butter-master, hollow handle, 7 1/4 in.........$26
Fork, 7 1/2 in...............................$50
Fork-cocktail, 5 7/8 in.......................$25
Fork-cold meat/serving, medium, solid,
    8 1/2 in..................................$70
Fork-pickle/olive, short handle, 5 7/8 in. $24
Fork-salad, individual, 6 3/4 in...............$40
Knife-cheese, stainless blade, 7 5/8 in.......$45
Knife-modern, hollow handle, 9 in............$34
Ladle-gravy, solid piece, 6 7/8 in. $65
Server-jelly, 6 1/2 in. $28
Server-pastry, stainless bowl, 10 1/2 in. $55
Server-pie and cake, stainless blade,
    11 1/8 in. $55
Spoon-dessert/oval soup, 7 1/8 in...........$34
Spoon-sugar, 6 1/4 in.......................$26
Spoon-teaspoon, 6 1/8 in. $20
Tablespoon, (serving spoon),
    8 5/8 in..................................$70
Tablespoon, (serving spoon), pierced,
    8 5/8 in..................................$80

Fleury by Gorham, 1909

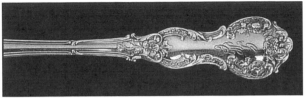

Carving set, 2 pieces, small, stainless blade,
    steak $140
Fork, 7 1/2 in. $70
Fork, 7 in..................................$50
Fork-cocktail, 5 3/8 in. $30
Fork-cold meat/serving, small, solid,
    6 3/8 in.................................$110
Fork-youth, 6 in. $53
Knife-old french, hollow handle, 9 3/4 in. $60
Spoon-baby, straight handle, 4 5/8 in.........$40
Spoon-dessert/oval soup, 7 in...............$50
Spoon-soup, round bowl, bouillon,
    5 1/8 in.................................$38
Spoon-soup, round bowl, gumbo,
    6 3/4 in.................................$60
Spoon-sugar, gold wash, 5 7/8 in............$48
Spoon-teaspoon, (five o'clock), 5 1/4 in.......$28
Spoon-teaspoon, 5 3/4 in...................$30
Tablespoon, (serving spoon), 8 1/2 in. $95

Florentine/Florenz by Gorham, 1901

Fork, 7 1/8 in. $90
Fork, fish/salad, solid, individual, large,
    7 1/8 in.................................$110
Knife-new french, hollow handle,
    9 5/8 in.................................$140
Spoon-demitasse, 4 1/4 in..................$50
Spoon-soup, round bowl, bouillon,
    5 3/8 in.................................$70

The following pieces have monograms:
Fork, 7 1/8 in. $70
Fork-pickle/olive, short handle, 5 3/4 in.......$70
Knife-old french, hollow handle,
    8 5/8 in.................................$80
Knife-pie, solid, large, 9 1/8 in..............$280
Spoon-teaspoon, 5 7/8 in..................$40

Fontainebleau by Gorham, 1880

Fork, 7 5/8 in. $200
Spoon-teaspoon, 6 in. $60
Tablespoon, (serving spoon), 8 1/4 in. $150

Gold Tip by Gorham, 1952

Butter spreader, hollow handle, modern, stainless
    paddle, 6 1/2 in. $30
Butter-master, flat handle, 7 in. $40
Fork-cocktail, 5 7/8 in. $30
Fork-pickle/olive, short handle,
    5 7/8 in. $35
Fork-salad serving, solid piece,
    9 1/8 in. $110
Server-cheese, stainless blade, 7 in. $50
Server-pastry, stainless bowl,
    10 1/8 in. $70
Spoon-sugar, 6 in. $40

Golden Wheat by Gorham, 1952

Butter spreader, hollow handle, modern, stainless
    paddle, 6 1/2 in. $30
Butter spreader, flat handle, 6 in. $30
Butter-master, flat handle, 7 1/2 in. $44
Butter-master, flat handle, 7 in. $44
Carving set, 2 pieces, small, stainless blade,
    steak $150
Fork, 7 1/2 in. $55
Fork-cold meat/serving, medium, solid,
    8 3/8 in. $94
Fork-pie, 6 3/4 in. $50. 9
Fork-salad, individual, 7 1/8 in. $55
Knife-new french, hollow handle,
    9 1/4 in. $50
Ladle-gravy, solid piece, 6 3/4 in. $94
Salad set, 2 pieces, solid piece $220
Server-pie, stainless blade,
    10 in. $75

Server-tomato, solid piece,
    6 3/8 in. $100
Spoon-dessert/oval soup, 7 in. $60
Spoon-iced tea, 7 1/2 in. $40
Spoon-sugar, 6 1/2 in. $48
Spoon-teaspoon, 6 in. $30
Tablespoon, (serving spoon),
    8 1/2 in. $90

Gorham-Plain by Gorham, 1933

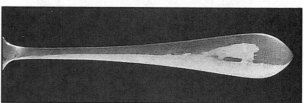

Butter spreader, hollow handle, modern, stainless
    paddle, 6 1/4 in. $17
Butter spreader, flat handle, 5 1/2 in. $20
Butter-master, flat handle, 7 1/8 in. $33
Fork, 7 7/8 in. $40
Fork, 7 in. $35
Fork-baby, 4 1/4 in. $30
Fork-cocktail, 5 1/2 in. $15
Fork-salad, individual, 6 3/8 in. $30
Fork-youth, 6 in. $36
Knife-fish, solid, individual, 7 7/8 in. $50
Knife-fruit, stainless blade, individual,
    7 in. $30
Knife-new french, hollow handle,
    9 1/2 in. $40
Knife-old french, hollow handle,
    9 1/2 in. $40
Ladle-cream, solid piece, 5 in. $30
Ladle-cream, solid piece, gold wash,
    5 in. $30
Ladle-gravy, solid piece, gold wash, 7 in. $70
Spoon-casserole, smooth bowl, solid,
    8 3/4 in. $70
Spoon-demitasse, gold wash, 4 1/4 in. $16
Spoon-iced tea, 8 1/8 in. $26
Spoon-soup, round bowl, bouillon,
    5 1/4 in. $18
Spoon-soup, round bowl, cream,
    6 1/8 in. $34
Spoon-soup, round bowl, gumbo,
    6 7/8 in. $40
Spoon-sugar, 5 7/8 in. $30
Spoon-teaspoon, (five o'clock), 5 3/8 in. $18
Spoon-teaspoon, 5 7/8 in. $20
Tablespoon, (serving spoon), 8 1/2 in. $60
Tongs-sugar, 3 7/8 in. $50

Gossamer by Gorham, 1965

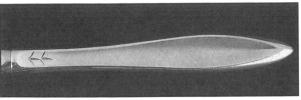

Butter spreader, hollow handle, modern, stainless paddle, 6 7/8 in..........................$35
Butter-master, hollow handle, no notch, 7 1/4 in.................................$35
Fork, 7 1/2 in...............................$45
Fork-cocktail, 5 7/8 in......................$40
Fork-salad, individual, 6 3/4 in..............$50
Napkin clip (made for teaspoons)............$26
Spoon-dessert/oval soup, 6 7/8 in...........$56
Spoon-sugar, 6 in...........................$35
Spoon-teaspoon, 6 in.......................$22
Tablespoon, (serving spoon), 8 5/8 in........$80
Tablespoon, (serving spoon), pierced, 8 5/8 in.................................$95

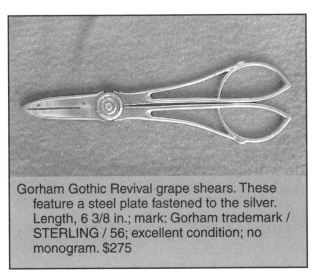

Gorham Gothic Revival grape shears. These feature a steel plate fastened to the silver. Length, 6 3/8 in.; mark: Gorham trademark / STERLING / 56; excellent condition; no monogram. $275

Governor's Lady by Gorham, 1937

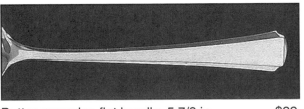

Butter spreader, flat handle, 5 7/8 in..........$22
Carving set, 2 pieces, small, stainless blade, steak....................................$90
Fork, 7 1/4 in...............................$40
Fork, 7 7/8 in...............................$60

Fork-carving, small, stainless prongs, steak, 8 1/2 in.................................$45
Fork-cocktail, 5 1/2 in......................$30
Fork-cold meat/serving, small, solid, 7 5/8 in.................................$70
Fork-lemon, 5 in............................$30
Fork-pickle/olive, short handle, 5 3/4 in.......$28
Fork-salad serving, solid piece, 9 in..........$90
Fork-salad, individual, 6 1/2 in. $40
Knife-new french, hollow handle, 9 in. $33
Ladle-cream, solid piece, 5 3/8 in............$40
Ladle-gravy, solid piece, 6 3/8 in.............$80
Server-jelly, 6 3/8 in. $30
Server-pie, stainless blade, 9 7/8 in..........$55
Spoon-casserole, smooth, solid, 8 5/8 in. $96
Spoon-demitasse, 4 1/4 in..................$20
Spoon-iced tea, 7 5/8 in....................$30
Spoon-soup, round bowl, gumbo, 6 3/4 in.....$37
Spoon-sugar, 6 in. $38
Spoon-teaspoon, (five o'clock), 5 5/8 in.......$18
Spoon-teaspoon, 6 in.......................$22
Tablespoon, (serving spoon), 8 1/2 in. $70

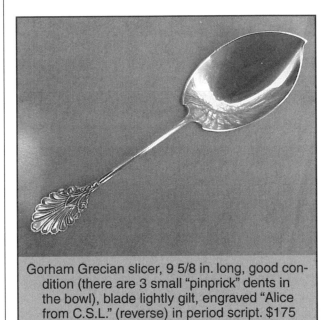

Gorham Grecian slicer, 9 5/8 in. long, good condition (there are 3 small "pinprick" dents in the bowl), blade lightly gilt, engraved "Alice from C.S.L." (reverse) in period script. $175

Greenbrier by Gorham, 1938

Butter spreader, hollow handle, modern, stainless paddle, 6 1/4 in......................... $22

Butter spreader, flat handle, 5 7/8 in..........$15
Butter-master, flat handle, 7 1/8 in............$35
Butter-master, hollow handle, 6 3/4 in.........$40
Carving set, 2 pieces, large, stainless blade,
    roast $130
Carving set, 2 pieces, small, stainless blade,
    steak...................................$120
Fork, 7 3/8 in...............................$30
Fork, 8 in...................................$55
Fork-baby, 4 3/8 in..........................$40
Fork-carving, large, stainless prongs,
    roast, 11 in. $64
Fork-carving, small, stainless prongs,
    steak, 9 in. $60
Fork-cocktail, 5 1/2 in......................$22
Fork-lemon, 4 1/2 in.........................$30
Fork-pickle/olive, short handle,
    5 7/8 in.................................$30
Fork-salad serving, solid piece,
    8 7/8 in................................$100
Fork-salad, individual, 6 3/4 in..............$32
Fork-serving, solid, no bevel, 4 tines,
    8 1/8 in.................................$90
Knife-modern, hollow handle, 8 7/8 in........$36
Knife-new french, hollow handle,
    8 7/8 in.................................$36
Knife-new french, hollow handle,
    9 5/8 in.................................$46
Knife-sharpener/steel, large, roast,
    13 5/8 in. $64
Ladle-cream, solid piece, 5 1/4 in. $45
Ladle-gravy, solid piece, 6 1/4 in. $80
Napkin clip (made for teaspoons)............$24
Salad set, 2 pieces, wooden bowl,
    10 3/4 in. $100
Server-cheese, stainless blade,
    6 5/8 in.................................$50
Server-jelly, 6 1/4 in. $34
Server-pie, stainless blade, 10 1/8 in. $60
Spoon-baby, straight handle, 4 1/2 in. $40
Spoon-bon-bon, 5 in. $38
Spoon-demitasse, 4 1/4 in. $22
Spoon-iced tea, 7 5/8 in. $34
Spoon-soup, round bowl, bouillon,
    5 1/2 in.................................$34
Spoon-soup, round bowl, cream,
    6 3/8 in.................................$30
Spoon-soup, round bowl, gumbo,
    6 7/8 in.................................$44
Spoon-sugar, 6 in...........................$28
Spoon-teaspoon, (five o'clock),
    5 5/8 in.................................$20
Spoon-teaspoon, 5 7/8 in. $17
Tablespoon, (serving spoon), 8 1/2 in........$70

Henry II by Gorham, 1900

Fork-cocktail, 5 5/8 in......................$70
Knife-new french, hollow handle,
    9 3/4 in................................$120
Knife-old french, hollow handle, 9 3/4 in.....$120
Spoon-fruit, 5 3/4 in. $60

The following pieces have monograms:
Fork-7 1/8 in...............................$80
Spoon-demitasse, 4 1/4 in...................$45

Hispana/Sovereign by Gorham, 1968

Butter-master, hollow handle, 7 3/8 in........$50
Fork, 7 1/2 in. $50
Knife-modern, hollow handle, 9 in. $50
Spoon-sugar, 6 1/8 in.......................$40
Spoon-teaspoon, 6 in........................$36

Hunt Club by Gorham, 1930

Butter spreader, flat handle, 5 1/2 in. $20
Butter-master, flat handle, 6 7/8 in...........$34
Carving set, 2 pieces, small, stainless blade,
    steak $100
Fork, 7 1/4 in. $34
Fork, 7 3/4 in. $50
Fork-baby, 4 3/8 in..........................$34
Fork-carving, small-stainless prongs, steak,
    8 5/8 in.................................$50
Fork-cocktail, 5 3/8 in......................$17
Fork-ice cream, 3 tines, 5 1/2 in. $36
Fork-lemon, 5 1/8 in. $24

Fork-pickle/olive, short handle, 6 in...........$25
Fork-salad, individual, 6 1/2 in...............$30
Fork-youth, 6 in.............................$36
Knife-new french, hollow handle,
    8 3/4 in.................................$28
Knife-new french, hollow handle,
    9 5/8 in.................................$40
Knife-orange, stainless blade, 7 in...........$45
Knife-youth, 7 5/8 in........................$32
Ladle-cream, solid piece, 5 1/4 in. $40
Ladle-cream, solid piece, 6 in...............$40
Ladle-gravy, solid piece, 7 1/4 in. $80
Server-cheese, stainless blade, 6 1/2 in......$40
Server-jelly, 6 1/4 in........................$24
Server-pastry, stainless bowl, 8 5/8 in. $60
Server-pie and cake, stainless blade,
    10 3/8 in. $60
Server-pie, stainless blade, 9 1/4 in. $58
Spoon-bon-bon, 4 5/8 in. $33
Spoon-demitasse, 4 1/2 in. $16
Spoon-demitasse, gold wash, 4 1/2 in. $16
Spoon-iced tea, 7 1/2 in. $33
Spoon-soup, round bowl, bouillon,
    5 1/2 in.................................$23
Spoon-soup, round bowl, cream,
    6 3/8 in.................................$36
Spoon-soup, round bowl, gumbo, 7 in. $40
Spoon-sugar, 5 7/8 in........................$30
Spoon-teaspoon, (five o'clock), 5 3/4 in. $16
Spoon-teaspoon, 6 in........................$18
Tablespoon, (serving spoon), tear bowl,
    8 1/2 in.................................$70

Imperial Chrysanthemum by Gorham, 1894

Fish-fork/salad, solid, individual, large, 4
    tines, no bevel, 6 7/8 in.................$120
Fork, 6 7/8 in...............................$50
Fork, 7 1/2 in...............................$80
Fork-carving, small, stainless prongs, steak,
    8 1/2 in.................................$86
Fork-cocktail, 5 1/2 in.......................$40
Fork-ice cream, gold wash, 4 3/4 in. $100
Ladle-soup, solid piece, 12 in..............$800
Spoon-demitasse, 4 in.......................$34
Spoon-demitasse, gold wash, 4 in...........$34

Spoon-fruit, 5 1/2 in. $60
Spoon-soup, round bowl, bouillon,
    4 3/4 in................................. $60
Spoon-teaspoon, (five o'clock), 5 in.......... $30
Spoon-teaspoon, 5 3/4 in.................... $40
Tablespoon, (serving spoon), 8 3/8 in. $100
Tongs-sugar, 4 in........................... $100

The following pieces have monograms:
Fish-fork/salad, solid, individual, large,
    6 5/8 in................................. $100
Fish-fork/salad, solid, individual, large,
    6 7/8 in................................. $100
Fork, 6 7/8 in. $40
Fork, 7 1/2 in. $70
Fork-strawberry, 4 5/8 in.................... $40
Spoon-dessert/oval soup, 7 in............... $60
Spoon-soup, round bowl, bouillon, 4 3/4 in.... $50
Spoon-soup, round bowl, cream,
    6 5/8 in................................. $60
Spoon-teaspoon, (five o'clock), 5 in.......... $23
Spoon-teaspoon, 5 3/4 in.................... $32

Jefferson by Gorham, 1907

Fork, 6 7/8 in. $45
Fork, 7 3/4 in. $70
Fork-cocktail, 5 1/2 in...................... $35
Fork-cold meat/serving, small, solid,
    7 1/8 in. $90
Fork-salad, individual, 6 1/2 in. $70
Knife-blunt, hollow handle, 8 1/2 in........... $38
Knife-old french, hollow handle, 9 7/8 in. $50
Ladle-cream, solid piece, 5 1/4 in............ $50
Ladle-gravy, solid piece, 6 1/2 in............ $94
Pick-butter, 1 tine, 5 7/8 in................. $50
Sardine-tined fork, serving, solid, large,
    5 1/2 in................................. $90
Spoon-casserole, smooth, solid, gold wash,
    9 1/8 in. $110
Spoon-demitasse, 4 1/8 in.................. $26
Spoon-dessert/oval soup, 7 in............... $50
Spoon-ice cream, 5 1/2 in. $55
Spoon-jelly, large, gold wash, 7 1/8 in........ $60
Spoon-preserve, gold wash, 9 in. $70
Spoon-soup, round bowl, bouillon,
    5 3/8 in................................. $48

Spoon-sugar, gold wash, 6 in................$60
Spoon-teaspoon, (five o'clock), 5 3/4 in. $20
Spoon-teaspoon, 6 in.......................$28
Tablespoon, (serving spoon), 8 5/8 in........$85
Tongs-sugar, 3 3/4 in......................$60

The following pieces have monograms:
Butter spreader, flat handle, 5 3/4 in.........$22
Fork, 6 7/8 in..............................$34
Fork, 7 3/4 in..............................$53
Fork-chipped beef, small, 6 7/8 in. $53
Fork-cocktail, 5 1/2 in......................$27
Fork-cold meat/serving, small, solid,
    7 1/8 in.................................$70
Fork-ice cream, 5 3/8 in....................$45
Fork-salad, individual, 6 1/2 in..............$45
Knife-blunt, hollow handle, 8 1/2 in..........$30
Knife-blunt, hollow handle, 9 7/8 in. $38
Knife-fruit, silver plate blade, individual,
    6 7/8 in.................................$29
Knife-new french, hollow handle, 9 3/4 in.....$38
Spoon-fruit, 5 7/8 in. $33
Spoon-iced tea, 7 1/2 in. $32
Spoon-soup, round bowl, bouillon,
    5 3/8 in.................................$36
Spoon-soup, round bowl, cream, 6 in........$45
Spoon-soup, round bowl, gumbo,
    6 7/8 in.................................$53
Spoon-teaspoon, (five o'clock), 5 3/4 in. $16
Spoon-teaspoon, 6 in.......................$20
Tablespoon, (serving spoon), 8 5/8 in........$64

King Edward by Gorham, 1936

Butter spreader, hollow handle, stainless paddle,
    6 in...................................$26
Butter spreader, flat handle, 5 3/4 in.........$26
Butter-master, flat handle, 6 3/4 in...........$45
Butter-master, hollow handle, 6 3/4 in........$45
Carving set, 2 pieces, small, stainless blade,
    steak.................................$120
Fork, (place size), 2 in. tines, 7 1/2 in. $42
Fork, 2 1/8 in. tines, 7 3/4 in................$44
Fork, 7 1/8 in..............................$32
Fork-cocktail, 7/8 in. tines, 5 1/2 in. $27
Fork-cold meat/serving, medium, solid,
    8 1/8 in.................................$90

Fork-salad serving, solid, 8 3/4 in...........$120
Fork-salad, individual, 6 1/4 in. $36
Fork-strawberry, 4 3/4 in....................$30
Knife-carving, small, stainless blade, steak,
    10 in..................................$60
Knife-modern, hollow handle, (place size),
    4 1/4 in. handle, 9 1/8 in. $35
Knife-modern, hollow handle, 3 3/4 in. handle,
    9 in...................................$35
Knife-modern, hollow handle, 9 5/8 in........$45
Knife-new french, hollow handle, 8 7/8 in. $34
Knife-steak, individual, 9 1/4 in...............$50
Ladle-gravy, solid piece, 6 3/8 in.............$80
Napkin clip (made for teaspoons) $24
Opener-bottle, stainless bowl, 5 1/4 in........$40
Salad set, 2 pieces, solid piece,
    3/4 in.................................$240
Scoop-ice, silver plate bowl, 8 5/8 in. $60
Server-asparagus, hollow handle, silver
    plate hood, 9 1/2 in....................$60
Server-pie and cake, stainless blade,
    10 1/2 in..............................$55
Server-pie, stainless blade, 9 7/8 in..........$60
Server-tomato, solid piece, 7 1/2 in. $100
Spoon-bon-bon, 4 3/4 in. $40
Spoon-iced tea, 7 1/2 in....................$37
Spoon-oval soup (place size), 2 3/8 in. long
    bowl, 6 7/8 in..........................$46
Spoon-salad serving, solid piece,
    8 3/4 in................................$120
Spoon-soup, round bowl, cream,
    6 1/4 in................................$42
Spoon-sugar, 5 3/4 in......................$35
Spoon-teaspoon, (five o'clock), 5 3/4 in.......$20
Spoon-teaspoon, 6 in.......................$18
Tablespoon, (serving spoon), 8 3/8 in. $80
Tablespoon, (serving spoon), pierced,
    8 3/8 in................................$100

King George by Gorham, 1894

Butter spreader, flat handle, 6 1/2 in. $50
Fork, 7 in..................................$60
Fork-cocktail, 5 3/4 in......................$48
Fork-ice cream, gold wash, 4 3/4 in..........$90
Knife-blunt, hollow handle, 8 5/8 in...........$70
Knife-blunt, hollow handle, 9 5/8 in...........$90

Knife-fish, solid, individual, 8 in. $100
Knife-fruit, silver plate blade, individual,
    7 in. $66
Knife-new french, hollow handle, 8 3/4 in......$70
Spoon-demitasse, gold wash, 4 1/4 in. $40
Spoon-demitasse/coffee, 4 7/8 in. $40
Spoon-dessert/oval soup, 7 1/8 in............$90
Spoon-soup, round bowl, cream, 6 in.........$90
Spoon-teaspoon, 5 7/8 in. $45
Tablespoon, (serving spoon), 8 5/8 in........$120

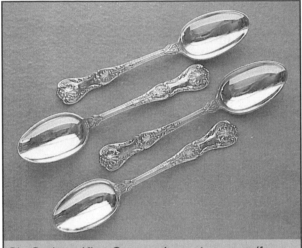

Six Gorham King George dessert spoons (four shown). These are "h" weight, for extra heavy. There is some minor wear (reverse) where spoon meets table, but the overall condition is fine. Length, 7 1/8 in.; monogram "EW" in script. Six for $300

Kings II by Gorham, 1885

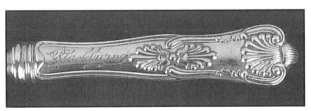

The following pieces have monograms:
Fork, 7 3/4 in. $110
Fork, 7 1/8 in. $80

Kings III by Gorham, 1885

Fork, 7 1/8 in. $50
Spoon-teaspoon, 5 7/8 in. $34
Tablespoon, (serving spoon), 8 3/8 in. $80
Tongs-sugar, 3 3/8 in. $83

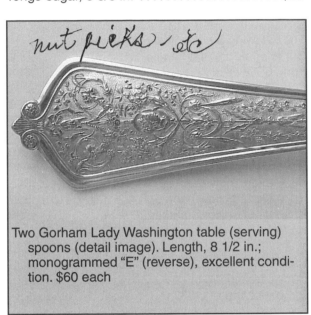

Two Gorham Lady Washington table (serving) spoons (detail image). Length, 8 1/2 in.; monogrammed "E" (reverse), excellent condition. $60 each

La Scala by Gorham, 1964

Butter-master, hollow handle, 7 in. $42
Fork, 7 1/2 in. $37
Fork-carving, small, stainless prongs, steak,
    8 5/8 in. $60
Fork-salad, individual, 6 3/8 in. $50
Knife-carving, small, stainless blade, steak,
    10 1/2 in. $60
Knife-modern, hollow handle, 9 1/8 in. $40
Ladle-gravy, solid piece, 7 in. $110
Scoop-ice/silver plate bowl, 9 in. $60
Server-pie and cake, stainless blade,
    10 7/8 in. $55
Spoon-demitasse, 4 3/8 in. $34
Spoon-dessert/oval soup, 6 7/8 in. $54
Spoon-soup, round bowl, cream, 6 1/8 in. $60
Spoon-sugar, 6 3/8 in. $44
Spoon-teaspoon, 6 1/4 in. $27
Tablespoon, (serving spoon), pierced,
    8 3/4 in. $110
Tablespoon, (serving spoon), 8 7/8 in. $100
Tongs-sugar, 3 7/8 in. $60

Gorham sterling silver cake or pie lifter in the La Scala pattern, designed by Peter C. Gavette. Measures 10 5/8 in. long. Generous handle decorated top and bottom with repoussé roses, primroses, and curls. Marked GORHAM Sterling on handle, stainless blade. Like new. $250

Lancaster by Gorham, 1897

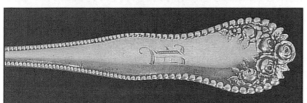

Butter-master, hollow handle, 6 3/4 in........$40
Fish-fork/salad, solid, individual, 7 in. $80
Fork, 7 5/8 in..............................$56
Fork, 7 in..................................$28
Fork-cocktail, 5 5/8 in......................$28
Fork-cold meat/serving, small, solid,
    6 3/8 in.................................$80
Fork-ice cream, 5 in........................$60
Fork-lettuce serving, large, 9 1/4 in.........$120
Fork-oyster, short handle, 5 5/8 in...........$26
Fork-pickle/olive, long handle, gold wash,
    8 1/8 in.................................$70
Fork-salad, individual, 6 in. $100
Knife-blunt, hollow handle, 8 1/2 in. $90
Knife-blunt, hollow handle, 8 7/8 in. $90
Knife-blunt, hollow handle, silver plate blade,
    9 5/8 in.................................$100
Knife-new french, hollow handle, place,
    9 1/8 in.................................$90
Knife-new french, hollow handle,
    8 3/4 in.................................$90
Knife-old french, hollow handle, 8 1/2 in.......$90
Ladle-cream, solid piece, not pierced,
    4 7/8 in.................................$50
Ladle-gravy, solid, 6 7/8 in. $100
Ladle-relish, 5 1/4 in.......................$50
Napkin clip (made for five o'clock) $24
Spoon-casserole, shell, solid,
    7 7/8 in.................................$140
Spoon-casserole, shell, solid, 9 in...........$140
Spoon-demitasse, gold wash,
    3 7/8 in.................................$24
Spoon-dessert/oval soup, 7 in. $38
Spoon-fruit, 5 5/8 in........................$44
Spoon-soup, round bowl, bouillon,
    5 1/8 in.................................$36

Spoon-soup, round bowl, gumbo,
    6 7/8 in.................................$48
Spoon-sugar shell, 6 in. $38
Spoon-teaspoon, (five o'clock),
    5 1/4 in.................................$18
Spoon-teaspoon, (five o'clock), no stamp,
    5 1/4 in.................................$18
Spoon-teaspoon, 5 7/8 in....................$20
Tablespoon, (serving spoon), pierced,
    8 1/2 in.................................$90
Tablespoon, (serving spoon), 8 1/2 in........$60
Tongs-sugar, 4 1/8 in. $60

Gorham Lancaster asparagus serving fork, 9 1/4 in. long, fine condition, pierced with florettes and asparagus tips. The front is engraved with a decorative three-letter art nouveau script monogram, "RHW." $325

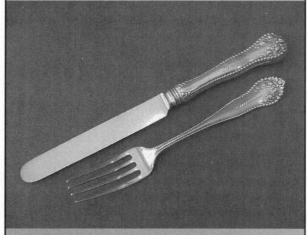

American silver youth knife and fork in the Lancaster pattern (1897); made by Gorham. Engraved "Truitt." Knife 7 5/8 in., fork 5 7/8 in. Silver plated blunt knife blade, some dings to knife handle. $40

Lansdowne by Gorham, 1917

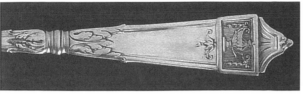

Butter spreader, flat handle, 5 3/4 in..........$30
Carving set, 2 pieces, small, stainless blade,
   steak...................................$160
Fork, 7 3/4 in...............................$90
Fork, 7 in...................................$44
Fork-carving, small, stainless prongs, steak,
   8 7/8 in..................................$70
Fork-cocktail, 5 3/8 in.......................$30
Fork-ice cream, 5 1/4 in.....................$60
Fork-salad, individual, diamond slot,
   6 1/8 in..................................$55
Knife-baby, 5 1/4 in.........................$42
Knife-new french, hollow handle, 9 1/2 in.....$50
Knife-old french, hollow handle, 8 1/2 in......$40
Knife-old french, hollow handle, 8 7/8 in......$40
Napkin clip (made for five o'clock) $22
Server-jelly, 6 1/8 in. $40
Spoon-demitasse, 4 3/8 in. $28
Spoon-five o'clock/youth, 1 3/4 in. bowl,
   5 1/2 in..................................$25
Spoon-fruit, no ribbing, 5 3/4 in. $40
Spoon-fruit, rib bowl, 5 3/4 in. $40
Spoon-soup, round bowl, bouillon,
   5 1/4 in..................................$40
Spoon-soup, round bowl, cream, 6 1/4 in......$70
Spoon-soup, round bowl, gumbo, 6 3/4 in. $60
Spoon-sugar, 5 7/8 in.......................$48
Spoon-teaspoon, (five o'clock), 2 in. long
   bowl, 5 5/8 in. $16
Tablespoon, (serving spoon), 8 1/2 in.........$90

Lily by Gorham, 1870

Spoon-berry, casserole, solid, gold wash,
   8 1/4 in.................................$500
Spoon-fruit, 5 1/4 in.......................$100

The following piece has a monogram:
Spoon-berry, casserole, solid, 9 in. $370

Lily of the Valley by Gorham, 1950

Butter spreader, hollow handle, modern,
   stainless paddle, 6 3/8 in................$23
Butter spreader, hollow handle, stainless
   paddle, 6 1/2 in.........................$23
Butter spreader, hollow handle, stainless
   paddle, 6 1/8 in.........................$23
Butter spreader, flat handle, 5 3/4 in. $16
Butter-master, flat handle, 7 1/8 in...........$40
Butter-master, hollow handle, 6 3/4 in........$40
Fork, 7 1/4 in. $36
Fork-cocktail, 5 5/8 in......................$28
Fork-cold meat/serving, medium, solid,
   8 1/4 in.................................$90
Fork-lemon, 5 in...........................$30
Fork-pickle/olive, short handle, 5 3/4 in.......$30
Fork-salad serving, solid, 8 7/8 in...........$120
Fork-salad, individual, 6 1/2 in. $40
Knife-modern, hollow handle, 9 in. $38
Ladle-cream, solid, 5 3/8 in. $50
Ladle-gravy, solid, 6 3/8 in.................$80
Napkin clip (made for teaspoons) $22
Salad set, 2 pieces, plastic bowl $90
Server-jelly, 6 1/4 in. $34
Spoon-bon-bon, 4 7/8 in. $45
Spoon-demitasse, 4 3/8 in..................$28
Spoon-soup, round bowl, cream,
   6 3/8 in.................................$27
Spoon-sugar, 6 in. $34
Spoon-teaspoon, 5 7/8 in...................$18
Tablespoon, (serving spoon), 8 1/2 in. $80

Louis XIV by Gorham, 1870

Fork, 7 1/2 in. $50
Fork, 7 in..................................$45
Spoon-dessert/oval soup, 7 in...............$60
Spoon-teaspoon, 5 7/8 in...................$30
Tablespoon, (serving spoon), 8 3/4 in. $80

Louis XV by Gorham, 1891

Knife-modern, hollow handle, 8 1/2 in........$100
Spoon-teaspoon, (five o'clock), 5 1/4 in......$19
Tablespoon, (serving spoon), 8 1/4 in. $60

Luxembourg by Gorham, 1893

Butter spreader, flat handle, 5 3/8 in. $46
Butter-master, flat handle, 7 3/4 in. $70
Fish-fork/salad, solid, individual, 5 3/4 In. $80
Fork, 6 7/8 in. $58
Fork, 7 1/2 in. $90
Fork-cocktail, 5 3/8 in. $50
Fork-cold meat/serving, small, solid,
    7 1/8 in. $130
Fork-ice cream, 4 7/8 in. $90
Fork-ice cream, gold wash, 4 7/8 in. $90
Fork-pastry, 5 7/8 in. $100
Knife-new french, hollow handle, 9 1/2 in. $90
Spoon-casserole, smooth, solid, gold
    wash, 8 3/4 in. $160
Spoon-dessert/oval soup, 7 1/2 in. $70
Spoon-fruit, gold wash, 5 3/4 in. $60
Spoon-place/oval soup, 7 in. $85
Spoon-soup, round bowl, cream, 5 7/8 in. $90
Spoon-sugar, 6 in. $70
Spoon-sugar, gold wash, 6 in. $70
Spoon-teaspoon, (five o'clock), 5 in. $28
Spoon-teaspoon, 5 3/4 in. $30
Tablespoon, (serving spoon), 8 3/8 in. $120
Tongs-sugar, 3 1/4 in. $80

Lyric by Gorham, 1940

Butter spreader, hollow handle, modern, stainless
    paddle, 6 1/4 in. $20
Butter spreader, flat handle, 5 3/4 in. $15
Butter-master, flat handle, 7 in. $36
Butter-master, hollow handle, notch blade,
    6 3/4 in. $40
Carving set, 2 pieces, small, stainless blade,
    steak $120
Fork, 7 3/8 in. $26
Fork, 8 in. $40
Fork-cocktail, 5 5/8 in. $26
Fork-cold meat/serving, medium, solid,
    8 1/8 in. $80
Fork-ice cream, 5 5/8 in. $44
Fork-lemon, 4 7/8 in. $30
Fork-salad serving, solid, 9 in. $110
Fork-salad, individual, 6 1/2 in. $27
Fork-youth, 6 1/8 in. $42
Knife-modern, hollow handle, stainless blade,
    8 7/8 in. $40
Knife-new french, hollow handle, 8 7/8 in. $40

Knife-new french, hollow handle, 9 1/2 in. $50
Ladle-gravy, solid, 6 1/4 in. $70
Napkin clip (made for teaspoons) $20
Server-cheese, stainless blade, 6 5/8 in. $50
Server-jelly, 6 1/4 in. $32
Server-pie, stainless blade, 10 1/4 in. $60
Spoon-soup, round bowl, cream, 6 1/4 in. $28
Spoon-sugar, 6 in. $30
Spoon-teaspoon, 6 in. $16
Tablespoon, (serving spoon), 8 1/2 in. $60
Tablespoon, (serving spoon), pierced,
    8 1/2 in. $90

Madam Jumel by Gorham/Whiting, 1908

Set — 2003 - Butterfields + more

Butter spreader, flat handle, 5 5/8 in. $18
Butter spreader, flat handle, 5 in. $18
Carving set, 2 pieces, small, stainless blade,
    steak $130
Fork, 6 7/8 in. $38
Fork-cocktail, 5 1/2 in. $26
Fork-fish, solid, individual, 1 of 4 beveled tines,
    6 1/8 in. $58
Fork-salad, 3 tines, 2 of 3 beveled, 6 1/8 in. . . $50
Knife-blunt, hollow handle, 8 7/8 in. $40
Knife-blunt, hollow handle, 9 3/4 in. $50
Knife-blunt, hollow handle, bolster, silver plate
    blade, 9 5/8 in. $50
Knife-new french, hollow handle, 8 7/8 in. $40
Knife-new french, hollow handle, 9 1/4 in. $40
Knife-old french, hollow handle, 9 1/4 in. $40
Knife-old french, hollow handle, bolster,
    stainless blade, 9 1/4 in. $40
Spoon-dessert/oval soup, 7 in. $50
Spoon-soup, round bowl, bouillon, 5 in. $26
Spoon-soup, round bowl, cream, 5 7/8 in. $37
Spoon-soup, round bowl, gumbo, 6 3/4 in. $55
Spoon-teaspoon, 5 7/8 in. $24
Tablespoon, (serving spoon), 8 1/8 in. $70

The following pieces have monograms:
Butter spreader, flat handle, 5 in. $15
Butter-master, flat handle, 6 1/4 in. $30
Fork, 6 7/8 in. $30
Fork-cold meat/serving, medium, solid,
    8 3/4 in. $60

Fork-ice cream, 5 in. $36
Fork-salad, 3 tines, 6 1/8 in. $40
Knife-carving, small, stainless blade, steak,
   9 3/4 in. $48
Knife-old french, hollow handle, bolster,
   8 3/4 in. $30
Ladle-cream, solid, 5 5/8 in. $36
Server-jelly, 6 1/4 in. $24
Server-pie, stainless blade, 9 1/2 in. $57
Spoon-bon-bon, 4 3/8 in. $30
Spoon-soup, round bowl, bouillon, 5 in. $20
Spoon-soup, round bowl, gumbo,
   6 3/4 in. $45
Spoon-teaspoon, 5 7/8 in. $19
Tablespoon, (serving spoon), 8 1/8 in. $53
Tablespoon, (serving spoon), pierced,
   8 1/8 in. $75
Tongs-sugar, 4 in. $53

Marguerite by Gorham, 1901

Tablespoon, (serving spoon), 8 3/8 in. $70

The following pieces have monograms:
Fork, 7 5/8 in. $53
Fork, 7 in. $32
Fork-cocktail, 5 3/8 in. $23
Fork-salad, individual, 6 in. $40
Spoon-teaspoon, (five o'clock), 5 3/8 in. $14
Spoon-teaspoon, 5 7/8 in. $18

Marie Antoinette by Gorham, 1890

Fork, 7 5/8 in. $55
Fork-ice cream, gold wash, 5 in. $60
Fork-pie, 1 of 3 bevel, 6 in. $58
Knife-sharpener/steel, small, steak,
   13 1/2 in. $85
Spoon-demitasse, 4 3/8 in. $30
Spoon-dessert/oval soup, 7 1/8 in. $65
Spoon-fruit, gold wash, 5 7/8 in. $45
Spoon-sugar, 5 7/8 in. $50

Spoon-teaspoon, (five o'clock), 5 1/4 in. $32
Spoon-teaspoon, 5 7/8 in. $30
Tongs-sugar, 3 7/8 in. $83

The following pieces have monograms:
Fork, 6 5/8 in. $30
Spoon-dessert/oval soup, 7 1/8 in. $50

Medallion by Gorham, 1864

Fork, 6 7/8 in. $140

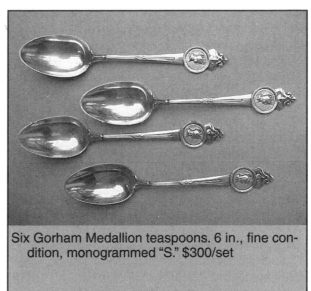

Six Gorham Medallion teaspoons. 6 in., fine condition, monogrammed "S." $300/set

Medici-Old by Gorham, 1880

Fork, 6 3/4 in. $60
Fork, 7 5/8 in. $90
Fork-cocktail, 5 3/4 in. $50
Spoon-demitasse, 4 1/4 in. $40
Spoon-demitasse, gold wash, 4 1/4 in. $40
Spoon-dessert/oval soup, 7 in. $100
Spoon-teaspoon, 5 7/8 in. $46
Tablespoon, (serving spoon), 8 3/8 in. $100

The following pieces have monograms:
Fork, 6 3/4 in. $54
Fork, 7 5/8 in. $80.5
Spoon-demitasse, 4 1/4 in. $36
Spoon-dessert/oval soup, 7 in. $90
Spoon-teaspoon, 5 7/8 in. $42
Tablespoon, (serving spoon), 8 3/8 in. $90

Six Gorham Medici-Old dinner forks (detail). Length, 7 5/8 in.; no monogram; some slight wear to the highest points but the tines are excellent and overall condition is fine. $450/set

Melrose by Gorham, 1948

Butter spreader, hollow handle, modern,
  stainless, 6 1/4 in. $28
Butter spreader, hollow handle, stainless
  paddle, 6 1/8 in. $28
Butter spreader, flat handle, 5 3/4 in. $30
Butter-master, flat handle, 7 in. $36
Butter-master, hollow handle, 6 3/4 in. $36
Carving set, 2 pieces, small, stainless blade,
  steak $140
Fork, (place size), 2 in. tines, 7 1/2 in. $60
Fork, 2 1/8 in. tines, 7 1/4 in. $35
Fork, 2 1/8 in. tines, 7 3/4 in. $65
Fork-carving, small, stainless prongs, steak,
  8 7/8 in. $70
Fork-cold meat/serving, medium, solid,
  8 1/8 in. $100

Fork-ice cream, 5 1/2 in. $60
Fork-lemon, 4 1/2 in. $38
Fork-pickle/olive, short handle, 2 tines,
  5 3/4 in. $35
Fork-salad serving, solid, 8 7/8 in. $140
Fork-salad, individual, 4 3/8 in. handle,
  6 5/8 in. $40
Fork-strawberry, 4 3/4 in. $36
Knife-cheese, stainless blade,
  7 1/8 in. $53
Knife-modern, hollow handle, 4 3/8 in. handle,
  9 5/8 in. $50
Knife-modern, hollow handle, 4 in. handle,
  8 7/8 in. $30
Knife-new french, hollow handle, 4 1/4 in. handle,
  9 1/2 in. $50
Knife-new french, hollow handle, 4 in. handle,
  8 7/8 in. $32
Knife-steak, individual, 9 1/4 in. $58
Knife-wedding cake, stainless blade,
  12 1/8 in. $50
Knife-youth, replacement blade,
  7 5/8 in. $50
Ladle-cream, solid, 5 1/2 in. $60
Ladle-cream, solid, 5 in. $60
Ladle-gravy, solid, 6 1/2 in. $100
Ladle-punch, stainless bowl, 13 5/8 in. $80
Ladle-soup, stainless bowl, 11 in. $70
Salad set, 2 pieces, solid $280
Salad set, 2 pieces, stainless bowl,
  11 3/8 in. $90
Salad set, 2 pieces, wooden bowl,
  11 in. $120
Scoop-ice, silver plate bowl, 9 in. $60
Server-asparagus, hollow handle, silver plate
  hood, 9 1/2 in. $65
Server-cheese, stainless blade,
  6 5/8 in. $55
Server-jelly, 6 1/8 in. $50
Server-lasagna, stainless blade, 12 in. $50
Server-pasta, stainless bowl, 11 1/8 in. $60
Server-pie and cake, stainless blade,
  10 3/4 in. $50
Server-tomato, solid, 8 1/8 in. $120
Spoon-bon-bon, 4 7/8 in. $50
Spoon-casserole, smooth, solid,
  8 3/4 in. $130
Spoon-dessert/oval soup, 6 7/8 in. $50
Spoon-fruit, 5 7/8 in. $50
Spoon-iced tea, 7 5/8 in. $37
Spoon-salad serving, solid, 8 3/4 in. $140
Spoon-salt, individual, 2 7/8 in. $12
Spoon-soup, round bowl, cream,
  6 1/4 in. $46

Gorham

Spoon-sugar shell, scallop bowl,
6 1/8 in.................................$40
Spoon-teaspoon, 6 in.......................$20
Tablespoon, (serving spoon), pierced,
8 1/2 in.................................$90
Tablespoon, (serving spoon), 8 1/2 in.........$85
Tongs-sugar, 4 in. $68

Melrose by Gorham, 1908

Spoon-teaspoon, (five o'clock), 5 3/8 in. $18

The following piece has a monogram:
Spoon-teaspoon, (five o'clock), 5 3/8 in. $14

Mothers-New by Gorham, 1926

Butter-master, flat handle, 7 in...............$33
Fork, 7 3/4 in...............................$55
Fork, 7 in.................................. $25
Fork-cold meat/serving, small, solid,
7 1/4 in.................................$75
Fork-salad, individual, 6 1/2 in. $32
Knife-new french, hollow handle, no bolster,
8 5/8 in.................................$30
Knife-new french, hollow handle, bolster,
8 5/8 in.................................$30
Knife-sharpener/steel, small, steak,
13 1/2 in. $50
Ladle-gravy, solid, 7 in......................$70
Server-pie and cake, stainless blade,
10 1/2 in. $55
Spoon-dessert/oval soup, 7 in. $34
Spoon-fruit, 5 7/8 in. $34
Spoon-iced tea, 7 1/2 in. $34
Spoon-soup, round bowl, bouillon,
5 1/8 in.................................$30
Spoon-soup, round bowl, cream,
6 in. $40
Spoon-soup, round bowl, gumbo,
6 7/8 in.................................$42
Spoon-sugar, 6 in..........................$36
Spoon-teaspoon, 5 5/8 in. $20
Tablespoon, (serving spoon),
8 1/2 in.................................$70
Tongs-sugar, 4 1/4 in......................$60

Mothers-Old by Gorham, 1875

Butter spreader, flat handle, 5 3/4 in. $15
Fork, 7 3/4 in. $46
Fork, 7 in................................. $36
Fork-carving, small, stainless prongs, steak,
9 in. $40
Fork-chipped beef, small, 7 in............... $48
Fork-cocktail, 5 5/8 in. $15
Fork-cold meat/serving, small, solid,
7 3/8 in................................. $60
Fork-salad, individual, 5 5/8 in. $30
Fork-youth, 5 3/4 in........................ $35
Knife-bar, hollow handle, 8 1/2 in. $24
Knife-carving, small, stainless blade, steak,
10 3/8 in................................ $40
Knife-new french, hollow handle,
9 3/4 in................................. $50
Knife-old french, hollow handle,
8 5/8 in................................. $40
Knife-wedding cake, stainless blade,
12 5/8 in................................ $60
Knife-youth, 7 1/2 in. $30
Ladle-cream, solid, 5 1/8 in................. $38
Ladle-mayonnaise, gold wash,
5 3/8 in................................. $35
Napkin clip (made for teaspoons) $20
Server-cheese, silver plate blade,
6 in. $50
Spoon-baby, straight handle,
4 1/2 in................................. $30
Spoon-bon-bon, gold wash, 5 in............. $35
Spoon-demitasse, 4 1/8 in.................. $15
Spoon-demitasse, gold wash, 4 1/8 in........ $15
Spoon-dessert/oval soup, 7 in............... $30
Spoon-fruit, 5 5/8 in. $30
Spoon-relish, 5 7/8 in. $28
Spoon-soup, round bowl, bouillon,
5 1/8 in................................. $28
Spoon-sugar, 5 5/8 in. $28
Spoon-teaspoon, (five o'clock),
5 3/8 in................................. $10
Spoon-teaspoon, 5 5/8 in.................. $18
Spoon-youth, 4 3/4 in...................... $30
Tablespoon, (serving spoon),
8 1/2 in................................. $50
Tongs-sugar, 4 7/8 in. $44

Mythologique by Gorham, 1894

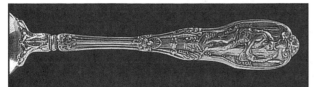

There are newer examples of this pattern; the following piece has a monogram:
Knife-old french, hollow handle, 8 5/8 in.....$110

New Tipt by Gorham, 1871

Spoon-teaspoon, (five o'clock), 5 3/8 in. $28
Tablespoon, (serving spoon), 8 in. $90

The following pieces have monograms:
Fork, 6 3/4 in. $44
Spoon-dessert/oval soup, 6 5/8 in. $45
Spoon-sugar, 5 5/8 in.........................$36
Spoon-teaspoon, (five o'clock), 5 3/8 in. $21
Spoon-teaspoon, 5 5/8 in. $22

Newcastle by Gorham, 1895

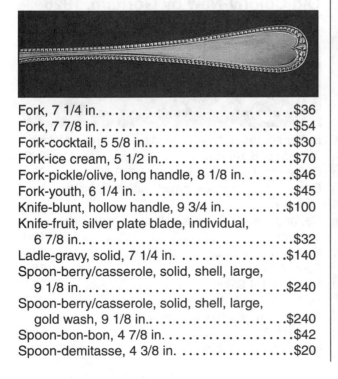

Fork, 7 1/4 in. $36
Fork, 7 7/8 in. $54
Fork-cocktail, 5 5/8 in........................$30
Fork-ice cream, 5 1/2 in......................$70
Fork-pickle/olive, long handle, 8 1/8 in. $46
Fork-youth, 6 1/4 in. $45
Knife-blunt, hollow handle, 9 3/4 in. $100
Knife-fruit, silver plate blade, individual,
    6 7/8 in...................................$32
Ladle-gravy, solid, 7 1/4 in. $140
Spoon-berry/casserole, solid, shell, large,
    9 1/8 in...................................$240
Spoon-berry/casserole, solid, shell, large,
    gold wash, 9 1/8 in........................$240
Spoon-bon-bon, 4 7/8 in. $42
Spoon-demitasse, 4 3/8 in. $20

Spoon-fruit, 5 1/2 in. $38
Spoon-fruit, 6 1/4 in. $38
Spoon-preserve, gold wash, 7 3/8 in. $100
Spoon-soup, round bowl, gumbo,
    6 7/8 in..................................$45
Spoon-teaspoon, (five o'clock), 5 3/8 in....... $16
Spoon-teaspoon, 3 3/4 in. handle,
    5 7/8 in..................................$24
Spoon-teaspoon, 4 in. handle, 6 1/8 in. $24
Tablespoon, (serving spoon), 8 5/8 in. $70

The following pieces have monograms:
Ladle-cream, solid, 5 3/4 in..................$40
Ladle-oyster, solid, 12 1/2 in. $400
Spoon-fruit, 6 1/4 in. $30
Spoon-teaspoon, (five o'clock), 5 3/8 in....... $12
Spoon-teaspoon, 5 7/8 in....................$18
Spoon-teaspoon, 6 1/8 in....................$18

Gorham Newcastle long-handle (10 5/8 in.) salad serving set. Gilt tines; excellent condition; engraved "AGL" (front) and "from Susie, 1902" reverse. $375/set

Gorham Newcastle lettuce fork (photo also includes nut picks). Excellent condition, no monogram, 9 1/4 in. $75

Gorham

Nocturne by Gorham, 1938

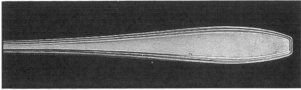

Butter spreader, hollow handle, modern, stainless
  paddle, 6 5/8 in................................$20
Butter spreader, hollow handle, stainless
  paddle, 6 1/2 in................................$19
Butter spreader, flat handle, 5 3/4 in...........$14
Butter-master, flat handle, 7 1/8 in.............$28
Butter-master, hollow handle, 7 in...............$28
Carving set, 2 pieces, small, stainless blade,
  steak..$110
Fork, 7 1/4 in....................................$24
Fork, 7 3/4 in....................................$36
Fork-salad, individual, 6 5/8 in.................$26
Knife-new french, hollow handle, stainless
  blade, 8 7/8 in.................................$30
Ladle-cream, solid, 5 3/8 in.....................$40
Ladle-gravy, solid, 6 3/4 in.....................$70
Server-jelly, 6 3/8 in...........................$30
Spoon-dessert/oval soup, 6 7/8 in................$40
Spoon-iced tea, 7 5/8 in.........................$28
Spoon-soup, round bowl, cream,
  6 3/8 in..$24
Spoon-sugar shell, 6 in..........................$32
Spoon-teaspoon, (five o'clock), 5 5/8 in.........$16
Spoon-teaspoon, 6 in.............................$18
Tablespoon, (serving spoon), 8 5/8 in............$70
Tablespoon, (serving spoon), pierced,
  8 5/8 in..$85

Norfolk/Villa Norfolk by Gorham, 1904

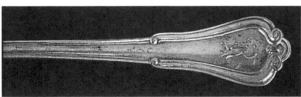

Butter spreader, flat handle, 5 3/4 in...........$22
Butter-master, flat handle, 6 3/4 in.............$36
Fork, 6 7/8 in....................................$30
Fork, 7 5/8 in....................................$34
Fork-chipped beef, small, 5 7/8 in...............$60
Fork-chipped beef, small, 6 5/8 in...............$60
Fork-cocktail, 5 3/8 in..........................$18
Fork-cold meat/serving, small, solid, 1 of 4
  tines beveled, 6 1/4 in.........................$65

Fork-cold meat/serving, small, solid, 7 in. $65
Fork-pickle/olive, short handle, 5 5/8 in........ $30
Knife-blunt, hollow handle, 9 3/4 in............. $45
Knife-fish, solid, individual, 7 3/4 in. $60
Knife-jelly, large, 7 7/8 in. $120
Knife-modern, hollow handle, 8 5/8 in......... $33
Knife-old french, hollow handle,
  8 7/8 in....................................... $36
Ladle-cream, solid, 4 7/8 in.................. $44
Ladle-cream, solid, 5 5/8 in.................. $44
Ladle-cream, solid, gold wash, 5 5/8 in....... $44
Ladle-gravy, solid, gold wash, 6 7/8 in........ $80
Sardine-tined fork, serving, solid, large,
  5 1/8 in....................................... $80
Spoon-baby, straight handle, 4 5/8 in......... $36
Spoon-bon-bon, 4 3/8 in. $38
Spoon-casserole, smooth, solid,
  8 3/4 in...................................... $100
Spoon-demitasse, 3 3/4 in.................... $18
Spoon-five o'clock/youth, 5 1/8 in............ $20
Spoon-preserve, 7 in. $55
Spoon-relish, 5 1/2 in....................... $38
Spoon-soup, round bowl, bouillon, 5 in....... $24
Spoon-soup, round bowl, gumbo,
  6 3/4 in....................................... $36
Spoon-sugar, 5 5/8 In........................ $35
Spoon-teaspoon, (five o'clock), 5 1/2 in...... $16
Spoon-teaspoon, 5 3/4 in.................... $24
Tablespoon, (serving spoon), 8 1/4 in. $60
Tongs-sugar, 4 1/4 in. $56

Old Colony-New by Gorham, 1926

Butter spreader, hollow handle, modern, stainless
  paddle, 6 1/4 in.......................... $26
Butter-master, hollow handle, 6 5/8 in........ $34
Carving set, 2 pieces, small, stainless blade,
  steak $120
Carving set, 3 pieces, small, stainless blade,
  steak $180
Fork, 7 1/8 in. $45
Fork, 7 7/8 in. $58
Fork-baby, 4 3/8 in.......................... $34
Fork-cocktail, 5 3/8 in...................... $28
Fork-cold meat/serving, medium, solid,
  8 1/4 in..................................... $80
Fork-lemon, 4 1/2 in. $26

Gorham

Fork-pickle/olive, short handle, 6 in..........$26
Fork-salad serving, solid, 8 7/8 in. $100
Fork-salad, individual, 6 5/8 in...............$43
Fork-youth, 6 1/8 in. $45
Knife-carving, small, stainless blade, steak,
   10 in.....................................$60
Knife-new french, hollow handle, 9 5/8 in......$48
Knife-new french, hollow handle, 9 in. $35
Ladle-cream, solid, 5 1/4 in...................$36
Ladle-gravy, solid, 6 1/8 in. $75
Ladle-gravy, solid, gold wash, 6 1/8 in. $75
Ladle-mayonnaise, 4 7/8 in....................$45
Server-cheese, stainless blade, 6 1/2 in.......$40
Server-cucumber, large, 6 in. $90
Server-jelly, 6 1/4 in. $30
Server-pie and cake, stainless blade,
   10 3/8 in. $50
Server-pie, stainless blade, 9 7/8 in. $50
Spoon-chocolate, short handle, large,
   5 3/8 in..................................$28
Spoon-demitasse, 4 1/4 in. $17
Spoon-dessert/oval soup, 6 7/8 in............$44
Spoon-fruit, 5 7/8 in.........................$32
Spoon-iced tea, 7 5/8 in. $30
Spoon-preserve, 8 in........................$48
Spoon-soup, round bowl, bouillon,
   5 1/4 in..................................$34
Spoon-soup, round bowl, cream,
   6 3/8 in..................................$36
Spoon-sugar, 5 7/8 in........................$34
Spoon-teaspoon, 6 in........................$24
Tablespoon, (serving spoon), 8 1/2 in........$80
Tongs-sugar, 4 5/8 in.......................$50

Old English Tipt by Gorham, 1870

Butter spreader, flat handle, 6 in. $32
Butter-master, hollow handle, 6 5/8 in........$48
Carving set, 2 pieces, large, stainless blade,
   roast $200
Fork, (place size), 7 1/2 in..................$60
Fork, 7 1/8 in...............................$45
Fork, 7 3/4 in...............................$60
Fork-carving, large, stainless prongs, roast,
   9 3/4 in.................................$100

Fork-cold meat/serving, large, solid,
   9 1/8 in.................................$105
Fork-lemon, 4 1/2 in. $36
Fork-pickle/olive, short handle, 5 5/8 in.......$30
Fork-salad (place size), 4 1/2 in. handle,
   6 3/4 in.................................$44
Fork-salad, individual, 4 1/4 in. handle,
   6 1/2 in.................................$40
Knife-carving, large, stainless blade, roast,
   12 1/4 in................................$100
Knife-modern, hollow handle, 3 7/8 in. handle,
   8 3/4 in.................................$40
Knife-modern, hollow handle, 4 1/2 in. handle,
   9 1/8 in.................................$40
Knife-new french, hollow handle, 8 3/4 in. $45
Ladle-gravy, solid, 6 5/8 in.................$120
Server-jelly, 6 3/8 in. $48
Server-pie and cake, stainless blade,
   10 5/8 in................................$75
Spoon-iced tea, 7 1/2 in....................$40
Spoon-place/oval soup, 6 3/4 in. $60
Spoon-soup, round bowl, cream, 6 1/8 in. $50
Spoon-sugar, 6 1/4 in......................$35
Spoon-teaspoon, 6 in.......................$28
Tablespoon, (serving spoon), pierced,
   9 1/8 in.................................$100
Tablespoon, (serving spoon), 9 1/8 in. $85

Fifty pieces Gorham Old English Tipt: 8 luncheon and 2 dinner forks, 8 luncheon and 2 dinner knives, 10 salad forks, 10 teaspoons, and 10 cream soup spoons. No monogram. C. 1950-1980. $1,200

Old French by Gorham, 1905

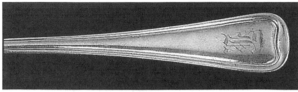

Butter spreader, hollow handle, modern, stainless
    paddle, 6 1/4 in............................$32
Butter-master, hollow handle, 6 5/8 in.........$45
Carving set, 2 pieces, small, stainless blade,
    steak.....................................$140
Carving set, 3 piece, small, stainless blade,
    steak.....................................$200
Fork, (place size), 2 in. tines, 7 1/2 in.........$44
Fork, 7 1/8 in.................................$35
Fork-baby, 4 1/2 in. $40
Fork-carving, small, stainless prongs, steak,
    8 5/8 in....................................$70
Fork-carving, small, stainless prongs, steak,
    9 in.......................................$70
Fork-cocktail, 3 7/8 in. handle, 5 1/8 in........$24
Fork-lemon, 4 3/8 in...........................$40
Fork-pickle/olive, short handle, 5 3/4 in. $40
Knife-carving, large, stainless blade, roast,
    13 1/4 in. $100
Knife-carving, small, stainless blade, steak,
    10 1/4 in. $70
Knife-carving, small, stainless blade, steak,
    9 3/4 in....................................$70
Knife-fruit, silver plate blade, individual,
    7 in. $38
Knife-fruit, stainless blade, individual,
    6 5/8 in....................................$38
Knife-modern, hollow handle, stainless blade,
    8 5/8 in....................................$40
Knife-new french, hollow handle, stainless
    blade, 8 5/8 in.............................$40
Knife-old french, hollow handle, stainless
    blade, 8 1/2 in.............................$40
Ladle-gravy, solid, 6 7/8 in. $100
Poultry shears, 10 1/4 in. $180
Scoop-ice, silver plate bowl, 8 1/2 in..........$50
Server-asparagus, hollow handle, silver plate
    hood, 9 3/4 in.............................$65
Spoon-fruit, no rim, 5 5/8 in. $34
Spoon-iced tea, 7 1/2 in. $36
Spoon-place/oval soup, 7 in.................$50
Spoon-soup, round bowl, cream,
    6 3/8 in....................................$45
Spoon-sugar, 5 7/8 in..........................$42
Spoon-teaspoon, 5 7/8 in. $28
Tongs-sugar, 4 in. $50

The following pieces have monograms:
Bone holder, silver plate tines, 8 1/2 in. $160
Fork-salad, individual, 6 in..................$40
Knife-orange, silver plate blade, 7 3/8 in...... $40
Pick-nut, 4 5/8 in. $50
Spoon-five o'clock/youth, 5 1/2 in............$20
Spoon-teaspoon, 5 7/8 in...................$18
Tablespoon, (serving spoon), 8 1/2 in. $58

Old London-Plain by Gorham, 1916

Butter spreader, flat handle, 5 1/2 in. $20
Fork, 7 5/8 in. $50
Fork, 7 in....................................$33
Fork-cocktail, 5 3/8 in. $24
Fork-ice cream, 5 1/4 in. $36
Fork-pickle/olive, short handle, 5 7/8 in....... $26
Fork-pie, 3 tines, 6 1/2 in. $36
Fork-salad, individual, 4 tines, 6 1/2 in. $40
Fork-salad, individual, 4 tines, 6 in...........$40
Knife-new french, hollow handle,
    8 1/2 in...................................$30
Knife-old french, hollow handle, 8 1/2 in...... $30
Knife-old french, hollow handle, 9 in. $30
Knife-old french, hollow handle, stainless
    blade, 9 1/2 in............................$40
Ladle-cream, solid, gold wash, 5 in. $38
Server-jelly, 6 1/4 in. $30
Spoon-casserole, smooth, solid, 8 3/4 in. $90
Spoon-demitasse, 4 1/4 in..................$18
Spoon-dessert/oval soup, 7 in..............$40
Spoon-fruit, 5 5/8 in. $34
Spoon-salad serving, solid, 9 in. $80
Spoon-soup, round bowl, bouillon,
    5 1/4 in..................................$28
Spoon-soup, round bowl, gumbo,
    6 7/8 in..................................$37
Spoon-teaspoon, (five o'clock), 5 3/8 in...... $17
Spoon-teaspoon, 5 5/8 in...................$15
Tablespoon, (serving spoon), 8 1/2 in. $60
Tongs-sugar, 4 3/8 in. $46

The following pieces have monograms:
Butter-master, flat handle, 7 in. $27
Fork, fish/salad, solid, individual, 6 5/8 in. $38
Fork-lemon, 4 3/8 in. $21
Fork-salad, individual, 6 in..................$30

Knife-old french, hollow handle, 8 1/2 in.......$23
Ladle-gravy, solid, 6 3/4 in. $53
Server-cheese, stainless blade, 6 1/2 in.......$30
Server-jelly, 6 1/4 in........................$24
Spoon-fruit, 5 5/8 in........................$24
Spoon-soup, round bowl, bouillon,
    5 1/4 in..................................$23
Spoon-sugar, 5 7/8 in.......................$27
Spoon-teaspoon, (five o'clock), 5 3/8 in. $13

Old Masters by Gorham, 1885

Ladle-cream, solid, 5 5/8 in.$500

Olive by Gorham, 1865

Fork-dessert/luncheon, solid, 6 3/4 in.........$60

Paris by Gorham, 1900

Fork, 7 3/4 in.............................$140
Knife-old french, hollow handle,
    8 1/2 in..................................$160
Spoon-soup, round bowl, bouillon,
    5 3/8 in..................................$90
Tablespoon, (serving spoon), 8 5/8 in........$140

The following pieces have monograms:
Fork, 7 in................................. $70
Fork-cocktail, 5 1/2 in......................$60
Knife-old french, hollow handle,
    8 1/2 in..................................$140
Knife-old french, hollow handle,
    9 3/4 in..................................$160
Spoon-demitasse, 4 1/4 in. $53
Spoon-dessert/oval soup, 6 7/8 in...........$90
Spoon-soup, round bowl, bouillon,
    5 3/8 in..................................$70
Spoon-teaspoon, 5 7/8 in. $60
Tablespoon, (serving spoon), 8 5/8 in.......$120

Perspective by Gorham, 1959

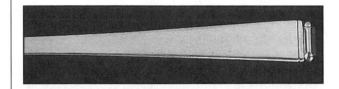

Antique American silver youth knife, fork, and spoon in the Piper pattern (1882); made by Gorham and residing in a Bailey, Banks & Biddle of Philadelphia, Pennsylvania red gift box. Engraved "Agnes 1893." Knife 7 1/8 in.; fork 5 7/8 in.; spoon 5 7/8 in. $350

Plymouth by Gorham, 1911

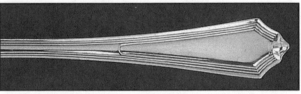

Butter spreader, flat handle, 5 7/8 in. $22
Butter-master, flat handle, 7 5/8 in........... $33
Butter-master, flat handle, 7 in. $33
Carving set, 2 pieces, small, stainless blade,
    steak $100
Fork, 7 5/8 in. $45
Fork, 7 in................................. $25
Fork-baby, 4 1/2 in........................ $36
Fork-carving, small, stainless prongs, steak,
    8 5/8 in.................................. $50
Fork-chipped beef, small, 6 1/8 in. $55
Fork-cocktail, 5 1/2 in...................... $20
Fork-cold meat/serving, small, solid, 4 tines,
    6 1/4 in.................................. $60
Fork-cold meat/serving, small, solid, 4 tines,
    7 1/4 in.................................. $60

Fork-fish/salad, solid, individual, large,
  heart slot, 6 1/2 in. $40
Fork-lemon, 4 3/8 in. $30
Fork-lemon, 5 1/8 in. $30
Fork-pastry, bar, pierced, 6 in. $35
Fork-pickle/olive, short handle, 5 1/2 in. $30
Fork-ramekin, 4 7/8 in. $40
Fork-sandwich, 7 in. $60
Knife-blunt, hollow handle, silver plate blade,
  9 3/4 in. $40
Knife-carving, small, stainless blade, steak,
  9 3/4 in. $50
Knife-orange, silver plate blade, serrated blade,
  6 7/8 in. $40
Knife-sharpener/steel, small, steak,
  10 1/2 in. $60
Knife-sharpener/steel, large, steak, 14 in. $60
Ladle-cream, solid, 5 1/8 in. $32
Ladle-cream, solid, gold wash, 5 1/8 in. $32
Ladle-gravy, solid, 7 in. $80
Napkin clip (made for teaspoons) $20
Napkin clip (made for five o'clock) $16
Server-cheese, silver plate blade, 6 in. $60
Server-jelly, not pierced, 6 1/4 in. $30
Server-pie, silver plate blade, 9 3/8 in. $60
Spoon-casserole, smooth, solid, 8 3/4 in. $95
Spoon-chocolate, short handle, 4 1/2 in. $24
Spoon-demitasse, gold wash, 4 1/4 in. $20
Spoon-dessert/oval soup, 7 1/8 in. $36
Spoon-fruit, 5 7/8 in. $28
Spoon-iced tea, 7 1/2 in. $35
Spoon-mustard, 4 5/8 in. $35
Spoon-olive, long handle, 7 3/8 in. $120
Spoon-olive, short-pierced bowl, gold wash,
  5 3/4 in. $80
Spoon-preserve, 7 1/8 in. $50
Spoon-salad serving, solid, 8 7/8 in. $80
Spoon-soup, round bowl, bouillon,
  5 3/8 in. $20
Spoon-soup, round bowl, gumbo,
  6 7/8 in. $36
Spoon-sugar, 6 in. $26
Spoon-teaspoon, (five o'clock), 3 3/4 in.
  handle, 5 1/2 in. $12
Spoon-teaspoon, 4 in. handle, 5 7/8 in. $18
Tablespoon, (serving spoon), 8 1/2 in. $50
Tablespoon, (serving spoon), pierced,
  8 1/2 in. $70
Tongs-sugar, 4 3/8 in. $45

Fork, 7 in. $50
Fork-cocktail, 5 5/8 in. $40
Fork-ice cream, 5 1/4 in. $70
Fork-salad, individual, 5 3/4 in. $80
Knife-blunt, hollow handle, 9 3/4 in. $90
Knife-carving, small, stainless blade, steak,
  9 1/2 in. $80
Ladle-gravy, solid, 7 in. $140
Spoon-demitasse, 3 7/8 in. $30
Spoon-fruit, 5 3/4 in. $50
Spoon-olive, short, pierced bowl,
  5 5/8 in. $100
Spoon-soup, round bowl, bouillon,
  5 1/4 in. $45
Spoon-teaspoon, (five o'clock), 5 1/2 in. $20
Tablespoon, (serving spoon), 8 1/2 in. $90
Tongs-sugar, 3 3/4 in. $90

The following pieces have monograms:
Fork, 7 5/8 in. $60
Fork, 7 in. $44
Knife-blunt, hollow handle, 8 1/2 in. $63
Knife-blunt, hollow handle, 9 3/4 in. $70
Ladle-gravy, solid, 7 in. $130
Server-pie, silver plate blade, 9 5/8 in. $70
Spoon-place/oval soup, 6 3/4 in. $54
Spoon-soup, round bowl, bouillon,
  5 1/4 in. $45
Spoon-soup, round bowl, bouillon,
  5 1/4 in. $45
Spoon-soup, round bowl, cream,
  6 5/8 in. $54
Spoon-teaspoon, (five o'clock), 5 1/2 in. $17
Spoon-teaspoon, 5 7/8 in. $25
Tablespoon, (serving spoon), 8 1/2 in. $80

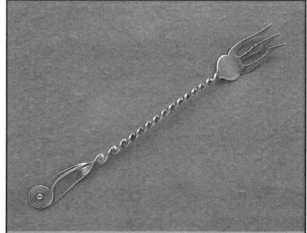

Whimsical Gorham olive fork. This is model 278, with applied wirework in the form of a watch-spring leading down into a twist handle. 7 3/8 in.; good condition, no monogram. $95

Poppy by Gorham, 1902

Portsmouth by Gorham, 1918

Butter spreader, flat handle, 5 3/4 in..........$24
Butter-master, flat handle, 6 3/4 in...........$38
Carving set, 2 pieces, small, stainless blade,
   steak...................................$120
Carving set, 3 pieces, small, stainless blade,
   steak...................................$180
Fork, 7 1/4 in................................$45
Fork, 8 1/8 in................................$60
Fork-baby, 3 1/4 in. $34
Fork-carving, small, stainless prongs, steak,
   9 1/8 in...................................$60
Fork-cocktail, 3 tines, not beveled,
   5 5/8 in...................................$20
Fork-cold meat/serving, small, solid,
   7 1/4 in...................................$80
Fork-ice cream, 5 1/4 in......................$48
Fork-lemon, 2 of 3 tines beveled, 6 in.........$30
Fork-pastry, pierced, 6 in....................$44
Fork-pickle/olive, short handle, 2 tines not
   beveled, 5 5/8 in..........................$30
Fork-pickle/olive, short handle, 2 of 3 tines
   beveled, 5 5/8 in..........................$30
Fork-youth, 6 1/8 in. $25
Knife-new french, hollow handle,
   9 7/8 in...................................$47
Knife-old french, hollow handle, 8 1/2 in.......$34
Knife-old french, hollow handle, 9 7/8 in.......$47
Knife-sharpener, steel, small, steak,
   10 1/2 in. $60
Server-cheese, stainless blade, 6 1/2 in.......$40
Spoon-demitasse, 4 1/4 in. $15
Spoon-dessert/oval soup, 7 in. $54
Spoon-five o'clock/youth, 5 1/4 in. $13
Spoon-iced tea, 8 1/8 in. $40
Spoon-olive, long handle, 8 1/4 in...........$160
Spoon-soup, round bowl, bouillon,
   5 1/8 in...................................$26
Spoon-soup, round bowl, cream, 6 in.........$36
Spoon-soup, round bowl, gumbo, 6 7/8 in. $45
Spoon-sugar, 6 in............................$36
Spoon-teaspoon, (five o'clock), 5 5/8 in. $16
Spoon-teaspoon, 6 in.........................$23
Tablespoon, (serving spoon), 8 3/4 in.........$50
Tablespoon, (serving spoon), pierced,
   8 3/4 in...................................$70

The following pieces have monograms:
Butter spreader, flat handle, 5 3/4 in. $21
Fork, 7 1/4 in. $36
Fork-cold meat/serving, small, solid,
   7 1/4 in.................................. $50
Knife-old french, hollow handle, 9 7/8 in. $36
Knife-old french, hollow handle, 9 in. $27
Ladle-mayonnaise, 5 in. $36
Spoon-dessert/oval soup, 7 in............... $40
Spoon-fruit, 5 5/8 in. $30
Spoon-iced tea, 8 1/8 in.................... $30
Spoon-soup, round bowl, bouillon,
   5 1/8 in.................................. $23
Spoon-soup, round bowl, gumbo,
   6 7/8 in.................................. $38
Spoon-sugar, 6 in. $30
Spoon-teaspoon, (five o'clock), 5 5/8 in....... $12
Spoon-teaspoon, 6 in........................ $18

Princess Patricia by Gorham, 1926

Butter spreader, flat handle, 5 1/2 in. $24
Butter-master, flat handle, 6 7/8 in........... $40
Carving set, 2 pieces, small, stainless blade,
   steak $130
Fork, 7 1/4 in. $34
Fork, 7 3/4 in. $48
Fork-carving, small, stainless prongs, steak,
   8 7/8 in.................................. $65
Fork-cocktail, 5 3/8 in. $30
Fork-cold meat/serving, medium, solid,
   8 in. $90
Fork-ice cream, 5 3/8 in. $50
Fork-lemon, 5 1/8 in. $30
Fork-salad, individual, 6 1/2 in. $40
Ladle-cream, solid, 6 in. $45
Napkin clip (made for five o'clock) $18
Server-jelly, 6 1/4 in. $34
Spoon-baby, straight handle, 4 5/8 in......... $40
Spoon-casserole, smooth, solid, 8 1/2 in. ... $110
Spoon-demitasse, 4 1/4 in................... $20
Spoon-fruit, 6 in............................ $34
Spoon-iced tea, 7 1/2 in..................... $40
Spoon-olive, short, pierced bowl, 5 3/4 in..... $90
Spoon-soup, round bowl, bouillon,
   5 1/2 in.................................. $34
Spoon-soup, round bowl, gumbo, 7 in........ $45

Spoon-sugar, 5 3/4 in........................$34
Spoon-teaspoon, (five o'clock), 5 1/2 in.......$18
Spoon-teaspoon, 5 7/8 in...................$24
Tablespoon, (serving spoon), 8 5/8 in.........$70

Providence by Gorham, 1920

Butter spreader, flat handle, 5 3/4 in..........$10
Carving set, 2 pieces, small, stainless blade,
    steak....................................$90
Fork, 7 1/8 in..............................$17
Fork, 7 3/4 in..............................$18
Fork-cocktail, 5 5/8 in........................$8
Fork-cold meat/serving, small, solid,
    7 3/8 in..................................$30
Fork-cold meat/serving, medium, solid,
    8 7/8 in..................................$30
Fork-ice cream, 5 3/8 in.....................$16
Fork-salad, individual, 6 1/8 in...............$16
Knife-carving, small, stainless blade, steak,
    10 in....................................$45
Knife-fish, solid, individual, 8 in.............$22
Knife-old french, hollow handle, 8 5/8 in.......$16
Knife-old french, hollow handle, 9 5/8 in.......$18
Ladle-cream, solid, 5 in.....................$27
Ladle-gravy, solid, 6 3/4 in. $30
Server-jelly, 6 3/8 in. $16
Server-pie, solid, 9 1/4 in. $55
Server-pie, solid, 9 3/4 in. $55
Spoon-casserole, smooth, solid, 8 3/4 in......$38
Spoon-fruit, 1 1/4 in. wide bowl, 5 7/8 in.......$15
Spoon-fruit, 1 in. wide bowl, 5 7/8 in..........$15
Spoon-fruit, gold wash, 5 7/8 in..............$15
Spoon-iced tea, 7 1/2 in. $10
Spoon-place/oval soup, 7 in. $13
Spoon-sherbet, egg bowl, 5 1/2 in............$10
Spoon-soup, round bowl, bouillon,
    5 3/8 in..................................$10
Spoon-soup, round bowl, gumbo,
    6 7/8 in..................................$13
Spoon-sugar, oval bowl, 6 in.................$15
Spoon-teaspoon, 5 3/4 in. $12
Tablespoon, (serving spoon), 8 5/8 in.........$23

Raphael by Gorham, 1875

Spoon-dessert/oval soup, 7 in. $80

Spoon-five o'clock/youth, 4 7/8 in............ $50
Spoon-salt, master, 3 1/2 in................. $40

The following pieces have monograms:
Fork, 7 1/2 in. $70
Fork, 7 in.................................. $53
Ladle-gravy, solid, 7 1/4 in................ $110
Spoon-demitasse, 4 1/4 in................. $30
Spoon-dessert/oval soup, 7 in.............. $60
Spoon-place/oval soup, 6 1/4 in. $60
Spoon-sugar, 6 1/8 in...................... $53
Spoon-teaspoon, (five o'clock), 5 1/2 in....... $30
Spoon-teaspoon, 6 in....................... $38
Tablespoon, (serving spoon), 7 7/8 in. $70
Tablespoon, (serving spoon), 8 1/2 in. $70

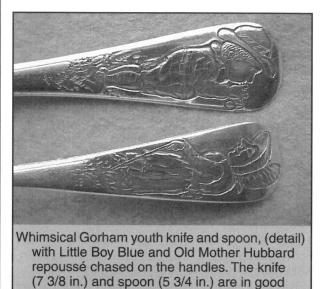

Whimsical Gorham youth knife and spoon, (detail) with Little Boy Blue and Old Mother Hubbard repoussé chased on the handles. The knife (7 3/8 in.) and spoon (5 3/4 in.) are in good condition. Both monogrammed "Roger from Auntie" (reverse). $185/pair

Roanoke by Gorham, 1913

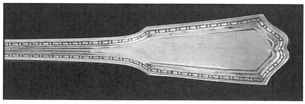

Butter spreader, hollow handle, modern,
    stainless paddle, 6 1/8 in................ $22
Butter spreader, flat handle, 5 1/2 in. $22
Fork, 7 3/4 in. $48
Fork-cold meat/serving, medium, solid,
    8 7/8 in................................. $80
Fork-salad, individual, 7 in.................. $50
Knife-old french, hollow handle, 9 5/8 in...... $43

Ladle-gravy, solid, 6 3/4 in. $70
Server-pie and cake, stainless blade,
   10 1/2 in. $55
Spoon-demitasse, 4 1/4 in. $22
Spoon-dessert/oval soup, 7 in. $40
Spoon-fruit, 5 3/4 in. $36
Spoon-soup, round bowl, bouillon,
   5 1/2 in. $30
Spoon-soup, round bowl, gumbo, 6 7/8 in. $38
Spoon-sugar, 6 in..........................$40
Spoon-teaspoon, 6 in.......................$26
Tablespoon, (serving spoon), 8 1/2 in........$70
Tablespoon, (serving spoon), pierced,
   8 3/8 in..................................$80
The following pieces have monograms:
Butter spreader, flat handle, 5 1/2 in.........$16
Butter spreader, flat handle, 6 in. $16
Fork, 7 3/4 in.............................$38
Fork, 7 in................................$32
Fork-cocktail, 5 5/8 in......................$22
Fork-salad, individual, 6 1/8 in. $30
Knife-old french, hollow handle, 8 1/2 in.......$30
Ladle-cream, solid, 5 1/8 in.................$35
Salad set, 2 pieces, solid, 8 3/4 in...........$140
Spoon-fruit, 5 3/4 in. $26
Spoon-iced tea, 8 1/8 in. $25
Spoon-soup, round bowl, bouillon,
   5 1/2 in..................................$23
Spoon-soup, round bowl, gumbo, 6 7/8 in. $30
Spoon-sugar, 6 in.........................$30
Spoon-teaspoon, (five o'clock), 5 1/2 in. $18
Spoon-teaspoon, 6 in.......................$20
Tablespoon, (serving spoon), 8 1/2 in........$53

Rondo by Gorham, 1951

Butter spreader, hollow handle, modern,
   stainless, 6 1/4 in.........................$27
Butter spreader, hollow handle, stainless paddle,
   6 1/4 in...................................$27
Butter spreader, flat handle, 5 7/8 in..........$30
Butter-master, flat handle, 6 7/8 in............$36
Butter-master, hollow handle, no notch,
   6 3/4 in...................................$36
Butter-master, hollow handle, notch blade,
   6 3/4 in...................................$36
Carving set, 2 pieces, small, stainless blade,
   steak....................................$150

Fork, (place size), 5 in. handle, 7 1/2 in....... $70
Fork, 4 3/4 in. handle, 7 1/4 in............... $40
Fork, 5 1/8 in. handle, 7 7/8 in.............. $70
Fork-cocktail, 5 3/4 in...................... $34
Fork-cold meat/serving, medium, solid,
   8 1/8 in............................... $110
Fork-lemon, 4 1/2 in. $36
Fork-pickle/olive, short handle, 2 tines,
   5 7/8 in................................ $36
Fork-salad (place size), 4 3/4 in. handle,
   6 3/4 in................................ $54
Fork-salad, individual, 4 1/4 in. handle,
   6 1/2 in................................ $46
Knife-carving, small, stainless blade, steak,
   10 1/2 in............................... $74
Knife-modern, hollow (place size), 4 1/4 in.
   handle, 9 1/8 in......................... $40
Knife-modern, hollow handle, 4 in. handle,
   9 in. $33
Knife-modern, hollow handle, 9 5/8 in........ $50
Ladle-cream, solid, 5 3/8 in................. $60
Ladle-gravy, solid, 6 3/8 in.................. $90
Salad set, 2 pieces, plastic bowl, 12 in. $100
Server-cheese, stainless blade, 6 3/4 in...... $55
Server-jelly, 6 1/4 in. $40
Server-pie and cake, stainless blade,
   10 5/8 in............................... $70
Server-pie, stainless blade, 10 1/8 in......... $80
Spoon-baby, straight handle, 4 1/2 in......... $50
Spoon-bon-bon, 4 7/8 in. $52
Spoon-demitasse, 4 1/4 in.................. $30
Spoon-dessert/oval soup, 2 1/2 in. bowl,
   7 in. $70
Spoon-iced tea, 7 1/2 in.................... $50
Spoon-infant feeding, 5 5/8 in. $50
Spoon-oval soup (place size), 2 1/4 in. bowl,
   6 7/8 in................................ $60
Spoon-soup, round bowl, cream, 6 1/2 in. $50
Spoon-sugar shell, 6 1/8 in. $30
Spoon-teaspoon, 5 7/8 in................... $22
Tablespoon, (serving spoon), 8 3/8 in. $95
Tablespoon, (serving spoon), pierced,
   8 3/8 in................................ $100

Rose Marie by Gorham, 1933

Butter spreader, flat handle, 5 3/4 in. $20

Rose Marie by Gorham, 1933

Butter-master, flat handle, 7 1/8 in...........$30
Fork, 7 1/4 in...............................$27
Fork, 7 7/8 in...............................$45
Fork-carving, small, stainless prongs, steak,
   8 3/4 in..................................$50
Fork-cocktail, 5 1/2 in......................$22
Fork-cold meat/serving, small, solid, gold
   wash, 7 7/8 in...........................$70
Fork-cold meat/serving, medium, solid,
   8 1/8 in.................................$70
Fork-ice cream, gold wash, 5 3/4 in. $34
Fork-lemon, 4 1/4 in.........................$26
Fork-salad serving, solid, gold wash, 9 in. $84
Fork-salad, individual, 6 5/8 in..............$30
Fork-salad, individual, gold wash,
   6 5/8 in.................................$30
Knife-new french, hollow handle, 9 5/8 in......$34
Knife-new french, hollow handle, 9 in.........$27
Ladle-cream, solid, 5 1/4 in..................$40
Ladle-gravy, solid, 6 1/2 in. $70
Ladle-gravy, solid, gold wash, 6 1/2 in. $70
Napkin clip (made for teaspoons)............$20
Server-cheese, stainless blade, 6 1/2 in.......$40
Server-jelly, 6 1/4 in. $24
Server-jelly, gold wash, 6 1/4 in..............$24
Spoon-bon-bon, 4 3/4 in. $27
Spoon-bon-bon, gold wash, 4 3/4 in..........$27
Spoon-demitasse, 4 1/4 in. $17
Spoon-demitasse, gold wash, 4 1/4 in. $17
Spoon-dessert/oval soup, 6 7/8 in............$48
Spoon-fruit, 6 in. $30
Spoon-fruit, gold wash, 6 in. $30
Spoon-iced tea, 7 1/2 in. $30
Spoon-preserve, 7 7/8 in.....................$40
Spoon-soup, round bowl, bouillon,
   5 1/2 in.................................$30
Spoon-soup, round bowl, cream, 6 1/4 in......$36
Spoon-sugar shell, 6 1/8 in..................$26
Spoon-sugar, 6 in...........................$26
Spoon-sugar, gold wash, 6 in.................$26
Spoon-teaspoon, (five o'clock), 5 5/8 in. $13
Spoon-teaspoon, 6 in........................$14
Tablespoon, (serving spoon), 8 1/2 in.........$60
Tongs-sugar, 4 3/4 in........................$50

Rose Tiara by Gorham, 1963

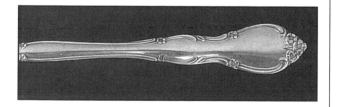

Butter spreader, hollow handle, modern,
   stainless paddle, 6 1/2 in.................$27
Butter-master, hollow handle, 7 in. $38
Fork, 7 1/2 in. $46
Fork-cold meat/serving, medium, solid,
   8 3/4 in..................................$90
Fork-pickle/olive, short handle, 5 7/8 in.......$34
Fork-salad, individual, 6 7/8 in. $45
Knife-modern, hollow handle, 9 in. $36
Ladle-gravy, solid, 6 3/4 in..................$90
Napkin clip (made for teaspoons) $30
Spoon-bon-bon, 5 in.........................$40
Spoon-dessert/oval soup, 6 1/2 in. $50
Spoon-iced tea, 7 5/8 in.....................$40
Spoon-infant feeding, 5 1/2 in...............$40
Spoon-sugar shell, 6 1/4 in. $40
Spoon-teaspoon, 6 in........................$20
Tablespoon, (serving spoon), 8 1/2 in. $90

Royal Oak by Gorham, 1904

Fish-fork/salad, solid, individual, small,
   5 3/4 in................................$100
Fork, 7 1/4 in. $60
Fork-cocktail, 5 5/8 in.......................$50
Spoon-dessert/oval soup, 7 1/4 in. $80
Spoon-soup, round bowl, gumbo, 6 3/4 in.....$80
Spoon-teaspoon, 5 7/8 in....................$40

Sea Rose by Gorham, 1958

Butter spreader, hollow handle, modern,
   stainless paddle, 6 1/2 in.................$24
Butter-master, hollow handle, no notch,
   7 in. $37
Fork, 7 1/2 in. $47
Fork-cocktail, 5 3/4 in.......................$34
Fork-cold meat/serving, medium, solid,
   8 5/8 in................................$100
Fork-lemon, 4 7/8 in.........................$38

Fork-pickle/olive, short handle, 5 7/8 in. $30
Fork-salad, individual, 6 3/4 in. $60
Knife-fruit, stainless blade, individual, 7 in. $35
Knife-modern, hollow handle, 9 1/4 in. $30
Ladle-cream, solid, 5 1/4 in. $50
Ladle-gravy, solid, 6 7/8 in. $90
Napkin clip (made for teaspoons) $22
Spoon-bon-bon, 4 3/4 in. $50
Spoon-demitasse, 4 3/8 in. $26
Spoon-dessert/oval soup, 7 in. $60
Spoon-sugar, 6 1/4 in. $27
Spoon-teaspoon, 6 in. $18

Secret Garden by Gorham, 1959

Butter spreader, hollow handle, modern,
   stainless, 6 1/2 in. $30
Butter-master, hollow handle, 7 in. $40
Fork, 7 1/2 in. $55
Fork-cocktail, 5 3/4 in. $35
Fork-salad, individual, 6 3/4 in. $50
Knife-modern, hollow handle, 9 1/4 in. $40
Spoon-dessert/oval soup, 6 7/8 in. $56
Spoon-sugar shell, 6 1/8 in. $40
Spoon-teaspoon, 6 in. $24
Tablespoon, (serving spoon), 8 1/2 in. $100
Tablespoon, (serving spoon), pierced,
   8 1/2 in. $110

Shamrock V by Gorham, 1931

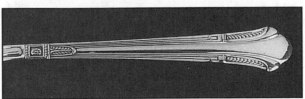

Butter spreader, hollow handle, modern, stainless
   paddle, 6 1/4 in. $25
Butter spreader, flat handle, 5 1/2 in. $22
Butter-master, flat handle, 7 in. $40
Fork, 7 1/8 in. $40
Fork, 7 7/8 in. $60
Fork-cocktail, 5 1/2 in. $22
Fork-lemon, 5 in. $32
Fork-salad, individual, 6 1/2 in. $44
Fork-salad, individual, gold wash,
   6 1/2 in. $44

Knife-new french, hollow handle,
   9 3/4 in. $50
Spoon-demitasse, 4 3/8 in. $20
Spoon-iced tea, 7 5/8 in. $40
Spoon-soup, round bowl, bouillon,
   5 1/2 in. $34
Spoon-soup, round bowl, cream, 6 1/4 in. $45
Spoon-sugar, 6 in. $35
Spoon-teaspoon, (five o'clock), 5 1/2 in. $20
Spoon-teaspoon, 6 in. $23
Tablespoon, (serving spoon), 8 5/8 in. $76

Sovereign-Old by Gorham, 1941

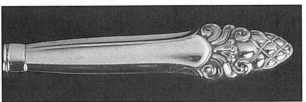

Butter spreader, flat handle, 5 5/8 in. $16
Butter spreader, hollow handle, modern, solid,
   6 in. $34
Butter-master, hollow handle, 6 3/4 in. $50
Fork, 7 3/8 in. $23
Fork-cocktail, 5 5/8 in. $32
Fork-salad, individual, 6 1/2 in. $45
Knife-new french, hollow handle, 9 3/4 in. $50
Ladle-gravy, solid, 6 3/4 in. $95
Spoon-casserole, smooth, solid, egg bowl,
   8 3/4 in. $90
Spoon-iced tea, 7 5/8 in. $54
Spoon-soup, round bowl, cream,
   6 3/8 in. $36
Spoon-sugar, 6 1/8 in. $40
Spoon-teaspoon, 6 in. $20
Tablespoon, (serving spoon), 8 1/2 in. $100

Spotswood by Gorham, 1912

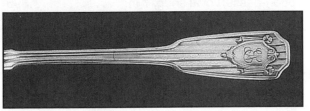

Butter spreader, flat handle, 5 3/4 in. $30
Spoon-soup, round bowl, bouillon,
   5 1/4 in. $50
Spoon-soup, round bowl, gumbo, 6 3/4 in. $65
Spoon-sugar, 5 7/8 in. $48
Spoon-teaspoon, (five o'clock), 5 1/2 in. $20
Spoon-teaspoon, 5 7/8 in. $26

Gorham

The following pieces have monograms:
Fork, 7 1/2 in. $60
Fork, 7 in. $40
Fork-cocktail, 5 1/2 in. $24
Fork-ice cream, 5 3/8 in. $45
Fork-pastry, 6 in. $42
Fork-salad, individual, 6 1/4 in. $50
Knife-fruit, silver plate blade, individual,
   6 7/8 in. $30
Knife-old french, hollow handle, 8 1/2 in. $50
Knife-old french, hollow handle, 9 3/4 in. $60
Ladle-gravy, solid, 7 1/8 in. $80
Server-pie, silver plate blade, 10 1/8 in. $60
Spoon-demitasse, 4 1/4 in. $20
Spoon-dessert/oval soup, 7 in. $50
Spoon-fruit, 5 3/4 in. $33
Spoon-soup, round bowl, bouillon,
   5 1/4 in. $38
Spoon-soup, round bowl, gumbo,
   6 3/4 in. $50
Spoon-teaspoon, 5 7/8 in. $20
Tablespoon, (serving spoon), 8 3/8 in. $70

St. Cloud by Gorham, 1885

Fork, 6 3/4 in. . . . .$80 ·
Fork, 7 5/8 in. $120
Spoon-demitasse, 4 3/8 in. $40
✓ Spoon-teaspoon, (five o'clock), 5 1/2 in. $40
Spoon-teaspoon, 6 in. $50

The following pieces have monograms:
Fork, 6 3/4 in. $70
Spoon-dessert/oval soup, 7 in. $90
Spoon-teaspoon, (five o'clock), 5 1/2 in. $36
Tablespoon, (serving spoon), 8 5/8 in. $120

St. Dunstan-chased by Gorham, 1917

Fork, 8 in. $65
Spoon-fruit, 5 3/4 in. $40

The following pieces have monograms:
Fork, 7 3/8 in. $38
Fork, 8 in. $50
Fork-cocktail, 5 3/4 in. $25
Fork-pastry, 6 3/8 in. $45
Knife-new french, hollow handle, 9 5/8 in. $40
Knife-old french, hollow handle, 9 in. $32
Spoon-fruit, 5 3/4 in. $30

Stardust by Gorham, 1957

Butter spreader, hollow handle, modern,
   stainless paddle, 6 1/2 in. $12
Butter-master, hollow handle, 7 in. $17
Fork, 7 1/2 in. $23
Fork-cocktail, 5 7/8 in. $27
Fork-cold meat/serving, medium, solid,
   8 1/2 in. $65
Fork-ice cream, 5 1/2 in. $36
Fork-ice cream, 5 5/8 in. $38
Fork-lemon, 4 7/8 in. $22
Fork-pickle/olive, short handle, 5 3/4 in. $20
Fork-salad server, plastic prongs,
   12 1/4 in. $40
Fork-salad, individual, 7 in. $27
Knife-bar, hollow handle, 8 1/2 in. $40
Knife-carving, small, stainless blade, steak,
   11 in. $64
Knife-cheese, stainless blade, 7 1/2 in. $40
Knife-modern, hollow handle, 9 in. $24
Ladle-cream, solid, 5 1/8 in. $38
Ladle-gravy, solid, 6 3/4 in. $60
Server-jelly, 6 3/8 in. $30
Server-pastry, stainless bowl, 10 1/2 in. $56
Server-pie and cake, stainless blade,
   11 1/8 in. $55
Spoon-baby, straight handle, 4 1/2 in. $40
Spoon-bon-bon, 4 3/4 in. $30
Spoon-demitasse, 4 3/8 in. $18
Spoon-dessert/oval soup, 7 1/8 in. $40
Spoon-iced tea, 7 1/2 in. $34
Spoon-infant feeding, 5 5/8 in. $40
Spoon-sugar, 6 1/8 in. $17
Spoon-teaspoon, 6 in. $15

Tablespoon, (serving spoon), 8 1/2 in.........$60
Tablespoon, (serving spoon), pierced,
    8 1/2 in.................................$70

Strasbourg by Gorham, 1897

Gorham's Strasbourg was first introduced in 1897. Pieces marked with "Gorham sterling" were produced after 1950. Pieces made prior to approximately 1950 will have the "lion/anchor/G" back stamp.

Butter spreader, flat handle, 6 in. $40
Butter-master, flat handle, 6 7/8 in...........$42
Carving set, 2 pieces, small, stainless blade,
    steak..................................$130
Fork, 7 5/8 in..............................$50
Fork, 7 in..................................$35
Fork-carving, small, stainless prongs, steak,
    9 in....................................$64
Fork-chipped beef, medium, 7 in...........$100
Fork-cocktail, 2 of 3 tines beveled,
    5 5/8 in................................$32
Fork-cocktail, 5 1/2 in.....................$32
Fork-cold meat/serving, medium, solid,
    8 1/2 in................................$100
Fork-salad, individual, 1 of 4 tines beveled,
    6 3/8 in................................$48
Knife-blunt, hollow handle, 8 1/2 in. $40
Knife-blunt, hollow handle, 9 3/4 in. $60
Knife-carving, small, stainless blade, steak,
    11 1/2 in. $64
Knife-modern, hollow handle, 9 in...........$40
Knife-new french, hollow handle, 8 1/2 in......$40
Knife-new french, hollow handle, 8 7/8 in......$40
Knife-new french, hollow handle, 9 5/8 in......$50
Knife-old french, hollow handle, 8 3/4 in......$40
Knife-old french, hollow handle, 9 5/8 in......$52
Knife-youth, 7 5/8 in.......................$45
Ladle-cream, solid, 5 1/4 in.................$50
Ladle-gravy, solid, 6 3/4 in. $110
Ladle-soup, solid, 12 in. $500
Napkin clip (made for teaspoons)...........$35
Pick-butter, two flared tines, 5 7/8 in.........$60
Salad set, 2 pieces, plastic bowl............$80
Server-pastry, stainless bowl, 10 1/8 in. $45
Server-pie, silver plate blade, 10 in..........$70
Spoon-bon-bon, 4 3/8 in. $44

Spoon-casserole, shell, solid, 8 3/4 in....... $160
Spoon-casserole, shell, solid, gold wash,
    8 3/4 in............................... $160
Spoon-casserole, smooth, solid, gold wash,
    8 1/2 in............................... $160
Spoon-demitasse, 4 in. $35
Spoon-dessert/oval soup, 7 1/8 in. $60
Spoon-fruit, 5 5/8 in. $48
Spoon-iced tea, 7 5/8 in.................... $45
Spoon-salad serving, plastic bowl, 12 in...... $40
Spoon-soup, round bowl, bouillon, 5 in. $40
Spoon-soup, round bowl, cream, 6 1/4 in. $50
Spoon-soup, round bowl, gumbo,
    6 7/8 in. $60
Spoon-sugar shell, 6 in. $40
Spoon-teaspoon, 5 7/8 in.................... $24
Tablespoon, (serving spoon), 8 1/2 in. $80
Tongs-sugar, small, 4 in.................... $60

FACE

Large Gorham punch ladle (two views). A long (15 3/8 in.) heavy ladle, decorated with grape clusters, leaves, and devil face at top of handle. Fine condition, with only light scratches on bottom of bowl. $750

Theme by Gorham, 1954

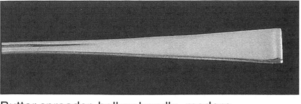

Butter spreader, hollow handle, modern,
  stainless paddle, 6 1/2 in. $20
Butter-master, hollow handle, 7 in. $25
Carving set, 2 pieces, small, stainless blade,
  steak $120
Fork, 7 5/8 in. $46
Fork-carving, large, stainless prongs, roast,
  9 1/2 in. $64
Fork-cocktail, 5 7/8 in. $32
Fork-cold meat/serving, medium, solid,
  2 tines, 8 1/2 in. $60
Fork-lemon, 4 in. $24
Fork-pickle/olive, short handle, 5 7/8 in. $24
Fork-salad serving, solid, 3 tines, 9 1/4 in. . . .$100
Fork-salad, individual, 7 in. $40
Knife-carving, small, stainless blade, steak,
  10 5/8 in. $60
Knife-modern, hollow handle, 9 1/4 in. $35
Ladle-gravy, solid, 6 7/8 in. $70
Napkin clip (made for teaspoons) $24
Server-jelly, 6 1/4 in. $35
Server-pie, stainless blade, 10 in. $70
Server-tomato, solid, 6 7/8 in. $100
Spoon-bon-bon, pierced, 4 1/8 in. $26
Spoon-bon-bon, solid, 4 1/8 in. $26
Spoon-dessert/oval soup, 7 in. $40
Spoon-sugar, 6 1/8 in. $24
Spoon-teaspoon, 6 in. $20
Tablespoon, (serving spoon), 8 1/2 in. $70
Tablespoon, (serving spoon), pierced,
  8 1/2 in. $90

Threaded Antique by Gorham, 1855

Butter spreader, hollow handle, modern,
  stainless, 6 1/8 in. $30
Butter spreader, flat handle, 6 in. $30
Fork, 6 3/4 in. $55
Fork, 7 1/2 in. $70

Fork-cocktail, 5 3/4 in. $32
Fork-salad, individual, 6 3/8 in. $60
Knife-new french, hollow handle,
  8 3/4 in. $50
Knife-new french, hollow handle,
  9 1/2 in. $70
Server-cheese, stainless blade, 6 1/2 in. $48
Spoon-demitasse, 4 3/8 in. $24
Spoon-dessert/oval soup, 6 7/8 in. $60
Spoon-soup, round bowl, cream, 6 1/4 in. $50
Spoon-teaspoon, 5 7/8 in. $30

Trilogy by Gorham, 1969

Butter spreader, hollow handle, modern,
  stainless paddle, 6 7/8 in. $30
Butter-master, hollow handle, 7 1/4 in. $40
Fork, 7 1/2 in. $45
Knife-modern, hollow handle, 8 7/8 in. $38
Spoon-sugar, 6 in. $35

Tuileries by Gorham, 1906

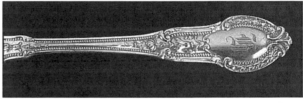

Fork, 7 1/8 in. $50
Fork, 7 3/4 in. $70
Fork-ice cream, 5 1/4 in. $70
Fork-salad, individual, 6 in. $55
Knife-blunt, hollow handle, 8 3/8 in. $50
Knife-new french, hollow handle,
  8 5/8 in. $50
Knife-new french, hollow handle, 9 5/8 in. $55
Knife-old french, hollow handle, 8 1/2 in. $50
Spoon-fruit, 5 3/4 in. $44
Spoon-soup, round bowl, bouillon,
  4 3/4 in. $44
Spoon-teaspoon, (five o'clock), 5 1/2 in. $25
Spoon-teaspoon, 5 3/4 in. $30
Spoon-teaspoon, 5 7/8 in. $30
Tablespoon, (serving spoon), 8 3/8 in. $70
Tablespoon, (serving spoon), pierced,
  8 3/8 in. $90

Set

Versailles by Gorham, 1888

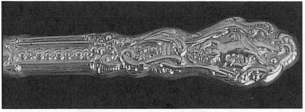

Butter spreader, flat handle, 5 7/8 in. $60
Carving set, 3 pieces, large, stainless blade,
   roast $530
Fish-fork/salad, solid, individual, large,
   2 of 4 beveled tines, 6 5/8 in. $100
Fish-fork/salad, solid, individual, small,
   1 beveled tine, pierced, 6 in. $80
Fork, 6 3/4 in. $55
Fork, 7 3/4 in. $110
Fork-cocktail, 5 7/8 in. $60
Fork-fruit, solid, individual, 6 in. $100
Fork-pastry, pierced, 6 in. $100
Fork-pickle/olive, long handle, 8 1/8 in. $180
Fork-salad, individual, 2 of 4 beveled tines,
   6 3/8 in. $100
Fork-vegetable/serving, solid, 7 7/8 in. $400
Knife-blunt, hollow handle, 3 3/4 in. handle,
   9 1/2 in. $120
Knife-new french, hollow handle,
   9 3/4 in. $120
Knife-old french, hollow handle,
   9 3/4 in. $120
Ladle-soup, solid, gold wash,
   12 1/4 in. $1,200
Salad set-2 pieces, solid, gold wash,
   8 3/4 in. $600
Spoon-berry/casserole, solid, shell bowl,
   gold wash, 9 1/8 in. $400
Spoon-demitasse, 4 1/4 in. $45
Spoon-demitasse, gold wash,
   4 1/4 in. $45
Spoon-dessert/oval soup, 4 3/4 in. handle,
   7 1/8 in. $90
Spoon-five o'clock/youth, 5 1/8 in. $30
Spoon-fruit, 5 7/8 in. $80
Spoon-jelly, large, 7 3/8 in. $150
Spoon-soup, round bowl, bouillon,
   5 in. $65
Spoon-soup, round bowl, gumbo,
   6 7/8 in. $120
Spoon-sugar shell, 6 1/8 in. $90
Spoon-sugar, gold wash, 6 1/4 in. $70
Spoon-teaspoon, 5 7/8 in. $38
Tablespoon, (serving spoon), 8 1/2 in. $90
Tongs-sugar, 5 1/8 in. $160

Gorham Versailles confection spoon. A rare piece with good detail and die-depth. Length, 5 1/8 in.; three letter conjoined script monogram. $195

Six Gorham Victorian-era demitasse spoons. Strong examples of 1880s Gorham design. Good condition, 4 1/4 in., no monogram. $75/ set

Violet by Gorham, 1890

Virginiana by Gorham, 1904/1905

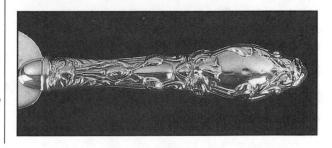

Virginiana by Gorham, 1904/1905

Butter spreader, flat handle, 5 7/8 in.........$50
Fork, 7 1/4 in...............................$46
Fork, 7 3/4 in...............................$90
Fork-cocktail, 5 1/2 in......................$44
Fork-salad, individual, 5 7/8 in.............$120
Fork-salad, individual, gold wash,
   5 7/8 in...............................$120
Knife-blunt, hollow handle, 8 1/2 in..........$60
Knife-blunt, hollow handle, 9 5/8 in..........$80
Knife-new french, hollow handle, 9 1/2 in......$80
Knife-orange, silver plate blade, 6 7/8 in......$60
Knife-orange, silver plate blade, 7 3/8 in......$60
Ladle-sugar, pierced, serving, 6 1/4 in. $200
Spoon-demitasse, 4 1/8 in. $35
Spoon-demitasse, gold wash, 4 1/8 in. $35
Spoon-dessert/oval soup, 7 1/4 in...........$80
Spoon-soup, round bowl, bouillon, 5 in........$50
Spoon-soup, round bowl, gumbo, 7 in. $80
Spoon-teaspoon, (five o'clock), 5 3/8 in. $32
Spoon-teaspoon, 5 7/8 in. $40
Tablespoon, (serving spoon), 8 1/2 in........$120

White Paisley by Gorham, 1966

Butter-master, hollow handle, 7 1/4 in.........$40
Fork, 7 1/2 in..............................$44
Fork-carving, large, stainless prongs, roast,
   10 1/4 in. $80
Fork-salad, individual, 6 3/4 in. $50
Knife-carving, large, stainless blade, roast,
   12 5/8 in. $80
Knife-modern, hollow handle, 9 in.............$36
Ladle-punch, stainless bowl, 14 3/4 in. $120
Server-pasta, stainless bowl, 11 3/4 in........$70
Spoon-dessert/oval soup, 6 7/8 in............$60
Spoon-iced tea, 7 3/4 in. $60
Spoon-sugar, 6 in...........................$35
Spoon-teaspoon, 6 in.......................$20

Willow by Gorham, 1954

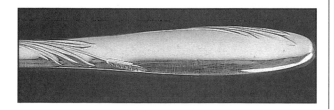

Butter spreader, hollow handle, modern, stainless,
   6 1/2 in...................................$12
Butter-master, hollow handle, 7 in. $27
Carving set, 2 pieces, small, stainless blade,
   steak $100
Fork, 7 1/2 in. $34
Fork-cocktail, 5 3/4 in. $18
Fork-cold meat/serving, medium, solid,
   8 1/2 in..................................$70
Fork-ice cream, 5 5/8 in.....................$34
Fork-lemon, 4 in............................$20
Fork-pickle/olive, short handle, 5 3/4 in.......$20
Fork-salad, individual, 7 in...................$30
Knife-cheese, stainless blade, 7 1/4 in. $36
Knife-modern, hollow handle, 9 1/4 in.........$27
Ladle-cream, solid, 5 1/4 in..................$40
Ladle-gravy, solid, 6 5/8 in...................$60
Server-cheese, stainless blade, 7 in. $40
Server-jelly, 6 1/4 in. $25
Server-pie and cake, stainless blade,
   10 1/2 in.................................$55
Spoon-bon-bon, pierced, 4 1/8 in............$27
Spoon-bon-bon, solid, 4 1/8 in. $27
Spoon-demitasse, 4 3/8 in...................$20
Spoon-dessert/oval soup, 7 1/8 in. $36
Spoon-iced tea, 7 1/2 in.....................$34
Spoon-sugar, 6 1/4 in.......................$25
Spoon-teaspoon, 6 in.......................$15
Tablespoon, (serving spoon), 8 5/8 in. $65
Tongs-sugar, 5 in...........................$50

Wreath by Gorham, 1911

Fork, 7 1/4 in. $50
Fork, 7 3/4 in. $60
Fork-salad, individual, 6 in...................$50
Fork-salad, individual, gold wash, 6 in........$50
Knife-new french, hollow handle,
   9 1/2 in..................................$50
Knife-old french, hollow handle,
   8 1/2 in..................................$40
Spoon-iced tea, 7 1/2 in.....................$40
Spoon-soup, round bowl, bouillon,
   5 3/8 in..................................$36
Spoon-teaspoon, (five o'clock), 5 3/8 in.......$18
Spoon-teaspoon, 5 5/8 in....................$25
Tablespoon, (serving spoon), 8 5/8 in. $80

The following pieces have monograms:

Butter spreader, flat handle, 5 3/4 in..........$19
Butter-master, flat handle, 8 1/4 in...........$33
Fork, 7 1/4 in.............................$38
Fork, 7 3/4 in.............................$45
Fork-cocktail, 5 3/8 in.....................$27
Fork-cold meat/serving, small, solid,
    7 1/2 in.................................$70
Fork-ice cream, 5 3/8 in....................$38
Fork-lemon, 5 7/8 in.......................$27
Knife-old french, hollow handle, 8 1/2 in.......$30
Knife-old french, hollow handle, 9 3/4 in.......$38

Spoon-dessert/oval soup, 7 1/4 in............$38
Spoon-fruit, 5 3/4 in.......................$30
Spoon-ice cream, 5 1/2 in..................$42

Spoon-soup, round bowl, bouillon,
    5 3/8 in. $30
Spoon-soup, round bowl, gumbo, 7 in........ $45
Spoon-sugar, 5 7/8 in. $36
Spoon-teaspoon, (five o'clock), 5 3/8 in....... $14
Spoon-teaspoon, 5 5/8 in.................... $20
Tablespoon, (serving spoon), 8 5/8 in. $60
Tablespoon, (serving spoon), 8 5/8 in. $60
Tongs-sugar, 4 1/8 in. $53

Gorham Zodiac child's cup. 2 3/4 in. high and 3 in. in diameter. The engraving: "Dorothy Whittemore Severn / Oct 2nd / 1908" is in script on the front panel. There are dents just above the base and also in the handle; die-rolled Zodiac sign border is in excellent condition. $195

Hallmark

HALLMARK

Hallmark Silversmiths Inc. of New York was active beginning in the first quarter of the 20th century. The firm became Hunt-Hallmark Co. in 1954.

Ballad by Hallmark, 1942

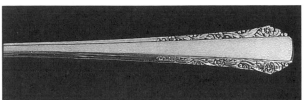

Butter spreader, flat handle, 5 3/4 in.. . . . . $20
Butter-master, flat handle, 6 7/8 in. $27
Fork, 7 1/8 in.. . . . . $30
Fork, 7 3/4 in.. . . . . $45
Fork-salad, individual, 6 1/4 in. $34
Knife-modern, hollow handle, 9 1/8 in. $30
Knife-modern, hollow handle, 9 3/8 in. $30
Knife-modern, hollow handle, 9 5/8 in. $40
Spoon-casserole, smooth bowl, solid,
    8 1/2 in. $80

Spoon-iced tea, 7 1/2 in. $33
Spoon-soup, round bowl, cream, 6 1/8 in. $30
Spoon-soup, round bowl, gumbo, 7 in.. . . . . . . $40
Spoon-sugar, 6 in. $27
Spoon-teaspoon, 6 in. $20

Ribbon Rose by Hallmark, 1942

Butter spreader, flat handle, 5 3/4 in.. . . . . $30
Fork, 7 1/8 in.. . . . . $48
Knife-modern, hollow handle, 9 1/8 in.. . . . . . . $36
Ladle-gravy, solid, 6 3/8 in.. . . . . $100
Spoon-soup, round bowl, cream, 6 in.. . . . . . . $48
Spoon-teaspoon, 6 in. $25

The following pieces have monograms:
Fork, 7 1/8 in.. . . . . $38
Spoon-casserole, smooth, solid, 8 1/2 in. $75
Spoon-soup, round bowl, gumbo,
    6 7/8 in. $38

INTERNATIONAL SILVER CO.

International Silver Co. was formed in Meriden, Connecticut, in 1898 by a group of independent silversmiths. This association came to include Rogers Bros. (and their famous 1847 trademark), Derby Silver, Meriden Britannia, Webster and Wilcox, among many others.

1810 by International, 1930

Butter spreader, hollow handle, paddle stainless, 6 in. $40
Butter spreader, flat handle, 6 in. $32
Butter-master, flat handle, 7 in. $38
Butter-master, hollow handle, 6 7/8 in. $40
Carving set, 2 pieces, small, stainless blade, steak $80
Fork, 7 1/4 in. $34
Fork, 7 7/8 in. $60
Fork-baby, 4 1/8 in. $30
Fork-cake, individual, 6 3/8 in. $40
Fork-carving small, stainless prongs, steak, 8 7/8 in. $40
Fork-cocktail, 5 5/8 in. $30
Fork-cold meat/serving, large, 5 stainless tines, 10 1/2 in. $40
Fork-cold meat/serving, medium, solid, 4 tines, 8 1/8 in. $90
Fork-cold meat/serving, medium, solid, 8 1/8 in. $90
Fork-fish, stainless tines, hollow handle, individual, 7 1/2 in. $45
Fork-pickle/olive, short handle, 5 3/4 in. $40
Fork-salad server, plastic prongs, 11 3/8 in. $45
Fork-salad serving, solid, 3 tines, 8 1/4 in. $160
Fork-salad serving, stainless prongs, not beveled, 10 7/8 in. $40
Fork-salad, individual, 6 3/8 in. $38
Knife-carving, small, stainless blade, steak, 10 in. $40
Knife-fish, stainless blade, individual, 7 7/8 in. $45
Knife-modern, hollow handle, 8 7/8 in. $45

Knife-new french, hollow handle, 9 1/8 in. $45
Knife-steak, individual, beveled blade, 8 1/8 in. $45
Knife-steak, individual, not beveled, 8 1/8 in. $45
Ladle-cream, solid, 5 1/2 in. $50
Ladle-gravy, hollow handle, stainless bowl, 7 5/8 in. $45
Ladle-gravy, solid, 6 3/8 in. $80
Ladle-punch, stainless bowl, 12 1/2 in. $60
Ladle-soup, stainless bowl, 10 3/4 in. $60
Napkin clip, (made for five o'clock) $24
Opener-bottle, stainless bowl, 5 3/4 in. $45
Scoop-ice cream, stainless bowl, 8 1/8 in. $45
Scoop-ice, silver plate bowl, 8 1/2 in. $50
Server-asparagus, solid, 9 3/8 in. $250
Server-cranberry, stainless bowl, 8 1/4 in. $45
Server-jelly, 6 1/2 in. $40
Server-lasagna, stainless blade, 9 3/8 in. $40
Server-pasta, stainless bowl, 10 in. $40
Server-pie, stainless blade, 10 1/8 in. $45
Spoon-bon-bon, 4 5/8 in. $48
Spoon-casserole, pierced, stainless bowl, 7 scallops, 9 in. $40
Spoon-casserole, shell, stainless bowl, 17 scallops, 9 3/4 in. $45
Spoon-casserole, smooth, solid, 8 1/4 in. $120
Spoon-demitasse, 4 1/4 in. $23
Spoon-dessert/oval soup, 6 7/8 in. $56
Spoon-dressing, stainless bowl, tear bowl, 10 5/8 in. $40
Spoon-fruit, 5 5/8 in. $45
Spoon-iced tea, 7 1/4 in. $40
Spoon-salad serving, stainless bowl, egg bowl, 10 7/8 in. $40
Spoon-soup, round bowl, bouillon, 5 1/2 in. $42
Spoon-sugar, 5 3/4 in. $38
Spoon-teaspoon, (five o'clock), 5 5/8 in. $20
Spoon-teaspoon, 6 1/8 in. $34
Spoon-utility/serving, stainless bowl, 7 scallops, 9 in. $45
Tablespoon (serving spoon), pierced, 7 3/4 in. $80
Tablespoon (serving spoon), 8 in. $70
Tongs-sugar, 4 1/8 in. $40

International Silver

Abbottsford by International, 1907

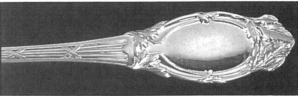

Butter spreader, flat handle, 5 7/8 in. $30
Fork, 6 7/8 in. $58
Fork, 7 1/4 in. $58
Fork-cold meat/serving, medium, solid,
   8 3/8 in. $100
Knife-old french, hollow handle,
   9 3/4 in. $70
Ladle-cream, solid, 5 1/2 in. $56
Ladle-gravy, solid, 7 in. $110
Spoon-demitasse, 4 1/2 in. $30
Spoon-dessert/oval soup, 6 7/8 in. $60
Spoon-soup, round bowl, bouillon, 5 in. $56
Spoon-soup, round bowl, gumbo,
   6 3/4 in. $70
Spoon-teaspoon, (five o'clock), 5 3/8 in. $27
Spoon-teaspoon, 5 7/8 in. $34
Tablespoon, (serving spoon), 7 7/8 in. $85
Tablespoon, (serving spoon), pierced,
   7 7/8 in. $110
Tongs-sugar, 4 3/4 in. $80

The following pieces have monograms:
Fork, 6 7/8 in. $46
Fork, 7 1/4 in. $46
Knife-old french, hollow handle, 9 in. $38
Ladle-gravy, solid, 7 in. $88
Spoon-demitasse, 3 7/8 in. $23
Spoon-dessert/oval soup, 6 7/8 in. $50
Spoon-teaspoon, 5 7/8 in. $26

Angelique by International, 1959

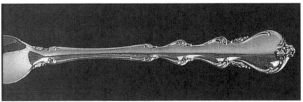

Butter spreader, hollow handle, stainless
   paddle, 6 3/8 in. $32
Butter-master, hollow handle, 7 in. $30
Carving set, 2 pieces, small, stainless blade,
   steak $80
Cleaver-cheese, stainless blade, 7 in. $40
Fork-baby, 4 1/8 in. $30

Fork-carving, small, stainless prongs, steak,
   9 5/8 in. $40
Fork-cocktail, 5 5/8 in. $32
Fork-cold meat/serving, large, 5 stainless tines,
   11 1/4 in. $40
Fork-cold meat/serving, large, solid, 9 in. $90
Fork-fish, stainless tines, hollow handle,
   individual, 8 3/8 in. $44
Fork-ice cream, 5 3/4 in. $45
Fork-lemon, 5 3/8 in. $23
Fork-salad serving, stainless prongs,
   4 tines, not beveled, 11 5/8 in. $45
Fork-salad, individual, 6 5/8 in. $42
Fork-youth, 6 in. $32
Knife-bar, hollow handle, 9 1/4 in. $45
Knife-carving, small, stainless blade, steak,
   10 3/4 in. $40
Knife-cheese, stainless blade, 7 1/4 in. $40
Knife-fish, stainless blade, individual,
   8 5/8 in. $45
Knife-fruit, stainless blade, individual,
   7 1/8 in. $40
Knife-modern, hollow handle, 9 1/4 in. $30
Knife-steak, individual, beveled blade,
   9 in. $45
Knife-steak, individual, not beveled,
   9 3/8 in. $45
Ladle-cream, solid, 5 3/8 in. $38
Ladle-gravy, hollow handle, stainless bowl,
   8 3/8 in. $40
Ladle-gravy, solid, 6 1/4 in. $90
Ladle-punch, stainless bowl, 13 1/4 in. $60
Ladle-soup, stainless bowl, 11 1/2 in. $60
Scoop-ice cream, stainless bowl,
   8 3/4 in. $45
Scoop-ice, silver plate bowl, 9 in. $50
Server/knife-fish, stainless blade, design in
   bowl, 11 3/4 in. $40
Server-cheese, stainless blade, 7 in. $45
Server-cranberry, stainless bowl,
   8 7/8 in. $40
Server-jelly, 6 3/8 in. $40
Server-lasagna, stainless blade,
   10 1/8 in. $40
Server-pasta, stainless bowl, 10 7/8 in. $40
Server-pie and cake, stainless blade,
   11 in. $45
Server-pie, stainless blade, 10 5/8 in. $44
Server-tomato, solid, 7 7/8 in. $100
Slicer-cake, stainless blade, wedding,
   13 in. $45
Spoon-baby, straight handle, 4 1/4 in. $30
Spoon-casserole, pierced, stainless bowl,
   7 scallops, 9 7/8 in. $40

Spoon-casserole, shell bowl, solid,
9 1/4 in.................................$140
Spoon-casserole, shell bowl, stainless bowl,
17 scallops, 10 1/2 in. $40
Spoon-demitasse, 4 in.....................$20
Spoon-dressing, stainless bowl, tear bowl,
11 1/2 in. $45
Spoon-iced tea, 7 3/8 in. $42
Spoon-salad serving, stainless bowl, egg
bowl, 12 in.............................$40
Spoon-sugar shell, 6 in. $30
Spoon-teaspoon, 6 in......................$18
Spoon-utility/serving, stainless bowl, 7
scallops, 9 7/8 in. $40
Tablespoon, (serving spoon), 8 3/8 in........$85
Tablespoon, (serving spoon), pierced,
8 3/8 in................................$90
Tongs-sugar, 5 in. $45

Avalon by International, 1900

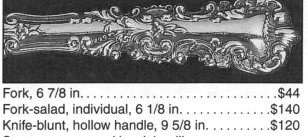

Fork, 6 7/8 in.............................$44
Fork-salad, individual, 6 1/8 in. $140
Knife-blunt, hollow handle, 9 5/8 in. $120
Spoon-soup, round bowl, bouillon,
4 3/4 in................................$38
Spoon-teaspoon, (five o'clock),
5 1/2 in................................$25
Spoon-teaspoon, 5 3/4 in. $36
Spoon-youth, 4 3/4 in......................$48
Tablespoon, (serving spoon), 8 1/4 in.........$85

Berkeley by International, 1915

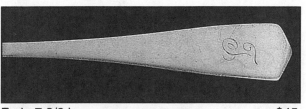

Fork, 7 3/8 in.............................$45
Fork-salad, individual, 4 tines, bar,
6 1/4 in................................$36
Server-pie, silver plate blade, 9 1/2 in........$60
Spoon-baby, straight handle, 4 1/8 in. $35
Spoon-dessert/oval soup, 7 1/8 in...........$40
Spoon-iced tea, 7 1/2 in. $35

Spoon-soup, round bowl, bouillon,
5 1/4 in................................$30
Tablespoon, (serving spoon), 8 1/4 in. $60

Blossom Time by International, 1950

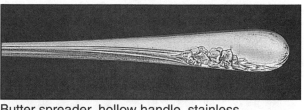

Butter spreader, hollow handle, stainless
paddle, 5 7/8 in.........................$13
Butter spreader, flat handle, 5 7/8 in. $13
Butter-master, flat handle, 7 1/4 in...........$27
Fork, 7 1/4 in............................$25
Fork, 7 3/4 in............................$60
Fork-baby, 4 1/8 in........................$36
Fork-cocktail, 5 5/8 in. $24
Fork-cold meat/serving, large, solid, 9 in. $90
Fork-pickle/olive, short handle, 5 7/8 in.......$40
Fork-salad, individual, 6 1/2 in. $32
Fork-youth, 6 3/8 in.......................$35
Knife-modern, hollow handle, 9 1/4 in........$30
Knife-modern, hollow handle, 9 5/8 in........$45
Ladle-gravy, solid, 6 1/2 in..................$70
Napkin clip, (made for teaspoons)...........$20
Salad set, 2 pieces, wooden bowl and
tines...................................$94
Server-cheese, stainless blade, 6 1/4 in......$44
Spoon-bon-bon, 5 in.......................$44
Spoon-dessert/oval soup, 6 7/8 in. $46
Spoon-iced tea, 7 3/8 in....................$50
Spoon-soup, round bowl, cream, 6 5/8 in.....$25
Spoon-sugar, 6 in. $20
Spoon-teaspoon, 6 in......................$15
Tablespoon, (serving spoon), 8 1/2 in. $80

Brandon by International, 1913

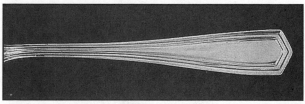

Butter spreader, flat handle, 5 1/4 in. $20
Butter spreader, flat handle, 5 5/8 in. $20
Butter-master, flat handle, 7 3/8 in...........$30
Fork, 7 1/4 in. $30
Fork, 7 3/4 in. $40
Fork-baby, 4 in...........................$36

Fork-cocktail, 5 1/2 in.......................$22
Fork-cold meat, serving, small, solid,
   7 3/8 in................................$80
Fork-pickle/olive, long handle, 7 in. $45
Fork-ramekin, large, 5 in....................$38
Fork-salad, individual, 4 tines, bar,
   6 1/8 in................................$36
Fork-youth, 6 in.............................$40
Knife-old french, hollow handle, 9 1/8 in......$30
Knife-old french, hollow handle, 9 7/8 in......$36
Knife-youth, 7 in............................$30
Ladle-cream, solid, 5 3/8 in..................$38
Ladle-gravy, solid, 6 3/8 in. $80
Spoon-baby, curved handle, 3 1/4 in..........$36
Spoon-baby, straight handle, 4 1/4 in. $36
Spoon-chocolate, short handle, 5 1/2 in......$26
Spoon-demitasse, 3 7/8 in. $20
Spoon-dessert/oval soup, 7 1/8 in............$40
Spoon-olive, long handle, 7 5/8 in. $130
Spoon-olive, short, pierced bowl, 6 1/4 in. $75
Spoon-soup, round bowl, bouillon,
   5 1/4 in................................$23
Spoon-soup, round bowl, gumbo, 7 in. $40
Spoon-sugar, 6 in...........................$38
Spoon-teaspoon, (five o'clock), 5 3/8 in. $14
Spoon-teaspoon, 5 3/4 in. $20
Tablespoon, (serving spoon), 8 3/8 in.........$50
Tablespoon, (serving spoon), pierced,
   8 1/8 in................................$80
Tongs-sugar, 3 3/4 in.......................$50
Tongs-sugar, 4 3/4 in.......................$50

Breton Rose by International, 1954

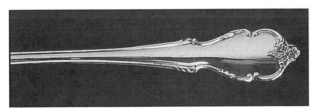

Butter spreader, hollow handle, stainless
   paddle, 6 1/4 in...........................$25
Butter-master, flat handle, 7 1/4 in............$33
Fork, 7 1/4 in................................$32
Fork-baby, 4 1/8 in. $36
Fork-salad, individual, 6 1/2 in...............$35
Fork-youth, 6 1/4 in. $44
Knife-modern, hollow handle, 9 1/4 in.........$33
Knife-youth, 7 1/4 in.........................$37
Napkin clip, (made for cream soup) $30
Spoon-baby, straight handle, 4 1/4 in. $35
Spoon-iced tea, 7 3/8 in. $40
Spoon-infant feeding, 5 5/8 in...............$27

Spoon-soup, round bowl, cream, 6 1/2 in. $27
Spoon-sugar, 5 7/8 in...................... $32
Spoon-teaspoon, 6 in....................... $16
Tablespoon, (serving spoon), 8 1/2 in........ $75

Bridal Veil by International, 1950

Butter spreader, hollow handle, stainless
   paddle, 5 7/8 in......................... $26
Butter spreader, flat handle, 5 3/4 in. $24
Butter-master, flat handle, 7 1/4 in........... $35
Carving set, 2 pieces, small, stainless blade,
   steak $120
Fork, 7 1/4 in. $23
Fork-baby, 4 1/8 in......................... $36
Fork-cocktail, 5 3/4 in...................... $22
Fork-cold meat/serving, large, solid,
   9 1/4 in................................. $90
Fork-salad, individual, 6 1/2 in. $27
Fork-youth, 6 3/8 in........................ $45
Knife-modern, hollow handle, 9 1/8 in........ $33
Knife-youth, 7 in............................ $37
Ladle-gravy, solid, 6 1/4 in.................. $80
Ladle-gravy, solid, 6 5/8 in.................. $80
Spoon-baby, straight handle, 4 1/4 in......... $36
Spoon-demitasse, 4 1/4 in................... $24
Spoon-iced tea, 7 1/2 in.................... $40
Spoon-infant feeding, 5 5/8 in............... $40
Spoon-soup, round bowl, cream, 6 1/2 in..... $24
Spoon-sugar, 6 in. $30
Spoon-teaspoon, 6 in....................... $16
Sugar sifter, 6 in. $34
Tablespoon, (serving spoon), 8 1/2 in........ $80

Brocade by International, 1950

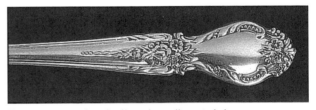

Butter spreader, hollow handle, stainless
   paddle, 5 7/8 in......................... $22
Butter spreader, flat handle, 5 3/4 in. $20
Butter-master, flat handle, 7 1/4 in........... $34
Fork, 7 3/4 in. $60

Fork, 7 3/8 in. $33
Fork-cocktail, 5 1/2 in. $24
Fork-lemon, 4 3/4 in. $30
Fork-lemon, 6 in. $30
Fork-salad, individual, 6 1/2 in. $44
Knife-modern, hollow handle, 9 1/4 in. $40
Knife-modern, hollow handle, 9 3/4 in. $50
Knife-steak, individual, not beveled,
   8 5/8 in. $56
Ladle-gravy, solid, 6 3/8 in. $80
Server-cheese, stainless blade, 6 3/8 in. $55
Server-jelly, 6 1/2 in. $40
Server-pasta, stainless bowl, 10 3/4 in. $60
Spoon-dessert/oval soup, 6 7/8 in. $46
Spoon-iced tea, 7 3/8 in. $40
Spoon-soup, round bowl, cream, 6 1/2 in. $34
Spoon-soup, round bowl, gumbo, 7 1/4 in. $55
Spoon-sugar shell, 6 in. $26
Spoon-teaspoon, 6 in. $20
Tablespoon, (serving spoon), 8 1/2 in. $76
Tablespoon, (serving spoon), pierced,
   8 1/2 in. $90

Cloeta by International, 1904

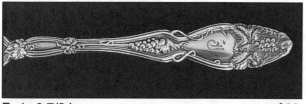

Fork, 6 7/8 in. $60
Spoon-demitasse, 4 1/2 in. $40
Spoon-dessert/oval soup, 7 in. $90

The following pieces have monograms:
Fork, 6 7/8 in. $54
Spoon-baby, curved handle, 3 1/2 in. $40
Spoon-teaspoon, 6 in. $36

Colonial Shell by International, 1941

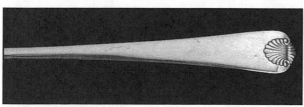

Butter spreader, hollow handle, solid paddle,
   6 in. $42
Butter spreader, flat handle, 5 3/4 in. $26
Fork, 7 3/8 in. $46
Fork-baby, 4 1/4 in. $33

Fork-cocktail, 5 5/8 in. $25
Fork-ice cream, 5 1/2 in. $50
Fork-pickle/olive, short handle, 5 7/8 in. $33
Fork-salad, individual, 6 1/2 in. $50
Knife-youth, 7 1/4 in. $34
Ladle-gravy, solid, 6 1/2 in. $100
Spoon-demitasse, 4 1/4 in. $24
Spoon-dessert/oval soup, 6 7/8 in. $70
Spoon-fruit, 6 in. $36
Spoon-iced tea, 7 1/2 in. $36
Spoon-soup, round bowl, cream, 6 1/2 in. $50
Spoon-soup, round bowl, gumbo, 7 1/4 in. $56
Spoon-sugar, 5 7/8 in. $40
Spoon-teaspoon, 6 1/8 in. $27
Tablespoon, (serving spoon), 8 3/4 in. $70
Tongs-sugar, 4 in. $58

Continental by International, 1934

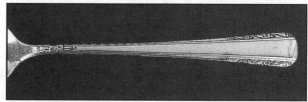

Butter spreader, hollow handle, paddle solid,
   6 in. $24
Butter spreader, flat handle, 5 3/4 in. $24
Fork, 7 1/4 in. $45
Fork-cocktail, 5 5/8 in. $36
Fork-salad, individual, 6 5/8 in. $55
Knife-new french, hollow handle, 8 3/4 in. $40
Knife-new french, hollow handle, 9 1/2 in. $60
Ladle-gravy, solid, 6 5/8 in. $100
Spoon-teaspoon, 6 in. $27
Tablespoon, (serving spoon), 8 3/8 in. $110

Courtship by International, 1936

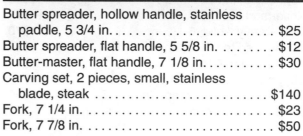

Butter spreader, hollow handle, stainless
   paddle, 5 3/4 in. $25
Butter spreader, flat handle, 5 5/8 in. $12
Butter-master, flat handle, 7 1/8 in. $30
Carving set, 2 pieces, small, stainless
   blade, steak $140
Fork, 7 1/4 in. $23
Fork, 7 7/8 in. $50

Fork-carving, small, stainless prongs, steak,
8 5/8 in................................$70
Fork-cocktail, 5 1/2 in.....................$23
Fork-cold meat, serving, small, solid,
7 3/4 in................................$90
Fork-grille (viand), 7 5/8 in. $40
Fork-ice cream, 3 3/4 in. handle, 5 1/2 in......$40
Fork-lemon, 4 5/8 in........................$32
Fork-pickle/olive, short handle, 5 7/8 in. $32
Fork-salad, individual, 6 3/8 in...............$25
Knife-new french, hollow handle,
9 1/2 in................................$40
Knife-new french, hollow handle, 9 1/8 in......$30
Ladle-gravy, solid, 6 1/8 in. $80
Napkin clip, (made for cream soup) $25
Server-cheese, stainless blade, 6 1/4 in.......$47
Server-jelly, 6 1/2 in.......................$30
Spoon-demitasse, 4 1/8 in. $22
Spoon-dessert/oval soup, 6 7/8 in............$46
Spoon-fruit, 5 3/4 in........................$40
Spoon-iced tea, 7 3/8 in. $24
Spoon-soup, round bowl, bouillon,
5 1/2 in................................$36
Spoon-soup, round bowl, cream, 6 3/8 in......$22
Spoon-soup, round bowl, gumbo, 7 1/8 in. $40
Spoon-sugar, 5 3/4 in.......................$24
Spoon-teaspoon, 6 in.......................$14
Tablespoon, (serving spoon), 8 1/2 in........$60

Dawn Rose by International, 1969

Butter spreader, hollow handle, modern,
stainless paddle, 6 3/4 in. $20
Butter-master, hollow handle, 7 1/4 in........$26
Fork, 7 3/8 in..............................$37
Fork-cold meat/serving, large, solid,
8 7/8 in................................$90
Fork-lemon, 5 1/2 in........................$26
Fork-salad, individual, 6 7/8 in...............$30
Knife-modern, hollow handle, 9 in............$27
Ladle-gravy, solid, 6 1/2 in. $70
Spoon-iced tea, 7 1/4 in. $34
Spoon-sugar, 6 in..........................$30
Spoon-teaspoon, 6 1/8 in. $23
Tablespoon, (serving spoon), 8 5/8 in........$60
Tablespoon, (serving spoon), pierced,
8 5/8 in................................$70

Deerfield/Beacon Hill by International, 1913

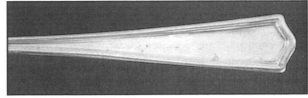

Butter-master, flat handle, 7 1/2 in........... $32
Carving set, 2 pieces, small, stainless blade,
steak $80
Fork, 7 1/4 in. $27
Fork, 7 7/8 in. $40
Fork-baby, 4 1/8 in........................ $30
Fork-cocktail, 5 5/8 in. $16
Fork-ice cream, 5 3/8 in. $26
Fork-salad, individual, bar, 6 1/4 in.......... $30
Knife-fruit, stainless blade, individual,
6 1/2 in................................ $23
Knife-old french, hollow handle,
10 3/8 in................................ $35
Knife-old french, hollow handle, 10 in. $35
Knife-old french, hollow handle, 9 3/8 in. $25
Knife-old french, hollow handle, 9 in. $25
Ladle-cream, solid, 5 3/8 in................. $26
Ladle-gravy, solid, 6 1/8 in................. $65
Ladle-mayonnaise $27
Spoon-demitasse, 4 1/2 in.................. $13
Spoon-demitasse, 4 in. $13
Spoon-fruit, 1 in. bowl, 5 3/4 in. $23
Spoon-iced tea, 7 1/2 in.................... $27
Spoon-relish, 6 3/8 in. $24
Spoon-soup, round bowl, bouillon,
5 1/4 in................................ $20
Spoon-soup, round bowl, gumbo,
7 1/8 in................................ $33
Spoon-sugar, 6 in. $26
Spoon-teaspoon, (five o'clock), 5 1/4 in...... $10
Spoon-teaspoon, 4 in. handle, 6 in.......... $20
Tablespoon, (serving spoon), 8 3/8 in. $45
Tongs-sugar, 3 1/2 in. $40

The following pieces have monograms:
Butter spreader, flat handle, 5 1/4 in. $12
Butter-master, flat handle, 7 1/2 in........... $23
Fork, 7 1/4 in. $22
Fork, 7 7/8 in. $30
Fork-lemon, 6 in.......................... $20
Fork-salad, individual, 6 1/4 in. $25
Knife-new french, hollow handle, 9 7/8 in..... $27
Knife-old french, hollow handle, 9 3/8 in. $19
Knife-sharpener/steel, small, steak, 14 in..... $30

Ladle-gravy, solid, 6 1/8 in. $48
Server-pie, stainless blade, 9 1/2 in. $34
Spoon-casserole, smooth bowl, solid,
  8 3/4 in. $60
Spoon-demitasse, 4 1/2 in. $10
Spoon-demitasse, 4 in. $10
Spoon-dessert/oval soup, 7 1/8 in. $27
Spoon-fruit, 5 1/2 in. $19
Spoon-fruit, 5 3/4 in. $19
Spoon-soup, round bowl, bouillon,
  5 1/4 in. $15
Spoon-soup, round bowl, cream,
  5 7/8 in. $24
Spoon-soup, round bowl, gumbo,
  7 1/8 in. $25
Spoon-sugar, 6 in. $23
Spoon-teaspoon, (five o'clock), 5 1/4 in. $10
Spoon-teaspoon, 5 3/4 in. $16
Tablespoon, (serving spoon), 8 3/8 in. $38
Tablespoon, (serving spoon), pierced,
  8 3/8 in. $53
Tongs-sugar, 4 3/4 in. $36

Devonshire by International, 1914

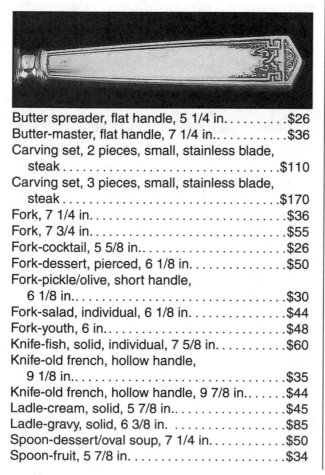

Butter spreader, flat handle, 5 1/4 in. $26
Butter-master, flat handle, 7 1/4 in. $36
Carving set, 2 pieces, small, stainless blade,
  steak $110
Carving set, 3 pieces, small, stainless blade,
  steak $170
Fork, 7 1/4 in. $36
Fork, 7 3/4 in. $55
Fork-cocktail, 5 5/8 in. $26
Fork-dessert, pierced, 6 1/8 in. $50
Fork-pickle/olive, short handle,
  6 1/8 in. $30
Fork-salad, individual, 6 1/8 in. $44
Fork-youth, 6 in. $48
Knife-fish, solid, individual, 7 5/8 in. $60
Knife-old french, hollow handle,
  9 1/8 in. $35
Knife-old french, hollow handle, 9 7/8 in. $44
Ladle-cream, solid, 5 7/8 in. $45
Ladle-gravy, solid, 6 3/8 in. $85
Spoon-dessert/oval soup, 7 1/4 in. $50
Spoon-fruit, 5 7/8 in. $34

Spoon-soup, round bowl, bouillon,
  5 3/8 in. $40
Spoon-soup, round bowl, gumbo, 7 in. $55
Spoon-sugar, 5 7/8 in. $36
Spoon-teaspoon, (five o'clock),
  5 5/8 in. $20
Spoon-teaspoon, 6 in. $25
Spoon-youth, 5 3/8 in. $38
Tablespoon, (serving spoon), 8 1/4 in. $70
Tongs-sugar, 4 5/8 in. $55

Du Barry by International, 1968

Baby set, 2 pieces $90
Butter spreader, hollow handle, modern,
  stainless paddle, 6 1/2 in. $44
Butter-master, hollow handle, 7 1/4 in. $36
Cleaver-cheese, stainless blade,
  7 1/4 in. $50
Fork, 7 3/8 in. $58
Fork, 7 7/8 in. $60
Fork-baby, 4 1/4 in. $45
Fork-cocktail, 5 1/2 in. $35
Fork-lemon, 5 1/2 in. $50
Fork-pickle/olive, short handle,
  6 in. $45
Fork-salad, individual, 6 5/8 in. $60
Knife-modern, hollow handle, 9 3/4 in. $56
Knife-modern, hollow handle, 9 in. $43
Knife-youth, 7 1/4 in. $48
Server-asparagus, hollow handle, silver
  plate hood, 10 in. $60
Server-jelly, 6 1/2 in. $50
Spoon-baby, straight handle, 4 1/4 in. $40
Spoon-bon-bon, 5 1/8 in. $44
Spoon-demitasse, 4 1/8 in. $27
Spoon-dessert/oval soup, 7 in. $50
Spoon-infant feeding, 5 1/2 in. $40
Spoon-sugar, 6 1/8 in. $40
Spoon-teaspoon, 6 in. $38
Tablespoon, (serving spoon), pierced,
  8 3/8 in. $100
Tongs-sugar, 4 1/2 in. $50

Edgewood by International, 1909

Spoon-dessert/oval soup, 6 7/8 in. $70

Spoon-soup, round bowl, bouillon, 5 in.........$55
Spoon-teaspoon, (five o'clock), 5 5/8 in.......$30
Spoon-teaspoon, 5 7/8 in.........................$32
Tablespoon, (serving spoon), 8 1/8 in.........$100
Tongs-sugar, 4 7/8 in.............................$90

The following pieces have monograms:
Fork, 7 1/2 in.....................................$70
Fork, 7 in...$50
Knife-old french, hollow handle, 9 7/8 in......$55
Knife-old french, hollow handle, 9 in..........$55
Spoon-dessert/oval soup, 6 7/8 in.............$53
Spoon-fruit, 5 5/8 in............................$40
Spoon-teaspoon, (five o'clock), 5 5/8 in.......$23
Spoon-teaspoon, 5 7/8 in........................$23
Tablespoon, (serving spoon), 8 1/8 in.........$75

Elegance by International, 1934

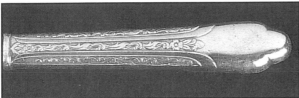

Butter spreader, flat handle, 6 1/8 in..........$20
Butter-master, flat handle, 7 in...............$38
Fork, 7 5/8 in.....................................$48
Fork, 7 in...$32
Fork-carving, small, stainless prongs, steak,
    8 5/8 in.......................................$45
Fork-cocktail, 5 1/2 in..........................$22
Fork-lemon, 6 in.................................$24
Fork-salad, individual, 6 1/2 in................$30
Knife-new french, hollow handle,
    8 3/4 in.......................................$27
Knife-new french, hollow handle,
    9 5/8 in.......................................$35
Ladle-gravy, solid, 6 3/8 in....................$75
Spoon-dessert/oval soup, 7 1/4 in...........$35
Spoon-soup, round bowl, cream, 6 in........$32
Spoon-soup, round bowl, gumbo, 7 in........$38
Spoon-teaspoon, 6 1/8 in.......................$18
Tablespoon, (serving spoon), 8 3/8 in........$60

Elsinore by International, 1931

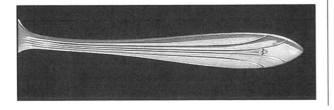

Butter-master, flat handle, 7 1/4 in...........$22
Carving set, 2 pieces, small, stainless blade,
    steak..$80
Fork, 7 1/4 in.....................................$35
Fork, 7 3/4 in.....................................$50
Fork-cocktail, 5 1/2 in..........................$15
Fork-grille (viand), 7 1/2 in....................$30
Fork-ice cream, 3 tines, 5 5/8 in..............$30
Fork-ice cream, 4 tines, 5 5/8 in..............$30
Fork-salad, individual, 6 3/8 in................$34
Knife-carving, small, stainless blade,
    steak, 10 in...................................$40
Ladle-gravy, solid, 6 3/8 in....................$63
Spoon-demitasse, 4 1/4 in......................$14
Spoon-fruit, 6 in.................................$20
Spoon-iced tea, 7 1/2 in........................$25
Spoon-soup, round bowl, bouillon, 1 3/4 in.
    bowl, 5 3/4 in.................................$24
Spoon-soup, round bowl, gumbo,
    7 1/8 in.......................................$36
Spoon-sugar, 2 in. bowl, 6 in..................$27
Spoon-teaspoon, 6 1/8 in.......................$20
Tablespoon, (serving spoon), 8 5/8 in........$55
Tongs-sugar, 4 in................................$40

Empress by International, 1932

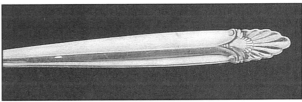

Butter spreader, hollow handle, stainless paddle,
    6 in...$40
Butter spreader, flat handle, 5 3/4 in.........$26
Butter-master, flat handle, 7 1/4 in...........$45
Butter-master, hollow handle, 6 5/8 in........$40
Carving set, 2 pieces, small, stainless blade,
    steak..$90
Cleaver-cheese, stainless blade,
    6 1/2 in.......................................$40
Fork, 7 1/4 in.....................................$40
Fork-carving, small, stainless prongs, steak,
    9 1/4 in.......................................$45
Fork-cocktail, 5 5/8 in..........................$22
Fork-cold meat/serving, small, solid,
    7 3/4 in.......................................$90
Fork-cold meat/serving, large, 5 stainless tines,
    11 in..$40
Fork-cold meat/serving, large, solid, 9 in. ...$100
Fork-grille (viand), 7 3/4 in....................$26
Fork-pickle/olive, short handle, 5 3/4 in.......$38

Fork-salad serving, stainless prongs, not
   beveled, 11 1/8 in. $40
Knife-cake, solid, 9 7/8 in. $160
Knife-carving, small, stainless blade, steak,
   10 1/2 in. $45
Knife-fruit, stainless blade, individual,
   6 3/4 in.. . . . .$40
Knife-grille, modern, hollow 5 1/8 in. handle,
   8 3/4 in.. . . . .$27
Knife-modern, hollow 3 5/8 in. handle,
   8 1/4 in.. . . . .$33
Knife-modern, hollow handle, 8 3/4 in.. . . . . . .$33
Knife-steak, individual, 8 5/8 in. $40
Knife-steak, individual, 9 in.. . . . .$40
Ladle-gravy, hollow handle, stainless bowl,
   7 3/4 in.. . . . .$40
Ladle-gravy, solid, 6 1/4 in. $80
Ladle-punch, stainless bowl, 13 in.. . . . .$55
Ladle-soup, stainless bowl, 11 1/4 in. $55
Server/knife-fish, stainless blade, design
   in bowl, 11 3/8 in. $45
Server-cranberry, stainless bowl, 8 5/8 in.. . . . .$45
Server-jelly, 6 3/8 in. $46
Server-lasagna, stainless blade, 9 7/8 in. $40
Server-pasta, stainless bowl, 10 1/2 in.. . . . . . .$45
Server-pie and cake, stainless blade,
   10 3/4 in. $45
Server-pie, stainless blade, 10 1/8 in. $40
Server-pie, stainless blade, 11 3/8 in. $40
Slicer-cake, stainless blade, wedding,
   12 1/2 in. $40
Spoon-bon-bon, 4 3/4 in. $50
Spoon-casserole, pierced, stainless bowl,
   7 scallops, 9 3/8 in.. . . . .$45
Spoon-casserole, shell bowl, stainless bowl,
   17 scallops, 10 in.. . . . .$45
Spoon-demitasse, 4 1/4 in. $20
Spoon-dessert/oval soup, 7 3/8 in.. . . . .$40
Spoon-dressing, stainless bowl, tear bowl,
   11 in.. . . . .$40
Spoon-fruit, 6 1/8 in. $34
Spoon-iced tea, 7 1/2 in. $32
Spoon-salad serving, stainless bowl, egg
   bowl, 11 1/8 in. $40
Spoon-soup, round bowl, cream, 6 in.. . . . .$34
Spoon-soup, round bowl, gumbo,
   7 1/4 in.. . . . .$40
Spoon-sugar shell, 6 1/4 in.. . . . .$37
Spoon-teaspoon, 6 in.. . . . .$23
Spoon-utility/serving, stainless bowl, 7
   scallops, 9 1/2 in. $45
Tablespoon, (serving spoon), 8 1/2 in.. . . . .$70
Tablespoon, (serving spoon), pierced,
   8 1/2 in.. . . . .$100

Enchanted Rose by International, 1954

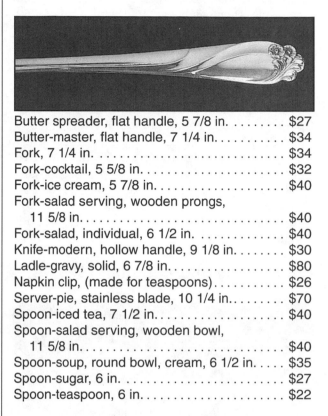

Butter spreader, flat handle, 5 7/8 in. $27
Butter-master, flat handle, 7 1/4 in.. . . . . $34
Fork, 7 1/4 in. $34
Fork-cocktail, 5 5/8 in. $32
Fork-ice cream, 5 7/8 in. $40
Fork-salad serving, wooden prongs,
   11 5/8 in.. . . . . $40
Fork-salad, individual, 6 1/2 in. $40
Knife-modern, hollow handle, 9 1/8 in.. . . . . . . $30
Ladle-gravy, solid, 6 7/8 in.. . . . . $80
Napkin clip, (made for teaspoons). $26
Server-pie, stainless blade, 10 1/4 in.. . . . . $70
Spoon-iced tea, 7 1/2 in.. . . . . $40
Spoon-salad serving, wooden bowl,
   11 5/8 in.. . . . . $40
Spoon-soup, round bowl, cream, 6 1/2 in.. . . . . $35
Spoon-sugar, 6 in.. . . . . $27
Spoon-teaspoon, 6 in.. $22

Enchantress by International, 1937

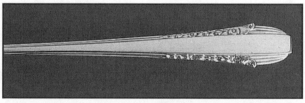

Butter spreader, hollow handle, modern, stainless
   paddle, 6 1/2 in.. . . . . $25
Butter spreader, flat handle, 5 3/4 in. $12
Butter-master, flat handle, 7 1/8 in.. . . . . $35
Fork, 7 1/4 in. $18
Fork, 7 7/8 in. $40
Fork-carving, small, stainless prongs, steak,
   8 1/2 in.. . . . . $64
Fork-cocktail, 5 1/2 in. $22
Fork-cold meat/serving, large, solid, 9 in. $90
Fork-ice cream, 3 tines, 5 1/2 in.. . . . . $40
Fork-ice cream, 3 tines, 5 in. $40
Fork-salad, individual, 6 1/2 in. $27
Knife-modern, hollow 3 3/4 in. handle,
   8 3/4 in.. . . . . $34
Knife-modern, hollow 4 in. handle, 8 7/8 in.. . . $34
Knife-new french, hollow handle, 9 1/2 in. $40

Knife-new french, hollow handle, 9 1/8 in......$33
Knife-wedding cake, stainless blade, 12 in.....$80
Ladle-gravy, solid, 6 1/4 in. $80
Server-pie, stainless blade, 10 1/8 in. $60
Spoon-demitasse, 4 1/4 in. $14
Spoon-fruit, 5 7/8 in.........................$32
Spoon-iced tea, 7 3/8 in. $34
Spoon-soup, round bowl, bouillon,
   5 5/8 in..................................$30
Spoon-soup, round bowl, cream, 6 1/2 in.....$16
Spoon-soup, round bowl, gumbo, 7 1/4 in. $36
Spoon-sugar, 5 7/8 in........................$20
Spoon-teaspoon, (five o'clock), 5 1/8 in. $18
Spoon-teaspoon, 6 in.........................$14
Tablespoon, (serving spoon), 8 5/8 in........$50
Tablespoon, (serving spoon), pierced,
   8 5/8 in..................................$80
Tongs-sugar, 4 1/8 in........................$60

Fontaine by International, 1924

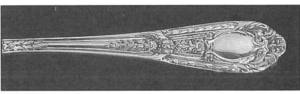

Butter spreader, flat handle, 6 in. $20
Carving set, 2 pieces, small, stainless blade,
   steak...................................$140
Fork, 7 1/4 in...............................$34
Fork-salad, individual, 6 1/4 in. $40
Knife-new french, hollow handle, 9 1/2 in.....$40
Knife-new french, hollow handle, 9 in........$40
Ladle-gravy, solid, 6 1/4 in. $95
Napkin clip, (made for teaspoons) $30
Spoon-demitasse, 4 1/4 in. $23
Spoon-iced tea, 7 3/8 in. $36
Spoon-soup, round bowl, bouillon,
   5 1/2 in.................................$34
Spoon-soup, round bowl, cream, 6 in........$55
Spoon-sugar, 6 1/8 in........................$45
Spoon-teaspoon, (five o'clock), 5 5/8 in. $20
Spoon-teaspoon, 6 in.........................$27
Tablespoon, (serving spoon), 8 1/2 in........$85

The following pieces have monograms:
Butter spreader, flat handle, 6 in. $14
Fork, 7 1/4 in...............................$25
Fork-ice cream, 5 3/8 in.....................$40
Fork-salad, individual, 6 1/4 in. $35
Knife-new french, hollow handle, 9 1/2 in.....$30
Knife-new french, hollow handle, 9 in........$27
Server-jelly, 6 1/2 in........................$30

Spoon-demitasse, 4 1/4 in...................$16
Spoon-fruit, 6 in............................$27
Spoon-ice cream, 5 3/8 in. $42
Spoon-soup, round bowl, bouillon,
   5 1/2 in.................................$24
Spoon-soup, round bowl, cream, 6 in. $45
Spoon-teaspoon, (five o'clock), 5 5/8 in......$15
Spoon-teaspoon, 6 in.......................$18

Frontenac by International, 1903

Fork, 7 1/2 in. $80
Fork-strawberry, 4 5/8 in...................$50
Fork-youth, 6 in. $60
Knife-old french, hollow handle, 5 1/8 in.
   blade, 9 in. $60
Spoon-chocolate, short handle, 3 3/4 in. $60
Spoon-sugar, 6 1/8 in.......................$60
Spoon-teaspoon, (five o'clock), 5 1/2 in......$22
Spoon-teaspoon, 5 7/8 in...................$34
Spoon-youth, 5 1/8 in......................$40
Tablespoon, (serving spoon), 8 3/8 in. $100

The following pieces have monograms:
Fork, 7 1/2 in. $53
Fork, 7 1/8 in. $40
Fork-cocktail, 5 1/2 in......................$30
Fork-salad, individual, 6 1/2 in. $80
Ice cream slicer, stainless blade,11 in........$80
Knife-old french, hollow handle, 9 7/8 in......$60
Knife-old french, hollow handle, 9 in. $45
Spoon-chocolate, short handle, 3 3/4 in. $50
Spoon-demitasse, 4 1/2 in...................$20
Spoon-demitasse, 4 in. $20
Spoon-soup, round bowl, bouillon, 5 in.......$35
Spoon-teaspoon, (five o'clock), 5 1/2 in......$18
Spoon-teaspoon, 5 7/8 in...................$22
Tablespoon, (serving spoon), 8 3/8 in. $75

Gadroon by International, 1933

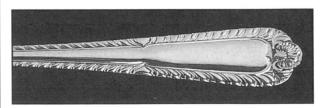

Butter spreader, flat handle, 5 3/4 in.........$24
Butter-master, flat handle, 7 1/8 in...........$44
Fork, 7 1/4 in...............................$44
Fork, 7 3/4 in...............................$50
Fork-cocktail, 5 1/2 in......................$27
Fork-cold meat/serving, small, solid,
    7 3/4 in..................................$70
Fork-grille (viand), 7 3/4 in. $34
Fork-ice cream, 5 1/2 in.....................$40
Fork-lemon, 4 3/4 in.........................$25
Knife-grille, modern, hollow handle,
    8 5/8 in..................................$26
Knife-modern, hollow handle, 8 3/4 in........$35
Knife-modern, hollow handle, 9 1/2 in........$46
Knife-modern, hollow handle, 9 1/4 in........$35
Ladle-gravy, solid, 6 1/2 in. $90
Server-jelly, 6 1/4 in.......................$34
Server-pie, stainless blade, 10 in...........$65
Server-pie, stainless blade, 9 3/8 in. $65
Server-tomato, solid, 8 in. $90
Spoon-fruit, 5 7/8 in........................$34
Spoon-iced tea, 7 1/2 in. $37
Spoon-soup, round bowl, bouillon,
    5 5/8 in..................................$30
Spoon-soup, round bowl, cream, 5 7/8 in......$34
Spoon-soup, round bowl, gumbo, 7 1/8 in. $48
Spoon-sugar shell, 6 in. $36
Tablespoon, (serving spoon), 8 1/2 in........$70
Tablespoon, (serving spoon), pierced,
    8 1/2 in..................................$80

Georgian Maid by International, 1923

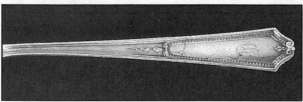

Butter spreader, hollow handle, stainless
    paddle, 5 1/4 in..........................$22
Butter spreader, flat handle, 5 1/2 in.........$16
Butter-master, flat handle, 7 1/4 in...........$34
Carving set, 2 pieces, small, stainless
    blade, steak $100
Fork, 7 1/4 in...............................$26
Fork, 7 5/8 in...............................$36
Fork-cocktail, 5 3/8 in......................$14
Fork-cold meat/serving, small, solid,
    7 1/8 in..................................$80
Fork-cold meat/serving, medium, solid,
    8 5/8 in..................................$90
Fork-pickle/olive, short handle, 5 3/4 in. $32

Fork-salad, individual, bar, 6 1/8 in.......... $34
Knife-new french, hollow handle,
    9 1/2 in..................................$38
Knife-new french, hollow handle, 9 in. $30
Ladle-gravy, solid, 6 3/4 in..................$80
Napkin clip (made for five o'clock) $20
Server-jelly, 6 3/8 in. $30
Spoon-dessert/oval soup, 7 1/8 in...........$40
Spoon-fruit, 5 7/8 in. $34
Spoon-iced tea, 7 3/8 in.....................$30
Spoon-soup, round bowl, bouillon,
    5 1/4 in..................................$25
Spoon-soup, round bowl, cream,
    5 7/8 in..................................$30
Spoon-soup, round bowl, gumbo, 7 in........$30
Spoon-sugar, 6 in. $34
Spoon-teaspoon, (five o'clock), 5 3/4 in......$12
Spoon-teaspoon, 6 in.........................$16
Tablespoon, (serving spoon), 8 1/4 in. $50
Tablespoon, (serving spoon), pierced,
    8 1/4 in..................................$80
Tongs-sugar, 3 1/4 in. $40

Governor Bradford by International, 1913

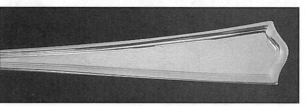

Fork, 7 1/2 in. $56
Fork, 7 in...................................$40
Fork-cocktail, 5 3/8 in. $22
Fork-cold meat/serving, medium, solid,
    8 1/4 in..................................$75
Fork-pickle/olive, short handle, 5 3/4 in.......$38
Fork-youth, 5 7/8 in.........................$38
Knife-new french, hollow handle, 8 3/4 in. $30
Knife-new french, hollow handle, 9 1/2 in. $42
Knife-old french, hollow handle, 9 in. $30
Ladle-gravy, solid, 6 1/4 in..................$85
Spoon-demitasse, 3 7/8 in...................$24
Spoon-fruit, 5 5/8 in. $36
Spoon-relish, 6 in. $38
Spoon-salt, individual, 2 3/8 in. $14
Spoon-soup, round bowl, gumbo,
    6 7/8 in..................................$55
Spoon-teaspoon, (five o'clock), 5 1/4 in......$16
Spoon-teaspoon, 5 3/4 in....................$20
Tablespoon, (serving spoon), 8 in. $70
Tongs-sugar, 4 7/8 in. $50

International Silver

Grande Regency by International, 1969

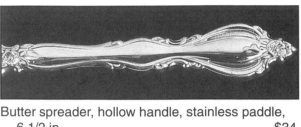

Butter spreader, hollow handle, stainless paddle,
6 1/2 in. $34
Butter-master, hollow handle, 7 1/4 in. $40
Carving set, 2 pieces, small, stainless blade,
steak $90
Cleaver-cheese, stainless blade, 7 1/8 in. $40
Fork, 7 1/2 in. $36
Fork, 8 in. $46
Fork-baby, 4 1/4 in. $30
Fork-carving, small, stainless prongs, steak,
9 7/8 in. $45
Fork-cold meat/serving, small, solid,
7 5/8 in. $95
Fork-cold meat/serving, large, stainless tines,
11 1/2 in. $40
Fork-fish, stainless tines, hollow handle,
individual, 8 3/4 in. $40
Fork-pickle/olive, short handle, 6 in. $36
Fork-salad serving, stainless prongs,
11 7/8 in. $45
Fork-salad, individual, 6 7/8 in. $36
Knife-bar, hollow handle, 9 1/2 in. $45
Knife-carving, large, stainless blade,
roast, 12 5/8 in. $50
Knife-carving, small, stainless blade, steak,
10 3/4 in. $45
Knife-cheese, stainless blade, 7 1/4 in. $45
Knife-cheese, stainless blade, 7 5/8 in. $45
Knife-fish, stainless blade, individual,
8 7/8 in. $40
Knife-fruit, stainless blade, individual,
7 3/8 in. $40
Knife-modern, hollow handle, 9 in. $34
Knife-steak, individual, 8 3/4 in. $44
Knife-steak, individual, 9 1/8 in. $44
Knife-steak, individual, 9 3/4 in. $44
Ladle-punch, stainless bowl, 13 1/4 in. $55
Ladle-soup, stainless bowl, 11 1/4 in. $60
Opener-bottle, stainless bowl, 6 3/4 in. $45
Salad set, 2 pieces, plastic bowl $90
Scoop-ice cream, stainless bowl,
8 7/8 in. $45
Scoop-ice, silver plate bowl, 9 1/2 in. $45
Server/knife-fish, stainless blade, 12 in. $40

Server-cranberry, stainless bowl, 9 in. $40
Server-lasagna, stainless blade,
10 3/8 in. $40
Server-pasta, stainless bowl, 11 1/4 in. $45
Server-pie and cake, stainless blade,
11 1/2 in. $45
Server-tomato, solid, 7 3/4 in. $100
Slicer-cake, stainless blade, wedding,
13 1/8 in. $40
Spoon-baby, straight handle, 4 1/4 in. $30
Spoon-casserole, pierced, stainless bowl,
9 7/8 in. $40
Spoon-casserole, shell bowl, solid,
8 3/4 in. $160
Spoon-casserole, stainless shell bowl,
10 3/4 in. $45
Spoon-demitasse, 4 1/8 in. $27
Spoon-dressing, stainless bowl, 11 5/8 in. $40
Spoon-infant feeding, 5 1/2 in. $30
Spoon-rice, stainless bowl, 10 in. $45
Spoon-salad serving, stainless bowl,
11 3/4 in. $45
Spoon-sugar shell, 6 1/8 in. $38
Tablespoon, (serving spoon), pierced,
8 1/2 in. $90
Tongs-sugar, 4 5/8 in. $45

Irene by International, 1902

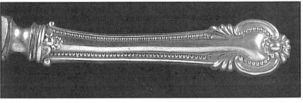

Butter spreader, flat handle, 6 in. $34
Fork, 7 1/2 in. $65
Fork, 7 in. $48
Fork-cold meat/serving, small, solid, 7 in. $90
Fork-cold meat/serving, medium, solid,
8 3/8 in. $100
Fork-salad, individual, 5 7/8 in. $57
Spoon-demitasse, 4 1/4 in. $26
Spoon-dessert/oval soup, 7 in. $50
Spoon-soup, round bowl, bouillon,
5 1/8 in. $45
Spoon-soup, round bowl, cream,
5 7/8 in. $58
Spoon-sugar, 5 3/4 in. $45
Spoon-teaspoon, (five o'clock), 5 3/8 in. $30
Spoon-teaspoon, 5 7/8 in. $30
Tablespoon, (serving spoon), 8 in. $90
Tongs-sugar, 5 1/8 in. $70

Joan of Arc by International, 1940

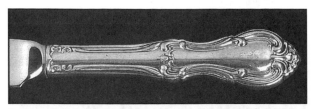

Butter spreader, hollow handle, modern, stainless paddle, 6 1/2 in. $30

Butter spreader, hollow handle, paddle stainless, 5 7/8 in. $30

Butter spreader, flat handle, no crimp, 5 3/4 in. $26

Butter-master, flat handle, 7 1/8 in. $35

Butter-master, hollow handle, no notch, 7 in. $35

Carving set, 2 pieces, small, stainless blade, steak $90

Cleaver-cheese, stainless blade, 6 5/8 in. $40

Fork, 7 3/4 in. $50

Fork, 7 3/8 in. $32

Fork-baby, 4 1/4 in. $32

Fork-carving, small, stainless prongs, steak, 8 7/8 in. $45

Fork-carving, small, stainless prongs, steak, 9 5/8 in. $45

Fork-cocktail, 5 1/2 in. $30

Fork-cold meat/serving, small, solid, 1 of 4 tines beveled, 7 5/8 in. $90

Fork-cold meat/serving, medium, solid, 1 of 4 tines beveled, 8 3/4 in. $90

Fork-fish, stainless tines, hollow handle, individual, 8 1/2 in. $45

Fork-lemon, 3 flared tines, 6 in. $40

Fork-lemon, 3 flared tines, 4 1/2 in. $40

Fork-pickle/olive, short handle, 3 flared tines, 5 7/8 in. $30

Fork-salad, individual, 4 tines, 6 1/8 in. $38

Knife-bar, hollow handle, 9 3/8 in. $44

Knife-carving, small, stainless blade, steak, 10 1/8 in. $45

Knife-carving, small, stainless blade, steak, 10 3/4 in. $45

Knife-cheese, stainless blade, 7 in. $45

Knife-fish, stainless blade, individual, 8 3/4 In. $45

Knife-modern, hollow handle, (place size), 4 1/2 in. handle, 9 1/4 in. $40

Knife-modern, hollow handle, 3 3/4 in. handle, 8 5/8 in. $32

Knife-new french, hollow handle, 9 1/4 in. $30

Knife-new french, hollow handle, 9 5/8 in. $40

Knife-steak, individual, 8 3/4 in. $45

Ladle-cream, solid, 5 1/2 in. $48

Ladle-gravy, hollow handle, stainless bowl, 8 3/8 in. $45

Ladle-gravy, solid, 6 1/2 in. $70

Ladle-punch, stainless bowl, 13 1/4 in. $60

Pick-butter, 1 tine, 5 1/4 in. $25

Scoop-ice cream, stainless bowl, 8 3/4 in. $45

Scoop-ice, silver plate bowl, 8 1/2 in. $50

Server/knife-fish, stainless blade, design in bowl, 11 3/4 in. $45

Server-asparagus, hollow handle, silver plate hood, 9 7/8 in. $60

Server-cheese, stainless blade, 6 1/4 in. $40

Server-cranberry, stainless bowl, 9 in. $45

Server-jelly, 6 3/8 in. $40

Server-lasagna, stainless blade, 10 1/4 in. $45

Server-macaroni, 10 3/8 in. $200

Server-pasta, stainless bowl, 11 in. $40

Server-pie, stainless blade, serrated, 10 1/4 in. $45

Server-tomato, solid, 7 7/8 in. $100

Spoon-baby, straight handle, 4 3/8 in. $32

Spoon-bon-bon, 4 5/8 in. $45

Spoon-cracker, 8 1/8 in. $150

Spoon-demitasse, 4 1/8 in. $24

Spoon-dessert/oval soup, 7 1/4 in. $44

Spoon-dressing, large, solid, with button, 14 1/4 in. $260

Spoon-dressing, stainless tear bowl, 11 3/8 in. $45

Spoon-five o'clock/youth, 5 1/2 in. $24

Spoon-iced tea, 7 1/2 in. $38

Spoon-infant feeding, 5 1/2 in. $32

Spoon-place/oval soup, 6 5/8 in. $40

Spoon-platter, solid, 13 3/4 in. $240

Spoon-salad serving, plastic bowl, 12 1/4 in. $40

Spoon-salt, individual, 2 3/8 in. $13

Spoon-soup, round bowl, cream, 6 in. $42

Spoon-sugar shell, 6 1/8 in. $34

Spoon-teaspoon, 5 7/8 in. $24

Tablespoon, (serving spoon), 8 1/4 in. $80

Tablespoon, (serving spoon), pierced, 8 1/4 in. $90

Tea, strainer, 7 3/8 in. $100

Tongs-sugar, 4 1/8 in. $45

International Silver

La Rochelle by International, 1909

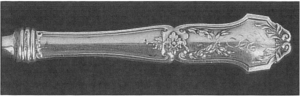

Fork, 6 7/8 in. $45
Fork, 7 1/2 in. $60
Knife-fish, solid, individual, 7 3/4 in. $75
Knife-old french, hollow handle, 9 7/8 in. $60
Spoon-soup, round bowl, gumbo,
   6 3/4 in. $70
Spoon-teaspoon, (five o'clock), 5 3/4 in. $24
Spoon-teaspoon, 6 in. $30
Spoon-youth, 5 3/8 in. $38

The following pieces have monograms:
Fork-ice cream, 5 3/4 in. $45
Fork-strawberry, 5 in. $40
Knife-old french, hollow handle, 9 7/8 in. $45
Spoon-demitasse, 4 1/2 in. $24
Spoon-dessert/oval soup, 7 1/8 in. $45
Spoon-fruit, 6 in. $38
Spoon-ice cream, 5 7/8 in. $45
Spoon-soup, round bowl, bouillon,
   5 1/2 in. $30
Spoon-youth, 5 3/8 in. $30
Tablespoon, (serving spoon), 8 1/4 in. $70

Lady Betty by International, 1920

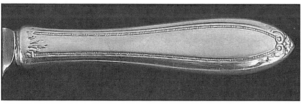

Butter spreader, flat handle, 5 1/2 in. $18
Butter-master, flat handle, 7 1/4 in. $30
Carving set, 2 pieces, small, stainless blade,
   steak $90
Fork, 7 1/4 in. $27
Fork, 7 3/4 in. $40
Fork-ice cream, 5 1/2 in. $35
Fork-salad, individual, 6 1/8 in. $28
Knife-old french, hollow handle, 9 7/8 in. $40
Server-jelly, 6 1/2 in. $30
Spoon-demitasse, 4 1/8 in. $18
Spoon-dessert/oval soup, 7 1/4 in. $36
Spoon-fruit, 6 in. $25
Spoon-iced tea, 8 in. $26

Spoon-soup, round bowl, bouillon,
   5 1/4 in. $22
Spoon-soup, round bowl, gumbo, 7 1/8 in. $34
Spoon-sugar, 5 7/8 in. $30
Spoon-teaspoon, (five o'clock), 5 1/2 in. $15
Spoon-teaspoon, 6 in. $17
Tablespoon, (serving spoon), 8 1/2 in. $50

Lambeth Manor by International, 1952

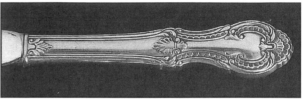

Butter spreader, flat handle, 5 3/4 in. $25
Carving set, 2 pieces, small, stainless blade,
   steak $130
Fork, 7 3/8 in. $48
Fork-salad, individual, 6 1/2 in. $34
Knife-modern, hollow handle, 9 1/8 in. $34
Spoon-teaspoon, 5 7/8 in. $18
Tablespoon, (serving spoon), 8 1/4 in. $80

Mademoiselle by International, 1964

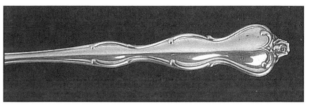

Butter spreader, hollow handle, stainless paddle,
   6 3/8 in. $26
Fork, 7 1/4 in. $40
Fork-salad, individual, 6 3/4 in. $58
Knife-modern, hollow handle, 9 1/4 in. $38
Spoon-dessert/oval soup, 6 5/8 in. $80
Spoon-sugar shell, 6 in. $40
Spoon-teaspoon, 6 in. $22

Maintenon by International, 1933

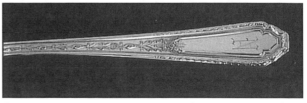

Butter spreader, flat handle, 5 3/4 in. $24

Carving set, 2 pieces, small, stainless blade,
  steak $140
Fork, 7 1/8 in. $40
Fork, 7 5/8 in. $60
Fork-cocktail, 5 3/8 in. $30
Fork-grille (viand), 7 5/8 in. $35
Fork-salad, individual, 6 1/4 in. $40
Knife-grille, new french, hollow handle,
  8 3/8 in. $33
Knife-new french, hollow handle, 9 5/8 in. $50
Knife-new french, hollow handle, 9 in. $35
Ladle-gravy, solid, 6 1/2 in. $90
Spoon-demitasse, 4 3/8 in. $28
Spoon-dessert/oval soup, 7 3/8 in. $60
Spoon-fruit, 5 7/8 in. $44
Spoon-soup, round bowl, bouillon,
  5 3/8 in. $30
Spoon-soup, round bowl, cream, 6 in. $60
Spoon-soup, round bowl, gumbo, 7 in. $60
Spoon-sugar, 5 3/4 in. $30
Spoon-teaspoon, 6 in. $28
Tablespoon, (serving spoon), 8 1/4 in. $80

Margaret-New by International, 1912

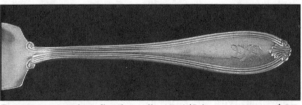

Butter spreader, flat handle, 5 1/2 in. $25
Butter-master, flat handle, 7 3/8 in. $40
Fork, 7 1/8 in. $40
Fork, 7 3/4 in. $55
Fork-chipped beef, small, 6 7/8 in. $60
Fork-cocktail, 5 5/8 in. $30
Fork-dessert, 2 of 4 tines beveled,
  6 1/8 in. $50
Fork-ice cream, 5 1/2 in. $45
Fork-ice cream, 5 in. $45
Fork-lemon, 5 1/2 in. $30
Fork-youth, 6 in. $48
Knife-old french, hollow handle, 9 7/8 in. $48
Ladle-cream, solid, 5 1/4 in. $48
Server-pie, silver plate blade, 10 1/4 in. $70
Spoon-bon-bon, 5 3/8 in. $40
Spoon-casserole, smooth bowl, solid,
  8 5/8 in. $100
Spoon-demitasse, 4 3/8 in. $24
Spoon-dessert/oval soup, 7 1/8 in. $40
Spoon-fruit, 5 5/8 in. $40
Spoon-iced tea, 7 in. $40

Spoon-place/oval soup, 6 3/4 in. $48
Spoon-soup, round bowl, bouillon,
  5 1/4 in. $40
Spoon-soup, round bowl, gumbo,
  7 in. $50
Spoon-sugar, 6 in. $44
Spoon-teaspoon, (five o'clock),
  5 5/8 in. $20
Spoon-teaspoon, 5 7/8 in. $30
Tablespoon, (serving spoon), 8 1/8 in. $85
Tongs-sugar, 4 3/4 in. $60

Margaret-Old by International, 1907

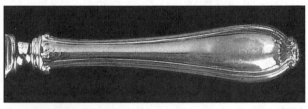

Fork, 6 7/8 in. $30
Fork, 7 1/4 in. $40
Fork-chipped beef, small, 6 1/4 in. $50
Fork-cocktail, 5 3/8 in. $28
Fork-cold meat/serving, medium, solid,
  8 1/4 in. $70
Fork-fish, solid, individual, 1 of 4 tines beveled,
  7 1/4 in. $40
Fork-salad, individual, no bevel, 6 1/4 in. $36
Fork-strawberry, 4 5/8 in. $34
Knife-old french, hollow handle, 9 in. $32
Ladle-cream, solid, 5 1/4 in. $36
Ladle-gravy, solid, 7 1/2 in. $70
Ladle-soup, solid, 9 3/8 in. $230
Server-cheese, silver plate blade,
  6 1/8 in. $55
Spoon-demitasse, 3 7/8 in. $16
Spoon-demitasse, 4 1/4 in. $16
Spoon-dessert/oval soup, 7 1/8 in. $30
Spoon-fruit, 5 7/8 in. $34
Spoon-iced tea, 7 1/8 in. $30
Spoon-olive, short, pierced bowl,
  5 3/4 in. $70
Spoon-place/oval soup, 6 3/4 in. $30
Spoon-preserve, 7 in. $60
Spoon-soup, round bowl, bouillon, 5 in. $25
Spoon-sugar, 5 7/8 in. $30
Spoon-teaspoon, 6 in. $20
Spoon-youth, 5 5/8 in. $36
Tablespoon, (serving spoon), 8 1/8 in. $50
Tablespoon, (serving spoon), pierced,
  8 1/8 in. $60
Tongs-sugar, 4 3/4 in. $60

International Silver

Masterpiece by International, 1963

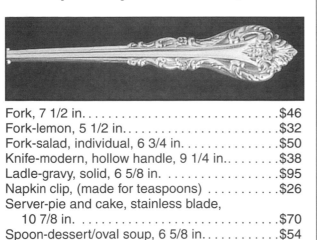

Fork, 7 1/2 in. $46
Fork-lemon, 5 1/2 in. $32
Fork-salad, individual, 6 3/4 in. $50
Knife-modern, hollow handle, 9 1/4 in. $38
Ladle-gravy, solid, 6 5/8 in. $95
Napkin clip, (made for teaspoons) $26
Server-pie and cake, stainless blade,
    10 7/8 in. $70
Spoon-dessert/oval soup, 6 5/8 in. $54
Spoon-iced tea, 7 1/4 in. $48
Spoon-sugar, 6 in. $36
Spoon-teaspoon, 6 in. $22
Tablespoon, (serving spoon), 8 1/4 in. $90
Tablespoon, (serving spoon), pierced,
    8 1/4 in. $100

May Melody by International, 1952

Butter spreader, flat handle, 5 7/8 in. $18
Butter-master, flat handle, 7 1/4 in. $35
Fork, 7 3/8 in. $34
Fork-cocktail, 5 5/8 in. $26
Fork-salad, individual, 6 1/2 in. $34
Ladle-gravy, solid, 6 5/8 in. $70
Spoon-demitasse, 4 1/8 in. $18
Spoon-iced tea, 7 3/8 in. $34
Spoon-soup, round bowl, cream, 6 5/8 in. $26
Spoon-sugar, 6 in. $34
Spoon-teaspoon, 6 in. $20
Tablespoon, (serving spoon), 8 1/2 in. $75
Tablespoon, (serving spoon), pierced,
    8 1/2 in. $80

Mille Fleurs by International, 1904

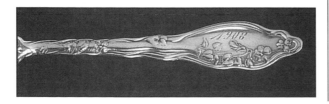

Masterpiece by International, 1963

Butter spreader, flat handle, 5 5/8 in. $30
Butter-master, flat handle, 7 1/4 in. $45
Fork, 7 1/2 in. $60
Fork, 7 1/8 in. $45
Fork-cocktail, 5 5/8 in. $30
Fork-salad, individual, gold wash, 6 3/8 in. . . . $70
Knife-old french, hollow handle, 9 in. $70
Spoon-berry/casserole, solid, 8 3/4 in. $200
Spoon-demitasse, 3 7/8 in. $26
Spoon-dessert/oval soup, 7 1/8 in. $60
Spoon-soup, round bowl, bouillon, 5 in. $36
Spoon-sugar, 6 1/8 in. $48
Spoon-teaspoon, (five o'clock), 5 1/2 in. $24
Spoon-teaspoon, 5 7/8 in. $30
Tablespoon, (serving spoon), 8 1/8 in. $80

Minuet by International, 1925

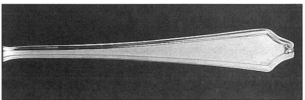

Butter spreader, flat handle, 5 5/8 in. $15
Butter-master, flat handle, 7 in. $30
Fork, 7 1/4 in. $26
Fork, 7 3/4 in. $50
Fork-baby, 4 1/8 in. $28
Fork-cocktail, 5 3/8 in. $24
Fork-grille (viand), 7 5/8 in. $28
Fork-lemon, 5 7/8 in. $34
Fork-pickle/olive, short handle, 3 tines,
    5 3/4 in. $28
Fork-salad, individual, 4 tines not beveled,
    6 in. $34
Fork-youth, 6 1/8 in. $35
Knife-carving, small, stainless blade, steak,
    9 3/4 in. $44
Knife-new french, hollow handle, 8 5/8 in. $30
Knife-new french, hollow handle, no notch,
    9 5/8 in. $40
Knife-new french, hollow handle, no notch,
    9 in. $30
Knife-new french, hollow handle, notch blade,
    9 in. $30
Knife-youth, 6 3/4 in. $30
Ladle-cream, solid, 5 1/2 in. $36
Ladle-gravy, solid, 6 1/2 in. $70
Napkin clip, (made for teaspoons) $22
Server-jelly, 6 1/4 in. $30
Spoon-bon-bon, 5 7/8 in. $34
Spoon-demitasse, 4 1/8 in. $18

Spoon-dessert/oval soup, 7 1/4 in............$44
Spoon-iced tea, 7 1/2 in. $32
Spoon-relish, 6 in. $32
Spoon-soup, round bowl, bouillon,
  5 3/8 in...............................$30
Spoon-soup, round bowl, cream, 5 7/8 in.....$34
Spoon-sugar, 5 7/8 in.....................$30
Spoon-teaspoon, (five o'clock), 5 5/8 in. $16
Spoon-teaspoon, 5 7/8 in. $18
Tablespoon, (serving spoon), 8 1/2 in........$55
Tongs-sugar, 4 1/8 in.....................$48

The following pieces have monograms:
Butter spreader, flat handle, 5 5/8 in.........$12
Butter-master, flat handle, 7 in..............$25
Carving set, 2 pieces, small, stainless blade,
  steak.................................$70
Fork, 7 1/4 in............................$22
Fork, 7 3/4 in............................$40
Fork-baby, 4 1/8 in. $24
Fork-cocktail, 5 3/8 in.....................$18
Fork-cold meat/serving, small, solid,
  7 1/4 in...............................$50
Fork-cold meat/serving, medium, solid,
  8 3/4 in...............................$55
Fork-dessert, 6 1/8 in.....................$30
Fork-grille (viand), 7 5/8 in. $28
Fork-lemon, 5 7/8 in......................$27
Fork-pickle/olive, short handle, 5 3/4 in. $23
Fork-salad, individual, 6 in. $28
Knife-new french, hollow handle,
  9 5/8 in...............................$30
Knife-new french, hollow handle, 9 in........$22
Knife-youth, 7 1/4 in......................$24
Ladle-cream, solid, 5 1/2 in................$32
Ladle-gravy, solid, 6 1/2 in. $50
Server-jelly, 6 1/4 in......................$24
Server-pie, stainless blade, 11 1/4 in. $40
Server-pie, stainless blade, 9 1/2 in. $40
Spoon-baby, straight handle, 4 1/4 in. $24
Spoon-bon-bon, 5 7/8 in. $27
Spoon-demitasse, 4 1/8 in. $14
Spoon-dessert/oval soup, 7 1/4 in............$30
Spoon-fruit, 5 3/4 in......................$26
Spoon-iced tea, 7 1/2 in. $24
Spoon-soup, round bowl, bouillon,
  5 3/8 in...............................$24
Spoon-soup, round bowl, cream,
  5 7/8 in...............................$25
Spoon-soup, round bowl, gumbo, 7 1/8 in. $30
Spoon-sugar, 5 7/8 in.....................$25
Spoon-teaspoon, 5 7/8 in. $14
Tablespoon, (serving spoon), 8 1/2 in........$45
Tongs-sugar, 4 1/8 in.....................$42

Moonbeam by International, 1948

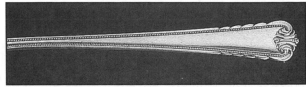

Butter spreader, flat handle, 5 3/4 in. $12
Fork, 7 1/4 in. $20
Fork-salad, individual, 6 1/2 in. $20
Spoon-soup, round bowl, cream, 6 1/2 in..... $20
Spoon-teaspoon, 6 in...................... $16

Moonglow by International, 1938

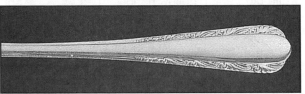

Butter spreader, flat handle, 5 5/8 in. $17
Butter-master, flat handle, 7 1/8 in. $17
Carving set, 2 pieces, small, stainless blade,
  steak $100
Fork, 7 1/8 in. $24
Fork, 7 3/4 in. $40
Fork-salad, individual, 6 1/8 in. $26
Knife-carving, small, stainless blade, steak,
  10 1/2 in................................ $50
Knife-new french, hollow handle, 8 3/4 in. $26
Knife-new french, hollow handle, 9 1/2 in. $35
Knife-new french, hollow handle, 9 1/8 in. $26
Ladle-gravy, solid, 6 in. $70
Napkin clip, (made for sugar) $25
Server-jelly, 5 in........................... $30
Spoon-bon-bon, 4 3/4 in. $33
Spoon-casserole, smooth, solid, 8 3/8 in. $96
Spoon-iced tea, 7 1/2 in.................... $30
Spoon-place/oval soup, 6 3/4 in. $32
Spoon-soup, round bowl, cream, 5 7/8 in..... $25
Spoon-sugar, 5 7/8 in...................... $18
Spoon-teaspoon, 6 in...................... $12
Tablespoon, (serving spoon), 8 1/8 in. $45

Napoleon by International, 1910

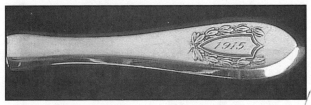

Butter spreader, flat handle, 5 7/8 in. $24
Butter-master, flat handle, 7 1/2 in. $40
Fork, 6 7/8 in. $44
Fork, 7 3/8 in. $70
Fork-carving, small, stainless prongs, steak,
   8 3/4 in. $75
Fork-cocktail, 5 3/8 in. $32
Fork-cocktail, 5 5/8 in. $32
Fork-dessert, 2 of 4 tines beveled,
   6 1/2 in. $50
Fork-fish, solid, individual, 1 of 4 tines beveled,
   7 1/8 in. $50
Fork-pickle/olive, short handle, 6 1/8 in. $33
Fork-salad, individual, 1 of 4 tines beveled,
   6 1/4 in. $50
Knife-old french, hollow handle, 10 in. $60
Knife-old french, hollow handle, 9 1/2 in. $60
Ladle-cream, solid, 5 3/4 in. $45
Server-cheese, silver plate blade,
   6 1/8 in. $70
Server-pie, silver plate blade, 10 1/2 in. $75
Spoon-casserole, smooth bowl, solid,
   8 3/4 in. $110
Spoon-demitasse, 4 in. $24
Spoon-dessert/oval soup, 7 1/8 in. $50
Spoon-fruit, 5 7/8 in. $38
Spoon-ice cream, 5 3/4 in. $50
Spoon-soup, round bowl, bouillon, 5 in. $30
Spoon-soup, round bowl, gumbo,
   6 7/8 in. $50
Spoon-sugar, 6 1/8 in. $40
Spoon-teaspoon, (five o'clock), 5 3/8 in. $22
Spoon-teaspoon, 5 3/4 in. $30
Tablespoon, (serving spoon), 8 1/8 in. $50
Tongs-sugar, 4 in. $60

The following pieces have monograms:
Butter spreader, flat handle, 5 7/8 in. $20
Fork, 6 7/8 in. $36
Fork, 7 3/8 in. $60
Fork-pickle/olive, short handle, 6 1/8 in. $28
Fork-salad, individual, 6 1/4 in. $40
Knife-carving, small, stainless blade, steak,
   10 1/2 in. $65
Knife-fruit, silver plate blade, individual,
   7 in. $35
Knife-new french, hollow handle, 9 3/8 in. $32
Knife-old french, hollow handle, 10 in. $40
Knife-old french, hollow handle, 8 7/8 in. $32
Knife-youth, 7 1/8 in. $35
Spoon-dessert/oval soup, 7 1/8 in. $48
Spoon-mustard, 4 1/2 in. $55
Spoon-soup, round bowl, gumbo, 7 in. $50

Spoon-teaspoon, (five o'clock), 5 3/8 in. $22
Spoon-teaspoon, 5 3/4 in. $23
Tablespoon, (serving spoon), 8 1/8 in. $55
Tablespoon, (serving spoon), pierced,
   8 1/8 in. $90

Norse by International, 1937

Butter spreader, flat handle, 5 3/4 in. $20
Butter-master, flat handle, 7 1/8 in. $28
Fork, 7 1/4 in. $34
Fork, 8 in. $56
Fork-cocktail, 5 1/2 in. $24
Fork-cold meat/serving, large, solid,
   9 1/4 in. $85
Fork-salad, individual, 6 1/2 in. $40
Knife-modern, hollow handle, 8 7/8 in. $32
Knife-modern, hollow handle, 9 7/8 in. $38
Knife-youth, 7 1/4 in. $28
Ladle-gravy, solid, 6 1/2 in. $80
Spoon-casserole, smooth, solid bowl,
   7 7/8 in. $100
Spoon-fruit, 6 in. $30
Spoon-iced tea, 7 3/8 in. $34
Spoon-soup, round bowl, bouillon,
   5 5/8 in. $26
Spoon-soup, round bowl, cream, 6 1/4 in. $33
Spoon-soup, round bowl, gumbo, 7 1/4 in. $33
Spoon-sugar, 6 in. $30
Spoon-teaspoon, 6 in. $24
Tablespoon, (serving spoon), 8 1/2 in. $70

Northern Lights by International, 1946

Butter spreader, hollow handle, solid paddle,
   6 in. $20
Butter-master, flat handle, 7 1/8 in. $47
Fork, 7 1/8 in. $50
Fork, 7 3/4 in. $70

Fork-cocktail, 5 5/8 in........................$28
Fork-cold meat/serving, medium, solid,
    8 7/8 in...................................$85
Fork-lemon, 4 3/4 in.........................$32
Fork-pickle/olive, short handle, 5 7/8 in. $36
Fork-salad, individual, 6 3/8 in. $40
Knife-modern, hollow handle, 9 3/4 in.........$55
Knife-modern, hollow handle, 9 in............$38
Ladle-cream, solid, 5 3/8 in..................$50
Ladle-gravy, solid, 6 1/4 in. $85
Salad set, 2 pieces, solid, 9 1/8 in..........$240
Salad set, 2 pieces, wooden bowl and
    tines $90
Server-jelly, 6 1/2 in.........................$40
Spoon-dessert/oval soup, 6 7/8 in...........$60
Spoon-iced tea, 7 3/8 in. $40
Spoon-soup, round bowl, cream,
    6 1/2 in...................................$43
Spoon-sugar, 5 7/8 in........................$38
Spoon-teaspoon, 6 in........................$26
Tablespoon, (serving spoon), 8 1/2 in........$80
Tongs-sugar, 4 1/4 in........................$56

Old Charleston by International, 1951

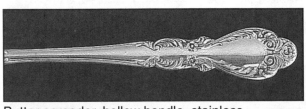

Butter spreader, hollow handle, stainless
    paddle, 5 7/8 in...........................$23
Butter spreader, flat handle, 5 3/4 in.........$18
Butter-master, flat handle, 7 1/8 in...........$35
Fork, 7 1/4 in................................$30
Fork-baby, 4 1/8 in. $40
Fork-cocktail, 5 3/4 in........................$28
Fork-ice cream, 5 3/4 in......................$40
Fork-salad, individual, 6 1/2 in. $38
Fork-youth, 6 1/4 in. $35
Knife-modern, hollow handle, 9 1/8 in.........$34
Knife-youth, 6 7/8 in.........................$30
Spoon-baby, straight handle, 4 1/4 in. $40
Spoon-demitasse, 4 1/8 in. $20
Spoon-infant feeding, 5 1/2 in...............$34
Spoon-soup, round bowl, cream,
    6 1/2 in...................................$38
Spoon-sugar, 5 7/8 in........................$33
Spoon-teaspoon, 6 in........................$18
Tablespoon, (serving spoon), 8 1/2 in........$90
Tongs-sugar, 4 in. $70

Orleans by International, 1936

Butter-master, flat handle, 7 in. $26
Fork, 7 1/8 in. $25
Fork-cocktail, 5 3/8 in........................$22
Fork-ice cream, 5 3/4 in.....................$30
Fork-salad, individual, 6 1/8 in. $26
Knife-new french, hollow handle, 9 in. $30
Spoon-demitasse, 4 1/2 in...................$20
Spoon-dessert/oval soup, 7 3/8 in. $34
Spoon-place/oval soup, 6 3/4 in. $30
Spoon-soup, round bowl, gumbo, 7 1/8 in.....$57
Spoon-sugar, 5 7/8 in........................$22
Spoon-teaspoon, 6 1/8 in....................$16

Pansy by International, 1909

Fork, 7 1/2 in. $95
Fork, 7 in...................................$80
Fork-cold meat/serving, small, solid, gold
    wash, 7 1/8 in. $180
Knife-new french, hollow handle, 9 1/8 in. $90
Knife-old french, hollow handle, 8 3/4 in......$90
Knife-old french, hollow handle, 9 1/4 in. $90
Spoon-soup, round bowl, gumbo, 6 3/4 in.....$90
Spoon-teaspoon, 5 7/8 in....................$70
Tablespoon, (serving spoon), 8 in. $100

The following pieces have monograms:
Fork, 7 in...................................$60
Spoon-teaspoon, (five o'clock), 5 1/2 in......$30
Spoon-teaspoon, 5 7/8 in....................$53

Pantheon by International, 1920

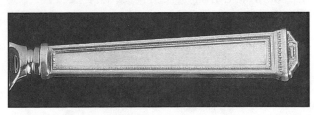

Pantheon by International, 1920

Butter spreader, flat handle, 5 5/8 in.........$30
Carving set, 2 pieces, small, stainless blade,
    steak.................................$150
Fork, 7 1/4 in...............................$40
Fork, 7 3/4 in...............................$60
Fork-salad, individual, 6 1/8 in...............$60
Knife-new french, hollow handle,
    9 3/4 in.................................$50
Knife-old french, hollow handle, 9 in.........$40
Knife-old french, hollow handle, silver plate
    blade, 9 7/8 in...........................$50
Knife-old french, hollow handle, stainless
    blade, 9 1/2 in...........................$50
Knife-orange, silver plate blade, 7 in.........$50
Knife-steak, individual, 8 1/4 in.............$53
Ladle-gravy, solid, 6 1/4 in. $100
Server-jelly, 6 3/8 in.......................$38
Spoon-casserole, smooth bowl, solid,
    7 5/8 in................................$120
Spoon-fruit, 5 7/8 in........................$40
Spoon-iced tea, 7 3/8 in. $48
Spoon-soup, round bowl, bouillon,
    5 1/2 in.................................$30
Spoon-soup, round bowl, gumbo, 7 1/8 in. $50
Spoon-teaspoon, (five o'clock),
    5 1/2 in.................................$20
Spoon-teaspoon, 6 in........................$30
Tablespoon, (serving spoon), 8 3/8 in.........$90

The following pieces have monograms:
Butter spreader, flat handle, 5 5/8 in..........$23
Carving set, 3 pieces, large, stainless blade,
    roast $220
Fork, 7 1/4 in...............................$30
Fork, 7 3/4 in...............................$42
Fork-cocktail, 5 5/8 in.......................$24
Fork-salad, individual, 6 1/8 in...............$45
Knife-new french, hollow handle,
    9 1/8 in.................................$30
Knife-new french, hollow handle,
    9 3/4 in.................................$38
Knife-old french, hollow handle, 9 7/8 in......$38
Knife-old french, hollow handle, 9 in.........$30
Knife-orange, silver plate blade, 7 in.........$38
Spoon-demitasse, 4 1/8 in. $19
Spoon-dessert/oval soup, 7 1/4 in...........$45
Spoon-fruit, 5 7/8 in........................$30
Spoon-iced tea, 7 3/8 in. $36
Spoon-soup, round bowl, gumbo,
    7 1/8 in.................................$38
Spoon-sugar, 5 7/8 in.......................$36
Spoon-teaspoon, 6 in........................$23
Tablespoon, (serving spoon), 8 3/8 in.........$70

Pine Spray by International, 1957

Butter spreader, hollow handle, modern, stainless
    paddle, not serrated, 6 3/8 in. $20
Butter spreader, hollow handle, modern,
    stainless paddle, serrated, 6 3/8 in. $20
Butter-master, hollow handle, 7 in. $35
Fork, 7 1/4 in. $35
Fork-salad, individual, 6 5/8 in. $33
Knife-modern, hollow handle, 9 1/4 in. $25
Ladle-gravy, solid, 6 1/4 in................. $90
Napkin clip, (made for teaspoons)........... $28
Spoon-demitasse, 4 1/8 in................. $30
Spoon-dessert/oval soup, 6 5/8 in. $40
Spoon-iced tea, 7 3/8 in.................... $50
Spoon-sugar, 6 in. $34
Spoon-teaspoon, (five o'clock), 5 1/2 in...... $22
Spoon-teaspoon, 6 in...................... $18
Tablespoon, (serving spoon), 8 1/2 in. $90
Tablespoon, (serving spoon), pierced, 3 tines,
    8 1/2 in................................ $100
Tablespoon, (serving spoon), pierced, no tines,
    8 1/2 in................................ $100

Pine Tree by International, 1927

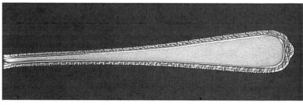

Butter spreader, flat handle, 5 5/8 in. $15
Carving set, 2 pieces, small, stainless blade,
    steak $120
Fork, 7 1/4 in. $20
Fork, 7 3/4 in. $40
Fork-baby, 4 1/4 in........................ $34
Fork-bird, silver plate, 3 prongs, individual,
    6 3/8 in................................ $50
Fork-carving, small, stainless prongs, steak,
    8 5/8 in................................ $60
Fork-cocktail, 5 1/2 in..................... $22
Fork-salad, individual, 6 1/8 in. $22
Knife-new french, hollow handle, 9 1/2 in. $45
Knife-new french, hollow handle, 9 1/8 in. $30
Ladle-gravy, solid, 6 1/4 in................. $80

Spoon-casserole, smooth bowl, solid,
   8 3/4 in.....................................$96
Spoon-demitasse, 4 in.....................$16
Spoon-fruit, 5 3/4 in.......................$34
Spoon-iced tea, 7 1/2 in. $34
Spoon-soup, round bowl, bouillon,
   5 5/8 in.....................................$20
Spoon-soup, round bowl, cream, 6 in........$26
Spoon-soup, round bowl, gumbo,
   7 1/4 in.....................................$40
Spoon-sugar, 5 7/8 in.....................$24
Spoon-teaspoon, (five o'clock), 5 in. $15
Spoon-teaspoon, 5 3/4 in. $16
Tablespoon, (serving spoon), 8 1/2 in........$50
Tablespoon, (serving spoon), pierced,
   8 1/2 in.....................................$70

The following pieces have monograms:
Butter spreader, flat handle, 5 5/8 in.........$10
Fork, 7 1/4 in................................$16
Fork-cold meat/serving, large, solid,
   9 1/8 in.....................................$64
Fork-ice cream, 5 1/2 in....................$30
Fork-salad, individual, 6 1/8 in...............$19
Knife-new french, hollow handle, 9 1/2 in......$35
Spoon-dessert/oval soup, 7 1/4 in...........$27
Spoon-fruit, 5 3/4 in.......................$28
Spoon-iced tea, 7 1/2 in. $27
Spoon-sugar, 5 7/8 in.....................$20
Spoon-teaspoon, 5 3/4 in. $14

Prelude by International, 1939

Baby set, 2 pieces..........................$60
Butter spreader, hollow handle, stainless
   paddle, 5 7/8 in...........................$30
Butter spreader, flat handle, 5 7/8 in.........$16
Butter-master, flat handle, 7 1/4 in...........$30
Carving set, 2 pieces, small, stainless blade,
   steak.....................................$90
Cheese grater, 9 3/8 in. $50
Cleaver-cheese, stainless blade, 6 1/2 in......$40
Fork, 7 1/4 in................................$20
Fork, 8 in...................................$50
Fork-baby, 4 1/4 in. $25
Fork-cake, individual, 6 1/2 in...............$50
Fork-carving, small, stainless prongs, steak,
   8 3/4 in...................................$45

Fork-carving, small, stainless prongs, steak,
   8 3/8 in................................... $45
Fork-cocktail, 5 5/8 in. $22
Fork-cold meat/serving, small, solid,
   7 3/4 in................................... $80
Fork-fish, stainless tines, hollow handle,
   individual, 8 3/8 in....................... $45
Fork-ice cream, 3 3/4 in. handle, 5 1/2 in. $40
Fork-ice cream, 4 in. handle, 5 3/4 in......... $40
Fork-lemon, 4 5/8 in. $30
Fork-pickle/olive, short handle, 5 7/8 in....... $30
Fork-salad server, plastic prongs,
   12 in....................................... $40
Fork-salad serving, solid, 3 tines,
   9 1/8 in................................... $120
Fork-salad serving, stainless prongs,
   4 tines not beveled, 11 5/8 in............. $45
Fork-salad, individual, 6 5/8 in. $36
Fork-strawberry, 4 5/8 in..................... $27
Fork-youth, 6 3/8 in......................... $30
Knife-bar, hollow handle, 9 1/4 in. $40
Knife-carving, small, stainless blade, steak,
   10 1/4 in.................................. $45
Knife-carving, small, stainless blade, steak,
   10 3/4 in.................................. $45
Knife-cheese, stainless blade, 6 7/8 in. $45
Knife-fish, stainless blade, individual,
   8 5/8 in................................... $40
Knife-fruit, stainless blade, individual,
   6 3/4 in................................... $45
Knife-modern, hollow handle, 4 1/2 in. handle,
   9 1/4 in................................... $30
Knife-modern, hollow handle, 5 1/8 in. blade,
   8 7/8 in................................... $30
Knife-new french, hollow handle, 9 1/2 in. $44
Knife-new french, hollow handle, 9 1/4 in. $25
Knife-new french, hollow handle, 9 in. $25
Knife-youth, 6 3/4 in. $32
Ladle-cream, solid, 4 in. $48
Ladle-cream, solid, 5 1/2 in................. $48
Ladle-gravy, hollow handle, stainless
   bowl, 8 3/8 in............................. $40
Ladle-gravy, solid, 6 1/2 in.................. $80
Ladle-punch, stainless bowl, 13 1/4 in........ $60
Ladle-soup, stainless bowl, 11 1/2 in........ $60
Napkin clip, (made for teaspoons),
   2 1/8 in................................... $25
Opener-bottle, stainless bowl, 6 1/2 in........ $40
Pick-butter, 1 tine, 5 5/8 in................. $30
Salad set, 2 pieces, solid, 9 1/8 in. $280
Salad set, 2 pieces, wooden bowl,
   10 5/8 in.................................. $90
Server/knife-fish, stainless blade, design in
   bowl, 11 3/4 in............................ $40

Server-asparagus, hollow handle, silver plate
hood $60
Server-asparagus, hollow handle, sterling
hood, 10 1/4 in. $330
Server-cheese, stainless blade, 6 1/4 in.. . . . . . .$45
Server-cranberry, stainless bowl, 8 7/8 in.. . . . .$40
Server-jelly, 5 1/8 in. $33
Server-jelly, 6 1/2 in. $33
Server-pasta, stainless bowl, 10 7/8 in. $45
Server-pie, stainless blade, 6 1/4 in. blade,
10 1/4 in. $44
Server-pie, stainless blade, 6 in. blade,
10 in. $44
Server-tomato, solid, 8 in. $110
Spoon-baby, straight handle, 4 3/8 in. $30
Spoon-bon-bon, 4 3/4 in. $40
Spoon-casserole, stainless shell bowl,
17 scallops, 10 3/8 in. $40
Spoon-demitasse, 4 1/8 in. $18
Spoon-dessert/oval soup, 6 7/8 in. $40
Spoon-dressing, stainless tear bowl,
11 3/8 in. $45
Spoon-iced tea, 7 3/8 in. $34
Spoon-infant feeding, 5 1/2 in.. . . . .$30
Spoon-salad serving, solid, 9 1/8 in. $130
Spoon-salad serving, stainless egg bowl,
11 5/8 in. $45
Spoon-salad serving, wooden bowl,
10 5/8 in. $44
Spoon-salad serving, wooden bowl, 11 in. $44
Spoon-salt, individual, 2 1/2 in. $13
Spoon-soup, round bowl, cream, 6 1/2 in.. . . . .$30
Spoon-soup, round bowl, gumbo, 7 1/4 in. $50
Spoon-sugar, 5 7/8 in.. . . . .$25
Spoon-teaspoon, (five o'clock), 5 3/4 in. $24
Spoon-teaspoon, 6 in.. . . . .$18
Spoon-utility/serving, stainless bowl, 7
scallops, 9 3/4 in. $45
Spoon-youth, 5 3/8 in.. . . . .$26
Tablespoon, (serving spoon), 8 1/2 in. $65
Tea strainer, 7 1/4 in.. . . . .$100
Tongs-sugar, 4 1/8 in. $45
Youth set, 3 pieces (spoon, knife, fork) $120

Primrose by International, 1936

Butter spreader, flat handle, 5 3/4 in. $25

Butter-master, flat handle, 7 1/4 in. $44
Fork, 7 3/4 in. $50
Fork-cocktail, 5 1/2 in. $34
Fork-grille (viand), 7 3/4 in. $50
Fork-salad, individual, 6 1/8 in. $44
Knife-grille, new french, hollow handle,
8 5/8 in. $38
Knife-new french, hollow handle,
8 5/8 in. $34
Knife-new french, hollow handle,
9 5/8 in. $50
Spoon-fruit, 5 7/8 in. $36
Spoon-iced tea, 7 3/8 in. $36
Spoon-soup, round bowl, gumbo,
7 1/8 in. $55
Spoon-sugar shell, 6 1/8 in. $46
Spoon-teaspoon, 5 7/8 in.. . . . . $28

Queen's Lace by International, 1949

Butter spreader, hollow handle, stainless
paddle, 5 7/8 in. $30
Butter spreader, flat handle, 5 7/8 in. $15
Butter-master, flat handle, 7 1/8 in. $35
Cleaver-cheese, stainless blade,
6 1/2 in. $45
Fork, 7 1/4 in. $30
Fork, 7 5/8 in. $56
Fork-baby, 4 1/4 in.. . . . . $40
Fork-carving, small, stainless prongs, steak,
9 in. $45
Fork-cocktail, 5 5/8 in. $30
Fork-cold meat/serving, large, 5 stainless
tines, 11 in. $40
Fork-cold meat/serving, large, solid,
9 1/8 in. $90
Fork-cold meat/serving, medium, solid,
8 in. $90
Fork-fish, stainless tines, hollow handle,
individual, 8 1/8 in.. . . . . $45
Fork-lemon, 4 3/4 in. $40
Fork-pickle/olive, short handle, 6 in. $40
Fork-salad serving, solid, 2 1/4 in. wide bowl,
9 1/8 in. $130
Fork-salad serving, stainless prongs, 4
tines not beveled, 11 1/4 in.. . . . . $40
Fork-salad serving, wooden prongs,
11 1/4 in. $40

Fork-salad, individual, 6 1/2 in. $40
Fork-youth, 6 3/8 in. $40
Knife-bar, hollow handle, 9 in. $45
Knife-carving, small, stainless blade, steak,
    10 1/2 in. $45
Knife-cheese, stainless blade, 7 1/8 in. $40
Knife-fish, stainless blade, individual,
    8 1/4 in.. . . . .$40
Knife-fruit, stainless blade, individual,
    6 3/8 in.. . . . .$45
Knife-modern, hollow handle, 9 1/2 in.. . . . .$44
Knife-modern, hollow handle, 9 1/8 in.. . . . .$40
Knife-steak, individual, bevel blade,
    8 1/2 in.. . . . .$45
Ladle-gravy, hollow handle, stainless bowl,
    7 7/8 in.. . . . .$40
Ladle-gravy, solid, 6 1/2 in. $90
Ladle-punch, stainless bowl, 13 1/4 in. $60
Ladle-soup, stainless bowl, 11 in.. . . . .$60
Napkin clip, (made for teaspoons) $25
Scoop-ice cream, stainless bowl,
    8 3/8 in.. . . . .$40
Scoop-ice, silver plate bowl, 8 5/8 in.. . . . .$45
Server/knife-fish, stainless blade, design
    in bowl, 11 3/8 in. $40
Server-cheese, stainless blade,
    6 1/8 in.. . . . .$40
Server-cranberry, stainless bowl,
    8 1/2 in.. . . . .$40
Server-jelly, 6 5/8 in. $40
Server-lasagna, stainless blade,
    9 3/4 in.. . . . .$40
Server-pasta, stainless bowl, 10 1/2 in.. . . . . . .$40
Server-pie and cake, stainless blade,
    10 3/4 in. $40
Server-pie, stainless blade, 10 5/8 in. $45
Spoon-demitasse, 4 1/8 in. $20
Spoon-dessert/oval soup, 6 7/8 in.. . . . .$50
Spoon-dressing, stainless tear bowl,
    11 in.. . . . .$45
Spoon-iced tea, 7 3/8 in. $38
Spoon-salad serving, stainless egg bowl,
    11 1/4 in. $45
Spoon-soup, round bowl, cream,
    6 1/2 in.. . . . .$28
Spoon-soup, round bowl, gumbo, 7 1/4 in. $44
Spoon-sugar, 5 7/8 in.. . . . .$28
Spoon-teaspoon, 6 in.. . . . .$20
Spoon-utility/serving, stainless bowl, 7 scallop,
    9 1/2 in.. . . . .$40
Tablespoon, (serving spoon), 8 1/2 in.. . . . .$80
Tablespoon, (serving spoon), pierced,
    8 1/2 in.. . . . .$95
Tongs-sugar, 4 1/8 in. $60

Radiant Rose by International, 1938

Butter spreader, flat handle, 5 5/8 in. $28
Butter-master, flat handle, 7 1/8 in. $35
Carving set, 2 pieces, small, stainless blade,
    steak $140
Fork, 7 1/8 in. $35
Fork, 7 3/4 in. $50
Fork-carving, small, stainless prongs, steak,
    9 in. $70
Fork-cocktail, 5 1/2 in. $30
Fork-cold meat/serving, medium, solid,
    8 5/8 in. $94
Fork-pickle/olive, short handle, 5 3/4 in. $35
Fork-salad, individual, 6 1/8 in. $45
Knife-modern, solid, 8 in. $40
Knife-new french, hollow handle, 9 1/2 in. $50
Ladle-cream, solid, 5 1/2 in. $53
Ladle-gravy, solid, 6 1/8 in. $90
Server-jelly, 5 in.. . . . . $38
Server-pie, stainless blade, 10 1/4 in.. . . . . $75
Spoon-bon-bon, 4 1/2 in. $46
Spoon-bon-bon, 4 3/4 in. $46
Spoon-iced tea, 7 1/2 in.. . . . . $40
Spoon-soup, round bowl, cream, 5 7/8 in. $40
Spoon-soup, round bowl, gumbo, 6 5/8 in.. . . . $70
Spoon-sugar, 5 7/8 in.. . . . . $38
Spoon-teaspoon, 6 in.. . . . . $26
Tablespoon, (serving spoon), 8 1/8 in. $90

Revere by International, 1898

Butter-master, flat handle, 7 1/4 in. $90
Fork, 6 1/2 in. $44
Fork, 7 1/2 in. $45
Fork-chipped beef, small, 5 tines, 6 in. $65
Fork-cocktail, 5 3/4 in. $33
Fork-cold meat/serving, medium, solid,
    8 5/8 in. $100
Fork-ice cream, 3 tines, 5 3/4 in. $60
Knife-blunt, hollow handle, 10 1/8 in. $56

Knife-blunt, hollow handle, 9 5/8 in. $56
Knife-breakfast, silver plate blade,
    8 1/8 in.. . . . .$60
Knife-old french, hollow handle, 10 in. $56
Ladle-gravy, solid, 7 1/8 in. $90
Spoon-demitasse, 4 3/4 in. $24
Spoon-demitasse, 4 in. $24
Spoon-dessert/oval soup, 6 7/8 in. $50
Spoon-ice cream, 5 3/4 in. $55
Spoon-soup, round bowl, bouillon,
    5 1/2 in.. . . . .$50
Spoon-soup, round bowl, cream, 6 5/8 in. $58
Spoon-sugar shell, 5 7/8 in. $44
Spoon-teaspoon, (five o'clock), 5 3/8 in. $22
Spoon-teaspoon, 5 5/8 in. $30
Tablespoon, (serving spoon), 8 in. $50
Tablespoon, (serving spoon), pierced,
    8 in.. . . . .$80

Rhapsody-New by International, 1957

Baby set, 2 pieces $60
Butter spreader, hollow handle, stainless paddle,
    notch blade, 6 1/2 in. $28
Butter-master, hollow handle, angle blade,
    7 in.. . . . .$30
Butter-master, hollow handle, taper blade,
    7 in.. . . . .$30
Fork, 7 1/4 in. $35
Fork-baby, 4 1/8 in. $30
Fork-cold meat/serving, large, 5 stainless
    tines, 11 3/8 in. $45
Fork-cold meat/serving, large, solid, 9 in. $90
Fork-fish, stainless tines, hollow handle,
    individual, 8 3/8 in. $40
Fork-lemon, 5 3/8 in. $24
Fork-salad serving, stainless prongs, 4
    tines not beveled, 11 3/8 in. $40
Fork-salad, individual, 6 1/2 in. $40
Knife-bar, hollow handle, 9 1/4 in. $40
Knife-cheese, stainless blade, 7 1/4 in. $40
Knife-fish, stainless blade, individual,
    8 3/4 ln. $40
Knife-fruit, stainless blade, individual,
    7 1/8 in.. . . . .$40
Knife-modern, hollow handle, 9 1/4 in. $28

Knife-modern, hollow handle, 9 3/4 in. $40
Knife-steak, individual, beveled blade,
    9 in. $45
Ladle-cream, solid, 5 1/2 in. $48
Ladle-gravy, solid, 6 1/4 in. $90
Ladle-soup, stainless bowl, 11 1/4 in. $50
Napkin clip, 2 in. $35
Scoop-ice, silver plate bowl, 9 in. $50
Server-cranberry, stainless bowl, 9 in. $45
Server-jelly, 6 1/2 in. $36
Server-pie and cake, stainless 6 1/4 in. blade,
    10 3/4 in.. . . . . $45
Server-tomato, solid, 7 7/8 in. $90
Slicer-cake, stainless blade, wedding,
    12 7/8 in.. . . . . $45
Spoon-baby, straight handle, 4 1/4 in. $30
Spoon-bon-bon, not pierced, 4 7/8 in. $40
Spoon-casserole, pierced, stainless bowl,
    7 scallops, 9 7/8 in. $40
Spoon-casserole, shell bowl, solid, 9 in.. . . . . . $120
Spoon-casserole, stainless shell bowl,
    17 scallops, 10 1/2 in. $40
Spoon-demitasse, 4 1/8 in. $20
Spoon-dessert/oval soup, 6 5/8 in. $44
Spoon-dressing, stainless tear bowl,
    11 3/8 in.. . . . . $40
Spoon-iced tea, 7 1/4 in. $42
Spoon-infant feeding, 5 1/2 in. $25
Spoon-salad serving, stainless egg bowl,
    11 3/4 in.. . . . . $45
Spoon-sugar shell, 6 in. $30
Spoon-teaspoon, 6 1/8 in.. . . . . $24
Spoon-utility/serving, stainless bowl, 7 scallops,
    9 7/8 in. $40
Sugar sifter, 3 pierce, 6 in. $25
Tablespoon, (serving spoon), 8 in. $80
Tablespoon, (serving spoon), pierced,
    8 in. $90
Tongs-sugar, 5 in. $40

Rhapsody-Old by International, 1931

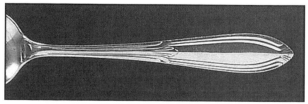

Butter spreader, flat handle, 5 3/4 in. $18
Butter-master, flat handle, 6 3/4 in. $40
Carving set, 2 pieces, small, stainless blade,
    steak $100
Fork, 7 1/2 in. $60

Fork, 7 in.............................. $34
Fork-cocktail, 3 tines, 5 1/2 in.............. $24
Fork-cold meat/serving, medium, solid,
   8 1/4 in................................ $90
Fork-ice cream, 5 1/2 in..................... $30
Fork-ice cream, 5 1/8 in..................... $30
Fork-pickle/olive, short handle, 3 tines,
   6 in................................ $32
Fork-salad, individual, 6 1/8 in.............. $36
Knife-new french, hollow handle,
   9 1/8 in................................ $30
Knife-new french, hollow handle, 9 5/8 in...... $46
Ladle-gravy, solid, 6 1/2 in. $80
Server-jelly, 6 1/2 in....................... $30
Server-pie, stainless blade, 9 1/2 in. $60
Server-tomato, solid, 7 1/2 in............... $90
Spoon-dessert/oval soup, 7 1/4 in........... $50
Spoon-soup, round bowl, bouillon,
   5 3/4 in................................ $26
Spoon-soup, round bowl, cream,
   6 1/4 in................................ $50
Spoon-soup, round bowl, gumbo,
   7 1/4 in................................ $50
Spoon-sugar, 6 in......................... $30
Spoon-teaspoon, 6 in....................... $18
Tablespoon, (serving spoon), 8 3/8 in........ $70
Tablespoon, (serving spoon), pierced,
   8 3/8 in................................ $80

Richelieu by International, 1935

Butter spreader, hollow handle, stainless paddle,
   5 7/8 in................................ $30
Butter spreader, flat handle, 6 in. $28
Butter-master, flat handle, 7 3/8 in........... $50
Fork, 7 1/4 in.............................. $50
Fork-carving, large, stainless prongs, roast,
   11 1/8 in. $105
Fork-cocktail, 5 1/2 in...................... $34
Fork-salad, individual, 6 5/8 in.............. $45
Knife-modern, hollow handle, 8 3/4 in........ $42
Ladle-gravy, solid, 6 1/2 in. $130
Spoon-iced tea, 7 1/4 in. $40
Spoon-soup, round bowl, cream, 6 1/2 in...... $53
Spoon-sugar, 5 7/8 in....................... $45
Spoon-teaspoon, 6 in....................... $25
Tablespoon, (serving spoon), 8 1/2 in........ $110

Riviera by International, 1936

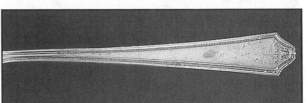

Butter spreader, flat handle, 5 3/4 in. $26
Fork, 7 1/4 in. $30
Fork, 7 7/8 in. $45
Fork-cocktail, 5 1/2 in. $23
Knife-modern, hollow handle, 8 1/2 in........ $28
Knife-new french, hollow handle, 9 1/4 in. $30
Knife-new french, hollow handle, 9 5/8 in. $35
Spoon-iced tea, 7 1/2 in.................... $36
Spoon-soup, round bowl, bouillon,
   5 1/2 in................................ $26
Spoon-soup, round bowl, cream, 6 3/8 in. $28
Spoon-soup, round bowl, gumbo, 7 1/8 in..... $40
Spoon-teaspoon, 5 7/8 in.................... $17

Rosalind-New by International, 1921

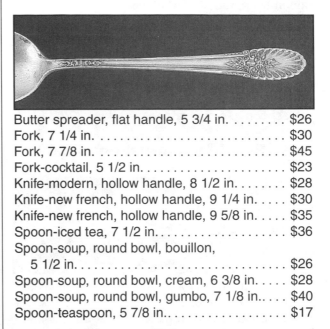

Butter spreader, flat handle, 5 3/8 in. $15
Butter-master, flat handle, 7 1/4 in........... $34
Fork, 7 1/4 in. $32
Fork, 7 5/8 in. $40
Fork-cocktail, 5 3/8 in...................... $22
Fork-cold meat, serving, small, solid,
   7 1/4 in................................ $65
Fork-ice cream, 5 1/2 in.................... $37
Fork-salad, individual, 6 1/8 in. $30
Knife-new french, hollow handle, 8 5/8 in. $26
Knife-new french, hollow handle, 9 1/2 in. $36
Knife-old french, hollow handle, 9 3/4 in. $36
Knife-youth, 7 in.......................... $36
Ladle-cream, solid, 5 5/8 in................ $45
Ladle-gravy, solid, 6 1/4 in................. $69
Ladle-gravy, solid, 6 5/8 in................. $69
Server-cheese, stainless blade, 6 1/4 in. $45
Server-jelly, 6 3/8 in. $32
Spoon-casserole, smooth bowl, solid,
   8 7/8 in................................ $90
Spoon-demitasse, 4 in...................... $15
Spoon-dessert/oval soup, 7 in............... $34
Spoon-fruit, 5 3/4 in. $28

International Silver

Spoon-iced tea, 7 3/8 in. $26
Spoon-soup, round bowl, bouillon,
   5 3/8 in. $25
Spoon-soup, round bowl, gumbo, 7 in. $40
Spoon-sugar, 5 7/8 in. $30
Spoon-teaspoon, (five o'clock), 5 3/8 in. $15
Spoon-teaspoon, 5 3/4 in. $20
Spoon-teaspoon, 6 in. $20
Tablespoon, (serving spoon), 8 1/4 in. $55

Rose Ballet by International, 1962

Butter spreader, hollow handle, modern, stainless
   paddle, no stamp, 6 1/4 in. $24
Butter spreader, hollow handle, modern, stainless
   paddle, point blade, 6 1/4 in. $24
Butter-master, hollow handle, 7 in. $26
Fork, 7 1/4 in. $30
Fork-cold meat/serving, medium, solid,
   8 5/8 in. $90
Fork-salad, individual, 6 3/4 in. $40
Knife-modern, hollow handle, 9 1/4 in. $25
Napkin clip (made for teaspoons) $20
Spoon-dessert/oval soup, 6 7/8 in. $46
Spoon-sugar, 6 in. $28
Spoon-teaspoon, 6 in. $15
Tablespoon, (serving spoon), 8 1/2 in. $70

Royal Danish by International, 1939

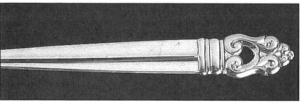

Butter spreader, hollow handle, solid paddle,
   insert blade, 6 in. $22
Butter-master, flat handle, 7 1/8 in. $40
Butter-master, hollow handle, 7 in. $40
Carving set, 2 pieces, small, stainless blade,
   steak $90
Cleaver-cheese, stainless blade, 6 1/2 in. $40
Food pusher, 3 3/4 in. $44
Fork, 7 1/4 in. $38
Fork, 7 3/4 in. $70
Fork-baby, 4 1/4 in. $35

Fork-carving, small, stainless prongs, steak,
   9 5/8 in. $45
Fork-carving, small, stainless prongs, steak,
   9 in. $45
Fork-cocktail, no notch, 5 5/8 in. $26
Fork-cold meat/serving, small, solid,
   7 3/4 in. $80
Fork-cold meat/serving, large, 5 stainless tines,
   11 1/8 in. $45
Fork-cold meat/serving, medium, solid,
   8 7/8 in. $90
Fork-fish, stainless tines, hollow handle,
   individual, 8 1/2 in. $45
Fork-ice cream, 5 1/2 in. $44
Fork-lemon, 4 3/4 in. $34
Fork-pickle/olive, short handle, 3 beveled tines,
   5 7/8 in. $30
Fork-salad serving, solid, 9 1/8 in. $130
Fork-salad serving, stainless prongs, 4 tines
   not beveled, 11 1/2 in. $45
Fork-salad, individual, 3 tines, no bevel,
   6 3/8 in. $42
Fork-strawberry, 5 in. $35
Fork-youth, 4 tines, not beveled, 6 1/4 in. $40
Knife-bar, hollow handle, 9 3/8 in. $40
Knife-carving, small, stainless blade, steak,
   10 1/2 in. $45
Knife-fish, stainless blade, individual,
   8 5/8 In. $45
Knife-fruit, stainless blade, individual,
   6 7/8 in. $45
Knife-modern, hollow handle, 3 3/4 in. handle,
   8 7/8 in. $33
Knife-modern, hollow handle, stainless blade,
   9 3/4 in. $50
Knife-new french, hollow handle, stainless
   blade, 9 1/2 in. $50
Knife-steak, individual, beveled blade,
   8 7/8 in. $45
Knife-steak, individual, not beveled,
   8 1/4 in. $45
Knife-youth, 7 in. $46
Ladle-cream, solid, 5 1/2 in. $45
Ladle-gravy, hollow handle, stainless bowl,
   8 1/4 in. $45
Ladle-gravy, solid, 6 1/2 in. $90
Ladle-punch, stainless bowl, 13 in. $60
Ladle-soup, stainless bowl, 11 3/8 in. $55
Napkin clip, (made for teaspoons) $24
Opener-bottle, stainless bowl, 6 1/2 in. $40
Salad set, 2 pieces, solid, 9 1/8 in. $310
Scoop-ice cream, stainless bowl,
   8 5/8 in. $45
Scoop-ice, silver plate bowl, 8 3/4 in. $45

International Silver

Server/knife-fish, stainless blade, design
in bowl, 11 3/4 in. $45
Server-asparagus, hollow handle, silver
plate hood, 9 3/4 in. $60
Server-cranberry, stainless bowl, 9 in. $45
Server-jelly, 6 1/2 in. $34
Server-lasagna, stainless blade, 10 in. $45
Server-pasta, stainless bowl, 10 7/8 in. $45
Server-pie and cake, stainless blade,
11 1/4 in. $45
Server-pie, stainless blade, 10 3/8 in. $45
Server-tomato, solid, 7 3/4 in. $100
Spoon-baby, straight handle, 4 3/8 in. $35
Spoon-bon-bon, 4 7/8 in. $42
Spoon-casserole, pierced bowl, stainless
bowl, 7 scallops, 9 3/4 in. $45
Spoon-casserole, stainless shell bowl, 17
scallops, 10 1/2 in. $45
Spoon-casserole, smooth, solid, 9 1/4 in. $140
Spoon-demitasse, 4 1/4 in. $25
Spoon-dessert/oval soup, 6 7/8 in. $45
Spoon-dressing, stainless tear bowl,
11 3/8 in. $45
Spoon-fruit, no rim, 6 in. $40
Spoon-fruit, rim bowl, 6 in. $40
Spoon-iced tea, tear bowl, 7 3/8 in. $35
Spoon-infant feeding, 5 5/8 in. $35
Spoon-salad serving, stainless egg bowl,
11 1/2 in. $45
Spoon-salt, individual, 2 3/8 in. $13
Spoon-soup, round bowl, cream, 6 1/2 in. $40
Spoon-sugar, 6 in. $36
Spoon-teaspoon, 6 in. $20
Spoon-utility/serving, stainless bowl, 7
scallops, 9 3/4 in. $45
Tablespoon, (serving spoon), 8 1/2 in. $75
Tablespoon, (serving spoon), pierced,
8 1/2 in. $90
Tongs-sugar, 4 in. $45

Royal Rose by International, 1938

Butter spreader, flat handle, 5 3/4 in. $20
Butter-master, flat handle, 6 7/8 in. $26
Fork, 7 1/8 in. $34
Fork-ice cream, 5 3/4 in. $40
Fork-salad, individual, 6 in. $44
Knife-new french, hollow handle, 9 in. $30
Spoon-dessert/oval soup, tear bowl,
7 1/4 in. $34
Spoon-place/oval soup, oval bowl,
6 5/8 in. $32
Spoon-soup, round bowl, gumbo, 7 in. $60
Spoon-sugar, 6 in. $26

Spoon-teaspoon, 6 in. $18
Tablespoon, (serving spoon), 8 1/2 in. $90

Sculptured Beauty by International, 1957

Butter-master, hollow handle, 7 in. . . . .$30.
Fork, 7 1/4 in. $28
Fork-cocktail, 5 5/8 in. $18
Fork-salad/individual, 6 1/2 in. $27
Knife-modern, hollow handle, 9 1/4 in. $28
Spoon-dessert/oval soup, 6 7/8 in. $30
Spoon-iced tea, 7 3/8 in. $28
Spoon-sugar, 6 in. $30
Spoon-teaspoon, 6 1/8 in. $18
Tablespoon, (serving spoon), 8 1/2 in. $60

Serenity by International, 1940

Butter spreader, flat handle, 5 3/4 in. $12
Butter spreader, hollow handle, stainless
paddle, 6 in. $20
Butter-master, flat handle, 7 1/4 in. $30
Fork, 7 1/4 in. $18
Fork, 7 3/4 in. $45
Fork-baby, 4 1/4 in. $30
Fork-carving, large, stainless prongs, roast,
11 in. $60
Fork-cocktail, 5 5/8 in. $18
Fork-cold meat/serving, large, solid,
9 1/8 in. $75
Fork-lemon, 4 3/4 in. $25
Fork-salad/individual, 6 1/2 in. $24
Knife-modern, hollow handle, 9 1/8 in. $30
Knife-new french, hollow handle, 9 1/8 in. $33
Knife-new french, hollow handle, 9 5/8 in. $42
Knife-youth, 6 7/8 in. $40
Ladle-cream, solid, 4 1/4 in. $40
Ladle-cream, solid, 5 1/2 in. $40
Ladle-gravy, solid, 6 3/8 in. $70

Napkin clip, (made for cream soup
  spoons)...................................$20
Salad set, 2 pieces, wooden bowl............$70
Server-cheese, stainless blade, 6 1/4 in.......$40
Server-jelly, 5 in. $22
Server-jelly, 6 5/8 in. $22
Spoon-bon-bon, 4 3/4 in. $40
Spoon-demitasse, 4 1/4 in. $20
Spoon-dessert/oval soup, 6 7/8 in...........$45
Spoon-iced tea, 7 3/8 in. $25
Spoon-soup, round bowl (cream),
  6 1/2 in..................................$18
Spoon-sugar, 5 7/8 in.......................$22
Spoon-teaspoon, 6 in.......................$14
Tablespoon, (serving spoon), 8 1/2 in.........$60
Tablespoon, (serving spoon), pierced,
  8 1/2 in.................................$80
Tongs-sugar, 4 1/8 in. $60

Shirley by International, 1910

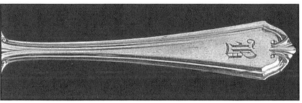

Butter spreader, flat handle, 6 in. $22
Fork, 7 in.................................$32
Fork-chipped beef, small, 6 1/8 in............$60
Fork-cocktail, 5 5/8 in.......................$24
Fork-dessert, 3 tines, 6 1/2 in................$40
Fork-pickle/olive, short handle, 5 3/4 in. $25
Fork-salad, individual, 6 3/8 in. $34
Fork-strawberry, 4 5/8 in. $26
Knife-new french, hollow handle,
  9 3/4 in.................................$40
Knife-old french, hollow handle,
  9 7/8 in.................................$40
Ladle-cream, solid, 5 1/4 in..................$38
Ladle-gravy, solid, gold wash, 5 5/8 in. $70
Server-cheese, silver plate blade,
  6 1/4 in.................................$50
Server-tomato, solid, 7 1/4 in. $80
Spoon-demitasse, 3 7/8 in. $18
Spoon-demitasse, 4 3/8 in. $18
Spoon-fruit, 5 3/4 in. $28
Spoon-iced tea, 6 3/8 in. $34
Spoon-olive, long handle, 7 7/8 in..........$120
Spoon-soup, round bowl (bouillon),
  5 1/8 in.................................$24
Spoon-teaspoon (five o'clock), 5 5/8 in........$13
Spoon-youth, 5 1/4 in......................$28

Silver Iris by International, 1955

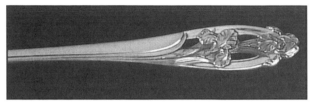

Note: Not all pieces in this pattern have pierced
  handles

Butter spreader, hollow handle, modern, stainless
  paddle, 6 1/4 in........................$34
Butter-master, hollow handle, 7 in. $35
Cleaver-cheese, stainless blade, 7 in. $40
Fork, 7 1/4 in. $45
Fork-carving, small, stainless prongs, steak,
  9 3/4 in...............................$45
Fork-cold meat/serving, large, 5 stainless
  tines, 11 1/4 in.......................$45
Fork-cold meat/serving, large, solid,
  9 1/4 in...............................$110
Fork-fish, stainless tines, hollow handle,
  individual, 8 3/8 in....................$40
Fork-salad serving, 4 stainless prongs, not
  beveled, 11 1/2 in.....................$40
Fork-salad, individual, 6 1/2 in. $50
Knife-carving, small, stainless blade, steak,
  10 3/4 in..............................$45
Knife-fish, stainless blade, individual,
  8 5/8 in...............................$45
Knife-fruit, stainless blade, individual,
  6 3/4 in...............................$45
Knife-modern, hollow handle, 9 1/4 in........$42
Knife-modern, hollow handle, 9 1/4 in........$42
Knife-steak, individual, 9 1/8 in.............$40
Ladle-gravy, hollow handle, stainless bowl,
  8 1/2 in...............................$45
Ladle-punch, stainless bowl, 13 ....$60
Opener-bottle, stainless bowl, 6 1/2 in........$45
Scoop-ice cream, stainless bowl,
  8 3/4 in...............................$45
Server/knife-fish, stainless blade, design on
  bowl, 11 3/4 in........................$45
Server-cheese, stainless blade, 7 1/8 in. $45
Server-lasagna, stainless blade, 10 in........$45
Server-pasta, stainless bowl, 11 1/8 in. $45
Server-pie and cake, stainless blade,
  11 1/4 in..............................$40
Slicer-cake, stainless blade, wedding,
  12 7/8 in..............................$45
Spoon-casserole, pierced stainless bowl,
  7 scallops, 9 3/4 in....................$40

Spoon-casserole, shell, stainless bowl,
17 scallops, 10 3/8 in. $40
Spoon-dessert/oval soup, 6 7/8 in. $45
Spoon-dressing, stainless tear bowl,
11 3/8 in. $45
Spoon-iced tea, 7 3/8 in. $40
Spoon-salad serving, stainless egg bowl,
11 1/2 in. $40
Spoon-sugar, 6 1/8 in. $40
Spoon-teaspoon, 6 in. $27
Spoon-utility/serving-stainless bowl, 7
scallops, 9 3/4 in. $40
Tablespoon, (serving spoon), 8 1/2 in. $100
Tablespoon, (serving spoon), pierced,
8 1/2 in. $90
Tongs-sugar, 5 . . . .$45

Silver Melody by International, 1955

Butter spreader, hollow handle, modern, stainless,
6 1/4 in. $22
Fork, 7 1/4 in. $32
Fork-cocktail, 5 5/8 in. $40
Fork-salad, individual, 6 1/2 in. $40
Knife-modern, hollow handle, 9 1/4 in. $34
Ladle-gravy, solid, 6 1/4 in. $90
Napkin clip, (made for teaspoons) $24
Spoon-dessert/oval soup, 6 7/8 in. $40
Spoon-sugar, 5 7/8 in. $30
Spoon-teaspoon, 6 in. $20
Tablespoon, (serving spoon), 8 1/2 in. $90
Tablespoon, (serving spoon), pierced,
8 1/2 in. $90

Silver Rhythm by International, 1953

Butter spreader, hollow handle, modern,
stainless paddle, 6 1/4 in. $16
Butter-master, hollow handle, 7 in. $24
Carving set, two pieces, small, stainless
blade, steak $120

Fork, 7 1/4 in. $30
Fork-cocktail, 5 5/8 in. $26
Fork-cold meat/serving, large, solid, 9 in. $80
Fork-joint/roast holder, large, 9 in. $90
Fork-pickle/olive, short handle, flared tines,
5 7/8 in. $22
Fork-salad, individual, 6 1/2 in. $37
Knife-modern, hollow handle, 9 1/4 in. $36
Ladle-cream, solid, 5 in. $40
Ladle-gravy, solid, 5 7/8 in. $60
Napkin clip, (made for sugar) $25
Salad set, 2 pieces, solid $170
Server-cheese, stainless blade, 7 1/8 in. $38
Server-jelly, 6 5/8 in. $28
Server-pie, stainless blade, 10 5/8 in. $50
Spoon-demitasse, 4 1/4 in. $30
Spoon-dessert/oval soup, 6 7/8 in. $34
Spoon-iced tea, 7 3/8 in. $38
Spoon-infant feeding, 5 5/8 in. $40
Spoon-sugar, 5 3/4 in. $20
Spoon-teaspoon, 6 in. $18
Tablespoon, (serving spoon), 8 1/2 in. $64
Tablespoon, (serving spoon), pierced,
8 1/2 in. $74

Sonja by International, 1937

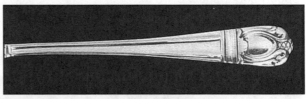

Butter spreader, flat handle, 5 5/8 in. $22
Butter-master, flat handle, 7 1/8 in. $34
Carving set, 2 pieces, small, stainless blade,
steak $130
Fork, 7 3/4 in. $57
Fork, 7 in. $35
Fork-cocktail, 5 1/2 in. $22
Fork-cold meat/serving, medium, solid,
8 1/2 in. $90
Fork-ice cream, 5 3/4 in. $44
Fork-salad, individual, 6 1/8 in. $35
Knife-carving, small, stainless blade,
steak $65
Knife-modern, hollow handle, 8 1/2 in. $34
Knife-new french, hollow handle, 8 3/4 in. $34
Knife-new french, hollow handle, 9 1/2 in. $45
Knife-new french, hollow handle, 9 1/8 in. $34
Ladle-gravy, solid, 6 1/4 in. $80
Server-jelly, 4 7/8 in. $35
Spoon-casserole, smooth bowl, solid,
8 1/4 in. $100

Spoon-dessert/oval soup, 6 7/8 in. $50
Spoon-iced tea, 7 1/2 in. $33
Spoon-soup, round bowl, cream,
    5 7/8 in. $34
Spoon-soup, round bowl, gumbo, 6 5/8 in. $57
Spoon-sugar, 5 3/4 in. $35
Spoon-teaspoon, 5 7/8 in. $18
Tablespoon, (serving spoon), 8 in. $80

Southern Treasure by International, 1953

Brush-lip, 5 1/2 in. $40
Butter spreader, flat handle, 5 7/8 in. $22
Butter-master, flat handle, 7 1/4 in. $36
Fork, 7 1/4 in. $50
Fork-cocktail, 5 5/8 in. $28
Fork-cold meat/serving, large, solid,
    9 1/8 in. $85
Fork-ice cream, 5 3/4 in. $46
Knife-modern, hollow handle, 9 1/4 in. $33
Knife-steak, individual, 8 1/8 in. $50
Knife-steak, individual, 9 in. $50
Ladle-gravy, solid, 6 1/2 in. $85
Spoon-iced tea, 7 3/8 in. $36
Spoon-soup, round bowl, cream, 6 5/8 in. $50
Spoon-sugar shell, 6 1/8 in. $38
Spoon-teaspoon, 6 in. $22

Splendor by International, 1939

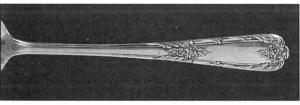

Butter spreader, flat handle, 5 5/8 in. $17
Butter-master, flat handle, 7 1/8 in. $26
Carving set, 2 pieces, small, stainless blade,
    steak $120
Fork, 7 1/8 in. $28
Fork, 7 3/4 in. $50
Fork-cocktail, 5 1/2 in. $23
Fork-cold meat/serving, medium, solid,
    8 3/4 in. $65
Fork-ice cream, 5 5/8 in. $38
Fork-lemon, 4 3/4 in. $28
Fork-salad, individual, 6 1/8 in. $34
Knife-carving, small, stainless blade, steak,
    10 1/4 in. $60
Knife-new french, hollow handle, 8 3/4 in. $34
Knife-new french, hollow handle, 9 5/8 in. $50

Knife-new french, hollow handle, silver plate
    blade, 8 3/4 in. $34
Knife-new french, hollow handle, stainless
    blade, 9 1/4 in. $34
Ladle-gravy, solid, 6 1/4 in. $60
Spoon-casserole, smooth, solid, 8 1/4 in. . . . $100
Spoon-dessert/oval soup, 6 7/8 in. $40
Spoon-iced tea, 7 1/2 in. $33
Spoon-soup, round bowl, cream, 5 7/8 in. $30
Spoon-soup, round bowl, gumbo, 6 7/8 in. $45
Spoon-sugar, 5 7/8 in. $26
Spoon-teaspoon, 5 7/8 in. $20
Tablespoon, (serving spoon), 8 1/8 in. $65
Tablespoon, (serving spoon), pierced,
    8 1/8 in. $85

Spring Bouquet by International, 1940

Butter spreader, flat handle, 5 5/8 in. $20
Butter-master, flat handle, 6 7/8 in. $35
Fork, 7 1/4 in. $28
Fork, 7 7/8 in. $45
Fork-cocktail, 5 3/8 in. $18
Fork-ice cream, 5 3/4 in. $36
Fork-salad, individual, 6 1/2 in. $43
Knife-modern, hollow handle, 8 7/8 in. $30
Knife-new french, hollow handle, 9 1/2 in. $40
Knife-new french, hollow handle, 9 1/4 in. $30
Spoon-dessert/oval soup, 6 7/8 in. $46
Spoon-fruit, 5 7/8 in. $40
Spoon-iced tea, 7 3/8 in. $28
Spoon-soup, round bowl, bouillon,
    5 5/8 in. $26
Spoon-soup, round bowl, cream, 6 1/2 in. $28
Spoon-soup, round bowl, gumbo, 7 1/4 in. $45
Spoon-teaspoon, 6 1/8 in. $15

Spring Glory by International, 1942

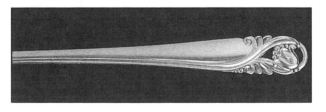

Butter spreader, flat handle, 5 3/4 in.........$15
Butter spreader, hollow handle, stainless
    paddle, 5 7/8 in.........................$24
Butter-master, flat handle, 7 1/8 in............$32
Carving set, 2 pieces, small, stainless blade,
    steak..................................$100
Fork, 7 1/4 in..............................$22
Fork, 7 3/4 in..............................$50
Fork-baby, 4 1/8 in.........................$30
Fork-cocktail, 5 5/8 in.......................$20
Fork-cold meat/serving, large, solid,
    9 1/8 in................................$90
Fork-salad, individual, 6 1/2 in...............$33
Fork-youth, 6 3/8 in........................$46
Knife-carving, small stainless blade, steak,
    10 1/2 in...............................$50
Knife-modern, hollow handle, 9 1/2 in........$50
Knife-modern, hollow handle, 9 1/4 in........$38
Knife-new french, hollow handle,
    9 1/2 in.................................$50
Ladle-gravy, solid, 6 3/8 in.................$70
Napkin clip, (made for teaspoons)..........$28
Napkin ring, (made for teaspoon),
    1 1/2 in................................$24
Server-jelly, 6 1/2 in........................$32
Spoon-bon-bon, 4 3/4 in....................$40
Spoon-demitasse, 4 1/4 in..................$20
Spoon-dessert/oval soup, 6 7/8 in..........$40
Spoon-five o'clock/youth, 5 3/4 in..........$22
Spoon-iced tea, 7 3/8 in....................$34
Spoon-soup, round bowl, cream, 6 1/2 in.....$25
Spoon-sugar, 5 7/8 in......................$28
Spoon-teaspoon, 6 in.......................$14
Tablespoon, (serving spoon), 8 1/2 in........$60
Tablespoon, (serving spoon), pierced,
    8 1/2 in................................$80

Springtime by International, 1935

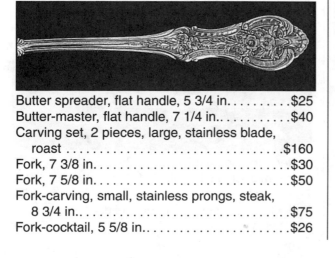

Butter spreader, flat handle, 5 3/4 in.........$25
Butter-master, flat handle, 7 1/4 in...........$40
Carving set, 2 pieces, large, stainless blade,
    roast..................................$160
Fork, 7 3/8 in..............................$30
Fork, 7 5/8 in..............................$50
Fork-carving, small, stainless prongs, steak,
    8 3/4 in................................$75
Fork-cocktail, 5 5/8 in.......................$26

Fork-cold meat/serving, medium, solid,
    8 3/4 in................................$90
Fork-cold meat/serving, small, solid,
    7 5/8 in................................$90
Fork-salad, individual, 6 1/8 in...............$40
Knife-grille, new french, hollow handle,
    8 5/8 in................................$40
Knife-new french, hollow handle, 8 5/8 in.....$40
Knife-new french, hollow handle, 9 1/2 in.....$53
Ladle-gravy, solid, 6 1/8 in.................$94
Napkin clip, (made for teaspoons)..........$25
Server-pie, stainless blade, 10 1/4 in.........$70
Spoon-soup, round bowl, cream, 6 in........$40
Spoon-soup, round bowl, gumbo, 7 in........$70
Spoon-teaspoon, 5 7/8 in...................$18
Tablespoon, (serving spoon), 8 3/8 in........$90

Stardust by International, 1937

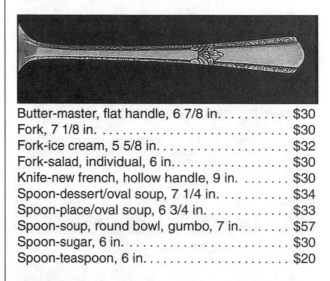

Butter-master, flat handle, 6 7/8 in..........$30
Fork, 7 1/8 in..............................$30
Fork-ice cream, 5 5/8 in....................$32
Fork-salad, individual, 6 in.................$30
Knife-new french, hollow handle, 9 in........$30
Spoon-dessert/oval soup, 7 1/4 in..........$34
Spoon-place/oval soup, 6 3/4 in............$33
Spoon-soup, round bowl, gumbo, 7 in........$57
Spoon-sugar, 6 in..........................$30
Spoon-teaspoon, 6 in.......................$20

Stratford by International, 1902

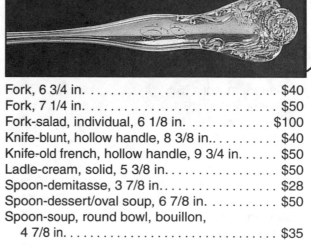

Fork, 6 3/4 in..............................$40
Fork, 7 1/4 in..............................$50
Fork-salad, individual, 6 1/8 in..............$100
Knife-blunt, hollow handle, 8 3/8 in..........$40
Knife-old french, hollow handle, 9 3/4 in......$50
Ladle-cream, solid, 5 3/8 in.................$50
Spoon-demitasse, 3 7/8 in..................$28
Spoon-dessert/oval soup, 6 7/8 in..........$50
Spoon-soup, round bowl, bouillon,
    4 7/8 in................................$35

Spoon-sugar, 6 1/8 in. $40
Spoon-teaspoon (five o'clock), 5 in. $28
Spoon-teaspoon, 5 3/4 in. $24
Tablespoon, (serving spoon), 7 3/4 in. $70
Tablespoon, (serving spoon), pierced,
    7 3/4 in. $90
Tongs-sugar, 4 5/8 in. $70

Swan Lake by International, 1960

Butter-master, hollow handle, 7 in. $34
Fork, 7 1/4 in. $34
Fork-salad, individual, 6 5/8 in. $46
Knife-modern, hollow handle, 9 in. $34
Ladle-gravy, solid, 6 in. $90
Napkin clip, (made for teaspoons) $25
Spoon-sugar, 6 in. $34

Theseum by International, 1922

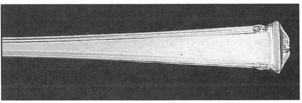

Butter-master, flat handle, 7 1/4 in. $40
Fork, 7 1/4 in. $33
Fork, 7 3/4 in. $40
Fork-cocktail, 5 3/8 in. $25
Fork-ice cream, 5 1/2 in. $50
Fork-salad, individual, 6 1/4 in. $32
Knife-new french, hollow handle,
    8 7/8 in. $30
Knife-new french, hollow handle, 9 1/2 in. $45
Knife-old french, hollow handle, 10 in. $45
Knife-old french, hollow handle, 9 in. $30
Ladle-cream, solid, 5 5/8 in. $48
Ladle-gravy, solid, 6 1/8 in. $90
Ladle-mayonnaise, 5 3/8 in. $48
Server-jelly, 6 3/8 in. $35
Spoon-casserole, smooth bowl, solid,
    8 5/8 in. $104
Spoon-demitasse, 4 1/8 in. $20
Spoon-dessert/oval soup, 7 1/4 in. $50
Spoon-fruit, 6 in. $38
Spoon-iced tea, 7 3/8 in. $38

Spoon-soup, round bowl, bouillon,
    5 1/2 in. $28
Spoon-soup, round bowl, cream, 6 in. $46
Spoon-soup, round bowl, gumbo,
    7 1/8 in. $46
Spoon-sugar, 5 5/8 in. $38
Spoon-teaspoon (five o'clock), 5 5/8 in. $12
Spoon-teaspoon, 6 in. $20
Spoon-youth, 5 1/8 in. $36
Tablespoon, (serving spoon), 8 3/8 in. $75

The following pieces have monograms:
Butter spreader, flat handle, 5 5/8 in. $18
Butter-master, flat handle, 7 1/4 in. $30
Fork, 7 1/4 in. $26
Fork, 7 3/4 in. $33
Fork-cocktail, 5 3/8 in. $18
Fork-cold meat/serving, small, solid,
    7 3/4 in. $60
Fork-salad, individual, 6 1/4 in. $26
Knife-new french, hollow handle,
    8 7/8 in. $22
Knife-old french, hollow handle, 10 in. $34
Knife-old french, hollow handle, 9 in. $23
Ladle-gravy, solid, 6 1/8 in. $70
Server-jelly, 6 3/8 in. $27
Spoon-dessert/oval soup, 7 1/4 in. $40
Spoon-fruit, 6 in. $30
Spoon-iced tea, 7 3/8 in. $28
Spoon-soup, round bowl, bouillon,
    5 1/2 in. $25
Spoon-soup, round bowl, gumbo,
    7 1/8 in. $36
Spoon-sugar, 5 5/8 in. $33
Spoon-teaspoon (five o'clock), 5 5/8 in. $10
Spoon-teaspoon, 6 in. $16
Tablespoon, (serving spoon), 8 3/8 in. $60
Tablespoon, (serving spoon), pierced,
    8 3/8 in. $70
Tongs-sugar, 4 1/4 in. $50

Torchlight by International, 1954

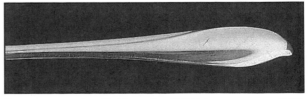

Butter spreader, flat handle, 5 3/4 in. $17
Butter-master, flat handle, 7 1/8 in. $28
Fork, 7 1/4 in. $26
Fork-cold meat/serving, large, solid,
    9 1/8 in. $80

Fork-salad, individual, 3 tines, 6 1/2 in. $24
Knife-carving, small, stainless blade, steak,
   10 3/4 in. $55
Knife-modern, hollow handle, 9 1/8 in. $23
Ladle-gravy, solid, 6 5/8 in. $70
Napkin clip (made for teaspoons) $16
Spoon-iced tea, 7 3/8 in. $26
Spoon-sugar, 5 3/4 in. $38
Spoon-teaspoon, 6 in. $14
Tablespoon, (serving spoon), 8 5/8 in. $70
Tablespoon, (serving spoon), pierced,
   8 5/8 in. $80

Trianon by International, 1921

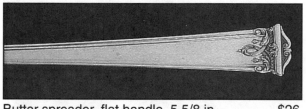

Butter spreader, flat handle, 5 5/8 in. $26
Butter-master, flat handle, 7 1/4 in. $48
Fork, 7 1/4 in. $25
Fork, 7 7/8 in. $50
Fork-cocktail, 5 3/8 in. $22
Fork-salad, individual, 6 1/8 in. $40
Knife-carving, small, stainless blade, steak,
   10 in. $70
Knife-carving, small, stainless blade, steak,
   11 in. $70
Knife-fruit, stainless blade, individual, 7 in. $37
Knife-new french, hollow handle, 9 1/2 in. $50
Knife-old french, hollow handle, 9 7/8 in. $50
Spoon-demitasse, 4 1/8 in. $26
Spoon-dessert/oval soup, 7 1/4 in. $55
Spoon-fruit, 6 in. $37
Spoon-iced tea, 7 3/8 in. $40
Spoon-olive, short, pierced bowl, 6 1/4 in. $90
Spoon-sugar, 5 5/8 in. $40
Spoon-teaspoon (five o'clock), 5 5/8 in. $16
Spoon-teaspoon, 6 in. $28
Tablespoon, (serving spoon), 8 3/8 in. $80

The following pieces have monograms:
Fork, 7 1/4 in. $20
Fork, 7 7/8 in. $40
Fork-carving, small, stainless prongs, steak,
   9 in. $55
Fork-cold meat/serving, medium, solid,
   8 in. $90
Ice cream slicer, silver plate blade,
   10 7/8 in. $70

Knife-new french, hollow handle,
   9 1/2 in. $42
Knife-new french, hollow handle, 9 1/8 in. $29
Knife-new french, hollow handle, 9 5/8 in. $42
Knife-old french, hollow handle, 9 7/8 in. $42
Knife-old french, hollow handle, 9 in. $30
Ladle-cream, solid, 5 1/2 in. $42
Ladle-gravy, solid, 6 1/4 in. $80
Spoon-demitasse, 4 1/8 in. $20
Spoon-dessert/oval soup, 7 1/4 in. $42
Spoon-fruit, 6 in. $30
Spoon-iced tea, 7 3/8 in. $30
Spoon-soup, round bowl, bouillon,
   5 1/2 in. $23
Spoon-soup, round bowl, gumbo, 7 in. $40
Spoon-sugar, 5 5/8 in. $30
Spoon-teaspoon (five o'clock), 5 5/8 in. $12
Spoon-teaspoon, 6 in. $18
Tablespoon, (serving spoon), 8 3/8 in. $70

Trousseau by International, 1934

Butter spreader, flat handle, 5 3/4 in. $18
Butter-master, flat handle, 7 1/4 in. $30
Carving set, 2 pieces, small, stainless blade,
   steak $100
Fork, 7 1/4 in. $30
Fork, 7 3/4 in. $40
Fork-cocktail, 5 1/2 in. $30
Fork-cold meat/serving, large, solid, 9 in. $85
Fork-cold meat/serving, small, solid,
   7 5/8 in. $70
Fork-grille (viand), 7 5/8 in. $34
Fork-lemon, 4 5/8 in. $30
Fork-pickle/olive, short handle, 5 7/8 in. $30
Fork-salad serving, solid, 8 3/4 in. $96
Fork-salad, individual, 6 1/2 in. $32
knife-fruit, stainless blade, individual,
   7 1/4 in. $30
knife-grille, new french, hollow handle,
   8 5/8 in. $33
Knife-new french, hollow handle, 8 3/4 in. $30
Knife-new french, hollow handle, 9 1/2 in. $40
Knife-new french, hollow handle, 9 in. $30
Ladle-cream, solid, 5 1/2 in. $40
Ladle-gravy, solid, 6 1/4 in. $80
Server-jelly, 6 3/8 in. $30

International Silver

International Silver

Spoon-casserole, smooth bowl, solid,
8 3/4 in.................................$96
Spoon-demitasse, 4 1/4 in. $20
Spoon-fruit, 6 in. $34
Spoon-iced tea, 7 1/2 in. $34
Spoon-soup, round bowl, bouillon,
5 5/8 in................................$24
Spoon-soup, round bowl, cream, 6 3/8 in......$30
Spoon-sugar, 5 3/4 in.....................$30
Spoon-teaspoon, 5 7/8 in. $18
Tablespoon, (serving spoon), 8 1/2 in........$70
Tablespoon, (serving spoon), pierced,
8 1/2 in................................$80
Tongs-sugar, 4 in. $50

Valencia by International, 1965

Butter-master, hollow handle, 7 3/8 in.........$34
Fork, 7 1/2 in.............................$40
Fork-cold meat/serving, large, solid,
9 1/8 in................................$100
Fork-salad, individual, 6 7/8 in. $50
Knife-modern, hollow handle, 9 1/8 in.........$36
Ladle-gravy, solid, 6 3/4 in. $100
Server-pie and cake, stainless blade,
11 1/4 in. $70
Spoon-iced tea, 7 1/2 in. $60
Spoon-sugar, 6 1/4 in.....................$32
Spoon-teaspoon, 6 1/4 in. $22
Tablespoon, (serving spoon), 8 3/4 in.........$80
Tablespoon, (serving spoon), pierced,
8 3/4 in................................$90

Vision by International, 1961

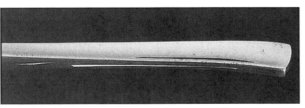

Butter spreader, flat handle, 6 3/4 in..........$46
Fork, 7 3/8 in.............................$36
Fork-pickle/lemon, 2 tines, 5 7/8 in. $50
Fork-serving, solid, 3 tines, 9 in.............$120
Knife-modern, hollow twisted handle,
8 1/2 in................................$35

Ladle-gravy, solid, 7 1/8 in..................$90
Spoon-dessert/oval soup, 7 3/8 in. $60
Spoon-serving, solid, 3 piercings, 9 in........$90
Spoon-serving, solid, 9 in. $90
Spoon-sugar, 6 3/8 in.....................$40
Spoon-teaspoon, 6 1/4 in...................$34

Warwick by International, 1898

Butter spreader, flat handle, 5 1/4 in. $30
Fork, 6 7/8 in. $44
Fork, 7 1/4 in. $60
Fork-chipped beef, small, 6 1/8 in. $70
Fork-cocktail, 5 1/4 in......................$34
Fork-cold meat/serving, medium, solid,
8 in. $94
Fork-pickle/olive, long handle, 7 in...........$53
Fork-youth, 6 1/8 in.......................$53
Knife-blunt, hollow handle, 9 5/8 in...........$80
Knife-old french, hollow handle, 8 5/8 in. $70
Ladle-cream, solid, 5 1/4 in. $50
Ladle-gravy, solid, 6 3/4 in.................$90
Spoon-casserole, smooth bowl, solid,
8 5/8 in.................................$100
Spoon-demitasse, 3 7/8 in..................$30
Spoon-demitasse, gold wash, 4 1/2 in........$30
Spoon-dessert/oval soup, 6 7/8 in. $40
Spoon-fruit, 5 7/8 in. $40
Spoon-soup, round bowl, bouillon,
5 3/4 in.................................$40
Spoon-soup, round bowl, cream, 6 5/8 in.....$44
Spoon-sugar shell, 6 in. $40
Spoon-teaspoon (five o'clock), 5 1/4 in.......$27
Spoon-teaspoon, 5 7/8 in...................$30
Tablespoon, (serving spoon), 7 7/8 in. $65
Tablespoon, (serving spoon), pierced,
7 7/8 in.................................$80
Tongs-sugar, 3 7/8 in. $70
Tongs-sugar, 4 5/8 in. $70

Wedding Bells by International, 1948

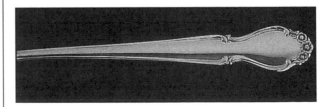

Butter spreader, flat handle, 5 3/4 in.........$14
Butter-master, flat handle, 7 1/4 in...........$35
Fork, 7 1/4 in...............................$23
Fork-baby, 4 1/4 in.........................$30
Fork-salad/individual, 6 1/2 in...............$23
Fork-youth, 6 1/4 in........................$40
Knife-modern, hollow handle, 9 1/8 in........$25
Knife-youth, 7 in............................$30
Ladle-gravy, solid, 6 3/8 in. $80
Spoon-baby, straight handle, 4 1/4 in. $30
Spoon-demitasse, 4 1/8 in. $18
Spoon-soup, round bowl, cream, 6 1/2 in......$20
Spoon-teaspoon (five o'clock), 5 3/4 in.......$20
Spoon-teaspoon, 6 in........................$16
Tablespoon, (serving spoon), 8 1/2 in.........$75

Wedgwood by International, 1924

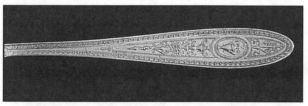

Butter spreader, flat handle, 5 3/4 in.........$18
Butter spreader, hollow handle, stainless paddle,
    5 3/4 in...................................$28
Butter-master, flat handle, 7 1/4 in...........$37
Butter-master, hollow handle, 6 1/2 in........$40
Carving set, 2 pieces, small, stainless blade,
    steak....................................$80
Cleaver-cheese, stainless blade, 6 1/2 in......$40
Fork, 7 1/4 in...............................$33
Fork, 7 3/4 in...............................$48
Fork-carving, small, stainless prongs, steak,
    8 5/8 in..................................$40
Fork-carving, small, stainless prongs, steak,
    9 1/8 in..................................$40
Fork-cocktail, 5 1/2 in.......................$25
Fork-cold meat/serving, large, five stainless
    tines, 10 3/4 in..........................$40
Fork-cold meat/serving, small, solid,
    7 3/8 in..................................$80
Fork-fish, stainless tines, hollow handle,
    individual, 7 7/8 in.......................$45
Fork-grille (viand), 7 5/8 in. $35
Fork-ice cream, 5 1/2 in......................$40
Fork-lemon, no bevel, 5 7/8 in. $42
Fork-pickle/olive, short handle, beveled tines,
    5 7/8 in..................................$42
Fork-salad serving, 4 stainless prongs, not bev-
    eled, 11 1/8 in...........................$40
Fork-salad, individual, bar, 6 1/4 in. $46

Knife-bar, hollow handle, 9 in. $40
Knife-carving, small, stainless blade, steak,
    9 7/8 in..................................$40
Knife-cheese, stainless blade, 7 in...........$40
Knife-fish, stainless blade, individual,
    8 1/4 in..................................$40
Knife-fruit, stainless blade, individual,
    6 5/8 in..................................$45
Knife-grille, new french, hollow handle,
    8 5/8 in..................................$44
Knife-modern, hollow handle, 4 3/8 in. handle,
    9 1/2 in..................................$50
Knife-modern, hollow handle, 9 in. $40
Knife-new french, hollow handle, 9 1/2 in. $50
Knife-new french, hollow handle, silver plate
    blade, 9 in...............................$40
Knife-new french, hollow handle, stainless
    blade, 9 in. $40
Knife-old french, hollow handle, 8 3/4 in. $40
Knife-steak, individual, beveled blade,
    8 1/2 in..................................$45
Knife-steak, individual, beveled blade, 9 in....$45
Ladle-gravy, hollow handle, stainless bowl,
    7 7/8 in..................................$45
Ladle-gravy, solid, 6 5/8 in..................$80
Ladle-punch, stainless bowl, 12 1/2 in........$55
Ladle-soup, stainless bowl, 11 1/4 in.........$55
Napkin clip, (made for teaspoons)...........$26
Opener-bottle, stainless bowl, 6 1/4 in........$40
Scoop-ice cream, stainless bowl, 8 1/8 in.....$45
Scoop-ice, silver plate bowl, 9 in. $50
Server/knife-fish, stainless blade, design on
    bowl, 11 1/4 in...........................$45
Server-asparagus, hollow handle, silver plate
    hood, 9 3/8 in............................$55
Server-cranberry, stainless bowl, 8 1/2 in.....$40
Server-jelly, 6 3/8 in. $50
Server-lasagna, stainless blade, 9 5/8 in. $40
Server-pasta, stainless bowl, 10 1/2 in. $45
Server-pie and cake, stainless blade,
    10 3/4 in.................................$45
Server-pie, stainless blade, 9 1/4 in..........$45
Slicer-cake, stainless blade, wedding,
    12 1/2 in.................................$45
Spoon-casserole, pierced stainless bowl,
    7 scallops, 9 3/8 in.......................$45
Spoon-casserole, shell, stainless bowl,
    17 scallops, 10 in. $45
Spoon-cracker, 8 1/8 in. $140
Spoon-demitasse, 4 in......................$20
Spoon-dressing, stainless tear-shaped bowl,
    11 in.....................................$40
Spoon-fruit, 5 7/8 in........................$40
Spoon-iced tea, 7 3/8 in.....................$30
Spoon-mustard, 5 5/8 in.....................$50
Spoon-relish, 6 in. $46

Spoon-salad serving, stainless egg-shaped
bowl, 11 1/8 in. $40
Spoon-soup, round bowl, bouillon,
5 1/2 in.. . . . .$34
Spoon-soup, round bowl, gumbo, 7 1/4 in. $48
Spoon-sugar shell, 6 1/4 in.. . . . .$36
Spoon-teaspoon, 6 in.. . . . .$20
Spoon-utility/serving, stainless bowl, 7
scallops, 9 3/8 in. $40
Tablespoon, (serving spoon), 8 5/8 in.. . . . .$60
Tablespoon, (serving spoon), pierced,
8 5/8 in.. . . . .$95

Wesley by International, 1912

Butter spreader, flat handle, 5 3/8 in.. . . . .$26
Butter-master, flat handle, 7 3/8 in.. . . . .$40
Carving set, 2 pieces, small, stainless blade,
steak $140
Fork, 7 1/2 in.. . . . .$50
Fork, 7 in.. . . . . $55
Fork-carving, large, stainless prongs, roast,
11 1/2 in. $80
Fork-carving, small stainless prongs, steak,
8 3/4 in.. . . . .$70
Knife-new french, hollow handle, 9 1/4 in.. . . . .$40
Knife-old french, hollow handle, 10 in.. . . . .$60
Knife-youth, 7 1/8 in.. . . . .$40
Spoon-demitasse, 3 7/8 in. $26
Spoon-dessert/oval soup, 6 7/8 in.. . . . .$55
Spoon-soup, round bowl, bouillon,
5 1/4 in.. . . . .$40
Spoon-sugar shell, 5 7/8 in.. . . . .$45
Spoon-teaspoon (five o'clock), 5 1/2 in.. . . . . . .$24
Spoon-teaspoon, 5 3/4 in. $30
Spoon-youth, 5 1/8 in.. . . . .$40
Tablespoon, (serving spoon), 8 in. $95

Westminster by International, 1915

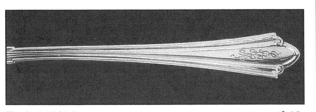

Fork, 7 3/4 in. $48

Fork, 7 in. $40
Fork-ice cream, 5 1/8 in. $50
Fork-ice cream, 5 3/8 in. $50
Knife-fruit, stainless blade, individual,
6 1/2 in. $38
Knife-new french, hollow handle, 9 1/2 in. $50
Knife-old french, hollow handle, 10 in. $50
Knife-old french, hollow handle, 9 1/4 in. $40
Napkin clip, (made for five o'clock) $24
Poultry shears, 10 3/8 in. $190
Server-pie, silver plate blade, 10 5/8 in. $70
Spoon-bon-bon, 4 3/4 in. $48
Spoon-demitasse, 4 1/8 in.. . . . . $24
Spoon-fruit, 5 3/4 in. $34
Spoon-soup, round bowl, bouillon,
5 3/8 in. $36
Spoon-soup, round bowl, gumbo, 7 1/8 in.. . . . $55
Spoon-sugar, 6 in. $38
Spoon-teaspoon (five o'clock), 5 1/2 in. $16
Tablespoon, (serving spoon), 8 3/8 in. $70
Tongs-sugar, 4 in.. . . . . $55

Whitewall-New by International, 1938

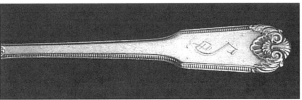

Butter spreader, flat handle, 5 3/4 in. $23
Butter spreader, hollow handle, stainless
paddle, 5 3/4 in.. . . . . $28
Fork, 7 1/4 in. $44
Fork, 7 7/8 in. $55
Fork-cold meat/serving, small, solid, 4 tines,
7 5/8 in. $80
Fork-salad, individual, 6 1/2 in. $45
Knife-carving, large, stainless blade, roast,
13 1/8 in.. . . . . $110
Knife-modern, hollow handle, 8 3/4 in. $35
Knife-new french, hollow handle, 9 1/8 in. $34
Knife-new french, hollow handle, 9 5/8 in. $48
Knife-youth, 6 5/8 in. $40
Salad set, 2 pieces, solid, 9 1/8 in. $210
Spoon-dessert/oval soup, 6 7/8 in. $50
Spoon-iced tea, 7 3/8 in.. . . . . $38
Spoon-iced tea, 7 7/8 in.. . . . . $38
Spoon-salad serving, solid, 9 1/8 in.. . . . . $104
Spoon-soup, round bowl, bouillon,
5 5/8 in. $40
Spoon-soup, round bowl, cream, 6 1/2 in. $44

Spoon-sugar, 5 7/8 in................$40
Spoon-teaspoon, 6 in................$24
Tablespoon, (serving spoon), 8 1/2 in........$85

Wild Rose-New by International, 1948

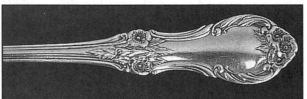

Butter spreader, flat handle, 5 3/4 in.........$20
Butter spreader, hollow handle, stainless
    paddle, 5 3/4 in...........................$28
Butter-master, flat handle, 7 1/8 in...........$30
Butter-master, hollow handle, 7 1/8 in........$32
Carving set, 2 pieces, small, stainless blade,
    steak....................................$80
Fork, 7 3/4 in..............................$43
Fork, 7 3/8 in..............................$24
Fork-baby, 4 1/4 in. $30
Fork-carving, small, stainless prongs, steak,
    8 5/8 in..................................$40
Fork-carving, small, stainless prongs, steak,
    9 5/8 in..................................$40
Fork-cocktail, 5 1/2 in......................$25
Fork-cold meat/serving, medium, solid,
    8 7/8 in..................................$90
Fork-cold meat/serving, small, solid,
    7 3/4 in..................................$80
Fork-fish, stainless tines, hollow handle,
    individual, 8 1/2 in. $40
Fork-lemon, 3 flared tines, 4 5/8 in. $27
Fork-lemon, 3 flared tines, 5 7/8 in. $27
Fork-pickle/olive, short handle, 2 of 3 beveled tines,
    5 7/8 in..................................$30
Fork-salad serving, four stainless prongs, no
    bevel, 11 5/8 in...........................$40
Fork-salad, individual, 6 1/8 in. $36
Fork-youth, 6 1/8 in. $40
Knife-bar, hollow handle, 9 3/8 in.............$40
Knife-carving, small, stainless blade, steak,
    10 1/4 in. $40
Knife-carving, small, stainless blade, steak,
    10 7/8 in. $40
Knife-carving, small, stainless blade, steak,
    9 7/8 in..................................$40
Knife-fruit, stainless blade, individual,
    6 3/4 in..................................$40
Knife-modern, hollow handle, 9 1/2 in.........$40
Knife-modern, hollow handle, 9 1/4 in.........$32

Knife-new french, hollow handle,
    9 1/4 in................................ $32
Knife-new french, hollow handle,
    9 5/8 in................................ $38
Knife-steak, individual, 9 in. $45
Ladle-cream, solid, 5 3/8 in............... $40
Ladle-gravy, hollow handle, stainless bowl,
    8 3/8 in................................ $45
Ladle-gravy, shell bowl, 6 3/8 in. $60
Ladle-soup, stainless bowl, 11 3/8 in........ $55
Napkin clip, (made for teaspoons).......... $30
Scoop-ice cream, stainless bowl,
    8 1/2 in................................ $40
Scoop-ice, silver plate bowl, 8 3/4 in. $50
Server/knife-fish, stainless blade, design on
    bowl, 11 7/8 in.......................... $40
Server-asparagus, hollow handle, silver plate
    hood, 9 3/4 in. $55
Server-cheese, stainless blade, 6 1/4 in. $45
Server-cranberry, stainless bowl, 9 in. $40
Server-jelly, 6 1/2 in. $28
Server-lasagna, stainless blade,
    10 1/4 in................................ $45
Server-pasta, stainless bowl, 11 in.......... $40
Server-pie, stainless blade, 10 1/4 in........ $45
Server-tomato, solid, 7 7/8 in. $90
Slicer-cake, stainless blade, wedding,
    12 7/8 in................................ $45
Spoon-baby, straight handle, 4 3/8 in......... $30
Spoon-bon-bon, 4 5/8 in. $35
Spoon-casserole, pierced stainless bowl,
    7 scallops, 9 7/8 in...................... $40
Spoon-casserole, shell, stainless bowl,
    17 scallops, 10 1/2 in.................... $40
Spoon-demitasse, 4 1/8 in................. $24
Spoon-dressing, stainless tear-shaped bowl,
    11 1/2 in................................ $40
Spoon-infant feeding, 5 1/2 in............... $30
Spoon-jam, smooth bowl, 6 in.............. $40
Spoon-salad serving, plastic bowl,
    11 3/4 in................................ $40
Spoon-salad serving, stainless egg-shaped
    bowl, 11 5/8 in.......................... $45
Spoon-salad serving, wooden bowl,
    10 3/4 in................................ $40
Spoon-salad/berry, solid, 9 1/4 in........... $120
Spoon-sugar shell, 6 1/8 in. $25
Spoon-teaspoon, 5 7/8 in................. $17
Spoon-utility/serving, stainless bowl, 7
    scallops, 9 7/8 in........................ $45
Tablespoon, (serving spoon), 8 1/4 in. $70
Tea strainer, 7 1/4 in..................... $100

Wild Rose-Old/Rosalind by International, 1908

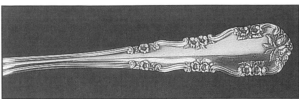

Butter spreader, flat handle, 6 1/8 in.........$24
Carving set, 2 pieces, small, stainless blade,
     steak $130
Fork, 7 1/2 in.............................$46
Fork, 7 in................................$22
Fork-chipped beef, small, 6 1/2 in...........$70
Fork-cocktail, 5 1/2 in.
Fork-cold meat/serving, medium, solid,
     8 3/4 in..................................$70
Fork-cold meat/serving, small, solid,
     6 1/2 in..................................$60
Fork-dessert, bar, 6 1/4 in..................$50
Fork-fish, solid, individual, not beveled,
     6 1/8 in..................................$48
Fork-ice cream, 5 1/4 in.....................$50
Fork-ice cream, gold wash, 5 1/4 in. $50
Fork-youth, 6 1/4 in. $48
Knife-new french, hollow handle, 9 1/8 in.....$32
Knife-new french, hollow handle, 9 5/8 in.....$42
Knife-old french, hollow handle, 8 7/8 in.......$34
Pick-butter, 1 tine, 6 1/8 in..................$55
Server-pie, stainless blade, 9 1/2 in. $50
Spoon-casserole, smooth, solid, 8 5/8 in.....$90
Spoon-casserole, smooth, solid, 9 in. $90
Spoon-chocolate, short handle, large,
     4 5/8 in..................................$32

Spoon-demitasse, 3 7/8 in.................. $24
Spoon-dessert/oval soup, 7 in.............. $38
Spoon-fruit, 6 in.......................... $40
Spoon-ice cream, 5 3/8 in. $48
Spoon-preserve, 7 3/8 in. $70
Spoon-soup, round bowl, bouillon, 5 in....... $24
Spoon-soup, round bowl, cream, 5 7/8 in..... $46
Spoon-soup, round bowl, gumbo, 6 5/8 in..... $40
Spoon-sugar, 6 in. $34
Spoon-teaspoon (five o'clock), 5 5/8 in....... $24
Spoon-teaspoon, 6 in....................... $16
Spoon-youth, 5 3/8 in...................... $28
Tablespoon, (serving spoon), 8 3/8 in. $60
Tablespoon, (serving spoon), pierced,
     8 3/8 in............................... $90

Windermere by International, 1939

Butter spreader, flat handle, 5 5/8 in. $16
Butter-master, flat handle, 7 1/8 in........... $28
Fork, 7 1/8 in. $32
Fork, 7 3/4 in. $45
Fork-cocktail, 5 1/2 in. $20
Fork-salad, individual, 6 1/8 in. $30
Knife-new french, hollow handle, 9 1/8 in. $30
Server-pie, stainless blade, 9 1/2 in.......... $55
Spoon-dessert/oval soup, 6 7/8 in. $34
Spoon-soup, round bowl, cream, 5 7/8 in..... $36
Spoon-sugar, 5 3/4 in...................... $36
Spoon-teaspoon, 6 in....................... $20

JENKINS & JENKINS

Jenkins & Jenkins, established in 1908 in Baltimore, Maryland, was the successor to a silver manufacturer known as A. Jacobi, which was started in 1879. The Schofield Co. of Baltimore bought the tools and dies of Jenkins & Jenkins in about 1915.

Repoussé by Jenkins & Jenkins

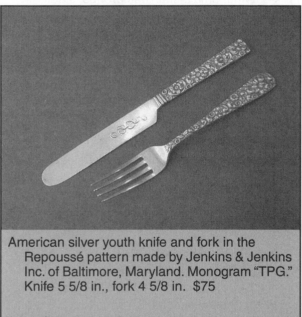

American silver youth knife and fork in the Repoussé pattern made by Jenkins & Jenkins Inc. of Baltimore, Maryland. Monogram "TPG." Knife 5 5/8 in., fork 4 5/8 in. $75

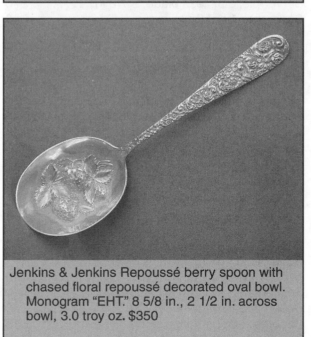

Jenkins & Jenkins Repoussé berry spoon with chased floral repoussé decorated oval bowl. Monogram "EHT." 8 5/8 in., 2 1/2 in. across bowl, 3.0 troy oz. $350

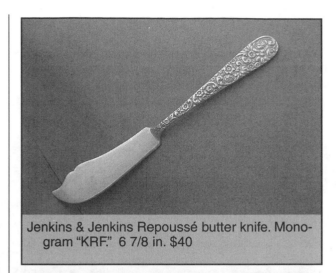

Jenkins & Jenkins Repoussé butter knife. Monogram "KRF." 6 7/8 in. $40

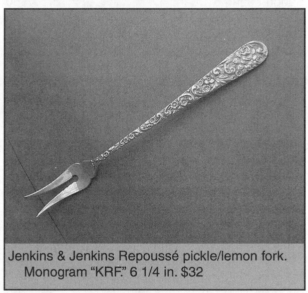

Jenkins & Jenkins Repoussé pickle/lemon fork. Monogram "KRF." 6 1/4 in. $32

Jenkins & Jenkins Repoussé large serving spoon with ovoid bowl. No monogram. 9 1/8 in., 2 1/8 in. across bowl. Some dings in bowl. $125

Courtesy: Imperial Half Bushel

KIRK STIEFF CORP.

Kirk Stieff Corp. began in Baltimore, Maryland, in 1815 as Kirk & Smith, and for the next 100 years, generations of the Kirk family operated the firm. Founder Samuel Kirk introduced the Repoussé pattern in 1828. The Stieff Co. of Baltimore acquired the Kirk Co. in 1979.

Betsy Patterson- Engraved by Kirk Stieff, 1932

Fork, 6 7/8 in.	$54
Fork-salad, individual, 6 1/8 in.	$70
Knife-new french, hollow handle, 9 in.	$40
Spoon-sugar, 6 1/8 in.	$50

The following pieces have monograms:

Butter spreader, flat handle, 6 in.	$22
Butter-master, flat handle, 7 1/8 in.	$35
Fork, 6 7/8 in.	$44
Fork, 7 3/8 in.	$60
Fork-cold meat/serving, small, solid, 7 5/8 in.	$110
Fork-ice cream, 5 3/4 in.	$50
Fork-lemon, 4 3/4 in.	$30
Fork-salad, individual, 6 1/8 in.	$50
Knife-modern, hollow handle, 9 in.	$30
Knife-new french, hollow handle, 9 1/2 in.	$40
Knife-new french, hollow handle, 9 in.	$30
Ladle-gravy, solid, 6 1/4 in.	$100
Spoon-bon-bon, 5 1/4 in.	$38
Spoon-demitasse, 4 3/8 in.	$23
Spoon-fruit, 5 7/8 in.	$40
Spoon-iced tea, 7 1/2 in.	$60
Spoon-serving, solid, 8 1/2 in.	$90
Spoon-soup, round bowl, gumbo, 6 5/8 in.	$60
Spoon-sugar, 6 1/8 in.	$40
Spoon-teaspoon (five o'clock), 5 5/8 in.	$16
Spoon-teaspoon, 6 in.	$22
Tablespoon, (serving spoon), 7 3/4 in.	$90

Betsy Patterson-Plain by Kirk Stieff, 1932

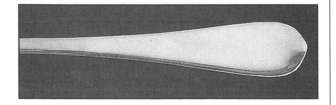

Butter spreader, flat handle, 6 in.	$25
Butter spreader, hollow handle, modern, stainless paddle, 6 in.	$28
Butter-master, flat handle, 7 1/8 in.	$40
Butter-master, hollow handle, 6 7/8 in.	$40
Butter-master, hollow handle, 7 3/4 in.	$40
Carving set, 2 pieces, small, stainless blade, steak	$120
Fork, 6 7/8 in.	$35
Fork, 7 3/8 in.	$50
Fork-carving, small, stainless prongs, steak, 8 1/2 in.	$60
Fork-carving, small, stainless prongs, steak, 9 1/2 in.	$60
Fork-cocktail, 5 5/8 in.	$23
Fork-cold meat/serving, medium, solid, 8 5/8 in.	$90
Fork-cold meat/serving, small, solid, 7 5/8 in.	$80
Fork-lemon, 4 3/4 in.	$30
Fork-pickle/olive, short handle, 6 1/8 in.	$30
Fork-salad, individual, indented, 6 1/8 in.	$37
Knife-carving, small stainless blade, steak, 11 3/8 in.	$60
Knife-new french, hollow handle, 8 7/8 in.	$34
Knife-new french, hollow handle, 9 1/2 in.	$50
Ladle-gravy, solid, 6 3/8 in.	$90
Salad set, 2 pieces, wooden bowl, 11 1/4 in.	$80
Salad set, 2 pieces, solid, 8 in.	$200
Server-pie, stainless blade, 9 7/8 in.	$70
Spoon-bon-bon, 5 1/4 in.	$40
Spoon-casserole, smooth bowl, solid, 8 1/2 in.	$110
Spoon-casserole, smooth bowl, solid, 8 in.	$110
Spoon-demitasse, 4 1/4 in.	$20
Spoon-dessert/oval soup, 6 5/8 in.	$46
Spoon-fruit, 6 in.	$28
Spoon-iced tea, 7 1/2 in.	$35
Spoon-olive, short, pierced bowl, 5 3/4 in.	$40
Spoon-olive, short, solid bowl, 5 3/4 in.	$30
Spoon-soup, round bowl, bouillon, 5 1/2 in.	$35
Spoon-soup, round bowl, cream, 6 1/8 in.	$47
Spoon-soup, round bowl, gumbo, 6 1/2 in.	$40
Spoon-soup, round bowl, gumbo, 7 in.	$40
Spoon-sugar, 6 1/8 in.	$30
Spoon-teaspoon (five o'clock), 5 5/8 in.	$15
Spoon-teaspoon (five o'clock), 5 in.	$15

Spoon-teaspoon, 5 7/8 in. $23
Tablespoon, (serving spoon), 7 5/8 in. $75

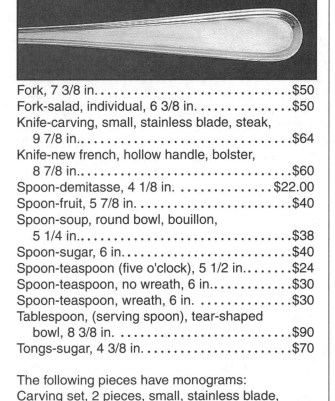

Sixty pieces Stieff Betsy Patterson Plain (1932): 8 luncheon knives, 8 luncheon forks, 8 tea-spoons, 8 salad forks, 8 cream soup spoons, 8 butter spreaders, 8 iced teaspoons, 1 medium serving spoon, 1 butter knife, 1 sauce ladle, and 1 lemon fork. Monogram "V." $1,200

Calvert by Kirk Stieff, 1927

Fork, 7 3/8 in. $50
Fork-salad, individual, 6 3/8 in. $50
Knife-carving, small, stainless blade, steak,
    9 7/8 in. $64
Knife-new french, hollow handle, bolster,
    8 7/8 in. $60
Spoon-demitasse, 4 1/8 in. $22.00
Spoon-fruit, 5 7/8 in. $40
Spoon-soup, round bowl, bouillon,
    5 1/4 in. $38
Spoon-sugar, 6 in. $40
Spoon-teaspoon (five o'clock), 5 1/2 in. $24
Spoon-teaspoon, no wreath, 6 in. $30
Spoon-teaspoon, wreath, 6 in. $30
Tablespoon, (serving spoon), tear-shaped
    bowl, 8 3/8 in. $90
Tongs-sugar, 4 3/8 in. $70

The following pieces have monograms:
Carving set, 2 pieces, small, stainless blade,
    steak $100

Fork, 7 7/8 in. $57
Fork-pickle/olive, short handle,
    5 3/4 in. $24
Fork-salad, individual, 6 3/8 in. $35
Knife-new french, hollow handle, bolster,
    9 3/4 in. $40
Spoon-bon-bon, 5 in. $33
Spoon-demitasse, 4 1/8 in. $18
Spoon-dessert/oval soup,
    7 3/8 in. $40
Spoon-fruit, 5 7/8 in. $30
Spoon-iced tea, 7 3/4 in. $38
Spoon-soup, round bowl, bouillon,
    5 1/4 in. $30
Spoon-soup, round bowl, cream,
    6 1/4 in. $40
Spoon-teaspoon, 6 in. $22

Carrollton by Kirk Stieff, 1961

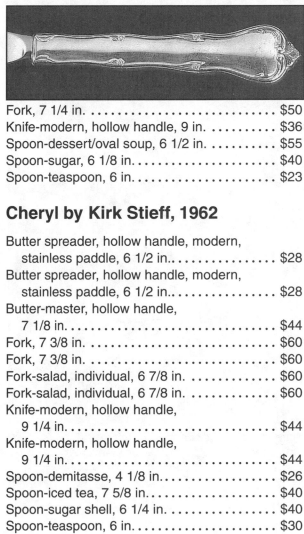

Fork, 7 1/4 in. $50
Knife-modern, hollow handle, 9 in. $36
Spoon-dessert/oval soup, 6 1/2 in. $55
Spoon-sugar, 6 1/8 in. $40
Spoon-teaspoon, 6 in. $23

Cheryl by Kirk Stieff, 1962

Butter spreader, hollow handle, modern,
    stainless paddle, 6 1/2 in. $28
Butter spreader, hollow handle, modern,
    stainless paddle, 6 1/2 in. $28
Butter-master, hollow handle,
    7 1/8 in. $44
Fork, 7 3/8 in. $60
Fork, 7 3/8 in. $60
Fork-salad, individual, 6 7/8 in. $60
Fork-salad, individual, 6 7/8 in. $60
Knife-modern, hollow handle,
    9 1/4 in. $44
Knife-modern, hollow handle,
    9 1/4 in. $44
Spoon-demitasse, 4 1/8 in. $26
Spoon-iced tea, 7 5/8 in. $40
Spoon-sugar shell, 6 1/4 in. $40
Spoon-teaspoon, 6 in. $30

Chrysanthemum by Kirk Stieff, 1904

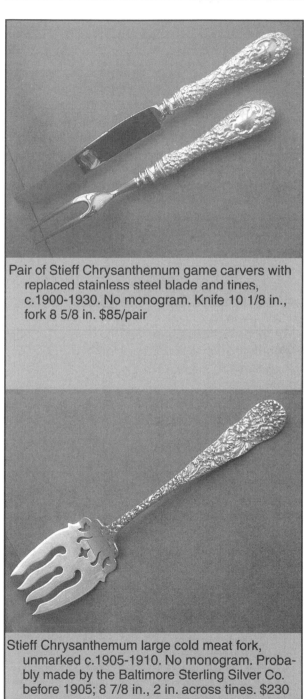

Pair of Stieff Chrysanthemum game carvers with replaced stainless steel blade and tines, c.1900-1930. No monogram. Knife 10 1/8 in., fork 8 5/8 in. $85/pair

Stieff Chrysanthemum large cold meat fork, unmarked c.1905-1910. No monogram. Probably made by the Baltimore Sterling Silver Co. before 1905; 8 7/8 in., 2 in. across tines. $230

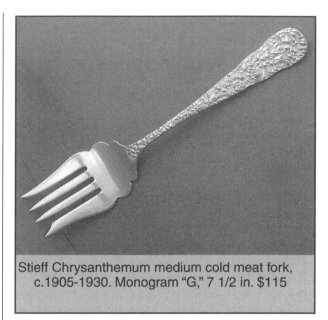

Stieff Chrysanthemum medium cold meat fork, c.1905-1930. Monogram "G," 7 1/2 in. $115

Clinton Engraved by Kirk Stieff, 1925

Butter spreader, flat handle, 6 in. $18
Butter-master, flat handle, 7 in. $28
Carving set, 2 pieces, small, stainless blade,
    steak $100
Fork, 6 7/8 in. $32
Fork, 7 1/2 in. $50
Fork, 8 in. $50
Fork-baby, 4 1/2 in. $36
Fork-cocktail, 5 5/8 in. $18
Fork-cold meat/serving, medium, solid,
    8 3/4 in. $75
Fork-cold meat/serving, medium, solid,
    8 3/8 in. $75
Fork-lettuce serving, large, 9 1/8 in. $80
Fork-pickle/olive, short handle, 6 in. $30
Fork-salad serving, solid, 8 1/8 in. $96
Fork-salad, individual, 6 in. $34
Knife-new french, hollow handle, bulge
    handle, 9 5/8 in. $43
Ladle-gravy, solid, 6 3/8 in. $75
Server-cheese, stainless blade, 6 1/4 in. $45
Server-hot cake, solid, 7 1/2 in. $80
Server-jelly, 6 1/4 in. $30
Spoon-casserole, smooth, solid,
    8 5/8 in. $90
Spoon-demitasse, 4 3/8 in. $16

Kirk Stieff

Spoon-dessert/oval soup, 7 1/8 in............$40
Spoon-fruit, 5 7/8 in........................$37
Spoon-soup, round bowl, bouillon,
    5 1/2 in..................................$28
Spoon-soup, round bowl, gumbo, 7 in. $38
Spoon-sugar, 6 1/8 in.......................$30
Spoon-teaspoon (five o'clock), 5 5/8 in.......$18
Tablespoon, (serving spoon), 7 3/4 in.........$60
Tablespoon, (serving spoon), 8 1/2 in.........$60

Sixty-two pieces Stieff Clinton (c.1920): 12 each
dinner forks, dinner knives, salad forks, teaspoons, and iced teaspoons; also 2 tablespoons. Monogram "CRC." $1,400

Corsage by Kirk Stieff, 1935

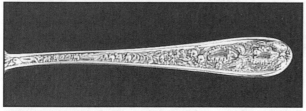

Butter spreader, flat handle, 6 in. $25
Butter spreader, hollow handle, modern,
    stainless paddle, 5 7/8 in. $30
Butter-master, flat handle, 7 1/8 in...........$40
Butter-master, hollow handle, 7 1/8 in........$40
Fork, 7 1/8 in..............................$42
Fork-bacon, solid, 8 1/4 in.................$120
Fork-cocktail, 5 3/4 in.....................$30
Fork-lemon, 4 3/4 in.......................$32
Fork-pickle/olive, short handle, 6 in..........$32

Fork-salad, individual, 6 in.................. $45
Knife-new french, hollow handle,
    8 7/8 in. $34
Ladle-gravy, solid, 6 1/2 in.................. $90
Ladle-gravy, solid, 6 1/8 in.................. $90
Napkin clip, (made for five o'clock) $18
Server-jelly, 6 1/4 in. $40
Server-pie, stainless blade, 9 7/8 in.......... $70
Spoon-casserole, smooth bowl, solid,
    8 1/8 in................................. $120
Spoon-demitasse, 4 1/4 in.................. $30
Spoon-fruit, 6 in........................... $40
Spoon-iced tea, 7 1/2 in.................... $42
Spoon-olive, short, pierced bowl,
    5 7/8 in................................. $80
Spoon-pea, solid, serving, 8 1/8 in.......... $200
Spoon-serving, solid, 8 5/8 in. $110
Spoon-soup, round bowl, cream, 1 5/8 in.
    bowl, 6 in. $60
Spoon-soup, round bowl, cream,
    6 1/2 in................................. $60
Spoon-sugar, 1 1/4 in. bowl, 6 1/8 in. $34
Spoon-teaspoon, 5 7/8 in................... $25
Tablespoon, (serving spoon),
    7 3/4 in................................. $75
Tablespoon, (serving spoon), pierced,
    7 3/4 in................................. $100

Thirty-four pieces Stieff Corsage (1935): 6 each
luncheon forks, luncheon knives, salad forks,
butter spreaders, and teaspoons; also 4 extra
teaspoons. Monogram "H." $850

American silver baby spoon in the Corsage pattern (1935) with loop handle; made by the Stieff Co. of Baltimore, Maryland. No monogram. 3 1/8 in. $35

Cynthia by Kirk Stieff, 1957

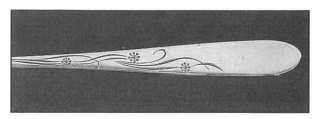

Butter spreader, hollow handle, modern,
  stainless paddle, 6 1/2 in. $20
Butter-master, hollow handle,
  7 1/8 in. $30
Fork, 7 1/4 in. $40
Fork-carving, small, stainless prongs,
  steak, 9 1/4 in. $50
Fork-salad, individual, 6 7/8 in. $40
Knife-carving, small, stainless blade, steak,
  10 5/8 in. $50
Knife-modern, hollow handle,
  9 1/8 in. $34
Ladle-gravy, solid, 6 7/8 in. $70
Server-jelly, 6 1/2 in. $35
Spoon-demitasse, 4 1/4 in. $20
Spoon-sugar shell, 6 in. $30
Spoon-teaspoon, 6 1/8 in. $20
Tablespoon, (serving spoon),
  8 5/8 in. $65
Tablespoon, (serving spoon), pierced,
  8 5/8 in. $80

Diamond Star by Kirk Stieff, 1958

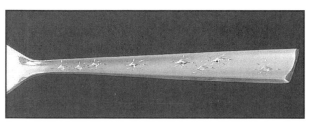

Butter spreader, hollow handle, modern,
  stainless paddle, 6 1/4 in. $18
Fork, 7 5/8 in. $50
Fork-salad, individual, 6 5/8 in. $34
Spoon-sugar, 6 1/4 in. $34
Spoon-teaspoon, 6 1/4 in. $20

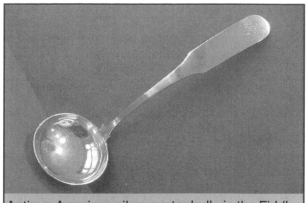

Antique American silver oyster ladle in the Fiddle pattern; original mark of Littleton Holland(?) over struck by Samuel Kirk, Baltimore assay marks of 1817 or 1823. Monogram "WMW," 9 1/2 in., 2 7/8 in. across bowl, 7/8 in. bowl depth, 2.4 troy oz. $400

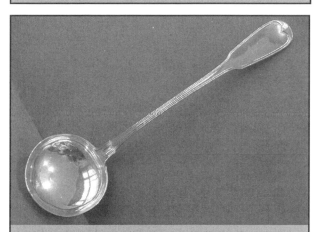

Antique American silver soup ladle in the single struck Fiddle Thread pattern; made by Samuel Kirk of Baltimore, Maryland, c.1835-1846. Engraved halberd crest on front and monogram "J" on back, 12 5/8 in., 3 1/2 in. across bowl, 5.5 troy oz. $450

Florentine by Kirk Stieff, 1962

Butter spreader, hollow handle, modern,
  stainless paddle, 6 1/2 in. $30
Butter-master, hollow handle, 7 1/4 in. $40
Fork, 7 1/2 in. $50

Fork-salad, individual, 7 1/8 in. $54
Knife-modern, hollow handle, 9 in. $34
Ladle-gravy, solid, 7 1/4 in. $85
Spoon-dessert/oval soup, 7 1/8 in. $64
Spoon-sugar, 6 1/4 in. $42
Spoon-teaspoon, 6 1/4 in. $24
Tablespoon, (serving spoon), 8 3/4 in. $90

Forget-Me-Not by Kirk Stieff, 1910

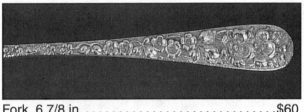

Fork, 6 7/8 in. $60
Fork-cold meat/serving, medium, solid,
   8 3/4 in. $100
Fork-cold meat/serving, small, solid,
   7 1/2 in. $90
Fork-ice cream, 5 3/4 in. $55
Fork-lettuce serving, large, 9 1/4 in. $90
Fork-salad, individual, 6 in. $70
Sardine fork, serving, solid, 6 in. $94
Spoon-iced tea, 5 7/8 inhandle, 7 1/2 in. $38
Spoon-iced tea, 6 1/2 in. handle,
   8 1/8 in. $38
Spoon-jelly, egg bowl, 6 in. $60
Spoon-serving, solid, 8 5/8 in. $100
Spoon-soup, round bowl, bouillon,
   5 1/2 in. $45
Spoon-soup, round bowl, gumbo, 7 in. $58
Spoon-teaspoon (five o'clock), 5 1/2 in. $30
Spoon-teaspoon, 5 7/8 in. $32

Golden Winslow by Kirk Stieff, 1850

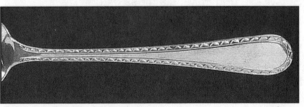

Butter-master, flat handle, 7 in. $44
Butter-master, hollow handle, 7 in. $44
Fork, 7 1/4 in. $50
Fork, 7 3/4 in. $70
Fork-baby, 3 3/4 in. $40
Fork-cocktail, 5 3/8 in. $40
Fork-cold meat/serving, medium, solid,
   8 5/8 in. $120
Fork-salad, individual, 6 1/8 in. $50

Knife-cheese, stainless blade, 7 1/4 in. $48
Knife-modern, hollow handle, 9 7/8 in. $60
Knife-modern, hollow handle, 9 in. $45
Knife-new french, hollow handle,
   9 3/4 in. $60
Knife-wedding cake, stainless blade,
   11 7/8 in. $80
Server-pie and cake, stainless blade,
   10 3/8 in. $70
Spoon-baby, straight handle, 3 3/4 in. $40
Spoon-dessert/oval soup, 7 3/8 in. $60
Spoon-fruit, 6 in. $44
Spoon-place/oval soup, 6 1/8 in. $50
Spoon-sugar, 6 in. $50
Tablespoon, (serving spoon), 8 1/4 in. $110
Tablespoon, (serving spoon), pierced,
   8 1/4 in. $100

Homewood by Kirk Stieff, 1938

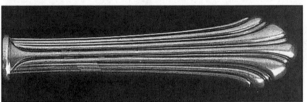

Butter spreader, flat handle, 6 in. $24
Butter-master, flat handle, 7 1/8 in. $33
Butter-master, hollow handle, 7 5/8 in. $34
Fork, 7 1/8 in. $30
Fork-cocktail, 5 3/4 in. $28
Fork-cold meat/serving, small, solid,
   7 7/8 in. $65
Fork-lemon, 4 3/4 in. $28
Fork-salad, individual, 6 1/8 in. $36
Ice cream slicer, stainless blade,
   10 1/8 in. $80
Knife-modern, hollow handle, 9 in. $35
Knife-new french, hollow handle, 9 in. $35
Ladle-cream, solid, 5 1/8 in. $45
Ladle-gravy, solid, 6 1/4 in. $80
Server-cheese, stainless blade,
   6 1/2 in. $45
Server-jelly, 6 1/4 in. $34
Server-pie, stainless blade, 9 7/8 in. $58
Spoon-bon-bon, 5 3/8 in. $40
Spoon-casserole, smooth bowl, solid,
   8 1/2 in. $100
Spoon-casserole, smooth bowl, solid,
   8 in. $100
Spoon-demitasse, 4 1/4 in. $22
Spoon-fruit, 6 in. $40
Spoon-iced tea, 7 1/2 in. $42
Spoon-sugar, 6 1/8 in. $30

Spoon-teaspoon, 6 in.........................$17
Tablespoon, (serving spoon), 7 3/4 in.........$65
Tablespoon, (serving spoon), pierced,
7 3/4 in...................................$80

King by Kirk Stieff, 1825

Fork, 7 1/2 in..............................$80
Fork, 7 1/4 in..............................$58
Fork, lion emblem, 7 1/4 in..................$58
Fork-carving, small stainless prongs, steak,
8 7/8 in..................................$80
Fork-cocktail, 5 7/8 in......................$34
Fork-salad serving, stainless prongs,
10 5/8 in. $60
Fork-salad, individual, 6 5/8 in..............$60
Knife-modern, hollow handle, 9 5/8 in.........$60
Knife-modern, hollow handle, 9 in............$44
Knife-new french, hollow handle, 9 5/8 in.....$60
Knife-new french, hollow handle, 9 in.........$44
Knife-old french, hollow handle, 8 5/8 in......$44
Ladle-gravy, solid, 6 5/8 in. $120
Scoop-ice, silver plate bowl, 8 1/4 in..........$60
Server-asparagus, hollow handle, silver
plate hood, 9 1/4 in. $60
Server-pie and cake, stainless blade,
10 3/8 in. $80
Spoon-casserole, smooth, stainless bowl,
10 1/2 in. $55
Spoon-iced tea, 7 1/4 in. $50
Spoon-salad serving, stainless bowl,
10 5/8 in. $60
Spoon-soup, round bowl, bouillon,
5 1/4 in..................................$50
Spoon-soup, round bowl, cream, 6 1/8 in......$65
Spoon-teaspoon, 5 3/4 in. $34
Tablespoon, (serving spoon), 8 1/2 in.........$110

Kingsley by Kirk Stieff, 1959

Butter spreader, hollow handle, modern,
stainless paddle, 6 1/2 in.................$18
Butter-master, hollow handle, 7 1/4 in........$34
Fork, 7 5/8 in. $43
Fork-cold meat/serving, medium, solid,
8 7/8 in..................................$80
Fork-pickle/olive, short handle, 6 1/8 in.......$30
Fork-salad, individual, 7 1/8 in. $35
Knife-modern, hollow handle, 9 in. $32
Server-pie and cake, stainless blade,
11 1/8 in.................................$60
Spoon-bon-bon, 5 1/8 in. $40
Spoon-demitasse, 4 1/4 in...................$20
Spoon-dessert/oval soup, 7 1/8 in. $35
Spoon-sugar, 6 1/4 in.......................$30
Spoon-teaspoon, 6 1/4 in....................$22
Tablespoon, (serving spoon), 8 7/8 in. $70

Lady Claire-Hand Engraved by Kirk Stieff, 1925

Fork, 1 7/8 in. tines, 6 3/4 in. $56
Fork, 2 1/8 in. tines, 7 in....................$56
Fork, 7 1/2 in. $65
Fork-grille (viand), 7 1/4 in..................$58
Fork-ice cream, 5 7/8 in....................$60
Fork-salad serving, wooden prongs,
10 3/8 in.................................$50
Knife-modern, hollow handle, 9 in. $42
Knife-new french, hollow handle, 9 1/2 in. $54
Server-cheese, stainless blade, 6 3/4 in......$54
Server-pie and cake, stainless blade,
10 1/4 in.................................$75
Spoon-bon-bon, 5 1/4 in. $50
Spoon-dessert/oval soup, 6 5/8 in. $70
Spoon-iced tea, 7 1/2 in....................$50
Spoon-salad serving, wooden bowl,
10 7/8 in.................................$50
Spoon-sugar, 6 in. $45
Spoon-teaspoon, 5 7/8 in...................$28
Tablespoon, (serving spoon), 7 3/4 in. $100

The following pieces have monograms:
Butter spreader, flat handle, 6 in.............$30
Butter-master, flat handle, 7 in. $34
Fork, 7 1/2 in. $50
Fork, 7 in.................................$40

Fork-cocktail, 5 3/4 in........................$30
Fork-cold meat/serving, medium, solid,
    8 in.....................................$84
Fork-cold meat/serving, small, solid,
    7 1/2 in.................................$76
Fork-salad, individual, 6 in. $40
Knife-blunt, hollow handle, 9 5/8 in. $40
Knife-blunt, hollow handle, 9 in. $30
Knife-modern, hollow handle, 9 in............$30
Knife-new french, hollow handle, 8 3/4 in......$30
Server-pie, stainless blade, 10 in.............$58
Spoon-iced tea, 7 1/2 in. $40
Spoon-soup, round bowl, cream, 6 1/8 in......$46
Spoon-soup, round bowl, gumbo, 7 in. $44
Spoon-sugar, 6 in.............................$34
Spoon-teaspoon, 5 7/8 in. $20
Tablespoon, (serving spoon), 7 3/4 in........$76
Tablespoon, (serving spoon), 8 1/2 in........$76

Mayflower by Kirk Stieff, 1846

Carving set, 2 pieces, small, stainless blade,
    steak....................................$150
Fork, 7 3/8 in...............................$54
Fork, 7 5/8 in...............................$80
Fork, 8 in...................................$80
Fork-carving, small, stainless prongs, steak,
    8 3/4 in.................................$75
Fork-salad serving, stainless prongs $60
Fork-salad, individual, 6 1/2 in...............$60
Fork-salad, individual, 6 1/8 in..............$60
Knife-carving, small, stainless blade, steak,
    11 1/2 in. $75
Knife-modern, hollow handle, 8 7/8 in.........$50
Knife-modern, hollow handle, 9 5/8 in.........$60
Ladle-gravy, solid, 7 1/8 in. $115
Ladle-soup, stainless bowl, 10 3/4 in. $100
Server-pie and cake, stainless blade,
    10 3/8 in. $80
Spoon-casserole, smooth, stainless bowl,
    10 1/4 in. $60
Spoon-iced tea, 7 5/8 in. $50
Spoon-place/oval soup, 6 3/4 in..............$60
Spoon-salad serving, stainless bowl $60
Spoon-sugar shell, 6 1/4 in...................$50
Spoon-teaspoon, 6 in.........................$34
Tablespoon, (serving spoon), 8 1/2 in.........$90

Old Maryland-Engraved by Kirk Stieff, 1936

Baby set, 2 pieces $75
Butter-master, hollow handle, no notch,
    6 7/8 in.................................$50
Carving set, 2 pieces, small, stainless blade,
    steak...................................$110
Fork, 7 1/4 in. $54
Fork, 7 7/8 in. $75
Fork-baby, 4 3/8 in..........................$40
Fork-carving, small, stainless prongs, steak,
    8 in. $55
Fork-cold meat/serving, medium, solid, 1 of
    4 tines beveled, 8 1/2 in...............$120
Fork-cold meat/serving, small, solid,
    7 5/8 in................................$110
Fork-ice cream, 5 1/2 in. $54
Fork-salad serving, stainless prongs, 3 tines,
    10 3/4 in................................$47
Fork-salad, individual, 6 3/8 in. $50
Knife-carving, small, stainless blade, steak,
    10 in. $55
Knife-cheese, stainless blade, 7 1/8 in. $50
Knife-modern, hollow handle, 9 5/8 in........$50
Knife-modern, hollow handle, 9 in. $45
Knife-new french, hollow handle, 8 7/8 in. $47
Knife-new french, hollow handle, 9 5/8 in. $50
Knife-steak, individual, beveled blade,
    8 5/8 in.................................$50
Ladle-gravy, solid, 7 1/8 in..................$110
Ladle-mayonnaise, 5 1/2 in. $60
Salad set, 2 pieces, solid $300
Server-asparagus, hollow handle, silver
    plate hood, 9 1/4 in.....................$55
Server-cheese, stainless blade, 6 1/2 in. $60
Server-pasta, stainless bowl, 10 3/8 in. $47
Server-pie and cake, stainless blade,
    3 5/8 in. handle, 10 in..................$46
Server-tomato, solid, 7 3/4 in. $120
Slicer-cake, stainless blade, ice cream,
    10 1/4 in................................$46
Slicer-cake, stainless blade, wedding,
    11 3/4 in................................$46
Spoon-baby, curved handle, 3 1/2 in. $50
Spoon-berry/casserole, solid, shell,
    9 1/4 in.................................$190

Kirk Stieff

Kirk Stieff

Spoon-dessert/oval soup, 7 3/8 in. $60
Spoon-fruit, 5 7/8 in. $50
Spoon-iced tea, 7 3/4 in. $54
Spoon-infant feeding, 5 5/8 in. $40
Spoon-place/oval soup, 6 5/8 in. $60
Spoon-salad serving, solid, 9 3/8 in. $150
Spoon-serving, stainless bowl, 5 scallops,
    9 3/8 in. $50
Spoon-soup, round bowl, cream, 6 3/8 in. $56
Spoon-sugar shell, 6 1/4 in. $50

Thirty-six pieces Kirk Stieff Old Maryland Engraved (1936): 6 each luncheon forks, luncheon knives, salad forks, teaspoons, dessert spoons, and butter spreaders. No monogram except one teaspoon marked "S." $1,260

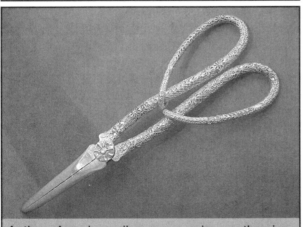

Antique American silver grape scissors, the sinuous tapering whipcord handles chased with floral repoussé decoration, inset steel cutting edges; made by S. Kirk & Son of Baltimore, Maryland, c.1885-1896. No monogram. "11 OZ" silver standard, 7 1/2 in., 2 5/8 in. across handles, 5.5 troy oz. gross. Hinge weak with some soft solder repair. $650

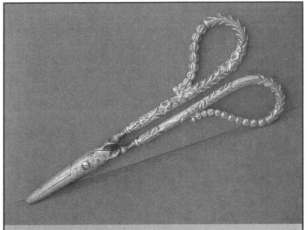

Antique American silver-handled grape scissors with steel blades, the hollow handles chased with floral and foliate decoration; made by S. Kirk & Son of Baltimore, Maryland, c.1885-1896. No monogram. "11 OZ" silver standard, 6 1/2 in., 2 3/4 in. across handles. Some surface corrosion to steel blades. $350

Old Maryland-Plain by Kirk Stieff, 1850

Butter spreader, flat handle, 5 3/8 in. $30
Fork, 7 1/4 in. $50
Fork, 7 7/8 in. $60
Fork-cocktail, 5 3/4 in. $28
Fork-cold meat/serving, small, solid, 4 tines,
    7 5/8 in. $80
Fork-salad, individual, 6 3/8 in. $40
Knife-modern, hollow handle, 8 7/8 in. $36
Knife-new french, hollow handle, 8 7/8 in. $38
Knife-youth, 7 1/4 in. $36
Ladle-cream, solid, 5 1/2 in. $45
Ladle-gravy, solid, 7 in. $80
Server-pie and cake, stainless blade,
    10 1/4 in. $60
Spoon-demitasse, 4 1/8 in. $22
Spoon-dessert/oval soup, 7 3/8 in. $54
Spoon-fruit, 5 7/8 in. $35
Spoon-place/oval soup, 6 5/8 in. $46
Spoon-soup, round bowl, bouillon,
    5 5/8 in. $32

Spoon-sugar shell, 6 1/4 in. $37
Spoon-teaspoon (five o'clock), 5 5/8 in. $18
Spoon-teaspoon, 5 7/8 in. $30
Tablespoon, (serving spoon), 8 3/8 in. $90

Personna by Kirk Stieff, 1959

Butter spreader, hollow handle, modern,
    stainless paddle, 6 1/4 in. $25
Fork, 7 5/8 in. $55
Fork-salad, individual, 6 5/8 in. $50
Knife-fish, stainless blade, individual,
    8 1/8 in. $38
Knife-modern, hollow handle, 9 in. $40
Server-pie and cake, stainless blade,
    10 3/4 in. $70
Spoon-dessert/oval soup, 6 7/8 in. $50
Spoon-iced tea, 7 1/4 in. $40
Spoon-sugar, 6 1/4 in. $40
Spoon-teaspoon, 6 1/4 in. $20
Tablespoon, (serving spoon), pierced,
    tear-shaped bowl, 8 1/2 in. $100

Primrose by Kirk Stieff, 1933

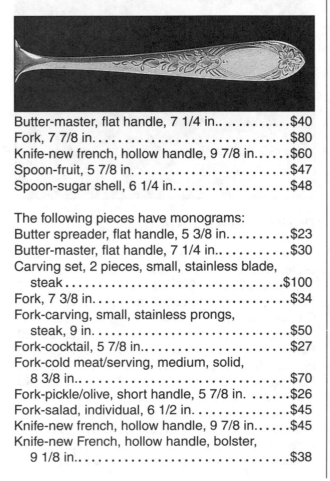

Butter-master, flat handle, 7 1/4 in. $40
Fork, 7 7/8 in. $80
Knife-new french, hollow handle, 9 7/8 in. $60
Spoon-fruit, 5 7/8 in. $47
Spoon-sugar shell, 6 1/4 in. $48

The following pieces have monograms:
Butter spreader, flat handle, 5 3/8 in. $23
Butter-master, flat handle, 7 1/4 in. $30
Carving set, 2 pieces, small, stainless blade,
    steak $100
Fork, 7 3/8 in. $34
Fork-carving, small, stainless prongs,
    steak, 9 in. $50
Fork-cocktail, 5 7/8 in. $27
Fork-cold meat/serving, medium, solid,
    8 3/8 in. $70
Fork-pickle/olive, short handle, 5 7/8 in. $26
Fork-salad, individual, 6 1/2 in. $45
Knife-new french, hollow handle, 9 7/8 in. $45
Knife-new French, hollow handle, bolster,
    9 1/8 in. $38

Ladle-gravy, solid, 6 7/8 in. $75
Spoon-casserole, smooth bowl, solid,
    8 1/2 in. $90
Spoon-iced tea, 7 3/4 in. $38
Spoon-serving, solid, 8 1/2 in. $90
Spoon-soup, round bowl, bouillon,
    5 3/8 in. $38
Spoon-soup, round bowl, cream, 6 3/8 in. $45
Spoon-sugar shell, 6 1/4 in. $38
Spoon-teaspoon, 6 in. $23
Tablespoon, (serving spoon), 8 1/2 in. $70

Princess-Hand Chased by Kirk Stieff, 1915

Fork-salad, individual, 6 1/4 in. $70

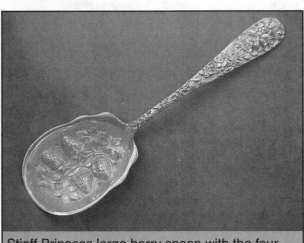

Stieff Princess large berry spoon with the four berry chased bowl, c.1915-1930. Monogram "W," 9 1/4 in., 2 3/4 in. across bowl, 4.7 troy oz. $900

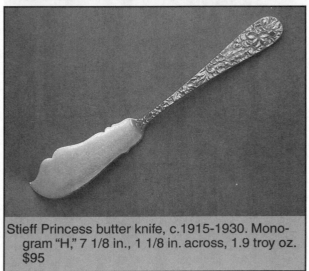

Stieff Princess butter knife, c.1915-1930. Monogram "H," 7 1/8 in., 1 1/8 in. across, 1.9 troy oz. $95

Kirk Stieff

Stieff Princess large cold meat fork, c.1915-1930. Monogram "W," 8 7/8 in., 1 5/8 in. across tines, 3.5 troy oz. $225

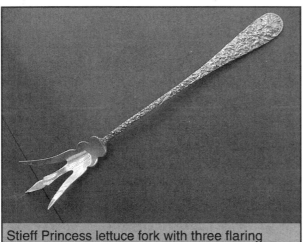

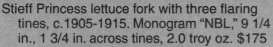

Stieff Princess lettuce fork with three flaring tines, c.1905-1915. Monogram "NBL," 9 1/4 in., 1 3/4 in. across tines, 2.0 troy oz. $175

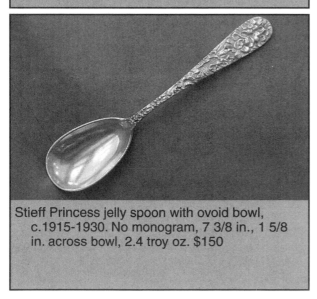

Stieff Princess jelly spoon with ovoid bowl, c.1915-1930. No monogram, 7 3/8 in., 1 5/8 in. across bowl, 2.4 troy oz. $150

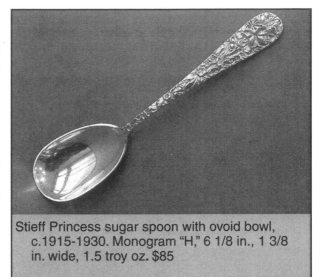

Stieff Princess sugar spoon with ovoid bowl, c.1915-1930. Monogram "H," 6 1/8 in., 1 3/8 in. wide, 1.5 troy oz. $85

Stieff Princess large tomato server, c.1915-1930. No monogram, 9 1/4 in., 3 1/2 in. across blade, 5.1 troy oz. $750

Puritan by Kirk Stieff, 1922

Butter spreader, flat handle, 6 in. $20
Butter spreader, hollow handle, modern,
    stainless paddle, 6 3/8 in. $25
Butter-master, flat handle, 7 in. $40
Carving set, 2 pieces, small, stainless blade,
    steak $120
Fork, 6 7/8 in. $28
Fork, 7 1/2 in. $60
Fork-baby, 4 1/2 in. $40
Fork-bacon, solid, 8 1/8 in. $100
Fork-carving, small stainless prongs, steak,
    8 5/8 in. $60
Fork-cocktail, 5 5/8 in. $26
Fork-cold meat/serving, large, solid, 9 in. $90

Fork-cold meat/serving, small, solid,
7 3/4 in.....................................$80
Fork-ice cream, 5 3/4 in....................$46
Fork-lemon, 4 3/4 in........................$30
Fork-pickle/olive, short handle, 5 7/8 in. $30
Fork-salad, individual, 6 1/8 in..............$35
Knife-blunt, hollow handle, 8 7/8 in. $35
Knife-new french, hollow handle,
8 7/8 in.....................................$36
Knife-new french, hollow handle,
9 5/8 in.....................................$45
Ladle-gravy, solid, 6 3/8 in. $70
Pick-butter, 1 tine, 5 3/4 in..................$48
Server-cheese, stainless blade, 6 3/8 in......$45
Server-pastry, stainless bowl, 9 1/2 in. $70
Server-pie, stainless blade, 9 7/8 in. $65
Server-tomato, solid, 7 1/2 in. $100
Spoon-baby, straight handle, 4 3/8 in. $40
Spoon-bon-bon, 5 1/2 in. $38
Spoon-casserole, smooth bowl, solid,
8 1/8 in.....................................$90
Spoon-demitasse, 4 3/8 in. $18
Spoon-egg, 6 1/8 in. $40
Spoon-fruit, 6 in. $35
Spoon-iced tea, 7 1/2 in. $35
Spoon-jam, 6 1/8 in. $38
Spoon-olive, short, pierced bowl, 5 3/4 in. $90
Spoon-soup, round bowl, bouillon,
5 5/8 in.....................................$40
Spoon-soup, round bowl, cream, 6 1/8 in......$45
Spoon-soup, round bowl, gumbo, 7 in. $50
Spoon-sugar, 6 1/8 in........................$30
Spoon-teaspoon (five o'clock), 5 5/8 in........$13
Spoon-teaspoon, 6 in........................$23
Tablespoon, (serving spoon), 7 3/4 in.........$70
Tablespoon, (serving spoon), pierced,
7 3/4 in.....................................$80

Quadrille by Kirk Stieff, 1950

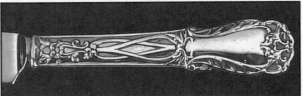

Fork, 7 1/4 in...............................$45
Fork-salad, individual, 6 3/4 in. $40
Knife-new french, hollow handle, 9 1/4 in......$34
Knife-new french, hollow handle, 9 7/8 in......$46
Spoon-soup, round bowl, cream, 6 3/8 in......$48
Spoon-sugar shell, 5 1/2 in..................$35
Spoon-teaspoon, 6 in........................$22

Repoussé by Kirk Stieff, 1828

Butter spreader, flat handle, design on 2 sides,
5 1/4 in. $30
Butter spreader, hollow handle, modern,
stainless paddle, 6 1/4 in.................. $32
Butter-master, flat handle, 7 1/4 in........... $40
Butter-master, hollow handle, 6 7/8 in........ $40
Carving set, 2 pieces, small, stainless blade,
steak, no rest $100
Carving set, 2 pieces, small, stainless blade,
steak, with rest.......................... $100
Fork, 7 1/4 in. $40
Fork, 7 7/8 in. $80
Fork-carving, small stainless prongs, steak,
8 1/2 in.................................... $50
Fork-carving, small stainless prongs, steak,
with rest, 9 in............................. $50
Fork-cocktail, 1 1/8 in. tines, 5 3/8 in. $30
Fork-cold meat/serving, medium, solid,
8 1/2 in.................................... $90
Fork-cold meat/serving, small, solid,
7 1/2 in.................................... $90
Fork-ice cream, smooth bowl, 5 1/2 in........ $50
Fork-lemon, 2 tines, 4 1/2 in. $30
Fork-oyster, short handle, 7/8 in. tines,
5 3/8 in. $40
Fork-pickle/olive, short handle, 3 tines,
6 in. $34
Fork-salad, individual, 6 1/4 in. $40
Knife-carving, large-stainless blade, roast,
12 3/8 in................................... $120
Knife-carving, small, stainless blade, steak,
no rest, 10 in. $50
Knife-carving, small, stainless blade, steak,
no rest, 9 1/2 in........................... $50
Knife-cheese, stainless blade, 7 in........... $50
Knife-fish, stainless blade, individual,
8 in. $64
Knife-modern, hollow handle, 9 3/4 in........ $54
Knife-modern, hollow handle, 9 in. $50
Knife-new french, hollow handle,
8 7/8 in. $44
Knife-new french, hollow handle, bolster,
8 7/8 in. $44
Knife-old french, hollow handle, full repousse,
8 3/4 in.................................... $100
Knife-old french, hollow handle, 8 5/8 in. $55

Kirk Stieff

Knife-steak, individual, beveled blade,
8 3/4 in...................................$50
Ladle-gravy, solid, 7 in....................$90
Ladle-mayonnaise, 4 1/8 in. handle,
5 1/2 in...................................$60
Ladle-punch, stainless bowl,
13 1/8 in. $100
Napkin clip, (made for five o'clock)...........$30
Napkin clip, (made for teaspoons)...........$30
Pick-butter, 2 tines, 6 in....................$50
Salad set, 2 pieces, solid $280
Salad set, 2 pieces, stainless bowl...........$90
Salad set, 2 pieces, wooden bowl............$90
Scoop-ice, silver plate bowl, 8 1/2 in..........$60
Server-asparagus, hollow handle, silver plate
hood, 9 1/4 in. $55
Server-cheese, stainless blade,
6 1/2 in...................................$50
Server-cheese, stainless blade,
6 3/4 in...................................$50
Server-lasagna, stainless blade,
11 3/8 in. $45
Server-pasta, stainless bowl, 10 1/2 in........$45
Server-pastry, stainless bowl, 10 in..........$70
Server-tomato, solid, 7 5/8 in. $120
Spoon-berry/casserole, solid, shell bowl,
crimped edge, 7 1/2 in. $120
Spoon-berry/casserole, solid, shell bowl,
large, crimped edge, 9 1/8 in.............$140
Spoon-bon-bon, berry bowl, 5 1/8 in..........$36
Spoon-casserole, smooth bowl, solid,
smooth edge, 8 3/8 in..................$130
Spoon-casserole, smooth stainless bowl,
10 1/4 in. $45
Spoon-demitasse, 2 3/4 in. handle,
4 1/8 in...................................$24
Spoon-iced tea, 7 5/8 in. $40
Spoon-infant feeding, 5 3/4 in................$40
Spoon-place/oval soup, 6 3/8 in..............$45
Spoon-salad serving, solid, 8 3/8 in. $140
Spoon-salad serving, solid, 9 1/8 in. $140
Spoon-salt, master, 3 in....................$28
Spoon-serving, solid, egg-shaped bowl,
8 1/2 in...................................$100
Spoon-soup, round bowl, cream,
6 1/8 in...................................$46
Spoon-sugar shell, shell-shaped bowl,
6 in.......................................$42
Spoon-sugar, smooth bowl, 6 in.............$43
Spoon-teaspoon (five o'clock), 3 7/8 in.
handle, 5 5/8 in..........................$24
Spoon-teaspoon, 4 in. handle, 5 7/8 in........$24
Tablespoon, (serving spoon), pierced,
8 3/8 in...................................$100
Tablespoon, (serving spoon), tear-shaped
bowl, 8 3/8 in. $85

Tongs-sugar, 3 1/4 in. $66
Tongs-sugar, 4 1/8 in. $66
Youth set, 3 pieces (spoon, knife, fork)......$140

Kirk Repoussé napkin ring. 1 3/4 in. wide by 15/16 in. high, no monogram, good condition, mark ("S. KIRK & SON CO. / 925 / 111") $250

Kirk Repoussé asparagus fork with four flattened tines (#2), c.1900-1925. No monogram, 8 5/8 in., 2 1/3 in. across tines. $400

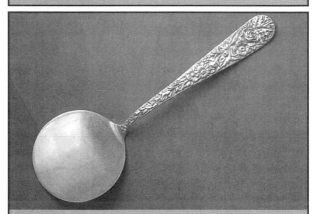

Kirk Repoussé cake lifter (#74C) with flat circular blade, c.1900-1925. No monogram, 6 1/3 in., 2 1/3 in. across blade. $145

Kirk Repoussé large serving spoon with ovoid bowl, c.1890-1895 (10.15 quality mark). Monogram "BHG," 9 3/4 in., 2 1/8 in. across bowl. $160

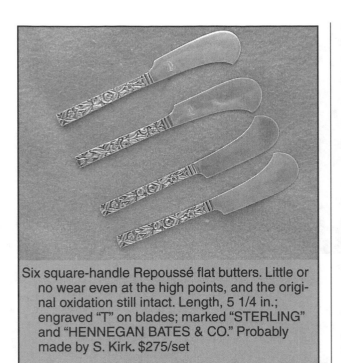

Six square-handle Repoussé flat butters. Little or no wear even at the high points, and the original oxidation still intact. Length, 5 1/4 in.; engraved "T" on blades; marked "STERLING" and "HENNEGAN BATES & CO." Probably made by S. Kirk. $275/set

Repoussé by S. Kirk & Son Inc., 1924

Butter-master, flat handle, 7 1/8 in............$50
Carving set, 2 pieces, small, stainless blade,
   steak....................................$120
Fork, 7 1/4 in..................................$45
Fork, 7 7/8 in..................................$90
Fork-chipped beef, small, 7 5/8 in............$84
Fork-cocktail, 1 1/8 in. tines, 5 1/4 in........$30
Fork-cold meat/serving, medium, solid,
   8 1/2 in....................................$100
Fork-lemon, 2 tines, 4 3/8 in.................$35
Fork-lemon, 2 tines, 5 3/4 in.................$35
Fork-oyster, short handle, 7/8 in. tines,
   5 3/8 in....................................$45
Fork-pickle/olive, short handle, 6 in...........$35
Fork-salad serving, solid, 5 tines,
   9 1/2 in....................................$160
Fork-salad, individual, 6 1/4 in...............$44
Fork-youth, 5 1/2 in. $55
Knife-modern, hollow handle, 9 in............$50
Knife-new french, hollow handle, bolster,
   8 7/8 in....................................$50

Knife-new french hollow handle, bolster,
   9 3/4 in....................................$70
Ladle-cream, solid, 5 in. handle, 6 1/2 in......$60
Ladle-gravy, solid, 7 in. $100
Ladle-mayonnaise, 4 1/8 in. handle,
   5 3/8 in....................................$70
Napkin clip, (made for five o'clock) $32
Server-jelly, 6 3/4 in. $50
Server-pie, stainless blade, 10 3/8 in.........$80
Server-pie, stainless blade, 9 7/8 in..........$80
Spoon-baby, straight handle, 3 3/4 in.........$40
Spoon-demitasse, 4 3/8 in..................$28
Spoon-fruit, 6 1/8 in. $48
Spoon-iced tea, 7 5/8 in.....................$44
Spoon-salt, individual, 2 1/2 in. $19
Spoon-serving, solid, egg-shaped bowl,
   8 1/2 in....................................$110
Spoon-soup, round bowl, bouillon,
   5 1/8 in....................................$45
Spoon-soup, round bowl, cream, 5 7/8 in.....$50
Spoon-sugar shell, 6 in. $40
Spoon-sugar, smooth bowl, 6 in.............$40
Spoon-teaspoon (five o'clock), 3 7/8 in.
   handle, 5 5/8 in.............................$28
Spoon-teaspoon, 4 in. handle, 5 7/8 in. $24
Tablespoon, (serving spoon), tear-shaped
   bowl, 8 3/8 in..............................$90

Kirk Repoussé bon bon spoon with embossed fruit decorated bowl (#29), c.1900-1925. Monogram "EN." 5 1/8 in., 2 in. across bowl. $60

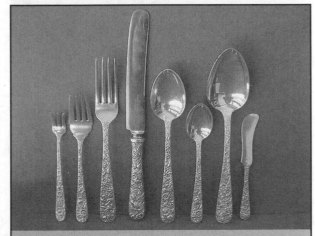

Eighty-eight pieces Kirk Steiff Repoussé: 12 each dinner forks, dinner knives, salad forks, teaspoons, dessert spoons, cocktail forks, and butter spreaders; also 4 tablespoons. c.1920-1940. Monogram "MLeM" except 2 teaspoons. $3,600

Kirk Repoussé medium cold meat fork, c.1925-1950. Monogram "MCC," 7 5/8 in., 1 1/2 in. wide. $68

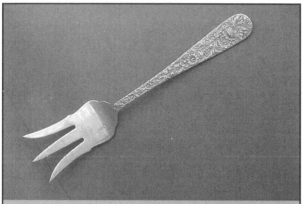

Kirk Repoussé relish fork with three tines, c.1925-1950. Monogram "HPS," 7 5/8 in., 1 5/8 in. across tines. $85

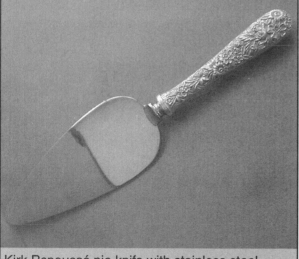

Kirk Repoussé pie knife with stainless steel blade, c.1925-1950. No monogram, 10 in., 2 1/4 in. across blade. $60

Kirk Repoussé bacon fork, c.1950-1980. Monogram "ALS," 7 5/8 in., 2 3/4 in. across tines. $120

Kirk Repoussé large berry spoon with floral embossed bowl, c.1950-1980. No monogram, 9 1/8 in., 3 1/8 in. across bowl, 3.8 troy oz. $190

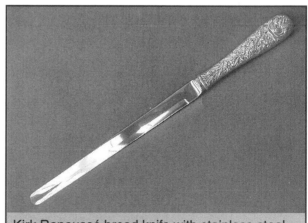

Kirk Repoussé bread knife with stainless steel blade, c.1950-1980. No monogram, 14 in. $100

Kirk Repoussé large cold meat fork, c.1950-1980. No monogram, 8 1/2 in., 1 5/8 in. wide. $95

Fork-salad, individual, 6 1/4 in.	$50
Spoon-bon-bon, berry bowl, 5 1/8 in.	$50
Spoon-fruit, 6 1/8 in.	$50
Spoon-iced tea, 7 5/8 in.	$50
Spoon-soup, round bowl, bouillon, 5 3/8 in.	$45
Spoon-sugar shell, 6 1/8 in.	$44
Spoon-sugar, 6 in.	$44
Spoon-teaspoon (five o'clock), 5 5/8 in.	$28
Spoon-teaspoon, 5 7/8 in.	$30
Tablespoon, (serving spoon), 8 3/8 in.	$100
Tea strainer, 6 7/8 in.	$480
Tongs-sugar, 3 1/4 in.	$90

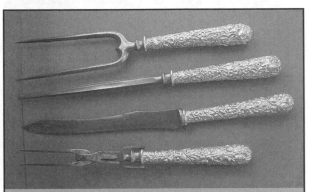

Four Kirk Repoussé roast carvers consisting of knife, fork, sharpener, and holder, c.1890-1900. Monogram "JAH." Two pieces marked "11 OZ," 2 "925." Hand chased rather than stamped. Knife 13 5/8 in., fork 11 1/2 in., sharpener 13 1/4 in., holder 12 1/8 in. Knife blade worn, knife handle over-polished. $600/set

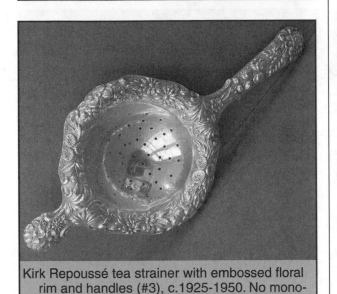

Kirk Repoussé tea strainer with embossed floral rim and handles (#3), c.1925-1950. No monogram, 6 5/8 in., 3 in. across bowl. $280

Kirk Repoussé large cold meat fork, c.1897-1910. Monogram "EMM," 9 3/8 in., 1 1/2 in. across bowl. $200

Repoussé by Kirk Stieff, 1896 — 925/100 back stamp

Butter-master, flat handle, 7 1/4 in.	$50
Fork, 7 1/4 in.	$50
Fork, 7 3/4 in.	$90
Fork-pickle/olive, short handle, 3 tines, 6 in.	$40

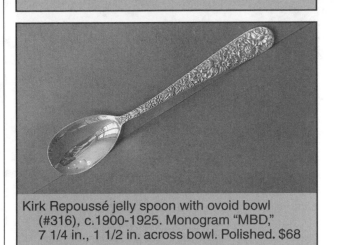

Kirk Repoussé jelly spoon with ovoid bowl (#316), c.1900-1925. Monogram "MBD," 7 1/4 in., 1 1/2 in. across bowl. Polished. $68

Kirk Repoussé large salad serving fork with five tines (#405), c.1900-1925. Monogram "LGK," 9 1/3 in., 2 in. wide. $210

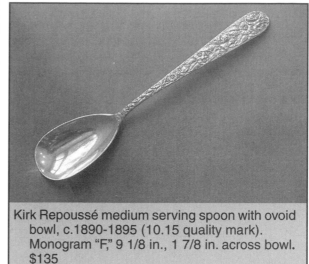

Kirk Repoussé medium serving spoon with ovoid bowl, c.1890-1895 (10.15 quality mark). Monogram "F," 9 1/8 in., 1 7/8 in. across bowl. $135

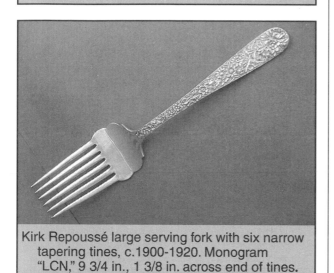

Kirk Repoussé large serving fork with six narrow tapering tines, c.1900-1920. Monogram "LCN," 9 3/4 in., 1 3/8 in. across end of tines. $230

Kirk Repoussé soup ladle, c.1896-1905. Monogram "M," 11 1/8 in., 3 5/8 in. across bowl. $500

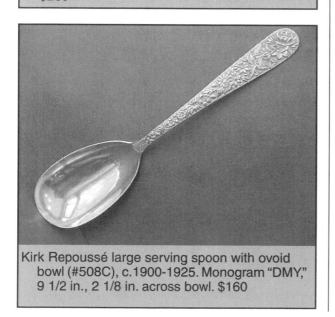

Kirk Repoussé large serving spoon with ovoid bowl (#508C), c.1900-1925. Monogram "DMY," 9 1/2 in., 2 1/8 in. across bowl. $160

Kirk Repoussé tea strainer with applied floral rim (#1), c.1900-1920. Monogram "HWK," 7 7/8 in., 3 1/4 in. across bowl. $350

Kirk Stieff

Rose by Kirk Stieff, 1937

Butter spreader, flat handle,
  5 3/8 in...............................$36
Fork, 7 3/8 in...............................$45
Fork-salad, individual,
  6 3/8 in...............................$55
Ladle-gravy, solid, 7 1/4 in. $120
Napkin clip, (made for teaspoons) $35
Spoon-bon-bon, 4 7/8 in. $60
Spoon-demitasse, 4 1/8 in. $32
Spoon-iced tea, 7 5/8 in. $50
Spoon-soup, round bowl, cream,
  6 in...............................$70
Spoon-sugar shell,
  6 1/4 in...............................$44
Spoon-teaspoon, 6 in......................$28
Tablespoon, (serving spoon),
  8 3/8 in...............................$90

Forty-one pieces Kirk Stieff Rose (1937): 8 each luncheon forks, luncheon knives, salad forks, and teaspoons; also 6 cream soup spoons, 1 tablespoon, 1 sugar spoon, and 1 butter knife. No monogram. $1,350

Seventy-two pieces Stieff Rose: 12 each luncheon forks, luncheon knives, salad forks, cream soup spoons, teaspoons, and butter spreaders. Monogram "MHL" except 1 salad fork "MH," 1 luncheon fork "DJD," and 6 cream soup spoons, no monogram. $2,100

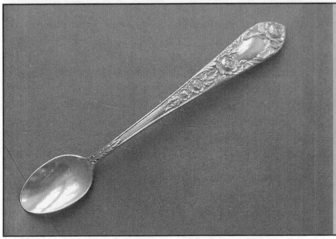

American silver infant feeding spoon in the Rose pattern (1937) made by S. Kirk & Son Inc. of Baltimore, Maryland. No monogram. 5 5/8 in. $35

American silver baby fork and spoon in the Rose pattern made by the Stieff Co. of Baltimore, Maryland, c.1940-1980. Monogram removed and polished. Fork 4 5/8 in., spoon 4 3/8 in. $75

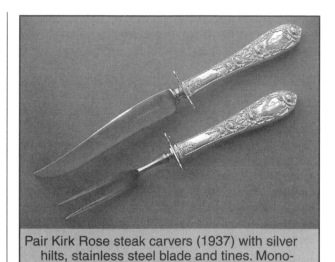

Pair Kirk Rose steak carvers (1937) with silver hilts, stainless steel blade and tines. Monogram "Z." Knife 10 1/8 in.; fork 8 7/8 in. $100

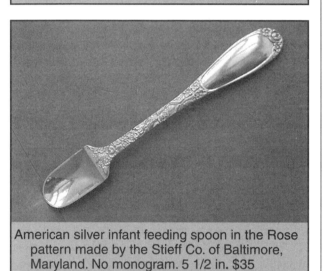

American silver infant feeding spoon in the Rose pattern made by the Stieff Co. of Baltimore, Maryland. No monogram. 5 1/2 in. $35

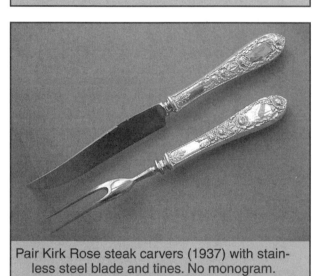

Pair Kirk Rose steak carvers (1937) with stainless steel blade and tines. No monogram. Knife 10 in., fork 9 in. $85

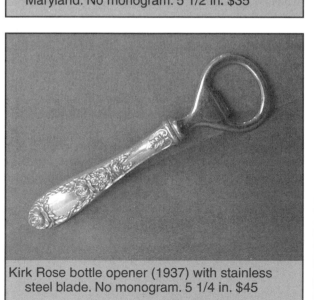

Kirk Rose bottle opener (1937) with stainless steel blade. No monogram. 5 1/4 in. $45

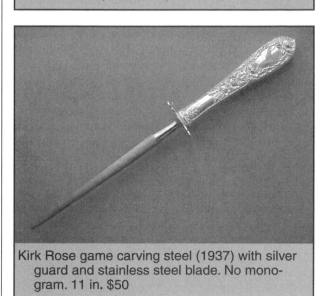

Kirk Rose game carving steel (1937) with silver guard and stainless steel blade. No monogram. 11 in. $50

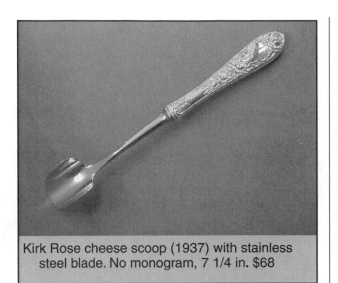

Kirk Rose cheese scoop (1937) with stainless steel blade. No monogram, 7 1/4 in. $68

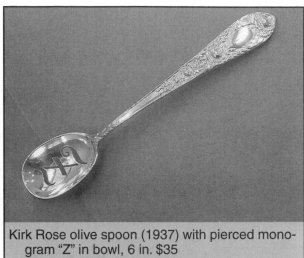

Kirk Rose olive spoon (1937) with pierced monogram "Z" in bowl, 6 in. $35

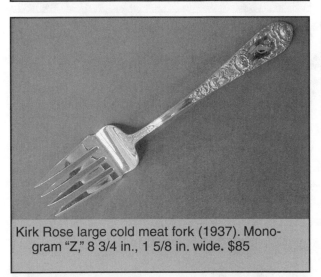

Kirk Rose large cold meat fork (1937). Monogram "Z," 8 3/4 in., 1 5/8 in. wide. $85

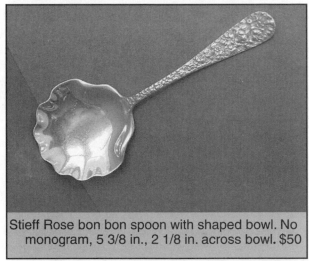

Stieff Rose bon bon spoon with shaped bowl. No monogram, 5 3/8 in., 2 1/8 in. across bowl. $50

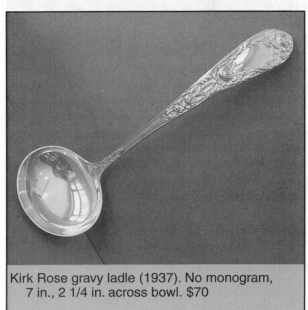

Kirk Rose gravy ladle (1937). No monogram, 7 in., 2 1/4 in. across bowl. $70

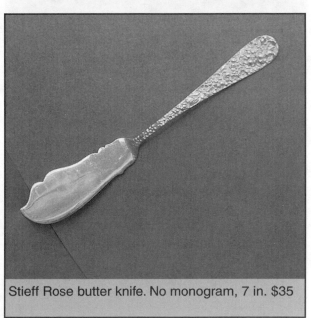

Stieff Rose butter knife. No monogram, 7 in. $35

Kirk Stieff

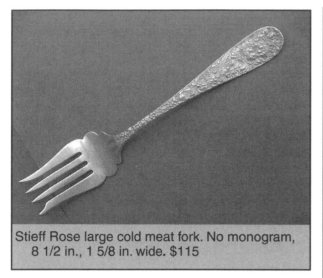

Stieff Rose large cold meat fork. No monogram, 8 1/2 in., 1 5/8 in. wide. $115

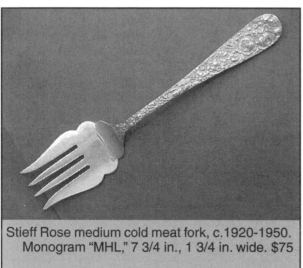

Stieff Rose medium cold meat fork, c.1920-1950. Monogram "MHL," 7 3/4 in., 1 3/4 in. wide. $75

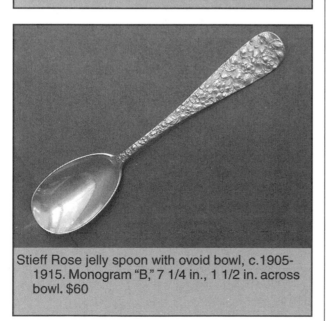

Stieff Rose jelly spoon with ovoid bowl, c.1905-1915. Monogram "B," 7 1/4 in., 1 1/2 in. across bowl. $60

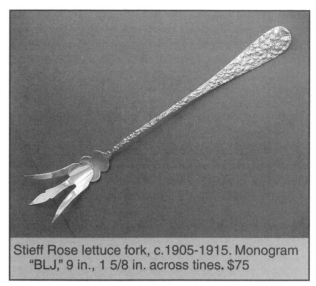

Stieff Rose lettuce fork, c.1905-1915. Monogram "BLJ," 9 in., 1 5/8 in. across tines. $75

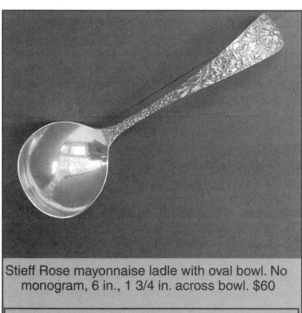

Stieff Rose mayonnaise ladle with oval bowl. No monogram, 6 in., 1 3/4 in. across bowl. $60

Stieff Rose medium napkin ring. No monogram, 1 1/4 in. high, 1 3/4 in. diameter. $230

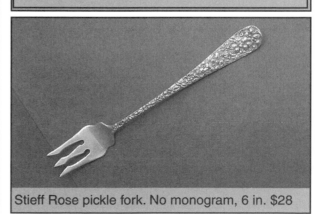

Stieff Rose pickle fork. No monogram, 6 in. $28

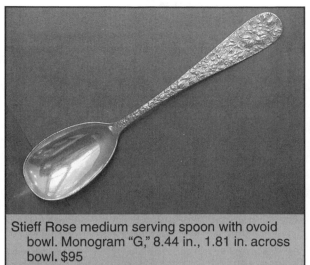

Stieff Rose medium serving spoon with ovoid bowl. Monogram "G," 8.44 in., 1.81 in. across bowl. $95

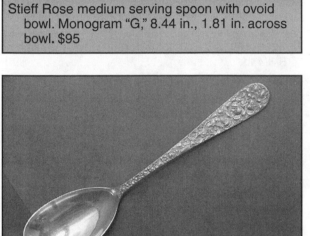

Stieff Rose medium serving spoon with ovoid bowl, c.1930-1970. No monogram, 8 in., 1 3/4 in. across bowl. $80

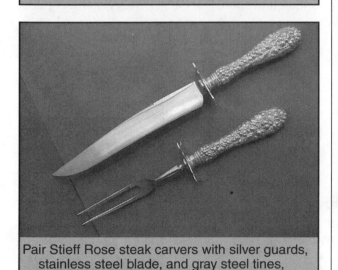

Pair Stieff Rose steak carvers with silver guards, stainless steel blade, and gray steel tines, c.1925-1935. No monogram. Knife 11 1/2 in., fork 9 1/2 in. $150

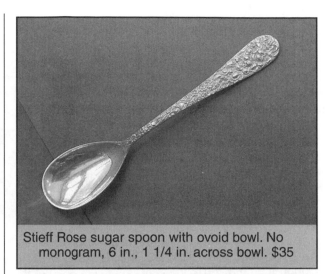

Stieff Rose sugar spoon with ovoid bowl. No monogram, 6 in., 1 1/4 in. across bowl. $35

Stieff Rose sugar tongs with claw grips. Script monogram "D," 4 1/4 in. $50

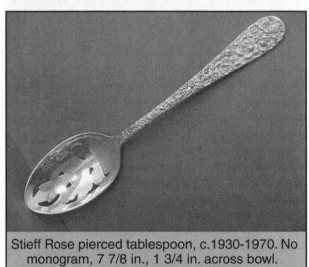

Stieff Rose pierced tablespoon, c.1930-1970. No monogram, 7 7/8 in., 1 3/4 in. across bowl. Piercing probably later. $75

Rose Motif by Kirk Stieff, 1954

Butter spreader, flat handle, 6 in............. $20
Butter spreader, hollow handle, modern, stainless paddle, 6 1/4 in................. $24
Butter-master, hollow handle, 7 in. $34

Fork, 7 3/8 in.............................$40
Fork-cocktail, 5 5/8 in.......................$32
Fork-cold meat/serving, medium, solid,
   8 1/2 in...................................$80
Fork-lemon, 4 3/4 in........................$28
Fork-pickle/olive, short handle, 6 in..........$28
Fork-salad, individual, 6 1/2 in...............$60
Knife-modern, hollow handle, 9 in............$34
Knife-youth, 7 1/4 in........................$38
Ladle-gravy, solid, 7 1/8 in. $80
Server-cheese, stainless blade, 6 3/4 in......$46
Server-jelly, 6 1/8 in........................$33
Server-pie, stainless blade, 10 in............$70
Spoon-casserole, smooth bowl, solid,
   8 1/2 in.................................$100
Spoon-dessert/oval soup, 6 7/8 in...........$50
Spoon-iced tea, 7 1/2 in. $40
Spoon-pea, solid, serving, 8 3/4 in. $85
Spoon-soup, round bowl, cream,
   6 3/8 in..................................$50
Spoon-sugar, 6 in...........................$34
Spoon-teaspoon, 6 in........................$20
Tablespoon, (serving spoon), 8 1/4 in.........$70

Royal Dynasty by Kirk Stieff, 1966

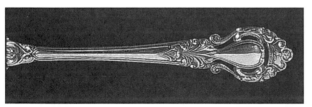

Fork, 7 1/2 in..............................$80
Fork-baby, 5 1/8 in. $60
Knife-modern, hollow handle, 9 1/8 in.........$70
Knife-steak, individual, 9 1/4 in. $70
Spoon-sugar shell, 6 1/8 in..................$60
Spoon-teaspoon, 6 1/4 in. $60

Severn by Kirk Stieff, 1940

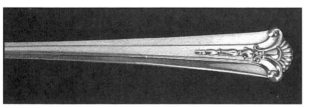

Butter spreader, flat handle, 5 3/4 in..........$20
Butter-master, flat handle, 7 in...............$40
Fork, 7 3/8 in..............................$34
Fork, 7 7/8 in..............................$50
Fork-ice cream, 5 1/2 in....................$38
Fork-salad, individual, 6 3/4 in...............$43

Knife-modern, hollow handle, no stamp,
   9 3/4 in..................................$46
Knife-new french, hollow handle, stamped
   S. Kirk & Son, 9 in. $33
Ladle-gravy, solid, 6 3/4 in..................$80
Ladle-gravy, solid, 7 1/8 in..................$80
Server-pie and cake, stainless blade,
   10 1/2 in.................................$60
Spoon-baby, straight handle, 3 7/8 in.........$34
Spoon-sherbet, large, 5 1/4 in...............$36
Spoon-soup, round bowl, cream,
   6 1/2 in..................................$46
Spoon-sugar shell, 6 1/4 in. $40
Spoon-teaspoon, 5 7/8 in...................$22
Spoon-youth, 5 1/2 in......................$20
Tablespoon, (serving spoon), 8 3/4 in. $90
Tablespoon, (serving spoon), pierced,
   8 3/4 in..................................$90

Signet-Plain by Kirk Stieff, 1958

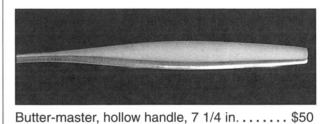

Butter-master, hollow handle, 7 1/4 in........$50
Fork, 7 1/2 in. $50
Fork-cold meat/serving, medium, solid,
   8 7/8 in.................................$105
Fork-pickle/olive, short handle, 6 in. $36
Ladle-gravy, solid, 7 in. $105
Spoon-sugar, 6 1/4 in.......................$40
Spoon-teaspoon, 6 1/4 in....................$30

The following pieces have monograms:
Butter spreader, hollow handle, modern,
   stainless, 6 1/2 in. $27
Fork, 7 1/2 in. $45
Fork-salad, individual, 7 1/8 in. $43
Knife-modern, hollow handle, 9 in. $35
Spoon-demitasse, 4 1/4 in..................$22
Spoon-teaspoon, 6 1/4 in...................$23

Silver Surf by Kirk Stieff, 1956

Butter spreader, hollow handle, modern, stainless
    paddle, 6 1/4 in..........................$27
Butter-master, hollow handle, 7 1/8 in.........$38
Fork, 7 1/2 in...............................$50
Fork-lemon, 4 3/4 in.........................$34
Knife-modern, hollow handle, 9 in............$38
Knife-steak, individual, 9 3/8 in. $50
Salad set, 2 pieces, solid...................$220
Server-cheese, stainless blade, 6 7/8 in.......$50
Server-pie and cake, stainless blade,
    10 3/4 in. $55
Spoon-dessert/oval soup, 6 7/8 in............$50
Spoon-olive, short, pierced bowl, 5 5/8 in. $80
Spoon-sugar, 6 1/8 in.......................$40
Spoon-teaspoon, 6 1/8 in. $28
Spoon-vegetable/serving, pierced,
    8 1/2 in..................................$130
Tablespoon, (serving spoon), pierced,
    8 1/2 in..................................$100

Stieff Rose by Kirk Stieff, 1892

Butter spreader, flat handle, 6 in. $24
Butter spreader, hollow handle, modern,
    stainless paddle, 6 in.....................$34
Butter-master, flat handle, 7 1/8 in...........$34
Carving set, 2 pieces, small, stainless blade,
    steak...................................$120
Fork, 6 7/8 in..............................$38
Fork-cocktail, 5 3/4 in......................$30
Fork-cold meat/serving, medium, solid, not
    pierced, 8 3/4 in.........................$90
Fork-cold meat/serving, small, solid,
    7 5/8 in..................................$80
Fork-lemon, 4 3/4 in........................$26
Fork-lettuce serving, large, 9 1/4 in...........$80
Fork-pickle/olive, short handle, 5 7/8 in. $26
Fork-relish, 6 in............................$60
Fork-salad serving, solid, 3 tines, 8 in.......$100
Fork-salad, individual, 6 in. $32
Fork-youth, 6 1/8 in. $46
Knife-blunt, hollow handle, 8 1/2 in. $34
Knife-blunt, hollow handle, 8 7/8 in. $34
Knife-blunt, hollow handle, 9 1/2 in. $54
Knife-dessert, stainless blade, 7 1/2 in........$36
Knife-wedding cake, stainless blade,
    12 1/8 in. $70

Ladle-gravy, solid, 5 3/4 in..................$80
Ladle-gravy, solid, 6 3/8 in..................$80
Napkin clip, (made for five o'clock) $25
Opener-bottle, stainless bowl, 5 1/2 in........$40
Server-asparagus, hollow handle, silver
    plate hood, 9 1/2 in......................$60
Server-jelly, flat bowl, 6 1/4 in. $30
Server-pie and cake, stainless blade,
    10 1/8 in.................................$55
Server-pie, silver plate blade, 9 3/4 in. $55
Server-pie, stainless blade, 10 1/8 in.........$55
Server-pie, stainless blade, 9 3/4 in..........$55
Spoon-bon-bon, 5 3/8 in. $35
Spoon-demitasse, 4 3/8 in...................$22
Spoon-egg, 2 in. bowl, 6 in. $38
Spoon-fruit, 6 in...........................$40
Spoon-iced tea, 7 1/2 in....................$32
Spoon-olive, short, pierced bowl, 7 piercings,
    5 3/4 in..................................$70
Spoon-place/oval soup, 6 5/8 in. $60
Spoon-salt, master, 2 7/8 in.................$30
Spoon-soup, round bowl, bouillon,
    5 1/2 in..................................$30
Spoon-soup, round bowl, cream, 6 in. $50
Spoon-soup, round bowl, gumbo, 7 in........$50
Spoon-sugar, 2 1/4 in. bowl, 6 1/4 in. $30
Spoon-teaspoon, (five o'clock), 5 5/8 in.......$14
Spoon-teaspoon, 5 7/8 in...................$20
Tablespoon, (serving spoon), 7 3/4 in. $60

Wadefield by Kirk Stieff, 1850

Butter spreader, flat handle, 5 3/8 in. $27
Butter-master, flat handle, no notch, 7 in......$36
Butter-master, flat handle, notch, 7 1/8 in.....$36
Carving set, 2 pieces, small, stainless blade,
    steak...................................$120
Fork, 7 3/8 in. $44
Fork-baby, 3 7/8 in.........................$40
Fork-baby, 4 3/8 in.........................$40
Fork-bacon, solid, 7 3/4 in..................$110
Fork-cocktail, 3 tines, 5 3/4 in...............$30
Fork-cocktail, 5 1/4 in......................$30
Fork-cold meat/serving, medium, solid,
    8 3/8 in..................................$90
Fork-cold meat/serving, small, solid,
    7 5/8 in..................................$90

Kirk Stieff

Fork-joint/roast holder, large, 10 1/2 in.......$100
Fork-lemon, 2 tines, 5 3/4 in.................$30
Fork-lemon, 4 5/8 in.........................$30
Fork-salad, individual, 6 3/8 in. $50
Knife-carving, small, stainless blade, steak,
    10 1/4 in. $60
Knife-new french, hollow handle, 9 3/4 in......$50
Knife-new french, hollow handle, 9 in. $40
Ladle-cream, solid, 5 1/8 in..................$40
Ladle-cream, solid, 6 in.....................$40
Ladle-gravy, solid, 6 7/8 in. $90
Napkin clip, (made for teaspoons) $30
Scoop-cheese, solid, 6 7/8 in................$80
Server-cheese, stainless blade, 6 1/2 in.......$48
Server-jelly, 6 3/4 in. $36
Server-pie, stainless blade, 10 1/8 in. $70
Spoon-baby, straight handle, 3 3/4 in. $42
Spoon-berry/casserole, solid, shell bowl,
    9 1/4 in..................................$140
Spoon-bon-bon, 5 1/8 in. $40
Spoon-casserole, smooth bowl, solid,
    8 1/2 in..................................$110
Spoon-demitasse, 4 1/4 in. $26
Spoon-dessert/oval soup, 7 3/8 in...........$70
Spoon-fruit, 5 7/8 in. $42
Spoon-iced tea, 7 3/4 in. $38
Spoon-olive, short, pierced bowl, 6 in.........$70
Spoon-salad serving, solid, 9 1/2 in. $130
Spoon-salt, individual, 2 1/2 in...............$16
Spoon-sherbet, 5 3/8 in.....................$40
Spoon-soup, round bowl, bouillon,
    5 1/2 in..................................$40
Spoon-soup, round bowl, cream,
    6 1/4 in..................................$50
Spoon-sugar shell, 6 1/4 in..................$34
Spoon-teaspoon, 6 in.......................$22
Tablespoon, (serving spoon), 8 1/2 in........$80
Tongs-sugar, 3 3/4 in.......................$50

Williamsburg Queen Anne by Kirk Stieff, 1940

Fork, no wing, 7 3/4 in.......................$50
Fork-baby, no wing, 4 5/8 in. $30
Fork-cocktail, no wing, 5 3/8 in..............$37
Fork-cold meat/serving, medium, solid, 4 tines,
    8 1/2 in..................................$120

Fork-salad, individual, 3 narrow tines,
    6 1/2 in.................................. $60
Knife-blunt/pistol, stainless blade,
    10 1/8 in................................. $65
Knife-blunt/pistol, stainless blade,
    8 1/2 in.................................. $48
Knife-blunt/pistol, stainless blade,
    9 1/4 in.................................. $48
Knife-fruit, stainless blade, individual, pistol grip,
    7 1/4 in. $45
Spoon-demitasse, wing handle, 4 1/2 in..... $32
Spoon-sugar, no wing, 5 5/8 in.............. $47
Spoon-teaspoon, no wing, 5 3/4 in........... $36
Tablespoon, (serving spoon), no wing,
    7 7/8 in.................................. $110

Winslow by Kirk Stieff, 1850

Butter spreader, flat handle, design on one
    side, 5 3/4 in. $30
Butter spreader, flat handle, design on two
    sides, 5 1/2 in. $30
Butter spreader, hollow handle, modern,
    stainless paddle, 6 3/8 in................ $30
Butter-master, flat handle, 7 in. $40
Butter-master, hollow handle, 7 in. $37
Carving set, 3 pieces, small, stainless blade,
    steak $170
Carving set, 2 pieces, small, stainless blade,
    steak $110
Fork, 7 1/4 in. $44
Fork-baby, 3 3/4 in........................ $40
Fork-cocktail, 5 3/8 in. $30
Fork-cold meat/serving, medium, solid,
    8 1/2 in.................................. $90
Fork-salad serving, solid, 9 3/8 in............ $96
Fork-salad, individual, 6 1/4 in. $50
Fork-youth, 6 1/4 in........................ $45
Knife-new french, hollow handle, 9 in. $35
Knife-youth, 5 3/4 in. $40
Ladle-gravy, solid, 7 in. $80
Server-pie and cake, stainless blade,
    10 1/2 in................................. $60
Spoon-bon-bon, 4 3/4 in. $40
Spoon-fruit, 6 in........................... $40
Spoon-place/oval soup, 6 1/4 in. $58
Spoon-soup, round bowl, bouillon, 5 in. $40

Spoon-soup, round bowl, cream, 6 in. $44
Spoon-soup, round bowl, gumbo, 7 1/4 in. $45
Spoon-sugar, 6 in. $38
Spoon-teaspoon, 5 7/8 in. $24
Spoon-youth, 5 1/2 in. $40
Tablespoon, (serving spoon), 8 1/4 in. $80

Thirty-two pieces Kirk Steiff Winslow: 8 each luncheon forks, luncheon knives, salad forks, and teaspoons. c.1900-1925. Monogram "C." $1,000

KNOWLES

Victorian tomato server by Knowles & Ladd, the gilt bowl engraved with foliate scrolls. Length 9 1/4 in.; monogrammed "G"; marked "900/ 1000 A. STOWELL K& L"; fine condition. $165

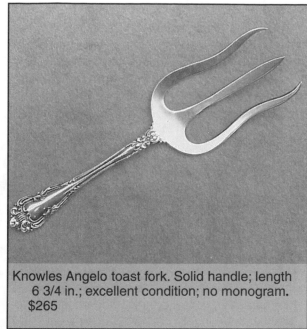

Knowles Angelo toast fork. Solid handle; length 6 3/4 in.; excellent condition; no monogram. $265

Knowles Trianon vegetable fork. A large server with gilt, matte finish tines and bowl. Excellent condition. Just under 9 1/8 in., monogrammed "B" (reverse). $250

LUNT SILVERSMITHS

Lunt Silversmiths was established in 1901 in Greenfield, Massachusetts as Rogers, Lunt & Bowlen Co., after the failure of the A.F. Towle & Son. Co., and began using the Lunt Silversmiths trademark in 1935. It later acquired the assets of the King Silver Co. and the Richard Dimes Co.

Alexandra by Lunt, 1961

Butter spreader, hollow handle, modern, stainless
  paddle, 6 1/4 in.. . . . .$40
Butter-master, hollow handle, 6 3/4 in.. . . . . . .$45
Fork, 7 3/8 in.. . . . .$50
Fork-cocktail, 5 7/8 in.. . . . .$46
Fork-cold meat/serving, small, solid,
  7 7/8 in.. . . . .$100
Fork-salad, individual, 6 5/8 in. $50
Knife-modern, hollow handle, 9 in.. . . . .$50
Knife-steak, individual, 5 3/8 in. blade,
  9 5/8 in.. . . . .$60
Ladle-gravy, solid, 6 1/4 in. $100
Napkin clip, (made for teaspoons) $35
Spoon-demitasse, 4 3/8 in. $40
Spoon-dessert/oval soup, 6 7/8 in.. . . . .$60
Spoon-iced tea, 7 3/8 in. $60
Spoon-sugar, 6 1/8 in.. . . . .$50
Spoon-teaspoon, 6 1/8 in. $30
Tablespoon, (serving spoon), 8 1/4 in.. . . . . . .$100
Tablespoon, (serving spoon), pierced,
  8 1/4 in.. . . . .$100

American Directoire by Lunt, 1931

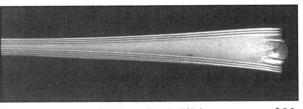

Butter spreader, flat handle, 5 7/8 in.. . . . .$30
Fork, 7 3/4 in.. . . . .$50
Fork-baby, 4 1/8 in. $40
Fork-cocktail, 5 5/8 in.. . . . .$20

Fork-salad, individual, 6 1/4 in. $50
Knife-new french, hollow handle,
  9 1/2 in.. . . . . $36
Knife-new french, hollow handle, bolster,
  9 3/4 in.. . . . . $36
Knife-youth, 8 in.. . . . . $30
Spoon-baby, straight handle, 4 1/4 in.. . . . . . . $40
Spoon-demitasse, 4 3/8 in.. . . . . $16
Spoon-dessert/oval soup, 7 1/8 in. $45
Spoon-sugar, 6 1/8 in.. . . . . $28
Spoon-teaspoon (five o'clock), 5 5/8 in. $18

The following pieces have monograms:
Butter spreader, flat handle, 5 7/8 in. $23
Fork-ice cream, 5 3/4 in.. . . . . $34
Fork-salad, individual, 6 1/4 in. $38
Knife-new french, hollow handle,
  9 1/8 in.. . . . . $27
Pick-butter, 1 tine, 6 in. $34
Spoon-soup, round bowl, cream,
  6 1/2 in.. . . . . $28
Spoon-sugar, 6 1/8 in.. . . . . $22
Tablespoon, (serving spoon), 8 5/8 in. $55

American Victorian by Lunt, 1941

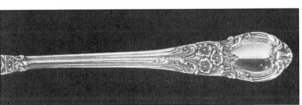

Butter spreader, flat handle, 5 7/8 in. $18
Butter spreader, hollow handle, stainless paddle,
  6 1/8 in.. . . . . $26
Butter-master, flat handle, 6 7/8 in.. . . . . $30
Fork, 7 1/4 in.. . . . . $26
Fork, 7 5/8 in.. . . . . $60
Fork-cocktail, 5 3/4 in. $25
Fork-cold meat/serving, small, solid,
  7 1/2 in.. . . . . $80
Fork-lemon, 4 7/8 in. $30
Fork-pickle/olive, short handle, 5 5/8 in.. . . . . . $32
Fork-salad, individual, 6 3/8 in. $36
Knife-cheese, stainless blade, 7 1/8 in. $44
Knife-modern, hollow handle, 9 in. $36
Knife-new french, hollow handle, silver plate
  blade, 8 3/4 in. $36
Knife-new french, hollow handle, stainless
  blade, 8 3/4 in. $36
Knife-steak, individual, serrated, 9 3/8 in. $48
Ladle-gravy, solid, 5 7/8 in. $80
Server-jelly, 6 1/8 in. $40

Lunt Silversmiths

Server-pie, stainless blade, 10 in............$60
Spoon-demitasse, 4 3/8 in. $20
Spoon-dessert/oval soup, 6 5/8 in...........$40
Spoon-fruit, 5 3/4 in. $40
Spoon-iced tea, 7 3/8 in. $36
Spoon-soup, round bowl, cream,
  6 1/4 in...................................$38
Spoon-sugar, 5 7/8 in..........................$35
Spoon-teaspoon, 5 3/4 in. $18
Tablespoon, (serving spoon), 8 3/8 in........$75
Tablespoon, (serving spoon), pierced,
  8 3/8 in.................................$85

Belle Meade by Lunt, 1967

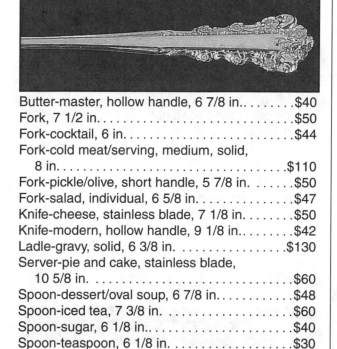

Butter-master, hollow handle, 6 7/8 in........$40
Fork, 7 1/2 in.............................$50
Fork-cocktail, 6 in.........................$44
Fork-cold meat/serving, medium, solid,
  8 in.....................................$110
Fork-pickle/olive, short handle, 5 7/8 in. $50
Fork-salad, individual, 6 5/8 in...............$47
Knife-cheese, stainless blade, 7 1/8 in.......$50
Knife-modern, hollow handle, 9 1/8 in........$42
Ladle-gravy, solid, 6 3/8 in. $130
Server-pie and cake, stainless blade,
  10 5/8 in. $60
Spoon-dessert/oval soup, 6 7/8 in...........$48
Spoon-iced tea, 7 3/8 in. $60
Spoon-sugar, 6 1/8 in.......................$40
Spoon-teaspoon, 6 1/8 in. $30
Tablespoon, (serving spoon), 8 1/4 in........$90
Tablespoon, (serving spoon), pierced,
  8 3/8 in.................................$90

Carillon by Lunt, 1957

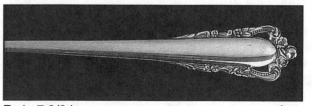

Fork, 7 3/8 in.............................$43
Fork-cocktail, 5 5/8 in......................$40
Fork-pickle/olive, short handle, 5 5/8 in. $33
Fork-salad, individual, 6 1/2 in..............$54

Knife-modern, hollow handle, 9 in. $40
Knife-steak, individual, 9 1/8 in.............$60
Spoon-place/oval soup, 6 1/2 in. $54
Spoon-sugar, 6 in. $40
Spoon-teaspoon, 6 in.......................$26
Tablespoon, (serving spoon), 8 3/8 in. $80
Tablespoon, (serving spoon), pierced,
  8 3/8 in. $90

Charles II by Lunt, 1934

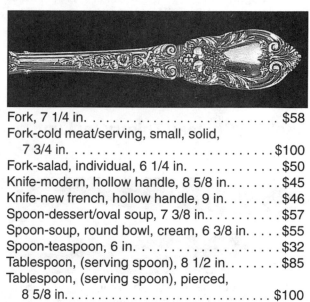

Fork, 7 1/4 in. $58
Fork-cold meat/serving, small, solid,
  7 3/4 in. $100
Fork-salad, individual, 6 1/4 in. $50
Knife-modern, hollow handle, 8 5/8 in........$45
Knife-new french, hollow handle, 9 in. $46
Spoon-dessert/oval soup, 7 3/8 in...........$57
Spoon-soup, round bowl, cream, 6 3/8 in. $55
Spoon-teaspoon, 6 in. $32
Tablespoon, (serving spoon), 8 1/2 in........$85
Tablespoon, (serving spoon), pierced,
  8 5/8 in.................................$100

Chased Classic by Lunt, 1936

Butter spreader, flat handle, 6 in............$18
Butter-master, flat handle, 7 1/8 in..........$34
Carving set, 2 pieces, small, stainless blade,
  steak $130
Fork, 7 1/8 in. $30
Fork, 7 5/8 in. $48
Fork-baby, 4 in............................$40
Fork-cocktail, 5 1/2 in.....................$22
Fork-cold meat/serving, medium, solid,
  8 in. $90
Fork-ice cream, 5 3/4 in....................$36
Fork-lemon, 4 7/8 in. $30
Fork-pickle/olive, short handle, 5 1/2 in.......$32
Fork-salad, individual, 6 3/8 in. $38
Knife-modern, hollow handle, 8 7/8 in........$26

Lunt Silversmiths

Knife-new french, hollow handle, 9 in. $30
Ladle-gravy, solid, 5 3/4 in. $80
Ladle-gravy, solid, 6 1/2 in. $80
Server-cheese, stainless blade, 6 5/8 in. $47
Server-jelly, 6 1/4 in. $34
Spoon-casserole, smooth bowl, solid,
    9 in. $104
Spoon-demitasse, 4 1/2 in. $20
Spoon-dessert/oval soup, 7 1/4 in. $50
Spoon-iced tea, 7 3/8 in. $40
Spoon-sugar, 6 in. $36
Spoon-teaspoon (five o'clock), 5 3/4 in. $16
Spoon-teaspoon, 6 in. $20
Tablespoon, (serving spoon), 8 1/2 in. $75
Tablespoon, (serving spoon), pierced,
    8 3/8 in. $90
Tongs-sugar, 4 1/4 in. $66

Chateau/Chateau Thierry by Lunt, 1919

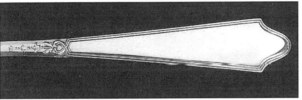

Butter spreader, flat handle, 5 1/2 in. $16
Carving set, 2 pieces, small, stainless blade,
    steak $100
Fork, 7 1/4 in. $22
Fork, 7 7/8 in. $36
Fork-baby, 4 1/8 in. $34
Fork-carving, large, stainless prongs, roast,
    10 3/4 in. $60
Fork-carving, small, stainless prongs, steak,
    8 1/2 in. $50
Fork-chipped beef, small, 6 1/8 in. $58
Fork-cocktail, no notch, 3 tines, 5 7/8 in. $23
Fork-cocktail, notch, 3 tines, 5 7/8 in. $23
Fork-ice cream, 5 5/8 in. $36
Fork-lemon, 4 7/8 in. $30
Fork-pickle/olive, short handle, 2 tines,
    5 7/8 in. $28
Fork-salad, individual, 6 in. $24
Fork-youth, 6 1/4 in. $38
Knife-baby, 5 in. $34
Knife-blunt, hollow handle, 8 5/8 in. $27
Knife-blunt, hollow handle, 9 1/2 in. $33
Knife-new french, hollow handle, 8 7/8 in. $26
Knife-old french, hollow handle, 8 5/8 in. $26
Knife-old french, hollow handle, silver plate
    blade, 9 1/2 in. $33

Knife-old french, hollow handle, stainless
    blade, 9 1/2 in. $33
Knife-sharpener, steel, small, steak,
    13 3/8 in. $50
Ladle-gravy, solid, 6 5/8 in. $80
Napkin clip (made for teaspoons) $18
Sardine-tined fork/serving, solid, large,
    4 3/4 in. $80
Server-jelly, 5 7/8 in. $28
Server-pie, silver plate blade, 10 1/4 in. $60
Spoon-baby, straight handle, 4 1/4 in. $34
Spoon-bon-bon, 5 in. $36
Spoon-casserole, smooth, solid,
    9 1/4 in. $100
Spoon-demitasse, 4 3/8 in. $18
Spoon-dessert/oval soup, 7 3/8 in. $30
Spoon-fruit, 5 7/8 in. $34
Spoon-iced tea, 7 1/2 in. $26
Spoon-soup, round bowl, bouillon,
    5 3/8 in. $22
Spoon-soup, round bowl, cream,
    6 1/2 in. $30
Spoon-soup, round bowl, gumbo, 7 in. $34
Spoon-sugar, 6 1/8 in. $26
Spoon-teaspoon (five o'clock), 5 1/2 in. $12
Spoon-teaspoon, 5 7/8 in. $13
Tablespoon, (serving spoon), 8 5/8 in. $50
Tablespoon, (serving spoon), pierced,
    8 5/8 in. $70
Tongs-sugar, 3 7/8 in. $58
Tongs-sugar, 4 1/4 in. $58

Chatelaine by Lunt, 1894

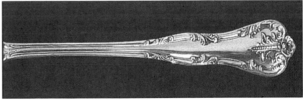

Butter spreader, flat handle, 6 1/8 in. $26
Butter-master, flat handle, 6 1/2 in. $30
Fork, 7 1/2 in. $50
Fork, 7 1/4 in. $36
Fork-carving, small, stainless prongs, steak,
    8 1/2 in. $70
Fork-chipped beef, medium, 7 in. $80
Fork-salad, individual, 6 in. $45
Knife-new french, hollow handle,
    9 5/8 in. $45
Knife-new french, hollow handle, 9 in. $37
Spoon-dessert/oval soup, 7 1/2 in. $40
Spoon-place/oval soup, 7 in. $48

Spoon-soup, round bowl, bouillon,
5 1/4 in. $40
Spoon-soup, round bowl, cream,
6 1/4 in. $60
Spoon-soup, round bowl, gumbo,
6 7/8 in. $50
Spoon-sugar, 5 7/8 in. $40
Spoon-teaspoon (five o'clock), 5 1/2 in. $17
Spoon-teaspoon, 5 7/8 in. $27
Tablespoon, (serving spoon), 8 1/4 in. $80

Colonial Manor by Lunt, 1940

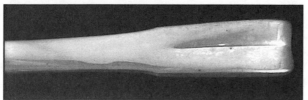

Butter spreader, flat handle, 5 3/4 in. $17
Butter-master, flat handle, 7 1/8 in. $35
Carving set, 2 pieces, small, stainless blade,
steak $110
Fork, 7 1/4 in. $45
Fork, 7 5/8 in. $50
Fork-cocktail, 5 5/8 in. $28
Fork-cold meat/serving, small, solid,
7 5/8 in. $70
Fork-lemon, 5 in. $28
Fork-pickle/olive, short handle, 5 3/4 in. $30
Fork-salad, individual, 6 1/4 in. $32
Knife-new french, hollow 4 1/2 in. handle,
9 1/2 in. $42
Ladle-gravy, solid, 5 5/8 in. $75
Server-pie, stainless blade, 10 1/2 in. $55
Spoon-demitasse, 4 1/2 in. $22
Spoon-iced tea, 7 3/8 in. $32
Spoon-soup, round bowl, cream,
6 3/8 in. $33
Spoon-sugar, 6 in. $28
Spoon-teaspoon, 6 in. $22
Tablespoon, (serving spoon), 8 3/8 in. $70

Colonial Theme by Lunt, 1964

Butter spreader, hollow handle, modern,
stainless paddle, 6 1/4 in. $25

Butter-master, hollow handle, 6 5/8 in. $36
Fork-cocktail, 6 in. $44
Fork-cold meat/serving, medium, solid,
8 1/8 in. $80
Knife-modern, hollow handle, 9 in. $34
Knife-steak, individual, 9 1/8 in. $48
Ladle-gravy, solid, 6 3/8 in. $80
Salad set, 2 pieces, plastic bowl $80
Spoon-dessert/oval soup, 6 7/8 in. $44
Spoon-iced tea, 7 3/8 in. $48
Spoon-sugar, 6 1/8 in. $34
Spoon-teaspoon, 6 in. $28
Tablespoon, (serving spoon), 8 1/4 in. $80
Tablespoon, (serving spoon), pierced,
8 1/4 in. $90

Contrast by Lunt, 1956, Black Nylon Handle

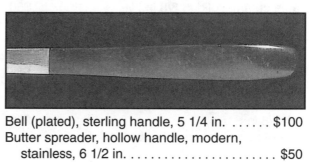

Bell (plated), sterling handle, 5 1/4 in. $100
Butter spreader, hollow handle, modern,
stainless, 6 1/2 in. $50
Butter-master, hollow handle, 7 in. $55
Carving set, 2 pieces, small, stainless blade,
steak $240
Fork, 7 5/8 in. $65
Fork-carving, small, stainless prongs, steak,
8 3/4 in. $120
Fork-cocktail, 6 1/8 in. $50
Fork-cold meat/serving, large, solid,
9 5/8 in. $140
Fork-pickle/olive, short handle, 2 tines,
6 1/8 in. $50
Fork-salad, individual, 6 5/8 in. $70
Knife-cheese, stainless blade, 7 1/4 in. $60
Knife-modern, hollow handle, 9 3/8 in. $65
Knife-steak, individual, 9 1/2 in. $70
Ladle-gravy, solid, 6 3/4 in. $130
Scoop-cheese, sterling scoop,
6 7/8 in. $70
Server-pie and cake, stainless blade,
11 in. $100
Spoon-dessert/oval soup, 7 1/4 in. $90
Spoon-teaspoon, 6 3/8 in. $50
Tablespoon, (serving spoon), 9 1/8 in. $130
Tablespoon, (serving spoon), pierced,
9 1/8 in. $130

Lunt Silversmiths

Coronet by Lunt, 1932

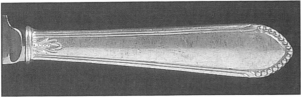

Butter spreader, flat handle, 5 7/8 in. $26
Fork, 7 5/8 in. $55
Fork-baby, 4 1/8 in. $40
Fork-cocktail, 5 5/8 in. $32
Fork-ice cream, 5 3/4 in. $55
Fork-lemon, 5 in. $30
Fork-pickle/olive, short handle, 5 5/8 in. $34
Fork-salad, individual, 6 3/8 in. $48
Knife-new french, hollow handle,
    9 3/4 in. $48
Ladle-cream, solid, 5 3/8 in. $50
Ladle-gravy, solid, 6 1/2 in. $90
Server-cheese, stainless blade,
    6 1/2 in. $50
Server-jelly, 6 in. $36
Spoon-bon-bon, 4 7/8 in. $50
Spoon-casserole, smooth bowl, solid,
    7 5/8 in. $90
Spoon-casserole, smooth bowl, solid,
    9 1/8 in. $90
Spoon-demitasse, 4 3/8 in. $26
Spoon-iced tea, 7 3/4 in. $38
Spoon-soup, round bowl, bouillon,
    5 1/4 in. $38
Spoon-soup, round bowl, cream, 6 1/2 in. $48
Spoon-soup, round bowl, gumbo, 7 in. $55
Spoon-sugar, 6 1/8 in. $45
Spoon-teaspoon (five o'clock), 5 3/4 in. $24
Spoon-teaspoon, 6 in. $26
Tablespoon, (serving spoon), 8 3/4 in. $90

Counterpoint by Lunt, 1969

Butter spreader, hollow handle, modern,
    stainless paddle, 6 1/4 in. $28
Butter-master, hollow handle, 6 3/4 in. $32
Fork, 7 1/2 in. $44
Fork-fish, stainless tines, hollow handle,
    individual, 7 7/8 in. $40

Knife-fish, stainless blade, individual,
    8 3/8 in. $40
Knife-fruit, stainless blade, individual,
    6 3/4 in. $38
Spoon-sugar shell, 6 1/8 in. $32
Spoon-teaspoon, 6 1/8 in. $20

Delacourt by Lunt, 1966

Fork, 7 1/2 in. $50
Fork-salad, individual, 6 5/8 in. $46
Knife-modern, hollow handle, 9 1/8 in. $44
Server-pie and cake, stainless blade,
    10 3/4 in. $70
Spoon-dessert/oval soup, 6 7/8 in. $40
Spoon-sugar shell, 6 1/4 in. $47
Tablespoon, (serving spoon), 8 3/8 in. $90
Tablespoon, (serving spoon), pierced,
    8 3/8 in. $90

Early American-Engraved by Lunt, 1926

Butter spreader, flat handle, 5 7/8 in. $30
Butter spreader, hollow handle, modern,
    stainless paddle, 6 1/4 in. $30
Butter spreader, hollow handle, stainless paddle,
    6 in. $30
Carving set, 2 pieces, large, stainless blade,
    roast. $180
Carving set, 2 pieces, small, stainless blade,
    steak $90
Fork, 7 1/4 in. $34
Fork, 7 5/8 in. $48
Fork-cocktail, 5 5/8 in. $24
Fork-cold meat/serving, medium, solid,
    8 in. $85
Fork-lemon, 4 7/8 in. $30
Fork-salad, individual, 6 1/4 in. $43
Knife-carving, small, stainless blade, steak,
    10 1/4 in. $45

Knife-new french, hollow handle,
9 5/8 in. $42
Knife-wedding cake, stainless blade,
11 7/8 in. $80
Ladle-gravy, solid, 6 1/4 in. $90
Server-jelly, 6 in. $30
Spoon-demitasse, 4 3/8 in. $24
Spoon-dessert/oval soup, 7 3/8 in. $60
Spoon-five o'clock/youth, 5 3/4 in. $17
Spoon-soup, round bowl, bouillon,
5 3/8 in. $36
Spoon-sugar, 6 1/8 in. $40
Spoon-teaspoon, 6 in. $20
Tablespoon, (serving spoon), 8 5/8 in. $85
Tongs-sugar, 3 3/4 in. $55

Early American-Plain by Lunt, 1926

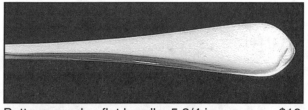

Butter spreader, flat handle, 5 3/4 in. $16
Carving set, 2 pieces, small, stainless blade,
steak $100
Fork, 7 1/2 in. $45
Fork, 7 1/4 in. $30
Fork-baby, 4 1/4 in. $40
Fork-carving, small, stainless prongs, steak,
8 3/8 in. $50
Fork-cocktail, 5 5/8 in. $20
Fork-ice cream, 5 3/4 in. $38
Fork-lemon, 4 7/8 in. $28
Fork-salad, individual, 6 1/4 in. $38
Knife-breakfast, stainless blade, 7 3/8 in. $32
Knife-cheese, stainless blade, 7 1/8 in. $40
Knife-new french, hollow handle,
9 1/8 in. $35
Ladle-cream, solid, 5 1/2 in. $50
Ladle-gravy, solid, 6 3/8 in. $80
Server-jelly, 6 in. $34
Server-pie, stainless blade, 10 3/8 in. $58
Server-pie, stainless blade, 9 5/8 in. $58
Spoon-bon-bon, 4 3/4 in. $36
Spoon-casserole, smooth bowl, solid,
9 in. $100
Spoon-demitasse, 4 1/4 in. $16
Spoon-fruit, 5 3/4 in. $30
Spoon-iced tea, 7 3/4 in. $34
Spoon-infant feeding, 5 3/8 in. $36
Spoon-salt/master, 3 1/2 in. $24

Spoon-soup, round bowl, bouillon,
5 3/8 in. $25
Spoon-soup, round bowl, gumbo, 7 in. $50
Spoon-sugar, 6 1/8 in. $32
Spoon-teaspoon (five o'clock), 5 3/4 in. $16
Spoon-teaspoon, 6 in. $18
Tablespoon, (serving spoon), 8 3/4 in. $70
Tongs-sugar, 3 5/8 in. $55

Early Colonial by Lunt, 1930

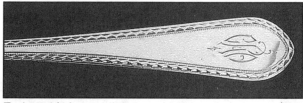

Fork, 7 1/4 in. $35
Fork, 7 5/8 in. $60
Fork-cocktail, 5 5/8 in. $24
Fork-cold meat/serving, small, solid,
7 3/4 in. $80
Knife-modern, hollow handle, 9 1/8 in. $40
Ladle-gravy, solid, 6 1/2 in. $80
Salad set, 2 pieces, plastic bowl,
10 5/8 in. $90
Spoon-dessert/oval soup, 7 1/4 in. $50
Spoon-soup, round bowl, cream,
6 1/2 in. $45
Spoon-sugar, 6 1/8 in. $28
Spoon-teaspoon, 6 in. $30

Eloquence by Lunt, 1953

Baby set, 2 pieces. $84
Butter spreader, hollow handle, modern,
stainless paddle, 6 1/4 in. $36
Butter spreader, hollow handle, stainless paddle,
6 1/8 in. $36
Butter-master, hollow handle, 6 7/8 in. $40
Carving set, 2 pieces, small, stainless blade,
steak $150
Fork, 7 3/8 in. $37
Fork, 7 7/8 in. $70
Fork-baby, 4 1/4 in. $42
Fork-cocktail, 5 7/8 in. $40
Fork-cold meat/serving, small, solid,
7 3/4 in. $90

Fork-ice cream, 5 7/8 in. $56
Fork-pickle/olive, short handle, 5 7/8 in. $40
Fork-salad serving, solid, 9 1/4 in. $120
Fork-salad, individual, 6 1/2 in. $44
Knife-cheese, stainless blade, 7 in. $55
Knife-modern, hollow handle, 9 3/4 in. $50
Knife-modern, hollow handle, 9 in. $38
Knife-steak, individual, 9 5/8 in. $50
Ladle-gravy, solid, 6 1/4 in. $95
Salad set, 2 pieces, plastic bowl,
 11 1/8 in. $90
Server-pie and cake, stainless blade,
 10 5/8 in. $50
Slicer-cake, stainless blade, wedding,
 12 1/4 in. $60
Spoon-baby, straight handle, 4 3/8 in. $42
Spoon-casserole, smooth bowl, solid,
 9 1/4 in. $140
Spoon-demitasse, 4 3/8 in. $36
Spoon-dessert/oval soup, 6 1/2 in. $40
Spoon-ice, 9 3/8 in. $140
Spoon-iced tea, 7 3/8 in. $48
Spoon-infant feeding, 5 1/2 in. $40
Spoon-salt, individual, 2 5/8 in. $14
Spoon-soup, round bowl, cream,
 6 1/4 in. $50
Spoon-sugar, 6 1/4 in. $36
Spoon-teaspoon, 6 1/8 in. $25
Tablespoon, (serving spoon), 8 1/2 in. $90
Tablespoon, (serving spoon), pierced,
 8 1/2 in. $100

English Shell by Lunt, 1937

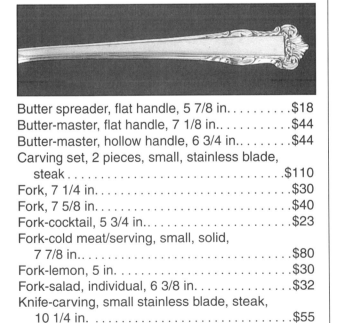

Butter spreader, flat handle, 5 7/8 in. $18
Butter-master, flat handle, 7 1/8 in. $44
Butter-master, hollow handle, 6 3/4 in. $44
Carving set, 2 pieces, small, stainless blade,
 steak $110
Fork, 7 1/4 in. $30
Fork, 7 5/8 in. $40
Fork-cocktail, 5 3/4 in. $23
Fork-cold meat/serving, small, solid,
 7 7/8 in. $80
Fork-lemon, 5 in. $30
Fork-salad, individual, 6 3/8 in. $32
Knife-carving, small stainless blade, steak,
 10 1/4 in. $55

Knife-modern, hollow handle, 9 in. $35
Knife-new french, hollow handle, 9 1/2 in. $50
Knife-new french, hollow handle, stainless
 blade, 9 in. $35
Knife-youth, 7 1/4 in. $40
Ladle-cream, solid, 5 3/8 in. $40
Ladle-gravy, solid, 5 7/8 in. $80
Server-cheese, stainless blade, 6 1/2 in. $48
Server-pie, stainless blade, 10 in. $70
Spoon-demitasse, 4 1/2 in. $20
Spoon-fruit, 6 in. $40
Spoon-iced tea, 7 1/2 in. $30
Spoon-soup, round bowl, bouillon,
 5 3/8 in. $38
Spoon-soup, round bowl, cream,
 6 3/8 in. $34
Spoon-sugar, 6 in. $34
Spoon-teaspoon, 6 in. $20
Tablespoon, (serving spoon), 8 1/4 in. $65
Tablespoon, (serving spoon), pierced,
 8 1/4 in. $90

Festival by Lunt, 1936

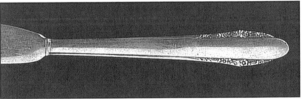

Butter spreader, flat handle, 5 7/8 in. $16
Butter-master, flat handle, 7 1/8 in. $30
Fork, 7 1/2 in. $55
Fork, 7 1/4 in. $35
Fork-carving, small, stainless prongs, steak,
 8 1/2 in. $50
Fork-cocktail, 5 3/4 in. $22
Fork-cold meat/serving, small, solid,
 7 3/4 in. $60
Fork-lemon, 5 in. $28
Fork-pickle/olive, short handle, 2 tines,
 5 3/4 in. $28
Fork-pickle/olive, short handle, 3 tines,
 5 3/4 in. $28
Fork-salad, individual, 6 1/4 in. $35
Knife-breakfast, stainless blade, 8 in. $28
Knife-carving, small, stainless blade, steak,
 10 1/4 in. $50
Knife-modern, hollow handle, 8 5/8 in. $33
Knife-new french, hollow handle,
 9 5/8 in. $40
Knife-new french, hollow handle, 9 in. $33
Ladle-cream, solid, 5 1/4 in. $38

Sterling Silver Flatware Gallery

Asparagus server in a rococo open-work pattern, by Durgin, with five square barred tines, monogrammed with the letter "K," marked on the reverse with a script "D" and "Sterling," 10 in. by 3 1/4 in.

Southern Grandeur pattern by Easterling.

Tiffany asparagus server with pierced upper blade, handle decorated with art nouveau scrolls and tendrils, marked "Tiffany Co. Sterling Pat. 1890" and "1246," 7 5/8 in. by 3 in.

Gorham fish serving set in the Versailles pattern, gold wash, both monogrammed "Thomas," fork measures 9 1/8 in. by 2 3/4 in., server measures 11 1/2 in. by 3 in.

Du Barry pattern by International Silver.

Tiffany & Co. serving spoon with putti on handle, gold wash, also marked on reverse "40," 9 1/8 in. by 2 1/8 in.

Grande Baroque pattern from Wallace Silver.

Reed & Barton pierced server (waffle?) in the La Comtesse pattern, 8 3/4 in. by 3 3/8 in.

Gorham macaroni server, marked on reverse with 1907 patent, sterling and "lion/anchor/G," 8 3/4 in. by 2 1/2 in.

Whiting berry spoon in the Imperial Queen pattern, gold wash and crimped bowl, 8 3/4 in. by 2 5/8 in.

Towle sliced lemon server in Old Colonial pattern, pierced and scalloped bowl, 5 5/8 in. by 1 3/8 in.

Bigelow Kennard & Co. pierced berry spoon, gold wash, monogrammed "B," 8 3/4 in. by 2 5/8 in.

Whiting soup ladle in Lily pattern, scalloped bowl, 11 7/8 in. by 4 1/8 in.

Royal Windsor pattern by Towle.

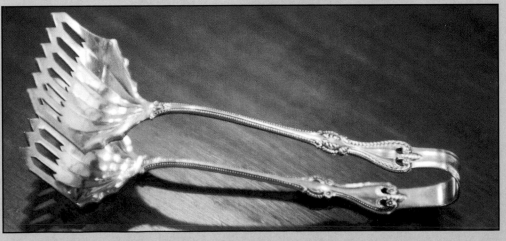

Towle bacon server in Old Colonial pattern, pierced tongs, 5 3/4 in. by 1 7/8 in.

Master butter knife by Wallace in the Grande Baroque pattern, 7 1/2 in. by 1 in.

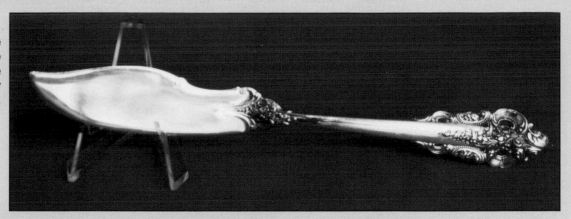

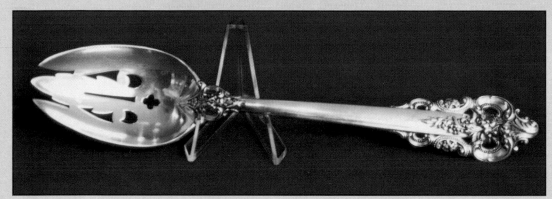

Serving spoon by Wallace in the Grande Baroque pattern, with pierced bowl and tines, 8 5/8 in. by 1 3/4 in.

King Albert by Whiting, later advertised as a Gorham pattern.

Fish serving set in the Les Cinq Fleurs pattern by Reed & Barton.

Cracker serving spoon in a floral pattern, maker unknown, monogrammed "HK," gold wash and scalloped bowl, 8 1/8 in. by 3 1/2 in.

Royal Danish pattern by International Silver.

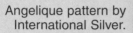

Angelique pattern by International Silver.

Cake/pie server by International in the Springtime pattern, stainless paddle, 10 in. by 2 in.

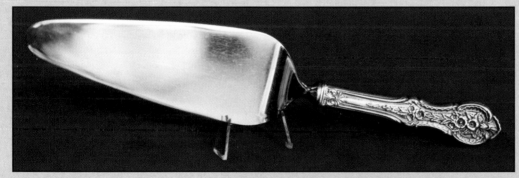

Berry spoon by S. Kirk & Son in the Repoussé pattern, scalloped bowl decorated with mixed fruit, strawberry, grapes, pineapple and apple, 5 1/8 in. by 2 in.

Pastry server in the fiddle, thread, and shell pattern, marked on reverse "B.B. & B. Co." for Bailey, Banks & Biddle Co. Jewelers, hallmarked, 8 in. by 2 7/8 in.

King Edward pattern by Gorham.

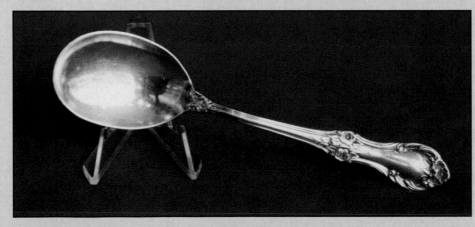

Sugar spoon by International in the Wild Rose pattern, 5 7/8 in. by 1 3/8 in.

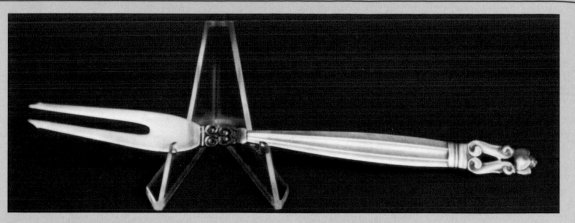

Olive fork by
Georg Jensen in
the Acorn pattern,
6 1/2 in. by 3/8 in.

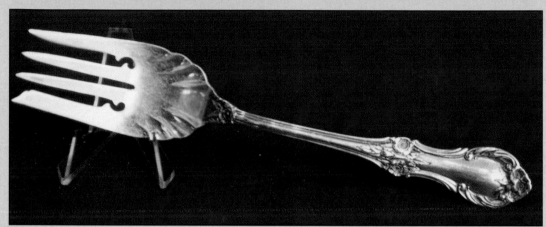

Cold meat fork by
International in the
Wild Rose pattern,
one beveled tine,
7 5/8 in. by 1 1/2 in.

Joan of Arc pattern by
International Silver.

Georgian Rose pattern by
Reed & Barton.

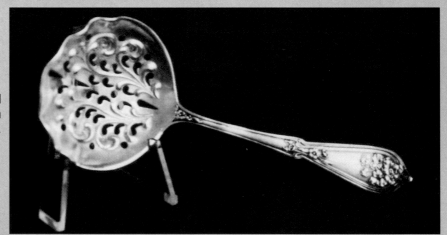

Bonbon/nut spoon with pierced and
scalloped bowl, marked "Sterling" on
reverse, 4 3/4 in. by 2 in.

Serving spoon by
S. Kirk & Son in the
Repoussé pattern, with
pierced bowl, 8 1/8 in.
by 2 14 in.

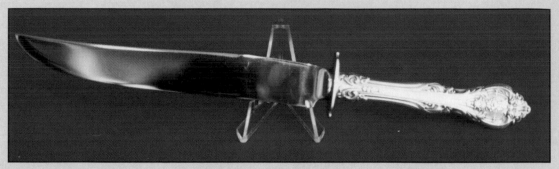

Small carving knife by Gorham in the King Edward pattern, with built-in rest, 10 1/4 in. by 1 1/2 in.

Prelude pattern by International Silver.

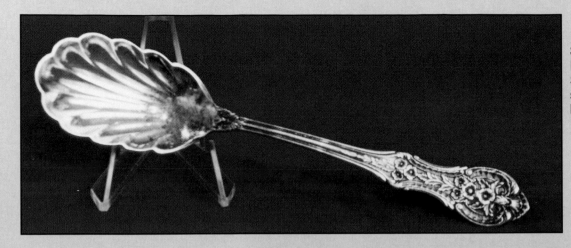

Sugar spoon by International in the Springtime pattern, scalloped bowl, 6 in. by 1 1/4 in.

Wild Rose pattern by International Silver.

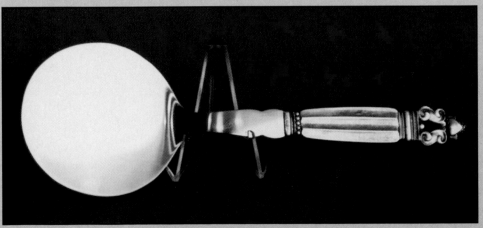

Tomato server by Georg Jensen in the Acorn pattern, 8 in. by 2 5/8 in.

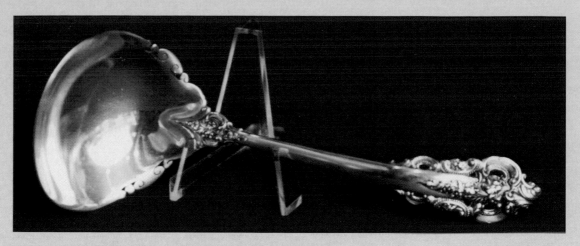

Sauce ladle by Wallace in the Grande Baroque pattern, with cutout scroll decoration on bowl, 6 1/4 in. by 2 3/8 in.

Towle bonbon server in Old Colonial pattern, pierced and faceted bowl with gold wash, 5 1/2 in. by 2 in.

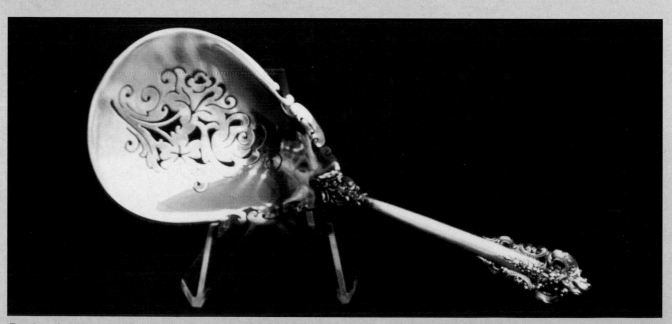

Bonbon/nut spoon by Wallace in the Grande Baroque pattern, with pieced bowl, 5 1/4 in. by 1 7/8 in.

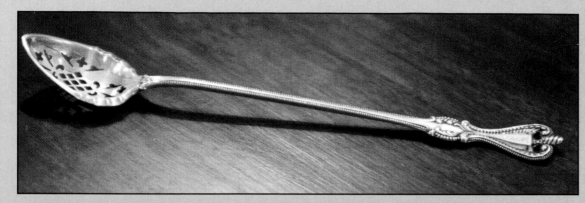

Towle olive spoon in Old Colonial pattern, pierced and crimped bowl, 8 1/2 in. by 1 1/8 in.

Serving/tablespoon by Wallace in the Grande Baroque pattern, 8 3/4 in. by 1 3/4 in.

Towle tomato server in Old Colonial pattern, pierced and scalloped, 8 1/8 in. by 2 3/8 in.

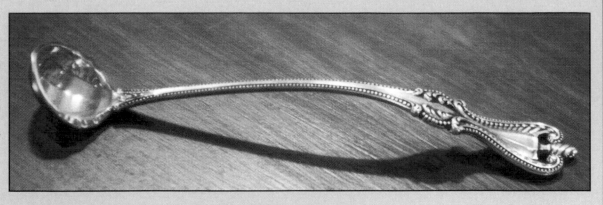

Towle mustard spoon in Old Colonial pattern, gold wash on faceted and crimped bowl, 5 1/4 in. by 7/8 in.

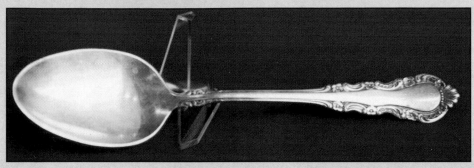

Serving spoon by Reed & Barton in the Georgian Rose pattern, 8 3/8 in. by 1 7/8 in.

Towle almond server in Old Colonial pattern, pierced and crimped bowl with gold wash, 4 5/8 in. by 2 in.

Berry spoon in the Lily pattern by Whiting.

Ladle-gravy, solid, 6 3/8 in. $80
Server-cheese, stainless blade, 6 1/2 in. $38
Server-jelly, 6 3/8 in. $30
Server-pastry, stainless bowl, 9 1/4 in. $60
Server-pie, stainless blade, 9 7/8 in. $60
Spoon-bon-bon, 4 7/8 in. $38
Spoon-casserole, smooth bowl, solid,
   8 5/8 in. $90
Spoon-fruit, 6 in. $37
Spoon-iced tea, 7 1/2 in. $32
Spoon-relish, 6 in. $36
Spoon-soup, round bowl, bouillon,
   5 3/8 in. $30
Spoon-soup, round bowl, cream,
   6 1/4 in. $30
Spoon-soup, round bowl, gumbo,
   6 7/8 in. $40
Spoon-sugar, 6 1/8 in. $30
Spoon-teaspoon (five o'clock), 5 3/4 in. $22
Spoon-teaspoon, 6 in. $16
Tablespoon, (serving spoon), 8 1/4 in. $60
Tablespoon, (serving spoon), pierced,
   8 1/4 in. $70
Tongs-sugar, 4 1/8 in. $50

Floral Lace by Lunt, 1967

Butter-master, hollow handle, 6 3/4 in. $28
Fork, 7 1/2 in. $50
Fork-pickle/olive, short handle, 5 5/8 in. $20
Fork-salad, individual, 6 5/8 in. $40
Knife-carving, large, stainless blade, roast,
   11 3/4 in. $60
Knife-modern, hollow handle, 9 1/8 in. $32
Server-pie and cake, stainless blade,
   10 5/8 in. $50
Spoon-bon-bon, 4 3/4 in. $38
Spoon-sugar, 6 1/8 in. $30
Spoon-teaspoon, 6 in. $24
Tablespoon, (serving spoon), 8 3/8 in. $80

Granado by Lunt, 1929

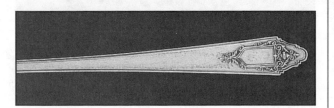

Butter spreader, flat handle, 5 7/8 in. $26
Butter spreader, hollow handle, stainless
   paddle, 6 1/2 in. $28
Butter-master, flat handle, 7 in. $34
Carving set, 2 pieces, small, stainless blade,
   steak $100
Fork, 7 1/4 in. $25
Fork, 7 5/8 in. $50
Fork-baby, 4 in. $38
Fork-cocktail, 5 5/8 in. $30
Fork-ice cream, 5 7/8 in. $45
Fork-lemon, 5 in. $32
Fork-salad, individual, 6 3/8 in. $35
Knife-carving, small, stainless blade, steak,
   10 1/4 in. $50
Knife-new french, hollow handle,
   9 in. $30
Ladle-cream, solid, 5 3/8 in. $45
Ladle-gravy, solid, 5 3/4 in. $85
Server-jelly, 6 1/4 in. $22
Spoon-demitasse, 4 1/4 in. $22
Spoon-fruit, 5 3/4 in. $37
Spoon-iced tea, 7 5/8 in. $30
Spoon-soup, round bowl, bouillon,
   5 1/2 in. $26
Spoon-soup, round bowl, gumbo, 7 in. $48
Spoon-sugar, 6 1/4 in. $36
Spoon-teaspoon, 5 7/8 in. $20
Tablespoon, (serving spoon), 8 5/8 in. $80

Sixty pieces Lunt Jefferson: 12 each luncheon
knives, luncheon forks, teaspoons, cream
soup spoons, and butter spreaders. Monogram "C." c.1930-1970. $800

Lace Point by Lunt, 1965

Butter-master, hollow handle, notch blade,
6 3/4 in..................................$34
Fork, 7 1/2 in............................$48
Fork-cocktail, 5 5/8 in....................$44
Fork-cold meat/serving, medium, solid,
8 in....................................$100
Fork-pickle/olive, short handle, 5 5/8 in. $44
Fork-salad, individual, 6 5/8 in. $48
Knife-modern, hollow handle, 9 in...........$40
Knife-steak, individual, 5 3/8 in. blade,
9 5/8 in.................................$54
Napkin clip (made for teaspoons)...........$30
Server-pie and cake, stainless blade,
10 5/8 in. $60
Spoon-dessert/oval soup, 6 7/8 in...........$50
Spoon-iced tea, 7 3/8 in. $60
Spoon-sugar, 6 1/8 in......................$25
Spoon-teaspoon, 6 in......................$22
Tablespoon, (serving spoon), 8 1/2 in.......$100
Tablespoon, (serving spoon), pierced,
8 1/2 in................................$110

Madrigal by Lunt, 1962

Fork, 7 1/2 in.............................$38
Fork-cold meat/serving, medium, solid,
8 1/8 in.................................$100
Fork-salad, individual, 6 7/8 in. $50
Knife-modern, hollow handle, 9 in...........$42
Spoon-dessert/oval soup, 6 7/8 in...........$50
Spoon-sugar, 6 in..........................$33
Spoon-teaspoon, 6 in......................$26
Tablespoon, (serving spoon), 8 1/4 in........$90

Mary II by Lunt, 1923

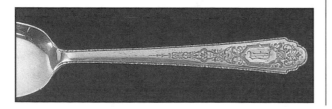

Butter spreader, flat handle, 5 7/8 in. $18
Butter-master, flat handle, 7 in. $37
Carving set, 2 pieces, small, stainless blade,
steak $120
Fork, 7 1/4 in. $23
Fork, 7 5/8 in. $35
Fork-cold meat/serving, small, solid,
7 3/8 in................................ $75
Fork-lemon, 4 7/8 in. $25
Fork-pickle/olive, short handle, 2 of 3 tines
beveled, 5 5/8 in. $25
Fork-pickle/olive, short handle, 2 tines,
5 5/8 in. $25
Fork-salad, individual, 6 in................. $32
Knife-new french, hollow handle, 9 5/8 in. $40
Knife-new french, hollow handle, 9 in. $30
Knife-youth, 8 in.......................... $40
Ladle-gravy, solid, 5 3/4 in................. $75
Napkin clip (made for five o'clock)........... $13
Pick-butter, 2 tines, 6 1/8 in................ $48
Server-jelly, 6 in.......................... $30
Server-pie, stainless blade, 10 1/4 in........ $60
Spoon-demitasse, 4 1/4 in.................. $18
Spoon-fruit, 5 3/4 in. $40
Spoon-iced tea, 7 5/8 in.................... $40
Spoon-soup, round bowl, bouillon,
5 3/8 in................................ $28
Spoon-soup, round bowl, cream,
6 1/2 in................................ $45
Spoon-soup, round bowl, gumbo, 7 in........ $50
Spoon-sugar, 5 3/4 in..................... $35
Spoon-teaspoon (five o'clock), 3 7/8 in.
handle, 5 3/4 in......................... $10
Spoon-teaspoon, 4 1/8 in. handle, 6 in. $20
Spoon-youth, 5 3/8 in...................... $15
Tablespoon, (serving spoon), 8 5/8 in. $65
Tablespoon, (serving spoon), pierced,
8 5/8 in................................ $90
Tongs-sugar, 3 1/2 in. $40

Memory Lane by Lunt, 1949

Butter spreader, flat handle, 5 3/4 in. $23
Butter spreader, hollow handle, stainless
paddle, 6 in. $27
Butter-master, hollow handle, 6 3/4 in. $40
Fork, 7 1/4 in. $25

Fork, 7 3/4 in. $40
Fork-cocktail, 5 7/8 in. $22
Fork-pickle/olive, short handle, 5 7/8 in. $32
Fork-salad, individual, 6 1/2 in. $34
Knife-new french, hollow handle,
    8 3/4 in. $34
Knife-new french, hollow handle,
    9 1/4 in. $34
Ladle-gravy, solid, 5 5/8 in. $60
Server-cheese, stainless blade, 6 1/2 in. $50
Server-jelly, 6 1/4 in. $35
Spoon-demitasse, 4 1/2 in. $24
Spoon-dessert/oval soup, 7 in. $40
Spoon-soup, round bowl, cream, 6 1/4 in. $40
Spoon-sugar, 6 in. $35
Spoon-teaspoon, 5 7/8 in. $22
Tablespoon, (serving spoon), 8 1/4 in. $70

Mignonette by Lunt, 1960

Butter spreader, hollow handle, modern,
    stainless paddle, 6 1/4 in. $32
Butter-master, hollow handle, 6 3/4 in. $35
Carving set, 2 pieces, small, stainless blade,
    steak. $120
Fork, 7 1/2 in. $42
Fork-cocktail, 5 7/8 in. $44
Fork-cold meat/serving, small, solid,
    7 7/8 in. $80
Fork-salad, individual, 6 5/8 in. $46
Knife-carving, large, stainless blade,
    roast, 12 in. $60
Knife-carving, small, stainless blade, steak,
    10 in. $60
Knife-carving, medium, stainless blade,
    steak, 11 5/8 in. $60
Knife-modern, hollow handle, 8 3/4 in. $37
Knife-modern, hollow handle, 9 1/8 in. $37
Knife-steak, individual, 5 3/8 in. blade,
    9 5/8 in. $60
Ladle-cream, solid, 5 1/2 in. $60
Ladle-gravy, solid, 6 1/2 in. $90
Napkin clip, (made for teaspoons) $28
Spoon-dessert/oval soup, 6 7/8 in. $40
Spoon-iced tea, 7 3/8 in. $60
Spoon-sugar, 6 1/4 in. $30
Spoon-teaspoon, 6 1/8 in. $20

Tablespoon, (serving spoon), 8 1/4 in. $85
Tablespoon, (serving spoon), pierced,
    8 1/4 in. $90

Modern Classic by Lunt, 1934

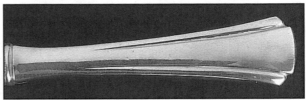

Butter spreader, flat handle, 6 in. $18
Butter spreader, hollow handle, modern,
    stainless 3 3/8 in. paddle, 6 3/4 in. $25
Butter spreader, hollow handle, stainless
    paddle, 6 1/8 in. $25
Butter-master, flat handle, 7 1/8 in. $28
Butter-master, hollow handle, 6 7/8 in. $28
Carving set, 2 pieces, small, stainless blade,
    steak $100
Fork, 2 1/8 in. tines, 7 1/8 in. $32
Fork, 7 5/8 in. $45
Fork-baby, 4 in. $40
Fork-carving, small stainless prongs, steak,
    8 3/4 in. $50
Fork-cocktail, 5 5/8 in. $18
Fork-cold meat/serving, small, solid,
    7 7/8 in. $70
Fork-lemon, 4 7/8 in. $24
Fork-pickle/olive, short handle, 2 tines,
    5 1/2 in. $28
Fork-pickle/olive, short handle, 3 tines,
    5 1/2 in. $28
Fork-salad, individual, 6 1/4 in. $32
Fork-youth, 6 1/2 in. $40
Knife-carving, small stainless blade, steak,
    10 3/8 in. $50
Knife-modern, hollow handle, 4 7/8 in. blade,
    8 5/8 in. $33
Knife-new french, hollow handle, 8 3/8 in. $32
Knife-new french, hollow handle, 8 7/8 in. $32
Knife-youth, 7 1/4 in. $30
Ladle-cream, solid, 5 1/8 in. $44
Ladle-cream, solid, 6 in. $44
Ladle-gravy, solid, 6 3/8 in. $70
Ladle-gravy, solid, 6 in. $70
Server-jelly, 6 3/8 in. $30
Server-pie, stainless blade, 10 in. $48
Server-pie, stainless blade, 9 5/8 in. $48
Spoon-baby, straight handle, 4 1/4 in. $40
Spoon-bon-bon, 4 7/8 in. $40
Spoon-iced tea, 7 1/2 in. $30

Spoon-soup, round bowl, bouillon,
5 1/2 in.................................$30
Spoon-soup, round bowl, cream,
6 3/8 in................................$38
Spoon-soup, round bowl, gumbo, 7 in. $50
Spoon-sugar, 6 in........................$24
Spoon-teaspoon, 6 1/8 in. $16
Spoon-youth, 5 3/4 in.....................$18
Tablespoon, (serving spoon), 8 1/2 in.........$55
Tongs-sugar, 4 1/4 in.....................$46

Modern Victorian by Lunt, 1941

Butter spreader, flat handle, 5 7/8 in..........$18
Butter spreader, hollow handle, stainless paddle,
double bolster, 6 1/8 in...................$24
Butter spreader, hollow handle, stainless paddle,
no bolster, 6 1/8 in......................$24
Butter-master, flat handle, 6 3/4 in............$36
Butter-master, hollow handle, 6 7/8 in.........$30
Carving set, 2 pieces, small, stainless blade,
steak....................................$110
Fork, 7 1/4 in............................$30
Fork, 7 5/8 in............................$54
Fork-baby, 4 1/8 in. $34
Fork-cocktail, 5 7/8 in.....................$22
Fork-cold meat/serving, small, solid,
7 1/2 in.................................$75
Fork-fish/serving, solid, large, 9 1/8 in. $115
Fork-ice cream, 5 7/8 in....................$40
Fork-lemon, 5 in. $28
Fork-pickle/olive, short handle, 2 tines,
5 7/8 in.................................$28
Fork-salad serving, solid, 9 in................$80
Fork-salad, individual, 6 3/8 in. $40
Fork-strawberry, 4 7/8 in. $30
Knife-carving, small, stainless blade, steak,
10 1/8 in. $55
Knife-carving, medium, stainless blade,
steak, 11 5/8 in..........................$55
Knife-fish/serving, solid, large,
10 7/8 in. $115
Knife-modern, hollow handle, 9 3/4 in.........$45
Knife-modern, hollow handle, 9 in.............$35
Knife-new french, hollow handle,
10 1/8 in. $45
Knife-new french, hollow handle,
8 5/8 in.................................$30

Knife-new french, hollow handle,
9 1/2 in. $45
Knife-new french, hollow handle,
9 1/4 in. $30
Ladle-gravy, solid, 6 in. $75
Napkin clip, (made for five o'clock) $22
Server-cheese, stainless blade, 6 5/8 in......$45
Server-jelly, 6 1/8 in. $30
Server-pie and cake, stainless blade,
10 1/2 in................................$60
Server-tomato, solid, 7 3/4 in. $90
Serving set, 2 pieces, fish, solid, large......$230
Spoon-baby, straight handle, 4 1/4 in.........$35
Spoon-bon-bon, 5 in.......................$40
Spoon-cracker, 7 1/2 in. $80
Spoon-dessert/oval soup, 6 5/8 in. $40
Spoon-dressing, large, solid, 10 3/4 in. $160
Spoon-iced tea, 7 3/8 in....................$38
Spoon-infant feeding, 5 3/8 in...............$40
Spoon-soup, round bowl, cream,
6 1/4 in.................................$33
Spoon-sugar, 5 7/8 in......................$26
Spoon-teaspoon (five o'clock), 3 7/8 in.
handle, 5 3/4 in..........................$12
Spoon-teaspoon, 4 1/8 in. handle, 6 in. $32
Tablespoon, (serving spoon), 8 3/8 in. $70
Tablespoon, (serving spoon), pierced,
8 3/8 in.................................$90
Tablespoon, (serving spoon), pierced,
8 3/8 in.................................$90
Tongs-sugar, 4 3/8 in. $60

Monticello by Lunt, 1908

Fork, 7 1/4 in. $37
Fork-salad, individual, 6 in.................$66
Napkin clip, (made for youth spoon) $35
Spoon-baby, straight handle, 4 3/8 in.........$50
Spoon-bon-bon, 5 1/8 in. $60
Spoon-teaspoon (five o'clock), 5 3/4 in.......$18
Spoon-youth, 5 3/8 in......................$32

The following pieces have monograms:
Butter spreader, flat handle, 5 1/2 in. $29
Fork, 7 1/4 in. $28
Fork-cocktail, 6 in. $30
Fork-salad, individual, 6 in.................$50

Knife-old french, hollow handle, 8 5/8 in.......$60
Spoon-demitasse, 4 5/8 in. $27
Spoon-iced tea, 7 3/8 in. $70
Spoon-soup, round bowl, bouillon,
    4 7/8 in..$34
Spoon-soup, round bowl, bouillon,
    5 1/4 in..$34
Spoon-teaspoon (five o'clock), 5 3/4 in.......$13
Spoon-teaspoon, 6 in........................$22
Spoon-youth, 5 3/8 in........................$30
Tablespoon, (serving spoon), 8 1/4 in........$83

Mount Vernon by Lunt, 1905

Butter-master, flat handle, 6 7/8 in...........$33
Fork, 7 1/2 in...............................$40
Fork, no design, 7 1/8 in. $20
Fork-cocktail, 6 in..........................$20
Fork-pickle/olive, short handle, 2 tines,
    6 in...$30
Fork-pickle/olive, short handle, 3 tines,
    6 in...$30
Fork-salad, individual, 6 1/8 in. $40
Fork-youth, 6 1/4 in. $45
Knife-new french, hollow handle, stainless
    blade, 9 1/2 in............................$45
Knife-old french, hollow handle, silver plate
    blade, 8 3/8 in............................$34
Knife-old french, hollow handle, silver plate
    blade, 8 5/8 in............................$34
Knife-old french, hollow handle, stainless
    blade, 8 3/8 in............................$34
Knife-old french, hollow handle, stainless
    blade, 8 5/8 in............................$34
Ladle-cream, solid, 5 1/2 in..................$36
Ladle-gravy, solid, 6 1/2 in. $85
Napkin clip, (made for teaspoons) $20
Server-jelly, 5 5/8 in. $37
Spoon-chocolate, short handle, large,
    5 1/4 in.....................................$28
Spoon-demitasse, 4 1/2 in. $22
Spoon-dessert/oval soup, 7 1/4 in...........$45
Spoon-ice cream, 5 1/4 in...................$50
Spoon-olive, short, pierced bowl, 6 1/8 in. $90
Spoon-olive, short, pierced bowl, gold wash,
    6 1/8 in.....................................$90
Spoon-soup, round bowl, bouillon,
    5 1/2 in.....................................$30

Spoon-sugar, 6 in. $37
Spoon-teaspoon (five o'clock), 3 1/2 in.
    handle, 5 1/4 in............................$10
Spoon-teaspoon (place size), 3 7/8 in. handle,
    6 in...$24
Spoon-teaspoon, 3 5/8 in. handle,
    5 5/8 in.....................................$15
Tablespoon, (serving spoon), 8 3/8 in. $70
Tongs-sugar, 3 3/4 in. $50

Nellie Custis by Lunt, 1915

Butter spreader, hollow handle, plate paddle,
    6 1/4 in.....................................$30
Butter-master, flat handle, 6 3/4 in. $35
Fork, 7 1/4 in. $34
Fork, 7 5/8 in. $47
Fork-lemon, 4 7/8 in. $34
Fork-pickle/olive, short handle, 5 7/8 in.......$34
Fork-ramekin, 5 1/4 in......................$35
Fork-salad, individual, 6 in..................$44
Fork-youth, 6 1/8 in........................$50
Ladle-cream, solid, 5 in. $53
Server-jelly, 5 3/4 in. $38
Spoon-demitasse, 4 1/8 in..................$25
Spoon-iced tea, 7 1/2 in....................$44
Spoon-relish, 5 3/4 in. $40
Spoon-sugar, 5 7/8 in.......................$40
Spoon-teaspoon (five o'clock), 5 3/8 in. $14
Spoon-teaspoon, 5 3/4 in...................$18
Tablespoon, (serving spoon), 8 3/8 in. $80
Tongs-sugar, 4 1/4 in. $70

Pendant of Fruit by Lunt, 1939

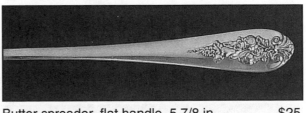

Butter spreader, flat handle, 5 7/8 in. $25
Butter spreader, hollow handle, stainless
    paddle, 6 1/2 in............................$28
Butter spreader, hollow handle, stainless
    paddle, 6 1/8 in............................$28
Butter-master, flat handle, 7 in. $42

Fork, 7 1/4 in. $35
Fork, 7 5/8 in. $50
Fork-cold meat/serving, small, solid,
    7 3/4 in.. . . . .$70
Fork-salad, individual, 6 1/4 in. $36
Knife-modern, hollow handle, 8 3/4 in. $28
Knife-new french, hollow handle,
    9 5/8 in.. . . . .$40
Spoon-demitasse, 4 1/2 in. $20
Spoon-dessert/oval soup, 6 7/8 in. $40
Spoon-fruit, 5 7/8 in. $30
Spoon-preserve, 7 1/2 in.. . . . .$80
Spoon-soup, round bowl, cream,
    6 3/8 in.. . . . .$45
Spoon-sugar, 5 7/8 in.. . . . .$27
Spoon-teaspoon, 5 7/8 in. $22
Tablespoon, (serving spoon), 8 1/4 in. $70

Raindrop by Lunt, 1959

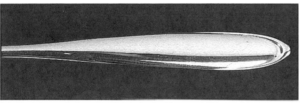

Butter spreader, hollow handle, modern, stainless
    paddle, 6 1/4 in.. . . . .$22
Butter-master, hollow handle, 6 3/4 in. $30
Fork, 7 1/2 in. $50
Fork-carving, small stainless prongs, steak,
    8 7/8 in.. . . . .$55
Fork-cold meat/serving, medium, solid,
    8 3/8 in.. . . . .$90
Fork-pickle/olive, short handle, 5 3/4 in. $28
Fork-salad, individual, 6 3/4 in. $40
Knife-modern, hollow handle, 9 1/4 in. $37
Ladle-gravy, solid, 6 1/2 in. $80
Napkin clip, (made for teaspoons) $28
Scoop-cheese, solid, 6 1/2 in. $40
Spoon-sugar, 6 1/8 in.. . . . .$30
Spoon-teaspoon, 6 1/4 in. $22
Tablespoon, (serving spoon), 8 3/8 in. $80
Tablespoon, (serving spoon), pierced,
    8 3/8 in.. . . . .$90

Rapallo by Lunt, 1968

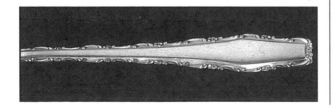

Butter spreader, hollow handle, modern, stainless
    paddle, 6 1/4 in.. . . . . $38
Butter-master, hollow handle, no notch,
    6 7/8 in.. . . . . $40
Butter-master, hollow handle, notch blade,
    6 7/8 in.. . . . . $40
Fork, 7 1/2 in. $46
Fork-cold meat/serving, medium, solid,
    8 in. $90
Fork-pickle/olive, short handle, 5 5/8 in. $30
Fork-salad, individual, 6 3/4 in. $58
Knife-cheese, stainless blade, 7 in. $50
Knife-modern, hollow handle, 9 1/8 in. $40
Ladle-cream, solid, 5 1/2 in. $50
Ladle-gravy, solid, 6 3/8 in. $90
Salad set, 2 pieces, plastic bowl $90
Server-pie and cake, stainless blade,
    10 1/2 in.. . . . . $70
Spoon-dessert/oval soup, 6 7/8 in. $70
Spoon-iced tea, 7 3/8 in.. . . . . $60
Spoon-sugar, 6 1/8 in.. $34
Spoon-teaspoon, 6 in.. $20
Tablespoon, (serving spoon), 8 3/8 in. $70
Tablespoon, (serving spoon), pierced,
    8 3/8 in.. . . . . $70

Regency by Lunt, 1935

Butter spreader, hollow handle, modern, stainless
    paddle, 6 1/4 in.. . . . . $28
Butter spreader, hollow handle, stainless
    paddle, no notch, 6 1/2 in. $28
Fork, 7 1/4 in. $50
Fork-cocktail, 5 5/8 in. $30
Fork-cold meat/serving, small, solid,
    7 7/8 in.. . . . . $80
Fork-salad, individual, 6 1/4 in. $50
Knife-modern, hollow handle, 8 7/8 in. $36
Ladle-gravy, solid, 6 3/8 in. $80
Server-jelly, 6 1/4 in. $35
Spoon-salad serving, solid, 8 7/8 in.. . . . . $100
Spoon-soup, round bowl, cream,
    6 1/2 in.. . . . . $50
Spoon-sugar, 6 1/8 in.. $44
Spoon-teaspoon, 6 in.. $24
Tablespoon, (serving spoon), 8 1/2 in. $80

Rondelay by Lunt, 1963

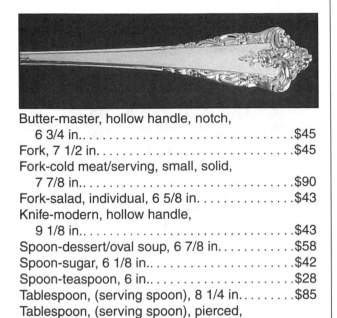

Butter-master, hollow handle, notch,
6 3/4 in..$45
Fork, 7 1/2 in.............................$45
Fork-cold meat/serving, small, solid,
7 7/8 in....................................$90
Fork-salad, individual, 6 5/8 in...............$43
Knife-modern, hollow handle,
9 1/8 in.....................................$43
Spoon-dessert/oval soup, 6 7/8 in...........$58
Spoon-sugar, 6 1/8 in.......................$42
Spoon-teaspoon, 6 in........................$28
Tablespoon, (serving spoon), 8 1/4 in........$85
Tablespoon, (serving spoon), pierced,
8 1/4 in....................................$85

Rose Elegance by Lunt, 1958

Butter spreader, hollow handle, modern,
stainless paddle, 6 1/4 in. $24
Butter-master, hollow handle,
6 3/4 in....................................$32
Fork, 7 1/2 in.............................$60
Fork-salad, individual, 6 3/4 in...............$44
Knife-modern, hollow handle, 9 1/8 in.........$40
Spoon-sugar, 6 in..........................$33
Tablespoon, (serving spoon),
8 1/4 in....................................$85

Spring Serenade by Lunt, 1957

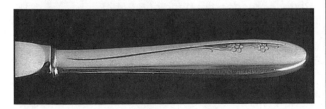

Butter spreader, hollow handle, modern, stainless
paddle, 6 1/4 in.........................$20

Butter-master, hollow handle,
6 3/4 in..................................$34
Fork, 7 1/2 in..............................$56
Fork-cocktail, 5 3/4 in......................$36
Fork-cold meat/serving, medium, solid,
8 in.......................................$95
Fork-pickle/olive, short handle, 5 3/4 in.......$30
Fork-salad, individual, 6 3/4 in..............$55
Knife-carving, small stainless blade, steak,
10 in......................................$64
Knife-modern, hollow handle, 9 1/8 in........$34
Ladle-gravy, solid, 6 1/4 in.................$90
Scoop-cheese, solid, 6 3/8 in..............$44
Server-pie and cake, stainless blade,
10 3/4 in...................................$70
Spoon-cheese, 6 1/2 in. $48
Spoon-dessert/oval soup, 6 7/8 in. $42
Spoon-sugar, 6 1/8 in......................$30
Spoon-teaspoon, 6 in.......................$18
Tablespoon, (serving spoon),
8 1/4 in....................................$90

Starfire by Lunt, 1955

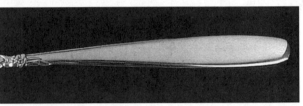

Butter spreader, hollow handle, modern, stainless
paddle, 6 1/4 in...........................$27
Butter-master, hollow handle, 6 3/4 in........$32
Carving set, 2 pieces, small, stainless blade,
steak $130
Fork, 7 3/8 in..............................$40
Fork-cocktail, 5 5/8 in......................$27
Fork-cold meat/serving, medium, solid,
8 in.......................................$85
Fork-pickle/olive, short handle, 5 5/8 in.......$30
Fork-salad, individual, 6 1/2 in..............$45
Knife-modern, hollow handle, 9 1/8 in........$40
Knife-steak, individual, 9 1/4 in.............$48
Ladle-gravy, solid, 6 1/2 in.................$80
Scoop-cheese, solid, 6 1/2 in...............$48
Server-pie and cake, stainless blade,
10 1/2 in...................................$70
Spoon-demitasse, 4 3/8 in..................$30
Spoon-dessert/oval soup, 6 1/2 in. $40
Spoon-iced tea, 7 3/8 in....................$40
Spoon-sugar, 6 in. $40
Spoon-teaspoon, 6 in.......................$20
Tablespoon, (serving spoon), 8 1/4 in........$80

Summer Song by Lunt, 1954

Butter spreader, flat handle, 5 7/8 in. $20
Butter spreader, hollow handle, modern, stainless
    paddle, 6 1/4 in. $20
Butter spreader, hollow handle, stainless paddle,
    6 1/8 in. $20
Butter-master, hollow handle, 6 3/4 in. $25
Carving set, 2 pieces, small, stainless blade,
    steak $120
Fork, 7 3/4 in. $60
Fork, 7 3/8 in. $36
Fork-cold meat/serving, medium, solid,
    8 in. $80
Fork-pickle/olive, short handle, 5 3/4 in. $30
Fork-salad, individual, 6 5/8 in. $44
Knife-carving, large, stainless blade, roast,
    12 in. $60
Knife-cheese, stainless blade, 7 1/8 in. $37
Knife-modern, hollow handle, 9 3/4 in. $50
Ladle-gravy, solid, 6 1/4 in. $80
Napkin clip, (made for teaspoons) $22
Salad set, 2 pieces, plastic bowl $80
Scoop-cheese, solid, 6 1/2 in. $35
Server-pie and cake, stainless blade,
    10 1/2 in. $70
Spoon-dessert/oval soup, 6 1/2 in. $34
Spoon-sugar, 6 1/8 in. $23
Spoon-teaspoon, 6 in. $15
Tablespoon, (serving spoon), 8 1/4 in. $60
Tablespoon, (serving spoon), pierced, 3 tines,
    8 1/4 in. $80

Sweetheart Rose by Lunt, 1951

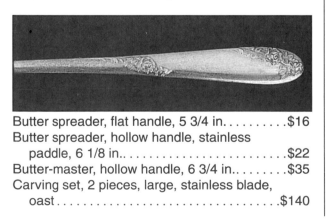

Butter spreader, flat handle, 5 3/4 in. $16
Butter spreader, hollow handle, stainless
    paddle, 6 1/8 in. $22
Butter-master, hollow handle, 6 3/4 in. $35
Carving set, 2 pieces, large, stainless blade,
    oast $140

Carving set, 2 pieces, small, stainless blade,
    steak $120
Fork, 7 1/4 in. $36
Fork-baby, 4 in. $40
Fork-cocktail, 5 7/8 in. $23
Fork-cold meat/serving, small, solid,
    7 5/8 in. $85
Fork-lemon, 5 in. $26
Fork-pickle/olive, short handle, 5 7/8 in. $24
Fork-salad, individual, 6 5/8 in. $40
Fork-youth, 6 1/4 in. $44
Knife-carving, large, stainless blade, roast
    13 1/8 in. $70
Knife-modern, hollow handle, 8 7/8 in. $34
Ladle-cream, solid, 5 in. $45
Ladle-gravy, solid, 5 3/4 in. $80
Napkin clip, (made for sugar) $28
Server-cheese, stainless blade, 6 1/2 in. $45
Server-jelly, 6 3/8 in. $34
Server-pie and cake, stainless blade,
    10 1/2 in. $70
Server-pie, stainless blade, 9 3/4 in. $70
Server-tomato, solid, 7 5/8 in. $110
Spoon-bon-bon, 5 in. $34
Spoon-demitasse, 4 3/8 in. $24
Spoon-dessert/oval soup, 6 7/8 in. $46
Spoon-iced tea, 7 1/2 in. $43
Spoon-soup, round bowl, cream,
    6 1/4 in. $36
Spoon-sugar, 6 in. $24
Spoon-teaspoon, 6 in. $18
Tablespoon, (serving spoon), 8 1/4 in. $85
Tablespoon, (serving spoon), pierced,
    8 1/4 in. $90
Tongs-sugar, 4 3/8 in. $70

William & Mary by Lunt, 1921

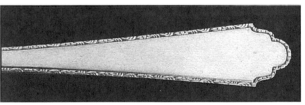

Butter spreader, flat handle, 5 3/4 in. $18
Butter spreader, hollow handle, modern,
    stainless paddle, 6 1/4 in. $24
Butter spreader, hollow handle, stainless
    paddle, 6 1/2 in. $24
Butter-master, flat handle, 7 in. $30
Fork, 7 1/8 in. $30
Fork, 7 5/8 in. $43
Fork-cocktail, 5 5/8 in. $25

Agnes Vanden Bosch's (Anderson) Set [handwritten annotation]

Fork-cold meat/serving, small, solid,
7 1/2 in................................$80
Fork-ice cream, 5 3/4 in....................$40
Fork-pickle/olive, short handle, 3 tines,
5 5/8 in.................................$32
Fork-salad, individual, 6 in. $34
Fork-strawberry, 4 7/8 in. $25
Knife-baby, 5 in...........................$34
Knife-blunt, hollow handle, 5 in. blade,
8 7/8 in.................................$36
Knife-modern, hollow handle (place size),
4 1/4 in. handle, 9 in....................$40
Knife-modern, hollow handle, 8 5/8 in.........$35
Knife-new french, hollow handle, 9 1/2 in......$45
Knife-new french, hollow handle, 9 3/4 in......$45
Knife-new french, hollow handle, 9 in.........$35
Knife-old french, hollow handle, 8 7/8 in.......$35
Knife-steak, individual, 9 1/4 in. $44
Ladle-cream, solid, 5 in.....................$38
Ladle-gravy, solid, 5 7/8 in. $80
Napkin clip, (made for five o'clock) $18
Server-jelly, 6 in. $30
Server-pie and cake, stainless blade,
10 5/8 in. $60

Server-pie, stainless blade, 10 in............$60
Slicer-cake, stainless blade,
12 1/2 in................................$60
Spoon-baby, straight handle, 4 1/4 in.........$40
Spoon-bon-bon, 4 3/4 in. $40
Spoon-cracker, 7 5/8 in. $80
Spoon-demitasse, 4 3/8 in...................$20
Spoon-dessert/oval soup, 7 1/4 in...........$48
Spoon-fruit, 5 3/4 in. $35
Spoon-iced tea, 7 3/4 in....................$34
Spoon-place/oval soup, 6 7/8 in.............$40
Spoon-soup, round bowl, bouillon,
5 1/2 in.................................$23
Spoon-soup, round bowl, cream,
6 1/2 in.................................$34
Spoon-soup, round bowl, gumbo,
6 7/8 in.................................$40
Spoon-sugar, 5 3/4 in......................$35
Spoon-teaspoon (five o'clock), 3 3/4 in.
handle, 5 3/4 in.........................$10
Spoon-teaspoon, 4 in. handle,
6 in.....................................$20
Spoon-youth, 3 5/8 in. handle, 5 1/2 in. $30
Tablespoon, (serving spoon), 8 5/8 in........$70

Lunt Silversmiths

Manchester Silver

MANCHESTER SILVER CO.

Manchester Silver Co. was established in 1887 in Providence, Rhode Island, and adopted the slogan, "If it's Manchester, it's sterling." The company mark was a cross surrounded by a crown, and the letter M.

Amaryllis by Manchester, 1951

Butter spreader, flat handle,
5 7/8 in. . . . .$20.
Butter spreader, hollow handle, stainless
paddle, 5 7/8 in. $20
Fork, 7 in. $40
Fork-baby, 4 7/8 in. $32
Fork-chipped beef, 5 3/4 in. $53
Fork-cocktail, 5 3/8 in. $22
Fork-lemon, 4 5/8 in. $22
Fork-salad, individual, 6 1/4 in. $30
Fork-youth, 6 1/8 in. $40
Knife-carving, small, stainless blade, steak,
9 3/4 in. $50
Knife-modern, hollow 3 3/4 in. handle,
8 5/8 in. $30
Knife-modern, hollow 4 in. handle,
8 7/8 in. $30
Knife-modern, hollow handle,
9 1/4 in. $30
Ladle-cream, solid, 5 1/4 in. $40
Ladle-gravy, solid, 6 in. $70
Sardine-tined fork/serving, solid, large,
5 1/2 in. $60
Server-cheese, stainless blade,
5 7/8 in. $36
Server-pie, solid, 9 3/8 in. $110
Spoon-bon-bon, 4 7/8 in. $36
Spoon-infant feeding, 5 5/8 in. $32
Spoon-soup, round bowl, cream,
6 1/4 in. $32
Spoon-soup, round bowl, gumbo,
6 7/8 in. $37
Spoon-sugar, 6 in. $30
Spoon-teaspoon (five o'clock),
5 3/8 in. $20
Spoon-teaspoon, 6 1/8 in. $20
Tongs-sugar, 4 in. $54

The following piece has a monogram:
Server-cheese, stainless blade,
5 7/8 in. $30

American Beauty by Manchester, 1935

Butter spreader, flat handle, 5 7/8 in. $16
Butter-master, flat handle, 7 1/8 in. $26
Carving set, 2 pieces, small, stainless blade,
steak $120
Fork, 7 1/2 in. $43
Fork, 7 1/8 in. $26
Fork-baby, 4 3/4 in. $40
Fork-cocktail, 4 1/8 in. handle,
5 3/8 in. $20
Fork-cocktail, 4 3/8 in. handle, 5 5/8 in. $20
Fork-cold meat/serving, medium, solid,
8 in. $90
Fork-cold meat/serving, small, solid,
7 in. $80
Fork-lemon, 4 1/2 in. $25
Fork-pickle/olive, short handle,
6 1/4 in. $30
Fork-salad, individual, 6 1/4 in. $38
Knife-new french, hollow handle,
8 7/8 in. $33
Knife-new french, hollow handle,
9 5/8 in. $45
Ladle-gravy, solid, 6 in. $85
Salad set, 2 pieces, solid $210
Server-jelly, 6 3/8 in. $30
Server-pie, solid, 9 3/8 in. $140
Spoon-casserole, smooth, solid, square
bowl, 8 1/2 in. $90
Spoon-demitasse, 4 3/8 in. $20
Spoon-iced tea, 7 3/8 in. $30
Spoon-soup, round bowl, bouillon,
5 1/4 in. $30
Spoon-soup, round bowl, cream,
6 1/4 in. $35
Spoon-soup, round bowl, gumbo,
6 5/8 in. $46
Spoon-sugar, 5 7/8 in. $28
Spoon-teaspoon (five o'clock),
5 1/4 in. $17
Spoon-teaspoon, 6 in. $20
Tablespoon, (serving spoon),
8 in. $70
Tongs-sugar, 3 7/8 in. $66

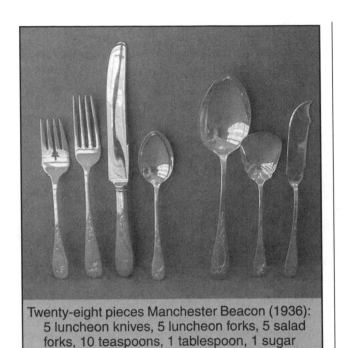

Twenty-eight pieces Manchester Beacon (1936): 5 luncheon knives, 5 luncheon forks, 5 salad forks, 10 teaspoons, 1 tablespoon, 1 sugar spoon, and 1 butter knife. No monogram. Handle engraved with possibly unique floral design. $325

Copenhagen by Manchester, 1936

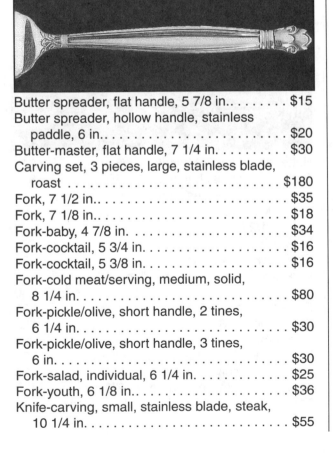

Butter spreader, flat handle, 5 7/8 in.......... $15
Butter spreader, hollow handle, stainless
   paddle, 6 in........................... $20
Butter-master, flat handle, 7 1/4 in. $30
Carving set, 3 pieces, large, stainless blade,
   roast $180
Fork, 7 1/2 in.......................... $35
Fork, 7 1/8 in.......................... $18
Fork-baby, 4 7/8 in. $34
Fork-cocktail, 5 3/4 in. $16
Fork-cocktail, 5 3/8 in. $16
Fork-cold meat/serving, medium, solid,
   8 1/4 in. $80
Fork-pickle/olive, short handle, 2 tines,
   6 1/4 in. $30
Fork-pickle/olive, short handle, 3 tines,
   6 in. $30
Fork-salad, individual, 6 1/4 in. $25
Fork-youth, 6 1/8 in..................... $36
Knife-carving, small, stainless blade, steak,
   10 1/4 in............................ $55

Knife-modern, hollow handle, 8 3/4 in........ $26
Knife-new french, hollow handle,
   8 7/8 in. $28
Knife-new french, hollow handle,
   9 5/8 in. $40
Knife-youth, 7 1/4 in. $34
Ladle-cream, solid, 5 1/2 in............... $45
Ladle-gravy, solid, 5 3/4 in.............. $70
Sardine-tined fork, serving, solid,
   5 3/8 in. $80
Server-cheese, stainless blade,
   5 7/8 in. $45
Server-jelly, 6 3/8 in..................... $30
Server-pie, stainless blade, 9 7/8 in. $60
Spoon-bon-bon, 4 7/8 in. $38
Spoon-casserole, smooth bowl, solid,
   8 7/8 in. $90
Spoon-demitasse, 4 1/2 in. $16
Spoon-fruit, 6 in........................ $28
Spoon-iced tea, 7 3/8 in. $18
Spoon-olive, long handle, 7 1/2 in.......... $120
Spoon-salad serving, solid, 8 1/2 in. $90
Spoon-soup, round bowl, bouillon,
   4 7/8 in. $20
Spoon-soup, round bowl, bouillon,
   5 1/4 in. $20
Spoon-soup, round bowl, cream,
   6 1/4 in. $20
Spoon-soup, round bowl, gumbo,
   6 7/8 in. $30
Spoon-sugar, 6 in. $20
Spoon-teaspoon, 6 1/8 in. $20
Tablespoon, (serving spoon), 8 1/8 in........ $60

Duke of Windsor by Manchester, 1937

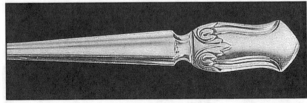

Butter spreader, flat handle, 5 7/8 in......... $22
Butter-master, flat handle, 7 1/4 in. $30
Carving set, 2 pieces, small, stainless blade,
   steak $100
Fork, 7 1/2 in........................... $44
Fork, 7 1/8 in........................... $32
Fork-cocktail, 5 3/8 in. $24
Fork-cold meat/serving, medium, solid,
   8 1/4 in. $70
Fork-salad, individual, 6 3/8 in. $32

Knife-modern, hollow handle, 8 3/4 in. $26
Knife-modern, hollow handle, 9 1/2 in. $36
Knife-new french, hollow handle,
   9 3/4 in. $36
Spoon-demitasse, 4 1/2 in. $18
Spoon-iced tea, 7 1/2 in. $30
Spoon-soup, round bowl, bouillon,
   5 1/4 in. $30
Spoon-soup, round bowl, cream,
   6 1/4 in. $32
Spoon-soup, round bowl, gumbo,
   6 3/4 in. $40
Spoon-sugar, 6 in. $32
Spoon-teaspoon, 6 1/8 in. $22
Sugar shovel, 6 1/8 in. $30
Tablespoon, (serving spoon), 8 in. $60

Eighteen pieces Manchester Duke of Windsor (1937): 6 each luncheon knives, luncheon forks, and teaspoons. No monogram. $250

Fleetwood by Manchester, 1910

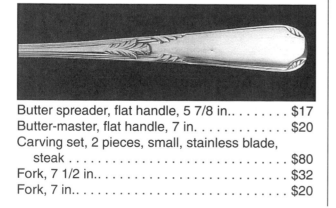

Butter spreader, flat handle, 5 7/8 in. $17
Butter-master, flat handle, 7 in. $20
Carving set, 2 pieces, small, stainless blade,
   steak $80
Fork, 7 1/2 in. $32
Fork, 7 in. $20

Fork-baby, 4 3/4 in. $34
Fork-cold meat/serving, small, solid,
   7 1/2 in. $70
Fork-cold meat/serving, small, solid,
   7 in. $70
Fork-grille (viand), 7 5/8 in. $30
Fork-salad, individual, 6 in. $30
Knife-carving, small, stainless blade, steak,
   10 1/4 in. $40
knife-grille, new french, hollow handle,
   8 1/2 in. $28
Knife-modern, hollow handle, 8 5/8 in. $24
Knife-new french, hollow handle,
   9 5/8 in. $40
Knife-new french, hollow handle, 9 in. $24
Ladle-gravy, solid, 5 7/8 in. $70
Napkin clip, (made for teaspoons) $16
Server-pie, stainless blade, 9 1/2 in. $50
Server-pie, stainless blade, 9 7/8 in. $50
Spoon-iced tea, 7 3/8 in. $23
Spoon-soup, round bowl, cream,
   6 1/8 in. $30
Spoon-soup, round bowl, gumbo,
   6 7/8 in. $34
Spoon-sugar, 5 5/8 in. $16
Spoon-teaspoon, 5 7/8 in. $14
Tablespoon, (serving spoon), 8 in. $47

Gadroonette by Manchester, 1938

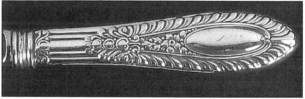

Butter spreader, flat handle, 5 7/8 in. $16
Butter-master, flat handle, 7 3/8 in. $25
Carving set, 2 pieces, small, stainless blade,
   steak $100
Fork, 7 1/2 in. $30
Fork, 7 in. $20
Fork-cocktail, 5 5/8 in. $22
Fork-cold meat/serving, medium, solid,
   8 1/4 in. $90
Fork-ice cream, 5 3/4 in. $36
Fork-lemon, 4 3/4 in. $25
Fork-lemon, 5 1/8 in. $25
Fork-pickle/olive, short handle, 6 1/8 in. $28
Fork-salad, individual, 6 1/4 in. $30
Knife-bread, stainless blade, 12 7/8 in. $110
Knife-carving, small, stainless blade, steak,
   9 7/8 in. $50

Knife-modern, hollow handle, no serrations,
8 5/8 in. $20
Knife-new french, hollow handle,
8 3/4 in. $20
Knife-new french, hollow handle,
9 5/8 in. $24
Ladle-cream, solid, 5 3/8 in. $36
Ladle-gravy, solid, 6 1/4 in. $80
Ladle-mayonnaise, 4 1/2 in. $35
Ladle-mayonnaise, 4 in. $35
Napkin clip, (made for teaspoons) $20
Poultry shears, 11 1/4 in. $140
Salad set, 2 pieces, solid, 8 3/4 in. $170
Server-cheese, stainless blade, 5 7/8 in. $34
Server-cheese, stainless blade, 6 3/8 in. $34
Server-cheese, stainless blade, 7 1/8 in. $34
Server-pie, stainless blade, 9 3/8 in. $50
Spoon-demitasse, 4 1/2 in. $16
Spoon-dessert/oval soup, 7 in. $36
Spoon-fruit, 6 1/8 in. $28
Spoon-iced tea, 7 1/2 in. $30
Spoon-soup, round bowl, bouillon,
5 1/4 in. $24
Spoon-soup, round bowl, cream,
6 1/4 in. $20
Spoon-sugar. 6 in. $24
Spoon-teaspoon (five o'clock), 5 3/8 in. $16
Spoon-teaspoon, 6 1/8 in. $16
Tablespoon, (serving spoon), 8 1/8 in. $55
Tongs-sugar, 4 in. $54

Fork-cold meat/serving, medium, solid,
8 1/8 in. $75
Fork-lemon, 5 1/8 in. $24
Fork-salad, individual, 6 1/4 in. $27
Fork-youth, 6 1/8 in. $35
Knife-carving, small, stainless blade, steak,
10 1/4 in. $50
Knife-modern, hollow handle, 5 1/4 in. blade, 9 1/4
in. $27
Knife-new french, hollow handle,
8 1/2 in. $26
Knife-new french, hollow handle,
8 7/8 in. $26
Knife-new french, hollow handle,
9 5/8 in. $34
Spoon-baby, straight handle, 4 7/8 in. $34
Spoon-demitasse, 4 1/2 in. $18
Spoon-dessert/oval soup, 7 in. $35
Spoon-iced tea, 7 1/2 in. $30
Spoon-soup, round bowl, bouillon,
5 1/2 in. $30
Spoon-soup, round bowl, cream,
6 1/8 in. $17
Spoon-soup, round bowl, gumbo,
6 7/8 in. $34
Spoon-sugar, 5 7/8 in. $16
Spoon-teaspoon (five o'clock), 5 1/2 in. $15
Spoon-teaspoon, 6 1/8 in. $16
Tablespoon, (serving spoon), 8 1/8 in. $50

Manchester by Manchester, 1932

Butter spreader, flat handle, 5 3/8 in. $12
Butter spreader, hollow handle, stainless
paddle, 5 3/4 in. $20
Butter-master, flat handle, 6 7/8 in. $20
Carving set, 2 pieces, small, stainless blade,
steak $90
Fork, 7 1/2 in. $34
Fork, 7 1/8 in. $20
Fork-baby, 4 1/4 in. $34
Fork-baby, 4 3/4 in. $34
Fork-carving, small stainless prongs, steak,
8 5/8 in. $45
Fork-cocktail, 5 5/8 in. $16
Fork-cold meat/serving, medium, solid,
8 1/4 in. $60

Leonore by Manchester, 1939

Butter spreader, flat handle, 5 3/4 in. $16
Butter spreader, hollow handle, modern,
stainless paddle, 6 in. $19
Butter spreader, hollow handle, stainless
paddle, 5 7/8 in. $19
Butter-master, flat handle, 7 1/8 in. $15
Carving set, 2 pieces, small, stainless blade,
steak $100
Fork, 7 1/2 in. $37
Fork, 7 in. $18
Fork-baby, 5 in. $34
Fork-carving, small stainless prongs, steak,
8 5/8 in. $50
Fork-cocktail, 5 5/8 in. $20

Manchester Silver

Fork-cold meat/serving, small, solid,
7 3/4 in. $48
Fork-cold meat/serving, small, solid, pierced,
7 1/4 in. $48
Fork-dessert, 4 tines bar, 5 3/4 in. $40
Fork-fish, solid, individual, 3 piercings,
5 7/8 in. $42
Fork-grille (viand), 7 5/8 in. $20
Fork-ice cream, 3 pierced tines, 5 1/8 in. $28
Fork-lemon, 4 7/8 in. $26
Fork-pickle/olive, long handle, 7 1/8 in. $40
Fork-pickle/olive, short handle, 6 1/8 in. $26
Fork-salad, individual, clover shape,
5 7/8 in. $24
Knife-carving, small, stainless blade,
steak $45
Knife-fruit, stainless blade, individual,
6 1/2 in. $30
Knife-grille, new french-hollow handle,
8 1/2 in. $25
Knife-new french, hollow handle,
8 3/4 in. $27
Knife-new french, hollow handle,
8 3/8 in. $27
Knife-new french, hollow handle,
9 3/4 in. $34
Ladle-cream, solid, 5 3/8 in. $40
Ladle-gravy, solid, 6 1/8 in. $60
Server-jelly, crimped edge, 6 in. $22
Server-jelly, no crimp, 6 1/4 in. $22
Server-pie, stainless blade, 10 3/8 in. $50
Server-pie, stainless blade, 9 5/8 in. $50
Spoon-bon-bon, 13 piercings, 4 7/8 in. $34
Spoon-bon-bon, no crimp, 5 5/8 in. $34
Spoon-demitasse, 4 1/4 in. $18
Spoon-dessert/oval soup, 7 in. $26
Spoon-fruit, pointed bowl, 5 5/8 in. $28
Spoon-iced tea, 7 1/2 in. $22
Spoon-preserve, 7 1/8 in. $60
Spoon-salad serving, solid, 8 1/2 in. $80
Spoon-soup, round bowl, bouillon,
5 in. $20
Spoon-soup, round bowl, cream,
6 1/8 in. $20
Spoon-soup, round bowl, gumbo,
6 7/8 in. $30
Spoon-sugar shell, crimped edge,
5 5/8 in. $17
Spoon-teaspoon (five o'clock), 5 1/8 in. $18
Spoon-teaspoon, tear-shaped bowl,
5 3/4 in. $12
Sugar shovel, 5 7/8 in. $34
Tablespoon, (serving spoon), 8 in. $40
Tongs-sugar, 4 in. $48

Mary Warren by Manchester, 1910/1932

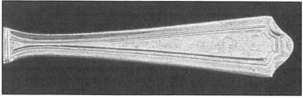

Butter spreader, flat handle, 5 3/8 in. $23
Butter-master, flat handle, 7 in. $33
Fork, 7 3/8 in. $32
Fork, 8 in. $46
Fork-baby, 4 3/4 in. $28
Fork-chipped beef, medium, 7 1/4 in. $56
Fork-chipped beef, medium, 7 3/4 in. $56
Fork-chipped beef, small, 6 5/8 in. $46
Fork-cocktail, 5 5/8 in. $22
Fork-cocktail, 5 in. $22
Fork-cold meat/serving, small, solid,
7 1/2 in. $60
Fork-dessert, 3 oval piercings, 5 7/8 in. $42
Fork-fish, solid, individual, 3 tear-shaped
piercings, 6 1/8 in. $40
Fork-lemon, 4 7/8 in. $22
Fork-lettuce serving, large, 8 1/4 in. $70
Fork-pickle/olive, short handle, 2 tines,
6 in. $22
Fork-pickle/olive, short handle, 6 1/4 in. $22
Fork-salad, individual, slotted tines, 6 in. $33
Knife-carving, small, stainless blade, steak,
10 in. $50
Knife-new french, hollow handle,
8 3/4 in. $30
Knife-new french, hollow handle,
9 3/4 in. $40
Knife-old french, hollow handle,
8 1/2 in. $30
Knife-old french, hollow handle,
9 3/4 in. $40
Ladle-cream, solid, 5 7/8 in. $28
Ladle-cream, solid, 5 in. $28
Ladle-gravy, solid, 6 1/2 in. $60
Ladle-mayonnaise, 4 7/8 in. $36
Pick-butter, 1 tine, 6 3/8 in. $40
Pick-cheese, 6 in. $35
Salad set, 2 pieces, solid $170
Sardine fork, serving, solid, 5 1/2 in. $60
Server-cheese, silver plate blade,
5 3/4 in. $50
Server-cheese, stainless blade,
5 3/4 in. $38
Server-cucumber, small, 6 1/8 in. $50

Server-jelly, 5 7/8 in. $24
Server-tomato, solid, 7 5/8 in. $65
Server-tomato, solid, 8 1/4 in. $65
Spoon-baby, straight handle, 4 5/8 in. $28
Spoon-bon-bon, 4 3/4 in. $28
Spoon-bon-bon, 5 3/4 in. $28
Spoon-casserole, smooth bowl, solid,
 7 3/8 in. $75
Spoon-demitasse, 4 3/8 in. $20
Spoon-dessert/oval soup, 7 1/8 in. $35
Spoon-fruit, no piercings, 5 7/8 in. $30
Spoon-iced tea, 7 3/4 in. $30
Spoon-infant feeding, 5 1/4 in. $30
Spoon-olive, long handle, tear-shaped bowl,
 7 1/2 in. $100
Spoon-olive, short, pierced bowl,
 5 1/2 in. $50
Spoon-olive, short, pierced bowl, egg-shaped
 bowl, 6 1/4 in. $50
Spoon-relish, square bowl, 6 in. $30
Spoon-soup, round bowl, bouillon,
 5 1/4 in. $22
Spoon-soup, round bowl, cream,
 6 1/4 in. $28
Spoon-soup, round bowl, gumbo,
 7 in. $38
Spoon-sugar, 6 in. $34
Spoon-teaspoon (five o'clock),
 5 3/8 in. $20
Spoon-teaspoon, 6 in. $20
Tablespoon, (serving spoon),
 8 1/8 in. $60
Tongs-sugar, 4 in. $40

Fork-carving, small, stainless prongs, steak,
 9 1/4 in. $40
Fork-cocktail, 5 1/8 in. $22
Fork-grille (viand), 7 5/8 in. $28
Fork-lemon, 4 1/2 in. $26
Fork-salad, individual, 6 in. $24
Knife-carving, small, stainless blade, steak,
 10 in. $40
Knife-new french, hollow handle,
 8 3/4 in. $34
Knife-new french, hollow handle,
 9 5/8 in. $50
Ladle-cream, solid, 5 in. $35
Ladle-gravy, solid, 5 7/8 in. $70
Poultry shears, 9 3/4 in. $130
Server-jelly, 5 7/8 in. $25
Server-jelly, 6 1/4 in. $25
Server-pie, stainless blade, 9 5/8 in. $50
Spoon-bon-bon, 4 7/8 in. $26
Spoon-demitasse, 4 3/8 in. $15
Spoon-dessert/oval soup, 7 in. $24
Spoon-iced tea, 7 5/8 in. $25
Spoon-soup, round bowl, bouillon,
 5 3/4 in. $22
Spoon-soup, round bowl, cream,
 6 1/8 in. $25
Spoon-soup, round bowl, gumbo,
 6 7/8 in. $34
Spoon-sugar, 5 3/4 in. $16
Spoon-teaspoon, 5 7/8 in. $14
Tablespoon, (serving spoon), 8 in. $55
Tongs-sugar, 4 in. $50

Polly Lawton by Manchester, 1935

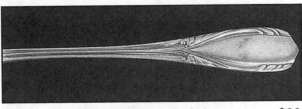
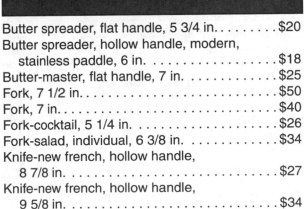

Butter spreader, flat handle, 5 3/4 in. $20
Butter spreader, hollow handle, modern,
 stainless paddle, 6 in. $18
Butter-master, flat handle, 7 in. $25
Fork, 7 1/2 in. $50
Fork, 7 in. $40
Fork-cocktail, 5 1/4 in. $26
Fork-salad, individual, 6 3/8 in. $34
Knife-new french, hollow handle,
 8 7/8 in. $27
Knife-new french, hollow handle,
 9 5/8 in. $34

Park Avenue by Manchester, 1931

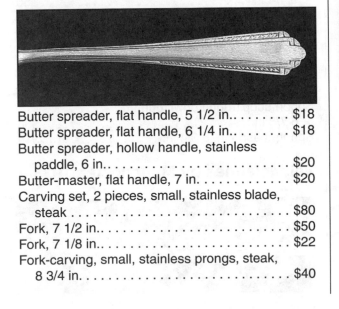

Butter spreader, flat handle, 5 1/2 in. $18
Butter spreader, flat handle, 6 1/4 in. $18
Butter spreader, hollow handle, stainless
 paddle, 6 in. $20
Butter-master, flat handle, 7 in. $20
Carving set, 2 pieces, small, stainless blade,
 steak $80
Fork, 7 1/2 in. $50
Fork, 7 1/8 in. $22
Fork-carving, small, stainless prongs, steak,
 8 3/4 in. $40

Manchester Silver

Spoon-dessert/oval soup, 7 in. $36
Spoon-iced tea, 7 3/8 in. $30
Spoon-soup, round bowl, cream 6 in. $35
Spoon-soup, round bowl, gumbo,
   6 7/8 in. $40
Spoon-sugar, 5 3/4 in. $30
Spoon-teaspoon, 5 7/8 in. $20
Spoon-teaspoon, 6 1/8 in. $20
Tablespoon, (serving spoon), 8 in. $60

Silver Stream by Manchester, 1934

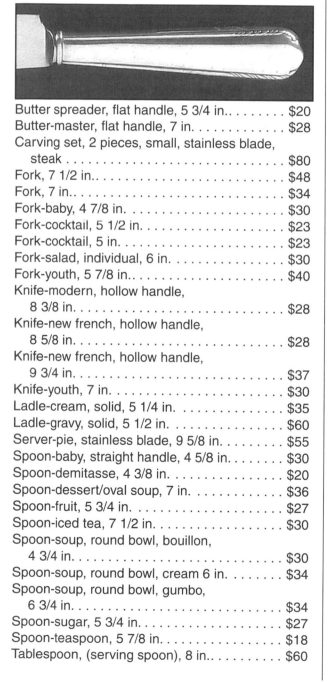

Butter spreader, flat handle, 5 3/4 in. $20
Butter-master, flat handle, 7 in. $28
Carving set, 2 pieces, small, stainless blade,
   steak $80
Fork, 7 1/2 in. $48
Fork, 7 in. $34
Fork-baby, 4 7/8 in. $30
Fork-cocktail, 5 1/2 in. $23
Fork-cocktail, 5 in. $23
Fork-salad, individual, 6 in. $30
Fork-youth, 5 7/8 in. $40
Knife-modern, hollow handle,
   8 3/8 in. $28
Knife-new french, hollow handle,
   8 5/8 in. $28
Knife-new french, hollow handle,
   9 3/4 in. $37
Knife-youth, 7 in. $30
Ladle-cream, solid, 5 1/4 in. $35
Ladle-gravy, solid, 5 1/2 in. $60
Server-pie, stainless blade, 9 5/8 in. $55
Spoon-baby, straight handle, 4 5/8 in. $30
Spoon-demitasse, 4 3/8 in. $20
Spoon-dessert/oval soup, 7 in. $36
Spoon-fruit, 5 3/4 in. $27
Spoon-iced tea, 7 1/2 in. $30
Spoon-soup, round bowl, bouillon,
   4 3/4 in. $30
Spoon-soup, round bowl, cream 6 in. $34
Spoon-soup, round bowl, gumbo,
   6 3/4 in. $34
Spoon-sugar, 5 3/4 in. $27
Spoon-teaspoon, 5 7/8 in. $18
Tablespoon, (serving spoon), 8 in. $60

Southern Rose by Manchester, 1933

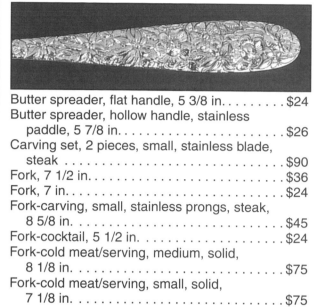

Butter spreader, flat handle, 5 3/8 in. $24
Butter spreader, hollow handle, stainless
   paddle, 5 7/8 in. $26
Carving set, 2 pieces, small, stainless blade,
   steak $90
Fork, 7 1/2 in. $36
Fork, 7 in. $24
Fork-carving, small, stainless prongs, steak,
   8 5/8 in. $45
Fork-cocktail, 5 1/2 in. $24
Fork-cold meat/serving, medium, solid,
   8 1/8 in. $75
Fork-cold meat/serving, small, solid,
   7 1/8 in. $75
Fork-ice cream, not pierced, 5 1/2 in. $40
Fork-ice cream, pierced, 5 1/2 in. $40
Fork-salad, individual, 5 7/8 in. $34
Knife-carving, small, stainless blade, steak,
   10 5/8 in. $45
Knife-new french, hollow handle,
   8 5/8 in. $30
Knife-new french, hollow handle,
   9 5/8 in. $40
Ladle-cream, solid, 4 3/8 in. $40
Poultry shears, 9 3/4 in. $190
Server-cheese, stainless blade, 5 3/4 in. $48
Server-jelly, 6 1/8 in. $34
Server-pie, stainless blade, 9 5/8 in. $60
Server-pie, stainless blade, no serrations,
   9 1/4 in. $60
Spoon-fruit, 5 3/4 in. $28
Spoon-iced tea, 7 3/8 in. $27
Spoon-soup, round bowl, bouillon, 3 3/8 in.
   handle, 4 7/8 in. $28
Spoon-soup, round bowl, bouillon, 3 in.
   handle, 4 3/4 in. $28
Spoon-soup, round bowl, gumbo,
   6 7/8 in. $36
Spoon-teaspoon, 5 3/4 in. $14

Valenciennes by Manchester, 1938

Fork, 7 1/2 in............................. $50
Fork, 7 in................................. $34
Fork-cocktail, 5 3/4 in..................... $24
Fork-cocktail, 5 3/8 in..................... $24
Fork-ice cream, 5 3/4 in................... $38
Fork-salad, individual, 6 3/8 in............ $34
Knife-modern, hollow handle, 8 5/8 in. $30
Knife-modern, hollow handle, 9 1/4 in. $30
Knife-new french, hollow handle,
   9 5/8 in.............................. $45

Spoon-demitasse, 4 5/8 in. $18
Spoon-dessert/oval soup, 6 7/8 in.......... $33
Spoon-fruit, 6 1/8 in....................... $32
Spoon-iced tea, 7 1/2 in. $28
Spoon-soup, round bowl, bouillon,
   5 1/4 in. $30
Spoon-soup, round bowl, gumbo,
   6 3/4 in. $40
Spoon-sugar, 6 1/8 in. $36
Spoon-teaspoon, 6 1/4 in. $17

Manchester Silver

NATIONAL SILVER CO.

National Silver Co. of New York began in 1904, and later acquired the F.B. Rogers Co., and the Ontario Manufacturing Co. of Muncie, Indiana, in the mid-1950s. No flatware has been produced since the mid-1940s.

Intermezzo by National, 1940

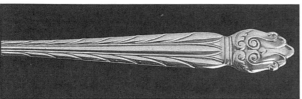

Butter-master, flat handle, 7 in.	$40
Fork, 7 1/2 in.	$50
Fork, 7 in.	$30
Fork-grille (viand), 7 3/4 in.	$34
Fork-salad, individual, 6 5/8 in.	$38
Knife-grille, modern, hollow handle, 8 3/8 in.	$28
Knife-modern, hollow handle, 9 1/2 in.	$45
Knife-modern, hollow handle, 9 1/4 in.	$35
Ladle-gravy, solid, 6 in.	$85
Spoon-demitasse, 4 1/2 in.	$22
Spoon-dessert/oval soup, 7 1/4 in.	$40
Spoon-iced tea, 7 5/8 in.	$38
Spoon-soup, round bowl, cream, 6 3/8 in.	$36
Spoon-soup, round bowl, gumbo, 7 in.	$50
Spoon-sugar, 6 in.	$35
Spoon-teaspoon, 6 in.	$17
Tablespoon, (serving spoon), 8 in.	$80

Margaret Rose by National, 1938

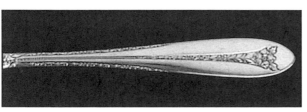

Butter spreader, flat handle, 5 7/8 in.	$18
Carving set, 2 pieces, small, stainless blade, steak	$100
Fork, 7 1/4 in.	$25
Fork, 7 5/8 in.	$40
Fork-baby, 4 1/2 in.	$30
Fork-cocktail, 6 in.	$15
Fork-grille (viand), 7 3/4 in.	$25

Fork-ice cream, 5 3/8 in.	$20
Fork-salad, individual, 6 1/2 in.	$24
Fork-youth, 6 1/4 in.	$30
Knife-grille, new french, hollow handle, 8 1/2 in.	$22
Knife-new french, hollow handle, silver plate blade, 8 7/8 in.	$26
Knife-new french, hollow handle, stainless blade, 8 7/8 in.	$26
Knife-new french, hollow handle, stainless blade, 9 1/2 in.	$40
Knife-sharpener, steel, small, steak, 13 3/4 in.	$55
Knife-youth, 7 in.	$35
Napkin clip, (made for teaspoons)	$20
Spoon-baby, straight handle, 4 3/8 in.	$30
Spoon-bon-bon, 4 3/4 in.	$40
Spoon-casserole, smooth bowl, solid, 8 1/2 in.	$100
Spoon-dessert/oval soup, 6 7/8 in.	$35
Spoon-fruit, 5 7/8 in.	$36
Spoon-iced tea, 7 in.	$22
Spoon-soup, round bowl, bouillon, 5 1/4 in.	$24
Spoon-soup, round bowl, cream, 6 3/8 in.	$16
Spoon-sugar, 5 3/4 in.	$35
Spoon-teaspoon, 6 in.	$14
Tablespoon, (serving spoon), 8 in.	$80

Narcissus by National, 1936

Butter-master, flat handle, 7 in.	$38
Fork, 7 in.	$45
Fork-cocktail, 6 1/8 in.	$34
Fork-salad, individual, 5 7/8 in.	$48
Knife-new french, hollow handle, 8 3/4 in.	$36
Spoon-dessert/oval soup, 7 in.	$50
Spoon-iced tea, 6 7/8 in.	$36
Spoon-soup, round bowl, bouillon, 5 1/8 in.	$36
Spoon-soup, round bowl, cream, 6 1/8 in.	$40
Spoon-sugar, 6 in.	$38
Spoon-teaspoon, 6 in.	$30
Tablespoon, (serving spoon), 7 7/8 in.	$90

Overture by National, 1936

Butter spreader, flat handle, 5 7/8 in.. . . . . $14
Butter-master, flat handle, 7 in.. . . . . $20
Fork, 7 1/4 in.. . . . . $18
Fork, 7 5/8 in.. . . . . $25
Fork-baby, 4 1/2 in.. . . . . $28
Fork-grille (viand), 7 5/8 in.. . . . . $18
Fork-salad, individual, 6 1/2 in.. . . . . $24
Fork-youth, 6 1/4 in.. . . . . $35
Knife-grille, new french, hollow handle,
   8 1/2 in.. . . . . $24
Knife-new french, hollow handle,
   8 7/8 in.. . . . . $24
Knife-new french, hollow handle,
   9 5/8 in.. . . . . $26
Napkin clip, (made for teaspoons). $18
Spoon-demitasse, 4 1/2 in.. . . . . $16
Spoon-fruit, 6 in.. . . . . $26
Spoon-iced tea, 7 1/8 in.. . . . . $26
Spoon-sherbet/large, 5 3/8 in.. . . . . $28
Spoon-soup, round bowl, bouillon,
   5 1/4 in.. . . . . $28
Spoon-soup, round bowl, cream,
   6 1/2 in.. . . . . $20
Spoon-soup, round bowl, gumbo,
   6 7/8 in.. . . . . $34
Spoon-sugar, 5 5/8 in.. . . . . $20
Spoon-teaspoon (five o'clock), 5 5/8 in.. . . . . . $16
Spoon-teaspoon, 6 in.. . . . . $14
Tablespoon, (serving spoon), 8 in.. . . . . $60

Princess Elizabeth by National, 1942

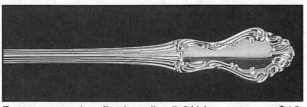

Butter spreader, flat handle, 5 3/4 in.. . . . . $18
Butter-master, flat handle, 6 7/8 in.. . . . . $40

Carving set, 3 pieces, large, stainless
   blade, roast $200
Carving set, 2 pieces, small, stainless
   blade, steak $100
Fork, 7 1/4 in.. . . . . $22
Fork, 7 7/8 in.. . . . . $45
Fork-cocktail, 6 in. $24
Fork-cold meat/serving, small, solid,
   7 3/4 in. $75
Fork-salad, individual, square bowl,
   6 1/8 in. $30
Knife-bread, stainless blade, 10 7/8 in. $90
Knife-new french, hollow handle,
   8 7/8 in.. . . . . $18
Knife-new french, hollow handle,
   9 5/8 in. $34
Ladle-gravy, solid, 6 1/4 in.. . . . . $90
Server-jelly, 6 1/4 in.. $33
Spoon-casserole, smooth bowl, solid,
   8 7/8 in. $90
Spoon-demitasse, 4 3/8 in. $20
Spoon-iced tea, 7 in. $40
Spoon-soup, round bowl, cream,
   6 1/8 in. $17
Spoon-soup, round bowl, gumbo, 7 in.. . . . . . . $44
Spoon-sugar, 5 7/8 in. $30
Spoon-teaspoon, 5 7/8 in. $15
Tablespoon, (serving spoon), 8 3/8 in.. . . . . . . $80

NORTHUMBRIA

Normandy Rose by Northumbria, date unknown

Butter spreader, hollow handle, modern,
   stainless paddle, 6 3/4 in. $28
Butter-master, flat handle, 7 in. $45
Fork, 7 5/8 in.. . . . . $70
Fork, 7 in.. . . . . $50
Fork-salad, individual, 6 1/4 in. $50
Knife-modern, hollow handle, 9 in.. . . . . $35
Knife-new french, hollow handle,
   9 7/8 in. $48
Knife-new french, hollow handle, 9 in. $35
Server-pie, stainless blade, 10 in. $70
Spoon-five o'clock/youth, 5 3/8 in. $28
Spoon-soup, round bowl, cream, 6 in. $50
Spoon-sugar, 6 in. $44
Spoon-teaspoon, 6 in. $30

OLD NEWBURY

Old Newbury Crafters of Newburyport and Amesbury, Massachusetts, was formally established in 1932, but began as a joint venture in 1915. They specialized in hand-wrought patterns, including Moulton and Old Newbury. All hand-wrought pieces have been marked by the craftsmen who made them since 1965.

Moulton by Old Newbury

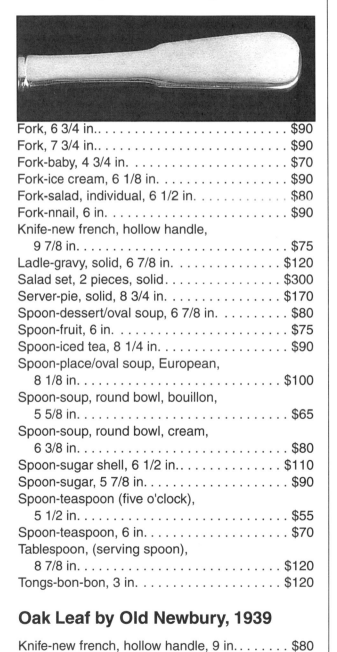

Fork, 6 3/4 in.	$90
Fork, 7 3/4 in.	$90
Fork-baby, 4 3/4 in.	$70
Fork-ice cream, 6 1/8 in.	$90
Fork-salad, individual, 6 1/2 in.	$80
Fork-nnail, 6 in.	$90
Knife-new french, hollow handle, 9 7/8 in.	$75
Ladle-gravy, solid, 6 7/8 in.	$120
Salad set, 2 pieces, solid.	$300
Server-pie, solid, 8 3/4 in.	$170
Spoon-dessert/oval soup, 6 7/8 in.	$80
Spoon-fruit, 6 in.	$75
Spoon-iced tea, 8 1/4 in.	$90
Spoon-place/oval soup, European, 8 1/8 in.	$100
Spoon-soup, round bowl, bouillon, 5 5/8 in.	$65
Spoon-soup, round bowl, cream, 6 3/8 in.	$80
Spoon-sugar shell, 6 1/2 in.	$110
Spoon-sugar, 5 7/8 in.	$90
Spoon-teaspoon (five o'clock), 5 1/2 in.	$55
Spoon-teaspoon, 6 in.	$70
Tablespoon, (serving spoon), 8 7/8 in.	$120
Tongs-bon-bon, 3 in.	$120

Oak Leaf by Old Newbury, 1939

Knife-new french, hollow handle, 9 in.	$80

Old Newbury by Old Newbury

Butter spreader, flat handle, 5 1/2 in.	$50
Carving set, 2 pieces, small, stainless blade, steak	$190
Fork, 4 tines, 7 in.	$85
Fork, 7 3/4 in.	$110
Fork-baby, curved handle, 3 5/8 in.	$80
Fork-carving, small, stainless prongs, steak, 8 1/2 in.	$95
Fork-cold meat/serving, small, solid, 7 3/4 in.	$170
Fork-dessert, 5 5/8 in.	$65
Fork-ice cream, 6 in.	$85
Fork-luncheon, 3 tines, 7 1/4 in.	$90
Fork-salad, individual, 6 3/4 in.	$75
Knife-fruit, stainless blade, individual, 7 1/8 in.	$70
Knife-new french, hollow handle, 9 1/2 in.	$70
Knife-old french, hollow handle, 8 5/8 in.	$65
Server-jelly, 6 1/2 in.	$90
Server-jelly, 6 1/8 in.	$90
Server-petite, 6 in.	$70
Spoon-bon-bon, 5 in.	$55
Spoon-dessert/oval soup, 7 7/8 in.	$85
Spoon-dressing, large, solid, 12 1/2 in.	$190
Spoon-iced tea, 8 in.	$90
Spoon-olive, short, pierced bowl, 6 in.	$110
Spoon-place/oval soup, European, 8 in.	$100
Spoon-salad serving, solid, 8 3/4 in.	$160
Spoon-soup, round bowl, bouillon, 5 3/4 in.	$75
Spoon-teaspoon (five o'clock), 5 1/2 in.	$60
Spoon-teaspoon, 6 1/4 in.	$70
Tablespoon, (serving spoon), 9 1/8 in.	$150

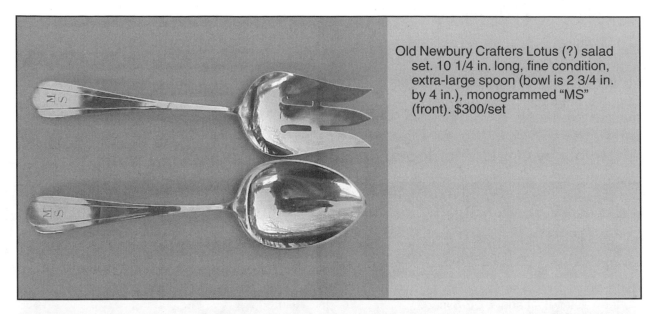

Old Newbury Crafters Lotus (?) salad set. 10 1/4 in. long, fine condition, extra-large spoon (bowl is 2 3/4 in. by 4 in.), monogrammed "MS" (front). $300/set

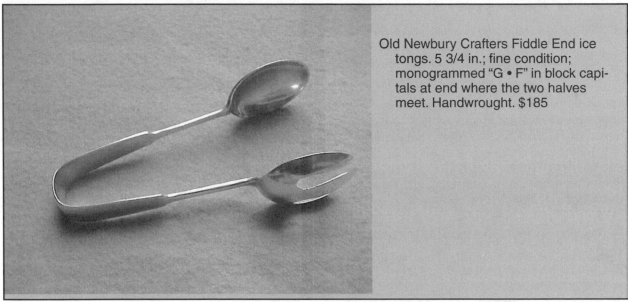

Old Newbury Crafters Fiddle End ice tongs. 5 3/4 in.; fine condition; monogrammed "G • F" in block capitals at end where the two halves meet. Handwrought. $185

ONEIDA

Oneida Silversmiths was incorporated in 1880 near Sherrill, New York as Oneida Community Limited. It became Oneida Ltd. in 1935 and began producing sterling flatware in 1946, marked Oneida Sterling or Heirloom Sterling.

Afterglow by Oneida/Heirloom, 1956

Butter spreader, flat handle, 5 3/4 in......... $20
Butter-master, flat handle, 6 7/8 in.......... $34
Carving set, 2 pieces, small, stainless blade,
    steak $130
Fork, 7 1/4 in............................ $20
Fork-salad, individual, 6 1/2 in. $30
Knife-modern, hollow handle, 8 7/8 in. $33
Ladle-gravy, solid, 6 1/4 in. $70
Spoon-demitasse, 4 1/8 in. $24
Spoon-iced tea, 7 1/2 in. $34
Spoon-soup, round bowl, cream,
    6 1/2 in............................ $43
Spoon-sugar, 6 in......................... $28
Spoon-teaspoon, 6 in...................... $20
Tablespoon, (serving spoon), 8 1/4 in........ $70

Belle Rose by Oneida/Heirloom, 1963

Butter spreader, hollow handle, modern, stainless
    paddle, 6 5/8 in........................ $18
Butter-master, hollow handle, 6 3/4 in. $23
Fork, 7 1/2 in............................ $40
Fork-pickle/olive, short handle, 2 tines,
    5 1/2 in.............................. $20
Fork-salad, individual, 6 7/8 in. $30
Knife-cheese, stainless blade, 7 3/8 in....... $38
Knife-modern, hollow handle, 9 in. $26
Ladle-cream, solid, 5 1/4 in. $24
Server-jelly, 6 1/2 in. $30

Server-pie and cake, stainless blade,
    10 5/8 in. $60
Spoon-bon-bon, 5 3/8 in. $30
Spoon-dessert/oval soup, 6 7/8 in.......... $40
Spoon-iced tea, 7 1/2 in. $34
Spoon-sugar, 5 1/2 in. $26
Spoon-teaspoon, 6 1/8 in. $14
Tablespoon, (serving spoon),
    8 1/4 in. $50
Tablespoon, (serving spoon), pierced,
    8 1/4 in. $55

Bountiful by Oneida/Heirloom, 1967

Fork, 7 1/4 in............................ $40
Fork-cocktail, 5 1/2 in. $28
Fork-salad, individual, 6 1/2 in. $40
Knife-modern, hollow handle,
    9 in. $33
Spoon-iced tea, 7 1/2 in. $33
Spoon-teaspoon, 6 in. $22

Damask Rose by Oneida/Heirloom, 1946

Butter spreader, flat handle, 5 7/8 in......... $16
Butter spreader, hollow handle, modern,
    stainless paddle, 6 3/8 in. $20
Butter spreader, hollow handle, stainless
    paddle, 6 1/4 in....................... $20
Butter-master, flat handle, 6 7/8 in. $23
Butter-master, hollow handle,
    6 3/8 in. $26
Fork, (place size), slotted tines,
    7 5/8 in. $40
Fork, no slotted tines, 7 1/4 in............. $23
Fork, no slotted tines, 7 7/8 in............. $40
Fork-baby, 4 3/8 in....................... $36
Fork-cocktail, 3/4 in. tines, 5 1/2 in. $24
Fork-cold meat/serving, medium, solid,
    8 1/4 in. $65
Fork-lemon, 5 3/8 in. $20
Fork-pickle/olive, short handle, 1 in. tines,
    5 3/4 in. $28
Fork-salad, individual, no slot,
    6 1/2 in. $26
Fork-salad, individual, slotted tines,
    6 1/2 in. $26
Fork-youth, 5 7/8 in...................... $36
Knife-modern, hollow 4 1/2 in. handle, (place
    size), 9 1/8 in. $30
Knife-modern, hollow 3 7/8 in. handle,
    8 7/8 in. $27

Knife-modern, hollow 4 1/2 in. handle,
8 7/8 in. $27
Knife-modern, hollow handle, 9 1/2 in. $34
Knife-youth, 3 7/8 in. handle, 7 1/2 in. $34
Ladle-gravy, solid, no spout, 6 1/2 in. $60
Napkin clip, (made for teaspoons) $24
Server-jelly, 6 3/8 in. $28
Server-tomato, solid, 7 3/4 in. $96
Spoon-casserole, smooth bowl, solid,
serving spoon, 8 1/2 in. $110
Spoon-dessert/oval soup, 7 in. $40
Spoon-iced tea, 7 1/2 in. $38
Spoon-place/oval soup, 6 5/8 in. $36
Spoon-soup, round bowl, cream,
6 1/2 in. $28
Spoon-soup, round bowl, gumbo, 7 in. $36
Spoon-sugar shell, ridged bowl,
6 1/8 in. $20
Spoon-sugar, smooth bowl, 6 1/8 in. $20
Spoon-teaspoon, 6 1/8 in. $15
Tablespoon, (serving spoon), 8 1/4 in. $65
Tablespoon, (serving spoon), pierced,
8 1/4 in. $80

Dover by Oneida/Heirloom, 1968

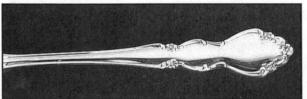

Butter spreader, hollow handle, stainless paddle,
6 1/2 in. $20
Butter-master, hollow handle, 6 3/4 in. $34
Carving set, 2 pieces, small, stainless blade,
steak $120
Fork, 7 3/8 in. $30
Fork-cocktail, 6 in. $24
Fork-cold meat/serving, medium, solid,
8 1/2 in. $70
Fork-pickle/olive, short handle, 6 in. $30
Fork-salad, individual, 6 3/4 in. $30
Knife-modern, hollow handle,
9 in. $25
Ladle-gravy, solid, 6 3/8 in. $70
Napkin clip, (made for teaspoons) $22
Spoon-demitasse, 4 1/4 in. $20
Spoon-iced tea, 7 3/8 in. $36
Spoon-teaspoon, 6 in. $16
Tablespoon, (serving spoon), 8 1/4 in. $65
Tablespoon, (serving spoon), pierced,
8 1/4 in. $65

Du Maurier by Oneida/Heirloom, 1967

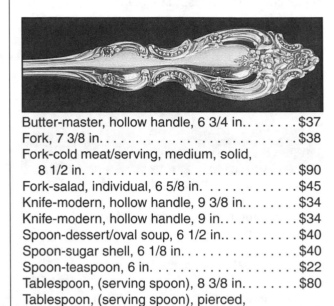

Butter-master, hollow handle, 6 3/4 in. $37
Fork, 7 3/8 in. $38
Fork-cold meat/serving, medium, solid,
8 1/2 in. $90
Fork-salad, individual, 6 5/8 in. $45
Knife-modern, hollow handle, 9 3/8 in. $34
Knife-modern, hollow handle, 9 in. $34
Spoon-dessert/oval soup, 6 1/2 in. $40
Spoon-sugar shell, 6 1/8 in. $40
Spoon-teaspoon, 6 in. $22
Tablespoon, (serving spoon), 8 3/8 in. $80
Tablespoon, (serving spoon), pierced,
8 3/8 in. $85

Engagement by Oneida/Heirloom, 1952

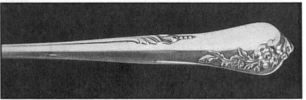

Butter spreader, flat handle, 5 3/4 in. $20
Butter spreader, hollow handle, stainless
paddle, 6 1/4 in. $18
Butter-master, flat handle, 6 7/8 in. $32
Butter-master, hollow handle, 6 3/4 in. $34
Butter-master, hollow handle, 6 3/8 in. $34
Fork, 7 1/4 in. $23
Fork-baby, 4 1/4 in. $30
Fork-cold meat/serving, medium, solid,
8 1/8 in. $80
Fork-salad, individual, 6 1/2 in. $23
Fork-youth, 5 7/8 in. $38
Knife-modern, hollow handle, 8 7/8 in. $27
Knife-youth, 6 1/4 in. $30
Ladle-gravy, solid, 6 3/8 in. $80
Spoon-baby, straight handle, 4 3/8 in. $34
Spoon-iced tea, 7 1/2 in. $30
Spoon-infant feeding, 5 5/8 in. $30
Spoon-sugar, 6 1/8 in. $25
Spoon-teaspoon, 6 1/8 in. $20

Spoon-youth, 5 1/4 in. $20
Tablespoon, (serving spoon), 8 1/4 in. $70
Tablespoon, (serving spoon), pierced,
   8 1/4 in. $85

First Frost by Oneida/Heirloom, 1965

Butter spreader, hollow handle, modern,
   stainless paddle, 6 5/8 in. $14
Butter-master, hollow handle, 6 3/4 in. $20
Fork, 7 1/2 in. $30
Fork-cocktail, 5 1/2 in. $20
Fork-cold meat/serving, medium, solid,
   8 3/8 in. $60
Fork-pickle/olive, short handle, 5 1/2 in. $20
Fork-salad, individual, 7 in. $28
Knife-cheese, stainless blade, 7 3/8 in. $30
Knife-modern, hollow handle, 9 1/8 in. $24
Ladle-cream, solid, 5 3/8 in. $20
Ladle-gravy, solid, 6 5/8 in. $60
Server-jelly, 6 1/2 in. $22
Server-tomato, solid, 8 in. $70
Spoon-bon-bon, 5 3/8 in. $28
Spoon-dessert/oval soup, 6 7/8 in. $32
Spoon-fruit, 6 1/8 in. $30
Spoon-iced tea, 7 1/2 in. $28
Spoon-sugar, 5 1/2 in. $18
Spoon-teaspoon, 6 1/4 in. $16
Tablespoon, (serving spoon), 8 1/4 in. $50
Tablespoon, (serving spoon), pierced,
   8 1/4 in. $55

Flower Lane by Oneida/Heirloom, 1957

Butter spreader, hollow handle, stainless
   paddle, 6 1/2 in. $16
Butter-master, hollow handle, 6 5/8 in. $24
Fork, 7 3/8 in. $30
Fork-cocktail, 5 3/8 in. $24

Fork-cold meat/serving, medium, solid,
   8 1/4 in. $70
Fork-lemon, 5 1/2 in. $20
Fork-salad, individual, 6 5/8 in. $30
Knife-modern, hollow handle, 9 1/8 in. $32
Knife-youth, 6 5/8 in. $34
Ladle-gravy, solid, 6 1/2 in. $70
Spoon-bon-bon, 4 7/8 in. $36
Spoon-dessert/oval soup, 6 1/2 in. $30
Spoon-soup, round bowl, cream, 6 1/2 in. $34
Spoon-sugar, 5 1/4 in. $30
Spoon-teaspoon, 6 in. $20
Tablespoon, (serving spoon), 8 1/8 in. $70
Tablespoon, (serving spoon), pierced,
   8 1/8 in. $80

Grandeur by Oneida/Heirloom, 1960

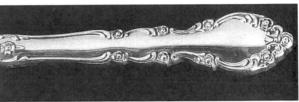

Butter spreader, hollow handle, stainless
   paddle, 6 1/2 in. $20
Butter-master, hollow handle, 6 3/4 in. $28
Fork, 7 3/8 in. $28
Fork-lemon, 5 3/8 in. $23
Knife-carving, small, stainless blade, steak,
   11 1/2 in. $50
Server-jelly, 6 1/2 in. $23
Spoon-bon-bon, 4 3/4 in. $33
Spoon-iced tea, 7 1/2 in. $35
Spoon-soup, round bowl, cream,
   6 1/2 in. $40
Spoon-sugar shell, 6 in. $28
Spoon-sugar, 5 1/4 in. $28
Spoon-teaspoon, 6 in. $22
Sugar sifter, 6 1/8 in. $30
Tablespoon, (serving spoon), 8 1/4 in. $70
Tablespoon, (serving spoon), pierced,
   8 1/4 in. $70

Heiress by Oneida/Heirloom, 1942

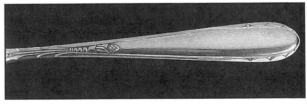

Butter spreader, flat handle, 5 3/4 in. $12

Oneida

Fork, 7 1/8 in.. . . . . $20
Fork-cocktail, 5 1/2 in.. . . . . $20
Fork-cold meat/serving, medium, solid,
    8 1/8 in.. . . . . $70
Fork-grille (viand), 7 5/8 in.. . . . . $15
Fork-salad, individual, 6 1/4 in.. . . . . $20
Knife-grille, modern, hollow handle,
    8 3/8 in.. . . . . $25
Knife-modern, hollow handle,
    9 1/8 in.. . . . . $20
Ladle-gravy, solid, 6 3/8 in.. . . . . $60
Server-pie, stainless blade,
    9 3/4 in.. . . . . $56
Spoon-demitasse, 4 1/8 in.. . . . . $16
Spoon-iced tea, 7 1/2 in.. . . . . $20
Spoon-soup, round bowl, cream,
    6 in.. . . . . $22
Spoon-teaspoon, 6 in.. . . . . $12
Tablespoon, (serving spoon),
    8 1/2 in.. . . . . $40

King Cedric by Oneida/Heirloom, 1949

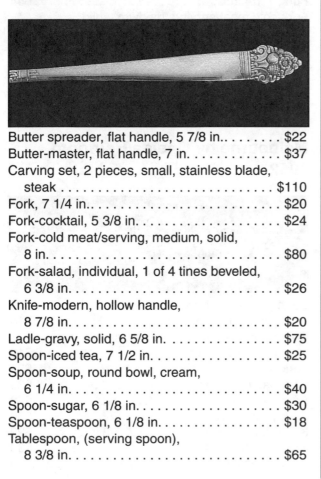

Butter spreader, flat handle, 5 7/8 in.. . . . . $22
Butter-master, flat handle, 7 in.. . . . . $37
Carving set, 2 pieces, small, stainless blade,
    steak $110
Fork, 7 1/4 in.. . . . . $20
Fork-cocktail, 5 3/8 in.. . . . . $24
Fork-cold meat/serving, medium, solid,
    8 in.. . . . . $80
Fork-salad, individual, 1 of 4 tines beveled,
    6 3/8 in.. . . . . $26
Knife-modern, hollow handle,
    8 7/8 in.. . . . . $20
Ladle-gravy, solid, 6 5/8 in.. . . . . $75
Spoon-iced tea, 7 1/2 in.. . . . . $25
Spoon-soup, round bowl, cream,
    6 1/4 in.. . . . . $40
Spoon-sugar, 6 1/8 in.. . . . . $30
Spoon-teaspoon, 6 1/8 in.. . . . . $18
Tablespoon, (serving spoon),
    8 3/8 in.. . . . . $65

Lasting Spring by Oneida/Heirloom, 1949

Butter spreader, flat handle, 6 1/8 in.. . . . . $18
Butter spreader, hollow handle, stainless
    paddle, 6 1/4 in.. . . . . $17
Butter-master, flat handle, 6 7/8 in.. . . . . $18
Butter-master, hollow handle, 6 3/8 in.. . . . . . . $22
Carving set, 2 pieces, small, stainless blade,
    steak $100
Fork, 7 7/8 in.. . . . . $45
Fork, round bowl, 7 1/4 in.. . . . . $27
Fork, square bowl, 7 1/4 in.. . . . . $27
Fork-baby, 4 1/4 in.. $30
Fork-cocktail, 5 3/8 in.. . . . . $24
Fork-cold meat/serving, medium, solid,
    8 1/8 in.. . . . . $60
Fork-dessert, 4 tines, not beveled,
    6 5/8 in.. . . . . $35
Fork-lemon, 5 3/8 in.. . . . . $20
Fork-pickle/olive, short handle, 5 7/8 in.. . . . . . $22
Knife-carving, large, stainless blade, roast,
    11 3/8 in.. . . . . $50
Knife-modern, hollow handle, 8 7/8 in.. . . . . . . $27
Knife-modern, hollow handle, 9 5/8 in.. . . . . . . $40
Knife-sharpener, steel, small, steak,
    11 1/4 in.. . . . . $45
Ladle-cream, solid, 5 3/8 in.. . . . . $38
Ladle-gravy, solid, 6 3/8 in.. . . . . $58
Napkin clip, (made for sugar) $20
Salad set, 2 pieces, plastic bowl $60
Server-cheese, stainless blade,
    6 1/2 in.. . . . . $38
Server-jelly, 6 1/4 in.. . . . . $27
Server-pie and cake, stainless blade,
    10 1/2 in.. . . . . $55
Server-pie, stainless blade, 10 in.. . . . . $45
Spoon-casserole, smooth bowl, solid,
    8 1/2 in.. . . . . $85
Spoon-demitasse, 4 1/8 in.. . . . . $20
Spoon-iced tea, 7 1/2 in.. . . . . $30
Spoon-soup, round bowl, cream,
    6 1/2 in.. . . . . $30
Spoon-teaspoon (five o'clock), 5 1/4 in.. . . . . . $18
Spoon-teaspoon, 6 1/8 in.. . . . . $18
Tablespoon, (serving spoon), 8 1/4 in.. . . . . . . $55
Tongs-sugar, 3 5/8 in.. . . . . $50

Mansion House by Oneida/Heirloom, 1948, Bright Finish

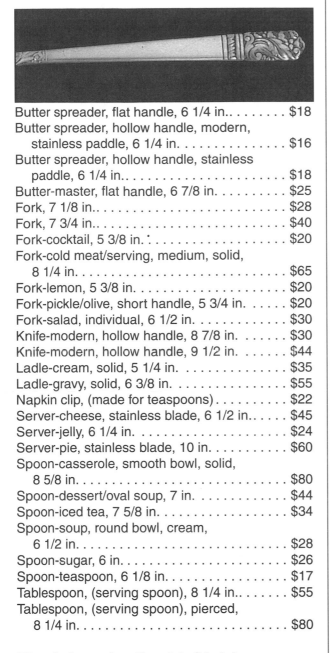

Butter spreader, flat handle, 6 1/4 in.. . . . . $18
Butter spreader, hollow handle, modern,
    stainless paddle, 6 1/4 in. $16
Butter spreader, hollow handle, stainless
    paddle, 6 1/4 in.. $18
Butter-master, flat handle, 6 7/8 in. $25
Fork, 7 1/8 in.. . . . . $28
Fork, 7 3/4 in.. . . . . $40
Fork-cocktail, 5 3/8 in. $20
Fork-cold meat/serving, medium, solid,
    8 1/4 in. $65
Fork-lemon, 5 3/8 in. $20
Fork-pickle/olive, short handle, 5 3/4 in. $20
Fork-salad, individual, 6 1/2 in. $30
Knife-modern, hollow handle, 8 7/8 in. $30
Knife-modern, hollow handle, 9 1/2 in. $44
Ladle-cream, solid, 5 1/4 in. $35
Ladle-gravy, solid, 6 3/8 in. $55
Napkin clip, (made for teaspoons) $22
Server-cheese, stainless blade, 6 1/2 in.. . . . $45
Server-jelly, 6 1/4 in. $24
Server-pie, stainless blade, 10 in. $60
Spoon-casserole, smooth bowl, solid,
    8 5/8 in. $80
Spoon-dessert/oval soup, 7 in. $44
Spoon-iced tea, 7 5/8 in. $34
Spoon-soup, round bowl, cream,
    6 1/2 in. $28
Spoon-sugar, 6 in. $26
Spoon-teaspoon, 6 1/8 in. $17
Tablespoon, (serving spoon), 8 1/4 in.. . . . . . $55
Tablespoon, (serving spoon), pierced,
    8 1/4 in. $80

Martinique by Oneida/Heirloom, 1967

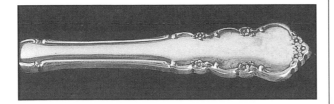

Butter spreader, hollow handle, stainless
    paddle, 6 1/2 in. $30
Butter-master, hollow handle, 6 7/8 in. $45
Fork, 7 3/8 in. $48
Fork-salad, individual, 6 5/8 in. $60
Knife-modern, hollow handle, 9 in. $44
Spoon-iced tea, 7 1/2 in. $56
Spoon-sugar, 6 in. $44
Tablespoon, (serving spoon), 8 3/8 in.. . . . . . $150
Tablespoon, (serving spoon), pierced,
    8 3/8 in. $150

Mediterranea by Oneida/Heirloom, 1967

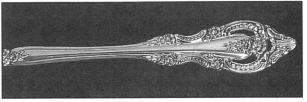

Butter spreader, hollow handle, stainless
    paddle, 6 1/2 in.. . . . . $25
Fork, 7 1/4 in. $44
Fork-cold meat/serving, medium, solid,
    8 1/2 in. $80
Fork-salad, individual, 6 3/4 in. $44
Knife-modern, hollow handle, 9 in. $36
Spoon-dessert/oval soup, 6 1/2 in.. . . . . $40
Spoon-sugar shell, 6 1/8 in. $36
Spoon-teaspoon, 6 in. $18

Melbourne by Oneida/Heirloom, 1952

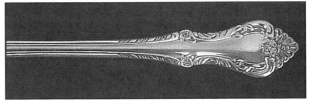

Butter spreader, hollow handle, modern,
    stainless paddle, 6 1/4 in. $18
Butter spreader, hollow handle, stainless
    paddle, 6 1/4 in.. . . . . $18
Fork, 7 1/8 in.. . . . . $22
Fork-baby, 4 3/8 in.. . . . . $30
Fork-salad, individual, 6 1/2 in. $28
Fork-youth, 5 7/8 in. $30
Knife-modern, hollow handle, 8 7/8 in. $22
Knife-youth, 6 1/4 in. $30
Spoon-baby, straight handle, 4 3/8 in. $30

Oneida

Spoon-infant feeding, 5 5/8 in............. $30
Spoon-soup, round bowl, cream, 6 1/2 in..... $30
Spoon-teaspoon, 6 in.................... $20

Reigning Beauty by Oneida/Heirloom, 1953

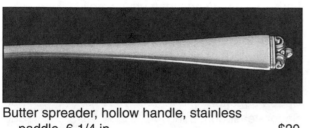

Butter spreader, hollow handle, stainless
    paddle, 6 1/4 in....................... $20
Butter-master, flat handle, 6 7/8 in. $15
Carving set, 2 pieces, small, stainless blade,
    steak $90
Fork, 7 1/4 in.......................... $40
Fork, 7 7/8 in.......................... $50
Fork-baby, 4 1/4 in. $34
Fork-carving, small, stainless prongs, steak,
    9 in. $45
Fork-cold meat/serving, medium, solid,
    8 1/8 in. $45
Fork-lemon, 5 3/8 in. $18
Fork-pickle/olive, short handle, 5 7/8 in. $24
Fork-salad, individual, 6 5/8 in. $32
Fork-youth, 5 7/8 in...................... $38
Knife-carving, small stainless blade, steak ... $45
Knife-modern, hollow handle, 8 7/8 in. $30
Knife-modern, hollow handle, 9 1/2 in. $40
Knife-youth, 6 3/8 in. $30
Ladle-cream, solid, 5 1/4 in. $40
Ladle-gravy, solid, 6 3/8 in. $48
Salad set, 2 pieces, plastic bowl $70
Server-cheese, stainless blade, 6 1/2 in...... $40
Server-jelly, 6 1/4 in. $28
Server-pie and cake, stainless blade,
    10 5/8 in. $50
Server-pie, stainless blade, 10 in. $45
Spoon-bon-bon, 4 7/8 in.................. $28
Spoon-demitasse, 4 1/8 in. $20
Spoon-iced tea, 7 1/2 in. $23
Spoon-soup, round bowl, cream,
    6 1/2 in. $32
Spoon-sugar, 6 1/8 in. $18
Spoon-teaspoon (five o'clock), 5 1/4 in....... $16
Spoon-teaspoon, 6 in..................... $20
Tablespoon, (serving spoon), 8 1/4 in........ $36
Tablespoon, (serving spoon), pierced,
    8 1/4 in. $60
Tongs-sugar, 3 5/8 in. $50

Rubaiyat by Oneida/Heirloom, 1969

Butter spreader, hollow handle, stainless
    paddle, 6 1/2 in....................... $28
Butter-master, hollow handle, 6 3/4 in........ $45
Fork, 7 1/2 in........................... $42
Fork-salad, individual, 6 7/8 in. $46
Knife-modern, hollow handle, 9 1/8 in........ $26
Spoon-sugar, 6 1/8 in. $44
Spoon-teaspoon, 6 1/4 in. $20

Satin Beauty by Oneida/Heirloom, 1966

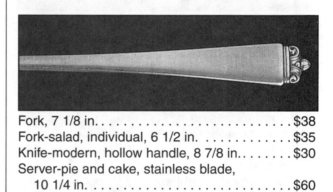

Fork, 7 1/8 in........................... $38
Fork-salad, individual, 6 1/2 in. $35
Knife-modern, hollow handle, 8 7/8 in........ $30
Server-pie and cake, stainless blade,
    10 1/4 in. $60
Spoon-teaspoon, 6 1/8 in. $25

Sentimental by Oneida/Heirloom, 1960

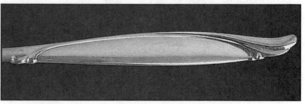

Butter spreader, hollow handle, stainless
    paddle, 6 1/2 in....................... $20
Butter-master, hollow handle, 6 3/4 in........ $20
Fork, 7 5/8 in........................... $40
Fork-cocktail, 5 1/2 in. $28
Fork-cold meat/serving, medium, solid,
    8 1/4 in. $70
Fork-lemon, 5 3/8 in. $24
Fork-pickle/olive, short handle, 5 1/2 in....... $24
Fork-salad, individual, 6 5/8 in. $40

Knife-modern, hollow handle, 9 1/8 in. $24
Ladle-gravy, solid, 6 5/8 in. $70
Napkin clip (made for teaspoons) $22
Server-jelly, 6 3/8 in. $30
Spoon-iced tea, 7 1/2 in. $45
Spoon-sugar, 5 1/4 in. $24
Spoon-teaspoon, 6 1/8 in. $20
Tablespoon, (serving spoon), 8 1/4 in.. . . . . . $80
Tablespoon, (serving spoon), pierced,
    8 1/4 in. $85

Silver Rose by Oneida/Heirloom, 1956

Butter spreader, hollow handle, modern,
    stainless paddle, 6 1/2 in. $12
Butter spreader, hollow handle, stainless paddle,
    6 1/2 in. $12
Butter-master, hollow handle, 6 5/8 in. $20
Fork, 7 3/8 in.. . . . . $33
Fork-cocktail, 5 1/2 in. $24
Fork-cold meat/serving, medium, solid,
    8 1/4 in. $64
Fork-lemon, 5 3/8 in. $20
Fork-pickle/olive, short handle, 2 tines,
    5 1/2 in. $25
Fork-salad, individual, 6 5/8 in. $34
Knife-modern, hollow handle, 8 1/2 in. $26
Ladle-gravy, solid, 6 5/8 in. $60
Napkin clip, (made for teaspoons) $20
Spoon-dessert/oval soup, 6 1/2 in. $34
Spoon-sugar shell, ribbed bowl, 5 1/4 in. $22
Spoon-teaspoon, 6 in. $14
Tablespoon, (serving spoon), 8 1/4 in.. . . . . . $60
Tablespoon, (serving spoon), pierced,
    8 1/4 in. $70

Stanton Hall by Oneida/Heirloom, 1951

Butter spreader, flat handle, 6 1/4 in. $20
Butter spreader, hollow handle, stainless
    paddle, 6 1/4 in. $20
Butter-master, flat handle, 7 in. $30
Fork, 7 1/4 in. $35
Fork, 7 7/8 in. $60
Fork-cocktail, 3/4 in. tines, 5 3/8 in. $30
Fork-cold meat/serving, medium, solid,
    8 1/4 in. $75
Fork-salad, individual, pierced, 6 5/8 in. $40
Knife-modern, hollow handle, 8 3/4 in. $32
Ladle-gravy, solid, 6 5/8 in.. . . . . $80
Spoon-soup, round bowl, cream, 6 1/2 in. . . . $32
Spoon-sugar shell, 6 in. $30
Spoon-teaspoon, 6 in. $20
Tablespoon, (serving spoon), 8 5/8 in. $74

Twilight by Oneida/Heirloom, 1942

Butter spreader, hollow handle, stainless
    paddle, 6 1/2 in. $20
Butter-master, hollow handle, 6 3/4 in. $25
Fork, 7 5/8 in. $30
Fork-salad, individual, 6 5/8 in. $30
Knife-modern, hollow handle, 9 1/8 in. $22
Ladle-gravy, solid, 6 3/4 in.. . . . . $65
Spoon-dessert/oval soup, 6 1/2 in.. . . . . $30
Spoon-sugar, 5 3/8 in. $24
Spoon-teaspoon, 6 in. $16
Tablespoon, (serving spoon), 8 1/4 in. $60

Virginian by Oneida/Heirloom, 1942

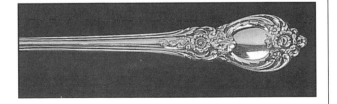

Butter spreader, flat handle, 5 3/4 in. $16
Butter-master, flat handle, 6 7/8 in. $36
Fork, 7 1/4 in. $20
Fork-cocktail, 5 3/8 in. $20
Fork-cold meat/serving, medium, solid,
    8 1/8 in. $70
Fork-grille (viand), 7 1/2 in. $20
Fork-salad, individual, 6 3/8 in. $20

Knife-grille, modern, hollow handle,
  8 1/2 in. $20
Knife-modern, hollow handle, 9 1/4 in. $24
Ladle-gravy, solid, 6 3/8 in. $60
Napkin clip, (made for teaspoons) $24
Spoon-casserole, smooth bowl, solid,
  8 5/8 in. $60
Spoon-iced tea, 7 1/2 in. $23
Spoon-soup, round bowl, cream, 6 1/4 in. $24
Spoon-sugar, 6 1/8 in. $22
Spoon-teaspoon, 6 in. $16

Vivant by Oneida/Heirloom, 1961

Butter spreader, hollow handle, modern,
  stainless paddle, 6 5/8 in. $17
Butter-master, hollow handle, 6 3/4 in. $25
Carving set, 2 pieces, small, stainless blade,
  steak $120
Fork, 7 1/2 in. $35
Fork-cold meat/serving, medium, solid,
  8 1/4 in. $65
Fork-lemon, 5 1/4 in. $17
Fork-pickle/olive, short handle, 5 1/2 in. $20
Fork-salad, individual, 7 in. $38
Knife-modern, hollow handle, 9 in. $25
Ladle-gravy, solid, 6 3/4 in. $70
Napkin clip, (made for sugar). $22
Server-jelly, 5 3/8 in. $24
Server-pie and cake, stainless blade,
  10 3/4 in. $58
Spoon-sugar, 5 1/2 in. $18
Spoon-teaspoon, 6 1/4 in. $18
Tablespoon, (serving spoon), 8 1/4 in. $55
Tablespoon, (serving spoon), pierced,
  8 1/4 in. $65

Will O' Wisp by Oneida/Heirloom, 1968

Butter spreader, hollow handle, stainless paddle,
  6 1/2 in. $17
Butter-master, hollow handle, 6 3/4 in. $28
Fork, 7 1/2 in. $34
Fork-cocktail, 6 1/8 in. $22
Fork-pickle/olive, short handle, 6 in. $24
Fork-salad, individual, 6 3/4 in. $27
Knife-modern, hollow handle,
  9 1/4 in. $25
Ladle-cream, solid, 5 3/4 in. $37
Ladle-gravy, solid, 6 1/2 in. $65
Spoon-dessert/oval soup, 6 7/8 in. $28
Spoon-sugar, 6 1/8 in. $26
Spoon-teaspoon, 6 1/4 in. $17
Tablespoon, (serving spoon),
  8 1/2 in. $55
Tablespoon, (serving spoon), pierced,
  8 1/2 in. $65

Young Love by Oneida/Heirloom, 1958

Butter spreader, hollow handle, stainless
  paddle, 6 1/2 in. $15
Butter-master, hollow handle, 6 5/8 in. $16
Fork, 7 5/8 in. $33
Fork-baby, 4 1/2 in. $40
Fork-cold meat/serving, medium, solid,
  8 3/8 in. $80
Fork-lemon, 5 3/8 in. $20
Fork-pickle/olive, short handle,
  5 1/2 in. $25
Fork-salad, individual, 6 5/8 in. $34
Knife-modern, hollow handle,
  9 1/8 in. $25
Ladle-gravy, solid, 7 in. $80
Napkin clip, (made for teaspoons) $20
Server-jelly, 6 1/2 in. $33
Spoon-bon-bon, 4 7/8 in. $26
Spoon-sugar, 5 1/4 in. $18
Spoon-teaspoon (five o'clock),
  5 1/4 in. $20
Spoon-teaspoon, 6 1/8 in. $15
Tablespoon, (serving spoon),
  8 1/4 in. $70
Tablespoon, (serving spoon), pierced,
  8 1/4 in. $76

REED & BARTON

Reed & Barton of Taunton, Massachusetts began in 1824 as the partnership of Babbitt & Crossman. Isaac Babbitt and William Crossman began a small Brittania ware firm that went through several incarnations and almost collapsed, but was saved by the work of three employees: Charles E. Barton (the brother-in-law of William Crossman), Henry Good Reed, and Benjamin Pratt. By 1840, the Reed & Barton firm was established.

Reed & Barton has produced more than 100 flatware patterns, including Francis I, which has been a popular pattern since its introduction in 1907. The firm acquired Dominick & Haff in 1928 and the Wester Co. in 1949, although Reed & Barton later sold that company to Towle in the 1960s. Initially, Reed & Barton produced Brittania ware, which resembles pewter but is more durable. Silver plated flatware was added in 1848 and sterling silverware introduced in 1889. The firm's marks on sterling feature the letter "R" in a shield flanked by an eagle on the left and a rearing lion on the right.

Amaryllis by Reed & Barton, 1901

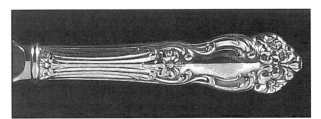

Knife-new french, hollow handle, 9 5/8 in......$70

Autumn Leaves by Reed & Barton, 1957

Butter spreader, hollow handle, modern, stainless, 6 3/4 in......................$20
Butter-master, hollow handle, 7 3/8 in........$36

Carving set, 2 pieces, small, stainless blade, steak $140
Fork, 7 1/2 in. $44
Fork-cold meat/serving-medium, solid, 8 1/4 in.. $90
Fork-pickle/olive, short handle, 5 3/4 in....... $34
Knife-modern, hollow handle, 9 in. $40
Ladle-gravy, solid, 6 3/4 in.................... $80
Napkin clip, (made for teaspoons)........... $28
Spoon-dessert/oval soup, 6 7/8 in. $40
Spoon-iced tea, 7 1/2 in..................... $44
Spoon-sugar, 6 1/4 in....................... $32
Spoon-teaspoon, 6 in....................... $20
Tablespoon, (serving spoon), 8 5/8 in. $90

Burgundy by Reed & Barton, 1949

Butter spreader, flat handle, 5 7/8 in. $34
Butter spreader, hollow handle, stainless paddle, 6 1/4 in......................... $34
Butter-master, hollow handle, 7 in. $40
Carving set, 2 pieces, small, stainless blade, steak $140
Fork, 7 1/8 in. $44
Fork, 7 7/8 in. $68
Fork-baby, 4 1/2 in........................... $36
Fork-cocktail, 5 5/8 in. $32
Fork-cold meat/serving, medium, solid, 8 in. $100
Fork-ice cream, 5 1/4 in.................... $52
Fork-salad serving, solid, 3 tines, 9 1/2 in................................. $180
Fork-salad serving, wooden prongs, 10 1/2 in................................. $50
Fork-salad, individual, 6 1/2 in. $40
Fork-serving, stainless tines, 8 5/8 in. $50
Knife-carving, small, stainless blade, steak, 11 1/2 in................................. $65
Knife-modern, hollow handle, 8 7/8 in........ $36
Knife-modern, hollow handle, 9 1/2 in........ $50
Knife-new french, hollow handle, 9 1/8 in..... $35
Knife-new french, hollow handle, 9 5/8 in..... $50
Knife-steak, individual, beveled blade, 9 in..................................... $45
Knife-youth, 3 1/2 in. blade, 7 in. $33
Ladle-cream, solid, 5 5/8 in................. $55
Ladle-gravy, solid, 6 1/2 in................. $100

Salad set, 2 pieces, solid, 9 1/2 in..........$360
Server-asparagus, hollow handle, silver
    plate hood, 9 1/4 in. $70
Server-cake, solid, 9 1/2 in...............$100
Server-lasagna, stainless blade, 10 in. $50
Server-pasta, stainless bowl, 10 5/8 in.......$50
Server-pastry, stainless bowl, 9 3/4 in. $50
Server-pie and cake, stainless blade,
    10 3/8 in. $50
Server-pie, stainless blade, 10 1/8 in. $58
Server-tomato, solid, 8 1/4 in..............$110
Spoon-bonbon, 4 3/4 in.....................$46
Spoon-chocolate, short handle, 4 1/4 in......$40
Spoon-demitasse, 4 3/8 in. $28
Spoon-dessert/oval soup, 7 1/4 in...........$50
Spoon-ice cream, 5 1/4 in..................$40
Spoon-iced tea, 7 3/4 in. $50
Spoon-infant feeding, 5 5/8 in...............$40
Spoon-mustard, gold wash, 4 7/8 in. $44
Spoon-pierced/serving, stainless bowl,
    8 1/2 in....................................$50
Spoon-place/oval soup, 6 3/4 in.............$42
Spoon-salad serving, wooden bowl,
    10 1/2 in. $50
Spoon-salt, individual, 2 3/8 in..............$15
Spoon-serving, stainless bowl, 8 1/2 in. $50
Spoon-soup, round bowl, cream, 6 3/8 in......$42
Spoon-soup, round bowl, gumbo, 7 1/4 in. $56
Spoon-sugar shell, 6 1/8 in..................$40
Spoon-teaspoon, 6 in........................$24
Tablespoon, (serving spoon), 8 3/8 in.........$90
Tablespoon, (serving spoon), pierced,
    8 3/8 in...................................$100
Youth set, 3 pieces (spoon, knife, fork) $130

Cameo by Reed & Barton, 1959

Butter spreader, hollow handle, modern,
    stainless paddle, 6 7/8 in. $40
Butter-master, hollow handle, 7 3/8 in.........$43
Fork, 7 1/2 in................................$54
Fork-cocktail, 5 5/8 in.......................$44
Fork-cold meat/serving, medium, solid,
    8 5/8 in...................................$110
Fork-salad, individual, 6 5/8 in. $44
Knife-bar, hollow handle, 8 7/8 in.............$42
Knife-modern, hollow handle, 9 in............$43

Ladle-gravy, solid, 6 3/4 in..................$85
Server-pie and cake, stainless blade,
    11 in. $60
Spoon-dessert/oval soup, 6 7/8 in. $54
Spoon-iced tea, 7 1/4 in....................$58
Spoon-sugar shell, 6 1/2 in. $50
Spoon-teaspoon, 6 1/8 in....................$24
Tablespoon, (serving spoon), 8 1/2 in. $100
Tablespoon, (serving spoon), pierced,
    8 1/2 in...................................$120

Cellini by Reed & Barton, 1967

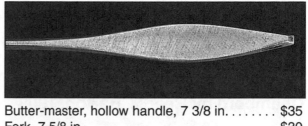

Butter-master, hollow handle, 7 3/8 in........$35
Fork, 7 5/8 in. $30
Fork-cold meat/serving, medium, solid,
    8 3/8 in....................................$80
Fork-salad, individual, 7 1/8 in. $35
Knife-modern, hollow handle, 9 in. $24
Ladle-gravy, solid, 7 1/8 in..................$80
Spoon-teaspoon, 6 1/4 in....................$20
Tablespoon, (serving spoon), 8 3/8 in. $90
Tablespoon, (serving spoon), pierced,
    8 3/8 in....................................$90

Cellini-Engraved by Reed & Barton, 1967

Butter spreader, hollow handle, modern,
    stainless paddle, 7 1/8 in..................$28
Butter-master, hollow handle, 7 3/8 in........$40
Carving set, 3 pieces, large, stainless blade,
    roast $210
Fork, 7 5/8 in. $55
Fork-cocktail, 6 in. $30
Fork-cold meat/serving, medium, solid,
    8 1/2 in....................................$85
Fork-lemon, 4 3/4 in. $30
Fork-pickle/olive, short handle, 6 1/4 in.......$30
Fork-salad, individual, 7 1/8 in. $46

Knife-cheese, stainless blade, 7 5/8 in. $44
Knife-modern, hollow handle, 9 in. $33
Ladle-gravy, solid, 7 1/4 in. $85
Salad set, 2 pieces, plastic bowl $80
Salad set, 2 pieces, solid $210
Server-jelly, 6 1/2 in. $33
Server-pie and cake, stainless blade,
    10 3/4 in. $70
Server-tomato, solid, 8 3/8 in. $90
Spoon-bonbon, 5 in. $40
Spoon-dessert/oval soup, 7 in. $50
Spoon-iced tea, 7 1/2 in. $40
Spoon-sugar, 6 1/8 in.. . . . .$37
Spoon-teaspoon, 6 3/8 in. $23
Tablespoon, (serving spoon), pierced,
    8 1/2 in.. . . . .$90
Tablespoon, (serving spoon,) 8 1/2 in. $80
Tongs-sugar, 4 1/2 in. $60

Chambord by Reed & Barton, 1909

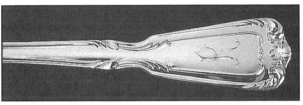

Butter spreader, flat handle, 5 5/8 in. $28
Carving set, 2 pieces, small, stainless blade,
    steak $150
Fork, 7 1/8 in. $40
Fork, 7 3/4 in. $50
Fork-cocktail, 5 3/8 in.. . . . .$28
Fork-ice cream, 5 1/4 in.. . . . .$50
Fork-lemon, 4 1/2 in. $40
Fork-salad, individual, 6 in. $42
Knife-new french, hollow handle,
    8 7/8 in.. . . . .$38
Knife-old french, hollow handle, 9 1/4 in. $38
Knife-old french, hollow handle, 9 5/8 in. $47
Ladle-cream, solid, 5 1/8 in.. . . . .$50
Spoon-bonbon, 4 3/4 in. $45
Spoon-casserole, smooth bowl, solid,
    7 7/8 in.. . . . .$110
Spoon-dessert/oval soup, 7 1/8 in. $50
Spoon-fruit, 5 1/2 in. $36
Spoon-iced tea, 7 1/8 in. $40
Spoon-soup, round bowl, bouillon,
    5 3/8 in.. . . . .$34
Spoon-soup, round bowl, cream,
    5 7/8 in.. . . . .$44
Spoon-sugar, 6 in. $45
Spoon-teaspoon (five o'clock), 5 1/4 in. $25

Spoon-teaspoon, 5 3/4 in.. . . . .$25
Tablespoon, (serving spoon), 8 3/8 in. $80
Tongs-sugar, 4 in.. . . . .$58

Classic Fashion by Reed & Barton, 1926

(Knife handle shown in profile.)

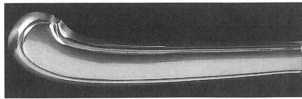

Fork, 8 in. $90
Fork-salad, individual, 6 5/8 in. $65
Knife-new french, pistol, 8 7/8 in.. . . . .$66
Knife-new french, pistol, 9 5/8 in.. . . . .$56
Ladle-gravy, solid, 6 in. $110
Spoon-demitasse, 4 1/4 in.. . . . .$38

Classic Rose by Reed & Barton, 1954

Baby set, 2 pieces. $80
Butter spreader, flat handle, 6 1/8 in. $32
Butter spreader, hollow handle, modern,
    stainless paddle, 6 3/8 in.. . . . .$30
Butter spreader, hollow handle, stainless
    paddle, 6 1/4 in.. . . . .$30
Butter-master, hollow handle, no notch,
    6 7/8 in.. . . . .$36
Butter-master, hollow handle, notch blade,
    6 7/8 in.. . . . .$36
Fork, 7 3/8 in. $46
Fork-baby, 4 1/2 in.. . . . .$40
Fork-cocktail, 5 5/8 in. $40
Fork-cold meat/serving, medium, solid,
    8 1/4 in.. . . . .$100
Fork-salad, individual, 6 5/8 in. $46
Knife-modern, hollow handle, 9 1/8 in. $40
Knife-steak, individual, 9 1/4 in. $60
Ladle-gravy, solid, 6 7/8 in. $100
Napkin clip, (made for teaspoons). $28
Server-pastry, stainless bowl, 9 7/8 in. $70
Spoon-bonbon, 5 in. $48

Spoon-dessert/oval soup, 6 5/8 in............$50
Spoon-iced tea, 7 1/2 in. $55
Spoon-infant feeding, 5 5/8 in..............$45
Spoon-sugar, 6 1/8 in........................$30
Spoon-teaspoon, 6 in........................$20
Tablespoon, (serving spoon), 8 5/8 in.......$100
Tablespoon, (serving spoon), pierced,
    8 5/8 in..................................$110
Tongs-sugar, 4 1/4 in. $70

Clovelly by Reed & Barton, 1912

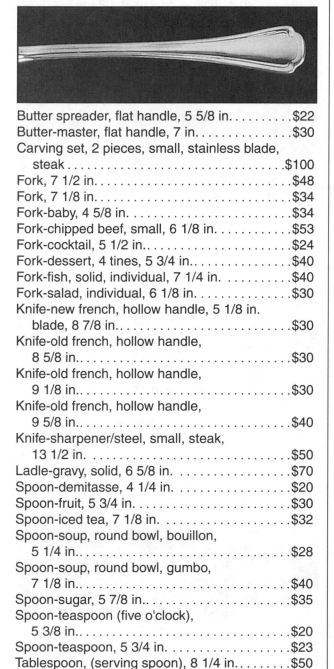

Butter spreader, flat handle, 5 5/8 in.........$22
Butter-master, flat handle, 7 in..............$30
Carving set, 2 pieces, small, stainless blade,
    steak $100
Fork, 7 1/2 in..............................$48
Fork, 7 1/8 in..............................$34
Fork-baby, 4 5/8 in. $34
Fork-chipped beef, small, 6 1/8 in. $53
Fork-cocktail, 5 1/2 in......................$24
Fork-dessert, 4 tines, 5 3/4 in..............$40
Fork-fish, solid, individual, 7 1/4 in. $40
Fork-salad, individual, 6 1/8 in. $30
Knife-new french, hollow handle, 5 1/8 in.
    blade, 8 7/8 in..........................$30
Knife-old french, hollow handle,
    8 5/8 in..................................$30
Knife-old french, hollow handle,
    9 1/8 in..................................$30
Knife-old french, hollow handle,
    9 5/8 in..................................$40
Knife-sharpener/steel, small, steak,
    13 1/2 in. $50
Ladle-gravy, solid, 6 5/8 in. $70
Spoon-demitasse, 4 1/4 in. $20
Spoon-fruit, 5 3/4 in........................$30
Spoon-iced tea, 7 1/8 in. $32
Spoon-soup, round bowl, bouillon,
    5 1/4 in..................................$28
Spoon-soup, round bowl, gumbo,
    7 1/8 in..................................$40
Spoon-sugar, 5 7/8 in.......................$35
Spoon-teaspoon (five o'clock),
    5 3/8 in..................................$20
Spoon-teaspoon, 5 3/4 in. $23
Tablespoon, (serving spoon), 8 1/4 in........$50

Columbia by Reed & Barton, 1912

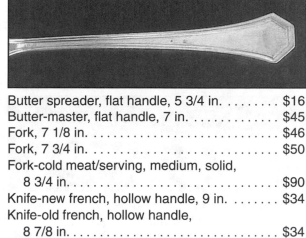

Butter spreader, flat handle, 5 3/4 in. $16
Butter-master, flat handle, 7 in. $45
Fork, 7 1/8 in. $46
Fork, 7 3/4 in. $50
Fork-cold meat/serving, medium, solid,
    8 3/4 in..................................$90
Knife-new french, hollow handle, 9 in. $34
Knife-old french, hollow handle,
    8 7/8 in..................................$34
Knife-old french, hollow handle,
    9 3/4 in..................................$44
Server-pie, silver plate blade, 10 5/8 in. $70
Spoon-bonbon, 4 5/8 in. $40
Spoon-demitasse, 4 1/8 in..................$20
Spoon-soup, round bowl, bouillon,
    5 1/4 in..................................$26
Spoon-soup, round bowl, gumbo,
    7 1/4 in..................................$44
Spoon-sugar, 6 in. $30
Spoon-teaspoon (five o'clock), 5 1/4 in. $22
Spoon-teaspoon, 5 3/4 in..................$20
Tablespoon, (serving spoon), 8 1/4 in. $70

Da Vinci by Reed & Barton, 1967

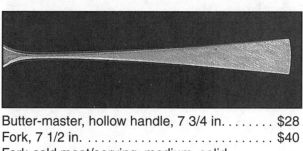

Butter-master, hollow handle, 7 3/4 in........$28
Fork, 7 1/2 in. $40
Fork-cold meat/serving, medium, solid,
    8 3/8 in..................................$70
Fork-pickle/olive, short handle, 6 in. $26
Fork-salad, individual, 7 in..................$32
Knife-modern, hollow handle, 9 1/4 in........$28
Ladle-gravy, solid, 7 1/8 in..................$70
Server-jelly, 6 1/4 in. $30
Server-tomato, solid, 8 1/4 in. $70
Spoon-bonbon, 5 in. $36
Spoon-dessert/oval soup, 7 in...............$38
Spoon-sugar, 5 3/4 in. $30

Spoon-teaspoon, 6 1/8 in. $18
Tablespoon, (serving spoon), 8 1/2 in. $65
Tablespoon, (serving spoon), pierced,
    8 1/2 in. $70

Dancing Flowers by Reed & Barton, 1950

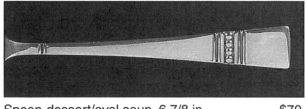

Butter spreader, flat handle, 5 3/4 in. $16
Butter spreader, hollow handle, modern,
    stainless paddle, 6 3/8 in. $20
Butter-master, flat handle, 7 1/4 in. $34
Carving set, 2 pieces, large stainless blade,
    roast $110
Carving set, 2 pieces, small, stainless blade,
    steak $110
Fork, 7 1/8 in. $36
Fork-cocktail, 5 5/8 in. $25
Fork-lemon, 5 3/4 in. $24
Fork-lemon, 5 in. $24
Fork-pickle/olive, short handle,
    5 7/8 in. $26
Fork-salad, individual, 6 1/2 in. $40
Knife-modern, hollow handle, 8 3/4 in. $36
Ladle-cream, solid, 5 3/8 in. $40
Ladle-gravy, solid, 6 1/2 in. $70
Napkin clip, (made for teaspoons) $20
Server-jelly, 6 1/4 in. $26
Server-pie, stainless blade, 10 in. $60
Server-tomato, solid, 8 1/8 in. $75
Spoon-soup, round bowl, cream,
    6 3/8 in. $34
Spoon-sugar, 6 1/8 in. $23
Spoon-teaspoon, 6 in. $20
Tablespoon, (serving spoon), 8 5/8 in. $60

Devon by Reed & Barton, 1911

Butter spreader, flat handle, 5 5/8 in. $26
Fork, 7 5/8 in. $55

Fork, 7 in. $45
Fork-cocktail, 5 5/8 in. $26
Fork-cold meat/serving, medium, solid, gold
    wash, 8 5/8 in. $80
Fork-cold meat/serving, small, solid,
    7 5/8 in. $70
Fork-dessert, 1 of 4 tines beveled,
    6 1/4 in. $50
Fork-salad, individual, 4 tines, not beveled,
    6 in. $45
Knife-old french, hollow handle, 3 7/8 in.
    andle, 9 1/2 in. $45
Knife-old french, hollow handle, 4 1/8 in.
    handle, 9 3/4 in. $45
Knife-old french, hollow handle, 9 in. $35
Ladle-cream, solid, 5 1/4 in. $40
Ladle-gravy, solid, 6 1/8 in. $90
Spoon-casserole, smooth, solid,
    7 3/4 in. $90
Spoon-casserole, smooth, solid,
    8 7/8 in. $90
Spoon-chocolate, short handle, large,
    gold wash, 4 1/8 in. $24
Spoon-demitasse, gold wash,
    4 1/4 in. $20
Spoon-dessert/oval soup, 7 1/8 in. $40
Spoon-fruit, 5 3/4 in. $30
Spoon-fruit, gold wash, 5 3/4 in. $30
Spoon-soup, round bowl, bouillon,
    5 1/4 in. $28
Spoon-soup, round bowl, gumbo,
    7 in. $44
Spoon-sugar, 6 in. $40
Spoon-teaspoon (five o'clock),
    5 3/8 in. $20
Spoon-teaspoon, 5 3/4 in. $30
Tablespoon, (serving spoon),
    8 1/4 in. $75
Tablespoon, (serving spoon), pierced,
    8 1/4 in. $90
Tongs-sugar, 4 1/2 in. $66

Diadem by Reed & Barton, 1967

Spoon-dessert/oval soup, 6 7/8 in. $70
Spoon-sugar, 6 in. $40
Spoon-teaspoon, 6 in. $32

Diamond by Reed & Barton, 1958

Butter spreader, hollow handle, modern,
  stainless paddle, 6 7/8 in. $25
Butter-master, hollow handle, 7 3/8 in. $36
Fork, 7 1/2 in. $42
Fork-salad, individual, 7 in. $50
Ladle-gravy, solid, 7 3/4 in. $85
Napkin clip, (made for teaspoons) $22
Spoon-dessert/oval soup, 6 7/8 in. $60
Spoon-salad serving, solid, 9 3/8 in. $140
Spoon-sugar, 6 1/8 in. $36
Spoon-teaspoon, 6 1/8 in. $20

Dimension by Reed & Barton, 1961

Butter spreader, hollow angled handle,
  modern, stainless paddle, 7 3/8 in. $26
Butter-master, hollow handle, 7 3/4 in. $35
Fork, 7 1/2 in. $60
Fork-cold meat/serving, medium, solid,
  8 1/4 in. $90
Fork-pickle/olive, short handle, 5 7/8 in. $30
Knife-modern, hollow angled handle,
  9 1/8 in. $35
Ladle-gravy, solid, 7 in. $80
Spoon-dessert/oval soup, 7 in. $56
Spoon-sugar, 5 7/8 in. $36
Spoon-teaspoon, 6 1/8 in. $27
Tablespoon, (serving spoon), 8 1/2 in. $80
Tablespoon, (serving spoon), pierced,
  8 1/2 in. $100

Dorothy Quincy by Reed & Barton, 1912

Butter spreader, flat handle, 5 3/4 in. $24
Butter-master, flat handle, 7 in. $45
Carving set, 3 pieces, large, stainless blade,
  roast $210
Carving set, 2 pieces, small, stainless blade,
  steak $120

Fork, 7 1/8 in. $35
Fork, 7 3/4 in. $56
Fork-cocktail, 5 1/2 in. $28
Fork-cold meat/serving, small, solid,
  7 3/4 in. $80
Fork-dessert, square slot, 6 in. $50
Fork-fish, solid, individual, square slot,
  6 1/4 in. $68
Fork-ice cream, 5 in. $50
Fork-pickle/olive, short handle, 6 in. $30
Knife-old french, hollow handle,
  8 7/8 in. $33
Knife-old french, hollow handle,
  9 5/8 in. $45
Ladle-cream, solid, 5 1/2 in. $45
Server-jelly, 6 in. $34
Spoon-demitasse, 4 1/4 in. $22
Spoon-dessert/oval soup, 7 1/4 in. $50
Spoon-iced tea, 7 1/8 in. $38
Spoon-soup, round bowl, bouillon,
  5 1/8 in. $28
Spoon-soup, round bowl, cream,
  5 7/8 in. $45
Spoon-soup, round bowl, gumbo,
  7 1/4 in. $50
Spoon-sugar, 6 in. $40
Spoon-teaspoon, 5 3/4 in. $23
Tablespoon, (serving spoon), 8 1/4 in. $80

Elegante/L'Elegante by Reed & Barton, 1900/1940

Butter spreader, flat handle, 5 7/8 in. $30
Fork, 7 in. $32
Fork-cocktail, 5 1/2 in. $26
Knife-new french, hollow handle, 9 3/4 in. $50
Knife-old french, hollow handle,
  10 1/8 in. $50
Spoon-demitasse, gold wash, 4 1/4 in. $26
Spoon-dessert/oval soup, 7 1/8 in. $50
Spoon-soup, round bowl, bouillon,
  5 1/4 in. $34
Spoon-soup, round bowl, cream,
  5 5/8 in. $60
Spoon-soup, round bowl, gumbo, 7 in. $60
Spoon-teaspoon, 5 3/4 in. $28
Tablespoon, (serving spoon), 8 1/4 in. $70

English Provincial by Reed & Barton, 1965

Butter spreader, hollow handle, modern, stainless
    paddle, 6 3/4 in............................$26
Butter-master, hollow handle, 7 3/8 in........$30
Fork, 7 5/8 in.................................$30
Knife-modern, hollow handle,
    9 1/8 in...................................$34
Spoon-dessert/oval soup, 6 7/8 in...........$50
Spoon-iced tea, 7 1/4 in. $50
Spoon-soup, round bowl, cream, 6 in........$46
Spoon-sugar shell, 6 1/4 in.................$35

Florentine Lace by Reed & Barton, 1951

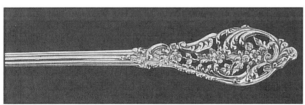

Butter spreader, hollow handle, modern,
    stainless paddle, 6 3/8 in. $37
Butter spreader, hollow handle, stainless
    paddle, 6 1/4 in...........................$37
Butter-master, flat handle, 7 3/8 in...........$55
Butter-master, hollow handle, 7 in............$50
Fork, 7 3/8 in.................................$50
Fork, 7 7/8 in.................................$68
Fork-cold meat/serving, medium, solid,
    8 in......................................$130
Fork-salad, individual, 6 1/2 in...............$60
Knife-modern, hollow handle, 9 1/2 in........$60
Knife-steak, individual, beveled blade,
    9 in......................................$60
Server-jelly, 6 3/8 in. $54
Server-pie, stainless blade, 10 1/8 in. $80
Spoon-dessert/oval soup, 7 1/4 in...........$60
Spoon-iced tea, 7 3/4 in. $60
Spoon-soup, round bowl, cream,
    6 1/4 in...................................$60
Spoon-sugar, 6 1/8 in........................$50
Spoon-teaspoon, 6 in........................$40
Tablespoon, (serving spoon), 8 1/2 in.......$120

Fragrance by Reed & Barton, 1941

Butter spreader, flat handle, 6 in............ $20
Carving set, 2 pieces, small, stainless blade,
    steak $140
Fork, 7 1/8 in. $30
Fork-cocktail, 5 1/2 in. $28
Fork-salad, individual, 6 1/8 in. $35
Spoon-dessert/oval soup, 6 7/8 in. $50
Spoon-iced tea, 7 5/8 in................... $38
Spoon-soup, round bowl, cream, 6 in. $30
Spoon-teaspoon, 6 in...................... $22

Francis I by Reed & Barton, 1907, "EAGLE/R/LION" stamp

Butter spreader, flat handle, 5 7/8 in. $44
Butter-master, flat handle, 7 1/8 in. $60
Carving set, 2 pieces, large stainless blade,
    roast................................... $300
Fork, 7 1/8 in. $50
Fork-carving, small stainless prongs, steak,
    8 7/8 in. $80
Fork-carving, small stainless prongs, steak,
    9 3/8 in. $80
Fork-cold meat/serving, small, solid,
    7 7/8 in. $120
Fork-salad serving, solid, 9 1/2 in........... $250
Fork-salad, individual, clover piercing,
    6 1/8 in. $50
Knife-new french, hollow handle, stainless blade,
    9 1/4 in. $50
Knife-youth, 7 7/8 in. $40
Knife-youth, french blade, 7 1/8 in. $40
Knife-youth, modern blade, 7 1/8 in. $40
Ladle-soup, solid, 11 1/2 in. $500
Salad set, 2 pieces, solid $600
Spoon-demitasse, 4 1/4 in.................. $44
Spoon-iced tea, 7 5/8 in................... $70
Spoon-soup, round bowl, cream, 6 in. $50
Spoon-sugar shell, 6 1/8 in. $60

Spoon-teaspoon, 6 in. $36
Tablespoon, (serving spoon) 7 piercings,
     8 3/8 in. $100
Tablespoon, (serving spoon), 8 3/8 in. $96
Tongs-sugar, 4 1/8 in. $80

Francis I by Reed & Barton, "PATENT PENDING" stamp

Butter spreader, flat handle, 5 7/8 in. $45
Fork, 7 1/8 in. $55
Fork, 7 7/8 in. $100
Fork-salad, individual, 6 1/4 in. $60
Spoon-soup, round bowl, cream,
     5 7/8 in. $55
Spoon-teaspoon, 5 7/8 in. $40
Spoon-youth, 5 3/8 in. $54
Tablespoon, (serving spoon), 8 1/2 in. $120

Vintage Reed & Barton flatware service in the
Francis I pattern, designed by Ernest Meyer in
1906. Sixty-one pieces. Knives measure 9 1/8
in. long; dinner fork is 7 1/8 in. long. Most of
the pieces are at least 50 years old. There is
one replacement setting. The set consists of:
9 dinner knives, 9 dinner forks, 9 soup spoons,
7 fish forks, 12 pickle forks, 9 fruit spoons, 9
teaspoons. Each piece is marked at the back
with the R&B R flanked by eagle and lion.
Word STERLING and PAT June 25, 07. Also
letter H. Very good condition. $3,200

Francis I by Reed & Barton, "REED & BARTON" stamp

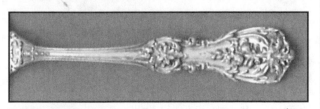

Baby set, 2 pieces. $80
Butter-master, hollow handle, 7 in. $35
Carving set, 2 pieces, large stainless
     blade, roast $240
Fork, 7 1/4 in. $40

Fork-asparagus/serving, solid, large, 4
     knobbed tines, 9 1/2 in. $280
Fork-baby, 4 3/8 in. $40
Fork-chipped beef, small, 6 1/8 in. $120
Fork-cocktail, 5 5/8 in. $40
Fork-cold meat/serving, small, solid,
     7 7/8 in. $90
Fork-fish, solid, individual, 4 tines, not beveled,
     7 1/4 in. $80
Fork-ice cream, 5 1/4 in. $40
Fork-salad, individual, clover piercing,
     6 1/8 in. $40
Fork-serving, stainless tines, 8 5/8 in. $50
Fork-strawberry, 4 3/4 in. $40
Knife-bar, hollow handle, 8 3/8 in. $48
Knife-crumber, hollow handle, stainless
     blade, 13 5/8 in. $70
Knife-modern, hollow handle, 9 1/2 in. $54
Knife-modern, hollow handle, stainless blade,
     8 7/8 in. $40
Knife-modern, hollow handle, stainless blade,
     9 1/4 in. $40
Knife-new french, hollow handle, stainless
     blade, 9 1/8 in. $40
Knife-sharpener/steel, large, roast,
     13 3/4 in. $110
Knife-steak, individual, beveled blade,
     9 in. $50
Knife-tea, stainless blade, french blade,
     7 3/4 in. $40
Knife-wedding cake, stainless blade,
     12 5/8 in. $55
Knife-youth, french blade, 7 1/8 in. $38
Knife-youth, modern blade, 7 1/8 in. $38
Ladle-cream, solid, 5 3/4 in. $58
Ladle-gravy, solid, 6 7/8 in. $100
Ladle-punch, solid, 15 in. $500
Ladle-soup, solid, 11 1/4 in. $300
Napkin clip, (made for teaspoons) $27
Napkin clip, (made for youth spoon) $40
Napkin ring, (made for teaspoon),
     1 1/2 in. $60
Pick-butter, 1 tine, 6 5/8 in. $80
Salad set, 2 pieces, wooden bowl $120
Salad set, 2 pieces, solid, 9 1/2 in. $380
Server-asparagus, hollow handle, silver
     plate hood, 9 1/8 in. $70
Server-asparagus, solid, 29 piercings,
     10 1/8 in. $280
Server-cake, solid, pie server,
     9 3/8 in. $130
Server-cheese, solid, 5 3/4 in. $70
Server-cheese, stainless blade,
     6 3/4 in. $50

Reed & Barton

Server-jelly/cake, 10 in. $240
Server-lasagna, stainless blade,
    10 in. $50
Server-macaroni, 10 3/8 in. $300
Server-pasta, stainless bowl,
    10 1/2 in. $50
Server-pastry, stainless bowl, 10 in. $50
Server-pie and cake, stainless blade,
    10 3/8 in. $44
Server-pie, stainless blade, 10 1/8 in. $70
Server-scalloped, solid, large,
    8 1/2 in. $200
Server-tomato, solid, 8 1/4 in. $120
Server-waffle, solid $300
Slicer-cake, stainless blade,
    10 1/2 in. $80
Spoon-baby, curved handle, 3 3/4 in. $48
Spoon-bonbon, 4 3/4 in. $50
Spoon-cracker, pierced, 8 7/8 in. $160
Spoon-dessert/oval soup, 7 1/4 in. $80
Spoon-ice, 9 1/2 in. $180
Spoon-iced tea, 7 3/4 in. $45
Spoon-infant feeding. 5 5/8 in. $35
Spoon-olive, short, pierced bowl,
    6 1/4 in. $90
Spoon-pierced/serving, stainless bowl,
    7 piercings, 8 1/2 in. $50
Spoon-place/oval soup, 6 5/8 in. $45
Spoon-platter, solid, 14 in. $270
Spoon-salad serving, plastic bowl ,
    11 3/4 in. $45
Spoon-salad serving, solid,
    9 1/2 in. $190
Spoon-salt, individual, 2 3/8 in. $18
Spoon-serving, stainless bowl,
    8 1/2 in. $50
Spoon-sherbet, 4 1/2 in. $50
Spoon-soup, round bowl, cream,
    6 in. $46
Spoon-soup, round bowl, gumbo,
    7 1/8 in. $88
Spoon-sugar shell, 6 1/8 in. $40
Spoon-teaspoon, 5 7/8 in. $27
Spoon-youth, 5 3/8 in. $40
Tea strainer, 7 1/8 in. $170
Tongs-asparagus, individual, solid,
    4 3/4 in. $90
Tongs-ice, serving, claw tip,
    6 1/2 in. $170
Tongs-sugar, 4 1/8 in. $60
Youth set, 3 pieces, (spoon, knife,
    fork) $140

Francis I, sterling and gold, by Reed & Barton, 1907

Fork, 7 1/4 in. $60
Fork, 7 7/8 in. $80
Fork-cocktail, 5 5/8 in. $44
Fork-salad, individual, 6 1/8 in. $60
Knife-modern, hollow handle, 8 7/8 in. $48
Knife-new french, hollow handle, 9 5/8 in. $60
Spoon-iced tea, 7 3/4 in. $50
Spoon-place/oval soup, 6 5/8 in. $60
Spoon-soup, round bowl, cream, 6 in. $70
Tablespoon, (serving spoon), pierced,
    8 3/8 in. $110

French Antique by Reed & Barton, 1901

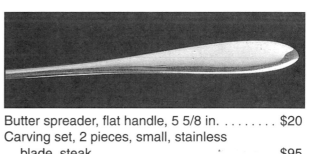

Butter spreader, flat handle, 5 5/8 in. $20
Carving set, 2 pieces, small, stainless
    blade, steak $95
Fork, 7 1/4 in. $35
Fork, 7 7/8 in. $40
Fork-cocktail, 5 3/8 in. $26
Fork-cold meat/serving, small, solid,
    7 3/4 in. $90
Fork-dessert, bar, 6 1/4 in. $40
Fork-fish, solid, individual, 1 piercing,
    6 in. $44
Fork-fish, stainless tines, hollow handle,
    individual, 7 3/4 in. $34
Fork-ice cream, 5 1/4 in. $34
Fork-ramekin, large, 5 in. $35
Fork-salad, individual, diamond slot,
    6 1/4 in. $34
Knife-new french, hollow handle, 9 1/8 in. $28
Knife-new french, hollow handle, 9 3/4 in. $37
Ladle-cream, solid, 5 1/4 in. $40
Ladle-gravy, solid, 6 1/8 in. $70
Server-pie, stainless blade, 10 1/8 in. $60

Spoon-demitasse, 4 in. $20
Spoon-dessert/oval soup, 7 1/4 in. $40
Spoon-fruit, 5 7/8 in. $37
Spoon-iced tea, 7 1/8 in. $33
Spoon-soup, round bowl, bouillon,
    5 1/4 in. $26
Spoon-soup, round bowl, cream,
    5 7/8 in. $32
Spoon-soup, round bowl, gumbo, 7 in. $36
Spoon-sugar shell, 6 1/4 in. $35
Spoon-teaspoon (five o'clock), 5 1/2 in. $20
Spoon-teaspoon, 6 in. $23
Tablespoon, (serving spoon), 8 1/4 in. $65

French Renaissance by Reed & Barton, 1941

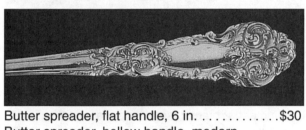

Butter spreader, flat handle, 6 in. $30
Butter spreader, hollow handle, modern,
    stainless paddle, 6 1/8 in. $30
Butter spreader, hollow handle, stainless
    paddle, 6 in. $32
Butter-master, flat handle, 7 1/4 in. $46
Butter-master, hollow handle, 6 3/4 in. $44
Fork, 7 1/8 in. $42
Fork, 7 7/8 in. $70
Fork-cocktail, 5 5/8 in. $32
Fork-cold meat/serving, small, solid,
    7 5/8 in. $110
Fork-ice cream, 5 1/2 in. $60
Fork-pickle/olive, short handle, 6 in. $44
Fork-salad, individual, 6 1/8 in. $46
Knife-modern, hollow handle, 9 1/2 in. $50
Knife-new french, hollow 3 3/4 in. handle,
    8 5/8 in. $42
Knife-new french, hollow 3 3/4 in. handle,
    9 in. $42
Knife-new french, hollow 4 in. handle,
    9 1/4 in. $42
Knife-new french, hollow handle,
    9 3/4 in. $50
Ladle-gravy, solid, 6 1/4 in. $110
Server-jelly, 5 7/8 in. $44
Server-pie and cake, stainless blade,
    10 1/4 in. $70
Server-pie, stainless blade, 10 1/8 in. $75
Spoon-dessert/oval soup, 6 7/8 in. $54

Spoon-iced tea, 7 1/2 in. $45
Spoon-soup, round bowl, cream,
    5 7/8 in. $44
Spoon-sugar shell, shell bowl,
    6 1/8 in. $48
Spoon-sugar, smooth bowl, 6 in. $48
Spoon-teaspoon, 5 7/8 in. $28
Tablespoon, (serving spoon),
    8 1/4 in. $100
Tablespoon, (serving spoon), pierced,
    8 1/4 in. $120
Tongs-sugar, 4 in. $70

Georgian Rose by Reed & Barton, 1941

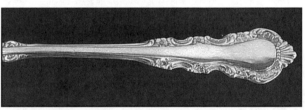

Butter spreader, flat handle, 6 in. $17
Butter spreader, hollow handle, stainless
    paddle, 6 1/8 in. $26
Butter-master, flat handle, 7 1/4 in. $40
Butter-master, hollow handle, 6 7/8 in. $40
Carving set, 2 pieces, small, stainless blade,
    steak $140
Fork, 7 1/8 in. $37
Fork, 7 3/4 in. $70
Fork-cocktail, 5 1/2 in. $26
Fork-cold meat/serving, small, solid,
    7 1/2 in. $90
Fork-salad, individual, 6 1/4 in. $30
Knife-new french, hollow handle, 9 5/8 in. $50
Knife-new french, hollow handle, silver plate
    blade, 9 1/8 in. $34
Knife-new french, hollow handle, stainless
    blade, 8 7/8 in. $34
Knife-new french, hollow handle, stainless
    blade, 9 1/8 in. $34
Server-jelly, 6 in. $40
Spoon-demitasse, 4 1/4 in. $25
Spoon-dessert/oval soup, 6 7/8 in. $60
Spoon-fruit, 6 in. $44
Spoon-iced tea, 7 1/2 in. $36
Spoon-soup, round bowl, cream, 6 in. $34
Spoon-sugar shell, 6 1/4 in. $35
Spoon-teaspoon (five o'clock), 5 1/2 in. $23
Spoon-teaspoon, 6 in. $16
Tablespoon, (serving spoon), 8 1/2 in. $70
Tongs-sugar, 4 in. $70

Grande Renaissance by Reed & Barton, 1967

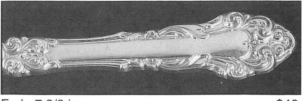

Fork, 7 3/8 in. $40
Fork, 8 in. $58
Fork-cold meat/serving, medium, solid,
   8 1/2 in. $90
Fork-salad, individual, 6 3/8 in. $44
Fork-youth, 6 1/4 in. $37
Knife-modern, hollow handle, 9 3/4 in. $40
Knife-modern, hollow handle, 9 in. $38
Knife-steak, individual, 9 1/8 in. $40
Napkin clip, (made for teaspoons) $34
Server-asparagus, hollow handle, silver
   plate hood, 9 3/8 in. $70
Server-pie and cake, stainless blade,
   10 1/2 in. $55
Spoon-dessert/oval soup, 6 7/8 in. $44
Spoon-iced tea, 7 1/4 in. $40
Spoon-soup, round bowl, cream, 6 1/4 in. $44
Spoon-sugar shell, 6 1/8 in. $38
Spoon-teaspoon, 6 in. $26
Tablespoon, (serving spoon), 8 5/8 in. $100
Tablespoon, (serving spoon), pierced,
   8 5/8 in. $100

Guildhall by Reed & Barton, 1941

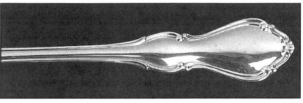

Butter spreader, flat handle, 6 in. $18
Butter spreader, hollow handle, solid paddle,
   notch blade, 6 1/8 in. $36
Butter-master, hollow handle, 6 7/8 in. $45
Fork, 7 5/8 in. $60
Fork, 7 in. $38
Fork-cocktail, 5 1/2 in. $30
Fork-salad, individual, 6 1/8 in. $40
Knife-new french, hollow handle, 9 3/4 in. $50
Knife-new french, hollow handle, silver
   plate blade, 9 in. $35
Knife-new french, hollow handle, stainless
   blade, 9 in. $35

Knife-youth, 7 in. $40
Spoon-demitasse, 4 1/4 in. $28
Spoon-iced tea, 7 1/2 in. $40
Spoon-soup, round bowl, cream, 5 7/8 in. $36
Spoon-sugar shell, 6 1/4 in. $38
Spoon-teaspoon, 6 in. $22
Tablespoon, (serving spoon), 8 3/8 in. $80

Hampton Court by Reed & Barton, 1964

Baby set, 2 pieces $80
Butter spreader, hollow handle, modern,
   stainless paddle, 6 3/8 in. $30
Butter-master, hollow handle, 7 in. $40
Carving set, 2 pieces, large stainless blade,
   roast $130
Carving set, 2 pieces, small, stainless blade,
   steak $120
Fork, 7 1/2 in. $47
Fork-baby, 4 3/8 in. $40
Fork-carving, small, stainless prongs, steak,
   9 1/8 in. $60
Fork-cocktail, 5 5/8 in. $35
Fork-cold meat/serving, medium, solid,
   8 5/8 in. $90
Fork-ice cream, 5 7/8 in. $46
Fork-lemon, 5 in. $34
Fork-pickle/olive, short handle, 5 3/4 in. $30
Fork-salad, individual, 6 5/8 in. $45
Fork-youth, 6 1/4 in. $42
Knife-modern, hollow handle, 9 1/8 in. $35
Knife-steak, individual, 9 1/4 in. $50
Knife-youth, 7 1/8 in. $33
Ladle-gravy, solid, 6 5/8 in. $90
Server-asparagus, hollow handle, silver plate
   hood, 9 5/8 in. $68
Server-pie and cake, stainless blade,
   10 1/2 in. $50
Spoon-baby, straight handle, 4 1/2 in. $40
Spoon-bonbon, 4 7/8 in. $44
Spoon-demitasse, 4 3/8 in. $26
Spoon-dessert/oval soup, 6 7/8 in. $45
Spoon-iced tea, 7 1/2 in. $46
Spoon-infant feeding, 5 3/4 in. $40
Spoon-soup, round bowl, cream, 6 in. $48
Spoon-sugar shell, 6 1/4 in. $40
Tablespoon, (serving spoon), 8 5/8 in. $96

Hawthorne by Reed & Barton, 1934

Butter spreader, flat handle, 6 3/8 in. $30
Carving set, 2 pieces, small, stainless blade,
    steak $150
Fork, 7 1/8 in. $55
Fork, 7 7/8 in. $60
Fork-cocktail, 5 3/4 in. $35
Fork-cold meat/serving, small, solid,
    7 5/8 in. $90
Fork-dessert, bar, pierced, 6 3/8 in. $58
Fork-ice cream, 5 3/8 in. $50
Fork-lemon, 5 in. $40
Fork-pickle/olive, short handle, 2 tines,
    6 in. $40
Fork-pickle/olive, short handle, 3 tines,
    6 in. $40
Fork-salad serving, solid $110
Fork-salad, individual, heart slot,
    6 3/8 in. $50
Knife-carving, large stainless blade, roast,
    13 1/4 in. $75
Knife-new french, hollow handle,
    9 5/8 in. $50
Knife-new french, hollow handle,
    9 in. $42
Ladle-cream, solid, 5 3/8 in. $53
Ladle-gravy, solid, 6 3/8 in. $90
Server-cheese, stainless blade, 6 5/8 in. $53
Server-jelly, 6 1/2 in. $40
Server-pie, stainless blade, 10 in. $75
Server-pie, stainless blade, 9 5/8 in. $75
Server-tomato, solid, 7 3/4 in. $100
Spoon-casserole, smooth, solid,
    7 5/8 in. $110
Spoon-demitasse, 4 1/2 in. $28
Spoon-fruit, 6 in. $40
Spoon-soup, round bowl, bouillon,
    5 3/8 in. $45
Spoon-soup, round bowl, gumbo,
    7 in. $60
Spoon-sugar shell, 6 3/8 in. $44
Spoon-teaspoon (five o'clock),
    5 1/4 in. $28
Spoon-teaspoon, 6 1/8 in. $30
Tablespoon, (serving spoon),
    8 3/8 in. $90

Hepplewhite-Chased by Reed & Barton, 1907

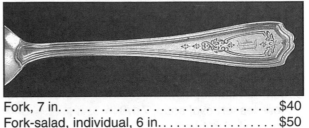

Fork, 7 in. $40
Fork-salad, individual, 6 in. $50
Spoon-teaspoon (five o'clock), 5 1/4 in. $20

Hepplewhite-Engraved by Reed & Barton, 1907

Fork, 7 in. $45
Fork-fish, solid, individual, 5 piercings,
    6 1/4 in. $58
Fork-salad, individual, clover slot, 6 in. $45
Fork-youth, 6 in. $50
Knife-modern, hollow handle, 8 3/4 in. $40
Knife-new french, hollow handle, 9 5/8 in. $50
Knife-old french, hollow handle, 9 3/8 in. $40
Knife-orange, silver plate blade, 7 7/8 in. $40
Spoon-teaspoon (five o'clock), 5 3/8 in. $28
Tongs-sugar, 3 3/4 in. $60

Hepplewhite-Plain by Reed & Barton, 1907

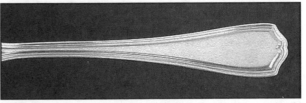

Butter spreader, flat handle, 5 5/8 in. $20
Carving set, 3 pieces, large, stainless blade,
    roast. $250
Fork, 7 5/8 in. $40
Fork, 7 in. $26
Fork-baby, 4 1/2 in. $28
Fork-cocktail, 5 1/2 in. $22
Fork-ice cream, 5 in. $36
Fork-pickle/olive, short handle, 5 7/8 in. $30

Fork-salad, individual, pierced, 6 in...........$44
Knife-new french, hollow handle,
   9 5/8 in....................................$44
Knife-old french, hollow handle, 8 7/8 in.......$30
Knife-old french, hollow handle, 9 3/8 in.......$30
Ladle-cream, solid, 5 3/8 in..................$40
Server-cheese, silver plate blade, 6 7/8 in.....$55
Server-jelly, 5 7/8 in.......................$30
Server-pie, silver plate blade, 10 7/8 in.......$55
Spoon-demitasse, 4 1/4 in. $16
Spoon-dessert/oval soup, 7 1/8 in...........$40
Spoon-fruit, 5 3/4 in.......................$25
Spoon-iced tea, 1 1/4 in. wide bowl,
   7 1/8 in...................................$32
Spoon-soup, round bowl, bouillon,
   5 1/4 in...................................$20
Spoon-soup, round bowl, cream,
   5 3/4 in...................................$35
Spoon-sugar, 6 in..........................$30
Spoon-teaspoon (five o'clock), 5 1/4 in.......$20
Spoon-teaspoon, 5 3/4 in. $22
Tablespoon, (serving spoon), 8 1/4 in.........$60

Heritage by Reed & Barton, 1924

Butter spreader, flat handle, 5 3/4 in..........$26
Carving set, 2 pieces, small, stainless blade,
   steak..................................$140
Fork, 7 1/8 in..............................$40
Fork, 7 3/4 in..............................$50
Fork-cocktail, 5 1/2 in......................$30
Fork-dessert, diamond slot, 6 1/4 in. $46
Fork-salad, individual, clover slot,
   6 1/4 in...................................$50
Knife-new french, hollow handle, 9 5/8 in......$50
Server-jelly, 6 in. $36
Spoon-demitasse, 4 1/4 in. $24
Spoon-fruit, 5 5/8 in.......................$34
Spoon-iced tea, 7 1/8 in. $38
Spoon-soup, round bowl, bouillon,
   5 1/4 in...................................$36
Spoon-soup, round bowl, cream,
   5 7/8 in...................................$38
Spoon-soup, round bowl, gumbo,
   7 1/4 in...................................$60
Spoon-teaspoon, 5 3/4 in. $28
Tablespoon, (serving spoon), 8 1/4 in.........$85

Intaglio by Reed & Barton, 1905

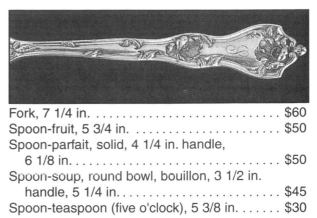

Fork, 7 1/4 in. $60
Spoon-fruit, 5 3/4 in. $50
Spoon-parfait, solid, 4 1/4 in. handle,
   6 1/8 in..................................$50
Spoon-soup, round bowl, bouillon, 3 1/2 in.
   handle, 5 1/4 in..........................$45
Spoon-teaspoon (five o'clock), 5 3/8 in. $30

Reed & Barton Intaglio berry spoon, 9 5/8 in., no
monogram, good condition, marked with
usual trademarks, sterling, etc. and "poppy" in
fine print. $350

Jubilee by Reed & Barton, 1936

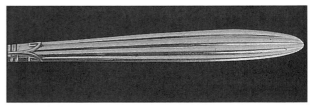

Butter spreader, hollow handle, stainless
   paddle, 6 in. $20
Butter-master, flat handle, 7 5/8 in. $35
Fork, 7 1/4 in. $40
Fork, 7 7/8 in. $54
Fork-carving, small stainless prongs,
   steak..................................$50
Fork-salad, individual, 6 3/8 in. $34

Knife-carving, small stainless blade,
   steak $50
Knife-modern, hollow handle,
   8 7/8 in.. . . . .$33
Knife-modern, hollow handle,
   9 1/2 in.. . . . .$45
Ladle-gravy, solid, 6 5/8 in. $80
Server-pie, stainless blade, 10 in.. . . . .$60
Spoon-soup, round bowl, cream,
   6 1/8 in.. . . . .$35
Spoon-soup, round bowl, gumbo,
   7 1/4 in.. . . . .$40
Spoon-teaspoon, 6 in.. . . . .$23
Tablespoon, (serving spoon),
   8 1/2 in.. . . . .$65

Kings by Reed & Barton, 1890

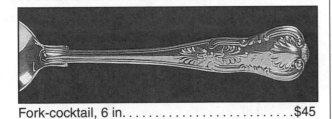

Fork-cocktail, 6 in.. . . . .$45

La Marquise by Reed & Barton, 1895

Fork, 7 7/8 in.. . . . .$80
Fork, 7 in.. . . . .$60
Spoon-demitasse, 4 1/8 in. $30
Spoon-dessert/oval soup, 7 3/8 in.. . . . .$46
Spoon-teaspoon (five o'clock),
   5 1/4 in.. . . . .$30
Spoon-teaspoon, raised back, 5 7/8 in.. . . . . . .$36
Tablespoon, (serving spoon),
   8 3/8 in.. . . . .$90

La Parisienne by Reed & Barton, 1902

Spoon-soup, round bowl, gumbo,
   7 1/8 in.. . . . .$100
Spoon-teaspoon, 6 in.. . . . .$50
Tablespoon, (serving spoon),
   8 1/4 in.. . . . .$150

La Perle-Engraved by Reed & Barton, 1902

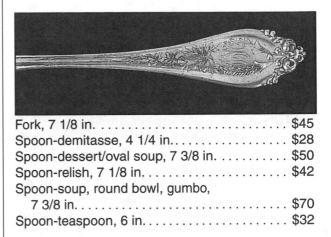

Fork, 7 1/8 in. $45
Spoon-demitasse, 4 1/4 in.. . . . . $28
Spoon-dessert/oval soup, 7 3/8 in. $50
Spoon-relish, 7 1/8 in.. . . . . $42
Spoon-soup, round bowl, gumbo,
   7 3/8 in.. . . . . $70
Spoon-teaspoon, 6 in.. . . . . $32

La Reine by Reed & Barton, 1893

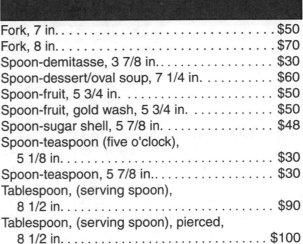

Fork, 7 in.. . . . .$50
Fork, 8 in.. . . . .$70
Spoon-demitasse, 3 7/8 in.. . . . . $30
Spoon-dessert/oval soup, 7 1/4 in. $60
Spoon-fruit, 5 3/4 in. $50
Spoon-fruit, gold wash, 5 3/4 in. $50
Spoon-sugar shell, 5 7/8 in. $48
Spoon-teaspoon (five o'clock),
   5 1/8 in.. . . . . $30
Spoon-teaspoon, 5 7/8 in.. . . . . $30
Tablespoon, (serving spoon),
   8 1/2 in.. . . . . $90
Tablespoon, (serving spoon), pierced,
   8 1/2 in.. . . . .$100

Lark by Reed & Barton, 1960

Butter spreader, hollow handle, modern,
   stainless paddle, 7 in.. $24
Butter-master, hollow handle, 7 3/8 in.. . . . . . . $37

Fork, 7 5/8 in. $50
Fork-cocktail, 6 1/8 in. $40
Fork-cold meat/serving, medium, solid,
    8 3/8 in. $90
Fork-salad, individual, 7 1/8 in. $50
Knife-modern, hollow handle, 9 1/8 in. $33
Ladle-gravy, solid, 7 1/8 in. $100
Napkin clip, (made for teaspoons) $28
Server-jelly, 6 1/2 in. $40
Server-pie and cake, stainless blade,
    10 3/4 in. $60
Spoon-dessert/oval soup, 7 in. $50
Spoon-sugar, 6 1/8 in. $37
Spoon-teaspoon, 6 1/4 in. $20
Tablespoon, (serving spoon), 8 1/2 in. $100
Tablespoon, (serving spoon), pierced,
    8 1/2 in. $110

Les Cinq Fleurs by Reed & Barton, 1900

Fork, 7 1/8 in. $50
Fork, 7 3/4 in. $65
Fork-fish/salad, solid, individual, not
    pierced, 7 in. $100
Fork-salad, individual, 1 1/8 in. bowl,
    6 1/4 in. $100
Knife-old french, hollow handle, 8 7/8 in. $100
Knife-old french, hollow handle, 9 7/8 in. $140
Spoon-chocolate, short handle, 4 3/8 in. $50
Spoon-teaspoon (five o'clock), 5 3/8 in. $30
Spoon-teaspoon, 5 3/4 in. $34
Tablespoon, (serving spoon), 8 1/4 in. $100

Les Six Fleurs by Reed & Barton, 1901

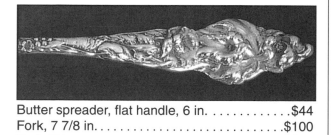

Butter spreader, flat handle, 6 in. $44
Fork, 7 7/8 in. $100
Fork, 7 in. $80

Fork-cocktail, 5 3/4 in. $50
Knife-new french, hollow handle, 9 in. $100
Spoon-demitasse, 4 1/4 in. $40
Spoon-dessert/oval soup, 7 1/4 in. $100
Spoon-fruit, 5 7/8 in. $60
Spoon-soup, round bowl, cream, 6 1/8 in. $70
Spoon-teaspoon (five o'clock), 5 3/8 in. $40
Spoon-teaspoon, 6 in. $48

Love Disarmed by Reed & Barton, 1899

The pieces listed here are newer examples of this
    pattern.
Baby cup, sterling. $150
Baby set, 2 pieces $120
Butter spreader, flat handle, 5 7/8 in. $90
Butter-master, flat handle, 7 1/2 in. $100
Fork, 7 3/4 in. $110
Fork, 7 in. $80
Fork-asparagus/serving, solid, large,
    4 knobbed tines, 10 7/8 in. $340
Fork-baby, 4 3/8 in. $60
Fork-cocktail, 5 5/8 in. $70
Fork-cold meat/serving, small, solid,
    7 7/8 in. $140
Fork-fish/serving, solid, large, 10 3/4 in. $380
Fork-ice cream, 5 1/4 in. $70
Fork-salad/individual, 6 in. $90
Fork-strawberry, 4 7/8 in. $50
Ice cream slicer, solid, 13 1/4 in. $380
Knife-crumber, hollow handle, stainless
    blade, 13 5/8 in. $80
Knife-new french, hollow handle,
    9 3/4 in. $100
Knife-steak, individual, beveled blade,
    9 1/8 in. $80
Ladle-gravy, solid, 6 3/4 in. $140
Salad set, 2 pieces, solid $550
Server-asparagus, hollow handle, silver
    plate hood, 9 1/2 in. $75
Server-asparagus, solid, 29 piercings,
    11 1/2 in. $350
Server-cake, solid, 9 1/2 in. $260
Server-ice cream, solid, large, 14 piercings,
    12 1/2 in. $330
Server-jelly/cake, 10 in. $300

Server-pie, stainless blade, serrated,
9 7/8 in. $80
Server-scalloped, solid, large, 8 7/8 in. $200
Server-toast, solid, 16 piercings,
11 1/4 in. $340
Server-tomato, solid, 8 1/8 in. $160
Server-waffle, solid, 16 piercings,
10 7/8 in. $380
Slicer-cake, stainless blade,
12 7/8 in. $90
Spoon-baby, straight handle,
4 1/2 in. $60
Spoon-chocolate, short handle,
4 1/4 in. $80
Spoon-cracker, 18 piercings,
8 3/4 in. $180
Spoon-demitasse, 4 1/4 in. $70
Spoon-dessert/oval soup, 7 1/4 in. $90
Spoon-fruit, 5 7/8 in. $90
Spoon-iced tea, 7 3/8 in. $90
Spoon-infant feeding, 5 5/8 in. $75
Spoon-salt, individual, 2 3/8 in. $20
Spoon-soup, round bowl, bouillon,
5 3/8 in. $56
Spoon-teaspoon (five o'clock), 5 in. $70
Spoon-teaspoon, 6 in. $80
Tablespoon, (serving spoon),
8 1/4 in. $130
Tablespoon, (serving spoon), 7 piercings,
8 1/4 in. $130
Tongs-asparagus, individual, solid,
5 1/8 in. $120
Tongs-sugar, 4 1/2 in. $100

Majestic by Reed & Barton, 1894

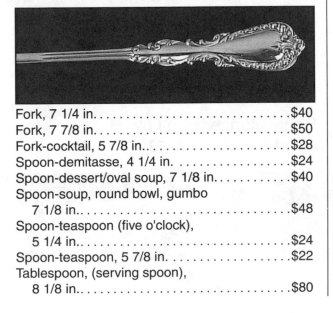

Fork, 7 1/4 in. $40
Fork, 7 7/8 in. $50
Fork-cocktail, 5 7/8 in. $28
Spoon-demitasse, 4 1/4 in. $24
Spoon-dessert/oval soup, 7 1/8 in. $40
Spoon-soup, round bowl, gumbo
7 1/8 in. $48
Spoon-teaspoon (five o'clock),
5 1/4 in. $24
Spoon-teaspoon, 5 7/8 in. $22
Tablespoon, (serving spoon),
8 1/8 in. $80

Marlborough by Reed & Barton, 1906

Baby set, 2 pieces. $80
Butter spreader, flat handle, 5 7/8 in. $23
Butter spreader, hollow handle, stainless
paddle, 6 1/4 in. $32
Butter-master, hollow handle, 7 1/8 in. $45
Fork, 7 1/4 in. $32
Fork, 7 3/4 in. $54
Fork-cocktail, 5 1/2 in. $22
Fork-pickle/olive, short handle, 5 5/8 in. $40
Fork-salad, individual, 6 1/8 in. $38
Knife-modern, hollow handle, 8 7/8 in. $38
Knife-modern, hollow handle, 9 1/2 in. $60
Knife-new french, hollow handle,
9 1/8 in. $37
Knife-steak, individual, 9 in. $45
Server-pie and cake, stainless blade,
10 3/8 in. $56
Spoon-demitasse, 4 1/4 in. $26
Spoon-dessert/oval soup, 7 1/4 in. $50
Spoon-iced tea, 7 5/8 in. $40
Spoon-infant feeding, 5 3/4 in. $40
Spoon-soup, round bowl, bouillon,
5 1/4 in. $45
Spoon-soup, round bowl, cream,
5 7/8 in. $50
Spoon-sugar, egg-shaped bowl,
5 7/8 in. $44
Spoon-teaspoon (five o'clock), 5 3/8 in. $24
Spoon-teaspoon, 5 3/4 in. $22
Tablespoon, (serving spoon), 8 1/4 in. $90
Tablespoon, (serving spoon), pierced,
8 1/4 in. $110

Petite Fleur by Reed & Barton, 1961

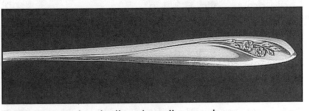

Butter spreader, hollow handle, modern,
stainless paddle, 6 3/4 in. $24
Butter-master, hollow handle, 7 3/8 in. $28

Fork, 7 3/8 in. $43
Fork-cocktail, 5 3/4 in. $30
Fork-cold meat/serving, medium, solid,
    8 1/4 in. $80
Fork-pickle/olive, short handle, 5 7/8 in. $30
Fork-salad, individual, 6 3/4 in. $46
Knife-modern, hollow handle, 9 in. $36
Ladle-gravy, solid, 6 3/4 in. $80
Spoon-dessert/oval soup, 6 7/8 in. $40
Spoon-sugar, 6 1/4 in. $34
Spoon-teaspoon, 6 1/8 in. $22

Pointed Antique by Reed & Barton, 1895

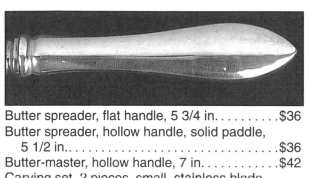

Butter spreader, flat handle, 5 3/4 in. $36
Butter spreader, hollow handle, solid paddle,
    5 1/2 in. $36
Butter-master, hollow handle, 7 in. $42
Carving set, 2 pieces, small, stainless blade,
    steak $140
Fork, 7 1/8 in. $60
Fork-baby, 4 1/4 in. $40
Fork-carving, small, stainless prongs, steak,
    8 7/8 in. $70
Fork-salad, individual, heart slot, 6 1/4 in. $60
Knife-carving, small stainless blade, steak,
    9 3/4 in. $70
Knife-cheese, stainless blade, 7 1/4 in. $50
Knife-modern, hollow handle, stainless blade,
    9 in. $40
Knife-new french, hollow handle, stainless
    blade, 8 3/4 in. $40
Knife-new french, hollow handle, stainless
    blade, 9 1/2 in. $60
Knife-steak, individual, 8 3/8 in. $55
Knife-wedding cake, 8 3/8 in. stainless blade,
    12 3/4 in. $70
Knife-youth, 7 3/4 in. $26
Ladle-gravy, solid, 6 3/8 in. $100
Salad set, 2 pieces, plastic bowl $90
Server-asparagus, hollow handle, silver
    plate hood, 9 3/8 in. $63
Server-cheese, stainless blade, 6 1/8 in. $55
Server-pastry, stainless bowl, 10 in. $70
Server-pastry, stainless bowl, 8 3/4 in. $70
Server-pastry, stainless bowl, 9 1/2 in. $70
Server-pie and cake, stainless blade,
    10 in. $60

Server-pie, stainless blade, 9 3/4 in. $80
Spoon-baby, straight handle, 4 1/4 in. $40
Spoon-infant feeding, 5 3/8 in. $40
Spoon-place/oval soup, oval bowl,
    6 3/4 in. $55
Spoon-soup, round bowl, bouillon,
    5 1/2 in. $48
Spoon-soup, round bowl, cream, 6 1/8 in. $55
Spoon-sugar shell, 6 1/2 in. $45
Spoon-teaspoon, 6 in. $36
Tablespoon, (serving spoon), 8 3/8 in. $100
Tablespoon, (serving spoon), 7 piercings,
    8 3/8 in. $100

Pointed Antique-Hammered by Reed & Barton, 1895

Fork, 7 3/4 in. $70
Fork-salad, individual, heart slot, 6 1/4 in. $60
Knife-modern, hollow handle, stainless blade,
    9 in. $44
Knife-new french, hollow handle, stainless
    blade, 9 1/2 in. $58
Knife-old french, hollow handle, 9 1/4 in. $45
Ladle-cream, solid, 5 1/8 in. $60
Server-lasagna, stainless blade, 10 1/8 in. $70
Server-pasta, stainless bowl, 10 5/8 in. $70
Server-pie and cake, stainless blade,
    10 1/2 in. $60
Spoon-dessert/oval soup, tear-shaped bowl,
    1/8 in. $60
Spoon-soup, round bowl, bouillon,
    5 1/2 in. $54
Spoon-sugar shell, 6 3/8 in. $48
Spoon-teaspoon, 6 1/8 in. $34
Tablespoon, (serving spoon), 8 1/4 in. $100

Renaissance Scroll by Reed & Barton, 1969

Butter spreader, hollow handle, modern,
    stainless, 6 7/8 in. $16

Butter-master, hollow handle, 7 3/8 in.........$20
Fork, 7 1/2 in..............................$34
Fork-cocktail, 5 5/8 in......................$25
Fork-salad, individual, 6 5/8 in.............$27
Knife-modern, hollow handle, 9 1/8 in........$28
Ladle-gravy, solid, 6 7/8 in. $80
Server-jelly, 6 1/4 in.......................$34
Spoon-demitasse, 4 3/8 in. $20
Spoon-dessert/oval soup, 6 5/8 in..........$38
Spoon-iced tea, 7 3/8 in. $30
Spoon-sugar shell, 6 1/4 in.................$22
Spoon-teaspoon, 6 in.......................$20
Tablespoon, (serving spoon), pierced,
    8 5/8 in.................................$80

Romaine/Monique by Reed & Barton, 1933

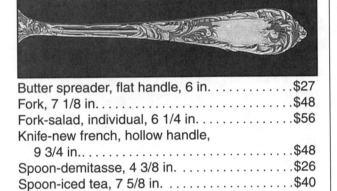

Butter spreader, flat handle, 6 in. $27
Fork, 7 1/8 in...............................$48
Fork-salad, individual, 6 1/4 in...............$56
Knife-new french, hollow handle,
    9 3/4 in.................................$48
Spoon-demitasse, 4 3/8 in. $26
Spoon-iced tea, 7 5/8 in. $40
Spoon-soup, round bowl, cream, 6 in........$46
Spoon-sugar shell, 6 1/4 in.................$48
Spoon-teaspoon, 6 in.......................$30

Rose Cascade by Reed & Barton, 1957

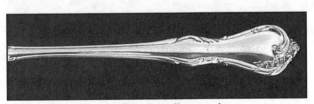

Butter spreader, hollow handle, modern,
    stainless, 6 3/8 in.......................$32
Butter-master, hollow handle,
    6 7/8 in.................................$45
Fork, 7 3/8 in..............................$60
Fork-salad, individual, 6 1/2 in..............$54
Fork-youth, 6 1/4 in. $55
Knife-modern, hollow handle,
    8 5/8 in.................................$44

Knife-steak, individual, serrated blade,
    9 1/4 in. $60
Server-pie and cake, stainless blade,
    10 5/8 in. $80
Spoon-dessert/oval soup, 6 5/8 in. $56
Spoon-iced tea, 7 3/8 in. $56
Spoon-sugar shell, 6 1/4 in. $43
Spoon-teaspoon, 6 in....................... $26

Savannah by Reed & Barton, 1962

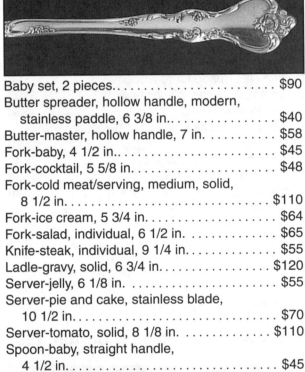

Baby set, 2 pieces......................... $90
Butter spreader, hollow handle, modern,
    stainless paddle, 6 3/8 in................. $40
Butter-master, hollow handle, 7 in. $58
Fork-baby, 4 1/2 in........................ $45
Fork-cocktail, 5 5/8 in. $48
Fork-cold meat/serving, medium, solid,
    8 1/2 in. $110
Fork-ice cream, 5 3/4 in. $64
Fork-salad, individual, 6 1/2 in. $65
Knife-steak, individual, 9 1/4 in.............. $55
Ladle-gravy, solid, 6 3/4 in................. $120
Server-jelly, 6 1/8 in. $55
Server-pie and cake, stainless blade,
    10 1/2 in................................ $70
Server-tomato, solid, 8 1/8 in. $110
Spoon-baby, straight handle,
    4 1/2 in................................. $45
Spoon-iced tea, 7 3/8 in.................... $58
Spoon-infant feeding, 5 3/4 in............... $50
Spoon-soup, round bowl, cream,
    5 7/8 in................................. $58
Spoon-sugar shell, 6 1/8 in. $60
Spoon-teaspoon, 6 in....................... $40
Tablespoon, (serving spoon), pierced,
    8 5/8 in................................ $120

Silver Sculpture by Reed & Barton, 1954

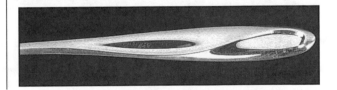

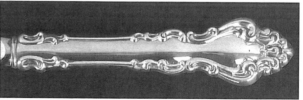

Reed & Barton

Butter spreader, hollow handle, modern, stainless paddle, 6 3/4 in..........................$24
Butter spreader, hollow handle, stainless paddle, 6 5/8 in....................................$24
Butter-master, hollow handle, 7 3/8 in.........$30
Fork, 7 3/8 in...............................$45
Fork-baby, 4 1/2 in..........................$50
Fork-cocktail, 5 5/8 in.......................$36
Fork-cold meat/serving, medium, solid, 8 1/4 in....................................$90
Fork-lemon, 2 tines, 4 3/4 in.................$30
Fork-pickle/olive, short handle, 5 3/4 in. $30
Fork-salad, individual, 6 5/8 in..............$54
Knife-cheese, stainless blade, 7 1/2 in.......$45
Knife-modern, hollow handle, 9 in.............$36
Ladle-cream, solid, 5 1/4 in..................$50
Ladle-gravy, solid, 6 5/8 in. $75
Napkin clip, (made for teaspoons) $28
Salad set, 2 pieces, plastic bowl............$100
Server-jelly, 6 1/2 in........................$34
Server-pie and cake, stainless blade, 11 in.....................................$70
Spoon-bonbon, 4 7/8 in........................$40
Spoon-demitasse, 4 1/2 in. $28
Spoon-dessert/oval soup, 6 5/8 in.............$46
Spoon-iced tea, 7 1/2 in. $56
Spoon-sugar, 6 1/4 in.........................$30
Spoon-teaspoon, 6 1/8 in......................$24
Tablespoon, (serving spoon), 8 5/8 in.........$80
Tablespoon, (serving spoon), pierced, 8 5/8 in....................................$90
Tongs-sugar, 4 1/4 in.........................$60

Silver Wheat by Reed & Barton, 1952

Butter spreader, flat handle, 5 3/4 in.........$16
Butter spreader, hollow handle, modern, stainless paddle, 6 3/8 in..............$18
Butter spreader, hollow handle, stainless paddle, 6 1/4 in...................$18
Butter-master, hollow handle, no notch, 7 in.....................................$28
Butter-master, hollow handle, notched blade, 7 in..................................$28
Carving set, 2 pieces, small, stainless blade, steak..................................$120
Fork, 7 3/8 in...............................$28

Fork, 7 5/8 in...............................$58
Fork-cocktail, 5 3/4 in.......................$28
Fork-cold meat/serving, medium, solid, 8 1/4 in....................................$70
Fork-lemon, 5 in.............................$25
Fork-pickle/olive, short handle, 5 3/4 in......$26
Fork-salad, individual, 6 5/8 in..............$38
Fork-youth, 6 3/8 in..........................$45
Knife-cake, stainless blade, 10 1/2 in.........$55
Knife-modern, hollow handle, 8 7/8 in.........$36
Knife-youth, 7 7/8 in.........................$42
Ladle-cream, solid, 5 1/4 in..................$45
Ladle-gravy, solid, 6 3/4 in..................$65
Server-cheese, stainless blade, 6 3/4 in......$45
Server-jelly, 6 1/2 in........................$30
Server-pastry, stainless bowl, 9 7/8 in.......$55
Server-pie and cake, stainless blade, 10 3/8 in...................................$60
Server-pie, stainless blade, 10 in............$60
Spoon-bonbon, 5 in...........................$30
Spoon-demitasse, 4 1/2 in.....................$20
Spoon-dessert/oval soup, 6 5/8 in.............$44
Spoon-iced tea, 7 1/2 in......................$40
Spoon-soup, round bowl, cream, 6 3/8 in....................................$33
Spoon-sugar shell, 6 3/8 in...................$27
Spoon-teaspoon, 6 1/8 in......................$16
Tablespoon, (serving spoon), 8 5/8 in.........$65
Tablespoon, (serving spoon), pierced, 8 5/8 in....................................$80

Spanish Baroque by Reed & Barton, 1965

Butter spreader, hollow handle, modern, stainless paddle, 6 3/8 in...............$32
Butter-master, hollow handle, 7 in............$33
Fork, 7 1/2 in...............................$30
Fork, 7 7/8 in...............................$68
Fork-cocktail, 5 1/2 in.......................$36
Fork-cold meat/serving, medium, solid, 8 1/2 in...................................$100
Fork-ice cream, 5 3/4 in......................$55
Fork-pickle/olive, short handle, 6 in.........$32
Fork-salad/individual, 6 1/2 in...............$44
Knife-modern, hollow handle, 9 1/4 in.........$33
Knife-modern, hollow handle, 9 3/4 in.........$54

Knife-steak, individual, 9 1/4 in. $40
Ladle-cream, solid, 5 1/2 in.. . . . .$50
Ladle-gravy, solid, 6 3/4 in. $90
Spoon-dessert/oval soup,
   6 7/8 in.. . . . .$38
Spoon-iced tea, 7 1/4 in. $46
Spoon-soup, round bowl, cream,
   5 7/8 in.. . . . .$50
Spoon-sugar shell, 6 1/4 in.. . . . .$35
Spoon-teaspoon, 6 in.. . . . .$24
Tablespoon, (serving spoon),
   8 5/8 in.. . . . .$100
Tablespoon, (serving spoon), pierced,
   8 5/8 in.. . . . .$100

Star by Reed & Barton, 1960

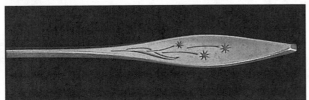

Butter spreader, hollow handle, modern,
   stainless paddle, 7 in.. . . . .$12
Butter-master, hollow handle, 7 3/8 in.. . . . .$23
Fork, 7 1/2 in.. . . . .$26
Fork-baby, 4 3/4 in. $34
Fork-cold meat/serving, medium, solid,
   8 3/8 in.. . . . .$60
Fork-lemon, 4 3/4 in.. . . . .$26
Fork-pickle/olive, short handle,
   6 3/8 in.. . . . .$26
Fork-salad, individual, 7 in. $26
Knife-bar, hollow handle, 8 3/4 in.. . . . .$34
Knife-modern, hollow handle, 9 in.. . . . .$22
Ladle-cream, solid, 5 7/8 in.. . . . .$40
Ladle-gravy, solid, 6 5/8 in.. . . . .$65
Ladle-gravy, solid, 7 in.. . . . .$65
Server-jelly, 6 1/2 in. $30
Spoon-bonbon, 5 in. $28
Spoon-casserole, smooth bowl, solid,
   8 1/2 in.. . . . .$80
Spoon-demitasse, 4 5/8 in. $20
Spoon-dessert/oval soup, 7 in. $33
Spoon-iced tea, 7 1/2 in. $30
Spoon-infant feeding, 5 7/8 in.. . . . .$34
Spoon-sugar, 6 1/8 in.. . . . .$26
Spoon-teaspoon, 6 1/4 in. $13
Tablespoon, (serving spoon),
   8 3/8 in.. . . . .$60
Tablespoon, (serving spoon), pierced,
   8 3/8 in.. . . . .$70

Tapestry by Reed & Barton, 1964

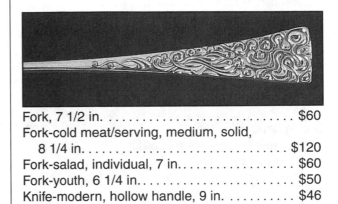

Fork, 7 1/2 in. $60
Fork-cold meat/serving, medium, solid,
   8 1/4 in.. . . . . $120
Fork-salad, individual, 7 in.. . . . . $60
Fork-youth, 6 1/4 in.. $50
Knife-modern, hollow handle, 9 in. $46
Knife-steak, individual, 9 1/2 in.. . . . . $56
Spoon-dessert/oval soup, 6 7/8 in. $60
Spoon-iced tea, 7 1/2 in.. . . . . $56
Spoon-sugar, 5 7/8 in.. . . . . $50
Spoon-teaspoon, 6 in.. . . . . $40
Tablespoon, (serving spoon), 8 1/2 in. $100
Tablespoon, (serving spoon), pierced,
   8 1/2 in.. . . . . $100

Tara by Reed & Barton, 1955

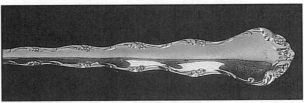

Butter spreader, hollow handle, modern,
   stainless paddle, 6 1/2 in.. . . . . $32
Butter spreader, hollow handle, stainless
   paddle, 6 1/4 in.. . . . . $32
Butter-master, hollow handle, 7 in. $40
Carving set, 2 pieces, small, stainless blade,
   steak $130
Fork, 7 1/2 in. $40
Fork-baby, 4 3/8 in.. $42
Fork-carving, small stainless prongs, steak,
   8 3/4 in.. . . . . $65
Fork-cold meat/serving, medium, solid,
   8 1/2 in.. . . . . $100
Fork-ice cream, pierced, 5 3/4 in. $50
Fork-pickle/olive, short handle, 5 7/8 in.. . . . . . $40
Fork-salad, individual, 6 1/2 in. $44
Fork-serving, stainless tines, 9 in.. . . . . $50
Fork-youth, 6 1/4 in.. $50
Knife-cheese, stainless blade, 7 3/8 in. $50
Knife-modern, hollow handle, 9 1/8 in.. . . . . . . $36
Knife-steak, individual, 9 in. $55
Knife-youth, 7 7/8 in. $40

Ladle-cream, solid, 5 1/2 in.. . . . .$55
Napkin clip, (made for teaspoons) $32
Salad set, 2 pieces, plastic bowl $100
Server-asparagus, hollow handle, silver
    plate hood, 9 3/8 in. $65
Server-lasagna, stainless blade, 10 1/4 in. $50
Server-pasta, stainless bowl, 10 3/4 in. $50
Server-pie and cake, stainless blade,
    10 1/2 in. $58
Spoon-bonbon, 4 3/4 in.. . . . .$50
Spoon-dessert/oval soup 6, 5/8 in. $54
Spoon-iced tea, 7 1/2 in. $54
Spoon-pierced/serving, stainless bowl,
    8 7/8 in.. . . . .$50
Spoon-serving, stainless bowl, 9 in.. . . . .$50
Spoon-soup, round bowl, cream, 6 in. $50
Spoon-sugar shell, 6 1/8 in.. . . . .$36
Spoon-teaspoon, 6 in.. . . . .$24
Tablespoon, (serving spoon), 8 1/2 in. $95

Tablespoon, (serving spoon), pierced,
    8 1/2 in. $110

Trajan by Reed & Barton, 1892

Butter-master, flat handle, 7 in. $50
Fork, 7 1/4 in. $60
Spoon-dessert/oval soup, 7 3/8 in. $70
Spoon-fruit, 5 3/4 in. $50
Spoon-soup, round bowl, gumbo,
    7 1/4 in.. . . . . $75
Spoon-teaspoon, 5 3/4 in.. . . . . $40
Tablespoon, (serving spoon), 8 3/8 in. $90

RICHARD DIMES CO.

The Richard Dimes Co. was founded in the first quarter of the 20th century (sources differ on the exact year) in South Boston, Massachusetts. In 1955, the firm was sold to King Silver Co., which in turn was taken over by Rogers, Lunt & Bowlen (later Lunt Silversmiths). Dimes' tools and dies were purchased by Manchester Silver Co. in the mid-1950s.

Debutante by Richard Dimes Co. 1918

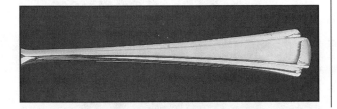

Butter spreader, flat handle,
5 7/8 in. $25
Butter spreader, hollow handle, stainless
paddle, 6 in. $26
Fork-cocktail, 6 1/4 in. $30
Fork-lemon, 5 in. $30
Fork-salad, individual, 6 1/2 in. $45
Knife-new french, hollow handle,
8 7/8 in. $35
Knife-new french, hollow handle,
9 3/8 in. $35
Ladle-cream, solid, 6 in. $45
Server-jelly, 7 in. $34
Spoon-demitasse, 4 3/8 in. $22
Spoon-soup, round bowl, bouillon,
5 1/2 in. $40
Spoon-soup, round bowl, cream,
6 in. $40
Spoon-sugar, 5 3/4 in. $40
Spoon-teaspoon, 5 7/8 in. $26
Tablespoon (serving spoon),
8 3/8 in. $80
Tongs-sugar, 4 in. $60

Richard Dimes

ROYAL CREST

Castle Rose by Royal Crest, 1942

Butter spreader, flat handle, 5 7/8 in.	$20
Butter-master, flat handle, 6 7/8 in.	$30
Carving set, 2 pieces, small, stainless blade, steak	$90
Fork, 7 1/4 in.	$30
Fork-cocktail, 5 3/8 in.	$23
Fork-cold meat/serving, medium, solid, 8 1/4 in.	$70
Fork-grille (viand), 7 5/8 in.	$17
Fork-lemon, 5 1/4 in.	$24
Fork-salad, individual, 6 3/8 in.	$22
Knife-grille, modern, hollow handle, 8 3/8 in.	$24
Knife-modern, hollow handle, 9 1/8 in.	$30
Ladle-gravy, solid, 6 1/4 in.	$70
Napkin clip, (made for teaspoons).	$20
Server-jelly, 6 1/4 in.	$30
Server-pie, stainless blade, 9 3/4 in.	$50
Spoon-casserole, smooth, solid, egg-shaped bowl, 8 1/2 in.	$70
Spoon-demitasse, 4 1/8 in.	$24
Spoon-dessert/oval soup 7.	$30
Spoon-ice cream, 6 in.	$30
Spoon-iced tea, 7 1/2 in.	$24
Spoon-soup, round bowl, cream, 6 1/4 in.	$20
Spoon-soup, round bowl, gumbo, 7 in.	$32
Spoon-sugar, 6 1/8 in.	$25
Spoon-teaspoon, 6 1/8 in.	$13
Tablespoon (serving spoon), 8 1/8 in.	$70

Promise by Royal Crest, 1948

Butter spreader, flat handle, 5 3/4 in.	$16
Fork, 7 1/8 in.	$25
Fork-cocktail, 5 3/8 in.	$22
Fork-grille (viand), 7 3/4 in.	$20
Fork-salad, individual, 6 3/8 in.	$25
Knife-grille, modern, hollow handle, 8 3/8 in.	$20
Knife-modern, hollow handle, 9 1/4 in.	$30
Spoon-demitasse, 4 1/8 in.	$17
Spoon-dessert/oval soup, 7 1/8 in.	$28
Spoon-iced tea, 7 1/2 in.	$28
Spoon-soup, round bowl, cream, 6 1/4 in.	$24
Spoon-sugar, 6 1/4 in.	$30
Spoon-teaspoon, 6 1/8 in.	$12

Wild Flower by Royal Crest, 1942

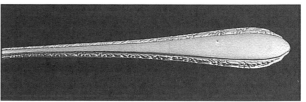

Butter spreader, flat handle, 5 7/8 in.	$12
Butter-master, flat handle, 6 7/8 in.	$30
Fork, 7 1/8 in.	$30
Fork-cocktail, 5 3/8 in.	$20
Fork-grille (viand), 7 5/8 in.	$14
Fork-salad, individual, 6 3/8 in.	$20
Knife-grille, modern, hollow handle, 8 3/8 in.	$22
Knife-modern, hollow handle, 9 1/4 in.	$26
Ladle-gravy, solid, 6 3/8 in.	$70
Napkin clip, (made for teaspoons).	$16
Spoon-casserole, smooth, solid, egg-shaped bowl, 8 1/2 in.	$80
Spoon-dessert/oval soup, 7 1/8 in.	$30
Spoon-iced tea, 7 1/2 in.	$24
Spoon-soup, round bowl, cream, 6 1/4 in.	$20
Spoon-sugar, 6 1/8 in.	$23
Spoon-teaspoon, 6 1/8 in.	$12
Tablespoon (serving spoon), tear-shaped bowl, 8 1/4 in.	$80

SCHOFIELD CO. INC.

Schofield Co. Inc. of Baltimore, Maryland began in 1903 as Baltimore Silversmiths Mfg. Co., and was known as Heer-Schofield Co. and Frank M. Schofield Co. until the late 1920s. The company purchased assets of Jenkins & Jenkins about 1915.

Baltimore Rose-Decor by Schofield Co., 1905

Image available but no priced examples.

Baltimore Rose-Plain, by Schofield Co., 1905

Butter-master, flat handle, 7 1/8 in. $50
Carving set, 2 pieces, small, stainless blade,
   steak. $180
Fork-cocktail, 5 1/2 in. $36
Fork-cold meat/serving, small, solid,
   7 5/8 in. $110
Fork-salad, individual, 6 1/4 in. $50
Ladle-cream, solid, 5 1/4 in. $60
Spoon-baby, straight handle, 4 in. $50
Spoon-dessert/oval soup, 7 1/8 in. $60
Spoon-olive, short, pierced bowl, 6 in. $100
Spoon-soup, round bowl, bouillon, 5 1/4 in. . . . $47
Spoon-soup, round bowl, cream, 6 in. $60
Spoon-teaspoon, 6 1/8 in. $26
Tablespoon (serving spoon), 8 1/2 in. $100

Sixty-one pieces Schofield Josephine (c. 1899): 8 luncheon knives, 8 luncheon forks, 8 salad forks, 10 teaspoons, 8 butter spreaders, 8 bouillon spoons, 8 citrus spoons, 1 sugar spoon, and 2 small carvers. Most monogram "W." A well-used set. $800

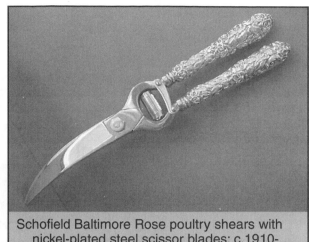

Schofield Baltimore Rose poultry shears with nickel-plated steel scissor blades; c.1910-1940. Monogram "PPP." 10 3/8 in. Some plated flecks off blades. $230

Forty pieces Schofield Elizabeth Tudor Hammered (c.1907): 10 each luncheon forks, luncheon knives, salad forks, and teaspoons. Monogram "CPA." $1,100

Lorraine by Schofield Co., 1896

Butter spreader, flat handle, 5 1/2 in.......... $40
Carving set, 2 pieces, small, stainless blade,
    steak................................ $210
Fork, 6 7/8 in............................ $90
Fork-salad, individual, 6 1/4 in. $100
Knife-new french, hollow handle, 8 5/8 in..... $80
Knife-new french, hollow handle, 9 in........ $80

Server-cheese, stainless blade, 6 7/8 in...... $75
Spoon-casserole, smooth bowl, solid,
    8 1/2 in. $180
Spoon-fruit, 6 in........................ $55
Spoon-iced tea, 8 in. $60
Spoon-soup, round bowl, cream, 6 1/4 in. $80
Spoon-soup, round bowl, gumbo, 6 7/8 in..... $90
Spoon-sugar shell, 6 1/8 in................ $70
Spoon-teaspoon, 6 1/8 in. $50

Thirty pieces Schofield Lorraine (1896): 6 each luncheon forks, luncheon knives, teaspoons, soup spoons, and salad forks. Monogram "DHW" except 4 teaspoons "K." $975

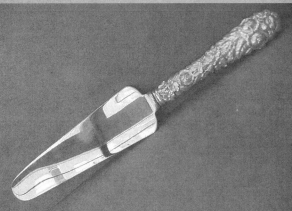

Schofield hand chased cake knife with new stainless steel blade; c.1905-1930. No monogram, 9 7/8 in., 1 5/8 in. across blade. $70

Schofield hand chased cake knife with new stainless steel blade; c.1905-1930. No monogram, 9 7/8 in., 2 1/8 in. across blade. $70

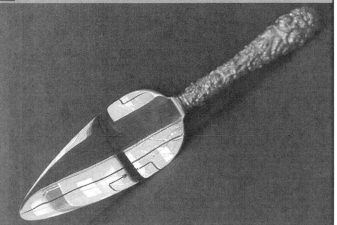

STATE HOUSE

Formality by State House, 1942

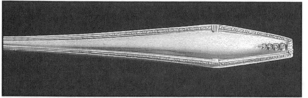

Butter spreader, flat handle, 5 7/8 in......... $16
Butter-master, flat handle, 7 in............. $20
Fork, 7 1/4 in.............................. $23
Fork-cocktail, 5 3/8 in.................... $22
Fork-cold meat/serving, medium, solid,
   8 1/8 in.............................. $70
Fork-grille (viand), 7 5/8 in. $14
Fork-salad, individual, 6 1/4 in. $24
Knife-grille, modern, hollow handle, 8 1/2 in... $25
Knife-modern, hollow handle, 9 1/4 in. $26
Knife-steak, individual, 9 in................ $40
Ladle-gravy, solid, 6 1/2 in. $60
Napkin clip, (made for teaspoons). $17
Spoon-casserole, smooth, solid, 8 1/2 in. $80
Spoon-dessert/oval soup, 7 in. $20
Spoon-iced tea, 7 1/2 in.................... $30
Spoon-soup, round bowl, cream, 6 1/4 in..... $20
Spoon-sugar, 6 in.......................... $23
Spoon-teaspoon, 6 1/8 in.................. $10

Inaugural by State House, 1942

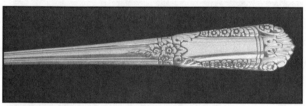

Butter spreader, flat handle, 5 3/4 in......... $20
Butter-master, flat handle, 7 in............. $16
Fork, 7 1/4 in.............................. $18
Fork-cocktail, 5 3/8 in.................... $22
Fork-cold meat/serving, medium, solid,
   8 1/4 in.............................. $70
Fork-grille (viand), 7 5/8 in. $15
Fork-lemon, 5 3/8 in. $24
Fork-salad, individual, 6 1/4 in. $24
Knife-grille, modern, hollow handle,
   8 3/8 in.............................. $20

Knife-modern, hollow handle, 9 1/4 in........ $26
Ladle-gravy, solid, 6 1/4 in................. $60
Napkin clip, (made for teaspoons).......... $18
Server-jelly, 6 1/4 in...................... $27
Spoon-casserole, smooth, solid, egg-shaped
   bowl, 8 1/2 in........................ $84
Spoon-dessert/oval soup, 7 in.............. $30
Spoon-iced tea, 7 1/2 in. $30
Spoon-soup, round bowl, cream, 6 1/4 in. $20
Spoon-sugar, 6 1/8 in. $17
Spoon-teaspoon, 6 in. $13

Stately by State House, 1948

Butter spreader, flat handle, 5 3/4 in........ $22
Butter-master, flat handle, 6 3/4 in. $14
Carving set, 3 pieces, small, stainless blade,
   steak................................ $160
Carving set, 2 pieces, small, stainless blade,
   steak................................ $110
Fork, 7 1/8 in............................. $22
Fork-carving, small stainless prongs, steak,
   8 3/4 in. $54
Fork-cocktail, 5 3/8 in. $24
Fork-cold meat/serving, medium, solid,
   8 1/8 in. $75
Fork-grille (viand), 7 5/8 in. $17
Fork-salad, individual, 6 3/8 in. $40
Knife-carving, small, stainless blade, steak,
   10 7/8 in. $54
Knife-grille, modern, hollow handle,
   8 3/8 in. $18
Knife-modern, hollow handle, 9 1/4 in........ $24
Knife-sharpener, steel, small, steak,
   10 3/4 in. $50
Ladle-gravy, solid, 6 1/4 in................. $60
Salad set, 2 pieces, wooden bowl........... $80
Spoon-casserole, smooth bowl, solid,
   8 1/2 in. $80
Spoon-dessert/oval soup, 7 1/8 in........... $33
Spoon-iced tea, 7 5/8 in. $28
Spoon-soup, round bowl, cream, 6 1/4 in. $26
Spoon-sugar, 6 1/8 in. $14
Spoon-teaspoon, 6 1/8 in. $16

Tiffany & Company

TIFFANY & COMPANY

Tiffany & Co. Inc. of New York began producing its own sterling flatware in the late 1800s, but as early as the 1850s had sold the wares of other makers that bore its name. The company introduced the English sterling silver standard (925/1000) in the United States in 1852, and this was later adopted as federal law to determine sterling silver purity.

Atlantis by Tiffany & Company, 1899

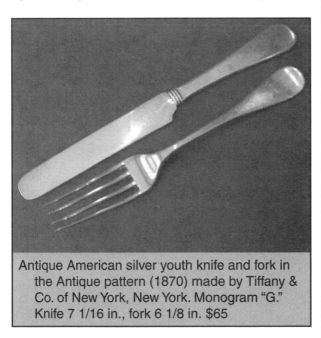

Fork, 6 7/8 in.. . . . . $160
Spoon-dessert/oval soup, 7 in. $200
Spoon-teaspoon, 5 7/8 in.. . . . . $100

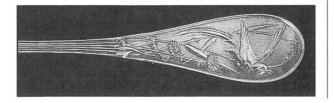

Antique American silver youth knife and fork in the Antique pattern (1870) made by Tiffany & Co. of New York, New York. Monogram "G." Knife 7 1/16 in., fork 6 1/8 in. $65

Audubon by Tiffany & Company, 1871

Bamboo by Tiffany & Company, 1961

Butter spreader, flat handle, 5 1/4 in. $64
Fork, 3 tine, 6 7/8 in. $90
Fork, 3 tine, 7 1/2 in. $130
Spoon-teaspoon, 5 3/4 in. $70

Beekman by Tiffany & Company, 1956

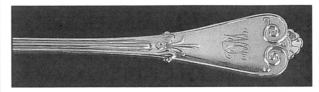

Spoon-place/oval soup, 7 in. $120

Broom Corn by Tiffany & Company, 1890

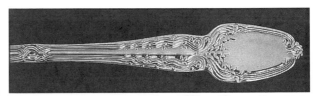

Spoon-teaspoon, 6 in. $60

Castilian by Tiffany & Company, 1929

Fork, 7 3/4 in.. . . . . $140
Fork-salad, individual, 6 5/8 in. $140
Spoon-fruit, 5 7/8 in.. . . . . $86
Spoon-sugar, 5 7/8 in. $95
Spoon-teaspoon, 5 7/8 in. $80
Tongs-sugar, 4 1/8 in.. . . . . $150

Century by Tiffany & Company, 1937

Butter spreader, flat handle, 6 1/8 in......... $50
Fork, 7 1/8 in............................. $90
Knife-blunt, hollow handle, 9 1/2 in......... $120
Knife-blunt, hollow handle, 9 1/8 in.......... $90
Spoon-soup, round bowl, cream, 6 3/4 in..... $90
Spoon-sugar, 5 3/4 in.................... $100
Tablespoon, (serving spoon), 8 5/8 in....... $200

Chrysanthemum by Tiffany & Company, 1880

Fork, 6 3/4 in............................ $140
Knife-blunt, hollow handle, 9 1/8 in........ $110

The following pieces have monograms:
Fork, 6 3/4 in........................... $130
Spoon-teaspoon, 5 3/4 in................ $80

Clinton by Tiffany & Company, 1912

Butter spreader, flat handle, 5 7/8 in........ $50
Butter-master, hollow handle, 7 in. $60
Fork, 7 1/2 in............................. $98
Fork, 7 in................................. $80
Fork-carving, large, stainless prongs, roast, 11 1/4
    in. $130
Fork-cocktail, 6 in. $60
Fork-cold meat/serving, medium, solid, 8 1/2 in...
    $160
Fork-salad, individual, 4 tines, 6 3/4 in....... $90
Knife-dessert, stainless blade, 7 3/4 in....... $60
Knife-fish, solid, individual, 8 1/8 in. $100
Knife-new french, hollow handle, 10 1/8 in.... $90
Spoon-demitasse, 4 3/8 in................ $40
Spoon-fruit, 5 7/8 in..................... $70
Spoon-place/oval soup, 7 1/8 in........... $90
Spoon-soup, round bowl, bouillon, 5 3/8 in.... $56
Spoon-soup, round bowl, gumbo, 7 1/2 in. ... $90
Spoon-sugar, 5 3/4 in.................... $70
Spoon-teaspoon, 5 7/8 in................ $44
Tablespoon, (serving spoon), 8 3/4 in....... $130

Colonial by Tiffany & Company, 1895

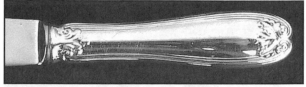

Butter-master, flat handle, 6 7/8 in. $100
Fork-pastry, 6 in. $90
Fork-salad, individual, 3 tine, 6 7/8 in. $100
Server-waffle, pierced, 8 7/8 in............ $500
Spoon-casserole, smooth bowl, solid,
    9 1/8 in. $190
Spoon-demitasse, 4 in. $50
Spoon-fruit, 5 5/8 in..................... $80
Spoon-fruit, gold wash, 5 5/8 in.......... $80
Spoon-soup, round bowl, gumbo,
    7 7/8 in............................. $120
Tongs-sugar, 4 1/4 in.................... $160

English King by Tiffany & Company, 1870

Fork, 7 in................................ $38
Fork-cocktail, 6 in. $32
Knife-fish, solid, individual, 7 7/8 in......... $50
Pick-nut, 4 7/8 in....................... $42
Spoon-place/oval soup, 7 1/8 in. $34
Tablespoon, (serving spoon),
    8 5/8 in. $45

English King by Tiffany & Company, 1885

Fork, 6 7/8 in........................... $120
Fork, 7 5/8 in........................... $150
Fork-cocktail, 6 in. $80
Fork-salad, individual, 2 of 4 tines beveled,
    6 3/4 in. $120
Knife-new french, hollow handle,
    10 1/4 in. $140
Knife-new french, hollow handle, 9 in. $120
Spoon-demitasse, 2 3/4 in. handle,
    4 in. $70
Spoon-iced tea, 7 1/2 in. $100
Spoon-soup, round bowl, bouillon,
    5 1/4 in. $100

Faneuil by Tiffany & Company, 1910

Butter spreader, flat handle, 5 7/8 in......... $45
Butter spreader, hollow handle, stainless
    paddle, 6 1/8 in...................... $60
Butter-master, hollow handle, 7 in. $100
Carving set, 2 pieces, large, stainless blade,
    roast $360
Carving set, 2 pieces, small, stainless blade,
    steak $340
Fork, 7 1/8 in.......................... $65
Fork, 7 5/8 in.......................... $110
Fork-cocktail, 3 tines, 6 in................ $48
Fork-cold meat/serving, large, solid,
    9 in.................................. $180
Fork-fish, solid, individual, 3 tines,
    6 3/4 in.............................. $95
Fork-ice cream, gold wash, 5 1/4 in. $80
Fork-salad, individual, 4 tines, 6 7/8 in....... $90
Fork-serving, solid, 8 3/4 in. $180
Knife-bar, hollow handle, 8 1/4 in. $60
Knife-blunt, hollow handle, 10 1/4 in........ $100
Knife-blunt, hollow handle, 9 3/8 in......... $70
Knife-carving, small stainless blade, steak,
    10 3/4 in............................. $170
Knife-cheese, stainless blade, 7 1/4 in....... $70
Knife-fish, solid, individual, 8 in. $140
Knife-fish, stainless blade, individual,
    8 1/8 in.............................. $100
Knife-new french, hollow handle,
    10 1/4 in............................. $100
Knife-new french, hollow handle, 9 1/4 in..... $75
Knife-orange, silver plate blade, 7 3/8 in...... $70
Knife-steak, individual, 9 in............... $100
Knife-youth, blunt blade, 7 3/4 in. $70
Ladle-cream, solid, 1 7/8 in. bowl,
    6 7/8 in.............................. $100
Ladle-gravy, solid, 2 3/8 in. bowl,
    7 1/4 in.............................. $175
Ladle-gravy, solid, 6 7/8 in. $175
Server-pie and cake, stainless blade,
    10 5/8 in............................. $100
Spoon-casserole, smooth, solid, 7 7/8 in. $220
Spoon-demitasse, 4 3/8 in. $38
Spoon-dessert/oval soup, gold wash,
    6 1/8 in.............................. $100
Spoon-fruit, blunt bowl, 5 7/8 in. $65

Spoon-fruit, point bowl, 5 7/8 in............ $65
Spoon-ice cream, 5 7/8 in................. $80
Spoon-ice cream, gold wash, 5 7/8 in........ $80
Spoon-iced tea, 7 5/8 in. $65
Spoon-infant feeding, 6 1/8 in.............. $65
Spoon-place/oval soup, 7 1/4 in. $90
Spoon-preserve, 7 1/4 in.................. $160
Spoon-salad serving, solid, 10 in. $250
Spoon-soup, round bowl, bouillon,
    5 1/2 in.............................. $45
Spoon-soup, round bowl, cream,
    6 3/4 in.............................. $100
Spoon-soup, round bowl, gumbo,
    7 1/2 in.............................. $100
Spoon-sugar, 4 1/4 in. handle, 6 in. $75
Spoon-sugar, 4 in. handle, 5 3/4 in. $75
Spoon-teaspoon, (five o'clock), 5 3/8 in. $44
Spoon-teaspoon, tear-shaped bowl, 6 in. $48
Spoon-vegetable, serving, solid, oval
    bowl, 9 5/8 in......................... $180
Tablespoon, (serving spoon), 8 3/4 in....... $130
Tongs-sugar, bowl tip, 4 in................ $130

Feather Edge by Tiffany & Company, 1901

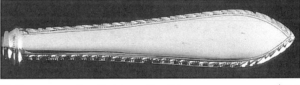

Butter spreader, flat handle, 6 in........... $60
Butter spreader, hollow handle, stainless
    paddle, 6 1/8 in...................... $80
Fork, 7 5/8 in.......................... $130
Fork-cold meat/serving, medium, solid,
    8 5/8 in.............................. $200
Fork-salad, individual, 6 3/4 in. $100
Knife-new french, hollow handle,
    10 1/4 in............................. $120
Spoon-teaspoon, 6 in. $70

Flemish by Tiffany & Company, 1911

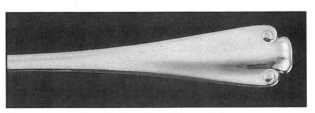

Butter spreader, hollow handle, stainless
    paddle, 6 1/8 in...................... $74

Carving set, 2 pieces, small, stainless blade,
　　steak $380
Fork, 7 in. $95
Fork-cocktail, 6 1/8 in. $64
Fork-cold meat/serving, medium, solid, flared
　　tines, 8 7/8 in. $180
Fork-fish, solid, individual, 4 tines, not
　　beveled, 7 1/8 in. $120
Fork-serving, solid, 8 5/8 in. $180
Knife-blunt, hollow handle, 9 1/4 in. $95
Knife-new french, hollow handle,
　　9 1/4 in. $95
Ladle-cream, solid, 7 in. $130
Ladle-gravy, solid, 7 5/8 in. $200
Spoon-demitasse, 4 5/8 in. $50
Spoon-demitasse, 4 in. $50
Spoon-fruit, 5 7/8 in. $80
Spoon-place/oval soup, 7 in. $110
Spoon-soup, round bowl, gumbo,
　　7 1/2 in. $120
Spoon-sugar, 5 3/4 in. $110
Spoon-sugar, gold wash, 5 3/4 in. $110
Spoon-teaspoon, 6 in. $60
Spoon-vegetable/serving, solid,
　　9 5/8 in. $300
Tablespoon, (serving spoon),
　　8 1/2 in. $160
Tongs-sugar, 4 1/8 in. $160

Hamilton by Tiffany & Company, 1938

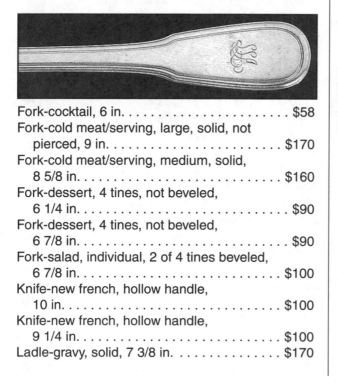

Fork-cocktail, 6 in. $58
Fork-cold meat/serving, large, solid, not
　　pierced, 9 in. $170
Fork-cold meat/serving, medium, solid,
　　8 5/8 in. $160
Fork-dessert, 4 tines, not beveled,
　　6 1/4 in. $90
Fork-dessert, 4 tines, not beveled,
　　6 7/8 in. $90
Fork-salad, individual, 2 of 4 tines beveled,
　　6 7/8 in. $100
Knife-new french, hollow handle,
　　10 in. $100
Knife-new french, hollow handle,
　　9 1/4 in. $100
Ladle-gravy, solid, 7 3/8 in. $170

Spoon-vegetable/serving, solid,
　　9 in. $200
Tablespoon, (serving spoon),
　　8 5/8 in. $140

Hampton by Tiffany & Company, 1934

Butter spreader, hollow handle, stainless
　　paddle, 6 1/8 in. $80
Fork-salad, individual, 6 7/8 in. $110
Knife-blunt, hollow handle, 9 1/4 in. $110

Japanese by Tiffany & Company, 1871

Spoon-cracker, gold wash, 9 1/2 in. $2,000

King William/Antique by Tiffany & Company, 1870

Butter spreader, hollow handle, stainless
　　paddle, 6 in. $60
Fork-cold meat/serving, medium, solid,
　　8 3/4 in. $150
Knife-new french, pistol, 10 in. $100
Knife-new french, pistol, 8 3/4 in. $80
Ladle-cream, solid, 5 3/4 in. $100
Spoon-demitasse, 4 1/8 in. $44
Spoon-teaspoon, (five o'clock),
　　4 3/4 in. $55
Spoon-teaspoon, 6 1/8 in. $60
Tablespoon, (serving spoon),
　　8 3/8 in. $140

Marquise by Tiffany & Company, 1902

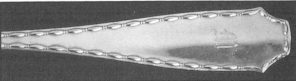

Butter spreader, flat handle, 5 7/8 in.. . . . . $50
Fork, 6 7/8 in.. . . . . $90
Fork-cocktail, 6 in. $55
Fork-youth, 6 1/8 in.. . . . . $80
Knife-blunt, hollow handle, 9 1/4 in.. . . . . . . $80
Knife-steak, individual, 9 in.. . . . . $90
Spoon-demitasse, 4 in. $36
Spoon-fruit, 5 3/4 in.. . . . . $60
Spoon-place/oval soup, 7 1/8 in. $100
Spoon-soup, round bowl, bouillon,
    5 in.. . . . . $70
Spoon-soup, round bowl, gumbo,
    8 in.. . . . . $110
Spoon-teaspoon, 5 7/8 in.. . . . . $45
Tablespoon, (serving spoon),
    8 1/2 in.. . . . . $130

Palm by Tiffany & Company, 1871

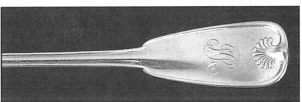

Fork, 8 in.. . . . . $100
Spoon-demitasse, 4 7/8 in.. . . . . $60
Spoon-place/oval soup, 7 1/4 in.. . . . . $110
Spoon-teaspoon, 6 1/8 in.. . . . . $65
Tablespoon, (serving spoon),
    8 1/2 in.. . . . . $130

Palmette by Tiffany & Company, 1947

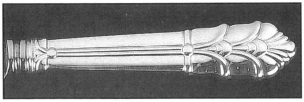

Butter spreader, flat handle, 6 1/8 in.. . . . . . . $70
Fork, 7 3/8 in.. . . . . $100

Fork-serving, solid, 8 3/4 in.. . . . . $210
Knife-blunt, hollow handle,
    9 1/4 in. $100
Knife-new french, hollow handle,
    8 3/4 in. $100
Spoon-sugar, 6 in. $100
Spoon-teaspoon, 6 1/8 in. $80
Tablespoon, (serving spoon),
    8 5/8 in. $180

Persian by Tiffany & Company, 1872

FORK & BUTTER Knife

Image available but no priced examples.

Provence by Tiffany & Company, 1961

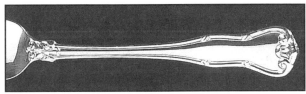

Butter spreader, flat handle, 6 in.. . . . . $60
Butter spreader, hollow handle, stainless
    paddle, 6 in.. . . . . $70
Fork, 6 7/8 in.. . . . . $96
Fork-cocktail, 6 in. $60
Fork-salad, individual, 6 5/8 in. $100
Knife-new french, hollow handle,
    10 3/8 in. $110
Knife-new french, hollow handle,
    9 in. $90
Server-pie and cake, stainless blade,
    11 in. $120
Spoon-demitasse, 4 1/8 in. $50
Spoon-place/oval soup, 7 1/8 in. $110
Spoon-soup, round bowl, bouillon,
    5 1/2 in. $95
Spoon-soup, round bowl, gumbo,
    7 in. $120
Spoon-sugar, 5 7/8 in. $100
Spoon-teaspoon, 6 in. $70
Tablespoon, (serving spoon),
    8 3/4 in. $170
Tablespoon, (serving spoon), pierced,
    8 3/4 in. $220

Queen Anne by Tiffany & Company, 1870

Butter spreader, flat handle,
  5 7/8 in. $60
Fork, 7 1/8 in. $80
Fork, 7 7/8 in. $100
Fork-cocktail, 6 in. $57
Fork-fish, solid, individual, 4 tines, not
  beveled, 6 7/8 in. $100
Fork-serving, solid, 8 5/8 in. $150
Knife-blunt, hollow handle, marked "New
  York," 9 3/8 in. $80
Scoop-cheese, solid, 7 3/8 in. $90
Spoon-demitasse, 4 1/4 in. $50
Spoon-place/oval soup,
  7 1/4 in. $100
Spoon-preserve, 7 1/4 in. $60
Spoon-sugar, 5 7/8 in. $80
Spoon-teaspoon, oval bowl, 6 in. $50
Tablespoon, (serving spoon), oval bowl,
  8 5/8 in. $140

Rat Tail by Tiffany & Company, 1958

Renaissance by Tiffany & Company, 1905

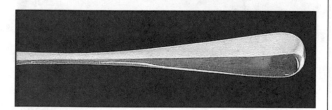

Spoon-teaspoon, 5 3/4 in. $130
Tablespoon, (serving spoon),
  8 1/2 in. $400

Richelieu by Tiffany & Company, 1892

Fork, 6 7/8 in. $90
Fork, 7 1/2 in. $140
Fork-cocktail, 5 7/8 in. $90
Ladle-gravy, solid, 7 5/8 in. $250
Spoon-fruit, 5 3/4 in. $80
Spoon-place/oval soup, 7 in. $130
Spoon-teaspoon, 6 in. $65

Salem by Tiffany & Company, 1956

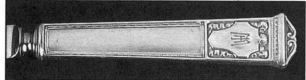

Butter spreader, flat handle, 5 3/4 in. $56
Fork, 6 7/8 in. $80
Fork-cocktail, 5 7/8 in. $60
Knife-new french, hollow handle,
  8 1/2 in. $80
Knife-youth 7 1/2 in. $66
Spoon-sugar, 5 5/8 in. $90

San Lorenzo by Tiffany & Company, 1916

2 Fish FORKS

Butter spreader, hollow handle, stainless paddle,
  6 in. $75
Fork, 4 straight tines, 7 in. $100
Fork-cocktail, 6 in. $65
Fork-salad, individual, 6 1/8 in. $100
Spoon-fruit, 5 3/4 in. $80
Spoon-iced tea, 7 1/2 in. $85
Spoon-place/oval soup, 7 1/8 in. $110
Spoon-soup, round bowl, bouillon,
  5 3/8 in. $80
Spoon-soup, round bowl, cream,
  6 3/4 in. $110

Spoon-soup, round bowl, gumbo,
7 1/4 in. $120
Spoon-teaspoon, 6 in. $70
Tablespoon, (serving spoon),
8 3/8 in. $170

Saratoga by Tiffany & Company, 1870

Fork, 8 in. $140
Spoon-place/oval soup,
7 1/8 in. $120
Spoon-teaspoon, 6 in. $60
Tablespoon, (serving spoon),
8 5/8 in. $160

Shell & Thread by Tiffany & Company, 1905

Butter-master, hollow handle,
6 7/8 in. $120
Fork, 6 3/4 in. $90
Fork, 7 1/2 in. $140
Fork-fish, solid, individual, 4 tines, not
beveled, 7 in. $120
Knife-fish, stainless blade, individual,
7 7/8 in. $120
Knife-new french, hollow handle,
10 1/8 in. $120
Knife-new french, hollow handle,
9 1/8 in. $100
Knife-steak, individual, 8 3/4 in. $130
Knife-youth, 7 1/2 in. $90
Spoon-demitasse, 4 1/8 in. $60
Spoon-iced tea, 7 1/2 in. $90
Spoon-place/oval soup, 7 1/8 in. $110
Spoon-soup, round bowl, bouillon,
5 1/4 in. $100
Tablespoon, (serving spoon),
8 5/8 in. $180

St. Dunstan by Tiffany & Company, 1909

Fork, 7 3/4 in. $100
Fork, 7 in. $90
Fork-ice cream, gold wash,
5 5/8 in. $90
Knife-blunt, hollow handle, 10 1/8 in. $100
Knife-blunt, hollow handle,
9 1/8 in. $90
Knife-fish, stainless blade, individual,
Sheffield plate blade, 8 1/8 in. $90
Knife-orange, silver plate blade,
7 1/4 in. $90
Spoon-fruit, point bowl, 5 5/8 in. $60
Spoon-soup, round bowl, bouillon,
5 3/8 in. $70
Spoon-soup, round bowl, gumbo,
7 1/4 in. $100
Spoon-teaspoon, 5 7/8 in. $60

St. James by Tiffany & Company, 1898

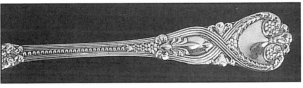

Spoon-soup, round bowl, bouillon,
5 1/2 in. $120
Tablespoon, (serving spoon),
8 1/2 in. $230

Tiffany by Tiffany & Company, 1869

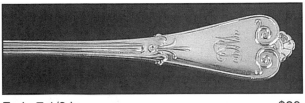

Fork, 7 1/8 in. $80
Tablespoon, (serving spoon),
8 5/8 in. $100
Tablespoon, (serving spoon), pierced,
8 1/2 in. $130

Vine/Fruits & Flowers by Tiffany & Company, 1892

(multiple motifs)

The following pieces have monograms:
Fork-cold meat/serving, medium, solid,
8 7/8 in. $540
Spoon-preserve, 8 3/4 in. $450

Wave Edge by Tiffany & Company, 1884

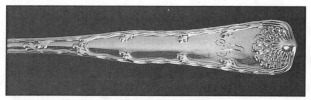

The following pieces have monograms:
Fork, 7 1/4 in. $90
Fork, 8 in. $130
Spoon-soup, round bowl, gumbo, 8 in. $110
Spoon-teaspoon, 6 1/8 in. $70
Tablespoon, (serving spoon), 8 5/8 in. $150

Windham by Tiffany & Company, 1923

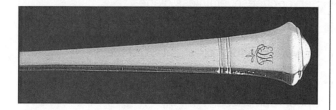

Butter spreader, flat handle, 6 in. $60
Fork, 7 in. $100
Fork-cold meat/serving, large, solid,
9 3/8 in. $200
Knife-new french, hollow handle,
10 in. $110
Knife-new french, hollow handle,
9 1/4 in. $90
Spoon-place/oval soup, 7 in. $100
Spoon-sugar, 5 7/8 in. $100
Tablespoon, (serving spoon),
8 5/8 in. $160

Winthrop by Tiffany & Company, 1909

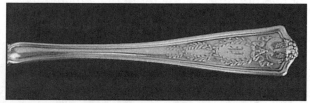

Butter-master, flat handle, 7 1/8 in. $100
Fork, 4 tines, not beveled,
6 3/4 in. $90
Fork, 7 1/2 in. $130
Fork-youth, 6 1/8 in. $80
Ladle-sauce, solid, 7 1/8 in. $240
Spoon-casserole, smooth, solid, gold
wash, 9 1/4 in. $300
Spoon-demitasse, 4 1/8 in. $50
Spoon-place/oval soup, 7 in. $120
Spoon-salt/master, gold wash,
3 5/8 in. $50
Spoon-teaspoon, 5 5/8 in. $60
Tablespoon, (serving spoon),
8 5/8 in. $150
Tongs-ice/serving, large,
7 1/8 in. $500
Tongs-sugar, 4 1/4 in. $150

Towle Silversmiths

TOWLE SILVERSMITHS

Towle Silversmiths of Newburyport, Massachusetts began in 1857 as Towle & Jones, but the company's heritage goes back to the 17th century. In 1679, William Mouton II left Hampton, New Hampshire and settled at Newbury (later Newburyport) where he became a trader and may have done some silversmithing

His son, Joseph, is generally recognized as the first silversmith of the Moulton line, which is said to have the longest continuous span of silversmithing of any American family. From father to son, this family produced silversmiths for two hundred years, more of its members entering the silver industry than from any other family in early American history. Even one woman in the Moulton clan—Lydia, daughter of William III—did some silversmithing. Although most of the Moultons carried on their craft in Newburyport, some went to other communities where they established themselves as silversmiths

The third William moved in a covered wagon to Marietta, Ohio, carrying his silversmith's tools with him. His son, Joseph, had four sons, all of whom were silversmiths. Ebenezer moved to Boston and Enoch to Portland, Maine, each of them continuing their crafts in their respective places. Abel inherited his father's business in Newburyport and the fourth William established his own shop in the same place

By this time, Anthony F. Towle went from Hampton to Newburyport where he became apprenticed to the fourth William Moulton. Anthony was a descendent of Philip Towle and the son of Jabez, who had purchased the General Moulton house in Hampton. Later Anthony joined with William P. Jones to establish a silversmith partnership. These two subsequently purchased the fourth Joseph Moulton's business and formed the firm of Towle and Jones in 1857

From this enterprise developed the silversmith establishment today known as The Towle Silversmiths. The company mark of a lion mounted on a script letter "T" was supposedly based on the family coat of arms.

Aristocrat by Towle, 1934

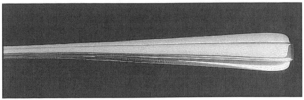

Butter spreader, flat handle, 5 7/8 in.	$22
Butter spreader, hollow handle, stainless paddle, 5 5/8 in.	$25
Butter-master, flat handle, 6 7/8 in.	$30
Butter-master, hollow handle, 6 5/8 in.	$30
Carving set, 2 pieces, small, stainless blade, steak	$70
Fork, 7 3/8 in.	$28
Fork, 7 7/8 in.	$45
Fork-carving, small stainless prongs, steak, 9 1/4 in.	$36
Fork-cocktail, 5 3/4 in.	$22
Fork-cold meat/serving, small, solid, 7 7/8 in.	$75
Fork-lemon, 5 1/2 in.	$30
Fork-salad, individual, 6 1/2 in.	$30
Knife-fruit, stainless blade, individual, 6 5/8 in.	$30
Knife-modern, hollow handle, 8 1/2 in.	$28
Knife-new french, hollow handle, 8 3/4 in.	$28
Ladle-gravy, solid, 6 5/8 in.	$80
Server-cheese, stainless blade, 6 1/8 in.	$34
Server-jelly, 6 5/8 in.	$36
Server-pie and cake, stainless blade, 10 5/8 in.	$40
Server-pie, stainless blade, 9 3/4 in.	$40
Spoon-demitasse, 4 1/4 in.	$17
Spoon-dessert/oval soup, 6 7/8 in.	$30
Spoon-iced tea, 8 1/8 in.	$26
Spoon-salad serving, solid, 9 1/8 in.	$100
Spoon-soup, round bowl, bouillon, 5 in.	$30
Spoon-soup, round bowl, gumbo, 7 in.	$44
Spoon-sugar, 5 3/4 in.	$28
Spoon-teaspoon (five o'clock), 5 3/4 in.	$19
Spoon-teaspoon, 6 in.	$15
Tablespoon, (serving spoon), 8 1/2 in.	$55
Tablespoon, (serving spoon), pierced, 8 1/2 in.	$80

Awakening by Towle, 1958

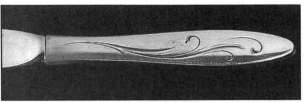

Butter spreader, hollow handle, modern, stainless
  paddle, 6 1/2 in.............................$22
Butter-master, hollow handle, 6 3/4 in.........$30
Carving set, 2 pieces, small, stainless blade,
  steak $80
Fork, 7 5/8 in.................................$40
Fork-carving, small stainless prongs, steak,
  9 3/8 in.....................................$40
Fork-cold meat/serving, large, solid,
  9 1/4 in.....................................$94
Fork-salad, individual, 6 5/8 in...............$40
Knife-carving, small stainless blade, steak,
  10 5/8 in....................................$40
Knife-fish, stainless blade, individual,
  8 1/2 in.....................................$35
Knife-modern, hollow handle, 8 7/8 in.........$30
Knife-steak, individual, 8 3/4 in. $35
Knife-utility/serving, stainless blade,
  11 1/4 in....................................$40
Ladle-cream, solid, 5 3/8 in..................$38
Ladle-gravy, solid, 6 3/4 in. $84
Server-pie and cake, stainless blade,
  10 3/4 in. $46
Slicer-cake, stainless blade, wedding,
  12 5/8 in. $40
Spoon-bonbon, 5 3/8 in........................$35
Spoon-dessert/oval soup, 6 5/8 in............$40
Spoon-fruit, 5 7/8 in.........................$34
Spoon-iced tea, 8 in..........................$28
Spoon-rice, stainless bowl, 9 7/8 in..........$45
Spoon-sugar, 5 1/2 in.........................$30
Spoon-teaspoon, 6 in..........................$20
Tablespoon, (serving spoon), 8 1/2 in.........$70
Tablespoon, (serving spoon), pierced,
  8 1/2 in.....................................$70

Benjamin Franklin by Towle, 1904

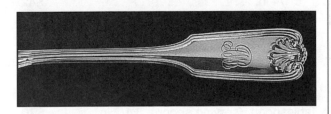

Butter spreader, flat handle, 6 in.............$30
Butter-master, hollow handle, 6 1/2 in. $40
Carving set, 2 pieces, small, stainless blade,
  steak $80
Cleaver-cheese, stainless blade, 6 5/8 in. $40
Fork, 7 1/8 in.................................$40
Fork, 7 3/4 in.................................$60
Fork-carving, small stainless prongs, steak,
  9 in...$40
Fork-cocktail, 6 1/8 in.......................$28
Fork-cold meat/serving, large, stainless
  tines, 9 1/4 in..............................$40
Fork-cold meat/serving, small, solid,
  7 7/8 in.....................................$90
Fork-fish, stainless tines, hollow handle,
  individual, 7 5/8 in.........................$40
Fork-ice cream, 5 1/2 in......................$40
Fork-lemon, 5 3/8 in..........................$30
Fork-pickle/olive, short handle, 6 1/4 in......$30
Fork-salad serving, stainless prongs,
  11 in..$40
Fork-salad, individual, 6 3/8 in. $45
Fork-strawberry, 5 1/2 in.....................$24
Fork-utility/serving, stainless tines,
  9 1/4 in.....................................$40
Fork-youth, 6 1/4 in..........................$40
Knife-bar, hollow handle, 8 5/8 in. $40
Knife-carving, small stainless blade, steak,
  10 in..$40
Knife-cheese, stainless blade, 7 in...........$45
Knife-fruit, stainless blade, individual,
  6 1/4 in.....................................$40
Knife-new french, hollow handle, 9 in. $35
Knife-steak, individual, 8 1/4 in.............$45
Knife-utility/serving, stainless blade,
  10 5/8 in....................................$40
Ladle-gravy, hollow handle, stainless bowl,
  7 1/2 in.....................................$40
Ladle-punch, stainless bowl, 12 1/4 in........$55
Ladle-soup, stainless bowl, 10 1/2 in.........$55
Opener-bottle, stainless bowl, 5 in...........$45
Scoop-ice cream, stainless bowl,
  7 7/8 in.....................................$40
Scoop-ice, silver plate bowl, 8 5/8 in. $50
Server-asparagus, hollow handle, silver
  plate hood, 9 1/4 in.........................$60
Server-cranberry, stainless bowl, 8 3/8 in.....$45
Server-lasagna, stainless blade, 9 1/4 in. $40
Server-pasta, stainless bowl, 10 1/4 in. $40
Server-pie and cake, stainless blade,
  10 3/8 in....................................$40
Server-pie and cake, stainless blade,
  10 in..$40
Spoon-bonbon, 5 1/8 in........................$44

Towle Silversmiths

Spoon-casserole, pierced, stainless bowl,
9 1/4 in.................................$45
Spoon-casserole, shell, stainless bowl,
9 7/8 in.................................$40
Spoon-dessert/oval soup, 7 in. $44
Spoon-dressing, stainless bowl, 10 1/2 in. $45
Spoon-iced tea, 8 1/8 in. $32
Spoon-mustard, 5 in.......................$45
Spoon-rice, stainless bowl, 9 1/2 in..........$45
Spoon-salad serving, stainless bowl,
10 3/4 in. $40
Spoon-salt, individual, 2 3/8 in..............$12
Spoon-teaspoon, 6 in......................$28

Candlelight by Towle, 1934

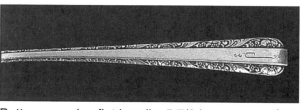

Butter spreader, flat handle, 5 7/8 in.........$18
Butter spreader/youth knife, 6 1/4 in.........$30
Butter spreader, hollow handle, stainless
paddle, 5 5/8 in........................$28
Butter-master, flat handle, 6 3/4 in..........$30
Butter-master, hollow handle, 6 5/8 in........$32
Carving set, 2 pieces, small, stainless blade,
steak...................................$80
Cheese grater, 8 3/8 in. $50
Cleaver-cheese, stainless blade, 6 3/8 in......$45
Fork, 7 1/4 in.............................$25
Fork-baby, 4 1/4 in. $30
Fork-carving, small stainless prongs, steak,
9 1/8 in.................................$40
Fork-cocktail, 5 3/4 in......................$24
Fork-cold meal/serving, small, solid,
7 7/8 in.................................$80
Fork-ice cream, 5 5/8 in....................$44
Fork-lemon, 5 3/8 in.......................$27
Fork-pickle/olive, short handle, 2 tines,
5 7/8 in.................................$30
Fork-salad server, plastic prongs,
11 5/8 in. $45
Fork-salad serving, stainless prongs,
11 in....................................$45
Fork-salad, individual, 6 3/8 in. $35
Fork-strawberry, 5 1/2 in. $30
Fork-youth, 6 in...........................$40
Knife-bar, hollow handle, 8 1/2 in............$40
Knife-carving, small, stainless blade,
steak, 9 3/4 in..........................$40

Knife-cheese, stainless blade, 6 7/8 in. $40
Knife-fish, stainless blade, individual,
7 3/4 in.................................$45
Knife-fruit, stainless blade, individual,
6 1/2 in.................................$44
Knife-modern, hollow handle, 8 1/2 in........$30
Knife-modern, hollow handle, 9 1/2 in........$44
Knife-new french, hollow handle, 9 1/2 in.....$44
Knife-new french, hollow handle, silver plate
blade, 8 1/2 in..........................$30
Knife-new french, hollow handle, stainless
blade, 8 3/4 in..........................$30
Knife-new french, hollow handle, stainless
blade, 9 1/4 in..........................$30
Knife-utility/serving, stainless blade, 11 in. ...$40
Ladle-cream, solid, 5 1/2 in.................$40
Ladle-gravy, solid, 6 3/4 in.................$75
Ladle-punch, stainless bowl, 12 3/4 in........$55
Ladle-soup, stainless bowl, 10 1/2 in.........$60
Opener-bottle, stainless bowl, 5 3/4 in.......$40
Pick-butter, 1 tine, 5 1/4 in.................$30
Scoop-ice cream, stainless bowl, 8 in. $40
Scoop-ice, silver plate bowl, 8 1/8 in. $50
Server-asparagus, hollow handle, silver plate
hood, 9 1/4 in. $53
Server-cranberry, stainless bowl, 8 3/8 in.....$40
Server-jelly, 6 1/2 in. $26
Server-lasagna, stainless blade, 9 5/8 in. $40
Server-pasta, stainless bowl, 10 1/4 in.......$45
Server-pastry, stainless bowl, 9 1/2 in........$45
Server-pie, stainless blade, 9 7/8 in..........$45
Spoon-baby, straight handle, 4 3/8 in........$30
Spoon-bonbon, 4 7/8 in. $40
Spoon-bonbon, 5 1/2 in. $40
Spoon-casserole, shell, stainless bowl,
9 7/8 in.................................$40
Spoon-casserole, smooth bowl, solid,
8 1/8 in................................$120
Spoon-demitasse, 4 1/4 in..................$22
Spoon-dessert/oval soup, 6 7/8 in. $46
Spoon-dressing, stainless bowl, 10 7/8 in.....$40
Spoon-fruit, no-rim bowl, 5 7/8 in............$36
Spoon-iced tea, 8 1/8 in....................$32
Spoon-salad serving, stainless bowl,
11 in....................................$40
Spoon-soup, round bowl, cream,
6 1/4 in.................................$42
Spoon-sugar, 5 7/8 in......................$23
Spoon-teaspoon (five o'clock), 3 7/8 in.
handle, 5 5/8 in.........................$15
Spoon-teaspoon, 6 in......................$15
Spoon-utility/serving, stainless bowl,
9 5/8 in.................................$45
Tablespoon, (serving spoon), 8 1/2 in. $70

Canterbury by Towle, 1893

Fork, 7 in. $34
Fork-chipped beef, small, 6 1/2 in. $70
Fork-cold meat/serving, small, solid,
   7 1/4 in. $100
Fork-youth, 6 in. $50
Ladle-cream, solid, 5 3/4 in. $50
Ladle-gravy, solid, 6 5/8 in. $100
Ladle-gravy, solid, gold wash, 6 5/8 in. $100
Ladle-soup, solid, 10 1/2 in. $400
Spoon-demitasse, 3 7/8 in. $20
Spoon-demitasse, gold wash, 3 7/8 in. $20
Spoon-dessert/oval soup, 7 in. $50
Spoon-jelly, large, gold wash, 6 3/8 in. $60
Spoon-olive, long handle, gold wash,
   8 1/2 in. $140
Spoon-preserve, gold wash, 7 3/4 in. $120
Spoon-preserve, shell bowl, 8 in. $120
Spoon-salad serving, solid, 8 3/4 in. $150
Spoon-soup, round bowl, gumbo,
   6 7/8 in. $50
Spoon-teaspoon (five o'clock), 5 1/2 in. $15
Spoon-teaspoon, 5 3/4 in. $22
Tablespoon, (serving spoon), 8 1/8 in. $80
Tablespoon, (serving spoon), pierced,
   8 1/8 in. $100

Cascade by Towle, 1933

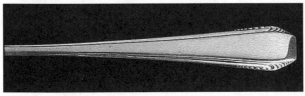

Butter spreader, flat handle, 5 7/8 in. $12
Butter-master, flat handle, 6 7/8 in. $30
Fork, 7 3/8 in. $18
Fork, 7 7/8 in. $30
Fork-cocktail, 5 3/4 in. $18
Fork-lemon, 5 1/2 in. $22
Fork-salad, individual, 6 3/8 in. $24
Server-cheese, stainless blade, 6 1/8 in. $40
Server-jelly, 6 3/4 in. $30
Server-pie and cake, stainless blade,
   10 3/4 in. $50

Spoon-bonbon, 4 7/8 in. $34
Spoon-demitasse, 4 1/4 in. $12
Spoon-dessert/oval soup, 6 7/8 in. $40
Spoon-fruit, 6 in. $26
Spoon-iced tea, 8 1/8 in. $30
Spoon-soup, round bowl, cream, 6 1/2 in. $28
Spoon-soup, round bowl, gumbo, 7 in. $36
Spoon-sugar, 5 7/8 in. $20
Spoon-teaspoon (five o'clock), 5 5/8 in. $12
Spoon-teaspoon, 6 in. $12
Tablespoon, (serving spoon), 8 1/2 in. $50
Tongs-sugar, 3 7/8 in. $48

Charlemagne by Towle, 1963

Butter spreader, hollow handle, modern, stainless
   paddle, 6 5/8 in. $45
Butter-master, hollow handle, 7 in. $40
Fork, 7 3/8 in. $34
Fork-cocktail, 5 1/2 in. $46
Fork-cold meat/serving, large, solid,
   9 1/8 in. $95
Fork-salad, individual, 6 3/4 in. $50
Knife-modern, hollow handle, 10 1/4 in. $50
Knife-modern, hollow handle, 9 1/8 in. $40
Ladle-gravy, solid, 6 3/4 in. $100
Scoop-ice, silver plate bowl, 9 1/8 in. $50
Server-jelly, 6 1/8 in. $50
Server-pie and cake, stainless blade,
   11 1/4 in. $55
Spoon-bonbon, 5 1/2 in. $50
Spoon-dessert/oval soup, 6 1/2 in. $55
Spoon-fruit, 6 in. $44
Spoon-soup, round bowl, cream, 6 1/2 in. $60
Spoon-sugar, 6 in. $36
Spoon-teaspoon, 6 in. $30
Tablespoon, (serving spoon), 8 1/2 in. $90
Tablespoon, (serving spoon), pierced,
   8 1/2 in. $90

Chased Diana by Towle, 1928

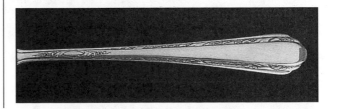

Butter spreader, flat handle, 6 in. $18
Butter-master, flat handle, 6 7/8 in. $36
Fork, 7 3/8 in. $24
Fork, 8 in. $40
Fork-lemon, 5 1/2 in. $24
Fork-pickle/olive, short handle, 6 in. $24
Fork-salad, individual, 6 3/8 in. $33
Knife-carving, small stainless blade, steak,
   9 3/4 in. $34
Knife-new french, hollow handle, 8 3/4 in. $30
Ladle-gravy, solid, 6 3/4 in. $80
Server-cheese, stainless blade, 6 1/8 in. $40
Server-jelly, 6 5/8 in. $38
Spoon-bonbon, 4 7/8 in. $40
Spoon-demitasse, 4 1/4 in. $15
Spoon-dessert/oval soup, 7 1/8 in. $44
Spoon-fruit, 5 7/8 in. $26
Spoon-iced tea, 8 1/8 in. $25
Spoon-relish, 6 in. $36
Spoon-soup, round bowl, bouillon, 5 in. $28
Spoon-soup, round bowl, cream, 6 3/8 in. $34
Spoon-sugar, 5 3/4 in. $23
Spoon-teaspoon (five o'clock), 5 5/8 in. $13
Spoon-teaspoon, 6 in. $18
Tablespoon, (serving spoon), 8 1/2 in. $70
Tongs-sugar, 3 7/8 in. $50

Chippendale by Towle, 1937

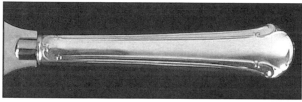

Butter spreader, flat handle, 5 7/8 in. $30
Butter spreader, hollow handle, stainless
   paddle, 5 5/8 in. $30
Butter-master, flat handle, 6 7/8 in. $33
Butter-master, hollow handle, blade angled,
   6 1/2 in. $35
Carving set, 2 pieces, small, stainless blade,
   steak $80
Cheese grater, 8 3/4 in. $50
Cleaver-cheese, stainless blade, 6 1/4 in. $40
Fork, 7 3/8 in. $34
Fork, 8 in. $56
Fork-baby, 4 1/4 in. $30
Fork-carving, small stainless prongs, steak,
   8 5/8 in. $40
Fork-cocktail, 5 3/4 in. $30
Fork-cold meat/serving, medium, solid,
   8 in. $85

Fork-fish, stainless tines, hollow handle,
   individual, 7 3/4 in. $40
Fork-ice cream, 5 5/8 in. $47
Fork-joint/roast holder, large, 11 1/4 in. $105
Fork-lemon, 5 1/2 in. $30
Fork-pickle/olive, short handle, 2 tines,
   5 7/8 in. $30
Fork-salad serving, stainless prongs,
   11 1/4 in. $40
Fork-salad, individual, 6 3/4 in. $36
Fork-strawberry, 5 1/2 in. $26
Fork-utility/serving, stainless tines, 2 of
   4 tines beveled, 9 7/8 in. $45
Fork-youth, 6 1/8 in. $40
Ice cream slicer, solid, 13 in. $270
Knife-bar, hollow handle, 9 in. $40
Knife-carving, small, stainless blade, steak,
   10 1/2 in. $40
Knife-carving, small, stainless blade, steak,
   10 in. $40
Knife-cheese, stainless blade, 6 7/8 in. $40
Knife-fish, stainless blade, individual, no
   notch, 8 in. $40
Knife-fish, stainless blade, individual, notch,
   8 1/2 in. $40
Knife-fruit, stainless blade, individual,
   3 1/2 in. blade, 6 1/2 in. $40
Knife-fruit, stainless blade, individual,
   3 1/4 in. blade, 6 1/4 in. $40
Knife-modern, hollow handle, 8 3/4 in. $30
Knife-modern, hollow handle, 9 5/8 in. $50
Knife-new french, hollow handle, 8 7/8 in. $33
Knife-new french, hollow handle, 9 1/4 in. $33
Knife-new french, hollow handle, 9 3/4 in. $50
Knife-steak, individual, 8 7/8 in. $40
Knife-steak, individual, beveled blade,
   8 3/8 in. $40
Knife-steak, individual, no bevel, 8 3/8 in. $40
Knife-utility/serving, stainless blade,
   11 1/4 in. $40
Knife-youth, 6 7/8 in. $40
Ladle-cream, solid, 5 1/2 in. $46
Ladle-gravy, hollow handle, stainless bowl,
   8 1/4 in. $45
Ladle-gravy, solid, 7 in. $80
Ladle-punch, solid, 15 1/4 in. $300
Ladle-punch, stainless bowl, 12 3/4 in. $60
Ladle-soup, stainless bowl, 11 in. $55
Opener-bottle, stainless bowl, 5 7/8 in. $40
Pick-butter, 1 tine, 5 1/4 in. $25
Scoop-ice cream, stainless bowl, 8 1/8 in. $40
Scoop-ice, silver plate bowl, 8 5/8 in. $50
Server-asparagus, hollow handle, silver
   plate hood, 9 1/2 in. $53

Server-cheese, stainless blade, 6 1/8 in.......$40
Server-cranberry, stainless bowl, 8 3/4 in.....$40
Server-fish, solid, large, 11 1/4 in. $130
Server-jelly, 6 5/8 in.......................$38
Server-lasagna, stainless blade, 9 7/8 in.....$45
Server-macaroni, 10 1/2 in................$200
Server-pasta, stainless bowl, 10 5/8 in.......$40
Server-pie and cake, stainless blade,
    10 3/8 in. $45
Server-pie, stainless blade, 10 1/2 in. $45
Slicer-cake, stainless blade, wedding,
    12 1/4 in. $45
Spoon-baby, straight handle, 4 3/8 in. $30
Spoon-bonbon, 4 7/8 in.....................$42
Spoon-casserole, pierced, stainless bowl,
    9 3/4 in.................................$45
Spoon-cracker, 8 in. $120
Spoon-demitasse, 4 1/4 in. $24
Spoon-dessert/oval soup, 6 7/8 in............$46
Spoon-dressing, stainless bowl, 11 1/4 in. $45
Spoon-five o'clock/youth, 5 3/8 in. $24
Spoon-fruit, rimmed bowl, 5 7/8 in............$40
Spoon-iced tea, 8 in.......................$38
Spoon-infant feeding, 5 in...................$32
Spoon-mustard, 5 1/4 in.....................$40
Spoon-salad serving, plastic bowl,
    11 7/8 in. $44
Spoon-salad serving, stainless bowl,
    11 3/8 in. $40
Spoon-salt, individual, 2 1/2 in...............$13
Spoon-soup, round bowl, bouillon,
    5 1/8 in.................................$40
Spoon-soup, round bowl, cream, 6 1/2 in.....$40
Spoon-sugar, 5 7/8 in......................$40
Spoon-teaspoon, 6 1/8 in. $24
Tablespoon, (serving spoon), 8 1/2 in........$80
Tea strainer, 7 1/4 in......................$100
Tongs-sugar, 4 in. $40

Colonial Thread by Towle, 1950

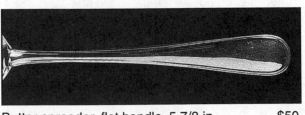

Butter spreader, flat handle, 5 7/8 in.........$50
Butter spreader/youth knife, 6 3/8 in.........$42
Butter-master, hollow handle, 6 5/8 in........$40
Carving set, 2 pieces, small, stainless blade,
    steak..................................$85
Fork, 7 1/4 in..............................$60

Fork-carving, small stainless prongs, steak,
    9 in. $40
Fork-salad serving, stainless prongs, 11 in. .. $45
Fork-salad, individual, 6 3/8 in. $55
Knife-new french, hollow handle, 8 3/4 in. $48
Knife-new french, hollow handle, 9 1/2 in. $50
Knife-old french, hollow handle, 9 1/2 in. $50
Knife-steak, individual, 8 in. $40
Knife-utility/serving, stainless blade,
    11 1/8 in................................$50
Ladle-gravy, hollow handle, stainless bowl,
    7 3/4 in.................................$45
Ladle-gravy, solid, 5 3/4 in..................$80
Ladle-gravy, solid, 6 1/2 in..................$80
Ladle-punch, stainless bowl, 12 5/8 in.......$60
Ladle-soup, stainless bowl, 10 7/8 in.........$55
Opener-bottle, stainless bowl, 5 3/4 in........$45
Server-cranberry, stainless bowl, 8 3/8 in.....$45
Server-pie and cake, stainless blade,
    10 3/4 in................................$40
Slicer-cake, stainless blade, wedding,
    11 3/4 in................................$40
Spoon-dessert/oval soup, 6 7/8 in. $50
Spoon-dressing, stainless bowl,
    10 3/4 in................................$45
Spoon-pierced rice, stainless bowl,
    9 1/2 in.................................$45
Spoon-rice, stainless bowl, 9 1/2 in. $45
Spoon-salad serving, stainless bowl,
    11 in. $45
Spoon-sugar, 5 7/8 in......................$40
Spoon-teaspoon, 6 in......................$40
Tablespoon, (serving spoon), pierced,
    8 1/2 in.................................$90
Tongs-sugar, 4 in..........................$70

Contessina by Towle, 1965

Butter spreader, hollow handle, modern, stainless
    paddle, 6 5/8 in........................$32
Butter-master, hollow handle, no notch,
    7 in. $35
Fork, 7 3/8 in. $40
Fork-carving, small stainless prongs, steak,
    9 7/8 in.................................$40
Fork-cold meat/serving, large, solid,
    9 1/4 in.................................$90

Towle Silversmiths

Fork-fish, stainless tines, hollow handle,
 individual, 8 1/2 in. $40
Fork-salad, individual, 6 5/8 in. $46
Knife-fish, stainless blade, individual,
 8 3/4 in. $40
Knife-modern, hollow handle, 9 1/8 in. $35
Ladle-gravy, solid, 6 3/4 in. $100
Scoop-ice, silver plate bowl, 9 1/4 in. $50
Server-pie and cake, stainless blade,
 11 1/8 in. $50
Spoon-sugar, 6 1/4 in. $32
Spoon-teaspoon, 6 1/8 in. $25
Tablespoon, (serving spoon), 8 5/8 in. $90
Tablespoon, (serving spoon), pierced,
 8 5/8 in. $90

Contour by Towle, 1950

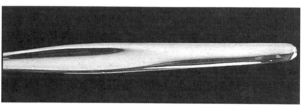

Butter spreader, hollow handle, stainless
 paddle, 6 in. $20
Butter-master, hollow handle, 7 in. $25
Fork, 7 3/4 in. $36
Fork-baby, 4 1/2 in. $34
Fork-cocktail, 6 1/8 in. $23
Fork-cold meat/serving, large, solid,
 9 1/2 in. $85
Fork-pickle/olive, short handle,
 6 1/4 in. $22
Fork-salad, individual, 6 3/4 in. $33
Fork-youth, 6 3/8 in. $40
Knife-modern, hollow handle, 8 3/4 in. $37
Knife-youth, 7 3/8 in. $34
Ladle-gravy, solid, 6 3/8 in. $63
Napkin clip, (made for teaspoons) $22
Server-jelly, 7 in. $28
Server-pie and cake, stainless blade,
 10 7/8 in. $55
Spoon-demitasse, 4 1/2 in. $20
Spoon-dessert/oval soup, 7 in. $38
Spoon-iced tea, 8 in. $40
Spoon-sugar, 5 7/8 in. $25
Spoon-teaspoon, 6 1/2 in. $18
Tablespoon, (serving spoon), 8 3/4 in. $65
Tablespoon, (serving spoon), pierced,
 8 3/4 in. $80
Toothbrush-baby, 4 5/8 in. $25

Country Manor by Towle, 1966

Butter spreader, hollow handle, modern,
 stainless paddle, 6 5/8 in. $28
Butter-master, hollow handle, 7 in. $34
Fork, 7 3/8 in. $38
Fork, 8 ln. $60
Fork-cold meat/serving, large, solid,
 9 1/8 in. $90
Knife-modern, hollow handle, 9 1/8 in. $36
Ladle-cream, solid, 5 1/2 in. $50
Ladle-gravy, solid, 6 3/4 in. $100
Server-jelly, 6 1/8 in. $44
Spoon-dessert/oval soup, 6 7/8 in. $60
Spoon-sugar, 6 1/8 in. $37
Spoon-teaspoon (five o'clock), 5 1/2 in. $20
Spoon-teaspoon, 6 1/4 in. $22

Craftsman by Towle, 1932

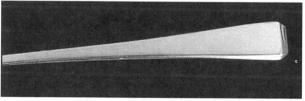

Baby set, 2 pieces $50
Butter spreader, flat handle, 6 in. $20
Butter spreader, hollow handle, modern,
 stainless paddle, 6 1/4 in. $24
Butter spreader, hollow handle, stainless
 paddle, 5 3/4 in. $24
Butter-master, flat handle, 7 in. $23
Butter-master, hollow handle, 6 5/8 in. $24
Carving set, 2 pieces, small, stainless blade,
 steak $80
Cleaver-cheese, stainless blade, 6 1/2 in. $40
Fork, 7 3/8 in. $27
Fork-baby, 4 1/8 in. $25
Fork-carving, small, stainless prongs, steak,
 8 3/4 in. $40
Fork-carving, small, stainless prongs, steak,
 8 3/8 in. $40
Fork-cocktail, 5 3/4 in. $24
Fork-cold meat/serving, medium, solid,
 8 in. $75

Fork-fish, stainless tines, hollow handle,
  individual, 7 5/8 in. $45
Fork-ice cream, 5 5/8 in. $40
Fork-lemon, 5 1/2 in. $23
Fork-pickle/olive, short handle, 6 in. $24
Fork-salad serving, stainless prongs,
  11 1/8 in. $40
Fork-salad, individual, 6 1/2 in. $34
Fork-utility/serving, stainless tines,
  9 5/8 in. $40
Fork-youth, 6 1/8 in. $40
Knife-bar, hollow handle, 8 5/8 in. $38
Knife-carving, small, stainless blade, steak,
  10 1/4 in. $40
Knife-carving, small, stainless blade, steak,
  11 in. $40
Knife-cheese, stainless blade, 6 7/8 in. $40
Knife-fish, stainless blade, individual,
  7 7/8 in. $45
Knife-fruit, stainless blade, individual,
  6 1/8 in. $40
Knife-modern, hollow handle, stainless blade,
  8 1/2 in. $30
Knife-modern, hollow handle, stainless blade,
  8 3/4 in. $30
Knife-new french, hollow handle, silver plate
  blade, 8 7/8 in. $30
Knife-new french, hollow handle, stainless
  blade, 8 7/8 in. $30
Knife-new french, hollow handle, stainless
  blade, 9 5/8 in. $40
Knife-steak, individual, 8 1/4 in. $45
Knife-utility/serving, stainless blade, no
  design, 11 in. $40
Ladle-cream, solid, 5 3/4 in. $30
Ladle-gravy, hollow handle, stainless bowl,
  8 in. $40
Ladle-gravy, solid, 6 5/8 in. $70
Ladle-punch, stainless bowl, 13 $60
Ladle-soup, stainless bowl, 10 3/4 in. $55
Opener-bottle, stainless bowl, 5 5/8 in. $45
Salad set, 2 pieces, plastic bowl $85
Scoop-ice cream, stainless bowl, 7 3/4 in. $40
Scoop-ice, silver plate bowl, 8 3/8 in. $50
Server-cranberry, stainless bowl, 8 1/2 in. $40
Server-jelly, 6 5/8 in. $33
Server-lasagna, stainless blade, 9 3/4 in. $40
Server-pasta, stainless bowl, 10 1/4 in. $40
Server-pie, stainless blade, 10 in. $40
Server-pie, stainless blade, 9 1/2 in. $40
Server-tomato, solid, 7 1/2 in. $80
Server-tomato, stainless blade, 8 3/8 in. $45
Slicer-cake, stainless blade, wedding,
  11 7/8 in. $40

Spoon-baby, straight handle, 4 1/4 in. $25
Spoon-bonbon, 5 1/2 in. $30
Spoon-bonbon, 5 in. $30
Spoon-casserole, shell, stainless bowl,
  10 in. $40
Spoon-demitasse, 4 1/4 in. $16
Spoon-dressing, stainless bowl, 11 in. $40
Spoon-fruit, 6 in. $40
Spoon-iced tea, 8 in. $32
Spoon-infant feeding, 5 in. $25
Spoon-mustard, 5 1/8 in. $35
Spoon-pierced rice, stainless bowl,
  9 1/2 in. $40
Spoon-relish, 6 in. $30
Spoon-rice, stainless bowl, 9 3/4 in. $40
Spoon-salad serving, plastic bowl,
  11 3/4 in. $43
Spoon-salad serving, stainless bowl,
  11 1/8 in. $40
Spoon-salt, individual, gold wash,
  2 1/2 in. $12
Spoon-soup, round bowl, bouillon,
  5 1/8 in. $40
Spoon-soup, round bowl, cream, 6 1/2 in. $40
Spoon-sugar, 6 in. $23
Spoon-teaspoon, 6 in. $18
Spoon-youth, 3 1/2 in. handle, 5 3/8 in. $30
Tablespoon, (serving spoon), 8 1/2 in. $65
Tongs-sugar, 4 in. $40

Debussy by Towle, 1959

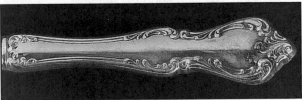

Butter spreader, hollow handle, modern,
  stainless paddle, 6 1/2 in. $38
Butter-master, hollow handle, 6 7/8 in. $38
Carving set, 2 pieces, small, stainless blade,
  steak $100
Fork, 7 3/8 in. $48
Fork, 8 in. $60
Fork-carving, small stainless prongs, steak,
  9 3/4 in. $50
Fork-cold meat/serving, large, stainless tines,
  11 1/8 in. $50
Fork-cold meat/serving, medium, solid,
  8 1/2 in. $100
Fork-lemon, 5 1/2 in. $36
Fork-pickle/olive, short handle, 5 3/4 in. $34

Fork-salad server, plastic prongs,
12 1/8 in. $50
Fork-salad, individual, 6 5/8 in. $48
Fork-youth, 6 1/4 in. $50
Jigger, double-wide, handle with silver plate
bowls, 6 3/8 in. $45
Knife-carving, small, stainless blade, steak,
10 3/4 in. $50
Knife-cheese, stainless blade, 7 1/8 in. $50
Knife-modern, hollow handle, 9 in. $40
Ladle-cream, solid, 5 3/4 in.................$65
Ladle-gravy, hollow handle, stainless bowl,
8 1/4 in.................................$50
Ladle-gravy, solid, 6 3/4 in. $90
Server/knife-fish, stainless blade,
11 3/4 in. $50
Server-jelly, 6 7/8 in. $40
Server-pie and cake, stainless blade,
11 1/2 in. $45
Server-pie and cake, stainless blade,
11 in....................................$45
Server-tomato, solid, 8 1/8 in. $90
Spoon-baby, straight handle, 4 1/2 in. $40
Spoon-bonbon, 5 1/2 in.....................$60
Spoon-demitasse, 4 3/8 in. $28
Spoon-dessert/oval soup, 6 5/8 in...........$48
Spoon-iced tea, 8 1/4 in. $60
Spoon-salt, individual, gold wash,
2 1/2 in.................................$14
Spoon-sugar, 5 5/8 in......................$34
Spoon-sugar, 6 in.........................$34
Tablespoon, (serving spoon), 8 3/4 in........$85
Tablespoon, (serving spoon), pierced,
8 3/4 in.................................$90

D'Orleans by Towle, 1923

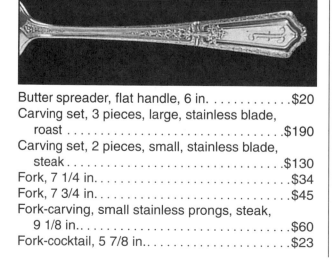

Butter spreader, flat handle, 6 in. $20
Carving set, 3 pieces, large, stainless blade,
roast $190
Carving set, 2 pieces, small, stainless blade,
steak...................................$130
Fork, 7 1/4 in.............................$34
Fork, 7 3/4 in.............................$45
Fork-carving, small stainless prongs, steak,
9 1/8 in.................................$60
Fork-cocktail, 5 7/8 in......................$23

Fork-cold meat/serving, medium, solid,
8 in. $90
Fork-ice cream, 1/4 in. tines, 5 1/2 in........$40
Fork-salad, individual, 6 1/8 in. $42
Knife-new french, hollow handle, 9 in. $34
Ladle-gravy, solid, 6 1/2 in.................$85
Server-cheese, stainless blade, 6 5/8 in......$50
Server-jelly, 6 7/8 in. $30
Server-pie, stainless blade, 9 5/8 in..........$60
Spoon-bonbon, 4 3/4 in. $44
Spoon-dessert/oval soup, 7 1/8 in. $45
Spoon-soup, round bowl, gumbo,
7 1/4 in.................................$50
Spoon-teaspoon, 4 in. handle, 6 in..........$24
Spoon-teaspoon, large, youth, 3 3/4 in.
handle, 5 3/4 in..........................$20
Tablespoon, (serving spoon), 8 5/8 in. $80
Tablespoon, (serving spoon), pierced,
8 5/8 in.................................$80

One hundred and four pieces Towle D'Orleans (1923): 8 each dinner knives, dinner forks, salad forks, dessert spoons, teaspoons, large soup spoons, bouillon spoons, cocktail forks, ice cream spoons, butter spreaders, citrus spoons, and demitasse spoons; 4 table-spoons, 2 pierced tablespoons, and pair medium carvers. Monogram "SHB." $1,700

Dorothy Manners by Towle, 1919

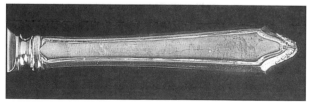

Butter spreader, flat handle, 6 in. $22
Fork, 7 1/4 in.. . . . .$30
Fork, 7 3/4 in.. . . . .$50
Fork-cocktail, 5 5/8 in.. . . . .$26
Fork-ice cream, 5 1/2 in.. . . . .$34
Fork-lemon, 5 1/2 in.. . . . .$28
Fork-pickle/olive, short handle, 5 7/8 in. $28
Fork-salad, individual, 6 1/4 in. $30
Knife-carving, small stainless blade, steak,
    10 in.. . . . .$55
Knife-old french, hollow handle, 8 3/4 in.. . . . . .$30
Knife-old french, hollow handle, 9 5/8 in.. . . . . .$40
Ladle-cream, solid, 5 1/2 in.. . . . .$38
Ladle-gravy, solid, 6 1/2 in. $80
Server-jelly, 6 3/4 in. $28
Server-tomato, solid, 7 5/8 in. $80
Spoon-casserole, smooth, solid, 8 1/8 in.. . . . . .$90
Spoon-demitasse, 4 1/4 in. $18
Spoon-dessert/oval soup, 7 1/8 in.. . . . .$36
Spoon-iced tea, 8 1/8 in. $34
Spoon-soup, round bowl, bouillon,
    5 1/8 in.. . . . .$28
Spoon-soup, round bowl, gumbo,
    7 1/4 in.. . . . .$38
Spoon-sugar, 5 7/8 in.. . . . .$38
Spoon-teaspoon (five o'clock), 5 3/4 in.. . . . . . .$16
Spoon-teaspoon, 6 in.. . . . .$26
Tablespoon, (serving spoon), 8 5/8 in.. . . . .$65
Tablespoon, (serving spoon), pierced,
    8 5/8 in.. . . . .$75

Drury Lane by Towle, 1939

Butter spreader, flat handle, 6 in. $26
Butter spreader, hollow handle, stainless
    paddle, 5 3/4 in.. . . . .$26
Butter-master, flat handle, 7 in.. . . . .$36
Fork, 7 3/8 in.. . . . .$40
Fork-cocktail, 5 3/4 in.. . . . .$24
Fork-cold meat/serving, small, solid,
    7 3/4 in.. . . . .$90
Fork-ice cream, 5 5/8 in.. . . . .$45
Fork-lemon, 5 1/2 in.. . . . .$34
Fork-pickle/olive, short handle, 5 3/4 in. $34
Fork-salad, individual, 6 1/2 in. $50
Knife-new french, hollow handle,
    8 3/4 in.. . . . .$34

Ladle-cream, solid, 5 3/4 in. $53
Ladle-gravy, solid, 6 1/2 in.. . . . . $90
Server-jelly, 6 3/4 in. $30
Server-tomato, solid, 7 1/2 in. $100
Spoon-demitasse, 4 1/4 in.. . . . . $26
Spoon-dessert/oval soup, 7 1/8 in. $56
Spoon-soup, round bowl, cream,
    6 1/2 in.. . . . . $48
Spoon-soup, round bowl, gumbo, 7 in.. . . . . . . $65
Spoon-sugar, 6 in. $34
Spoon-teaspoon (five o'clock), 5 3/4 in. $26
Spoon-teaspoon, 6 in.. . . . . $27
Tablespoon, (serving spoon), 8 1/2 in. $80
Tongs-sugar, 4 in.. . . . . $58

El Grandee by Towle, 1964

Butter spreader, hollow handle, modern,
    stainless paddle, 6 3/4 in.. . . . . $42
Butter spreader, hollow handle, stainless
    paddle, 6 1/4 in.. . . . . $40
Butter-master, hollow handle, no notch,
    6 7/8 in.. . . . . $36
Cheese grater, 9 1/4 in.. $55
Cleaver-cheese, stainless blade, 6 7/8 in. $50
Fork, 7 1/2 in. $36
Fork, 7 7/8 in. $60
Fork-baby, 4 1/4 in.. . . . . $35
Fork-carving, small stainless prongs, steak,
    9 5/8 in.. . . . . $40
Fork-cocktail, 5 5/8 in. $30
Fork-cold meat/serving, large, solid,
    9 1/8 in.. . . . . $100
Fork-fish, stainless tines, hollow handle,
    individual, 8 1/4 in.. . . . . $40
Fork-ice cream, 5 1/4 in. $40
Fork-lemon, 3 tines, 5 5/8 in. $34
Fork-pickle/olive, short handle, 2 tines,
    5 1/2 in.. . . . . $30
Fork-pickle/olive, short handle, 2 tines,
    5 7/8 in.. . . . . $30
Fork-salad serving, stainless prongs,
    11 3/4 in.. . . . . $40
Fork-salad, individual, 6 7/8 in. $50
Fork-strawberry, 5 5/8 in.. . . . . $30
Fork-youth, 6 3/8 in.. . . . . $40
Knife-bar, hollow handle, 9 3/8 in. $42

Towle Silversmiths

Knife-carving, small, stainless blade, steak,
10 5/8 in. $40
Knife-cheese, stainless blade, 7 3/8 in. $45
Knife-fish, stainless blade, individual,
8 1/2 in.................................$40
Knife-fish, stainless blade, individual, 9 in. $40
Knife-fruit, stainless blade, individual,
7 1/8 in.................................$40
Knife-modern, hollow handle, 8 3/4 in........$40
Knife-steak, individual, 8 7/8 in. $45
Knife-utility/serving, stainless blade,
11 1/2 in. $45
Knife-youth, 7 3/8 in........................$40
Ladle-cream, solid, 6 in.....................$50
Ladle-gravy, hollow handle, stainless
bowl, 8 1/2 in. $40
Ladle-gravy, solid, 7 1/8 in. $80
Ladle-punch, stainless bowl, 13 in............$55
Ladle-soup, stainless bowl, 11 1/2 in. $58
Opener-bottle, stainless bowl, 6 1/2 in. $40
Scoop-ice cream, stainless bowl,
8 1/2 in.................................$40
Scoop-ice, silver plate bowl $50
Server-asparagus, hollow handle, silver
plate hood, 9 7/8 in. $50
Server-cranberry, stainless bowl, 9 in.........$45
Server-lasagna, stainless blade,
10 1/4 in. $40
Server-pasta, stainless bowl, 10 7/8 in........$40
Server-pie and cake, stainless blade,
11 1/8 in. $44
Server-tomato, solid, 8 1/8 in. $120
Slicer-cake, stainless blade, wedding,
12 3/4 in. $40
Spoon-bonbon, 6 in. $50
Spoon-casserole, pierced stainless bowl,
7 scallops, 10 1/8 in.....................$40
Spoon-casserole, shell, stainless bowl,
10 1/2 in. $40
Spoon-demitasse, 4 1/2 in. $25
Spoon-dessert/oval soup, 6 5/8 in...........$45
Spoon-dressing, stainless bowl,
11 3/4 in. $40
Spoon-iced tea, 8 1/8 in. $50
Spoon-infant feeding, 5 1/2 in..............$30
Spoon-salad serving, stainless bowl,
11 3/4 in. $40
Spoon-sugar, 6 1/4 in.......................$40
Spoon-teaspoon, 6 1/8 in. $26
Spoon-utility/serving, stainless bowl, 7
scallops, 10 1/8 in. $40
Tablespoon, (serving spoon), 8 5/8 in........$100
Tablespoon, (serving spoon), pierced,
8 5/8 in.................................$100

Esplanade by Towle, 1952

Butter spreader, hollow handle, modern,
stainless paddle, 6 5/8 in................$26
Butter spreader, hollow handle, stainless
paddle, 6 in. $26
Butter-master, hollow handle, 7 in. $36
Fork, 7 3/8 in. $40
Fork, 7 7/8 in. $65
Fork-cocktail, 5 7/8 in......................$30
Fork-cold meat/serving, large, solid,
9 1/2 in.................................$80
Fork-salad, individual, 6 5/8 in. $40
Knife-fruit, stainless blade, individual,
6 7/8 in.................................$35
Knife-modern, hollow handle, 9 5/8 in. $40
Knife-modern, hollow handle, 9 in. $30
Ladle-gravy, solid, 6 1/4 in..................$90
Server-jelly, 7 1/8 in. $30
Spoon-demitasse, 4 1/2 in...................$24
Spoon-dessert/oval soup, 6 7/8 in. $44
Spoon-iced tea, 8 1/8 in....................$40
Spoon-sugar, 5 7/8 in. $28
Spoon-teaspoon, 6 1/8 in...................$28
Tablespoon, (serving spoon), 8 3/4 in. $76
Tablespoon, (serving spoon), pierced,
8 3/4 in.................................$80

Federal Cotillion by Towle, 1901

The following pieces are newer examples of this
pattern:
Butter spreader, flat handle, 5 3/4 in. $26
Butter spreader, hollow handle, modern,
stainless, 6 1/2 in.......................$40
Butter-master, flat handle, 7 in. $40
Butter-master, hollow handle, 6 1/2 in........$40
Carving set, 2 pieces, small, stainless blade,
steak stainless blade....................$90
Cleaver-cheese, stainless blade, 6 5/8 in. $45

Fork, 7 1/4 in............................$48
Fork, 7 5/8 in............................$70
Fork-carving, small stainless prongs, steak,
    9 1/8 in..............................$45
Fork-cold meat/serving, large, stainless tines,
    2 of 4 tines beveled, 9 5/8 in............$40
Fork-fish, stainless tines, hollow handle,
    individual, 7 1/2 in......................$40
Fork-salad serving, stainless prongs,
    11 in..................................$40
Fork-salad, individual, 1 of 4 tines beveled,
    6 1/4 in...............................$50
Knife-bar, hollow handle, 8 3/8 in..........$45
Knife-carving, small, stainless blade, steak,
    10 1/4 in.............................$45
Knife-cheese, stainless blade, 7 1/8 in.....$45
Knife-fish, stainless blade, individual,
    7 5/8 in..............................$45
Knife-modern, hollow handle, 9 1/2 in.......$50
Knife-modern, hollow handle, stainless blade,
    8 1/2 in..............................$40
Knife-new french, hollow handle, 8 1/2 in....$40
Knife-new french, hollow handle, 9 1/2 in....$50
Knife-steak, individual, 8 1/8 in............$45
Knife-utility/serving, stainless blade, no
    design, 11 in.........................$40
Ladle-gravy, hollow handle, stainless bowl,
    7 1/2 in..............................$45
Ladle-punch, stainless bowl, 12 3/4 in.......$60
Ladle-soup, stainless bowl, 10 3/4 in........$55
Opener-bottle, stainless bowl, 5 3/4 in.......$45
Salad set, 2 pieces, stainless bowl, 11 in.....$80
Scoop-ice cream, stainless bowl,
    8 1/8 in..............................$40
Server-asparagus, hollow handle, silver
    plate hood, 9 1/4 in...................$66
Server-cranberry, stainless bowl, 8 1/2 in.....$45
Server-lasagna, stainless blade, 9 5/8 in......$40
Server-pasta, stainless bowl, 10 1/4 in.......$40
Server-pie and cake, stainless blade,
    10 3/4 in.............................$45
Slicer-cake, stainless blade, wedding,
    12 1/2 in.............................$45
Spoon-dressing, stainless tear-shaped bowl,
    11 in.................................$45
Spoon-pierced rice, stainless bowl, 8 piercings,
    9 1/2 in..............................$45
Spoon-rice, stainless bowl, 7 scallops,
    9 1/2 in..............................$40
Spoon-salad serving, stainless bowl,
    11 in.................................$40
Spoon-soup, round bowl, cream, 6 in.........$50
Spoon-teaspoon, 5 3/4 in. $34
Tablespoon, (serving spoon), 8 1/8 in.......$100

Fiddle Thread by Towle, 1902

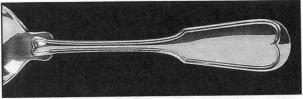

Butter spreader, hollow handle, modern, stainless
    paddle, 6 5/8 in.......................$40
Butter-master, hollow handle, 6 7/8 in.......$40
Carving set, 2 pieces, small, stainless blade,
    steak $80
Cleaver-cheese, stainless blade, 6 3/4 in.....$40
Fork-carving, small stainless prongs, steak,
    9 1/4 in..............................$40
Fork-salad, individual, 6 in................$60
Knife-carving, small stainless blade, steak,
    10 1/2 in.............................$40
Knife-cheese, stainless blade, 7 1/4 in.......$45
Knife-fish, stainless blade, individual,
    7 7/8 in..............................$40
Knife-modern, hollow handle, stainless blade,
    8 3/8 in..............................$40
Knife-new french, hollow handle, 9 5/8 in.....$55
Knife-old french, hollow handle, 8 5/8 in.....$45
Knife-steak, individual, 8 in................$46
Knife-utility/serving, stainless blade, no
    design, 11 in.........................$40
Ladle-gravy, hollow handle, stainless bowl,
    7 7/8 in..............................$45
Ladle-punch, stainless bowl, 12 3/4 in.......$60
Ladle-soup, stainless bowl, 11 1/8 in........$60
Scoop-ice cream, stainless bowl,
    7 7/8 in..............................$45
Scoop-ice, silver plate bowl $50
Server-asparagus, hollow handle, silver
    plate hood, 9 3/8 in...................$66
Server-cranberry, stainless bowl,
    8 1/2 in..............................$45
Server-lasagna, stainless blade, 9 3/4 in.....$40
Server-pasta, stainless bowl, 10 1/2 in.......$45
Server-pie and cake, stainless blade,
    3 5/8 in. handle, 10 1/4 in.............$44
Server-pie and cake, stainless blade,
    4 1/8 in. handle, 10 7/8 in.............$44
Slicer-cake, stainless blade, wedding,
    12 3/8 in.............................$45
Spoon-pierced rice, stainless bowl, 7 scallops,
    9 1/2 in..............................$40
Spoon-rice, stainless bowl, 7 scallops,
    9 1/2 in..............................$45
Tablespoon, (serving spoon), 8 in. $100

Fontana by Towle, 1957

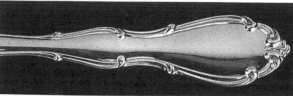

Butter spreader, hollow handle, modern, stainless, 6 5/8 in. $30

Butter-master, hollow handle, 6 7/8 in. $28

Carving set, 2 pieces, small, stainless blade, steak $80

Cleaver-cheese, stainless blade, 6 5/8 in. $40

Fork, 7 1/4 in. $38

Fork, 7 3/4 in. $48

Fork-baby, 4 1/8 in. $30

Fork-carving, small stainless prongs, steak, 9 1/4 in. $40

Fork-carving, small stainless prongs, steak, 9 3/4 in. $40

Fork-cocktail, 5 1/2 in. $30

Fork-cold meat/serving, large, solid, 9 1/4 in. $100

Fork-fish, stainless tines, hollow handle, individual, 8 1/8 in. $45

Fork-ice cream, 5 1/4 in. $44

Fork-lemon, 5 1/8 in. $30

Fork-pickle/olive, short handle, 5 5/8 in. $30

Fork-salad server, plastic prongs, 12 1/8 in. $44

Fork-salad serving, stainless prongs, 11 7/8 in. $40

Fork-salad, individual, 6 1/2 in. $40

Fork-utility/serving, stainless tines, 10 3/8 in. $40

Fork-youth, 6 1/4 in. $35

Knife-bar, hollow handle, 8 3/8 in. $45

Knife-bar, hollow handle, 9 1/4 in. $45

Knife-carving, small, stainless blade, steak, 11 in. $40

Knife-cheese, stainless blade, 7 1/8 in. $40

Knife-fish, stainless blade, individual, 8 5/8 in. $40

Knife-fruit, stainless blade, individual, 6 1/2 in. $40

Knife-fruit, stainless blade, individual, 7 in. $40

Knife-modern, hollow handle, 9 5/8 in. $44

Knife-modern, hollow handle, 9 in. $32

Knife-steak, individual, 3/8 5 in. blade, 9 in. $40

Knife-steak, individual, 4 1/2 in. blade, 9 in. $40

Knife-youth, 7 1/8 in. $40

Ladle-cream, solid, 5 3/8 in. $46

Ladle-gravy, hollow handle, stainless bowl, 8 5/8 in. $40

Ladle-gravy, solid, 6 1/4 in. $60

Ladle-punch, stainless bowl, 13 1/2 in. $55

Ladle-soup, stainless bowl, 11 1/2 in. $55

Opener-bottle, stainless bowl, 6 1/2 in. $45

Pick-butter, 1 tine, 4 7/8 in. $30

Salad set, 2 pieces, plastic bowl $90

Salad set, 2 pieces, stainless bowl $80

Scoop-ice cream, stainless bowl, 8 5/8 in. $45

Scoop-ice, silver plate bowl, 9 1/8 in. $50

Server/knife-fish, stainless blade, 11 5/8 in. $45

Server-cranberry, stainless bowl, 9 1/4 in. $40

Server-jelly, 6 3/8 in. $40

Server-lasagna, stainless blade, 10 1/4 in. $40

Server-pasta, stainless bowl, 11 1/8 in. $40

Server-pie and cake, stainless blade, 11 in. $45

Server-tomato, solid, 7 3/8 in. $100

Slicer-cake, stainless blade, wedding, 13 ....$40

Spoon-baby, straight handle, 4 1/8 in. $28

Spoon-bonbon, 5 3/8 in. $34

Spoon-casserole, pierced, stainless bowl, 10 3/8 in. $40

Spoon-casserole, shell, stainless bowl, 10 3/4 in. $40

Spoon-demitasse, 4 1/4 in. $20

Spoon-dessert/oval soup, 6 5/8 in. $45

Spoon-dressing, stainless bowl, 11 3/4 in. $40

Spoon-five o'clock/youth, 5 1/4 in. $30

Spoon-fruit, 6 1/8 in. $30

Spoon-iced tea, 7 7/8 in. $40

Spoon-infant feeding, 5 3/8 in. $32

Spoon-rice, stainless bowl, 10 1/4 in. $40

Spoon-salad serving, stainless bowl, 11 3/4 in. $40

Spoon-salt, individual, gold wash, 2 1/2 in. $10

Spoon-sugar, 5 1/4 in. $25

Spoon-teaspoon, 6 in. $18

Tablespoon, (serving spoon), 8 5/8 in. $80

Tablespoon, (serving spoon), pierced, 8 5/8 in. $90

Tongs-sugar, 4 in. $40

Towle Silversmiths

French Colonial by Towle, 1940

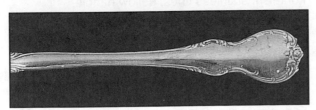

Butter spreader, flat handle, 5 7/8 in. $70
Butter spreader, hollow handle, stainless
    paddle, 6 in. $60
Butter-master, flat handle, 7 1/4 in. $55
Carving set, 2 pieces, small, stainless blade,
    steak $140
Fork, 7 1/4 in. $80
Fork, 7 5/8 in. $100
Fork-cocktail, 5 3/8 in. $60
Fork-cold meat/serving, small, solid,
    7 7/8 in. $140
Fork-fish, solid, individual, slotted tines,
    6 1/2 in. $65
Fork-lemon, 4 1/2 in. $55
Fork-pickle/olive, short handle, 5 3/4 in. $55
Ladle-gravy, solid, 6 1/4 in. $140
Ladle-mayonnaise, 5 1/4 in. $60
Server-cheese, stainless blade. 6 1/2 in. $50
Server-jelly, 6 1/4 in. $65
Server-pie, stainless blade, 9 5/8 in. $60
Server-tomato, solid, 7 5/8 in. $170
Spoon-bonbon, 4 3/4 in. $70
Spoon-casserole, smooth, solid,
    8 7/8 in. $130
Spoon-demitasse, 4 1/4 in. $35
Spoon-dessert/oval soup, 7 in. $75
Spoon-iced tea, 7 1/2 in. $80
Spoon-infant feeding, 5 3/8 in. $34
Spoon-soup, round bowl, bouillon,
    5 3/8 in. $60
Spoon-soup, round bowl, cream,
    6 1/4 in. $80
Spoon-sugar, 5 7/8 in. $75
Spoon-teaspoon, 6 in. $60
Tablespoon, (serving spoon), 8 5/8 in. $140

French Provincial by Towle, 1948

Baby set, 2 pieces $60

Butter spreader, hollow handle, stainless
    paddle, 6 in. $26
Butter spreader/youth knife, 6 1/2 in. $40
Butter-master, hollow handle, 6 7/8 in. $30
Carving set, 2 pieces, small, stainless blade,
    steak $85
Cheese grater, 8 3/4 in. $50
Cleaver-cheese, stainless blade, 6 5/8 in. $45
Fork, 7 1/4 in. $37
Fork-baby, 4 1/4 in. $30
Fork-carving, small, stainless prongs, steak,
    8 3/4 in. $45
Fork-carving, small, stainless prongs, steak,
    9 1/4 in. $45
Fork-cocktail, 5 5/8 in. $36
Fork-cold meat/serving, large, stainless tines,
    9 7/8 in. $40
Fork-cold meat/serving, medium, solid,
    8 1/4 in. $80
Fork-fish, stainless tines, hollow handle,
    individual, 7 3/4 in. $40
Fork-joint/roast holder, large, 11 1/8 in. $100
Fork-lemon, 5 1/2 in. $30
Fork-pickle/olive, short handle, 2 tines,
    6 in. $28
Fork-salad server, plastic prongs, 12 in. $45
Fork-salad server, stainless prongs,
    11 3/8 in. $45
Fork-salad, individual, 6 3/8 in. $44
Fork-strawberry, 5 1/2 in. $30
Fork-youth, 6 in. $40
Knife-carving, small, stainless blade, steak,
    10 1/4 in. $40
Knife-cheese, stainless blade, 7 1/8 in. $40
Knife-fish, stainless blade, individual,
    8 1/8 in. $40
Knife-fruit, stainless blade, individual,
    6 5/8 in. $40
Knife-modern, hollow handle, 8 7/8 in. $33
Knife-modern, hollow handle, 9 5/8 in. $40
Knife-new french, hollow handle, 8 7/8 in. $34
Knife-steak, individual, beveled, no rest,
    8 3/8 in. $45
Knife-steak, individual, no bevel, 8 3/8 in. $45
Knife-utility/serving, stainless blade, no
    design, 11 1/8 in. $40
Knife-youth, 7 1/8 in. $40
Ladle-cream, solid, 5 3/4 in. $40
Ladle-gravy, hollow handle, stainless bowl,
    7 7/8 in. $40
Ladle-gravy, solid, 6 3/4 in. $80
Ladle-punch, stainless bowl, 13 1/4 in. $50
Ladle-soup, stainless bowl, 10 7/8 in. $55
Ladle-soup, stainless bowl, 11 1/4 in. $55

Towle Silversmiths

Opener-bottle, stainless bowl, 6 in. $45
Pick-butter, 1 tine, , 5 1/4 in. $25
Salad set, 2 pieces, plastic bowl $90
Scoop-ice cream, stainless bowl,
    8 1/8 in.. . . . .$45
Scoop-ice, silver plate bowl, 8 1/2 in. $50
Server-asparagus, hollow handle,
    silver plate hood, 9 1/2 in. $55
Server-asparagus, hollow handle, sterling
    hood, 10 in. $300
Server-asparagus, solid, 9 3/4 in. $320
Server-cranberry, stainless bowl,
    8 3/4 in.. . . . .$40
Server-jelly, 6 1/2 in. $40
Server-lasagna, stainless blade, 10 in. $45
Server-macaroni, 10 1/2 in. $280
Server-pasta, stainless bowl, 10 5/8 in. $40
Server-pie and cake, stainless blade,
    10 3/8 in. $44
Server-tomato, solid, 7 3/8 in. $100
Slicer-cake, stainless blade, wedding,
    12 1/4 in. $45
Spoon-baby, straight handle, 4 1/4 in. $30
Spoon-bonbon, 5 1/2 in.. . . . .$40
Spoon-casserole, shell, stainless bowl,
    10 1/4 in. $40
Spoon-chocolate, short handle,
    4 1/8 in.. . . . .$40
Spoon-cracker, 7 7/8 in. $90
Spoon-demitasse, 4 1/4 in. $20
Spoon-dessert/oval soup, 6 1/2 in. $44
Spoon-dressing, shell, stainless bowl,
    11 1/4 in. $40
Spoon-five o'clock/youth, 5 3/8 in. $38
Spoon-iced tea, 7 7/8 in. $42
Spoon-infant feeding, 4 7/8 in.. . . . .$32
Spoon-mustard, 5 1/4 in. $35
Spoon-salad server, plastic bowl, 12 in. $45
Spoon-salad server, stainless bowl,
    11 3/8 in. $45
Spoon-salt, individual, 2 1/2 in. $13
Spoon-soup, round bowl, cream,
    6 1/4 in.. . . . .$46
Spoon-sugar, 5 7/8 in.. . . . .$30
Spoon-teaspoon, 6 in.. . . . .$22
Spoon-utility/serving, stainless bowl, 7
    scallops, 9 3/4 in. $40
Tablespoon, (serving spoon), 8 1/2 in. $80
Tablespoon, (serving spoon), pierced,
    8 1/2 in.. . . . .$90
Tea strainer, 7 1/8 in.. . . . .$100
Tongs-sugar, 4 in. $40
Youth set, 3 pieces (spoon, knife, fork) $120

Georgian by Towle, 1898

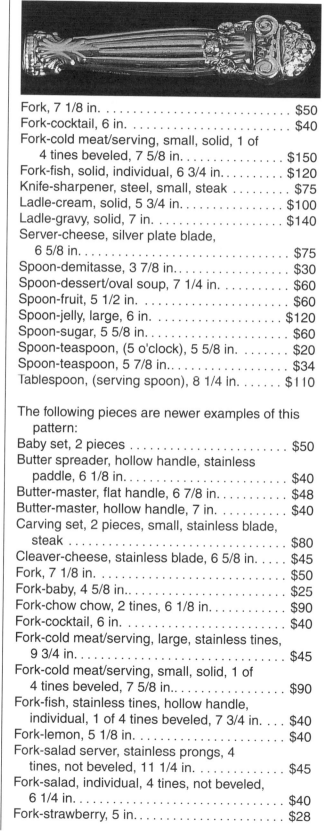

Fork, 7 1/8 in. $50
Fork-cocktail, 6 in. $40
Fork-cold meat/serving, small, solid, 1 of
    4 tines beveled, 7 5/8 in. $150
Fork-fish, solid, individual, 6 3/4 in. $120
Knife-sharpener, steel, small, steak $75
Ladle-cream, solid, 5 3/4 in. $100
Ladle-gravy, solid, 7 in. $140
Server-cheese, silver plate blade,
    6 5/8 in. $75
Spoon-demitasse, 3 7/8 in.. . . . . $30
Spoon-dessert/oval soup, 7 1/4 in. $60
Spoon-fruit, 5 1/2 in. $60
Spoon-jelly, large, 6 in. $120
Spoon-sugar, 5 5/8 in. $60
Spoon-teaspoon, (5 o'clock), 5 5/8 in. $20
Spoon-teaspoon, 5 7/8 in.. . . . . $34
Tablespoon, (serving spoon), 8 1/4 in. $110

The following pieces are newer examples of this
    pattern:
Baby set, 2 pieces $50
Butter spreader, hollow handle, stainless
    paddle, 6 1/8 in.. . . . . $40
Butter-master, flat handle, 6 7/8 in. $48
Butter-master, hollow handle, 7 in. $40
Carving set, 2 pieces, small, stainless blade,
    steak $80
Cleaver-cheese, stainless blade, 6 5/8 in. $45
Fork, 7 1/8 in. $50
Fork-baby, 4 5/8 in.. . . . . $25
Fork-chow chow, 2 tines, 6 1/8 in. $90
Fork-cocktail, 6 in. $40
Fork-cold meat/serving, large, stainless tines,
    9 3/4 in. $45
Fork-cold meat/serving, small, solid, 1 of
    4 tines beveled, 7 5/8 in.. . . . . $90
Fork-fish, stainless tines, hollow handle,
    individual, 1 of 4 tines beveled, 7 3/4 in. . . . $40
Fork-lemon, 5 1/8 in. $40
Fork-salad server, stainless prongs, 4
    tines, not beveled, 11 1/4 in. $45
Fork-salad, individual, 4 tines, not beveled,
    6 1/4 in.. . . . . $40
Fork-strawberry, 5 in.. . . . . $28

Towle Silversmiths

Fork-utility/serving, 2 of 4 beveled stainless tines, 9 3/4 in. $40

Jigger-double wide, handle, silver plate bowls, 6 1/4 in. $50

Knife-bar, hollow handle, 8 3/4 in. $40

Knife-carving, small, stainless blade, steak, 10 3/8 in. $40

Knife-cheese, stainless blade, 7 1/4 in. $40

Knife-fish, stainless blade, individual, 8 1/8 in. $45

Knife-fruit, stainless blade, individual, 6 1/2 in. $40

Knife-new french, hollow handle, 9 1/8 in. $40

Knife-steak, individual, 8 1/2 beveled blade $40

Knife-utility/serving, stainless blade, no design, 11 1/4 in. $45

Ladle-gravy, hollow handle, stainless bowl, 8 in. $45

Ladle-gravy, solid, 7 in. $100

Ladle-punch, stainless bowl, 12 3/4 in. $55

Ladle-soup, stainless bowl, 11 in. $55

Opener-bottle, stainless bowl, 6 in. $40

Sardine-flat server, solid, 6 1/2 in. $60

Scoop-ice cream, stainless bowl, 8 1/8 in. $40

Scoop-ice, silver plate bowl $50

Server-asparagus, hollow handle, silver plate hood $65

Server-asparagus, solid, 9 1/8 in. $200

Server-cranberry, stainless bowl, 8 3/8 in. $45

Server-dessert/pie, solid, 9 7/8 in. $160

Server-lasagna, stainless blade, 10 in. $40

Server-macaroni, 10 1/8 in. $240

Server-pasta, stainless bowl, 10 1/2 in. $40

Server-pie and cake, stainless blade, 10 3/4 in. $40

Server-pie, solid, 9 7/8 in. $150

Server-pie, stainless blade, 10 1/8 in. $45

Slicer-cake, stainless blade, wedding, 12 1/4 in. $45

Spoon-baby, straight handle, 5 in. $25

Spoon-bonbon, 5 3/8 in. $45

Spoon-casserole, pierced stainless bowl, 7 scallops, 9 3/4 in. $40

Spoon-casserole, shell, stainless bowl, 17 scallops, 10 1/4 in. $45

Spoon-chocolate, short handle, 4 1/2 in. $40

Spoon-demitasse, 3 7/8 in. $28

Spoon-dessert/oval soup, 7 1/8 in. $40

Spoon-dressing, shell, stainless tear bowl, 11 1/8 in. $40

Spoon-fruit, 5 1/2 in. $40

Spoon-iced tea, 8 3/8 in. $40

Spoon-infant feeding, 4 3/4 in. $30

Spoon-mustard, 5 1/2 in. $35

Spoon-platter, solid, tear bowl, 13 7/8 in. $260

Spoon-salad server, stainless egg bowl, 11 1/2 in. $45

Spoon-salt, individual, 2 3/8 in. $12

Spoon-soup, round bowl, cream, 6 1/8 in. $50

Spoon-sugar, 5 5/8 in. $40

Spoon-teaspoon, 5 7/8 in. $30

Spoon-utility/serving, stainless bowl, 7 scallops, 9 5/8 in. $45

Tablespoon, (serving spoon), 8 1/4 in. $90

Tablespoon, (serving spoon), 10 piercings, 8 1/4 in. $90

Tongs-asparagus, individual, solid, 5 1/2 in. $80

Tongs-ice/serving, large, bowl tip, 7 1/8 in. $150

King Richard by Towle, 1932

Butter spreader, hollow handle, modern, stainless paddle, 6 1/4 in. $40

Butter spreader, hollow handle, solid paddle, 5 3/4 in. $45

Butter spreader, hollow handle, stainless paddle, 5 3/4 in. $40

Butter-master, flat handle, 7 3/8 in. $44

Butter-master, hollow handle, 6 5/8 in. $42

Carving set, 2 pieces, small, stainless blade, steak $90

Cheese grater, 8 3/4 in. $55

Fork, 7 3/8 in. $42

Fork, 7 7/8 in. $70

Fork-baby, 4 1/4 in. $35

Fork-carving, small, stainless prongs, steak, 8 5/8 in. $45

Fork-chipped beef, small, 5 tines, 7 1/2 in. $100

Fork-cocktail, 5 3/4 in. $35

Fork-cold meat/serving, large, stainless tines, 2 of 4 tines beveled, 9 5/8 in. $45

Fork-cold meat/serving, medium, solid, 8 1/8 in. $90

Fork-fish, stainless tines, hollow handle, individual, 7 5/8 in. $45

Fork-ice cream, 5 5/8 in. $48

Fork-lemon, 5 in. $42

Towle Silversmiths

Fork-salad, individual, 6 1/2 in. $50
Fork-strawberry, 5 1/8 in. $35
Ice cream slicer, solid, 13 in. $240
Knife-bar, hollow handle, 8 3/4 in. $40
Knife-carving, small, stainless blade, steak,
   10 in. $45
Knife-cheese, stainless blade, 6 7/8 in. $40
Knife-fish, stainless blade, individual, 8 in. $40
Knife-fruit, stainless blade, individual,
   no bolster, 6 1/4 in. $40
Knife-modern, hollow handle, 8 3/4 in. $40
Knife-modern, hollow handle, 9 1/2 in. $55
Knife-new french, hollow handle, bolster,
   9 in. $40
Knife-new french, hollow handle,
   9 3/4 in. $60
Knife-new french, hollow handle, 9 in. $40
Knife-steak, individual, beveled blade,
   8 3/8 in. $40
Knife-steak, individual, not beveled,
   8 3/8 in. $40
Knife-utility/serving, stainless blade, no
   design, 11 in. $40
Knife-youth, 7 in. $40
Ladle-gravy, hollow handle, stainless bowl,
   8 in. $40
Ladle-gravy, solid, 7 1/4 in. $90
Ladle-punch, stainless bowl, 13 in. $60
Ladle-soup, solid, 14 1/4 in. $350
Ladle-soup, stainless bowl, 11 in. $60
Opener-bottle, stainless bowl, 5 7/8 in. $40
Salad set, 2 pieces, plastic bowl $100
Salad set, 2 pieces, wooden bowl, 11 in. $100
Sardine-flat server, solid, 6 1/4 in. $50
Scoop-ice cream, stainless bowl, 8 in. $40
Scoop-ice, silver plate bowl, 8 1/2 in. $50
Server-asparagus, hollow handle, silver plate
   hood, 9 3/8 in. $60
Server-asparagus, hollow handle, sterling
   hood, 10 in. $330
Server-cranberry, stainless bowl, 8 1/2 in. $40
Server-dessert/pie, solid, 10 3/8 in. $180
Server-jelly, 6 7/8 in. $50
Server-lasagna, stainless blade, 9 3/4 in. $45
Server-macaroni, 10 5/8 in. . . . .$250.
Server-pasta, stainless bowl, 10 1/8 in. $45
Server-pie and cake, stainless 5 1/2 in. blade,
   10 1/4 . . . .$45
Server-pie and cake, stainless 5 3/4 in. blade,
   10 5/8 . . . .$45
Spoon-baby, straight handle, 4 1/4 in. $35
Spoon-bonbon, 5 7/8 in. $45
Spoon-casserole, stainless shell bowl,
   16 scallops, 10 in. $40

Spoon-chocolate, short handle, large,
   4 1/8 in. $40
Spoon-demitasse, 4 1/2 in. $25
Spoon-dessert/oval soup, 7 1/4 in. $45
Spoon-dressing, stainless tear bowl,
   11 in. $40
Spoon-fruit, 5 7/8 in. $48
Spoon-iced tea, 8 1/4 in. $38
Spoon-infant feeding, 5 in. $35
Spoon-mustard, 5 1/4 in. $46
Spoon-pierced rice, stainless bowl,
   9 3/4 in. $45
Spoon-platter, solid, 13 1/2 in. $300
Spoon-rice, stainless bowl, 9 5/8 in. $45
Spoon-salt, individual, 2 1/2 in. $13
Spoon-soup, round bowl, cream, 6 1/8 in. $50
Spoon-soup, round bowl, gumbo,
   7 1/4 in. $60
Spoon-sugar, 5 3/4 in. $38
Spoon-teaspoon, 6 in. $22
Tablespoon, (serving spoon), 8 5/8 in. $90
Tablespoon, (serving spoon), pierced,
   8 5/8 in. $110
Tea strainer, 7 3/8 in. $100
Tongs-ice/serving, large, bowl tip,
   7 1/4 in. $180
Tongs-sugar, 4 in. $50

Lady Constance by Towle, 1922

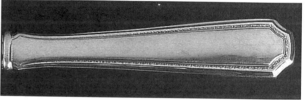

Butter spreader, flat handle, 6 in. $14
Butter-master, flat handle, 6 7/8 in. $30
Carving set, 2 pieces, small, stainless blade,
   steak $80
Fork, 7 3/8 in. $22
Fork, 7 7/8 in. $38
Fork-carving, small, stainless prongs, steak,
   9 1/8 in. $40
Fork-cocktail, 5 3/4 in. $16
Fork-cold meat/serving, medium, solid,
   8 in. $60
Fork-fish, solid, individual, 6 3/4 in. $40
Fork-fish, stainless tines, hollow handle,
   individual, 7 5/8 in. $36
Fork-lemon, 5 5/8 in. $20
Fork-pickle/olive, short handle, 6 1/8 in. $20
Fork-salad, individual, 6 1/4 in. $30

Knife-carving, small, stainless blade, steak, 10 1/8 in. $40

Knife-cheese, stainless blade, 7 1/4 in. $36

Knife-fish, stainless blade, individual, 7 7/8 in. $40

Knife-fruit, stainless blade, individual, 6 7/8 in. $32

Knife-new french, hollow handle, 9 1/8 in. $30

Knife-old french, hollow handle, 9 1/4 in. $30

Knife-old french, hollow handle, 9 5/8 in. $35

Knife-orange, silver plate blade, 7 3/4 in. $36

Knife-sharpener, steel, small, steak, 13 3/4 in. $40

Knife-steak, individual, beveled blade, 8 1/8 in. $36

Ladle-cream, solid, 6 in. $26

Ladle-gravy, solid, 6 3/4 in. $54

Server-cheese, stainless blade, 6 in. $40

Server-jelly, 6 1/2 in. $20

Server-pie and cake, stainless blade, 10 3/4 in. $45

Server-pie, silver plate blade, 9 5/8 in. $50

Server-pie, stainless blade, 10 in. $50

Spoon-baby, straight handle, 4 1/4 in. $32

Spoon-bonbon, 4 3/4 in. $28

Spoon-casserole, smooth bowl, solid, 8 1/4 in. $80

Spoon-demitasse, 4 3/8 in. $16

Spoon-dessert/oval soup, 7 1/8 in. $40

Spoon-fruit, 5 5/8 in. $30

Spoon-relish, 6 1/2 in. $30

Spoon-soup, round bowl, bouillon, 5 in. $16

Spoon-soup, round bowl, cream, 6 3/8 in. $36

Spoon-soup, round bowl, gumbo, 7 1/8 in. $34

Spoon-sugar, 5 3/4 in. $24

Spoon-teaspoon, (5 o'clock), 5 3/4 in. $8

Spoon-teaspoon, 6 in. $20

Spoon-youth, 5 3/8 in. $30

Tablespoon, (serving spoon), 8 5/8 in. $50

Tongs-sugar, 4 in. $48

Lady Diana by Towle, 1928

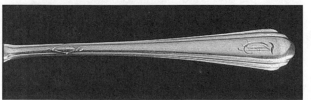

Butter spreader, flat handle, 5 7/8 in. $12

Butter spreader, hollow handle, stainless paddle, 6 in. $30

Butter spreader, hollow handle, stainless paddle, no notch, 5 5/8 in. $30

Butter-master, flat handle, 7 in. $30

Carving set, 2 pieces, small, stainless blade, steak $70

Fork, 7 3/8 in. $24

Fork, 7 7/8 in. $40

Fork-carving, small, stainless prongs, steak, 8 3/4 in. $35

Fork-cocktail, 5 3/4 in. $18

Fork-cold meat/serving, large, solid, 9 1/8 in. $90

Fork-cold meat/serving, small, solid, 7 7/8 in. $60

Fork-lemon, 5 5/8 in. $15

Fork-pickle/olive, short handle, 2 tines, 6 in. $24

Fork-pickle/olive, short handle, 3 tines, 6 in. $24

Fork-salad, individual, 6 3/8 in. $27

Knife-carving, large, stainless blade, roast, 11 1/4 in. $60

Knife-carving, small, stainless blade, steak, 10 in. $35

Knife-new french, hollow handle, 8 3/4 in. $30

Knife-new french, hollow handle, 9 3/4 in. $40

Knife-new french, hollow handle, 9 3/8 in. $30

Ladle-cream, solid, 5 1/2 in. $34

Ladle-gravy, solid, 6 3/4 in. $60

Server-cheese, stainless blade, 6 1/8 in. $35

Server-jelly, 6 5/8 in. $15

Server-pie and cake, stainless blade, 10 1/2 in. $50

Server-pie, stainless blade, 10 in. $50

Server-pie, stainless blade, 9 5/8 in. $50

Server-tomato, solid, 6 5/8 in. $80

Server-tomato, solid, 7 1/2 in. $80

Spoon-baby, straight handle, 4 1/4 in. $36

Spoon-bonbon, 4 3/4 in. $23

Spoon-casserole, smooth, solid, oval bowl, 8 1/4 in. $80

Spoon-demitasse, 4 1/4 in. $12

Spoon-fruit, 5 5/8 in. $30

Spoon-iced tea, 8 in. $28

Spoon-relish, 6 in. $30

Spoon-salad server, plastic bowl, 11 5/8 in. $34

Spoon-serving, solid, tear-shaped bowl, 8 3/4 in. $70

Spoon-soup, round bowl, bouillon, 5 in. $16

Spoon-soup, round bowl, cream,
6 3/8 in.................................$35
Spoon-sugar, 5 3/4 in....................$17
Spoon-teaspoon, (5 o'clock), 5 3/4 in.........$10
Spoon-teaspoon, 6 in.....................$16
Tablespoon, (serving spoon), pierced,
tear-shaped bowl, 8 3/8 in..............$70
Tablespoon, (serving spoon), tear bowl,
8 3/8 in................................$45
Tongs-sugar, 4 in. $35

Lady Mary by Towle, 1917

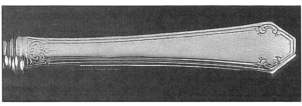

Butter spreader, flat handle, 5 7/8 in.........$14
Carving set, 2 pieces, small, stainless blade,
steak...................................$80
Fork, 7 1/8 in...........................$20
Fork, 7 3/4 in...........................$44
Fork-carving, small, stainless prongs, steak,
9 in....................................$40
Fork-cocktail, 5 5/8 in....................$13
Fork-cold meat/serving, small, solid,
7 7/8 in................................$80
Fork-fish, solid, individual, 6 3/4 in. $60
Fork-lemon, 5 1/2 in......................$22
Fork-pickle/olive, short handle, 6 1/4 in. $20
Fork-ramekin, 5 1/2 in. $36
Fork-salad, individual, 6 1/4 in..............$28
Knife-fish, silver plate blade, individual,
8 1/2 in................................$32
Knife-fruit, stainless blade, individual, 7 in.....$30
Knife-old french, hollow handle, 8 5/8 in......$28
Knife-old french, hollow handle, 9 1/2 in.......$40
Knife-orange, silver plate blade, 7 5/8 in......$30
Ladle-cream, solid, 5 3/8 in.................$40
Poultry shears, 10 in. $130
Server-cheese, silver plate blade, 6 in. $30
Server-jelly, 6 5/8 in......................$16
Server-pastry, silver plate blade, 8 5/8 in......$40
Server-pie, silver plate blade, 10 1/4 in........$40
Server-tomato, solid, 7 1/2 in...............$95
Spoon-casserole, smooth, solid, 7 7/8 in......$80
Spoon-demitasse, 4 1/4 in. $16
Spoon-dessert/oval soup, 7 in. $40
Spoon-fruit, 5 3/4 in......................$28
Spoon-iced tea, 7 7/8 in. $32
Spoon-olive, long handle, 8 in. $110

Spoon-soup, round bowl, bouillon, 5 in........$12
Spoon-soup, round bowl, gumbo, 7 in.........$40
Spoon-sugar, 5 3/4 in......................$15
Spoon-teaspoon (5 o'clock), 5 1/2 in..........$10
Spoon-teaspoon, 5 7/8 in...................$15
Tablespoon, (serving spoon), 8 1/2 in........$48
Tongs-sugar, 3 7/8 in. $38

Lafayette by Towle, 1905

Butter spreader, hollow handle, modern, stainless
paddle, 6 5/8 in.........................$24
Butter spreader, flat handle, round blade,
6 in....................................$20
Butter spreader, hollow handle, silver plate
blade, 6 1/4 in..........................$24
Butter-master, flat handle, 7 5/8 in...........$28
Fork, 7 3/4 in...........................$38
Fork, 7 3/8 in...........................$28
Fork-carving, small, stainless prongs, steak,
9 1/4 in................................$45
Fork-cocktail, 4 7/8 in.....................$20
Fork-cold meat/serving, medium, solid,
8 1/4 in................................$60
Fork-cold meat/serving, medium, solid,
8 5/8 in................................$60
Fork-cold meat/serving, small, solid,
7 1/8 in................................$60
Fork-lemon, 5 1/2 in......................$20
Fork-salad, individual, 6 3/8 in..............$35
Knife-carving, small, stainless blade, steak,
10 1/2 in...............................$45
Knife-modern, hollow handle, 8 3/4 in........$24
Knife-modern, hollow handle, 9 5/8 in........$40
Knife-new french, hollow handle, 8 7/8 in.....$23
Knife-new french, hollow handle, 9 7/8 in.....$35
Ladle-cream, solid, 6 1/4 in.................$32
Ladle-gravy, solid, 7 in....................$63
Ladle-sauce, solid, 5 in....................$32
Server-cheese, silver plate blade, 6 5/8 in. ...$42
Server-pie and cake, stainless blade,
10 5/8 in...............................$40
Server-pie, stainless blade, 10 1/8 in.........$45
Spoon-demitasse, 4 3/4 in..................$15
Spoon-demitasse, 4 3/8 in..................$15
Spoon-dessert/oval soup, 5 1/8 in. handle,
7 1/2 in................................$35

Spoon-fruit, 3 3/4 in. handle, 5 7/8 in. $30
Spoon-fruit, 4 1/8 in. handle, 6 1/8 in. $30
Spoon-lettuce, 9 5/8 in.. . . . .$80
Spoon-olive, short, pierced bowl, 6 3/4 in. $60
Spoon-place/oval bowl, 4 5/8 in. handle,
   7 in.. . . . .$40
Spoon-salad serving, solid, 10 1/8 in. $75
Spoon-soup, round bowl, bouillon, 5 3/8 in. . . .$24
Spoon-soup, round bowl, cream, 5 5/8 in.. . . . .$35
Spoon-soup, round bowl, gumbo, 7 1/2 in. $40
Spoon-sugar, 5 3/4 in.. . . . .$24
Spoon-teaspoon, (5 o'clock), 5 5/8 in. $14
Spoon-teaspoon, 6 1/8 in. $16
Tablespoon, (serving spoon), 5 1/4 in. handle,
   7 7/8 in.. . . . .$50
Tablespoon, (serving spoon), 6 in. handle,
   8 5/8 in.. . . . .$50
Tablespoon, (serving spoon), pierced, 6 in.
   handle, 8 5/8 in.. . . . .$60
Tongs-sugar, 4 in. $45

Fifty-seven pieces Towle Lafayette (1905): 8 luncheon knives, 8 luncheon forks, 8 salad forks, 9 small teaspoons, 8 dessert spoons, 8 bouillon spoons, and 8 fruit knives. Monogram "WW." One luncheon fork repaired. $950

Laureate by Towle, 1968

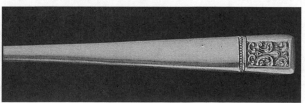

Butter-master, hollow handle, 7 in.. . . . .$60
Fork, 7 1/2 in.. . . . .$60

Fork-salad, individual, 6 5/8 in. $75
Knife-modern, hollow handle, 9 5/8 in.. . . . . . . $70
Server-pie and cake, stainless blade,
   10 7/8 in.. . . . . $90
Spoon-dessert/oval soup, 7 in.. . . . . $80
Spoon-sugar, 6 1/4 in.. . . . . $43
Spoon-teaspoon, 6 1/8 in.. . . . . $40
Tablespoon, (serving spoon), 8 5/8 in. $130

Legato by Towle, 1962

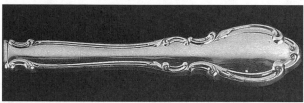

Butter-master, hollow handle, 6 7/8 in.. . . . . . . $34
Cleaver-cheese, stainless blade,
   6 7/8 in.. . . . . $40
Fork, 7 3/8 in. $36
Fork-baby, 4 1/8 in.. . . . . $30
Fork-carving, small, stainless prongs, steak,
   9 1/8 in.. . . . . $40
Fork-carving, small, stainless prongs, steak,
   9 7/8 in.. . . . . $40
Fork-cold meat/serving, large, solid,
   9 1/8 in.. . . . . $80
Fork-fish, stainless tines, hollow handle,
   individual, 8 3/8 in.. . . . . $45
Fork-ice cream, 5 1/8 in.. . . . . $40
Fork-lemon, 5 3/8 in. $30
Fork-pickle/olive, short handle, 5 3/4 in.. . . . . . $30
Fork-salad server, stainless prongs,
   11 3/4 in.. . . . . $45
Fork-salad, individual, 6 5/8 in. $48
Fork-strawberry, 5 1/2 in.. . . . . $30
Fork-utility/serving, stainless tines, 2 of 4
   tines beveled, 10 3/8 in. $45
Fork-youth, 6 1/4 in.. . . . . $40
Knife-bar, hollow handle, 9 3/8 in. $40
Knife-carving, small, stainless blade, steak,
   10 7/8 in.. . . . . $40
Knife-cheese, stainless blade, 7 1/8 in. $40
Knife-fish, stainless blade, individual,
   8 3/4 in.. . . . . $40
Knife-fruit, stainless blade, individual,
   6 1/2 in.. . . . . $45
Knife-fruit, stainless blade, individual,
   7 in. $45
Knife-modern, hollow handle, 9 in. $34
Knife-steak, individual, 9 1/2 in.. . . . . $44
Knife-steak, individual, 9 in. $44

Towle Silversmiths

Knife-utility/serving, stainless blade, no design,
11 3/4 in. $40
Knife-youth, 7 1/8 in. $40
Ladle-gravy, hollow handle, stainless bowl,
8 1/2 in. $40
Ladle-gravy, solid, 6 5/8 in. $80
Ladle-punch, stainless bowl, 13 1/4 in. $55
Ladle-soup, stainless bowl, 11 3/4 in. $55
Magnifying glass, sterling handle, 6 1/2 in. $45
Opener-bottle, stainless bowl, 5 3/8 in. $45
Opener-letter, stainless blade, 9 1/4 in. $40
Pick-butter, 1 tine, 5 in. $30
Plane-cheese, stainless plane, 9 3/4 in. $45
Scoop-ice cream, stainless bowl, 8 7/8 in. $40
Scoop-ice, silver plate bowl, 9 1/8 in. $50
Server-cranberry, stainless bowl, 9 in. $40
Server-jelly, 6 1/4 in. $36
Server-lasagna, stainless blade, 10 1/2 in. $40
Server-pasta, stainless bowl, 11 1/4 in. $40
Server-pie and cake, stainless blade,
11 3/8 in. $45
Server-tomato, solid, 7 1/2 in. $90
Spoon-baby, straight handle, 4 1/4 in. $30
Spoon-bonbon, 5 1/2 in. $32
Spoon-casserole, pierced stainless bowl,
7 scallops, 10 1/4 in. $40
Spoon-casserole, shell, stainless bowl,
17 scallops, 10 3/4 in. $45
Spoon-demitasse, 4 1/4 in. $24
Spoon-dressing, shell, stainless bowl,
11 3/4 in. $40
Spoon-infant feeding, 5 1/2 in. $30
Spoon-salad serving, stainless bowl,
11 7/8 in. $45
Spoon-salt, individual, gold wash,
2 1/2 in. $12
Spoon-sugar, 6 in. $26
Spoon-teaspoon, 6 1/8 in. $24
Spoon-utility/serving, stainless bowl,
7 scallops, 10 1/4 in. $40
Tablespoon, (serving spoon), 8 3/8 in. $80
Tablespoon, (serving spoon), pierced,
8 3/8 in. $80

Carving set, 2 pieces, small, stainless blade,
steak $90
Fork, 7 3/8 in. $28
Fork, 7 7/8 in. $50
Fork-carving, small, stainless prongs, steak,
8 7/8 in. $45
Fork-cocktail, 5 1/2 in. $20
Fork-cold meat/serving, small, solid,
7 5/8 in. $80
Fork-lemon, 5 3/8 in. $25
Fork-salad, individual, 6 1/4 in. $37
Knife-bar, hollow handle, 8 5/8 in. $40
Knife-carving, small, stainless blade, steak,
10 in. $45
Knife-new french, hollow handle, 3 5/8 in.
handle, 8 3/4 in. $34
Knife-new french, hollow handle, 9 1/2 in. $50
Knife-new french, hollow handle, plated
blade, 8 1/2 in. $34
Knife-old french, hollow handle, stainless
blade, 8 3/4 in. $35
Knife-steak, individual, 8 1/2 in. $50
Knife-steak, individual, beveled edge,
8 1/8 in. $50
Ladle-gravy, solid, 6 3/8 in. $75
Opener-letter, stainless blade, 7 5/8 in. $30
Salad set, 2 pieces, plastic bowl $80
Scoop-ice, silver plate bowl, 8 1/4 in. $50
Server-jelly, 6 1/2 in. $28
Spoon-dessert/oval soup, 7 in. $45
Spoon-fruit, 5 1/2 in. $30
Spoon-iced tea, 7 7/8 in. $30
Spoon-salt, individual, 2 5/8 in. $15
Spoon-soup, round bowl, bouillon, 5 in. $27
Spoon-soup, round bowl, cream, 6 1/4 in. $37
Spoon-sugar, 5 5/8 in. $32
Spoon-teaspoon (5 o'clock), 5 1/2 in. $14
Spoon-teaspoon, 5 7/8 in. $18
Spoon-youth, 5 1/4 in. $40
Tablespoon, (serving spoon), 8 1/4 in. $60
Tablespoon, (serving spoon), pierced,
8 1/4 in. $80
Tongs-sugar, 4 in. $60

Louis XIV by Towle, 1924

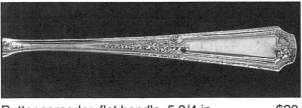

Butter spreader, flat handle, 5 3/4 in. $20
Butter spreader, hollow handle, stainless paddle,
6 in. $25

Madeira by Towle, 1948

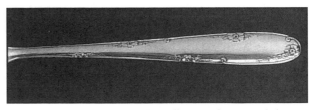

Butter spreader, hollow handle, modern, stainless
paddle, 6 1/2 in. $22

Butter spreader, flat handle, 5 3/4 in..........$18
Butter spreader, hollow handle, stainless
    paddle, 5 7/8 in..........................$22
Butter-master, flat handle, 6 7/8 in...........$28
Butter-master, hollow handle, 6 7/8 in........$30
Carving set, 2 pieces, small, stainless blade,
    steak.....................................$80
Cleaver-cheese, stainless blade, 6 3/4 in......$45
Fork, 7 3/8 in................................$38
Fork, 8 1/8 in................................$50
Fork-baby, 4 1/4 in..........................$25
Fork-carving, small, stainless prongs, steak,
    9 1/2 in..................................$40
Fork-cocktail, 5 5/8 in.......................$22
Fork-cold meat/serving, medium, solid, pierced,
    8 3/8 in..................................$75
Fork-fish, stainless tines, hollow handle,
    individual, 8 in. $40
Fork-ice cream, 5 5/8 in......................$40
Fork-lemon, 5 3/8 in.........................$22
Fork-olive, 3 tines, 5 7/8 in. $35
Fork-pickle/olive, short handle, 2 tines,
    5 7/8 in..................................$23
Fork-salad server, stainless prongs,
    11 1/2 in. $40
Fork-salad, individual, 6 1/2 in...............$38
Fork-strawberry, 5 5/8 in.....................$30
Knife-bar, hollow handle, 9 in................$40
Knife-carving, small, stainless blade, steak,
    10 5/8 in. $40
Knife-cheese, stainless blade, 7 in. $45
Knife-fish, stainless blade, individual,
    8 1/4 in..................................$45
Knife-fruit, stainless blade, individual,
    6 1/2 in..................................$45
Knife, modern, hollow handle, 9 7/8 in. $45
Knife, modern, hollow handle, 9 in...........$38
Knife-new french, hollow handle, 9 in........$40
Knife-steak, individual, 8 5/8 in..............$45
Ladle-cream, solid, 5 5/8 in..................$40
Ladle-gravy, hollow handle, stainless bowl,
    8 1/4 in..................................$40
Ladle-gravy, solid, 6 7/8 in. $60
Ladle-punch, stainless bowl, 12 3/4 in. $60
Opener-bottle, stainless bowl, 6 1/8 in. $40
Opener-letter, stainless blade, 7 5/8 in........$40
Pick-butter, 1 tine, 5 1/4 in..................$30
Scoop-ice, silver plate bowl, 8 7/8 in..........$50
Server/knife-fish, stainless blade, 11 3/8 in. ...$40
Server-cranberry, stainless bowl, 8
    5/8 in....................................$40
Server-jelly, 6 1/2 in.........................$30
Server-lasagna, stainless blade, 10 in. $40
Server-pasta, stainless bowl, 10 3/4 in........$40

Server-pie and cake, stainless blade,
    10 5/8 in.................................$40
Server-pie, stainless blade, 10 in............$45
Server-tomato, solid, 7 1/2 in. $95
Spoon-baby, straight handle, 4 3/8 in......... $25
Spoon-bonbon, 5 1/2 in. $40
Spoon-casserole, shell, stainless bowl,
    10 3/8 in.................................$45
Spoon-casserole, smooth, solid, 8 1/4 in. ... $110
Spoon-demitasse, 4 1/4 in....................$20
Spoon-dessert/oval soup, 6 7/8 in. $46
Spoon-dressing, stainless bowl, 11 in........$45
Spoon-fruit, 5 7/8 in. $36
Spoon-infant feeding, 4 7/8 in...............$25
Spoon-mustard, 5 1/4 in.....................$35
Spoon-pierced rice, stainless bowl, 10 in. $40
Spoon-rice, stainless bowl, 9 3/4 in.........$40
Spoon-salad server, stainless bowl,
    11 1/2 in.................................$40
Spoon-salt, individual, gold wash, 2 1/2 in. ... $10
Spoon-soup, round bowl, cream, 6 3/8 in. $38
Spoon-sugar, 5 7/8 in.......................$22
Spoon-teaspoon, 5 7/8 in....................$18
Tablespoon, (serving spoon), 8 1/2 in. $75
Tablespoon, (serving spoon), pierced,
    8 1/2 in..................................$90
Tongs-sugar, 4 in...........................$50

Marie Louise by Towle, 1939

Butter spreader, flat handle, 5 3/4 in. $28
Butter-master, flat handle, 7 1/8 in. $45
Butter-master, hollow handle, 6 3/4 in. $40
Carving set, 2 pieces, small, stainless blade,
    steak $90
Fork, 7 1/4 in. $40
Fork, 7 3/4 in. $60
Fork-cocktail, 5 3/8 in. $25
Fork-joint/roast holder, large, 10 in.......... $110
Fork-lemon, 4 5/8 in. $36
Fork-salad server, stainless prongs,
    11 1/8 in................................. $40
Fork-salad, individual, 1 of 4 tines beveled,
    6 1/4 in.................................. $46
Knife-carving, small, stainless blade, steak,
    10 1/4 in................................. $45
Knife-cheese, stainless blade, 7 1/8 in. $40

Towle Silversmiths

Knife-fish, stainless blade, individual,
7 7/8 in. $40
Knife-new french, hollow handle, 8 7/8 in. $40
Knife-new french, hollow handle, 9 1/2 in. $45
Knife-steak, individual, 8 1/4 in. $45
Knife-utility/serving, stainless blade,10 7/8 in. .$40
Ladle-cream, solid, 5 1/8 in. $60
Ladle-gravy, hollow handle, stainless bowl,
8 in. $40
Ladle-gravy, solid, 6 1/2 in. $90
Ladle-punch, stainless bowl, 13 1/4 in. $60
Ladle-soup, stainless bowl, 11 in. $55
Scoop-ice cream, stainless bowl, 8 1/4 in. $45
Server-cheese, stainless blade, 6 1/4 in. $60
Server-lasagna, stainless blade, 9 3/4 in. $40
Server-pasta, stainless bowl, 10 3/8 in. $40
Server-pie and cake, stainless blade,
10 3/4 in. $46
Slicer-cake, stainless blade, wedding,
12 in. $40
Spoon-bonbon, 4 3/4 in. $46
Spoon-casserole, shell, stainless bowl,
10 1/8 in. $40
Spoon-casserole, smooth, solid, 9 in. $130
Spoon-demitasse, 4 1/4 in. $24
Spoon-dessert/oval soup, 6 7/8 in. $46
Spoon-dressing, stainless bowl, 11 in. $45
Spoon-rice, stainless bowl, 9 5/8 in. $40
Spoon-salad server, stainless bowl, 11 1/4 in. . .$40
Spoon-soup, round bowl, bouillon, 5 1/2 in. . . .$38
Spoon-soup, round bowl, cream, 6 1/4 in. $45
Spoon-sugar, 6 in. $36
Spoon-teaspoon, 6 in. $28
Tablespoon, (serving spoon), 8 1/2 in. $80
Tablespoon, (serving spoon), oval bowl,
7 3/4 in. $80
Tablespoon, (serving spoon), pierced,
8 1/2 in. $90

Mary Chilton by Towle, 1912

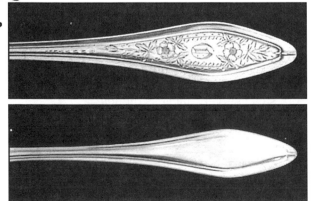

Butter spreader, flat handle, 6 in. $20
Butter-master, flat handle, 7 1/4 in. $32
Carving set, 2 pieces, small, stainless blade,
steak $100
Fork, 7 3/4 in. $50
Fork-carving, small, stainless prongs, steak,
8 5/8 in. $50
Fork-carving, small, stainless prongs, steak,
9 in. $50
Fork-chipped beef, medium, 7 1/2 in. $70
Fork-cocktail, 6 in. $20
Fork-cold meat/serving, large, solid,
9 1/8 in. $80
Fork-cold meat/serving, medium, solid,
8 in. $75
Fork-dessert/luncheon, solid, 7 1/4 in. $33
Fork-fish, solid, individual, 1 1/4 in. wide tines,
7 in. $50
Fork-lemon, 5 1/4 in. $24
Fork-lettuce serving, large, 9 1/4 in. $120
Fork-olive, 3 tines, 6 1/4 in. $25
Fork-salad, individual, 6 1/4 in. $34
Fork-sherbet, 4 3/4 in. $30
Fork-tea, 7/8 in. wide tines, 7 in. $35
Knife-blunt, hollow handle, silver plate blade,
9 in. $30
Knife-cheese, stainless blade, 7 3/8 in. $45
Knife-new french, hollow handle, stainless
blade, 9 3/4 in. $40
Knife-new french, hollow handle, stainless
blade, 9 in. $30
Knife-old french, hollow handle, plated blade,
9 3/4 in. $40
Knife-old french, hollow handle, plated blade,
9 in. $30
Knife-old french, hollow handle, stainless
blade, 9 3/4 in. $40
Knife-old french, hollow handle, stainless
blade, 9 in. $30
Knife-sharpener/steel, large, roast,
14 1/8 in. $65
Knife-utility/serving, stainless blade, no
design, 11 1/4 in. $45
Ladle-cream, solid, 1 7/8 in. wide bowl,
6 1/4 in. $30
Ladle-gravy, solid, 2 1/4 in. wide bowl,
6 3/8 in. $70
Opener-letter, stainless blade. $30
Server-cheese, silver plate blade, 6 in. $50
Server-cheese, stainless blade, 6 in. $45
Server-cucumber, large, 6 3/4 in. $70
Server-jelly, 6 7/8 in. $22
Server-lasagna, stainless blade,, 9 7/8 in. $45

Server-pie and cake, stainless blade,
 10 7/8 in. $50
Server-pie, silver plate blade, 10 1/2 in.. . . . . . .$50
Server-pie, silver plate blade, 9 3/4 in.. . . . .$50
Server-pie, stainless blade, 10 3/8 in. $50
Server-tomato, solid, 7 7/8 in. $90
Spoon-bonbon, 4 3/4 in.. . . . .$30
Spoon-casserole, smooth bowl, solid,
 7 7/8 in.. . . . .$80
Spoon-casserole, smooth bowl, solid,
 8 7/8 in.. . . . .$80
Spoon-demitasse, 4 in.. . . . .$20
Spoon-demitasse, 5 in.. . . . .$20
Spoon-dessert/oval soup, 7 1/2 in.. . . . .$44
Spoon-fruit, 1 1/8 in. bowl, 6 in.. . . . .$30
Spoon-ice cream, 1 3/4 in. bowl, 5 5/8 in.. . . . .$40
Spoon-iced tea, 8 1/8 in. $34
Spoon-lettuce, 8 3/4 in.. . . . .$100
Spoon-olive, long handle, 7 piercings,
 8 1/8 in.. . . . .$130
Spoon-preserve, 7 7/8 in.. . . . .$60
Spoon-relish, 6 3/8 in.. . . . .$36
Spoon-serving, stainless bowl, pierced,
 9 5/8 in.. . . . .$50
Spoon-soup, round bowl, bouillon, 1 3/4 in. bowl,
 square, 5 5/8 in. $28
Spoon-soup, round bowl, bouillon, 5 1/4 in. . . .$28
Spoon-soup, round bowl, gumbo, 3/8 in. square
 bowl, 7 in.. . . . .$36
Spoon-soup, round bowl, gumbo, 7 in. $36
Spoon-sugar, 2 in. bowl, 5 7/8 in. $23
Spoon-teaspoon, (5 o'clock), 5 3/4 in.. . . . .$12
Spoon-teaspoon, 6 1/8 in. $18
Spoon-utility/serving, stainless bowl, 7
 scallops, 9 5/8 in. $40
Tablespoon, (serving spoon), 2 3/4 in. bowl,
 8 1/4 in.. . . . .$50
Tablespoon, (serving spoon), pierced,
 8 3/8 in.. . . . .$80
Tongs-sugar, 3 3/4 in. $50
Tongs-sugar, 4 3/4 in.. . . . .$50

Meadow Song by Towle, 1967

Butter spreader, hollow handle, modern, stainless
 paddle, 6 3/4 in.. . . . .$22
Fork, 7 5/8 in.. . . . .$32

Fork, 8 in. $50
Fork-salad, individual, 6 7/8 in. $32
Knife, modern, hollow handle, 9 1/4 in.. . . . . . .$28
Server-pie and cake, stainless blade,
 11 1/8 in.. . . . .$46
Spoon-sugar, 6 1/4 in.. . . . .$30

Newport Shell by Towle, 1910

Butter spreader, hollow handle, modern, stainless
 paddle, 6 1/2 in.. . . . .$35
Butter-master, hollow handle, 7 in. $45
Fork-salad serving, stainless prongs,
 11 in. $50
Fork-salad, individual, 6 in.. . . . .$50
Fork-utility/serving, stainless tines,
 9 1/2 in. $50
Knife, modern, hollow handle, 8 1/2 in.. . . . . . .$40
Knife-steak, individual, 8 1/8 in.. . . . .$50
Knife-utility/serving, stainless blade, no design,
 10 7/8 in.. . . . .$50
Ladle-gravy, hollow handle, stainless bowl,
 7 3/4 in.. . . . .$45
Ladle-soup, stainless bowl, 11 in. $60
Server-cranberry, stainless bowl, 8 1/4 in.. . . . .$50
Server-pie and cake, stainless blade,
 10 7/8 in.. . . . .$45
Spoon-casserole, pierced stainless bowl,
 9 1/2 in.. . . . .$45
Spoon-dressing, stainless bowl, 10 7/8 in.. . . . .$45
Spoon-rice, stainless bowl, 9 1/2 in. $50
Spoon-teaspoon, (5 o'clock), 5 1/2 in. $24

Novantique by Towle, 1969

Fork, 7 3/4 in. $34
Fork, 8 1/8 in. $50
Knife, modern, hollow handle, 9 1/8 in.. . . . . . .$28
Ladle-gravy, solid, 6 7/8 in.. . . . .$90
Spoon-sugar, 6 3/8 in.. . . . .$35

Old Brocade by Towle, 1932

Butter spreader, flat handle, 5 7/8 in. $20
Butter spreader, hollow handle, stainless
    paddle, 5 5/8 in.. . . . .$25
Butter-master, flat handle, 6 7/8 in. $36
Butter-master, hollow handle, 6 1/2 in.. . . . .$37
Carving set, 2 pieces, small, stainless blade,
    steak $90
Fork, 7 3/8 in. $35
Fork-carving, small, stainless prongs, steak,
    8 1/2 in.. . . . .$45
Fork-cold meat/serving, medium, solid, 8 in. . .$80
Fork-cold meat/serving, small, solid,
    7 3/4 in.. . . . .$80
Fork-ice cream, 5 5/8 in.. . . . .$40
Fork-lemon, 5 1/2 in.. . . . .$30
Fork-pickle/olive, short handle, 2 tines,
    5 7/8 in.. . . . .$30
Fork-pickle/olive, short handle, 3 tines,
    5 3/4 in.. . . . .$30
Fork-salad, individual, 6 3/8 in. $40
Knife-cake, stainless blade, 12 1/4 in. $50
Knife-new french, hollow handle, 8 3/4 in.. . . . .$35
Knife-new french, hollow handle, 9 1/2 in.. . . . .$46
Ladle-cream, solid, 5 5/8 in.. . . . .$40
Ladle-gravy, solid, 6 5/8 in. $80
Scoop-ice, silver plate bowl, 8 1/8 in.. . . . .$45
Server-jelly, 6 5/8 in. $30
Server-pie, stainless blade, 9 1/2 in. $50
Spoon-demitasse, 4 1/4 in. $20
Spoon-fruit, 5 7/8 in.. . . . .$33
Spoon-iced tea, 8 in.. . . . .$35
Spoon-olive, short, pierced bowl, 6 in.. . . . .$90
Spoon-soup, round bowl, cream, 6 3/8 in.. . . . .$42
Spoon-sugar, 5 7/8 in.. . . . .$35
Spoon-teaspoon (5 o'clock), 5 5/8 in.. . . . .$16
Spoon-teaspoon, 5 7/8 in. $18
Tablespoon, (serving spoon), 8 1/2 in.. . . . . . .$70
Tongs-sugar, 3 3/4 in. $50

Old Colonial by Towle, 1895

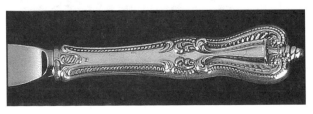

Baby set, 2 pieces $60
Butter spreader, flat handle, paddle blade,
    5 3/4 in.. . . . . $32
Butter spreader, flat handle, pointed blade,
    5 1/2 in.. . . . . $32
Butter spreader, hollow handle, stainless
    paddle, 5 7/8 in.. . . . . $30
Butter-master, hollow handle, 6 7/8 in. $40
Carving set, 2 pieces, small, stainless
    blade, steak $80
Cheese grater, 8 7/8 in.. . . . . $60
Cleaver-cheese, stainless blade, 6 5/8 in. . . . $45
Fork, 7 5/8 in. $70
Fork-baby, 4 5/8 in.. . . . . $30
Fork-baked potato, factory made, 7 in. $80
Fork-carving, small, stainless prongs,
    steak, 8 1/4 in. $40
Fork-carving, small, stainless prongs, steak,
    9 1/8 in. $40
Fork-cocktail, 6 1/4 in. $33
Fork-cold meat/serving, large, stainless tines,
    9 3/4 in. $40
Fork-cold meat/serving, small, solid, bar,
    7 3/4 in. $100
Fork-cold meat/serving, small, solid, no bar,
    7 1/4 in. $100
Fork-dessert/luncheon, solid, 2 in. wide tines,
    7 1/8 in. $48
Fork-fish, stainless tines, hollow handle,
    individual, 7 3/4 in.. $40
Fork-ice cream, no piercings, 5 1/8 in. $47
Fork-lemon, 5 in.. . . . . $40
Fork-olive, long handle, 8 1/4 in. $80
Fork-pickle/olive, long handle, 7 3/4 in. $65
Fork-salad server, stainless prongs,
    11 1/8 in. $40
Fork-salad, individual, 6 1/4 in. $46
Fork-strawberry, 5 1/8 in.. . . . . $30
Knife-bar, hollow handle, 8 5/8 in. $40
Knife-carving, small, stainless blade, steak,
    10 1/4 in.. . . . . $40
Knife-cheese, stainless blade, 7 1/8 in. $40
Knife-fish, stainless blade, individual, 8 in.. . . . $40
Knife-fruit, stainless blade, individual,
    bolster, 6 7/8 in.. . . . . $40
Knife-fruit, stainless blade, individual, no
    bolster, 6 1/2 in.. . . . . $40
Knife, modern, hollow handle, 9 5/8 in. $50
Knife-new french, hollow handle, 9 3/4 in. $50
Knife-new french, hollow handle, stainless
    blade, 8 3/4 in. $40
Knife-steak, individual, beveled blade,
    8 1/4 in. $45

Knife-youth, 7 1/8 in. $40
Ladle-cream, solid, 6 in. $48
Ladle-gravy, hollow handle, stainless bowl,
   8 in. $40
Ladle-gravy, solid, 7 3/8 in. $90
Ladle-punch, stainless bowl, 12 1/2 in. $53
Ladle-punch, stainless bowl, 13 3/8 in. $53
Ladle-soup, stainless bowl, 10 7/8 in. $55
Opener-bottle, stainless bowl, 5 7/8 in. $40
Opener-letter, stainless blade, 7 3/4 in. $40
Opener-letter, stainless blade, 9 3/8 in. $40
Salad set, 2 pieces, plastic bowl $100
Sardine-flat server, solid, 6 1/2 in. $50
Scoop-ice cream, stainless bowl, 8 in. $45
Scoop-ice, silver plate bowl, 8 3/4 in. $50
Scoop-ice, silver plate bowl, 8 3/8 in. $50
Server/knife-fish, stainless blade, 11 1/8 in. . . .$40
Server-asparagus, hollow handle, silver plate
   hood, 9 1/2 in. $60
Server-cranberry, stainless bowl, 8 5/8 in. $45
Server-dessert/pie, solid, 9 7/8 in. $160
Server-jelly, 5 7/8 in. $56
Server-lasagna, stainless blade, 9 7/8 in. $40
Server-pasta, stainless bowl, 10 3/8 in. $40
Server-pie and cake, stainless blade,
   10 1/2 in. $40
Slicer-cake, stainless blade, wedding,
   12 1/8 in. $40
Spoon-baby, straight handle, 4 1/4 in. $30
Spoon-bonbon, nut spoon, 5 1/2 in. $45
Spoon-casserole, pierced stainless bowl,
   9 3/4 in. $45
Spoon-chocolate, short handle, large, 4 in. $42
Spoon-cracker, 8 1/4 in. $160
Spoon-demitasse, 4 3/4 in. $25
Spoon-demitasse, 4 in. $25
Spoon-dessert/oval soup, 7 1/8 in. $48
Spoon-dressing, shell, stainless bowl,
   11 1/8 in. $40
Spoon-fruit, 5 7/8 in. $40
Spoon-infant feeding, 5 7/8 in. $30
Spoon-mustard, 5 3/8 in. $60
Spoon-pierced rice, stainless bowl, 9 5/8 in. . . .$40
Spoon-platter, solid, 14 1/4 in. $270
Spoon-salad server, stainless bowl,
   11 1/8 in. $40
Spoon-soup, round bowl, bouillon,
   5 1/4 in. $42
Spoon-soup, round bowl, cream, 6 in. $50
Spoon-soup, round bowl, gumbo, 6 7/8 in. $60
Spoon-sugar, 5 7/8 in. $36
Spoon-teaspoon, 3 3/4 in. handle, 5 5/8 in. $20
Spoon-utility/serving, stainless bowl,
   9 5/8 in. $40

Tablespoon, (serving spoon), 8 1/2 in. $95
Tablespoon, (serving spoon), 8 1/8 in. $95
Tablespoon, (serving spoon), pierced,
   8 1/2 in. $100
Tongs-asparagus, individual, solid,
   5 1/4 in. $90
Tongs-ice/serving, large, bowl tip,
   7 1/4 in. $150
Tongs-sugar, 4 in. $45

Towle Old Colonial pierced salad fork. Length,
6 5/8 in.; monogram "h"; fine condition. $75

Old English by Towle, 1892

Butter spreader, flat handle, 5 1/8 in. $30
Butter spreader, flat handle, 6 3/8 in. $30
Butter spreader, hollow handle, stainless paddle,
   5 7/8 in. $28
Butter-master, hollow handle, 6 7/8 in. $38
Cleaver-cheese, stainless blade, 6 3/4 in. $45
Fork, 7 1/2 in. $60
Fork, 7 in. $22
Fork-cocktail, 3 tines, no bevel, 6 1/8 in. $30
Fork-cold meat/serving, small, solid, design on
   bowl, 7 3/8 in. $60
Fork-dessert, 6 in. $50
Fork-fish, stainless tines, hollow handle,
   individual, 7 1/2 in. $36
Fork-salad, individual, 5 3/4 in. $45
Fork-strawberry, gold wash, 5 in. $50
Fork-youth, 6 in. $45

Old English by Towle, 1892

Knife-blunt, hollow handle, 9 1/2 in. $70
Knife-modern, hollow handle, 8 1/2 in. $50
Knife-modern, hollow handle, 8 3/4 in. $50
Knife-new french, hollow handle, 8 3/4 in. $50
Knife-new french, hollow handle, 9 1/2 in. $70
Ladle-cream, solid, gold wash, 5 7/8 in. $50
Ladle-gravy, solid, 6 1/2 in. $90
Opener-letter, stainless blade, 7 5/8 in. $30
Sardine fork/serving, solid, 5 5/8 in. $60
Server-pie and cake, stainless blade,
    10 3/4 in. $50
Spoon-berry/casserole, solid, 8 1/4 in. $150
Spoon-berry/casserole, solid, 9 1/4 in. $150
Spoon-demitasse, 3 7/8 in. $20
Spoon-demitasse, gold wash, 3 7/8 in. $20
Spoon-dessert/oval soup, 7 in. $40
Spoon-fruit, gold wash, 5 3/8 in. $40
Spoon-fruit, 5 3/8 in. $40
Spoon-iced tea, 8 1/2 in. $40
Spoon-olive, long handle, 8 1/2 in. $160
Spoon-olive, long handle, gold wash,
    8 1/2 in. $160
Spoon-soup, round bowl, cream, 5 5/8 in. $40
Spoon-sugar, design on bowl, 5 3/4 in. $36
Spoon-teaspoon (5 o'clock), 3 1/2 in. handle,
    5 1/2 in. $20
Spoon-youth, 4 7/8 in. $40
Spoon-youth, gold wash, 4 7/8 in. $40
Tablespoon, (serving spoon), 8 1/8 in. $60
Tablespoon, (serving spoon), pierced,
    8 1/8 in. $70
Tongs-sugar, 4 in. $60

Old Lace by Towle, 1939

Butter spreader, hollow handle, modern, stainless
    paddle, 6 1/4 in. $20
Butter spreader, flat handle, 5 7/8 in. $17
Butter spreader, hollow handle, stainless
    paddle, 5 3/4 in. $23
Butter-master, flat handle, 6 7/8 in. $32
Butter-master, hollow handle, 6 5/8 in. $34
Carving set, 2 pieces, small, stainless blade,
    steak $80
Cleaver-cheese, stainless blade, 6 5/8 in. $40
Fork, 7 3/8 in. $28
Fork, 7 7/8 in. $50

Fork-baby, 4 1/4 in. $32
Fork-carving, small, stainless prongs, steak,
    8 3/4 in. $40
Fork-carving, small, stainless prongs, steak,
    9 5/8 in. $40
Fork-cocktail, 5 3/4 in. $22
Fork-cold meat/serving, medium, solid, 8 in. . . . $80
Fork-fish, stainless tines, hollow handle,
    individual, 8 1/8 in. $45
Fork-ice cream, 5 1/2 in. $40
Fork-joint/roast holder, large, 11 1/4 in. $90
Fork-pickle/olive, short handle, 2 tines, 6 in. . . . $30
Fork-salad server, stainless prongs,
    11 1/2 in. $45
Fork-salad, individual, 6 3/4 in. $34
Fork-strawberry, square bowl, 5 1/2 in. $25
Fork-youth, 6 3/8 in. $40
Fork-youth, 6 in. $40
Knife-bar, hollow handle, 9 in. $40
Knife-carving, large, stainless blade, roast,
    13 3/8 in. $54
Knife-carving, small, stainless blade, steak,
    10 3/8 in. $40
Knife-cheese, stainless blade, 6 7/8 in. $45
Knife-fish, stainless blade, individual,
    8 1/4 in. $45
Knife-fruit, stainless blade, individual,
    3 1/4 in. stainless blade, 6 1/4 in. $45
Knife-fruit, stainless blade, individual,
    3 3/4 in. stainless blade, 6 3/4 in. $45
Knife, modern, hollow handle, 5 in. stainless
    blade, 8 7/8 in. $32
Knife, modern, hollow handle, stainless blade,
    9 7/8 in. $50
Knife-new french, hollow handle, 4 1/2 in.
    stainless blade, 8 3/4 in. $28
Knife-new french, hollow handle, 9 1/2 in. $50
Knife-steak, individual, no rest, 8 5/8 in. $45
Knife-utility/serving, stainless blade, no
    design, 11 3/8 in. $45
Knife-youth, 7 in. $40
Ladle-cream, solid, 5 3/4 in. $42
Ladle-gravy, hollow handle, stainless bowl,
    8 3/8 in. $40
Ladle-gravy, solid, 6 3/4 in. $70
Ladle-soup, stainless bowl, 11 1/4 in. $60
Opener-bottle, stainless bowl, 6 1/8 in. $40
Pick-butter, 1 tine, 5 1/4 in. $30
Plane-cheese, stainless plane, 9 1/4 in. $48
Scoop-ice cream, stainless bowl, 8 1/4 in. $40
Scoop-ice, silver plate bowl, 8 5/8 in. $50
Server-cranberry, stainless bowl, 8 7/8 in. $45
Server-jelly, 6 3/4 in. $32
Server-lasagna, stainless blade, 10 1/8 in. . . . $40

Server-pasta, stainless bowl, 10 3/4 in........$45
Server-pie and cake, stainless blade,
    10 5/8 in. $45
Server-tomato, solid, 7 1/2 in. $90
Slicer-cake, stainless blade, wedding,
    12 3/4 in. $45
Spoon-bonbon, 4 7/8 in....................$40
Spoon-bonbon, 5 1/2 in....................$40
Spoon-casserole, stainless shell bowl,
    10 1/2 in. $45
Spoon-demitasse, 4 1/4 in. $24
Spoon-dessert/oval soup, 6 7/8 in...........$50
Spoon-dressing, stainless bowl, 11 in........$45
Spoon-five o'clock/youth, 5 5/8 in. $22
Spoon-fruit, 6 in. $35
Spoon-iced tea, 8 1/8 in. $33
Spoon-infant feeding, 5 in.................$32
Spoon-mustard, 5 1/8 in. $44
Spoon-relish, 6 in.......................$40
Spoon-rice, stainless bowl, 10 in...........$40
Spoon-salad serving, stainless bowl,
    11 5/8 in. $40
Spoon-salt, individual, gold wash, 2 1/2 in.....$10
Spoon-soup, round bowl, cream, 6 1/2 in......$34
Spoon-sugar, 6 in.........................$34
Spoon-teaspoon, 6 1/8 in. $18
Tablespoon, (serving spoon), 8 1/2 in........$70
Tablespoon, (serving spoon), pierced,
    8 1/2 in...............................$100
Tongs-sugar, 4 in. $45

Old Master by Towle, 1942

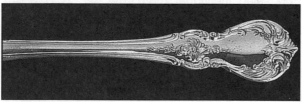

Butter spreader, hollow handle, modern, stainless
    paddle, 6 1/2 in.........................$36
Butter spreader, flat handle, 5 3/4 in.........$32
Butter spreader, hollow handle, stainless
    paddle, 5 7/8 in.........................$36
Butter-master, flat handle, 6 7/8 in...........$40
Butter-master, hollow handle, 6 1/2 in........$40
Butter-master, hollow handle, 6 7/8 in........$40
Carving set, 2 pieces, large, stainless blade,
    roast $110
Carving set, 2 pieces, small, stainless blade,
    steak..................................$90
Cheese grater, 8 7/8 in. $60
Cleaver-cheese, stainless blade, 6 1/2 in......$45

Fork, 7 1/4 in. $35
Fork, 7 3/4 in. $56
Fork-baby, 4 1/8 in........................$30
Fork-carving, small, stainless prongs, steak,
    8 5/8 in................................$45
Fork-cocktail, 5 3/4 in. $28
Fork-cold meat/serving, large, stainless tines,
    9 7/8 in. $45
Fork-cold meat/serving, medium, solid,
    8 1/4 in................................$100
Fork-fish, stainless tines, hollow handle,
    individual, 7 7/8 in......................$44
Fork-ice cream, 3/8 in. tines, 5 1/2 in.........$45
Fork-lemon, 5 1/4 in. $32
Fork-lemon, 5 5/8 in. $32
Fork-lettuce serving, large, 8 3/4 in. $100
Fork-pickle/olive, long handle, 8 in. $60
Fork-pickle/olive, short handle, 2 tines,
    5 7/8 in................................$36
Fork-salad server, plastic prongs, 12 in.......$44
Fork-salad server, stainless prongs,
    11 3/8 in...............................$45
Fork-salad serving, solid, no bar,
    9 1/8 in................................$120
Fork-salad, individual, pierced, 6 3/8 in.......$44
Fork-strawberry, 5 5/8 in...................$30
Fork-youth, 6 in. $40
Jigger-double wide, handle, silver plate bowls,
    6 1/8 in................................$50
Knife-bar, hollow handle, 8 7/8 in. $30
Knife-carving, small, stainless blade, steak,
    10 1/4 in...............................$45
Knife-cheese, stainless blade, 7 1/8 in. $40
Knife-fish, stainless blade, individual, no notch,
    8 1/8 in................................$40
Knife-fish, stainless blade, individual, notch,
    8 1/2 in................................$40
Knife-fruit, stainless blade, individual,
    6 7/8 in................................$40
Knife-ham slicer, stainless blade, 15 3/4 in.... $60
Knife, modern, hollow handle, 8 7/8 in........$32
Knife, modern, hollow handle, 9 5/8 in........$50
Knife-new french, hollow handle, 8 7/8 in. $32
Knife-new french, hollow handle, stainless
    blade, 9 5/8 in.........................$45
Knife-new french, sterling blade, 8 3/4 in. $70
Knife-steak, individual, no rest, 8 3/8 in.......$45
Knife-utility/serving, stainless blade,
    11 1/8 in...............................$40
Knife-youth, 7 1/8 in. $40
Ladle-gravy, hollow handle, stainless bowl,
    8 in...................................$45
Ladle-gravy, solid, 6 3/4 in. $90
Ladle-punch, stainless bowl, 12 7/8 in........$60

Old Master by Towle, 1942

Ladle-soup, solid, 15 1/8 in. $350
Ladle-soup, stainless bowl, 11 in. $60
Opener-letter, stainless blade, 7 5/8 in. $35
Pick-butter, 1 tine, 5 1/4 in. $30
Salad set, 2 pieces, plastic bowl, 12 in. $80
Salad set, 2 pieces, stainless bowl,
   11 3/8 in. $90
Sardine-flat server, solid, 6 3/8 in. $45
Scoop-cheese, solid, 6 1/4 in. $70
Scoop-coffee, silver plate bowl, 4 in. $44
Scoop-ice cream, stainless bowl, 8 in. $45
Scoop-ice, silver plate bowl, 8 1/2 in. $50
Server/knife-fish, stainless blade, 11 1/4 in. . . .$45
Server-asparagus, hollow handle, silver plate
   hood, 9 5/8 in. $60
Server-asparagus, solid, 9 1/2 in. $250
Server-cranberry, stainless bowl, 8 5/8 in. $45
Server-jelly, 6 1/2 in. $40
Server-lasagna, stainless blade, 10 in. $45
Server-lasagna, stainless blade, 9 5/8 in. $45
Server-macaroni, 10 3/8 in. $180
Server-pasta, stainless bowl, 10 1/2 in. $40
Server-pie and cake, stainless blade,
   10 3/4 in. $40
Server-pie, solid, 10 1/8 in. $150
Server-pie, stainless, oversize,
   12 1/4 in. $40
Spoon-baby, straight handle, 1 3/4 in. bowl,
   4 1/4 in. $30
Spoon-bonbon, 5 1/2 in. $44
Spoon-casserole, pierced stainless bowl,
   9 7/8 in. $45
Spoon-casserole, shell, stainless bowl,
   10 1/4 in. $45
Spoon-chocolate, short handle, large,
   4 in. $38
Spoon-demitasse, 4 1/4 in. $20
Spoon-dessert/oval soup, 6 5/8 in. $46
Spoon-dressing/shell, stainless bowl,
   11 1/4 in. $45
Spoon-five o'clock/youth, 5 3/8 in. $36
Spoon-iced tea, 7 7/8 in. $36
Spoon-infant feeding, 4 7/8 in. $34
Spoon-mustard, 5 1/8 in. $45
Spoon-platter, solid, 13 1/2 in. $250
Spoon-relish, not pierced, 5 7/8 in. $50
Spoon-salad server, stainless bowl,
   11 3/8 in. $45
Spoon-salad serving, solid, 9 1/8 in. $130
Spoon-salad serving, wooden bowl,
   10 3/4 in. $45
Spoon-salt, individual, 2 1/2 in. $13
Spoon-soup, round bowl, cream,
   6 1/4 in. $42

Spoon-sugar, 5 3/4 in. $30
Spoon-teaspoon, 6 in. $20
Spoon-utility/serving, stainless bowl,
   9 3/4 in. $40
Tablespoon, (serving spoon), 8 1/2 in. $80
Tea strainer, 7 1/8 in. $100
Tongs-asparagus, individual, solid,
   5 7/8 in. $90
Tongs-ice/serving, large, bowl tip,
   7 1/4 in. $160
Tongs-salad, 8 1/2 in. $260
Tongs-sugar, 4 in. $45
Youth set, 3 pieces (spoon, knife, fork) $120

Old Mirror by Towle, 1940

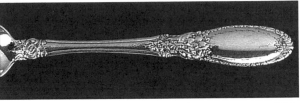

Butter spreader, flat handle, 5 3/4 in. $26
Butter spreader, hollow handle, stainless paddle,
   5 3/4 in. $28
Butter-master, flat handle, 7 in. $46
Butter-master, hollow handle, 6 3/8 in. $46
Fork, 7 1/8 in. $40
Fork, 7 3/4 in. $60
Fork-cocktail, 5 3/4 in. $28
Fork-cold meat/serving, small, solid,
   7 7/8 in. $85
Fork-salad, individual, 6 3/8 in. $40
Knife, modern, hollow handle, stainless
   blade, 8 1/4 in. $40
Knife, modern, hollow handle, stainless
   blade, 8 3/4 in. $40
Knife, modern, hollow handle, stainless
   blade, 9 5/8 in. $54
Knife-new french, hollow handle, stainless
   blade, 8 3/4 in. $40
Ladle-gravy, solid, 6 3/4 in. $95
Server-pie and cake, stainless blade,
   10 7/8 in. $60
Spoon-demitasse, 4 1/4 in. $28
Spoon-dessert/oval soup, 6 7/8 in. $40
Spoon-fruit, 5 7/8 in. $44
Spoon-iced tea, 7 7/8 in. $40
Spoon-soup, round bowl, cream,
   6 1/4 in. $44
Spoon-sugar, 6 in. $36
Spoon-teaspoon, 6 in. $22
Tablespoon, (serving spoon), 8 1/2 in. $75

Old Newbury/Newbury by Towle, 1900

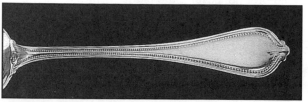

Butter spreader, flat handle, 5 3/4 in. $30
Butter spreader, hollow handle, stainless
    paddle, 6 1/8 in. $30
Butter-master, flat handle, 6 7/8 in. $40
Butter-master, flat handle, 7 3/8 in. $40
Cleaver-cheese, stainless blade, 6 7/8 in. $45
Fork, 6 3/4 in. $34
Fork, 7 1/2 in. $50
Fork, 7 1/8 in. $34
Fork-carving, small, stainless prongs, steak,
    9 1/4 in. $40
Fork-cold meat/serving, large, stainless tines,
    9 5/8 in. $40
Fork-cold meat/serving, small, solid,
    7 1/2 in. $90
Fork-fish, solid, individual, bar, 6 1/8 in. $58
Fork-fish, stainless tines, hollow handle,
    individual, 7 3/8 in. $40
Fork-oyster, short handle, 4 1/2 in. handle,
    5 3/4 in. $24
Fork-salad server, stainless prongs,
    11 1/8 in. $40
Fork-salad, individual, 6 3/8 in. $54
Knife-carving, small, stainless blade, steak,
    10 1/8 in. $40
Knife-cheese, stainless blade, 7 1/8 in. $45
Knife-fish, stainless blade, individual,
    8 3/8 in. $40
Knife-fruit, stainless blade, individual,
    7 1/8 in. $45
Knife-new french, hollow handle, silver plate
    blade, 8 7/8 in. $32
Knife-new french, hollow handle, stainless
    blade, 8 7/8 in. $32
Knife-old french, hollow handle, silver plate
    blade, 8 7/8 in. $32
Knife-old french, hollow handle, stainless
    blade, 8 7/8 in. $32
Knife-old french, hollow handle, stainless
    blade, 9 3/4 in. $40
Knife-orange, silver plate blade, 7 3/8 in. $38
Knife-utility/serving, stainless blade, no
    design, 11 in. $40
Ladle-cream, solid, 5 3/4 in. $48

Ladle-gravy, hollow handle, stainless bowl,
    7 7/8 in. $40
Ladle-gravy, solid, 6 3/4 in. $90
Ladle-punch, stainless bowl, 12 3/4 in. $55
Ladle-punch, stainless bowl, 13 3/4 in. $55
Ladle-soup, solid, 12 1/2 in. $250
Ladle-soup, stainless bowl, 10 5/8 in. $50
Salad set, 2 pieces, stainless bowl $80
Scoop-ice, silver plate bowl, 8 1/2 in. $50
Server-asparagus, hollow handle, silver plate
    hood, 9 3/8 in. $55
Server-cheese, stainless blade, 6 1/2 in. $45
Server-cranberry, stainless bowl,
    8 1/2 in. $45
Server-lasagna, stainless blade, 9 5/8 in. $40
Server-pasta, stainless bowl, 10 1/4 in. $40
Server-pie and cake, stainless blade,
    10 7/8 in. $45
Server-tomato, solid, 7 1/2 in. $90
Spoon-casserole, pierced stainless bowl,
    7 scallops, 9 1/2 in. $40
Spoon-casserole, shell, stainless bowl,
    10 1/8 in. $40
Spoon-chocolate muddler, long handle,
    7 1/2 in. $45
Spoon-chocolate, short handle, large,
    5 1/2 in. $25
Spoon-demitasse, 3 7/8 in. $20
Spoon-demitasse, 4 5/8 in. $20
Spoon-dessert/oval soup, 7 1/8 in. $40
Spoon-dressing/shell, stainless bowl,
    11 1/8 in. $40
Spoon-fruit, 5 5/8 in. $36
Spoon-iced tea, 5 3/4 in. handle, 7 1/2 in. $38
Spoon-parfait, solid, 4 1/2 in. handle,
    6 3/8 in. $40
Spoon-place/oval soup, tear-shaped bowl,
    6 5/8 in. $40
Spoon-salad server, stainless bowl,
    11 1/4 in. $40
Spoon-soup, round bowl, bouillon,
    5 1/2 in. $36
Spoon-soup, round bowl, cream, oval bowl,
    6 1/2 in. $38
Spoon-sugar, 5 7/8 in. $30
Spoon-teaspoon, (5 o'clock), 5 1/2 in. $18
Spoon-teaspoon, 5 7/8 in. $22
Spoon-utility/serving, stainless bowl, 7
    scallops, 9 1/2 in. $40
Spoon-youth, 5 3/8 in. $20
Tablespoon, (serving spoon), 5 1/2 in. handle,
    8 1/8 in. $60
Tablespoon, (serving spoon), 5 1/4 in. handle,
    7 7/8 in. $60

Towle Silversmiths

Towle Silversmiths

Tablespoon, (serving spoon), pierced,
8 1/8 in. $70
Tongs-sugar, 4 3/4 in. $60
Tongs-sugar, 4 in. $60

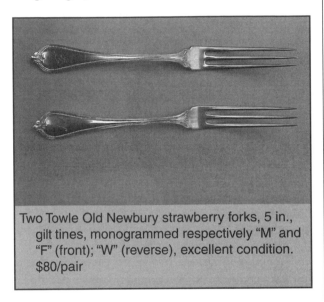

Two Towle Old Newbury strawberry forks, 5 in.,
gilt tines, monogrammed respectively "M" and
"F" (front); "W" (reverse), excellent condition.
$80/pair

Paul Revere by Towle, 1906

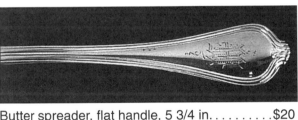

Butter spreader, flat handle, 5 3/4 in. $20
Butter spreader, hollow handle, stainless paddle,
no notch, 6 1/4 in. $20
Butter-master, flat handle, crimp in handle,
6 7/8 in. $34
Butter-master, hollow handle, 7 in. $28
Carving set, 2 pieces, small, stainless blade,
steak $110
Fork, 7 1/8 in. $34
Fork, 7 5/8 in. $40
Fork-chipped beef, small, 3 tines, 5 7/8 in. $70
Fork-cocktail, 5 5/8 in. $27
Fork-cold meat/serving, small, solid,
7 1/2 in. $60
Fork-lemon, 5 in. $28
Fork-salad, individual, pierced once,
5 3/4 in. $35
Fork-salad, individual, pierced once,
6 1/4 in. $35
Knife-blunt, hollow handle, 8 3/4 in. $30
Knife-new french, hollow handle, 8 7/8 in. $30
Knife-new french, hollow handle, 9 1/2 in. $40

Knife-new french, hollow handle, 9 3/4 in. $40
Knife-old french, hollow handle, 8 7/8 in. $30
Knife-old french, hollow handle, 9 5/8 in. $40
Knife-orange, silver plate blade, 7 1/2 in. $40
Ladle-cream, solid, 4 7/8 in. $35
Ladle-gravy, solid, 7 in. $60
Server-cranberry, stainless bowl, 8 1/2 in. $45
Server-pie and cake, stainless blade,
10 1/4 in. $40
Server-pie, silver plate blade, 9 7/8 in. $55
Spoon-baby, straight handle, 4 3/8 in. $37
Spoon-chocolate, short handle, oval bowl,
5 3/8 in. $25
Spoon-demitasse, 3 7/8 in. $20
Spoon-dessert/oval soup, 7 in. $35
Spoon-dressing, large, solid, with button,
12 in. $210
Spoon-dressing, stainless bowl, 10 7/8 in. $60
Spoon-fruit, 5 5/8 in. $35
Spoon-ice cream, egg-shaped bowl,
5 1/2 in. $34
Spoon-iced tea, 7 3/8 in. $35
Spoon-preserve, 7 3/8 in. $80
Spoon-soup, round bowl, cream, 1 1/2 in.
bowl, 5 1/2 in. $32
Spoon-soup, round bowl, cream, 1 3/4 in.
bowl, 5 3/4 in. $32
Spoon-soup, round bowl, gumbo, oval bowl,
7 .... $40
Spoon-sugar, 5 5/8 in. $26
Spoon-teaspoon (5 o'clock), 5 1/2 in. $15
Spoon-teaspoon, 5 7/8 in. $23
Tablespoon, (serving spoon), 8 1/2 in. $35
Tablespoon, (serving spoon), 8 in. $35

Peachtree Manor by Towle, 1956

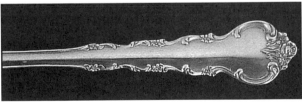

Butter spreader, hollow handle, modern, stainless
paddle, 6 1/2 in. $28
Butter-master, hollow handle, 6 7/8 in. $26
Fork, 7 1/4 in. $40
Fork, 7 3/4 in. $48
Fork-cold meat/serving, small, solid, 7 3/4 in. .. $90
Fork-pickle/olive, short handle, 5 3/4 in. $35
Fork-salad, individual, 6 1/2 in. $50
Knife-modern, hollow handle, 8 7/8 in. $34
Knife-modern, hollow handle, 9 3/4 in. $50

Ladle-gravy, solid, 6 1/2 in. $80
Server-jelly, 6 5/8 in. $38
Server-pie and cake, stainless blade,
10 7/8 in. $70
Spoon-dessert/oval soup, 6 5/8 in. $44
Spoon-sugar, 5 1/2 in. $32
Spoon-teaspoon, 5 7/8 in. $24
Tablespoon, (serving spoon), 8 5/8 in. $80
Tablespoon, (serving spoon), pierced,
8 5/8 in. $90

Petit Point by Towle, 1957

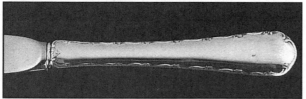

Butter spreader, hollow handle, modern, stainless
paddle, 6 1/2 in. $24
Butter-master, hollow handle, 6 7/8 in. $34
Fork, 7 1/4 in. $43
Fork-cold meat/serving, small, solid,
7 3/4 in. $90
Fork-lemon, 5 1/4 in. $27
Fork-pickle/olive, short handle, 5 3/4 in. $27
Fork-salad, individual, 6 1/2 in. $50
Knife-cheese, stainless blade, 7 in. $47
Knife-modern, hollow handle, 8 7/8 in. $40
Ladle-cream, solid, 5 5/8 in. $45
Ladle-gravy, solid, 6 1/2 in. $85
Server-pie and cake, stainless blade,
10 1/2 in. $70
Spoon-demitasse, 4 1/4 in. $26
Spoon-dessert/oval soup, 6 5/8 in. $50
Spoon-sugar, 5 3/8 in. $30
Spoon-sugar, 6 1/4 in. $30
Spoon-teaspoon, 5 7/8 in. $20
Tablespoon, (serving spoon), 8 1/2 in. $80
Tablespoon, (serving spoon), pierced,
8 1/2 in. $90

Pomona by Towle, 1887

(multiple motifs)

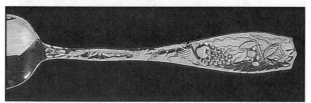

Spoon-demitasse, 3 7/8 in. $30

Spoon-teaspoon, 5 7/8 in. $36
Tablespoon, (serving spoon), 8 in. $100

R.S.V.P. by Towle, 1965

Butter spreader, hollow handle, modern, stainless
paddle, 6 5/8 in. $27
Butter-master, hollow handle, 6 7/8 in. $30
Fork, 7 1/2 in. $50
Fork-baby, 4 1/8 in. $36
Fork-carving, small, stainless prongs, steak,
9 5/8 in. $40
Fork-cold meat/serving, medium, solid,
8 3/8 in. $70
Fork-salad, individual, 7 in. $32
Knife-carving, small, stainless blade, steak,
10 3/4 in. $40
Knife-modern, hollow handle, 9 in. $24
Ladle-gravy, solid, 6 3/8 in. $70
Server-jelly, 6 1/8 in. $30
Server-pasta, stainless bowl, 10 3/4 in. $45
Slicer-cake, stainless blade, wedding,
12 7/8 in. $50
Spoon-baby, straight handle, 4 1/4 in. $36
Spoon-bonbon, teeth, 5 1/4 in. $30
Spoon-fruit, 6 1/8 in. $33
Spoon-iced tea, 7 3/4 in. $34
Spoon-infant feeding, 5 1/2 in. $36
Spoon-sugar, 5 1/8 in. $34
Spoon-teaspoon, 6 1/4 in. $20
Tablespoon, (serving spoon), 8 1/8 in. $70
Tablespoon, (serving spoon), pierced,
8 1/4 in. $80

Rambler Rose by Towle, 1937

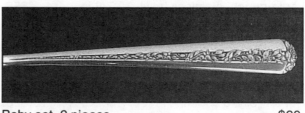

Baby set, 2 pieces $60
Butter spreader, flat handle, 5 7/8 in. $18
Butter spreader, hollow handle, stainless
paddle, 5 5/8 in. $22

Towle Silversmiths

Butter-master, flat handle, 6 7/8 in............$35
Butter-master, hollow handle, 6 3/8 in.........$35
Carving set, 2 pieces, small, stainless blade,
    steak....................................$90
Cleaver-cheese, stainless blade, 6 1/4 in......$40
Fork, 7 3/8 in................................$26
Fork, 8 in....................................$40
Fork-baby, 4 1/4 in...........................$30
Fork-cocktail, 5 3/4 in.......................$20
Fork-cold meat/serving, large, stainless tines,
    9 3/4 in.................................$40
Fork-cold meat/serving, small, solid,
    7 7/8 in.................................$80
Fork-lemon, 5 1/2 in..........................$28
Fork-salad server, stainless prongs,
    11 1/4 in................................$40
Fork-salad, individual, 6 5/8 in..............$30
Fork-youth, 6 1/8 in..........................$40
Knife-bar, hollow handle, 8 3/4 in............$45
Knife-carving, small, stainless blade, steak,
    9 5/8 in.................................$45
Knife-cheese, stainless blade, 6 3/4 in.......$40
Knife-fish, stainless blade, individual,
    7 7/8 in.................................$40
Knife-fish, stainless blade, individual,
    8 1/4 in.................................$40
Knife-fruit, stainless blade, individual,
    6 3/8 in.................................$45
Knife-modern, hollow handle, 9 1/2 in.........$40
Knife-new french, hollow handle, silver plate
    blade, 8 5/8 in..........................$30
Knife-new french, hollow handle, silver plate
    blade, 9 1/2 in..........................$40
Knife-new french, hollow handle, stainless
    blade, 8 5/8 in..........................$30
Knife-new french, hollow handle, stainless
    blade, 9 1/2 in..........................$40
Knife-steak, individual, beveled blade,
    8 3/8 in.................................$40
Knife-utility/serving, stainless blade, no
    design on bowl, 11 1/8 in................$45
Ladle-cream, solid, 5 3/4 in..................$40
Ladle-gravy, solid, 6 7/8 in..................$80
Ladle-punch, stainless bowl, 12 7/8 in........$55
Opener-bottle, stainless bowl, 5 7/8 in.......$40
Opener-letter, stainless blade, 7 1/4 in......$40
Scoop-ice cream, stainless bowl, 8 1/4 in.....$40
Scoop-ice, silver plate bowl, 8 1/4 in........$50
Server-cheese, stainless blade, 6 1/8 in......$45
Server-jelly, 6 3/4 in........................$28
Server-lasagna, stainless blade, 9 3/4 in.....$40
Server-pasta, stainless bowl, 10 1/2 in.......$45
Server-pie and cake, stainless blade,
    10 7/8 in................................$40

Server-pie, stainless blade, 10 in............$45
Slicer-cake, stainless blade, wedding,
    12 1/8 in................................$40
Spoon-baby, straight handle, 4 1/2 in.........$30
Spoon-bonbon, 4 7/8 in........................$40
Spoon-bonbon, 5 1/2 in........................$40
Spoon-casserole, pierced stainless bowl,
    9 5/8 in.................................$40
Spoon-casserole, stainless shell bowl,
    10 1/8 in................................$40
Spoon-casserole, smooth bowl, solid,
    8 1/8 in................................$120
Spoon-demitasse, 4 1/4 in.....................$22
Spoon-dessert/oval soup, 6 7/8 in.............$50
Spoon-dressing, shell, stainless bowl,
    11 1/4 in................................$45
Spoon-five o'clock/youth, 5 1/2 in............$23
Spoon-fruit, no rim, 6 in.....................$38
Spoon-iced tea, 8 1/8 in......................$33
Spoon-infant feeding, 5 in....................$28
Spoon-salad server, stainless bowl,
    11 1/4 in................................$40
Spoon-salt, individual, gold wash,
    2 1/2 in.................................$12
Spoon-soup, round bowl, cream, 6 3/8 in.......$36
Spoon-sugar, 5 7/8 in.........................$16
Spoon-teaspoon, 6 in..........................$16
Spoon-utility/serving, stainless bowl,
    9 5/8 in.................................$40
Tablespoon, (serving spoon), 8 1/2 in.........$65
Tongs-sugar, 4 in.............................$40

Rose Solitaire by Towle, 1954

Butter spreader, flat handle, 5 3/4 in.........$26
Butter spreader, hollow handle, stainless
    paddle, 5 7/8 in.........................$26
Butter-master, hollow handle, no notch,
    6 3/4 in.................................$26
Fork, 7 3/8 in................................$43
Fork, 8 1/8 in................................$54
Fork-baby, 4 1/8 in...........................$36
Fork-cold meat/serving, large, solid,
    9 1/4 in.................................$85
Fork-lemon, 5 1/4 in..........................$30
Fork-pickle/olive, short handle, 5 3/4 in.....$30
Fork-salad, individual, 6 1/2 in..............$48

Knife-modern, hollow handle, 9 in. $40
Ladle-cream, solid, 5 3/8 in. $40
Ladle-gravy, solid, 6 1/2 in. $75
Server-jelly, 6 1/2 in. $38
Server-pie and cake, stainless blade,
    11 1/8 in. $40
Spoon-baby, straight handle, 4 1/4 in. $36
Spoon-bonbon, 2 in. wide bowl,
    5 1/2 in. $38
Spoon-demitasse, 4 1/8 in. $28
Spoon-dessert/oval soup, 6 5/8 in. $50
Spoon-serving, pierced, 8 1/2 in. $90
Spoon-sugar, 3 1/2 in. handle,
    5 1/2 in. $23
Spoon-teaspoon, 5 7/8 in. $20
Tablespoon, (serving spoon), 8 1/2 in. $80

Royal Windsor by Towle, 1935

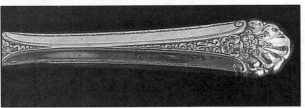

Butter spreader, flat handle, 6 in. $20
Butter-master, flat handle, 6 7/8 in. $40
Fork, 7 3/8 in. $33
Fork, 7 7/8 in. $45
Fork-carving, small, stainless prongs, steak,
    8 5/8 in. $60
Fork-cocktail, 5 5/8 in. $23
Fork-cold meat/serving, medium, solid,
    8 1/8 in. $90
Fork-lemon, 5 1/2 in. $36
Fork-salad, individual, 6 5/8 in. $40
Knife-modern, hollow handle,
    8 3/4 in. $32
Knife-modern, hollow handle,
    9 5/8 in. $45
Knife-new french, hollow handle,
    8 3/4 in. $32
Knife-new french, hollow handle,
    9 5/8 in. $40
Ladle-gravy, solid, 6 3/4 in. $85
Spoon-iced tea, 8 in. $34
Spoon-soup, round bowl, cream,
    6 3/8 in. $40
Spoon-sugar, 6 in. $30
Spoon-teaspoon, (5 o'clock),
    5 5/8 in. $15

Spoon-teaspoon, 6 in. $16
Tablespoon, (serving spoon),
    8 1/2 in. $75

Scroll & Bead by Towle, 1940

Butter-master, hollow handle, 6 3/4 in. $40
Fork, 7 1/8 in. $50
Fork-carving, small, stainless prongs, steak,
    9 1/8 in. $40
Fork-cold meat/serving, large, stainless tines,
    9 3/4 in. $45
Fork-cold meat/serving, small, solid,
    7 1/2 in. $95
Fork-salad server, stainless prongs,
    11 1/4 in. $40
Knife-carving, small, stainless blade, steak,
    10 1/4 in. $40
Knife-fish, stainless blade, individual,
    7 3/8 in. $45
Knife-modern, hollow handle, 8 3/4 in. $40
Knife-new french, hollow handle,
    8 3/4 in. $40
Knife-new french, hollow handle,
    9 1/2 in. $45
Knife-steak, individual, 8 3/8 in. $40
Knife-youth, 6 3/8 in. $48
Ladle-gravy, hollow handle, stainless bowl,
    7 3/4 in. $45
Ladle-punch, stainless bowl, 12 3/4 in. $60
Ladle-soup, stainless bowl, 11 in. $60
Opener-letter, stainless blade,
    7 1/2 in. $40
Server/knife-fish, stainless blade,
    11 3/8 in. $45
Server-cranberry, stainless bowl,
    8 1/2 in. $45
Server-lasagna, stainless blade,
    9 5/8 in. $40
Server-pasta, stainless bowl,
    10 3/8 in. $45
Server-pie and cake, stainless blade,
    10 7/8 in. $45
Slicer-cake, stainless blade, wedding,
    12 3/8 in. $40
Spoon-dressing, stainless bowl,
    11 in. $45
Spoon-salad server, stainless bowl,
    11 1/4 in. $40
Spoon-utility/serving, stainless bowl,
    9 3/4 in. $45
Tablespoon, (serving spoon), pierced,
    8 1/2 in. $96

Sculptured Rose by Towle, 1961

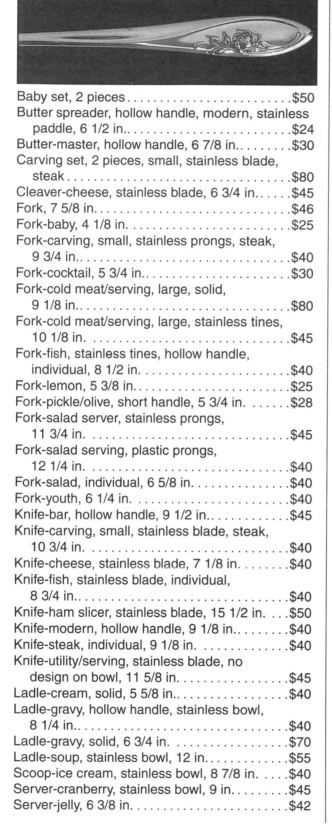

Baby set, 2 pieces..........................$50
Butter spreader, hollow handle, modern, stainless
    paddle, 6 1/2 in...........................$24
Butter-master, hollow handle, 6 7/8 in.........$30
Carving set, 2 pieces, small, stainless blade,
    steak....................................$80
Cleaver-cheese, stainless blade, 6 3/4 in......$45
Fork, 7 5/8 in................................$46
Fork-baby, 4 1/8 in..........................$25
Fork-carving, small, stainless prongs, steak,
    9 3/4 in..................................$40
Fork-cocktail, 5 3/4 in......................$30
Fork-cold meat/serving, large, solid,
    9 1/8 in..................................$80
Fork-cold meat/serving, large, stainless tines,
    10 1/8 in. $45
Fork-fish, stainless tines, hollow handle,
    individual, 8 1/2 in......................$40
Fork-lemon, 5 3/8 in.........................$25
Fork-pickle/olive, short handle, 5 3/4 in. $28
Fork-salad server, stainless prongs,
    11 3/4 in. $45
Fork-salad serving, plastic prongs,
    12 1/4 in. $40
Fork-salad, individual, 6 5/8 in...............$40
Fork-youth, 6 1/4 in. $40
Knife-bar, hollow handle, 9 1/2 in.............$45
Knife-carving, small, stainless blade, steak,
    10 3/4 in. $40
Knife-cheese, stainless blade, 7 1/8 in........$40
Knife-fish, stainless blade, individual,
    8 3/4 in..................................$40
Knife-ham slicer, stainless blade, 15 1/2 in. ...$50
Knife-modern, hollow handle, 9 1/8 in.........$40
Knife-steak, individual, 9 1/8 in. $40
Knife-utility/serving, stainless blade, no
    design on bowl, 11 5/8 in. $45
Ladle-cream, solid, 5 5/8 in..................$40
Ladle-gravy, hollow handle, stainless bowl,
    8 1/4 in..................................$40
Ladle-gravy, solid, 6 3/4 in. $70
Ladle-soup, stainless bowl, 12 in.............$55
Scoop-ice cream, stainless bowl, 8 7/8 in. $40
Server-cranberry, stainless bowl, 9 in.........$45
Server-jelly, 6 3/8 in........................$42

Server-lasagna, stainless blade, 10 3/8 in. ... $45
Server-pasta, stainless bowl, 10 3/4 in. $40
Server-pie and cake, stainless blade,
    11 1/8 in................................. $40
Slicer-cake, stainless blade, wedding,
    13 in. $40
Spoon-baby, straight handle, 4 1/8 in......... $25
Spoon-bonbon, 5 1/2 in. $38
Spoon-casserole, stainless shell bowl,
    10 1/2 in................................. $40
Spoon-demitasse, 4 1/8 in................. $20
Spoon-dressing, stainless bowl, 11 5/8 in..... $45
Spoon-infant feeding, 5 1/2 in............... $30
Spoon-pierced rice, stainless bowl,
    10 1/8 in................................. $45
Spoon-rice, stainless bowl, 10 in. $40
Spoon-salad serving, stainless bowl,
    11 5/8 in................................. $45
Spoon-sugar, 5 3/8 in...................... $25
Spoon-teaspoon, 6 in....................... $22
Tablespoon, (serving spoon), 8 1/2 in. $80
Tablespoon, (serving spoon), pierced,
    8 1/2 in................................. $90

Seville by Towle, 1926

Butter spreader, flat handle, 5 7/8 in. $15
Butter-master, flat handle, 6 7/8 in........... $28
Carving set, 2 pieces, small, stainless
    blade, steak $80
Fork, 7 3/8 in. $32
Fork-carving, small, stainless prongs, steak,
    9 1/2 in................................. $40
Fork-cocktail, 5 5/8 in...................... $20
Fork-cold meat/serving, small, solid,
    7 3/4 in................................. $55
Fork-ice cream, 5 3/8 in.................... $30
Fork-pickle/olive, short handle, 6 3/8 in....... $24
Fork-salad, individual, 6 3/8 in. $28
Knife-new french, hollow handle, 8 3/4 in. $24
Knife-old french, hollow handle, 8 5/8 in...... $25
Ladle-cream, solid, 5 1/2 in................ $35
Ladle-gravy, solid, 6 5/8 in................. $55
Server-cheese, stainless blade, 6 1/8 in...... $35
Server-jelly, 6 1/2 in. $25
Server-pie, stainless blade, 10 1/8 in........ $44
Server-tomato, solid, 6 1/4 in. $60

Spoon-bonbon, 4 7/8 in. $30
Spoon-casserole, smooth bowl, solid,
    8 1/8 in. $70
Spoon-demitasse, 4 1/8 in. $16
Spoon-dessert/oval soup, 7 in. $30
Spoon-iced tea, 7 7/8 in. $28
Spoon-soup, round bowl, bouillon, 5 in. $28
Spoon-soup, round bowl, cream, 6 1/4 in. $30
Spoon-soup, round bowl, gumbo, 7 in. $35
Spoon-sugar, 5 3/4 in. $28
Spoon-teaspoon (5 o'clock), 5 5/8 in. $17
Spoon-teaspoon, 6 in. $20
Tablespoon, (serving spoon), 8 1/4 in. $50
Tablespoon, (serving spoon), pierced,
    8 1/4 in. $60
Tongs-sugar, 4 1/4 in. $48

Silver Flutes by Towle, 1941

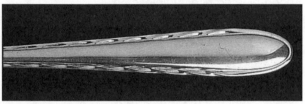

Butter spreader, flat handle, 5 3/4 in. $17
Butter spreader, hollow handle, stainless
    paddle, 5 7/8 in. $26
Butter-master, flat handle, 7 in. $32
Butter-master, hollow handle, 6 7/8 in. $32
Carving set, 2 pieces, small, stainless blade,
    steak $100
Fork, 7 3/8 in. $26
Fork, 8 in. $60
Fork-baby, 4 3/8 in. $40
Fork-carving, small, stainless prongs, steak,
    9 3/8 in. $50
Fork-cocktail, 5 3/4 in. $20
Fork-cold meat/serving, medium, solid,
    8 3/8 in. $70
Fork-fish, stainless tines, hollow handle,
    individual, 7 3/4 in. $40
Fork-ice cream, 5 5/8 in. $50
Fork-lemon, 5 1/2 in. $22
Fork-olive, 5 7/8 in. $26
Fork-pickle/olive, short handle, 2 tines,
    6 in. $26
Fork-salad server, stainless prongs,
    11 3/8 in. $40
Fork-salad serving, plastic prongs,
    12 1/8 in. $40
Fork-salad serving, wooden prongs,
    10 3/8 in. $40

Fork-salad, individual, pierced, 6 1/2 in. $38
Knife-bar, hollow handle, 8 7/8 in. $38
Knife-carving, small, stainless blade, steak,
    10 1/8 in. $50
Knife-cheese, stainless blade, 7 1/8 in. $43
Knife-fruit, stainless blade, individual,
    6 7/8 in. $37
Knife-modern, hollow handle, 8 7/8 in. $42
Knife-new french, hollow handle,
    8 7/8 in. $40
Knife-new french, hollow handle, 9 5/8 in. $57
Knife-steak, individual, beveled blade,
    8 1/2 in. $45
Knife-steak, individual, beveled blade,
    8 1/4 in. $45
Knife-steak, individual, no bevel, 8 1/2 in. $45
Knife-steak, individual, rest, 8 1/2 in. $45
Knife-utility/serving, stainless blade,
    11 1/4 in. $40
Ladle-cream, solid, 5 5/8 in. $48
Ladle-gravy, hollow handle, stainless bowl,
    7 3/4 in. $40
Ladle-gravy, solid, 7 in. $70
Salad set, 2 pieces, plastic bowl, black bowl,
    12 1/8 in. $80
Salad set, 2 pieces, wooden bowl $80
Scoop-ice, silver plate bowl, 8 5/8 in. $45
Server-cranberry, stainless bowl,
    8 5/8 in. $40
Server-jelly, 6 1/2 in. $30
Server-pasta, stainless bowl, 10 5/8 in. $44
Server-tomato, solid, 7 3/8 in. $100
Spoon-baby, straight handle, 4 1/2 in. $40
Spoon-bonbon, 5 5/8 in. $32
Spoon-bonbon, 5 in. $32
Spoon-casserole, smooth bowl, solid,
    8 1/8 in. $140
Spoon-demitasse, 4 1/4 in. $24
Spoon-dessert/oval soup, 6 7/8 in. $47
Spoon-dressing, shell, stainless bowl,
    11 1/4 in. $50
Spoon-fruit, 2 1/8 in. long bowl, 6 1/8 in. $36
Spoon-iced tea, 8 in. $34
Spoon-infant feeding, 5 in. $40
Spoon-relish, 1 3/4 in. bowl, 6 in. $40
Spoon-rice, stainless bowl, 9 7/8 in. $45
Spoon-soup, round bowl, cream,
    6 1/2 in. $34
Spoon-sugar, 6 in. $25
Spoon-teaspoon, 6 in. $16
Tablespoon, (serving spoon), 8 5/8 in. $60
Tablespoon, (serving spoon), pierced,
    8 5/8 in. $90
Tongs-sugar, 4 1/8 in. $54

Towle Silversmiths

Silver Plumes by Towle, 1939

Butter spreader, flat handle, 6 in. $24
Butter spreader, hollow handle, stainless
    paddle, 5 5/8 in. $26
Butter-master, flat handle, 6 7/8 in. $45
Butter-master, hollow handle, no notch,
    6 1/2 in. $40
Carving set, 2 pieces, small, stainless blade,
    steak $90
Cleaver-cheese, stainless blade, 6 3/8 in. $45
Fork, 7 3/8 in. $40
Fork, 8 in. $50
Fork-carving, small, stainless prongs, steak,
    9 1/2 in. $45
Fork-cold meat/serving, large, stainless tines,
    9 1/2 in. $45
Fork-fish, stainless tines, hollow handle,
    individual, 7 3/4 in. $40
Fork-lemon, 5 3/8 in. $30
Fork-pickle/olive, short handle, 2 tines,
    6 in. $30
Fork-pickle/olive, short handle, 3 tines,
    6 in. $30
Fork-salad serving, stainless prongs,
    11 in. $40
Fork-salad, individual, 6 3/4 in. $40
Knife-bar, hollow handle, 8 3/4 in. $45
Knife-carving, small, stainless blade, steak,
    10 1/2 in. $45
Knife-cheese, stainless blade, 6 7/8 in. $44
Knife-fish, stainless blade, individual,
    8 1/4 in. $40
Knife-fruit, stainless blade, individual,
    6 1/8 in. $40
Knife-new french, hollow handle, 8 3/4 in. $34
Knife-steak, individual, beveled blade,
    8 1/4 in. $40
Knife-utility/serving, stainless blade, no design on
    blade, 11 1/8 in. $40
Ladle-gravy, hollow handle, stainless bowl,
    8 in. $40
Ladle-gravy, solid, 7 in. $80
Ladle-punch, stainless bowl, 12 3/4 in. $55
Ladle-soup, stainless bowl, 10 7/8 in. $60
Magnifying glass, sterling handle, 6 1/4 in. $40
Opener-bottle, stainless bowl, 6 in. $45

Opener-letter, stainless blade, 7 3/8 in. $40
Scoop-ice, silver plate bowl, 8 1/2 in. $50
Server-cheese, stainless blade, 6 1/8 in. $44
Server-cranberry, stainless bowl, 8 3/4 in. $45
Server-jelly, 6 1/2 in. $40
Server-lasagna, stainless blade, 9 3/4 in. $40
Server-pasta, stainless bowl, 10 5/8 in. $45
Server-pie and cake, stainless blade,
    10 3/4 in. $40
Server-tomato, solid, 7 5/8 in. $90
Slicer-cake, stainless blade, wedding,
    11 7/8 in. $40
Spoon-casserole, shell, stainless bowl,
    10 1/4 in. $40
Spoon-demitasse, 4 1/4 in. $20
Spoon-dressing, shell, stainless tear-shaped
    bowl, 11 1/8 in. $45
Spoon-fruit, 5 7/8 in. $40
Spoon-iced tea, 8 in. $34
Spoon-pierced rice, stainless bowl,
    9 7/8 in. $40
Spoon-rice, stainless bowl, 9 3/4 in. $40
Spoon-salad server, stainless bowl,
    11 1/8 in. $40
Spoon-serving, pierced, 8 1/2 in. $90
Spoon-soup, round bowl, cream,
    6 1/2 in. $40
Spoon-teaspoon, 6 in. $22
Tablespoon, (serving spoon), 8 1/2 in. $80

Silver Spray by Towle, 1956

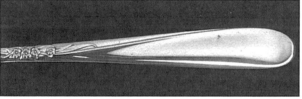

Butter spreader, hollow handle, modern, stainless
    paddle, 6 1/2 in. $18
Butter-master, hollow handle, 6 7/8 in. $18
Fork, 7 5/8 in. $30
Fork-baby, 4 1/8 in. $28
Fork-cold meat/serving, large, solid,
    9 1/8 in. $65
Fork-lemon, 5 1/8 in. $20
Fork-pickle/olive, short handle, 5 3/4 in. $20
Fork-salad, individual, 6 5/8 in. $30
Fork-youth, 6 1/8 in. $33
Knife-modern, hollow handle, 9 in. $25
Ladle-cream, solid, 5 1/2 in. $40
Ladle-gravy, solid, 6 3/8 in. $70
Napkin clip, (made for sugar spoons) $20

Napkin clip, (made for teaspoons) $20
Server-jelly, 6 1/2 in. $32
Server-pie and cake, stainless blade,
    10 7/8 in. $42
Spoon-bonbon, 5 1/2 in. $36
Spoon-demitasse, 4 1/8 in. $22
Spoon-dessert/oval soup, 6 7/8 in. $30
Spoon-sugar, 5 3/8 in. $18
Spoon-teaspoon, 6 in. $18
Tablespoon, (serving spoon), 8 1/2 in. $70
Tablespoon, (serving spoon), pierced,
    8 1/2 in. $70

Southwind by Towle, 1952

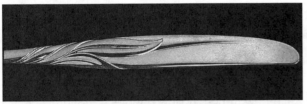

Butter spreader, flat handle, 5 7/8 in. $15
Butter spreader, hollow handle, stainless
    paddle, 6 1/8 in. $16
Butter-master, hollow handle, 7 in. $23
Carving set, 2 pieces, large, stainless blade,
    roast $100
Carving set, 2 pieces, small, stainless blade,
    steak. $90
Fork, 7 5/8 in. $26
Fork-cocktail, 5 5/8 in. $18
Fork-cold meat/serving, large, solid,
    9 1/2 in. $70
Fork-lemon, 5 3/4 in. $24
Fork-pickle/olive, short handle, 6 3/8 in. $22
Fork-salad, individual, 6 3/4 in. $30
Knife-carving, small, stainless blade, steak,
    10 3/4 in. $45
Knife-cheese, stainless blade, 7 1/4 in. $28
Knife-modern, hollow handle, 8 7/8 in. $27
Ladle-cream, solid, 6 1/8 in. $35
Ladle-gravy, solid, 6 1/2 in. $60
Napkin clip, (made for teaspoons) $22
Salad set, 2 pieces, plastic bowl. $80
Server-jelly, 6 1/2 in. $25
Server-pie and cake, stainless blade,
    10 3/4 in. $42
Server-tomato, solid, 7 1/2 in. $90
Spoon-bonbon, 6 1/2 in. $26
Spoon-casserole, smooth, solid, 9 1/2 in. $110
Spoon-demitasse, 4 1/2 in. $20
Spoon-dessert/oval soup, 7 1/8 in. $32
Spoon-iced tea, 8 1/4 in. $26

Spoon-jam, 6 1/2 in. $40
Spoon-sugar, 6 in. $18
Spoon-teaspoon, 6 in. $14
Tablespoon, (serving spoon), 8 3/4 in. $60
Tablespoon, (serving spoon), pierced,
    8 3/4 in. $80
Tongs-sugar, 4 in. $50

Spanish Provincial by Towle, 1967

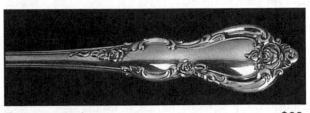

Baby set, 2 pieces $60
Butter spreader, hollow handle, modern,
    stainless paddle, 6 5/8 in. $30
Butter-master, hollow handle, 7 in. $34
Carving set, 2 pieces, small, stainless blade,
    steak $80
Cleaver-cheese, stainless blade, 6 7/8 in. $45
Fork, 7 3/8 in. $35
Fork, 7 7/8 in. $50
Fork-baby, 4 1/4 in. $30
Fork-carving, small, stainless prongs, steak,
    9 7/8 in. $40
Fork-cold meat/serving, large, solid,
    9 1/4 in. $100
Fork-cold meat/serving, large, stainless
    tines, 10 1/4 in. $45
Fork-fish, stainless tines, hollow handle,
    individual, 8 1/4 in. $45
Fork-pickle/olive, short handle, 5 7/8 in. $30
Fork-salad server, stainless prongs,
    11 3/4 in. $40
Fork-salad, individual, 6 1/2 in. $42
Fork-youth, 6 1/2 in. $35
Knife-bar, hollow handle, 9 1/4 in. $40
Knife-carving, small, stainless blade, steak,
    10 3/4 in. $40
Knife-cheese, stainless blade, 7 1/2 in. $40
Knife-fish, stainless blade, individual,
    8 1/2 in. $40
Knife-fruit, stainless blade, individual,
    7 1/4 in. $40
Knife-modern, hollow handle, 8 3/4 in. $28
Knife-modern, hollow handle, 9 1/2 in. $44
Knife-steak, individual, 9 3/8 in. $44
Knife-steak, individual, 9 in. $44
Knife-utility/serving, stainless blade, no
    design on bowl, 11 5/8 in. $40

Knife-youth, 7 1/4 in. $40
Ladle-gravy, hollow handle, stainless bowl,
    8 1/4 in. $40
Ladle-gravy, solid, 6 7/8 in. $90
Ladle-soup, stainless bowl, 11 3/8 in. $60
Magnifying glass, sterling handle, 6 5/8 in. $45
Opener-bottle, stainless bowl, 5 3/8 in. $40
Scoop-ice cream, stainless bowl, 8 1/2 in. $45
Scoop-ice, silver plate bowl, 8 7/8 in. $50
Server-cranberry, stainless bowl, 9 in. $40
Server-jelly, 6 1/4 in. $45
Server-lasagna, stainless blade,
    10 1/4 in. $45
Server-pie and cake, stainless blade,
    10 7/8 in. $44
Server-tomato, solid, 7 7/8 in. $100
Slicer-cake, stainless blade, 12 5/8 in. $45
Spoon-baby, straight handle, 4 1/4 in. $30
Spoon-casserole, stainless shell bowl,
    10 5/8 in. $40
Spoon-demitasse, 4 3/8 in. $24
Spoon-dessert/oval soup, 6 7/8 in. $44
Spoon-dressing, stainless shell bowl,
    11 3/4 in. $45
Spoon-fruit, 6 in. $36
Spoon-iced tea, 8 1/4 in. $40
Spoon-infant feeding, 5 1/2 in. $30
Spoon-pierced rice, stainless bowl,
    10 1/4 in. $40
Spoon-rice, stainless bowl, 10 1/4 in. $40
Spoon-salad serving, stainless bowl,
    11 5/8 in. $45
Spoon-sugar, 6 1/8 in. $26
Spoon-teaspoon (5 o'clock), 5 1/2 in. $20
Spoon-teaspoon, 6 in. $22
Tablespoon, (serving spoon), 8 3/4 in. $75
Tablespoon, (serving spoon), pierced,
    8 3/4 in. $90
Youth set, 3 pieces (spoon, knife, fork) $115

Symphony by Towle, 1931

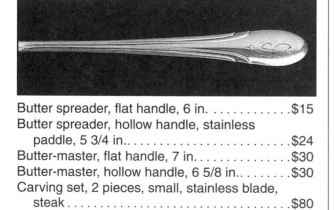

Butter spreader, flat handle, 6 in. $15
Butter spreader, hollow handle, stainless
    paddle, 5 3/4 in. $24
Butter-master, flat handle, 7 in. $30
Butter-master, hollow handle, 6 5/8 in. $30
Carving set, 2 pieces, small, stainless blade,
    steak $80

Fork, 7 3/4 in. $34
Fork, 7 3/8 in. $24
Fork, 8 in. $34
Fork-carving, small, stainless prongs, steak,
    9 1/4 in. $40
Fork-cocktail, 5 3/4 in. $18
Fork-cold meat/serving, medium, solid,
    8 1/8 in. $70
Fork-ice cream, 5 3/4 in. $30
Fork-lemon, 5 5/8 in. $24
Fork-pickle/olive, short handle, 2 tines,
    6 in. $26
Fork-pickle/olive, short handle, 3 tines,
    6 in. $26
Fork-salad server, stainless prongs,
    11 1/8 in. $45
Fork-salad, individual, 6 1/2 in. $30
Knife-baby, 6 3/8 in. $34
Knife-carving, small, stainless blade, steak,
    10 1/4 in. $40
Knife-new french, hollow handle, 3 3/4 in.
    handle, 8 7/8 in. $28
Knife-new french, hollow handle, 4 1/8 in.
    handle, 9 3/4. . . . .$38
Ladle-cream, solid, 5 3/4 in. $35
Ladle-gravy, solid, 6 3/4 in. $65
Napkin clip, (made for teaspoons) $15
Server-cheese, stainless blade, 6 1/4 in. $38
Server-jelly, 6 3/4 in. $24
Server-pie and cake, stainless blade,
    10 3/4 in. $44
Server-pie, stainless blade, 10 1/8 in. $50
Slicer-cake, stainless blade, wedding,
    12 3/8 in. $45
Spoon-bonbon, 4 7/8 in. $30
Spoon-casserole, smooth, solid, 8 7/8 in. $90
Spoon-demitasse, 4 1/4 in. $15
Spoon-dessert/oval soup, 7 1/4 in. $43
Spoon-dressing, shell, stainless bowl,
    11 1/8 in. $45
Spoon-fruit, 6 in. $32
Spoon-iced tea, 8 1/4 in. $30
Spoon-olive, short, pierced bowl, 6 1/8 in. $70
Spoon-salad server, stainless bowl,
    11 1/4 in. $45
Spoon-salad serving, solid, 9 1/4 in. $80
Spoon-soup, round bowl, bouillon,
    5 1/8 in. $35
Spoon-soup, round bowl, cream,
    6 1/2 in. $33
Spoon-soup, round bowl, gumbo, 7 1/8 in. $40
Spoon-sugar, 6 in. $23
Spoon-teaspoon, (5 o'clock), 5 3/4 in. $12
Spoon-teaspoon, 6 in. $14
Tablespoon, (serving spoon), 8 5/8 in. $60

Vespera by Towle, 1961

Butter spreader, hollow handle, modern, stainless
    paddle, 6 5/8 in................................$16
Butter-master, hollow handle, 6 7/8 in.........$28
Fork, 7 1/2 in....................................$34
Fork-cold meat/serving, medium, solid,
    8 3/8 in.....................................$80
Fork-lemon, 5 1/8 in.............................$30
Fork-pickle/olive, short handle, 5 3/4 in. $26
Fork-salad, individual, 7 in....................$36
Knife-modern, hollow handle, 8 7/8 in.........$30
Knife-steak, individual, 9 in...................$46
Ladle-cream, solid, 5 1/2 in....................$40
Ladle-gravy, solid, 6 1/4 in. $80
Server-jelly, 6 1/8 in. $30
Spoon-bonbon, teeth, 5 1/4 in. $36
Spoon-demitasse, 4 1/4 in......................$17
Spoon-dessert/oval soup, 7 1/8 in...........$40
Spoon-fruit, 6 in. $36
Spoon-sugar, 5 1/8 in..........................$32
Spoon-teaspoon, 6 1/4 in. $26
Tablespoon, (serving spoon), 8 1/8 in.........$70
Tablespoon, (serving spoon), pierced,
    8 1/8 in.....................................$80

Virginia Carvel by Towle, 1919

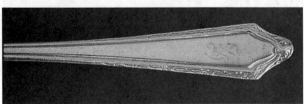

Butter spreader, flat handle, 6 in. $15
Butter-master, flat handle, 7 in...............$30
Carving set, 2 pieces, small, stainless blade,
    steak.......................................$80
Fork, 7 3/8 in....................................$20
Fork-carving, small, stainless prongs, steak,
    8 3/4 in.....................................$40
Fork-cocktail, 5 3/4 in..........................$20
Fork-ice cream, 3/8 in. long tines, 5 1/2 in. $35
Fork-ice cream, 5/8 in. long tines, 5 1/2 in. $30
Fork-lemon, 5 1/2 in.............................$30
Fork-pickle/olive, short handle, 2 tines,
    5 3/4 in.....................................$30

Fork-pickle/olive, short handle, 3 tines,
    6 3/8 in.....................................$30
Fork-salad, individual, 6 1/4 in. $24
Knife-carving, small, stainless blade, steak,
    10 1/4 in....................................$40
Knife-old french, hollow handle, 8 7/8 in......$30
Knife-old french, hollow handle, 9 3/8 in......$30
Ladle-cream, solid, 5 1/2 in.................$34
Ladle-cream, solid, 6 1/8 in.................$34
Ladle-gravy, solid, 6 3/4 in..................$77
Server-cheese, stainless blade, 6 in. $38
Server-jelly, 6 3/4 in. $24
Server-pie, stainless blade, 10 3/8 in........$40
Server-tomato, solid, 6 1/2 in. $95
Server-tomato, solid, 7 5/8 in. $95
Spoon-baby, straight handle, 4 1/4 in........$30
Spoon-bonbon, 5 in. $34
Spoon-casserole, smooth bowl, solid,
    8 1/8 in.....................................$95
Spoon-demitasse, 4 1/4 in....................$15
Spoon-dessert/oval soup, 7 in...............$38
Spoon-fruit, 5 1/2 in. $26
Spoon-iced tea, 8 1/8 in.....................$30
Spoon-olive, short, pierced bowl,
    6 1/2 in.....................................$90
Spoon-salad serving, solid, 9 1/4 in.........$105
Spoon-soup, round bowl, bouillon,
    5 1/8 in.....................................$18
Spoon-soup, round bowl, cream, 6 3/8 in.....$38
Spoon-soup, round bowl, gumbo, 7 1/4 in.....$40
Spoon-sugar, 5 7/8 in.........................$22
Spoon-teaspoon (5 o'clock), 5 3/4 in.........$10
Spoon-teaspoon, 6 in..........................$24
Spoon-youth, 5 3/8 in.........................$15
Tablespoon, (serving spoon), 8 5/8 in. $60

Virginia Lee by Towle, 1920

Butter spreader, flat handle, 5 7/8 in. $24
Carving set, 2 pieces, small, stainless blade,
    steak.......................................$150
Fork, 7 1/4 in....................................$50
Fork-cocktail, 5 5/8 in........................$34
Fork-salad, individual, 6 1/4 in. $45
Knife-old french, hollow 3 3/4 in. handle,
    9 3/8 in.....................................$38
Knife-old french, hollow handle, 8 3/4 in. $38
Knife-old french, hollow handle, 9 3/4 in......$50
Ladle-cream, solid, 5 1/2 in.................$45
Spoon-dessert/oval soup, 7 1/8 in. $45
Spoon-soup, round bowl, bouillon, 5 1/8 in....$44
Spoon-soup, round bowl, gumbo, 7 1/8 in.....$60
Spoon-teaspoon, 6 in..........................$28
Tablespoon, (serving spoon), 8 5/8 in. $80

Tuttle Silversmiths

TUTTLE SILVERSMITHS

Tuttle Silversmiths was established by Timothy Tuttle in Boston, Massachusetts in 1890. Wallace Silversmiths acquired it in 1955. Since the presidency of Calvin Coolidge, each piece bears the initials of the U.S. president during whose term it was produced.

Beauvoir by Tuttle, 1967

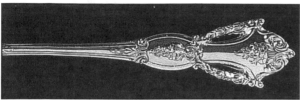

Cleaver-cheese, stainless blade,
6 3/4 in. $50
Fork-cold meat/serving, large, 5 stainless
tines, 11 3/8 in. $45
Fork-fish, stainless tines, hollow handle,
individual, 8 3/8 in. $45
Knife-bar, hollow handle, 9 1/4 in. $45
Knife-cheese, stainless blade,
7 1/8 in. $45
Knife-fruit, stainless blade/individual,
6 1/2 in. $45
Ladle-punch, stainless bowl, 14 in. $60
Scoop-ice cream, stainless bowl,
8 5/8 in. $45
Server-asparagus, hollow handle, silver
plate hood, 10 1/8 in. $60
Server-cranberry, stainless bowl, 9 in. $45
Server-lasagna, stainless blade,
10 1/8 in. $45
Server-pie and cake, stainless blade, no
stamp, 11 in. $44
Spoon-demitasse, no stamp,
4 1/8 in. $28

Colonial Fiddle by Tuttle, 1925

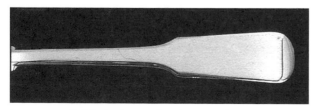

Image available but no priced examples.

Feather Edge by Tuttle, 1938

Butter spreader, hollow handle, modern, stainless
paddle, 6 1/8 in. $36
Butter spreader, flat handle, 6 in. $48
Fork, 7 1/4 in. $60
Fork-cold meat/serving, large, stainless tines,
10 5/8 in. $140
Fork-salad/individual, 6 3/8 in. $60
Knife-modern, hollow handle, 4 1/2 in. blade,
8 3/8 in. $60
Knife-steak, individual, 8 3/8 in. $60
Ladle-gravy, solid, 5 3/4 in. $150
Salad set, 2 pieces, solid $380
Spoon-rice, stainless bowl, 9 1/4 in. $120
Spoon-soup, round bowl, cream,
6 1/2 in. $70
Spoon-sugar, 5 3/4 in. $80
Spoon-teaspoon, 5 7/8 in. $50
Spoon-teaspoon, 5 7/8 in. $50
Tablespoon, (serving spoon), 8 1/4 in. $150

Hannah Hull by Tuttle, 1927

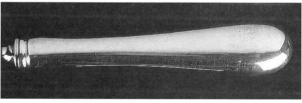

Butter spreader, flat handle, 5 3/8 in. $34
Fork, 7 1/2 in. $70
Fork, 7 1/8 in. $50
Fork, 7 3/4 in. $70
Fork-carving, small, stainless prongs,
steak, 9 in. $45
Fork-cocktail, 5 3/4 in. $38
Fork-ice cream, 5 in. $60
Knife-bar, hollow handle, 8 3/4 in. $45
Knife-carving, small, stainless blade, steak,
10 1/8 in. $45
Knife-new french, hollow handle,
8 3/4 in. $50
Knife-new french, hollow handle,
9 5/8 in. $60
Knife-steak, individual, 8 7/8 in. $45

Ladle-cream, solid, 5 1/4 in. $70
Scoop-ice cream, stainless bowl,
8 1/8 in. $45
Server-jelly, 6 3/8 in. $70
Spoon-demitasse, 4 1/4 in. $30
Spoon-fruit, 5 3/4 in. $50
Spoon-soup, round bowl, bouillon,
5 1/8 in. $48
Spoon-soup, round bowl, cream,
6 1/2 in. $55
Spoon-teaspoon, 5 7/8 in. $34
Tablespoon, (serving spoon),
8 1/8 in. $100

Lamerie by Tuttle, 1936

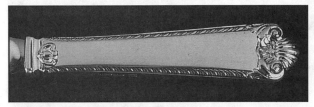

Fork-pickle/olive, short handle, 5 3/4 in. $50

Onslow by Tuttle, 1931

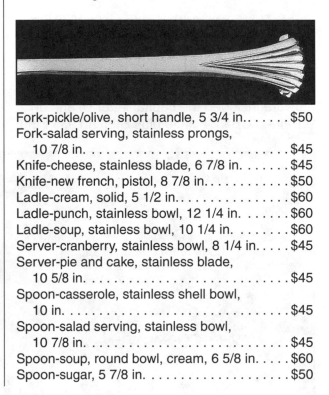

Fork-pickle/olive, short handle, 5 3/4 in.. . . . . . $50
Fork-salad serving, stainless prongs,
10 7/8 in. $45
Knife-cheese, stainless blade, 6 7/8 in. $45
Knife-new french, pistol, 8 7/8 in.. . . . . $50
Ladle-cream, solid, 5 1/2 in.. . . . . $60
Ladle-punch, stainless bowl, 12 1/4 in. $60
Ladle-soup, stainless bowl, 10 1/4 in. $60
Server-cranberry, stainless bowl, 8 1/4 in.. . . . $45
Server-pie and cake, stainless blade,
10 5/8 in. $45
Spoon-casserole, stainless shell bowl,
10 in. $45
Spoon-salad serving, stainless bowl,
10 7/8 in. $45
Spoon-soup, round bowl, cream, 6 5/8 in. $60
Spoon-sugar, 5 7/8 in. $50

Unger Brothers

UNGER BROS.

Unger Bros. was started in the late 1870s in Newark, New Jersey and made silver items until 1914. The firm's flatware patterns were also featured on other items, including desk sets, ashtrays, and letter openers. Marks on flatware included the capital letter U, and an entwined UB in a circle plus Sterling 935 Fine.

Douvaine by Unger Bros., 1890

The following piece has a monogram:
Spoon-teaspoon, 5 3/4 in. $80

American silver youth knife, fork, and spoon in the Cupid Sunbeam pattern (1904); made by Unger Bros. of Newark, New Jersey. No monogram. Knife 7 1/4 in., fork 6 in., spoon 5 7/8 in. Silver plated knife blade with slight wear. Wear to tines and bowl. $280

American silver youth spoon in the Cupid's Nosegay pattern (1904); made by Unger Bros. of Newark, New Jersey. No monogram, 5 3/4 in. $60

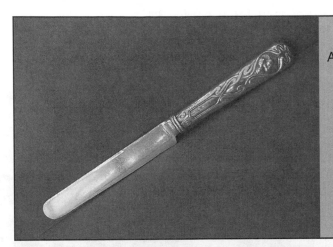

American silver-handled youth knife in the Love's Dream pattern (1904); made by Unger Bros. of Newark, New Jersey. No monogram, 7 1/4 in. Slight wear to silver plated blunt blade. $125

American silver youth spoon in the Love's Dream pattern (1904); made by Unger Bros. of Newark, New Jersey. Monogram "MMcD." 5 7/8 in. Some surface wear. $45

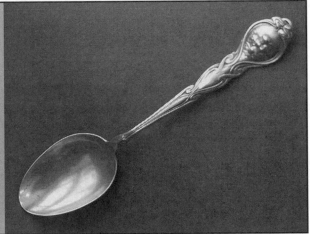

American silver youth spoon in the Secret of the Flowers pattern (1904); made by Unger Bros. of Newark, New Jersey. No monogram, 5 7/8 in. $85

WALLACE SILVERSMITHS INC.

Wallace Silversmiths Inc. began producing sterling flatware in Wallingford, Connecticut in 1871. Company founder Robert Wallace was apprenticed in 1831, when he was 16, to a maker of Britannia metal spoons. Two years later, he rented an old gristmill, powered by Connecticut's Quinnipiac River, and started to make spoons.

In 1835 Wallace learned of a new metal that had been developed in Germany. He traveled to New York City and purchased the formula from a German chemist for $20, then converted his gristmill to produce nickel-based silver spoons.

Under the name R. Wallace & Sons Mfg. Co., the firm introduced the sterling patterns Hawthorne, The Crown, and St. Leon. Designer William Warren's "three-dimensional" patterns included Sir Christopher and Grande Baroque. Wallace eventually acquired the Watson Co., Tuttle Silver Co., and Smith & Smith

America by Wallace, 1915

Butter-master, flat handle, 7 1/4 in.	$40
Fork, 7 1/2 in.	$40
Fork, 7 in.	$28
Fork-cocktail, 5 1/2 in.	$32
Fork-lemon, 5 3/8 in.	$28
Fork-pie, 6 in.	$48
Fork-salad, individual, 6 1/8 in.	$38
Knife-blunt, hollow handle, 9 5/8 in.	$45
Knife-new french, hollow handle, 8 7/8 in.	$35
Knife-old french, hollow handle, 8 1/2 in.	$35
Knife-old french, hollow handle, 9 5/8 in.	$45
Ladle-cream, solid, 5 1/2 in.	$40
Ladle-gravy, solid, 6 3/8 in.	$90
Spoon-5 o'clock/youth, 5 1/2 in.	$22
Spoon-demitasse, 4 1/8 in.	$22
Spoon-dessert/oval soup, 7 1/8 in.	$40

Spoon-fruit, 1 in. bowl, 5 3/4 in.	$34
Spoon-iced tea, 7 5/8 in.	$36
Spoon-soup, round bowl, bouillon, 5 in.	$40
Spoon-soup, round bowl, gumbo, 7 1/8 in.	$36
Spoon-sugar, 6 in.	$40
Tablespoon, (serving spoon), 8 1/4 in.	$80

Carnation by Wallace, 1909

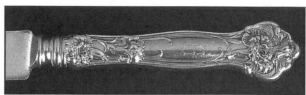

Butter spreader, flat handle, 5 in.	$30
Fork, 7 5/8 in.	$60
Fork-cocktail, 5 7/8 in.	$35
Spoon-5 o'clock/youth, 5 1/2 in.	$26
Spoon-teaspoon, 6 in.	$30

Carthage by Wallace, 1917

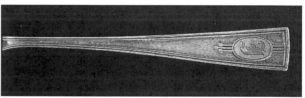

Butter spreader, flat handle, 5 1/2 in.	$22
Fork, 6 7/8 in.	$40
Fork-pickle/olive, short handle, 5 3/4 in.	$30
Fork-salad, individual, 5 5/8 in.	$50
Knife-carving, small, stainless blade, steak, 9 3/4 in.	$60
Ladle-gravy, solid, 5 3/4 in.	$85
Poultry shears, 10 1/2 in.	$160
Spoon-bonbon, gold wash, 4 1/2 in.	$40
Spoon-sugar, 5 5/8 in.	$40
Spoon-teaspoon, 5 5/8 in.	$20
Tablespoon, (serving spoon), 8 1/8 in.	$70
Tongs-sugar, 3 1/2 in.	$60
Tongs-sugar, 3 7/8 in.	$60

Corinthian by Wallace, 1911

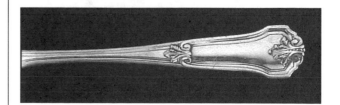

Butter spreader, flat handle, 5 1/2 in.........$28
Fork, 7 in..................................$44
Knife-new french, hollow handle, 9 5/8 in.....$45
Knife-old french, hollow handle, 8 3/4 in......$32
Knife-old french, hollow handle, 9 5/8 in......$45
Spoon-soup, round bowl, bouillon,
    5 3/8 in..................................$46

Dauphine by Wallace, 1916

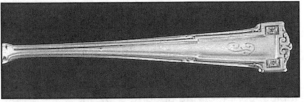

Butter spreader, flat handle, 5 7/8 in.........$18
Butter-master, flat handle, 7 1/8 in...........$37
Fork, 7 1/2 in..............................$60
Fork, 7 1/8 in..............................$38
Fork-cocktail, 5 5/8 in......................$32
Fork-dessert, four tines, 5 3/4 in. $45
Fork-ice cream, 5 1/2 in.....................$50
Fork-lemon, 5 3/8 in.........................$35
Fork-pickle/olive, long handle, 7 3/8 in. $53
Fork-ramekin, 5 in. $34
Knife-modern, hollow handle, 8 7/8 in.........$36
Knife-old french, hollow handle, 8 1/2 in......$37
Knife-old french, hollow handle, 9 1/2 in......$45
Spoon-5 o'clock/youth, 5 1/2 in. $18
Spoon-demitasse, 4 1/8 in. $26
Spoon-fruit, 5 3/4 in. $38
Spoon-soup, round bowl, bouillon,
    5 1/4 in..................................$35
Spoon-soup, round bowl, gumbo, 7 in. $55
Spoon-sugar, 6 in...........................$35
Spoon-teaspoon, 5 7/8 in. $24
Tablespoon, (serving spoon), 8 1/8 in........$60

Dawn Mist by Wallace, 1963

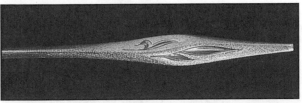

Butter spreader, hollow handle, modern
    stainless paddle, 7 in....................$20
Fork, 7 5/8 in..............................$34
Fork-lemon, 6 in............................$28
Knife-modern, hollow handle, 9 3/8 in........$24

Spoon-sugar, 6 1/2 in......................$28
Spoon-teaspoon, 6 5/8 in...................$16

Debutante by Wallace, 1960

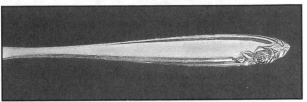

Butter spreader, hollow handle, modern
    stainless paddle, 6 5/8 in................$20
Butter-master, hollow handle, 7 in. $36
Fork, 7 3/8 in. $36
Fork-carving, small, stainless prongs, steak,
    9 3/4 in.................................$45
Fork-salad, individual, 6 3/8 in. $40
Knife-modern, hollow handle, 9 5/8 in........$40
Napkin clip, (made for teaspoons), ...$28
Server-pie and cake, stainless blade,
    11 1/4 in................................$50
Spoon-sugar, 6 1/4 in.......................$40
Spoon-teaspoon, 6 1/8 in....................$23

Discovery by Wallace, 1957

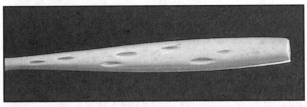

Baby set, 2 pieces $70
Butter spreader, hollow handle, modern
    stainless paddle, 6 5/8 in................$10
Butter-master, flat handle, 7 1/4 in...........$25
Butter-master, hollow handle, 7 1/8 in........$25
Fork, 7 1/2 in. $30
Fork-cocktail, 5 7/8 in......................$20
Fork-lemon, 5 1/8 in. $20
Fork-pickle/olive, short handle, 2 tines,
    5 3/4 in.................................$18
Fork-salad, individual, 6 7/8 in. $25
Knife-new french, hollow handle,
    9 1/2 in.................................$23
Ladle-gravy, solid, 7 1/8 in.................$60
Spoon-dessert/oval soup, 7 in..............$30
Spoon-soup, round bowl, cream,
    6 1/2 in.................................$34
Spoon-teaspoon, 6 1/2 in...................$15
Tablespoon, (serving spoon), 9 in. $60

Eton by Wallace, 1903

Fork, 7 1/2 in. $70
Fork, 7 in. $45
Fork-cocktail, 5 3/4 in. $30
Fork-salad, individual, 6 1/4 in. $70
Knife-blunt, hollow handle, 9 in. $50
Spoon-soup, round bowl, bouillon,
   5 1/8 in. $44
Spoon-sugar, 6 1/8 in. $44
Tablespoon, (serving spoon), 8 1/4 in. $80

Evening Mist by Wallace, 1963

Fork, 7 1/2 in. $34
Fork-salad, individual, 7 in. $35
Knife-modern, hollow handle, 9 3/8 in. $25
Spoon-dessert/oval soup, 7 3/8 in. $40
Spoon-sugar, egg-shaped bowl,
   6 1/2 in. $32
Spoon-teaspoon, 6 5/8 in. $20
Tablespoon, (serving spoon), 9 1/8 in. $80

Feliciana by Wallace, 1969

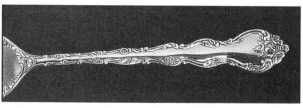

Butter-master, hollow handle, 6 5/8 in. $40
Fork, 7 3/8 in. $40
Fork-carving, small, stainless prongs, steak,
   9 1/2 in. $60
Fork-cold meat/serving, medium, solid,
   8 1/4 in. $80
Knife-carving, small, stainless blade, steak,
   10 1/2 in. $60
Knife-fruit, stainless blade, individual, 7 in. $40

Knife-modern, hollow handle, 9 7/8 in. $40
Knife-modern, hollow handle, 9 in. $40
Knife-steak, individual, 9 1/2 in. $45
Knife-steak, individual, beveled edge,
   8 7/8 in. $45
Ladle-gravy, hollow handle, stainless bowl,
   8 1/4 in. $40
Ladle-gravy, solid, 6 1/4 in. $90
Opener-letter, stainless blade, 7 5/8 in. $40
Server-pie and cake, stainless blade,
   11 in. $40
Slicer-cake, stainless blade, wedding,
   12 3/4 in. $50
Spoon-dessert/oval soup, 7 in. $80
Spoon-sugar shell, 6 1/8 in. $36
Spoon-teaspoon, 6 1/8 in. $37
Tablespoon, (serving spoon), 8 1/2 in. $80
Tablespoon, (serving spoon), pierced,
   8 1/2 in. $90

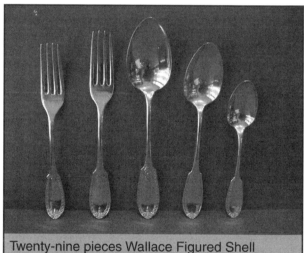

Twenty-nine pieces Wallace Figured Shell (1874): 6 tablespoons, 6 table forks, 6 dessert spoons, 5 dessert forks, and 6 teaspoons. Later monogram "LNN." $560

Georgian Colonial by Wallace, 1932

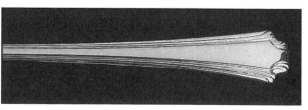

Butter spreader, flat handle, 5 7/8 in. $20
Fork, 7 1/4 in. $25
Fork, 7 7/8 in. $45
Fork-salad, individual, 6 1/4 in. $27
Knife-modern, hollow handle, 8 7/8 in. $30

Knife-modern, hollow handle, 9 5/8 in........$33
Knife-new french, hollow handle,
    8 7/8 in..............................$30
Knife-new french, hollow handle, 9 5/8 in.....$30
Spoon-soup, round bowl, cream, 6 in........$24
Spoon-teaspoon, 6 in.....................$23

Grand Colonial by Wallace, 1942

(Knife handle shown in profile.)

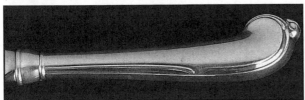

Butter spreader, flat handle, 6 in. $22
Butter spreader, hollow handle, modern
    stainless, 6 1/4 in.......................$25
Butter spreader, hollow handle, stainless
    paddle, no notch, 6 1/8 in...............$25
Butter-master, flat handle, 6 7/8 in...........$30
Butter-master, hollow handle, 6 5/8 in........$30
Cleaver-cheese, stainless blade, 6 5/8 in.....$45
Fork, 7 1/4 in.............................$30
Fork-baby, 4 1/2 in. $30
Fork-cake, individual, 3 tines, 5 3/4 in........$34
Fork-carving, small, stainless prongs, steak,
    9 1/2 in................................$45
Fork-cocktail, 5 5/8 in.....................$24
Fork-cold meat/serving, large, 5 stainless
    tines, 11 1/8 in. $45
Fork-cold meat/serving, medium, solid,
    8 in...................................$84
Fork-fish, stainless tines, hollow handle,
    individual, 8 1/4 in. $45
Fork-ice cream, 5 1/4 in....................$40
Fork-lemon, 5 1/2 in........................$30
Fork-salad serving, plastic prongs,
    12 1/2 in. $35
Fork-salad serving, solid, 9 in...............$135
Fork-salad serving, stainless prongs, 4 tines,
    11 3/8 in. $45
Fork-salad, individual, 6 3/8 in. $36
Fork-strawberry, 5 in. $28
Fork-youth, 5 3/4 in. $30
Knife-bar, hollow handle, 9 1/4 in............$40
Knife-carving, small, stainless blade, steak,
    10 1/2 in. $45
Knife-cheese, stainless blade, 7 1/8 in. $45
Knife-fish, stainless blade, individual,
    8 5/8 in.................................$40
Knife-fruit, stainless blade, individual,
    6 7/8 in.................................$30

Knife-modern, hollow handle, 8 7/8 in. $30
Knife-modern, hollow handle, 9 3/4 in. $46
Knife-modern, pistol grip, 8 7/8 in...........$30
Knife-steak, individual, 8 3/4 in..............$45
Knife-youth, 6 3/4 in. $30
Ladle-cream, solid, 5 1/2 in.................$48
Ladle-gravy, hollow handle, stainless bowl,
    8 1/4 in................................$40
Ladle-gravy, solid, 6 in. $75
Ladle-punch, stainless bowl, 13 1/8 in.......$58
Ladle-soup, stainless bowl, 11 1/2 in........$55
Opener-bottle, stainless bowl, 6 3/8 in.......$40
Salad set, 2 pieces, plastic bowl,
    12 1/2 in...............................$70
Scoop-ice cream, stainless bowl, 8 in. $40
Scoop-ice, silver plate bowl, 8 in. $45
Scoop-ice, silver plate bowl, 9 in. $45
Server/knife-fish, stainless blade,
    11 5/8 in...............................$45
Server-asparagus, hollow handle, silver plate
    hood, 10 in..............................$54
Server-cheese, stainless blade, 6 1/2 in......$35
Server-cranberry, stainless bowl, 8 3/4 in.....$40
Server-jelly, 6 1/4 in. $46
Server-lasagna, stainless blade, 10 in........$45
Server-pasta, stainless bowl, 10 5/8 in. $40
Server-pie and cake, stainless blade,
    11 in. $45
Server-tomato, solid, 7 5/8 in. $100
Spoon-baby, straight handle, 4 1/2 in.........$30
Spoon-bonbon, 5 in. $40
Spoon-demitasse, 4 1/8 in..................$25
Spoon-dessert/oval soup, 6 7/8 in. $50
Spoon-dressing, stainless tear bowl,
    11 1/4 in...............................$45
Spoon-fruit, 5 7/8 in. $42
Spoon-iced tea, 7 1/2 in....................$35
Spoon-infant feeding, 5 5/8 in...............$30
Spoon-pierced rice, stainless bowl,
    9 5/8 in................................$45
Spoon-salad serving, stainless egg-shaped
    bowl, 11 5/8 in.........................$40
Spoon-salt, individual, 2 1/2 in. $13
Spoon-soup, round bowl, bouillon,
    5 1/2 in................................$40
Spoon-soup, round bowl, cream, 6 in. $30
Spoon-sugar shell, 6 in. $30
Spoon-sugar, 5 7/8 in......................$30
Spoon-teaspoon, 6 in......................$24
Spoon-utility/serving, stainless bowl, 7
    scallops, 9 3/4 in.......................$40
Tablespoon, (serving spoon), 8 5/8 in. $80
Tablespoon, (serving spoon), pierced,
    8 5/8 in................................$95

Grande Baroque by Wallace, 1941

Brush-lip, 4 3/8 in. $25
Butter spreader, flat handle, 6 3/8 in. $42
Butter spreader, hollow handle, modern
    stainless paddle, 6 3/4 in. $38
Butter spreader, hollow handle, stainless
    paddle, no notch, 6 1/8 in. $38
Butter-master, flat handle, 7 1/2 in. $44
Butter-master, hollow handle, 6 3/4 in. $38
Caviar set, 2 pieces (scoop and
    spreader) $120
Cheese-grater, 9 1/4 in. $50
Cleaver-cheese, stainless blade, 6 7/8 in. $45
Fork, 7 1/2 in. $43
Fork, 8 in. $80
Fork-baby, 4 1/8 in. $35
Fork-carving, small, stainless prongs, steak,
    9 3/8 in. $45
Fork-chipped beef, small, 5 pierced tines,
    7 1/4 in. $90
Fork-cocktail, 5 1/2 in. $38
Fork-cold meat/serving, large, 5 stainless
    tines, 11 in. $45
Fork-cold meat/serving, medium, solid,
    8 1/8 in. $85
Fork-fish, stainless tines, hollow handle,
    individual, 8 3/8 in. $45
Fork-ice cream, no diamond slot, 5 1/2 in. $46
Fork-lettuce serving, large, 8 5/8 in. $90
Fork-pickle/olive, long handle, 7 1/2 in. $50
Fork-pickle/olive, short handle, 2 tines,
    5 1/2 in. $40
Fork-salad serving, solid, 9 3/8 in. $150
Fork-salad, individual, 6 1/2 in. $43
Fork-strawberry, 5 1/8 in. $30
Fork-youth, 5 7/8 in. $40
Knife-bar, hollow handle, 9 1/4 in. $40
Knife-carving, small, stainless blade, steak,
    10 3/4 in. $45
Knife-cheese, stainless blade, 7 in. $45
Knife-fish, stainless blade, individual,
    8 5/8 in. $45
Knife-fruit, stainless blade, individual,
    6 1/2 in. $45
Knife-fruit, stainless blade, individual, 7 in. $45
Knife-modern, hollow handle, 8 7/8 in. $37

Knife-modern, hollow handle, 9 3/4 in. $60
Knife-steak, individual, 8 3/4 in. $44
Ladle-gravy, hollow handle, stainless bowl,
    8 1/4 in. $45
Ladle-punch, stainless bowl, 13 in. $60
Magnifying glass, sterling handle, 6 3/8 in. . . . $50
Napkin clip, 2 3/8 in. $50
Opener-letter, stainless blade, 7 3/4 in. $45
Pick-butter, 1 tine, 5 1/8 in. $35
Poultry shears, 12 1/8 in. $200
Salad set, 2 pieces, wooden bowl,
    11 1/8 in. $100
Sardine server, solid, 6 1/2 in. $80
Scoop-caviar, sterling handle, pearl scoop,
    7 in. $60
Scoop-cheese, solid, 6 5/8 in. $70
Scoop-cheese, solid, large, 8 5/8 in. $90
Scoop-ice cream, stainless bowl, 8 1/2 in. $43
Scoop-ice, silver plate bowl, 9 in. $45
Server/knife-fish, stainless blade, design on
    bowl, 11 3/4 in. $45
Server-asparagus, hollow handle, silver plate
    hood, 10 in. $65
Server-asparagus, solid, 9 7/8 in. $240
Server-cheese, stainless blade, 6 1/2 in. $44
Server-jelly, 6 7/8 in. $60
Server-lasagna, stainless blade, 10 in. $45
Server-pasta, stainless bowl, 10 3/4 in. $45
Server-pie, stainless blade, 10 1/2 in. $46
Server-pie, stainless blade, oversize,
    12 3/4 in. $50
Slicer-ice cream, solid, 13 in. $240
Spoon-baby, straight handle, 4 in. $35
Spoon-bonbon, 5 3/8 in. $50
Spoon-casserole, pierced stainless bowl,
    7 scallops, 9 3/4 in. $45
Spoon-casserole, shell, stainless bowl,
    17 scallops, 10 1/2 in. $45
Spoon-casserole, smooth, solid,
    9 3/8 in. $150
Spoon-chocolate, short handle, large,
    4 3/8 in. $40
Spoon-cracker, 8 1/4 in. $120
Spoon-demitasse, 4 1/8 in. $28
Spoon-dressing, stainless bowl, tear-shaped
    bowl, 11 1/2 in. $40
Spoon-fruit, gold wash, 6 in. $48
Spoon-fruit, no wings, 6 in. $48
Spoon-fruit, wing bowl, 6 in. $48
Spoon-iced tea, 7 5/8 in. $40
Spoon-infant feeding, 5 5/8 in. $36
Spoon-mustard, 5 1/4 in. $35
Spoon-place or oval soup, 6 3/4 in. $50
Spoon-platter, solid, 13 3/4 in. $350

Spoon-salad serving, stainless bowl,
11 1/2 in. $45
Spoon-salt, individual, 2 1/2 in. $13
Spoon-soup, round bowl, gumbo,
6 3/4 in. $70
Spoon-sugar, 6 1/4 in. $40
Spoon-teaspoon, 6 1/4 in. $32
Spoon-utility/serving, stainless bowl, 7
scallops, 9 3/4 in. $45
Tablespoon, (serving spoon), 8 3/4 in. $90
Tablespoon, (serving spoon), pierced,
8 3/4 in. $100
Tongs-asparagus, individual, solid,
5 3/8 in. $100
Tongs-serving, with bowl tip, 8 3/4 in. $300
Tongs-sugar, 4 1/2 in. $50
Youth set, 3 pieces (spoon, knife, fork) $130

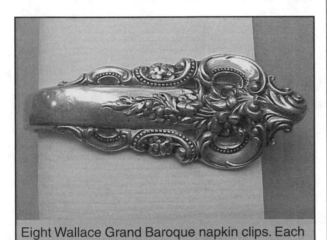

Eight Wallace Grand Baroque napkin clips. Each
is engraved with a different name. 2 1/8 in.
long, excellent condition. $250/set

Hampton by Wallace, 1904

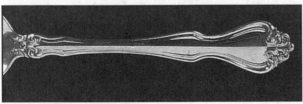

Butter-master, flat handle, 7 1/2 in. $40
Fork, 7 1/8 in. $38
Fork, 7 5/8 in. $55
Fork-cocktail, 5 5/8 in. $30
Fork-salad, individual, 6 1/8 in. $45
Knife-blunt, hollow handle, 8 7/8 in. $34
Knife-blunt, hollow handle, 9 3/4 in. $44
Knife-new french, hollow handle, 8 3/4 in. $34
Knife-old french, hollow handle, 9 3/4 in. $44

Knife-steak, individual, 9 in. $40
Ladle-cream, solid, 5 1/2 in. $45
Salad set, 2 pieces, plastic bowl $80
Server-pie, stainless blade, 9 7/8 in. $70
Server-tomato, solid, 7 3/4 in. $85
Spoon-5 o'clock/youth, 5 1/2 in. $18
Spoon-casserole, smooth bowl, solid,
9 1/8 in. $90
Spoon-fruit, 6 in. $34
Spoon-place or oval soup, tear-shaped bowl,
7 in. $44
Spoon-salt/master, 3 1/2 in. $24
Spoon-soup, round bowl, bouillon,
5 1/4 in. $40
Spoon-teaspoon, 6 in. $30
Tablespoon, (serving spoon), 8 1/4 in. $65
Tablespoon, (serving spoon)-pierced,
8 1/4 in. $70

Irian by Wallace, 1902

Carving set, 2 pieces, small, stainless blade,
steak $340
Fork, 7 1/2 in. $100
Fork, 7 in. $90
Fork, 8 in. $100
Fork-cold meat/serving, small, solid,
8 1/4 in. $250
Knife-blunt, hollow handle, 8 7/8 in. $160
Ladle-cream, solid, gold wash, 5 1/2 in. $120
Spoon-5 o'clock/youth, 5 1/2 in. $40
Spoon-bonbon, 5 1/8 in. $110
Spoon-casserole, smooth, solid,
7 3/4 in. $300
Spoon-sugar, 6 in. $100
Spoon-teaspoon, 6 in. $50
Tongs-sugar, 4 1/2 in. $160

Juliet by Wallace, 1924

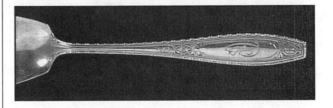

Butter spreader, flat handle, 5 5/8 in.........$20
Butter-master, flat handle, 6 3/4 in...........$40
Fork, 7 1/2 in...............................$60
Fork, 7 in..................................$36
Fork-carving, small, stainless prongs, steak,
   8 7/8 in....................................$55
Fork-cocktail, 5 1/2 in......................$20
Fork-cold meat/serving, small, solid,
   7 1/2 in..................................$70
Fork-cold meat/serving, small, solid,
   7 in......................................$70
Fork-lemon, 5 7/8 in........................$30
Fork-salad, individual, 5 7/8 in..............$42
Knife-carving, small, stainless blade, steak,
   10 1/4 in.................................$55
Knife-carving, small, stainless blade, steak,
   9 3/4 in..................................$55
Knife-new french, hollow handle,
   8 7/8 in..................................$34
Ladle-cream, solid, 5 1/8 in.................$40
Ladle-gravy, solid, 5 7/8 in.................$80
Server-jelly, 6 5/8 in........................$34
Server-tomato, solid, 7 in...................$90
Spoon-5 o'clock/youth, 5 3/8 in............$18
Spoon-casserole, smooth, solid,
   8 5/8 in..................................$85
Spoon-dessert/oval soup, 7 in..............$46
Spoon-fruit, 5 7/8 in........................$32
Spoon-iced tea, 7 5/8 in....................$30
Spoon-olive/short, pierced bowl, 6 in.......$80
Spoon-preserve, 7 in........................$45
Spoon-soup, round bowl, bouillon, 5 in......$25
Spoon-soup, round bowl, gumbo,
   6 5/8 in..................................$40
Spoon-sugar, 5 3/4 in.......................$34
Spoon-teaspoon, 5 7/8 in...................$30
Tablespoon, (serving spoon), 8 1/4 in.......$60
Tablespoon, (serving spoon), pierced,
   8 1/4 in..................................$80
Tongs-sugar, 4 1/2 in.......................$60

King Christian by Wallace, 1940

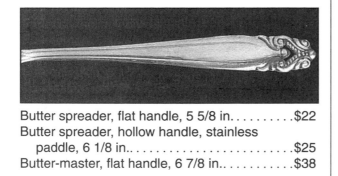

Butter spreader, flat handle, 5 5/8 in.........$22
Butter spreader, hollow handle, stainless
   paddle, 6 1/8 in..........................$25
Butter-master, flat handle, 6 7/8 in...........$38

Fork, 7 3/8 in...............................$26
Fork, 7 7/8 in...............................$45
Fork-cocktail, 5 3/4 in......................$23
Fork-cold meat/serving, medium, solid,
   8 1/8 in..................................$80
Fork-salad, individual, 6 3/8 in..............$36
Knife-modern, hollow handle, 9 5/8 in.......$30
Knife-modern, hollow handle, 9 in..........$34
Knife-new french, hollow handle,
   9 3/4 in..................................$30
Knife-new french, hollow handle, 9 in.......$34
Server-jelly, 6 3/8 in........................$34
Spoon-demitasse, 3 7/8 in..................$24
Spoon-dessert/oval soup, 7 1/4 in..........$40
Spoon-iced tea, 7 3/4 in....................$30
Spoon-soup, round bowl, cream, 6 in.......$36
Spoon-soup, round bowl, gumbo,
   6 7/8 in..................................$48
Spoon-sugar, 6 1/8 in.......................$33
Spoon-teaspoon, 6 1/8 in...................$18
Tablespoon, (serving spoon), 8 5/8 in.......$75

Kings by Wallace, 1903

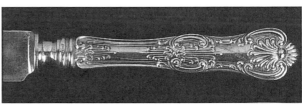

Fork, 6 7/8 in...............................$60
Fork, 7 5/8 in...............................$80
Spoon-demitasse, 4 1/4 in..................$30
Spoon-soup, round bowl, bouillon,
   5 in......................................$60

La Reine by Wallace, 1921

Butter spreader, flat handle, 6 1/4 in........$20
Butter spreader, hollow handle, modern
   stainless paddle, 3 3/8 in. blade,
   6 5/8 in..................................$30
Butter spreader, hollow handle, modern
   stainless paddle, 3 in. blade, 6 3/8 in......$30
Butter spreader, hollow handle, stainless
   paddle, no notch, 6 1/4 in...............$25

Butter spreader, hollow handle, stainless
    paddle, notch, 6 1/4 in. $25
Butter-master, flat handle, 7 5/8 in.. . . . .$46
Butter-master, hollow handle, 6 3/4 in.. . . . . . .$46
Carving set, 2 pieces, small, stainless blade,
    steak $140
Fork, 7 in.. . . . .$27
Fork-carving, small, stainless prongs/steak,
    9 1/4 in.. . . . .$70
Fork-cocktail, 3 tines, 5 3/4 in.. . . . .$28
Fork-cold meat/serving, medium, solid,
    8 1/2 in.. . . . .$95
Fork-fish, stainless tines, hollow handle,
    individual, 7 3/4 in. $40
Fork-ice cream, 5 5/8 in.. . . . .$60
Fork-pickle/olive, short handle, 2 tines,
    5 3/4 in.. . . . .$42
Fork-salad serving, stainless prongs,
    11 in.. . . . .$44
Fork-salad, individual, 6 1/4 in. $38
Knife-carving, small, stainless blade, steak,
    10 1/4 in. $70
Knife-fish, stainless blade, individual,
    8 in.. . . . .$48
Knife-modern, hollow handle, 9 5/8 in.. . . . .$56
Knife-modern, hollow handle, 9 in. $38
Knife-new french, hollow handle, 9 in. $40
Ladle-cream, solid, 5 1/4 in.. . . . .$50
Ladle-gravy, solid, 6 1/2 in. $90
Server-jelly, 6 3/4 in. $46
Server-pie and cake, stainless blade,
    10 1/8 in. $70
Server-pie, stainless blade, 9 7/8 in. $70
Spoon-5 o'clock/youth, 5 1/2 in. $22
Spoon-bonbon, 5 in. $50
Spoon-iced tea, 7 3/4 in. $38
Spoon-salad serving, stainless bowl,
    egg-shaped bowl, 10 7/8 in. $44
Spoon-soup, round bowl, bouillon,
    5 3/8 in.. . . . .$50
Spoon-soup, round bowl, cream, 6 in. $38
Spoon-sugar, 6 1/8 in.. . . . .$33
Spoon-teaspoon, 6 in.. . . . .$18
Tablespoon, (serving spoon), 8 3/8 in.. . . . . . .$70

Lamerie by Wallace, 1936

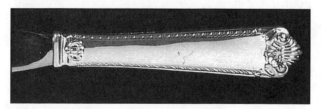

Image available but no priced examples

Larkspur by Wallace, 1939

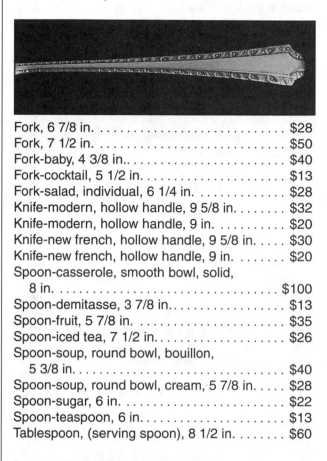

Fork, 6 7/8 in. $28
Fork, 7 1/2 in. $50
Fork-baby, 4 3/8 in.. . . . .$40
Fork-cocktail, 5 1/2 in. $13
Fork-salad, individual, 6 1/4 in. $28
Knife-modern, hollow handle, 9 5/8 in. $32
Knife-modern, hollow handle, 9 in. $20
Knife-new french, hollow handle, 9 5/8 in. $30
Knife-new french, hollow handle, 9 in. $20
Spoon-casserole, smooth bowl, solid,
    8 in. $100
Spoon-demitasse, 3 7/8 in.. . . . .$13
Spoon-fruit, 5 7/8 in. $35
Spoon-iced tea, 7 1/2 in.. . . . .$26
Spoon-soup, round bowl, bouillon,
    5 3/8 in.. . . . .$40
Spoon-soup, round bowl, cream, 5 7/8 in. $28
Spoon-sugar, 6 in. $22
Spoon-teaspoon, 6 in. $13
Tablespoon, (serving spoon), 8 1/2 in. $60

Lotus by Wallace, 1935

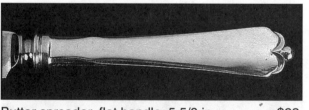

Butter spreader, flat handle, 5 5/8 in. $23
Butter spreader, hollow handle, modern
    stainless, 6 in. $28
Butter spreader, hollow handle, stainless
    paddle, 6 in. $28
Butter-master, flat handle, 7 1/8 in. $40
Butter-master, hollow handle, 6 1/2 in. $40
Carving set, 2 pieces, small, stainless blade,
    steak $140
Fork, 7 3/8 in. $45
Fork-carving, small, stainless prongs, steak,
    9 in. $70
Fork-cocktail, 5 3/4 in. $23
Fork-cold meat/serving, small, solid,
    7 3/4 in. $80

Fork-ice cream, 5 3/8 in....................$40
Fork-ice cream, 5 5/8 in....................$38
Fork-lemon, 4 5/8 in.......................$27
Fork-pickle/olive, short handle,
   6 1/8 in.................................$28
Fork-salad, individual, 6 1/2 in. $46
Knife-fruit, stainless blade, individual,
   6 3/4 in..................................$34
Knife-modern, hollow handle, 8 7/8 in........$34
Knife-new french, hollow handle, 9 in. $34
Ladle-gravy, solid, 6 1/4 in. $80
Server-pie and cake, stainless blade,
   10 5/8 in. $50
Server-pie, stainless blade, 10 1/4 in. $50
Spoon-5 o'clock/youth, 5 1/4 in. $18
Spoon-bonbon, 4 1/2 in....................$40
Spoon-casserole, smooth bowl, solid,
   7 3/4 in..................................$90
Spoon-casserole, smooth bowl, solid,
   8 1/8 in..................................$90
Spoon-demitasse, 4 1/4 in. $24
Spoon-dessert/oval soup, 7 3/8 in...........$48
Spoon-iced tea, 7 1/4 in. $33
Spoon-soup, round bowl, cream,
   6 5/8 in..................................$40
Spoon-soup, round bowl, gumbo,
   7 in......................................$50
Spoon-sugar, 5 7/8 in......................$28
Spoon-teaspoon, 5 7/8 in. $23
Tablespoon, (serving spoon), 8 1/2 in........$70
Tablespoon, (serving spoon), pierced,
   8 1/2 in..................................$80

Louvre by Wallace, 1893

Fork, 6 3/4 in...............................$45
Fork-chipped beef/small, 6 in...............$70
Fork-pie, 6 in..............................$55
Scoop-cheese, solid, 6 in. $70
Spoon-dessert or oval soup,
   6 7/8 in..................................$50
Spoon-sugar, 5 7/8 in......................$40
Spoon-teaspoon, (5 o'clock)
   5 1/4 in..................................$18
Spoon-teaspoon, 5 3/4 in. $23
Tablespoon, (serving spoon),
   8 1/8 in..................................$80

Lucerne by Wallace, 1896

Butter spreader, hollow handle, modern stainless,
   6 in. $30
Fork, 7 1/2 in. $47
Fork, 7 in.................................$40
Fork-cocktail, 5 7/8 in. $28
Fork-salad, individual, 5 3/4 in. $44
Knife-modern, hollow handle, 9 5/8 in........$50
Knife-modern, hollow handle, 9 in. $40
Knife-new french, hollow handle, 9 1/4 in. $40
Knife-old french, hollow handle, 9 1/4 in......$40
Ladle-gravy, solid, 7 1/4 in.................$120
Spoon-5 o'clock/youth, 5 in. $24
Spoon-demitasse, 4 1/4 in..................$30
Spoon-dessert/oval soup, 7 1/8 in. $47
Spoon-dressing, stainless bowl,
   10 3/4 in..................................$45
Spoon-soup, round bowl, bouillon,
   4 7/8 in..................................$40
Spoon-soup, round bowl, cream,
   5 7/8 in..................................$48
Spoon-sugar shell, 6 in. $37
Spoon-teaspoon, 6 in......................$20
Tablespoon, (serving spoon), 8 1/4 in. $70

Madison by Wallace, 1913

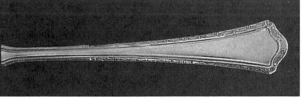

Butter spreader, flat handle, 6 in.............$18
Butter-master, flat handle, 7 in. $30
Carving set, 2 pieces, small, stainless blade,
   steak $90
Fork, 7 1/2 in. $40
Fork, 7 1/8 in. $30
Fork-cocktail, 5 1/2 in......................$30
Fork-fish, solid, individual, 7 in. $40
Fork-pickle/olive, long handle, 7 1/2 in........$40
Fork-salad, individual, 5 7/8 in. $32
Knife-old french, hollow handle, bolster,
   8 3/4 in..................................$30

Knife-old french, hollow handle, 8 1/2 in.......$30
Ladle-cream, solid, 5 3/8 in..................$34
Ladle-gravy, solid, 6 1/8 in. $70
Server-jelly, 6 5/8 in. $30
Server-pie, silver plate blade, 10 in..........$55
Server-pie, silver plate blade, 9 3/8 in........$55
Spoon-bonbon, 5 1/4 in....................$40
Spoon-demitasse, 4 1/4 in. $16
Spoon-dessert/oval soup, 7 1/8 in...........$34
Spoon-fruit, 5 3/4 in.......................$30
Spoon-soup, round bowl, cream,
  6 5/8 in..................................$30
Spoon-soup, round bowl, gumbo,
  6 7/8 in..................................$34
Spoon-sugar, 6 in..........................$35
Spoon-teaspoon, 5 7/8 in. $20
Tablespoon, (serving spoon), 8 3/8 in.........$60
Tablespoon, (serving spoon), pierced,
  8 3/8 in..................................$70
Tongs-sugar, 3 1/4 in......................$50

Meadow Rose by Wallace, 1907

Butter spreader, hollow handle, modern
  stainless paddle, 6 1/4 in. $32
Butter spreader, hollow handle, stainless paddle,
  6 1/8 in..................................$30
Carving set, 2 pieces, small, stainless blade,
  steak $80
Cleaver-cheese, stainless blade, 6 5/8 in......$40
Fork, 7 3/4 in.............................$50
Fork, thick tines, 7 3/8 in...................$34
Fork, thin tines, 7 1/8 in....................$34
Fork-carving, small, stainless prongs,
  steak, 8 3/4 in...........................$40
Fork-cocktail, 3 tines, 5 5/8 in...............$25
Fork-cold meat/serving, large, stainless tines,
  10 3/4 in. $40
Fork-cold meat/serving, small, solid,
  7 3/4 in..................................$80
Fork-fish, stainless tines, hollow handle,
  individual, 7 3/4 in. $45
Fork-salad serving, stainless prongs,
  10 7/8 in. $40
Knife-carving, small blade, steak, 10 in. $40
Knife-cheese, stainless blade, 7 in. $40
Knife-fish, stainless blade, individual, 8 in. $45

Knife-fruit, stainless blade, individual,
  6 7/8 in..................................$40
Knife-modern, hollow handle, 9 5/8 in........$46
Knife-modern, hollow handle, 9 in. $30
Knife-steak, individual, 8 3/4 in..............$45
Knife-steak, individual, 8 3/8 in..............$45
Ladle-cream, solid, 5 1/8 in..................$50
Ladle-gravy, hollow handle, stainless bowl,
  7 1/4 in..................................$40
Ladle-soup, stainless bowl, 10 5/8 in.........$55
Scoop-ice cream, stainless bowl,
  7 7/8 in..................................$45
Scoop-ice, silver plate bowl, 8 3/8 in. $50
Server/knife-fish, stainless blade,
  11 1/4 in.................................$45
Server-cranberry, stainless bowl,
  8 1/4 in..................................$40
Server-lasagna, stainless blade,
  9 1/2 in..................................$40
Server-pasta, stainless bowl, 10 1/4 in. $45
Server-pie and cake, stainless blade,
  10 3/4 in.................................$45
Slicer-cake, stainless blade, 12 1/8 in........$40
Spoon-5 o'clock/youth, 5 3/8 in..............$24
Spoon-baby/straight handle, 4 1/8 in.........$34
Spoon-demitasse, 4 1/4 in..................$20
Spoon-dessert/oval soup, 7 in...............$50
Spoon-dressing, stainless bowl,
  10 7/8 in.................................$40
Spoon-iced tea, 7 3/8 in....................$32
Spoon-pierced rice, stainless bowl,
  9 1/4 in..................................$40
Spoon-rice, stainless bowl, 9 1/4 in..........$40
Spoon-salad serving, stainless bowl,
  10 7/8 in.................................$40
Spoon-sugar, 5 3/8 in......................$30
Spoon-teaspoon, 5 7/8 in...................$20
Tablespoon, (serving spoon), 8 3/8 in. $80
Tablespoon, (serving spoon), pierced,
  8 3/8 in..................................$100

Melanie by Wallace, 1959

Butter spreader, hollow handle, modern stainless
  paddle, 6 1/2 in..........................$20
Butter-master, hollow handle, 7 in. $38
Fork, 7 3/8 in. $34

Fork-pickle/olive, short handle, 5 3/4 in. $30
Fork-salad, individual, 6 1/2 in. $40
Knife-modern, hollow handle, 9 1/2 in. $36
Knife-steak, individual, 9 1/4 in. $46
Spoon-dessert/oval soup, 6 7/8 in. $40
Spoon-sugar, 6 1/8 in. $35
Spoon-teaspoon, 6 in. $20

Michele by Wallace, 1968

Butter-master, hollow handle,
  6 3/4 in. $40
Fork, 7 5/8 in. $36
Fork-carving, small, stainless prongs, steak,
  9 1/2 in. $45
Fork-fish, stainless tines, hollow handle,
  individual, 8 1/2 in. $40
Fork-fruit, stainless tines, individual,
  6 1/2 In. $35
Fork-salad serving, stainless prongs,
  11 1/2 in. $40
Fork-salad, individual, 6 5/8 in. $40
Knife-bar, hollow handle, 9 1/2 in. $36
Knife-carving, small, stainless blade, steak,
  10 7/8 in. $45
Knife-fish, stainless blade, individual,
  8 5/8 in. $40
Knife-modern, hollow handle, 9 in. $28
Knife-steak, individual, beveled edge,
  9 in. $45
Knife-youth, 6 7/8 in. $38
Ladle-gravy, solid, 6 3/8 in. $87
Server-cheese, stainless blade,
  6 5/8 in. $50
Server-pasta, stainless bowl, 11 in. $45
Server-pie and cake, stainless blade,
  11 1/8 in. $45
Slicer-cake, stainless blade, wedding,
  12 7/8 in. $40
Spoon-dressing, stainless bowl,
  11 1/2 in. $50
Spoon-salad serving, stainless bowl,
  11 3/4 in. $40
Spoon-sugar, 6 1/4 in. $30
Spoon-teaspoon, 6 1/2 in. $24
Tablespoon, (serving spoon), pierced,
  8 5/8 in. $100

Sixty-four pieces Wallace Monterey (1922): 8 luncheon forks, 8 luncheon knives, 12 teaspoons, 7 salad forks, 8 bouillon spoons, 8 citrus spoons, 8 ice cream forks, 2 tablespoons, 1 cold meat fork, 1 butter knife, and 1 sugar spoon. Monogram "R." $825

My Love by Wallace, 1958

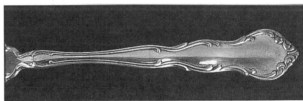

Butter spreader, hollow handle, modern
  stainless paddle, 6 1/2 in. $30
Butter-master, hollow handle, 6 7/8 in. $36
Fork, 7 1/2 in. $45
Fork-cold meat/serving, medium, solid,
  8 1/4 in. $90
Knife-modern, hollow handle, 9 1/2 in. $36
Knife-youth, 7 in. $30
Ladle-gravy, solid, 6 1/8 in. $90
Spoon-sugar, 6 1/4 in. $30
Spoon-teaspoon, 6 in. $30
Tablespoon, (serving spoon), pierced,
  8 1/2 in. $90

Nile by Wallace, 1908

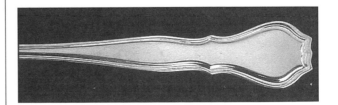

Fork, 7 1/2 in. $50
Fork, 7 1/8 in. $40
Fork-cold meat/serving, medium, solid,
    8 1/4 in. $90
Fork-salad, individual, not beveled,
    6 1/8 in. $50
Fork-youth, 6 1/8 in. $45
Knife-new french, hollow handle,
    9 1/2 in. $45
Knife-old french, hollow handle,
    9 1/2 in. $45
Ladle-cream, solid, 5 5/8 in. $45
Spoon-demitasse, 4 1/4 in. $20
Spoon-dessert/oval soup, 7 1/8 in. $40
Spoon-iced tea, 7 in. $40
Spoon-soup, round bowl, bouillon,
    5 1/4 in. $30
Spoon-soup, round bowl, gumbo, 7 in. $50
Spoon-sugar, 6 1/8 in. $28
Tablespoon, (serving spoon), 8 1/4 in. $55
Tongs-sugar, 3 3/8 in. $55
Tongs-sugar, 4 3/8 in. $55

Normandie by Wallace, 1933

Butter spreader, flat handle, 5 7/8 in. $17
Butter spreader, hollow handle, stainless
    paddle, 6 in. $20
Butter-master, flat handle, 6 7/8 in. $30
Fork, 7 1/4 in. $28
Fork, 7 7/8 in. $50
Fork-carving, small, stainless prongs, steak,
    8 3/4 in. $60
Fork-cocktail, 5 5/8 in. $17
Fork-cold meat/serving, small, solid,
    7 7/8 in. $80
Fork-grille (viand), 7 3/4 in. $30
Fork-ice cream, 5 3/8 in. $38
Fork-lemon, 5 1/2 in. $27
Fork-salad, individual, 6 3/8 in. $30
Knife-fruit, stainless blade, individual,
    6 5/8 in. $34
Knife-grille/new french, hollow handle,
    8 1/2 in. $30
Knife-modern, hollow handle, 8 3/4 in. $30
Knife-modern, hollow handle, 9 5/8 in. $45
Knife-new french, hollow handle, 8 3/4 in. $30

Knife-new french, hollow handle, 9
    5/8 in. $45
Ladle-cream, solid, 5 3/8 in. $44
Ladle-gravy, solid, 6 in. $70
Ladle-mayonnaise, 5 1/8 in. $45
Server-cheese, stainless blade,
    6 1/2 in. $50
Server-jelly, 6 3/8 in. $26
Server-pie, stainless blade, 9 3/8 in. $60
Server-pie, stainless blade, 9 7/8 in. $60
Spoon-5 o'clock/youth, 5 3/8 in. $16
Spoon-baby, straight handle,
    3 7/8 in. $40
Spoon-bonbon, 5 in. $36
Spoon-casserole, smooth bowl, solid,
    9 in. $100
Spoon-demitasse, 4 1/8 in. $20
Spoon-fruit, 6 in. $40
Spoon-iced tea, 7 1/2 in. $35
Spoon-relish, 5 5/8 in. $40
Spoon-soup, round bowl, cream,
    6 1/8 in. $36
Spoon-soup, round bowl, gumbo,
    6 5/8 in. $40
Spoon-sugar, 6 1/8 in. $25
Spoon-teaspoon, 6 1/8 in. $18
Tablespoon, (serving spoon),
    8 1/2 in. $70
Tongs-sugar, 4 in. $50

Orange Blossom by Wallace, 1923

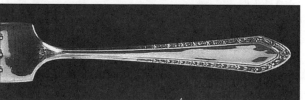

Butter spreader, flat handle, 5 3/4 in. $30
Butter-master, flat handle, 7 in. $44
Fork, 7 3/4 in. $65
Fork, 7 in. $48
Fork-cocktail, 5 1/2 in. $28
Fork-cold meat/serving, small, solid,
    7 3/4 in. $90
Fork-fish, solid, individual, 6 3/4 in. $58
Fork-salad, individual, 6 in. $50
Knife-fruit, stainless blade, individual,
    6 5/8 in. $34
Knife-old french, hollow handle,
    8 1/2 in. $42
Knife-old french, hollow handle,
    9 1/8 in. $42

Wallace Silversmiths

Ladle-cream, solid, 5 3/8 in.................\$53
Ladle-gravy, solid, 6 1/2 in. \$94
Server-pie, silver plate blade, 9 1/2 in........\$70
Spoon-5 o'clock/youth, 5 3/8 in. \$28
Spoon-demitasse, 4 in....................\$26
Spoon-dessert/oval soup, 7 1/8 in...........\$60
Spoon-fruit, 5 7/8 in. \$35
Spoon-iced tea, 7 5/8 in. \$40
Spoon-soup, round bowl, bouillon,
   5 1/4 in.................................\$50
Spoon-soup, round bowl, cream,
   5 7/8 in.................................\$60
Spoon-soup, round bowl, gumbo,
   6 7/8 in.................................\$60
Spoon-sugar, 5 7/8 in....................\$36
Spoon-teaspoon, 5 7/8 in. \$30
Tablespoon, (serving spoon),
   8 1/4 in.................................\$90

Orchid Elegance by Wallace, 1956

Butter spreader, hollow handle, stainless
   paddle, 6 1/4 in.........................\$24
Butter-master, flat handle, 7 in..............\$40
Butter-master, hollow handle,
   6 3/4 in.................................\$40
Fork, 7 1/4 in..........................\$40
Fork-cocktail, 5 3/4 in....................\$26
Fork-cold meat/serving, medium, solid,
   8 1/8 in.................................\$80
Fork-lemon, 5 1/8 in.....................\$28
Fork-pickle/olive, short handle,
   5 3/4 in.................................\$30
Fork-salad, individual, 6 1/2 in. \$45
Knife-modern, hollow handle, 9 in...........\$30
Ladle-cream, solid, 5 3/8 in................\$40
Ladle-gravy, solid, 6 1/2 in. \$80
Spoon-bonbon, 5 7/8 in...................\$36
Spoon-demitasse, 4 1/4 in. \$22
Spoon-dessert/oval soup, 6 3/8 in...........\$42
Spoon-iced tea, 7 5/8 in. \$36
Spoon-sugar, 6 1/8 in....................\$34
Spoon-teaspoon, 6 in....................\$20
Tablespoon, (serving spoon),
   8 1/2 in.................................\$80
Tablespoon, (serving spoon), pierced,
   8 1/2 in.................................\$90

Penrose by Wallace, 1962

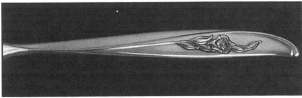

Butter spreader, hollow handle, modern
   stainless paddle, 6 5/8 in................\$16
Butter-master, hollow handle, 7 in. \$24
Fork, 7 5/8 in. \$30
Fork-cold meat/serving, medium, solid,
   8 1/4 in.................................\$58
Fork-salad, individual, 6 3/4 in. \$30
Knife-modern, hollow handle, 9 1/4 in. \$23
Ladle-cream, solid, 5 7/8 in................\$48
Ladle-gravy, solid, 6 1/2 in................\$58
Spoon-dessert/oval soup, 7 in..............\$33
Spoon-iced tea, 7 1/2 in...................\$36
Spoon-sugar, 6 in. \$25
Spoon-teaspoon, 6 1/8 in..................\$20
Tablespoon, (serving spoon), 8 1/2 in. \$65
Tablespoon, (serving spoon), pierced,
   8 1/2 in.................................\$65

Peony by Wallace, 1906

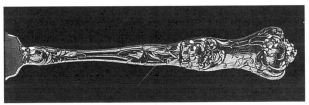

Butter spreader, flat handle, 6 1/8 in. \$40
Fork-salad, individual, 6 in.................\$120
Fork-youth, 5 7/8 in......................\$70

Princess Anne by Wallace, 1926

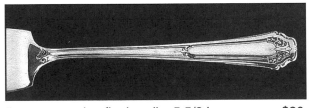

Butter spreader, flat handle, 5 5/8 in. \$20
Butter-master, flat handle, 6 7/8 in...........\$30
Carving set, 2 pieces, small, stainless blade,
   steak \$120
Fork, 7 1/8 in. \$37
Fork, 7 5/8 in. \$50

Fork-cocktail, 5 1/2 in..........................$24
Fork-cold meat/serving, small, solid,
   7 3/4 in.....................................$60
Fork-ice cream, 5 3/8 in...........................$38
Fork-salad, individual, 6 1/8 in..............$44
Knife-modern, hollow handle, 8 7/8 in.........$34
Knife-new french, hollow handle,
   8 3/4 in.....................................$34
Knife-new french, hollow handle,
   9 5/8 in.....................................$44
Knife-pie, solid, large, 9 1/4 in..............$130
Ladle-gravy, solid, 6 in.........................$70
Server-pie, stainless blade, 10 1/8 in.........$60
Spoon-bonbon, 4 7/8 in...........................$44
Spoon-casserole, smooth bowl, solid,
   8 3/4 in....................................$100
Spoon-demitasse, 4 1/8 in.......................$18
Spoon-fruit, 6 in...............................$30
Spoon-iced tea, 7 3/4 in.........................$34
Spoon-soup, round bowl, bouillon,
   5 1/2 in.....................................$25
Spoon-sugar, 5 7/8 in............................$28
Spoon-teaspoon, (5 o'clock) 5 5/8 in.........$18
Spoon-teaspoon, 6 in............................$23
Spoon-youth, 5 3/8 in............................$34
Tablespoon, (serving spoon), 8 1/4 in.........$60
Tablespoon, (serving spoon), pierced,
   8 1/4 in.....................................$70

Princess Mary by Wallace, 1922

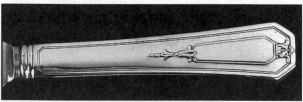

Butter-master, flat handle, 6 3/4 in...........$24
Carving set, 2 pieces, small, stainless blade,
   steak.......................................$80
Fork, 7 1/2 in..................................$38
Fork, 7 1/8 in..................................$28
Fork-baby, 4 in.................................$30
Fork-carving, small, stainless prongs, steak,
   8 7/8 in.....................................$40
Fork-cocktail, 5 1/2 in..........................$18
Fork-fish, solid, individual, 5 3/4 in.........$38
Fork-salad, individual, 6 1/4 in...............$34
Knife-new french, hollow handle, 8 7/8 in.....$24
Knife-old french, hollow handle, 8 5/8 in.....$24
Ladle-cream, solid, 5 3/8 in....................$35
Ladle-gravy, solid, 6 1/8 in....................$60
Ladle-mayonnaise, 5 1/4 in......................$34

Spoon-5 o'clock/youth, 5 3/4 in.............. $12
Spoon-casserole, smooth bowl, solid,
   8 7/8 in.................................... $80
Spoon-demitasse, 4 1/4 in.................. $15
Spoon-dessert/oval soup, 7 1/8 in.......... $34
Spoon-iced tea, 8 in...................... $30
Spoon-soup, round bowl, bouillon,
   5 1/2 in.................................... $24
Spoon-sugar, 6 in......................... $24
Tablespoon, (serving spoon), 8 3/8 in........ $50
Tablespoon, (serving spoon), pierced,
   8 3/8 in.................................... $65
Tongs-sugar, 3 7/8 in..................... $50

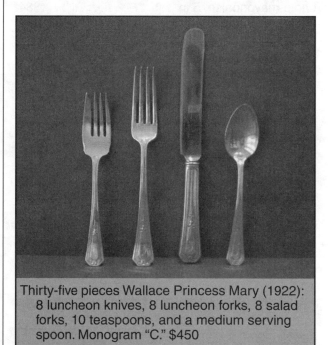

Thirty-five pieces Wallace Princess Mary (1922): 8 luncheon knives, 8 luncheon forks, 8 salad forks, 10 teaspoons, and a medium serving spoon. Monogram "C." $450

Puritan by Wallace, 1909

Butter spreader, flat handle, 5 5/8 in. $18
Butter-master, flat handle, 6 7/8 in........... $28
Fork, round bowl, 7 1/8 in. $35
Fork, round bowl, 7 3/4 in. $50
Fork, square bowl, 7 1/8 in. $35
Fork, square bowl, 7 3/4 in. $50
Fork-cold meat/serving, medium, solid,
   8 3/4 in.................................. $63

Fork-cold meat/serving, small, solid,
7 5/8 in. $60
Fork-dessert, 5 3/4 in. $34
Fork-lemon, 4 3/4 in. $20
Fork-salad, individual, 6 1/4 in. $30
Knife-carving, small, stainless blade, steak,
10 1/4 in. $40
Knife-new french, hollow handle,
9 5/8 in. $30
Knife-old french, hollow handle,
9 3/4 in. $30
Ladle-cream, solid, 5 3/8 in. $33
Ladle-gravy, solid, 6 1/4 in. $60
Ladle-mayonnaise, 5 in. $34
Server-tomato, solid, 7 3/4 in. $70
Spoon-5 o'clock/youth, 5 3/8 in. $14
Spoon-5 o'clock/youth, 5 5/8 in. $14
Spoon-casserole, smooth bowl, solid,
8 3/4 in. $75
Spoon-demitasse, 3 7/8 in. $16
Spoon-demitasse, 4 1/4 in. $16
Spoon-dessert/oval soup, 7 1/8 in. $30
Spoon-fruit, 6 in. $30
Spoon-iced tea, 8 in. $28
Spoon-sherbet, large, 6 in. $30
Spoon-soup, round bowl, cream, 6 in. $30
Spoon-soup, round bowl, gumbo,
7 1/4 in. $32
Spoon-teaspoon, 6 in. $17
Tablespoon, (serving spoon), 8 3/8 in. $50

Putnam by Wallace, 1912

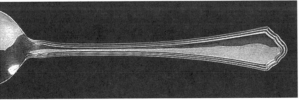

Butter spreader, flat handle, 5 3/4 in. $28
Butter-master, flat handle, 7 1/2 in. $35
Fork, 6 7/8 in. $47
Fork, 7 5/8 in. $60
Fork-cocktail, 5 1/2 in. $26
Fork-fish, solid, individual, 6 3/4 in. $58
Fork-ice cream, 5 1/4 in. $50
Fork-pickle/olive, long handle, 7 1/4 in. $45
Fork-salad, individual, 5 3/4 in. $48
Knife-old french, hollow handle, 8 1/2 in. $38
Knife-sharpener, steel, small, steak,
14 1/2 in. $70
Spoon-5 o'clock/youth, 5 5/8 in. $15
Spoon-bonbon, 4 3/4 in. $45

Spoon-casserole, smooth bowl, solid,
7 1/4 in. $110
Spoon-chocolate, short handle, 4 3/8 in. $30
Spoon-demitasse, 3 7/8 in. $28
Spoon-fruit, 5 3/4 in. $38
Spoon-iced tea, 7 3/8 in. $38
Spoon-salad serving, solid, 8 3/4 in. $100
Spoon-soup, round bowl, bouillon,
5 3/8 in. $35
Spoon-soup, round bowl, gumbo,
6 7/8 in. $46
Spoon-sugar, 5 7/8 in. $32
Spoon-teaspoon, 5 7/8 in. $28
Tablespoon, (serving spoon), 8 1/8 in. $70
Tablespoon, (serving spoon), pierced,
8 1/8 in. $100
Tongs-sugar, 3 3/8 in. $45
Tongs-sugar, 4 in. $45

Renaissance by Wallace, 1925

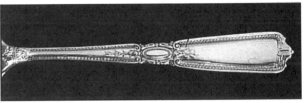

Butter spreader, flat handle, 5 5/8 in. $30
Butter-master, flat handle, 6 7/8 in. $38
Fork, 7 1/2 in. $55
Fork-carving, small, stainless prongs, steak,
9 in. $85
Fork-cocktail, 5 5/8 in. $24
Fork-cold meat/serving, small, solid,
7 3/4 in. $100
Fork-ice cream, 5 1/4 in. $60
Fork-pickle/olive, short handle, 5 1/2 in. $40
Fork-salad, individual, 6 in. $45
Knife-modern, hollow handle, 8 7/8 in. $47
Knife-new french, hollow handle, 8 7/8 in. $50
Knife-new french, hollow handle, 9 3/4 in. $60
Knife-old french, hollow handle, 8 1/2 in. $50
Ladle-cream, solid, 5 in. $60
Ladle-gravy, solid, 5 7/8 in. $75
Poultry shears, 10 1/8 in. $240
Server-cheese, silver plate blade,
6 3/8 in. $50
Server-jelly, 6 1/2 in. $40
Server-tomato, solid, 7 3/8 in. $120
Spoon-5 o'clock/youth, 5 5/8 in. $18
Spoon-bonbon, 4 7/8 in. $50
Spoon-dessert/oval soup, 7 1/8 in. $70
Spoon-fruit, 5 7/8 in. $48

Spoon-iced tea, 7 5/8 in. $38
Spoon-relish, 5 7/8 in. $50
Spoon-soup, round bowl, bouillon,
    5 1/2 in. $30
Spoon-soup, round bowl, cream, 5 7/8 in. $42
Spoon-soup, round bowl, gumbo, 6 7/8 in. $60
Spoon-sugar, 5 3/4 in. $40
Spoon-teaspoon, 5 7/8 in. $30
Tablespoon, (serving spoon), 8 1/4 in. $80
Tongs-sugar, 4 1/4 in. $80

Rheims by Wallace, 1919

Butter spreader, flat handle, 5 1/2 in. $26
Fork, 7 1/2 in. $65
Fork-salad, individual, 5 5/8 in. $50
Spoon-5 o'clock/youth, 5 5/8 in. $26
Spoon-sugar, 5 7/8 in. $45
Spoon-teaspoon, 5 7/8 in. $30
Tablespoon, (serving spoon), 8 1/4 in. $80

Rhythm by Wallace, 1929

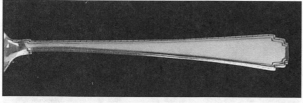

Butter spreader, flat handle, 5 5/8 in. $18
Butter-master, flat handle, 6 7/8 in. $30
Fork, 7 1/8 in. $30
Fork, 7 3/4 in. $50
Fork-carving, small, stainless prongs, steak,
    8 7/8 in. $50
Fork-cocktail, 5 1/2 in. $23
Fork-pickle/olive, short handle, 5 5/8 in. $27
Fork-salad, individual, 6 1/4 in. $30
Knife-new french, hollow handle, 8 3/4 in. $30
Knife-new french, hollow handle, 9 1/2 in. $40
Ladle-cream, solid, 5 in. $40
Ladle-gravy, solid, 6 1/8 in. $75
Server-cheese, stainless blade, 6 1/2 in. $32
Server-jelly, 6 1/4 in. $27
Server-pie, stainless blade, 10 in. $55
Server-pie, stainless blade, 9 1/2 in. $55

Spoon-5 o'clock/youth, 5 5/8 in. $16
Spoon-fruit, 6 in. $26
Spoon-olive, short, pierced bowl,
    5 7/8 in. $70
Spoon-soup, round bowl, cream, 6 in. $36
Spoon-soup, round bowl, gumbo,
    6 5/8 in. $40
Spoon-sugar, 6 1/8 in. $30
Spoon-teaspoon, 6 in. $17
Tablespoon, (serving spoon), 8 3/8 in. $60

Romance of the Sea by Wallace, 1950

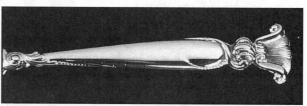

Butter spreader, flat handle, 6 1/4 in. $44
Butter spreader, hollow handle, modern
    stainless paddle, 6 1/4 in. $40
Butter spreader, hollow handle, stainless
    paddle, 6 1/4 in. $40
Butter-master, hollow handle, 6 7/8 in. $40
Carving set, 2 pieces, small, stainless blade,
    steak $90
Cheese-grater, 9 1/4 in. $50
Cleaver-cheese, stainless blade,
    6 3/4 in. $45
Fork, 7 1/4 in. $50
Fork, 7 3/4 in. $60
Fork-carving, small, stainless prongs, steak,
    9 1/2 in. $45
Fork-cocktail, 5 1/2 in. $40
Fork-cold meat/serving, large, stainless tines,
    11 1/4 in. $40
Fork-fish, stainless tines, hollow handle,
    individual, 8 3/8 in. $45
Fork-pickle/olive, short handle, 2 tines,
    5 1/2 in. $40
Fork-salad serving, stainless prongs,
    11 3/4 in. $40
Fork-salad, individual, 6 1/2 in. $45
Knife-bar, hollow handle, 9 3/8 in. $40
Knife-carving, small, stainless blade, steak,
    10 5/8 in. $45
Knife-cheese, stainless blade, 7 1/4 in. $45
Knife-fish, stainless blade, individual,
    8 5/8 in. $45
Knife-fruit, stainless blade, individual,
    6 1/2 in. $40

Knife-modern, hollow handle, 9 1/8 in.........$44
Knife-modern, hollow handle, 9 3/4 in.........$54
Knife-steak, individual, 9 in...................$45
Ladle-gravy, hollow handle, stainless bowl,
    8 3/8 in.....................................$40
Ladle-gravy, solid, 6 5/8 in. $100
Ladle-punch, stainless bowl,
    13 1/8 in. $50
Ladle-soup, stainless bowl, 11 in.............$60
Opener-bottle, stainless bowl,
    6 1/2 in.....................................$45
Opener-letter, stainless blade,
    7 3/4 in.....................................$45
Sardine server, solid, 6 1/4 in...............$60
Scoop-ice cream, stainless bowl,
    8 5/8 in.....................................$40
Scoop-ice, silver plate bowl, 9 1/8 in........$50
Server/knife-fish, stainless blade, engraved
    blade, 11 3/4 in............................$40
Server-asparagus, hollow handle, silver plate
    hood, 10 1/8 in.............................$54
Server-cheese, stainless blade,
    6 1/2 in.....................................$45
Server-cranberry, stainless bowl, 9 in........$40
Server-pasta, stainless bowl,
    10 7/8 in. $45
Server-pie and cake, stainless blade, plain
    blade, 10 7/8 in............................$45
Server-pie and cake, stainless blade, plain
    blade, 11 1/4 in............................$45
Server-tomato, solid, 8 1/4 in. $120
Slicer-cake, stainless blade, wedding,
    12 3/4 in. $45
Spoon-casserole, pierced stainless bowl,
    9 3/4 in.....................................$45
Spoon-casserole, shell, stainless bowl,
    10 1/2 in....................................$40
Spoon-chocolate, short handle, large,
    4 1/4 in.....................................$34
Spoon-demitasse, 4 in..........................$30
Spoon-dessert/oval soup, tear-shaped bowl,
    6 7/8 in.....................................$45
Spoon-dressing, stainless bowl, tear-shaped
    bowl, 11 1/2 in. $40
Spoon-mustard, 5 1/2 in. $35
Spoon-salad serving, stainless bowl,
    11 3/4 in. $40
Spoon-soup, round bowl, cream, 4 in. handle,
    6 in...$50
Spoon-sugar, 6 in..............................$40
Spoon-teaspoon, 6 in...........................$32
Tea strainer, 7 1/8 in.........................$140

Rose by Wallace, 1898/1888

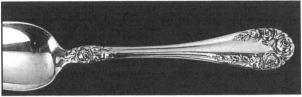

Fork, 7 1/2 in. $50
Fork, 7 in. $45
Fork-salad, individual, 6 1/8 in. $90
Knife-bar, hollow handle, 8 3/4 in. $40
Knife-blunt, hollow handle, 8 7/8 in........... $40
Ladle-cream, solid, 5 3/8 in. $48
Spoon-5 o'clock/youth, 5 3/8 in.............. $18
Spoon-demitasse, 3 7/8 in.................... $22
Spoon-demitasse, 4 1/4 in.................... $22
Spoon-dessert/oval soup, 7 in............... $50
Spoon-soup, round bowl, bouillon,
    4 7/8 in................................... $40
Spoon-soup, round bowl, cream, 6 in. $50
Spoon-soup, round bowl, gumbo, 7 in........ $50
Spoon-teaspoon, 6 in......................... $20
Tablespoon, (serving spoon), 8 3/8 in. $70
Tablespoon, (serving spoon), pierced,
    8 1/8 in................................... $90

Rose Point by Wallace, 1934

Baby set, 2 pieces $64
Butter spreader, flat handle, 5 1/2 in. $24
Butter spreader, hollow handle, modern
    stainless paddle, 6 1/4 in................. $30
Carving set, 2 pieces, small, stainless blade,
    steak $90
Cheese-grater, 8 3/4 in...................... $50
Cleaver-cheese, stainless blade, 6 5/8 in. $45
Fork, 7 5/8 in. $50
Fork, 7 in.................................... $30
Fork-baby, 4 3/8 in.......................... $32
Fork-cake, individual, 3 tines, 6 1/4 in. $40
Fork-carving, large, stainless prongs, roast,
    11 1/8 in................................. $75
Fork-carving, small, stainless prongs, steak,
    9 in. $45
Fork-cocktail, 5 5/8 in. $30

Fork-cold meat/serving, medium, solid, 8 1/8 in. ...$90

Fork-cold meat/serving, small, solid, 7 1/4 in. ...$90

Fork-fish, stainless tines, hollow handle, individual, 7 7/8 in. ...$40

Fork-lemon, 5 1/2 in. ...$35

Fork-lettuce serving/large, 8 3/8 in. ...$80

Fork-pickle/olive, long handle, 7 1/2 in. ...$58

Fork-pickle/olive, short handle, 2 tines, 5 5/8 in. ...$30

Fork-salad serving, solid, 8 1/8 in. ...$100

Fork-salad serving, solid, 8 3/4 in. ...$100

Fork-salad serving, wooden prongs, 11 in. ...$45

Fork-salad, individual, 6 3/8 in. ...$38

Fork-strawberry, 5 in. ...$30

Knife-bar, hollow handle, 8 3/4 in. ...$44

Knife-carving, small, stainless blade, steak, 10 1/4 in. ...$45

Knife-fish, stainless blade, individual, 8 1/8 in. ...$45

Knife-fruit, stainless blade, individual, 6 1/2 in. ...$40

Knife-fruit, stainless blade, individual, 7 in. ...$40

Knife-modern, hollow handle, 9 1/8 in. ...$30

Knife-modern, hollow handle, 9 3/4 in. ...$50

Knife-new french, hollow handle, 9 1/8 in. ...$30

Knife-new french, hollow handle, 9 3/4 in. ...$50

Knife-steak, individual, 8 1/8 in. ...$45

Knife-steak, individual, not beveled, 9 in. ...$45

Knife-youth, 4 1/8 in. blade, 7 3/8 in. ...$40

Ladle-gravy, hollow handle, stainless bowl, 7 1/2 in. ...$45

Ladle-gravy, solid, 6 1/4 in. ...$80

Ladle-punch, stainless bowl, 12 7/8 in. ...$60

Ladle-soup, solid, 14 5/8 in. ...$300

Ladle-soup, stainless bowl, 10 7/8 in. ...$50

Magnifying glass, sterling handle, 6 5/8 in. ...$45

Napkin clip, 2 1/8 in. ...$40

Opener-bottle, stainless bowl, 6 in. ...$45

Sardine server, solid, 6 1/4 in. ...$60

Scoop-ice cream, stainless bowl, 8 1/8 in. ...$45

Server/knife-fish, stainless blade, 11 1/8 in. ...$40

Server-asparagus, hollow handle, silver plate hood, 9 5/8 in. ...$66

Server-asparagus, hollow handle, sterling hood, 10 in. ...$300

Server-asparagus, solid, 9 3/8 in. ...$280

Server-cranberry, stainless bowl, 8 3/8 in. ...$40

Server-jelly, 6 3/8 in. ...$38

Server-macaroni, 10 3/8 in. ...$260

Server-pie and cake, stainless blade, 10 3/4 in. ...$45

Server-pie, stainless blade, 10 1/8 in. ...$45

Server-tomato, solid, 7 5/8 in. ...$100

Slicer-ice cream, solid, 12 3/4 in. ...$200

Spoon-5 o'clock/youth, 5 3/8 in. ...$23

Spoon-baby, straight handle, 4 1/2 in. ...$32

Spoon-casserole, pierced stainless bowl, 7 scallops, 9 1/4 in. ...$45

Spoon-casserole, shell, stainless bowl, 9 7/8 in. ...$45

Spoon-casserole, smooth, solid, 9 in. ...$130

Spoon-chocolate, short handle, large, 4 1/4 in. ...$35

Spoon-cracker, 8 1/8 in. ...$120

Spoon-demitasse, 4 in. ...$20

Spoon-dessert/oval soup, 7 1/8 in. ...$54

Spoon-dressing, stainless bowl, 1 0 3/4 in. ...$45

Spoon-fruit, 6 in. ...$34

Spoon-iced tea, 7 1/2 in. ...$32

Spoon-infant feeding, 5 5/8 in. ...$32

Spoon-salt, individual, 2 3/8 in. ...$13

Spoon-sherbet, large, 5 1/8 in. ...$40

Spoon-soup, round bowl, cream, 5 7/8 in. ...$40

Spoon-sugar, 6 1/8 in. ...$28

Spoon-teaspoon, 6 in. ...$22

Spoon-utility/serving, stainless bowl, 7 scallops, 9 1/4 in. ...$45

Tablespoon, (serving spoon), 8 3/8 in. ...$80

Tablespoon, (serving spoon), pierced, 8 1/4 in. ...$90

Tongs-asparagus, individual, solid, 5 1/4 in. ...$90

Tongs-ice/serving, large, bowl tip, 7 in. ...$180

Tongs-salad, 8 1/2 in. ...$170

Tongs-sugar, 4 in. ...$45

Royal Rose by Wallace, 1962

Fork, 7 3/8 in. ...$60

Fork-cocktail, 5 3/4 in........................$44
Fork-cold meat/serving, medium, solid,
   8 in.......................................$120
Fork-lemon, 5 1/4 in..........................$40
Fork-salad, individual, 6 1/2 in...............$70
Knife-modern, hollow handle, 9 in............$45
Knife-youth, 7 1/8 in..........................$38
Ladle-gravy, solid, 6 1/8 in...................$140
Spoon-sugar shell, 6 in.......................$45
Spoon-teaspoon, (5 o'clock), 5 3/8 in........$30
Spoon-teaspoon, 6 in..........................$33
Tablespoon, (serving spoon), 8 1/2 in........$120
Tablespoon, (serving spoon), pierced,
   8 1/2 in..................................$130

Knife-old french, hollow handle,
   9 3/4 in..................................$48
Server-tomato, solid, 7 5/8 in...............$90
Spoon-5 o'clock/youth, 5 1/2 in.............$22
Spoon-demitasse, 4 1/4 in...................$23
Spoon-dessert/oval soup, 7 in...............$50
Spoon-preserve, 7 1/8 in....................$50
Spoon-relish, 6 1/4 in.......................$40
Spoon-sugar, 5 1/2 in........................$35
Spoon-sugar, 6 in............................$35
Spoon-teaspoon, 5 3/4 in....................$25
Tablespoon, (serving spoon),
   8 1/4 in..................................$70
Tongs-sugar, 3 3/8 in........................$60

Royal Satin by Wallace, 1965

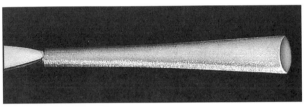

Butter-master, hollow handle, 7 3/8 in........$36
Fork, 7 3/4 in.................................$36
Fork-cold meat/serving, medium, solid,
   8 1/2 in..................................$80
Fork-pickle/olive, short handle, 5 7/8 in......$28
Fork-salad, individual, 6 7/8 in...............$36
Knife-modern, hollow handle, 9 in............$25
Ladle-gravy, solid, 6 1/2 in...................$80
Spoon-dessert/oval soup, 7 1/4 in...........$45
Spoon-iced tea, 7 3/8 in......................$40
Spoon-sugar, 6 3/8 in.........................$35
Spoon-teaspoon, 6 1/2 in.....................$18
Tablespoon, (serving spoon), 8 7/8 in........$80
Tablespoon, (serving spoon), pierced,
   8 7/8 in..................................$80

Saxon by Wallace, 1910

Butter-master, flat handle, 6 7/8 in...........$35
Butter-master, flat handle, 7 1/2 in...........$35
Fork, 7 1/2 in.................................$60
Fork, 7 in....................................$40
Fork-cocktail, 5 3/4 in........................$30
Fork-fish/serving, solid, large, 4 tines, bar,
   9 in.....................................$150
Fork-salad, individual, 1 wide tine,
   5 7/8 in..................................$45
Knife-new french, hollow handle,
   9 3/8 in..................................$38
Knife-old french, hollow handle, 8 3/4 in......$35

Shenandoah by Wallace, 1966

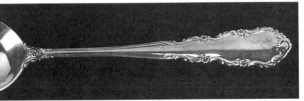

Butter spreader, hollow handle, modern
   stainless paddle, 6 1/4 in...............$30
Butter-master, hollow handle, 6 5/8 in.......$35
Carving set, 2 pieces, small, stainless blade,
   steak...................................$90
Cleaver-cheese, stainless blade,
   6 3/4 in..................................$40
Fork, 7 3/8 in................................$40
Fork, 7 7/8 in................................$50
Fork-cocktail, 5 5/8 in.......................$24
Fork-cold meat/serving, large, stainless tines,
   11 1/4 in.................................$40
Fork-cold meat/serving, medium, solid,
   8 in.....................................$90
Fork-fish, stainless tines, hollow handle,
   individual, 8 1/4 in......................$40
Fork-lemon, 5 5/8 in.........................$36
Fork-pickle/olive, short handle, 5
   5/8 in...................................$30
Fork-salad serving, stainless prongs,
   11 3/8 in.................................$40
Fork-salad, individual, 6 3/8 in..............$40
Knife-bar, hollow handle, 9 1/4 in...........$40
Knife-carving, small, stainless blade, steak,
   10 3/4 in.................................$45
Knife-cheese, stainless blade, 7 in..........$40
Knife-fish, stainless blade, individual,
   8 5/8 in..................................$40
Knife-fruit, stainless blade, individual,
   7 in.....................................$40

Knife-modern, hollow handle, 9 3/4 in..........$45
Knife-modern, hollow handle, 9 in............$32
Knife-steak, individual, 8 3/4 in. $40
Ladle-gravy, hollow handle, stainless bowl,
    8 1/4 in...................................$40
Ladle-gravy, solid, 6 1/4 in. $80
Ladle-punch, stainless bowl, 13 in...........$55
Ladle-soup, stainless bowl, 11 in............$55
Magnifying glass, sterling handle,
    6 1/2 in...................................$45
Napkin clip, (made for teaspoons), $28
Opener-letter, stainless blade, 7 5/8 in........$45
Salad set, 2 pieces, stainless bowl..........$80
Scoop-ice cream, stainless bowl, 8 5/8 in. $40
Scoop-ice, silver plate bowl, 9 in. $50
Server/knife-fish, stainless blade,
    11 5/8 in. $40
Server-cranberry, stainless bowl, 8 7/8 in.....$40
Server-lasagna, stainless blade,
    10 1/8 in. $40
Server-pasta, stainless bowl, 10 3/4 in.......$40
Server-pie and cake, stainless blade,
    10 7/8 in. $45
Server-pie and cake, stainless blade,
    11 1/4 in. $45
Spoon-bonbon, 5 1/2 in...................$40
Spoon-casserole, pierced stainless bowl,
    9 3/4 in..................................$45
Spoon-casserole, shell, stainless bowl,
    10 3/8 in. $40
Spoon-demitasse, 4 1/8 in. $20
Spoon-dessert/oval soup, 7 in. $40
Spoon-dressing, stainless bowl, 11 1/4 in. $40
Spoon-fruit, 6 7/8 in. $40
Spoon-iced tea, 7 3/4 in. $40
Spoon-salad serving, stainless bowl,
    11 5/8 in. $40
Spoon-sugar, 6 in.........................$32
Spoon-teaspoon, 6 in......................$25
Spoon-utility/serving, stainless bowl,
    7 scallops, 9 3/4 in.....................$40
Tablespoon, (serving spoon), 8 1/2 in........$85
Tablespoon, (serving spoon), pierced,
    8 1/2 in..................................$80

Silver Swirl by Wallace, 1955

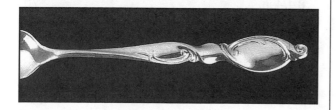

Butter spreader, hollow handle, modern stainless
    paddle, 6 1/4 in........................ $20
Butter spreader, hollow handle, stainless
    paddle, 6 1/4 in....................... $24
Butter-master, flat handle, 7 in. $35
Butter-master, hollow handle,
    6 5/8 in............................. $35
Fork, 7 1/4 in. $37
Fork-salad, individual, 6 3/8 in. $40
Knife-modern, hollow handle, 9 5/8 in....... $36
Knife-modern, hollow handle, 9 in. $30
Knife-wedding cake, stainless blade,
    13 1/8 in............................. $80
Server-jelly, 6 1/8 in. $30
Spoon-dessert/oval soup, 6 7/8 in. $45
Spoon-iced tea, 7 1/2 in.................... $41.
Spoon-soup, round bowl, cream, 6 in. $35
Spoon-sugar, 6 1/4 in...................... $35
Spoon-teaspoon, 6 in...................... $23
Tablespoon, (serving spoon), 8 3/8 in. $70
Tablespoon, (serving spoon), pierced,
    8 3/8 in.............................. $80

Sir Christopher by Wallace, 1936

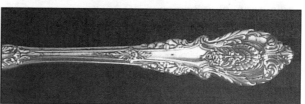

Baby set, 2 pieces $70
Butter spreader, flat handle, 6 3/8 in. $36
Butter spreader, hollow handle, modern
    stainless paddle, 3 in. blade, 6 1/4 in. $34
Butter spreader, hollow handle, stainless
    paddle, 6 in. $34
Butter-master, hollow handle, 6 5/8 in........ $40
Carving set, 2 pieces, small, stainless blade,
    steak $80
Food pusher, 3 3/4 in. $50
Fork, 7 1/4 in. $40
Fork, 7 3/4 in. $70
Fork-baby, 4 1/8 in........................ $36
Fork-carving, small, stainless prongs, steak,
    9 in. $40
Fork-cocktail, flared tines, 5 1/2 in. $30
Fork-ice cream, 5 1/2 in.................... $50
Fork-lemon, three 1 3/8 in. long tines,
    5 5/8 in............................... $35
Fork-pickle/olive, short handle, 2 tines,
    5 1/2 in............................... $30
Fork-salad serving, solid, 9 3/8 in.......... $180

Fork-salad serving, stainless prongs,
11 1/8 in. $40
Fork-salad, individual, 5 tines, 6 3/8 in. $50
Fork-strawberry, 5 in. $35
Knife-bar, hollow handle, 8 3/4 in.............$40
Knife-carving, small, stainless blade, steak,
10 1/4 in. $40
Knife-cheese, stainless blade, 7 1/8 in. $46
Knife-fish, stainless blade, individual,
8 in......................................$46
Knife-fruit, stainless blade, individual, bolster,
6 7/8 in. $40
Knife-fruit, stainless blade, individual, no
bolster, 6 5/8 in..........................$40
Knife-modern, hollow handle, 9 1/8 in.........$40
Knife-modern, hollow handle, 9 3/4 in.........$50
Knife-new french, hollow handle,
9 1/8 in..................................$40
Ladle-cream, solid, 5 5/8 in.................$60
Ladle-gravy, hollow handle, stainless bowl,
7 7/8 in..................................$40
Ladle-gravy, solid, 6 3/8 in. $94
Ladle-punch, stainless bowl, 12 1/2 in. $60
Ladle-punch, stainless bowl, 13 in...........$60
Ladle-soup, stainless bowl, 11 in............$55
Ladle-soup, stainless bowl, 10 1/2 in. $55
Napkin clip, 2 in...........................$40
Opener-bottle, stainless bowl, 6 1/8 in. $40
Opener-letter, stainless blade, 7 5/8 in. $46
Pick-butter, 1 tine, 5 1/8 in..................$25
Scoop-ice cream, stainless bowl,
8 1/4 in..................................$40
Scoop-ice, silver plate bowl, 8 1/2 in..........$50
Server/knife-fish, stainless blade,
11 1/8 in. $40
Server-asparagus, hollow handle, silver plate
hood, 9 5/8 in............................$60
Server-cheese, stainless blade, 6 1/2 in.......$46
Server-cranberry, stainless bowl,
8 1/2 in..................................$40
Server-jelly, 6 3/4 in. $60
Server-lasagna, stainless blade, 9 5/8 in......$46
Server-pasta, stainless bowl, 10 3/8 in........$40
Server-pie and cake, stainless blade,
10 3/4 in. $46
Server-pie, stainless blade, 10 in.............$50
Spoon-5 o'clock/youth, 5 5/8 in. $28
Spoon-baby, straight handle, 4 in. $36
Spoon-bonbon, 5 3/8 in....................$54
Spoon-casserole, pierced stainless bowl,
7 scallops, 9 3/8 in.......................$46
Spoon-casserole, shell, stainless bowl,
10 in....................................$40
Spoon-casserole, smooth, solid, 9 1/4 in.....$150

Spoon-demitasse, 4 1/8 in.................$25
Spoon-dessert/oval soup, 7 in..............$50
Spoon-dressing, stainless bowl,
11 in....................................$46
Spoon-fruit, no notch, 6 in. $48
Spoon-fruit, notch, 6 in.....................$48
Spoon-mustard, 5 1/2 in....................$35
Spoon-pierced rice, stainless bowl,
9 1/4 in..................................$40
Spoon-rice, stainless bowl, 7 scallops,
9 3/8 in..................................$40
Spoon-salad serving, stainless bowl,
11 1/8 in.................................$45
Spoon-salad serving, wooden bowl,
10 3/4 in.................................$50
Spoon-soup, round bowl, cream,
6 in. $50
Spoon-sugar, 6 in. $40
Spoon-teaspoon, 6 in.......................$30
Spoon-utility/serving, stainless bowl, 7
scallops, 9 1/4 in.........................$40
Tablespoon, (serving spoon), 8 1/2 in. $86
Tea strainer, 7 1/8 in......................$100

Spanish Lace by Wallace, 1964

Butter spreader, hollow handle, modern
stainless paddle, 3 in. blade, 6 3/4 in. $27
Butter-master, hollow handle, 7 1/4 in........$16
Carving set, 2 pieces, small, stainless blade,
steak $80
Cleaver-cheese, stainless blade,
7 3/8 in..................................$45
Fork, 7 5/8 in. $24
Fork-carving, small, stainless prongs, steak,
9 7/8 in. $40
Fork-cocktail, 3 flared tines, 5 7/8 in. $25
Fork-cold meat/serving, large, stainless tines,
11 1/2 in.................................$45
Fork-cold meat/serving, medium, solid,
8 1/4 in..................................$70
Fork-fish, stainless tines, hollow handle,
individual, 8 3/4 in........................$40
Fork-pickle/olive, short handle, 2 tines,
5 7/8 in..................................$22
Fork-salad serving, stainless prongs,
11 3/4 in.................................$40

Fork-salad, individual, 6 5/8 in. $30
Knife-bar, hollow handle, 9 5/8 in. $40
Knife-carving, small, stainless blade, steak,
    11 in. $40
Knife-cheese, stainless blade,
    7 5/8 in. $38
Knife-fish, stainless blade, individual,
    8 7/8 in. $40
Knife-fruit, stainless blade, individual,
    7 in. $44
Knife-modern, hollow handle, 10 1/4 in. $35
Knife-modern, hollow handle,
    8 7/8 in. $18
Knife-modern, hollow handle,
    9 1/4 in. $18
Knife-modern, hollow handle, 9 3/4 in. $35
Knife-steak, individual, 9 1/8 in. $40
Ladle-cream, solid, 5 3/4 in. $46
Ladle-gravy, hollow handle, stainless
    bowl, 8 1/2 in. $40
Ladle-gravy, solid, 6 1/2 in. $75
Ladle-punch, stainless bowl, 13 1/4 in. $55
Ladle-soup, stainless bowl, 11 1/2 in. $55
Salad set, 2 pieces, wooden bowl. $70
Scoop-ice cream, stainless bowl, 9 in. $45
Server/knife-fish, stainless blade, engraved
    blade, 12 in. $40
Server-cheese, stainless blade, 7 in. $33
Server-cranberry, stainless bowl,
    9 3/8 in. $40
Server-pasta, stainless bowl, 11 1/4 in. $45
Server-pie and cake, stainless blade,
    11 1/4 in. $40
Slicer-cake, stainless blade, wedding,
    13 1/4 in. $40
Spoon-bonbon, 6 1/4 in. $35
Spoon-casserole, pierced stainless bowl,
    7 scallops, 10 1/8 in. $40
Spoon-casserole, stainless shell bowl,
    10 3/4 in. $45
Spoon-demitasse, 4 1/8 in. $20
Spoon-dessert/oval soup, 7 1/8 in. $40
Spoon-dressing, stainless tear bowl,
    11 3/4 in. $40
Spoon-iced tea, 7 1/2 in. $34
Spoon-rice, stainless bowl, 10 in. $40
Spoon-salad serving, stainless bowl,
    egg-shaped bowl, 11 7/8 in. $40
Spoon-sugar, 6 1/4 in. $17
Spoon-teaspoon, 6 1/4 in. $12
Tablespoon, (serving spoon),
    8 5/8 in. $80
Tablespoon, (serving spoon), pierced,
    8 5/8 in. $80

Sterling Rose by Wallace, 1955

Butter spreader, flat handle, 5 7/8 in. $28
Butter spreader, hollow handle, modern
    stainless paddle, 6 in. $24
Butter spreader, hollow handle, stainless
    paddle, 6 in. $24
Butter-master, flat handle, 7 1/8 in. $33
Butter-master, hollow handle, 6 5/8 in. $34
Fork, 7 3/8 in. $43
Fork, 7 7/8 in. $75
Fork-cocktail, 5 3/4 in. $38
Fork-salad, individual, 6 1/2 in. $46
Knife-modern, hollow handle, 9 5/8 in. $45
Knife-modern, hollow handle, 9 in. $34
Ladle-cream, solid, 4 3/4 in. $60
Ladle-gravy, solid, 6 1/8 in. $100
Server-jelly, 6 7/8 in. $40
Spoon-demitasse, 4 1/8 in. $32
Spoon-dessert/oval soup, 7 3/8 in. $40
Spoon-iced tea, 7 3/8 in. $48
Spoon-soup, round bowl, cream,
    6 5/8 in. $44
Spoon-sugar, 5 7/8 in. $34
Spoon-teaspoon, 5 7/8 in. $30
Tablespoon, (serving spoon), 8 1/2 in. $90

Stradivari by Wallace, 1937

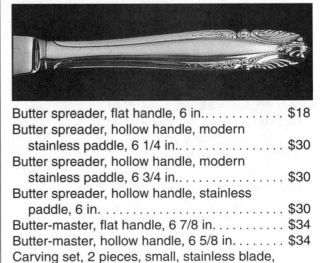

Butter spreader, flat handle, 6 in. $18
Butter spreader, hollow handle, modern
    stainless paddle, 6 1/4 in. $30
Butter spreader, hollow handle, modern
    stainless paddle, 6 3/4 in. $30
Butter spreader, hollow handle, stainless
    paddle, 6 in. $30
Butter-master, flat handle, 6 7/8 in. $34
Butter-master, hollow handle, 6 5/8 in. $34
Carving set, 2 pieces, small, stainless blade,
    steak $80

Wallace Silversmiths

Cleaver-cheese, stainless blade,
6 3/4 in.................................$40
Fork, 7 1/8 in..............................$33
Fork, 7 3/4 in..............................$47
Fork-carving, small, stainless prongs, steak,
8 7/8 in.................................$40
Fork-cocktail, 5 1/2 in.......................$22
Fork-cold meat/serving, large, stainless tines,
10 3/4 in. $40
Fork-cold meat/serving, medium, solid,
8 1/8 in................................$100
Fork-fish, stainless tines, hollow handle,
individual, 7 7/8 in.....................$40
Fork-lemon, 5 1/2 in.........................$22
Fork-pickle/olive, short handle, 5 1/2 in. $30
Fork-salad serving, stainless prongs,
11 in...................................$45
Fork-salad, individual, 6 3/8 in...............$34
Knife-bar, hollow handle, 8 7/8 in.............$40
Knife-carving, small, stainless blade, steak,
10 1/8 in. $40
Knife-cheese, stainless blade, 7 in.............$40
Knife-fish, stainless blade, individual,
8 1/8 in.................................$45
Knife-fruit, stainless blade, individual,
7 in....................................$45
Knife-modern, hollow handle, 4 1/4 in. handle,
9 1/2 in.................................$44
Knife-modern, hollow handle, 4 1/4 in. handle,
9 3/4 in.................................$44
Knife-modern, hollow handle, 4 in. handle,
9 1/2 in.................................$44
Knife-modern, hollow handle, 9 1/8 in.........$28
Knife-new french, hollow handle,
9 3/4 in.................................$45
Knife-steak, individual, 8 1/2 in. $45
Ladle-cream, solid, 5 1/2 in..................$45
Ladle-gravy, hollow handle, stainless bowl,
7 1/2 in.................................$40
Ladle-gravy, solid, 6 1/4 in. $80
Ladle-punch, stainless bowl, 13 in............$60
Ladle-soup, stainless bowl, 10 3/4 in. $60
Opener-bottle, stainless bowl, 6 in. $40
Salad set, 2 pieces, plastic bowl.............$76
Scoop-ice, silver plate bowl, 8 1/2 in..........$50
Server/knife-fish, stainless blade,
11 1/4 in. $40
Server-asparagus, hollow handle, silver
plate hood, 9 1/2 in.....................$54
Server-cranberry, stainless bowl,
8 3/8 in.................................$45
Server-jelly, 6 3/4 in........................$37
Server-lasagna, stainless blade,
9 5/8 in.................................$40

Server-pasta, stainless bowl, 10 1/2 in........$45
Server-pie, stainless blade, 9 7/8 in..........$44
Spoon-bonbon, 5 1/2 in. $45
Spoon-casserole, pierced stainless bowl,
9 3/8 in.................................$40
Spoon-casserole, stainless shell bowl,
9 7/8 in.................................$40
Spoon-demitasse, 3 7/8 in...................$20
Spoon-dressing, stainless bowl,
10 3/4 in................................$40
Spoon-fruit, 5 7/8 in. $40
Spoon-iced tea, 7 1/2 in.....................$38
Spoon-rice, stainless bowl, 9 3/8 in. $40
Spoon-salad serving, stainless bowl,
11 1/8 in................................$40
Spoon-salt, individual, 2 1/2 in. $12
Spoon-soup, round bowl, bouillon,
5 1/4 in.................................$40
Spoon-soup, round bowl, cream, 6 in. $38
Spoon-sugar, 6 in. $30
Spoon-teaspoon, 6 in........................$18
Tablespoon, (serving spoon), 8 1/2 in. $70
Tablespoon, (serving spoon), pierced,
8 1/2 in.................................$100

Violet by Wallace, 1904

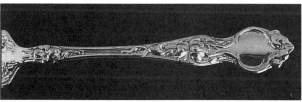

Butter spreader, flat handle, 5 1/8 in. $34
Butter spreader, hollow handle, modern
stainless paddle, 6 1/4 in................$34
Butter spreader, hollow handle, stainless
paddle, 6 1/8 in.........................$34
Fork, no indent, 7 1/4 in.....................$34
Fork-carving, small, stainless prongs, steak,
8 3/4 in. $60
Fork-cocktail, 5 7/8 in.......................$36
Fork-dessert, 6 in. $60
Fork-salad serving, solid, 8 3/4 in...........$104
Fork-salad serving, stainless prongs,
10 3/4 in................................$50
Knife-carving, small, stainless blade, steak,
9 3/4 in. $60
Knife-modern, hollow handle, 9 1/2 in. $46
Knife-new french, hollow handle,
8 3/4 in.................................$36
Knife-old french, hollow handle,
8 5/8 in.................................$36

Knife-sharpener, steel, small, steak,
15 1/4 in. $60
Knife-steak, individual, 8 3/4 in. $60
Server-pie and cake, stainless blade,
10 3/4 in. $60
Server-pie, stainless blade, 4 in. handle,
9 5/8 in. $46
Spoon-demitasse, 2 1/2 in. handle,
3 7/8 in. $30
Spoon-dessert/oval soup, 7 in. $46
Spoon-iced tea, 7 1/8 in. $48
Spoon-soup, round bowl, bouillon,
5 1/4 in. $40
Spoon-sugar, 6 1/8 in. $40
Spoon-teaspoon, 5 7/8 in. $28
Tablespoon, (serving spoon),
8 1/4 in. $70

Waltz of Spring by Wallace, 1952

Butter spreader, flat handle, 6 in. $28
Butter spreader, hollow handle, modern
stainless, 6 1/4 in. $28
Butter spreader, hollow handle, stainless
paddle, 6 1/8 in. $26
Butter-master, flat handle, 7 1/2 in. $50
Butter-master, hollow handle, 6 3/4 in. $46
Carving set, 2 pieces, small, stainless blade,
steak $120
Fork, 7 1/4 in. $45
Fork, 7 3/4 in. $70
Fork-carving, small, stainless prongs, steak,
9 1/2 in. $60
Fork-cocktail, 5 5/8 in. $36
Fork-cold meat/serving, medium, solid,
8 1/8 in. $90
Fork-fish, stainless tines, hollow handle,
individual, 8 1/4 in. $40
Fork-ice cream, 5 1/2 in. $70
Fork-ice cream, 5 5/8 in. $65
Fork-lemon, 5 3/8 in. $37
Fork-pickle/olive, short handle, 5 5/8 in. $37
Fork-salad serving, solid, 9 in. $170
Fork-salad serving, stainless prongs,
11 3/8 in. $40
Fork-salad, individual, 6 3/8 in. $54
Knife-bar, hollow handle, 9 1/4 in. $36

Knife-carving, small, stainless blade, steak,
10 5/8 in. $60
Knife-fish, stainless blade, individual,
8 1/2 in. $40
Knife-fruit, stainless blade, individual,
6 7/8 in. $38
Knife-modern, hollow handle, 9 3/4 in. $54
Knife-modern, hollow handle, 9 in. $33
Knife-steak, individual, beveled edge,
8 7/8 in. $50
Ladle-gravy, solid, 6 1/2 in. $110
Opener-bottle, stainless bowl,
6 3/8 in. $50
Opener-letter, stainless blade,
9 7/8 in. $35
Server/knife-fish, stainless blade,
11 1/2 in. $40
Server-cranberry, stainless bowl,
8 3/4 in. $40
Server-jelly, 6 7/8 in. $42
Server-lasagna, stainless blade, 10 in. $50
Server-pie and cake, stainless blade,
11 in. $60
Server-pie, stainless blade, 10 3/8 in. $70
Slicer-wedding cake, stainless blade,
12 3/4 in. $60
Spoon-bonbon, 6 in. $52
Spoon-casserole, stainless shell bowl,
10 3/8 in. $40
Spoon-demitasse, 4 in. $30
Spoon-dressing, stainless tear bowl,
11 3/8 in. $50
Spoon-iced tea, 7 5/8 in. $70
Spoon-rice, stainless bowl, 9 7/8 in. $40
Spoon-salad serving, solid, 9 in. $170
Spoon-salad serving, stainless egg bowl,
11 3/8 in. $40
Spoon-soup, round bowl, cream,
6 1/8 in. $44
Spoon-sugar, 6 1/4 in. $34
Spoon-teaspoon, 6 1/8 in. $24
Tablespoon, (serving spoon), 8 1/2 in. $80
Tablespoon, (serving spoon), pierced,
8 1/2 in. $90

Washington by Wallace, 1911

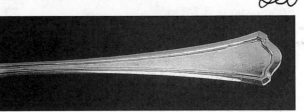

Wallace Silversmiths

Butter spreader, flat handle, 5 1/2 in.........$22
Butter spreader, flat handle, 5 7/8 in.........$22
Butter-master, flat handle, 6 7/8 in............$34
Carving set, 2 pieces, small, stainless blade,
    steak...................................$110
Fork, 7 1/8 in...............................$30
Fork-carving, small, stainless prongs, steak,
    10 5/8 in. $60
Fork-carving, small, stainless prongs, steak,
    8 3/4 in.................................$60
Fork-chipped beef, small, 5 7/8 in. $66
Fork-dessert, 3 3/4 in. handle,
    5 3/4 in.................................$36
Fork-ice cream, 5 1/4 in....................$38
Fork-pickle/olive, short handle,
    5 1/2 in.................................$30
Fork-salad, individual, 4 in. handle,
    5 7/8 in.................................$40
Fork-youth, 6 1/4 in. $42
Knife-carving, small, stainless blade, steak,
    10 in...................................$50
Knife-modern, hollow handle, 4 1/8 in.
    handle, 9 in.............................$36
Knife-new french, hollow handle,
    8 3/4 in.................................$36
Knife-old french, hollow handle,
    8 1/2 in.................................$36
Knife-wedding cake, stainless blade,
    12 1/8 in...............................$70
Knife-youth, 7 3/8 in........................$36
Ladle-cream, solid, 5 3/8 in.................$40
Ladle-gravy, solid, 6 in.....................$80
Poultry shears, 10 3/8 in. $160
Server-cheese, stainless blade,
    6 1/2 in.................................$44
Server-jelly, 5 7/8 in. $28
Server-pie and cake, stainless blade,
    10 1/2 in. $60
Spoon-5 o'clock/youth, 5 1/2 in. $18
Spoon-bonbon, 5 1/4 in.....................$40
Spoon-demitasse, 4 1/4 in. $18
Spoon-fruit, 5 3/4 in. $35
Spoon-iced tea, 7 3/4 in. $36
Spoon-soup, round bowl, bouillon,
    5 1/4 in.................................$20
Spoon-sugar, 5 7/8 in........................$30
Spoon-teaspoon, 5 7/8 in. $20
Tablespoon, (serving spoon), 8 1/4 in.........$55
Tablespoon, (serving spoon), pierced,
    8 1/4 in.................................$80
Tongs-sugar, 3 1/8 in.......................$40
Tongs-sugar, 3 7/8 in.......................$40

Waverly by Wallace, 1890

Butter-master, flat handle, 7 1/2 in........... $50
Fork, 7 1/2 in. $60
Fork, 7 in................................$48
Fork-carving, small, stainless prongs,
    steak, 8 3/8 in. $75
Fork-chipped beef, 6 in.................... $70
Fork-cocktail, 5 3/4 in. $35
Fork-pickle/olive, short handle, 2 tines,
    5 3/4 in. $35
Fork-pie, 6 1/4 in..........................$100
Knife-blunt, hollow handle, 9 5/8 in.. .... $70
Knife-modern, hollow handle, 9 3/8 in. $60
Server-pie, silver plate blade, 10 1/4 in. $75
Spoon-5 o'clock/youth, 5 1/2 in.............. $20
Spoon-demitasse, 3 7/8 in................. $28
Spoon-dessert/oval soup, 7 1/8 in. $60
Spoon-fruit, 5 3/4 in. $44
Spoon-ice cream, 5 in. $55
Spoon-soup, round bowl, bouillon,
    4 3/4 in. $47
Spoon-soup, round bowl, cream,
    6 1/2 in. $60
Spoon-sugar, design on bowl, 5 7/8 in....... $44
Spoon-teaspoon, 5 3/4 in.................. $30
Tablespoon, (serving spoon), 8 in. $60
Tablespoon, (serving spoon), pierced,
    8 in. $70
Tongs-sugar, 3 3/8 in. $70
Tongs-sugar, 4 in.......................... $70

Windsor/Victoria by Wallace, 1957

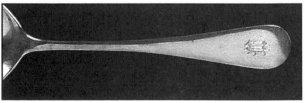

Butter spreader, flat handle, 5 3/4 in. $28
Butter-master, flat handle, 6 1/2 in........... $44
Fork, 7 1/4 in. $44
Fork, 7 7/8 in. $70
Fork-cocktail, 5 3/4 in. $32
Fork-salad, individual, 6 in.................. $45
Knife-modern, hollow handle, 8 7/8 in........ $35

Knife-old french, hollow handle,
8 3/4 in.................................$35
Ladle-cream, solid, 5 3/8 in.................$46
Ladle-gravy, solid, 6 in.....................$90
Server-pie, silver plate blade,
10 1/4 in. $65
Spoon-casserole, smooth, solid, 9 in. $100
Spoon-demitasse, 4 in.......................$22
Spoon-dessert or oval soup, 7 in.............$48
Spoon-fruit, 5 3/4 in. $38
Spoon-teaspoon, 5 3/4 in. $22
Tablespoon, (serving spoon), 8 3/8 in.........$90

Windsor Rose by Wallace, 1940

Butter spreader, flat handle,
5 5/8 in..................................$27
Fork, 7 1/4 in.............................$40
Fork, 7 3/4 in.............................$55
Fork-salad, individual, 6 1/2 in..............$43
Knife-modern, hollow handle,
9 3/4 in.................................$50
Knife-modern, hollow handle, 9 in............$40
Knife-new french, hollow handle,
9 1/8 in.................................$40
Ladle-gravy, solid, 6 1/8 in. $80
Scoop-ice cream, stainless bowl, 8 in.........$70
Spoon-soup, round bowl, cream,
6 1/2 in..................................$56
Spoon-sugar, 5 1/2 in......................$50
Spoon-teaspoon, 5 7/8 in. $26

Wishing Star by Wallace, 1954

Butter spreader, flat handle, 6 in............ $12
Butter spreader, hollow handle. modern
stainless paddle, 6 1/4 in.................. $12
Butter spreader, hollow handle, stainless
paddle, 6 1/8 in........................ $12
Butter-master, flat handle, 7 in. $23
Butter-master, hollow handle,
6 3/4 in............................... $23
Fork, 7 1/8 in. $20
Fork-carving, small, stainless prongs, steak,
9 1/2 in................................ $60
Fork-cocktail, 5 5/8 in. $30
Fork-cold meat/serving, medium, solid,
8 1/4 in................................ $70
Fork-salad, individual, 6 3/8 in. $34
Knife-modern, hollow handle, 9 3/4 in. $30
Knife-modern, hollow handle, 9 in. $20
Knife-youth, 7 3/8 in. $35
Ladle-gravy, solid, 6 1/8 in.................. $60
Server-cheese, stainless blade,
6 1/2 in................................ $40
Server-jelly, 6 1/4 in. $30
Server-tomato, solid, 7 3/4 in. $80
Spoon-bonbon, 5 5/8 in. $35
Spoon-casserole, smooth, solid,
8 7/8 in................................ $90
Spoon-soup, round bowl, cream, 6 in. $27
Spoon-sugar, 6 1/8 in...................... $18
Spoon-teaspoon, 6 in...................... $15
Tablespoon, (serving spoon),
8 1/4 in................................ $60

Wallace Silversmiths

WATSON CO.

Watson Co. began producing silver items in Attleboro, Massachusetts, in the late 1890s, and produced dozens of flatware patterns and hundreds of style of souvenir spoons.

Colonial Fiddle by Watson, 1925

Butter spreader, flat handle, 5 3/4 in.. . . . . $34
Butter spreader, hollow handle, modern
    stainless paddle, 6 1/8 in. $40
Butter spreader, hollow handle, stainless
    paddle, 6 in.. . . . . $38
Butter-master, flat handle, 7 in. $40
Fork, 7 1/4 in.. . . . . $60
Fork-cold meat/serving, small, solid,
    7 7/8 in. $100
Fork-lemon, 4 3/4 in. $45
Fork-salad, individual, 6 3/8 in. $60
Knife-new french, hollow handle,
    8 7/8 in. $44
Ladle-gravy, solid, 6 1/8 in. $110
Server-cheese, stainless blade,
    6 3/8 in. $80
Spoon-demitasse, 4 1/8 in. $35
Spoon-dessert/oval soup, 7 1/4 in. $60
Spoon-iced tea, 7 5/8 in. $60
Spoon-soup, round bowl, cream,
    6 3/8 in. $55
Spoon-sugar, 5 3/4 in.. . . . . $48
Spoon-teaspoon, 5 7/8 in. $30
Tablespoon, (serving spoon), 8 7/8 in.. . . . . . $120

Foxhall by Watson, 1942

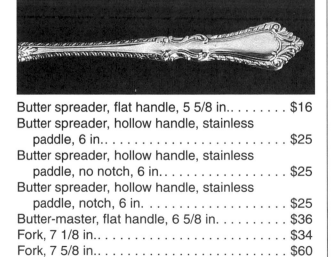

Butter spreader, flat handle, 5 5/8 in.. . . . . . . $16
Butter spreader, hollow handle, stainless
    paddle, 6 in.. . . . . $25
Butter spreader, hollow handle, stainless
    paddle, no notch, 6 in.. . . . . $25
Butter spreader, hollow handle, stainless
    paddle, notch, 6 in. $25
Butter-master, flat handle, 6 5/8 in. $36
Fork, 7 1/8 in.. . . . . $34
Fork, 7 5/8 in.. . . . . $60

Fork-cocktail, 5 5/8 in. $28
Fork-ice cream, 4 7/8 in. $40
Fork-salad, individual, 6 3/8 in. $40
Knife-new french, hollow handle,
    9 7/8 in. $40
Knife-new french, hollow handle, 9 in. $30
Spoon-fruit, 6 in.. . . . . $38
Spoon-soup, round bowl, cream, 6 in. $40
Spoon-soup, round bowl, gumbo,
    6 3/4 in. $48
Spoon-sugar, 5 7/8 in. $35
Spoon-teaspoon, 5 7/8 in. $20

George II by Watson, 1937

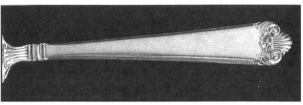

Butter spreader, flat handle, 5 5/8 in.. . . . . . . $22
Butter spreader, flat handle, 6 1/2 in.. . . . . . . $22
Butter spreader, hollow handle, modern
    stainless paddle, 6 in. $25
Butter-master, flat handle, 7 1/4 in. $45
Fork, 7 1/4 in.. . . . . $48
Fork, 7 7/8 in.. . . . . $70
Fork-cocktail, 5 3/8 in. $28
Fork-cold meat/serving, small, solid,
    7 3/4 in. $80
Fork-salad, individual, 6 5/8 in. $47
Knife-modern, hollow handle, 9 in.. . . . . $36
Knife-new french, hollow handle, 9 in. $36
Ladle-cream, solid, 5 in.. . . . . $46
Ladle-gravy, solid, 6 1/8 in.. . . . . $90
Spoon-demitasse, 4 1/8 in. $20
Spoon-soup, round bowl, cream,
    6 1/8 in. $46
Spoon-sugar shell, 6 in.. . . . . $42
Spoon-teaspoon, 6 in. $24
Tablespoon, (serving spoon), 8 1/2 in.. . . . . . $80

George II Rex by Watson, 1936, Hand Chased

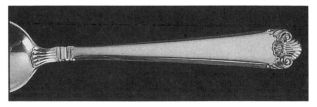

Butter spreader, hollow handle, stainless
paddle, 5 7/8 in......................... $26
Fork, 7 1/4 in............................. $60
Fork, 7 7/8 in............................. $80
Fork-salad, individual, 6 1/2 in. $60
Knife-modern, hollow handle, 9 in. $45
Knife-new french, hollow handle,
10 1/4 in............................... $55
Knife-new french, hollow handle,
9 3/8 in. $45
Knife-new french, hollow handle, 9 in....... $45
Spoon-soup, round bowl, cream,
6 1/8 in................................ $60
Spoon-soup, round bowl, gumbo, 7 in. $70
Spoon-sugar, 6 1/8 in..................... $48
Spoon-teaspoon, 6 in..................... $35

John Alden by Watson, 1911

Butter-master, flat handle, 6 1/2 in.......... $34
Carving set, 2 pieces, small, stainless blade,
steak $100
Fork, 7 1/4 in............................. $34
Fork, 8 in................................ $46
Fork-carving, small, stainless prongs, steak,
8 3/4 in................................ $50
Fork-chipped beef, small, 6 7/8 in.......... $48
Fork-cocktail, 5 3/8 in. $25
Fork-dessert, 1 of 4 tines beveled,
5 5/8 in................................ $40
Fork-dessert, not beveled, 5 7/8 in.......... $40
Fork-fish, solid, individual, 1 of 4 tines
beveled, 6 in........................... $50
Fork-ice cream, 5 1/2 in. $40
Fork-pickle/olive, short handle,
5 7/8 in................................ $28
Fork-salad, individual, not beveled,
6 3/8 in. $50
Knife-carving, small, stainless blade, steak,
10 3/8 in............................... $50
Knife-fish, solid, individual, 7 3/4 in. $56
Knife-new french, hollow handle,
8 7/8 in................................ $30
Knife-new french, hollow handle,
9 5/8 in................................ $44
Knife-old french, hollow handle,
9 1/8 in................................ $30

Knife-old french, hollow handle,
9 3/4 in. $44
Ladle-mayonnaise, 1 1/4 in. bowl,
5 1/8 in. $46
Server-jelly, 6 1/2 in...................... $30
Server-pie, silver plate blade, 10 in......... $58
Spoon-bonbon, 4 1/2 in................... $40
Spoon-casserole, smooth bowl, solid,
8 1/8 in. $90
Spoon-chocolate, short handle,
5 1/2 in. $24
Spoon-demitasse, 4 1/8 in. $18
Spoon-dessert/oval soup, 7 1/8 in.......... $46
Spoon-fruit, 5 3/4 in...................... $34
Spoon-iced tea, 7 3/8 in. $40
Spoon-iced tea, 7 in. $40
Spoon-relish, 5 3/4 in. $34
Spoon-soup, round bowl, bouillon,
4 5/8 in. $30
Spoon-soup, round bowl, bouillon,
5 1/8 in. $30
Spoon-soup, round bowl, cream,
6 1/4 in. $36
Spoon-sugar, 5 3/8 in. $40
Spoon-teaspoon, 5 3/4 in. $20
Spoon-youth, 5 in. $36
Tongs-sugar, 3 1/2 in..................... $60
Tongs-sugar, 4 in........................ $60

Juliana by Watson, 1938

Butter spreader, flat handle,
5 7/8 in. $28
Fork, 7 3/8 in............................ $45
Fork, 7 7/8 in............................ $60
Fork-salad, individual, 6 3/8 in. $48
Knife-modern, hollow handle,
8 7/8 in. $38
Ladle-gravy, solid, 6 in.................... $90
Spoon-dessert/oval soup, 7 1/8 in.......... $48
Spoon-iced tea, 7 3/8 in. $42
Spoon-soup, round bowl, cream,
6 1/2 in. $36
Spoon-sugar, 6 in. $38
Spoon-teaspoon, 6 1/8 in. $28
Tablespoon, (serving spoon),
8 1/2 in. $90

Lamerie by Watson, 1936

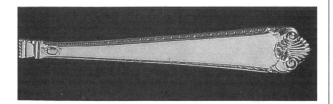

Lily by Watson, 1902

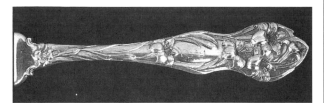

Spoon-teaspoon, (5 o'clock), 5 1/2 in. $50

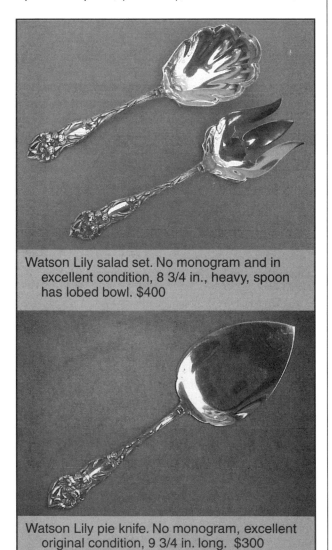

Watson Lily salad set. No monogram and in excellent condition, 8 3/4 in., heavy, spoon has lobed bowl. $400

Watson Lily pie knife. No monogram, excellent original condition, 9 3/4 in. long. $300

Lotus by Watson, 1935

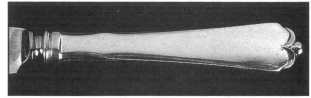

Butter spreader, hollow handle, modern
    stainless, 6 in. $26
Fork, 7 3/8 in. $50
Fork-lemon, 4 5/8 in. $28
Knife-modern, hollow handle, 8 3/4 in. $35
Knife-new french, hollow handle, 9 in. $35
Spoon-bonbon, 4 1/2 in. $45
Spoon-teaspoon, 5 7/8 in. $24

Martha Washington by Watson, 1912

Butter spreader, flat handle, 5 3/4 in. $26
Carving set, 2 pieces, small, stainless
    blade, steak $120
Carving set, 3 pieces, large, stainless
    blade, roast, ... $200
Fork, 7 1/4 in. $34
Fork, 8 in. $50
Fork-cocktail, 5 1/4 in. $28
Fork-ice cream, 5 1/4 in. $50
Fork-pickle/olive, short handle, 5 5/8 in. $32
Knife-old french, hollow handle, 9 3/4 in. $48
Ladle-cream, solid, 5 in. $48
Spoon-bonbon, 4 1/2 in. $40
Spoon-demitasse, 3 3/4 in. $22
Spoon-dessert/oval soup, 7 1/8 in. $50
Spoon-fruit, 5 5/8 in. $34
Spoon-iced tea, 7 in. $40
Spoon-soup, round bowl, bouillon,
    4 5/8 in. $28
Spoon-soup, round bowl, bouillon, 5 in. $28
Spoon-soup, round bowl, gumbo,
    6 7/8 in. $50
Spoon-sugar, 5 1/2 in. $40
Spoon-teaspoon, (5 o'clock), 5 3/8 in. $22
Spoon-teaspoon, (5 o'clock), 5 in. $22
Spoon-teaspoon, 5 7/8 in. $24
Tablespoon, (serving spoon), 8 3/8 in. $70
Tongs-sugar, 3 5/8 in. $66

Meadow Rose by Watson, 1907

Butter spreader, flat handle, 5 3/4 in.. . . . . $20
Butter spreader, hollow handle, modern
    stainless paddle, 6 1/4 in. $28
Butter spreader, hollow handle, stainless
    paddle, indented blade, 6 1/8 in. $30
Butter-master, hollow handle, no stamp,
    6 1/2 in. $32
Carving set, 2 pieces, small, stainless blade,
    steak $90
Fork, 7 3/4 in.. . . . . $50
Fork, no stamp, 7 3/8 in. $30
Fork, thick tines, 7 3/8 in.. . . . . $30
Fork, thin tines, 7 1/8 in. $30
Fork-carving, small, stainless prongs, steak,
    8 3/4 in. $45
Fork-cocktail, 3 tines, 5 5/8 in. $24
Fork-salad, individual, indented bowl,
    6 1/4 in. $40
Knife-carving, large, stainless blade, roast,
    13 1/2 in.. . . . . $55
Knife-modern, hollow handle, 8 3/4 in. $30
Knife-modern, hollow handle, no stamp,
    8 3/4 in. $30
Knife-modern, hollow handle, no stamp,
    9 5/8 in.. . . . . $46
Knife-modern, hollow handle, no stamp,
    9 in. $30
Knife-new french, hollow handle,
    8 3/4 in. $30
Knife-new french, hollow handle,
    9 3/4 in.. . . . . $45
Ladle-gravy, solid, 6 1/4 in. $90
Server-pie, stainless blade, 10 in. $44
Spoon-iced tea, 7 3/8 in. $30
Spoon-soup, round bowl, cream,
    6 1/4 in.. . . . . $38
Spoon-soup, round bowl, gumbo,
    6 3/4 in.. . . . . $50
Spoon-sugar, 5 3/8 in. $28
Spoon-teaspoon, 5 7/8 in. $18
Tablespoon, (serving spoon),
    8 3/8 in. $80

Mount Vernon by Watson, 1907

Fork, 7 in.. . . . . $50
Fork-pickle/olive, short handle,
    5 5/8 in. $35
Ladle-cream, solid, 5 3/8 in. $40
Server-cheese, solid, 5 3/4 in. $130
Spoon-baby, straight handle,
    4 1/4 in. $40
Spoon-demitasse, 4 1/4 in. $28
Spoon-ice cream, gold wash,
    4 3/8 in. $50
Spoon-ice cream, 4 3/8 in. $50
Spoon-iced tea, 7 1/8 in. $50
Spoon-infant feeding, 5 1/2 in. $40
Spoon-soup, round bowl, bouillon,
    4 1/2 in. $36
Spoon-soup, round bowl, gumbo,
    6 7/8 in. $70
Spoon-teaspoon, 5 7/8 in. $28
Tablespoon, (serving spoon), 8 1/2 in.. . . . . . $80
Tablespoon, (serving spoon), pierced,
    8 1/2 in. $100

Navarre by Watson, 1908

Butter spreader, flat handle, 5 7/8 in.. . . . . . . $26
Carving set, 2 pieces, small, stainless blade,
    steak $130
Fork, 7 1/8 in.. . . . . $40
Fork, 7 7/8 in.. . . . . $44
Fork-cocktail, 5 7/8 in. $28
Fork-cold meat/serving, large, solid, 9 in. $90
Fork-pickle/olive, short handle, 6 1/4 in.. . . . . . $30
Fork-salad, individual, 6 in. $45
Knife-new french, hollow handle,
    8 7/8 in. $35
Knife-old french, hollow handle,
    8 7/8 in. $35
Knife-old french, hollow handle,
    9 1/2 in. $45
Knife-youth, 7 3/8 in. $40
Ladle-cream, solid, 5 1/2 in. $46
Ladle-gravy, solid, 6 1/4 in.. . . . . $85
Salad set, 2 pieces, solid, 9 in.. . . . . $200
Spoon-bonbon, 6 1/8 in.. . . . . $44
Spoon-demitasse, 4 in. $22
Spoon-dessert/oval soup, 7 1/4 in.. . . . . $50
Spoon-iced tea, 7 1/2 in. $34

Spoon-soup, round bowl, bouillon,
5 1/4 in. $36
Spoon-soup, round bowl, cream,
6 1/2 in. $50
Spoon-soup, round bowl, gumbo, 7 in. $48
Spoon-sugar, 5 5/8 in. $44
Spoon-teaspoon, 5 3/4 in. $22
Tablespoon, (serving spoon), 8 3/8 in. $70
Tablespoon, (serving spoon), pierced,
8 1/2 in. $80

Watson Orchid serving fork. Fine condition,
just under 9 1/4 in., monogrammed "B."
$350

Wentworth by Watson, 1913

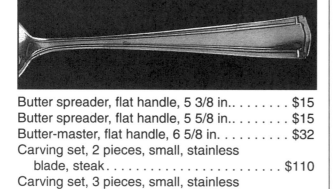

Butter spreader, flat handle, 5 3/8 in. $15
Butter spreader, flat handle, 5 5/8 in. $15
Butter-master, flat handle, 6 5/8 in. $32
Carving set, 2 pieces, small, stainless
blade, steak. $110
Carving set, 3 pieces, small, stainless
blade, steak. $170
Fork, 7 3/8 in. $34

Fork-baby, 3 1/2 in. $34
Fork-baby, 4 in. $34
Fork-cocktail, 5 1/4 in. $22
Fork-cold meat/serving, medium, solid,
8 1/2 in. $75
Fork-cold meat/serving, small, solid,
6 3/4 in. $65
Fork-pickle/olive, short handle, 5 3/4 in. $28
Fork-youth, 6 in. $40
Knife-fruit, stainless blade, individual,
6 5/8 in. $30
Knife-new french, hollow handle,
9 3/4 in. $45
Knife-old french, hollow handle,
8 5/8 in. $30
Knife-old french, hollow handle,
9 3/4 in. $45
Ladle-gravy, solid, 6 1/4 in. $80
Server-cheese, silver plate blade,
6 1/4 in. $50
Server-jelly, 7 in. $30
Server-pie, silver plate blade, 10 1/4 in. $55
Spoon-baby, straight handle, 3 7/8 in. $34
Spoon-baby, straight handle, 4 1/8 in. $34
Spoon-bonbon, 4 3/8 in. $35
Spoon-casserole, smooth bowl, solid,
8 1/2 in. $75
Spoon-casserole, smooth bowl, solid,
8 1/8 in. $75
Spoon-demitasse, 3 3/4 in. $17
Spoon-demitasse, 4 1/8 in. $17
Spoon-ice cream, 5 1/8 in. $34
Spoon-olive, short, pierced bowl,
5 3/4 in. $70
Spoon-sherbet, large, 4 1/4 in. $30
Spoon-soup, round bowl, bouillon, 5 in. $20
Spoon-soup, round bowl, gumbo,
7 in. $34
Spoon-sugar, 5 3/8 in. $34
Spoon-teaspoon, (5 o'clock), 5 3/8 in. $16
Spoon-teaspoon, 5 3/4 in. $18
Tablespoon, (serving spoon), pierced,
8 1/2 in. $80
Tongs-sugar, 3 1/2 in. $50

Windsor Rose by Watson, 1940

Butter spreader, flat handle, 5 5/8 in.. . . . . $18

Butter spreader, hollow handle, modern
stainless paddle, 6 1/8 in. $24

Butter spreader, hollow handle, stainless
paddle, 6 in.. . . . . $24

Butter-master, flat handle, 7 in. $40

Carving set, 2 pieces, small, stainless blade,
steak $120

Fork, 7 1/4 in.. . . . . $32

Fork, 7 7/8 in.. . . . . $46

Fork-carving, small, stainless prongs,
steak, 9 in.. . . . . $60

Fork-cocktail, 5 3/4 in. $26

Fork-pickle/olive, short handle, 3 tines,
5 7/8 in.. . . . . $30

Fork-pickle/olive, short handle, 5 7/8 in.. . . . . . $30

Knife-bar, hollow handle, 8 3/4 in. $40

Knife-modern, hollow handle, 9 1/2 in.. . . . . . . $40

Knife-new french, hollow handle,
9 7/8 in.. . . . . $36

Ladle-cream, solid, 5 1/4 in.. . . . . $48

Ladle-gravy, solid, 6 in.. . . . . $90

Server-pie, stainless blade, 10 1/4 in. $70

Spoon-dessert/oval soup, 7 in.. . . . . $44

Spoon-iced tea, 7 3/8 in. $36

Spoon-soup, round bowl, cream,
6 3/8 in. $33

Spoon-sugar, 5 1/2 in. $30

Tablespoon, (serving spoon), pierced,
8 1/4 in. $90

WEIDLICH BROS. MFG. CO.

Weidlich Bros. Mfg. Co. sterling silver was produced in Bridgeport, Connecticut between 1901 and 1950. Its marks on sterling included AVON.

Ancestry by Weidlich, 1940

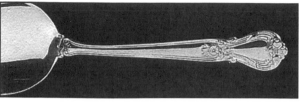

Butter spreader, flat handle, 6 in............ $20
Butter-master, flat handle, 7 in............. $45
Carving set, 2 pieces, small, stainless blade,
    steak.............................. $120
Fork, 7 1/8 in............................ $35
Fork, 7 3/4 in............................ $46
Fork-baby, 4 3/8 in....................... $40
Fork-bacon, solid, 6 3/4 in. $80
Fork-carving, small, stainless prongs, steak,
    8 3/4 in. $60
Fork-cold meat/serving, small, solid,
    7 3/8 in............................ $80
Fork-salad, individual, 6 1/8 in............ $34
Fork-youth, 5 3/4 in....................... $45
Knife-cake, stainless blade, 9 3/4 in........ $70
Knife-fruit, stainless blade, individual,
    7 in. $35
Knife-modern, hollow handle,
    9 1/4 in............................ $33
Knife-new french, hollow handle,
    9 1/2 in............................ $48
Knife-new french, hollow handle,
    9 1/4 in............................ $33
Knife-wedding cake, stainless blade,
    12 1/4 in........................... $80
Knife-youth, 6 7/8 in...................... $38
Knife-youth, 7 3/8 in...................... $38
Ladle-cream, solid, 5 1/4 in............... $40
Ladle-gravy, solid, 6 1/2 in............... $90
Salad set, 2 pieces, wooden bowl $70
Server-cheese, stainless blade,
    6 1/4 in............................ $40
Server-jelly, 6 1/8 in...................... $35
Server-pie, stainless blade, 9 1/2 in. $50
Spoon-baby, straight handle,
    4 1/4 in............................ $40
Spoon-demitasse, 4 1/4 in.................. $23

Spoon-iced tea, 7 3/8 in. $30
Spoon-infant feeding, 5 1/2 in.............. $36
Spoon-soup, round bowl, bouillon,
    5 5/8 in............................ $34
Spoon-soup, round bowl, cream,
    5 7/8 in............................ $38
Spoon-sugar, 2 1/4 in. long bowl,
    6 1/8 in............................ $38
Spoon-sugar, 2 in. long bowl,
    5 7/8 in............................ $38
Spoon-teaspoon, (5 o'clock),
    5 1/4 in............................ $18
Spoon-teaspoon, 5 7/8 in. $18
Tablespoon, (serving spoon), 8 in........... $80

Lady Sterling by Weidlich, 1925

Butter spreader, flat handle, 4 3/4 in........ $18
Butter spreader, flat handle, 5 7/8 in........ $18
Butter-master, flat handle, 6 7/8 in. $35
Carving set, 2 pieces, small, stainless blade,
    steak $120
Fork, 7 1/8 in............................ $26
Fork, 7 5/8 in............................ $40
Fork-carving, small, stainless prongs,
    steak, 9 in.......................... $60
Fork-cocktail, 5 1/2 in. $20
Fork-cold meat/serving, small, solid,
    7 1/2 in............................ $80
Fork-salad, individual, 5 7/8 in. $40
Knife-carving, small, stainless blade, steak,
    12 1/8 in........................... $60
Knife-new french, hollow handle,
    9 1/2 in............................ $36
Knife-new french, hollow handle,
    9 1/4 in............................ $35
Ladle-cream, solid, 5 1/8 in............... $48
Ladle-gravy, solid, 6 1/4 in................ $90
Spoon-demitasse, 4 1/4 in. $16
Spoon-dessert/oval soup, 7 1/8 in.......... $50
Spoon-iced tea, 7 1/2 in. $40
Spoon-soup, round bowl, bouillon, 5 in...... $36
Spoon-soup, round bowl, cream,
    5 5/8 in............................ $50
Spoon-soup, round bowl, gumbo,
    6 7/8 in............................ $50
Spoon-sugar, 5 3/4 in. $34

Spoon-teaspoon, 5 3/4 in. $20
Tablespoon, (serving spoon),
   8 1/4 in. $70

Virginia Sterling by Weidlich, 1929

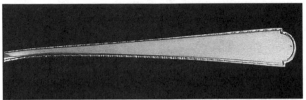

Butter spreader, flat handle, 5 3/4 in.. . . . . $17
Butter-master, flat handle, 7 in. $27
Fork, 7 1/4 in.. . . . . $30
Fork, 7 5/8 in.. . . . . $40
Fork-baby, 4 3/8 in. $26
Fork-cold meat/serving, medium, solid,
   8 3/8 in.. . . . . $75
Fork-salad, individual, 5 7/8 in. $32
Fork-youth, 5 1/2 in.. $34
Knife-baby, 5 7/8 in.. $36
Knife-modern, hollow handle, 9 1/8 in. $30
Knife-new french, hollow handle,
   9 1/4 in.. . . . . $30
Knife-youth, 7 1/2 in. $33

Ladle-gravy, solid, 6 5/8 in.. . . . . $75
Server-pie, stainless blade, 10 in. $60
Server-tomato, solid, 7 3/8 in. $80
Spoon-baby, straight handle, 4 3/8 in. $26
Spoon-bonbon, 4 3/4 in.. . . . . $40
Spoon-demitasse, 4 1/4 in. $18
Spoon-dessert/oval soup, 7 1/8 in.. . . . . $36
Spoon-fruit, 5 3/4 in.. $34
Spoon-iced tea, 7 1/2 in. $30
Spoon-infant feeding, 5 1/2 in.. . . . . $30
Spoon-soup, round bowl, bouillon,
   4 7/8 in. $24
Spoon-soup, round bowl, cream,
   5 5/8 in. $24
Spoon-soup, round bowl, gumbo,
   6 7/8 in. $40
Spoon-sugar, 5 7/8 in. $28
Spoon-teaspoon, (5 o'clock), oval bowl,
   5 1/8 in. $15
Spoon-teaspoon, (5 o'clock), pointed bowl,
   5 1/8 in. $15
Spoon-teaspoon, 5 3/4 in. $16
Tablespoon, (serving spoon),
   8 1/4 in. $60
Tablespoon, (serving spoon), pierced,
   8 1/4 in. $70
Tongs-sugar, 4 3/4 in.. . . . . $60

WESTMORLAND

Westmorland Sterling Co. of Wallingford, Connecticut began selling pieces in five patterns produced by Wallace Silversmiths in 1940. Its trademark was a ram's head in profile in a box.

Enchanting Orchid by Westmorland, 1950

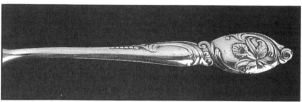

Butter spreader, hollow handle, stainless
    paddle, 6 1/4 in. $20
Butter-master, flat handle, 7 in. $24
Fork, 7 1/8 in. $30
Fork-carving, small, stainless prongs, steak,
    9 in. $45
Fork-cocktail, 5 5/8 in. $23
Fork-cold meat/serving, large, stainless tines,
    10 3/4 in. $45
Fork-cold meat/serving, small, solid,
    7 3/4 in. $70
Fork-fish, stainless tines, hollow handle,
    individual, 7 3/4 in. $40
Fork-salad, individual, 6 3/8 in. $40
Knife-carving, small, stainless blade, steak,
    10 1/4 in. $45
Knife-cheese, stainless blade, 7 1/4 in. $40
Knife-fish, stainless blade, individual,
    8 1/4 in. $35
Knife-fruit, stainless blade, individual,
    7 1/8 in. $40
Knife-modern, hollow handle, 9 1/8 in. $27
Knife-steak, individual, 9 in. $40
Ladle-gravy, hollow handle, stainless bowl,
    7 3/4 in. $40
Ladle-gravy, solid, 6 1/8 in. $60
Ladle-punch, stainless bowl, 13 1/8 in. $55
Ladle-soup, stainless bowl, 11 in. $60
Napkin clip, 2 in. $24
Salad set, 2 pieces, plastic bowl, clear
    bowl $70
Scoop-ice cream, stainless bowl, 8 in. $45
Server/knife-fish, stainless blade,
    11 1/8 in. $45
Server-cranberry, stainless bowl, 8 3/8 in. $45
Server-jelly, 6 1/4 in. $34

Server-lasagna, stainless blade,
    9 1/2 in. $40
Server-pasta, stainless bowl, 10 1/4 in. $40
Server-pie and cake, stainless blade,
    10 3/4 in. $40
Server-pie, stainless blade, 9 3/4 in. $45
Server-tomato, solid, 7 5/8 in. $70
Slicer-cake, stainless blade, wedding,
    12 1/8 in. $45
Spoon-casserole, pierced stainless bowl,
    7 scallops, 9 3/8 in. $40
Spoon-casserole, smooth, solid, 9 in. $100
Spoon-dessert/oval soup, 7 1/4 in. $45
Spoon-dressing, stainless bowl,
    10 7/8 in. $45
Spoon-fruit, 6 in. $25
Spoon-salt, individual, 2 3/8 in. $10
Spoon-soup, round bowl, cream, 6 in. $35
Spoon-sugar, 6 in. $20
Spoon-teaspoon, 6 in. $20
Spoon-utility/serving, stainless bowl,
    9 3/8 in. $45
Tablespoon, (serving spoon), 8 3/8 in. $65
Tablespoon, (serving spoon), pierced,
    8 3/8 in. $80

George & Martha Washington by Westmorland, 1940 *Set (12)*

Baby set, 2 pieces $60
Butter spreader, flat handle, 6 1/8 in. $24
Butter spreader, hollow handle, stainless
    paddle, 6 1/8 in. $26
Butter-master, flat handle, 7 in. $20
Butter-master, hollow handle, 6 7/8 in. $24
Fork, 7 1/2 in. $70
Fork, 7 1/8 in. $22
Fork-baby, 4 3/8 in. $30
Fork-carving, small, stainless prongs, steak,
    8 1/2 in. $40
Fork-carving, small, stainless prongs, steak,
    9 1/8 in. $40
Fork-cocktail, 5 5/8 in. $24
Fork-cold meat/serving, large, stainless tines,
    10 3/4 in. $40
Fork-cold meat/serving, medium, solid,
    8 3/8 in. $70

Fork-fish, stainless tines, hollow handle,
individual, 7 7/8 in. $40
Fork-salad, individual, 6 in. $35
Knife-carving, small, stainless blade, steak,
10 1/8 in. $40
Knife-cheese, stainless blade, 7 1/8 in. $40
Knife-fruit, stainless blade, individual,
6 1/2 in. $45
Knife-fruit, stainless blade, individual,
7 in. $45
Knife-modern, hollow handle, 9 in. $30
Knife-new french, hollow handle,
8 3/4 in. $30
Knife-new french, hollow handle, 9 1/2 in. $45
Knife-steak, individual, beveled blade,
8 3/8 in. $45
Knife-steak, individual, beveled blade,
9 in. $45
Ladle-gravy, hollow handle, stainless bowl,
7 7/8 in. $40
Ladle-gravy, solid, 7 in. $65
Ladle-punch, stainless bowl, 12 3/4 in. $50
Ladle-punch, stainless bowl, 12 3/8 in. $50
Ladle-soup, stainless bowl, 10 1/2 in. $55
Napkin clip, 2 1/4 in. $30
Salad set, 2 pieces, wooden bowl,
10 1/2 in. $70
Salad set, 2 pieces, clear plastic bowl,
10 3/4 in. $70
Scoop-ice cream, stainless bowl, 8 1/8 in. . . . $40
Scoop-ice, silver plate bowl, 8 1/2 in. $40
Server/knife-fish, stainless blade,
11 1/8 in. $40
Server-cranberry, stainless bowl,
8 3/8 in. $40
Server-lasagna, stainless blade,
9 1/2 in. $40
Server-pasta, stainless bowl, 10 1/2 in. $40
Server-pie, stainless blade, 9 3/4 in. $45
Server-tomato, solid, 7 7/8 in. $80
Slicer-cake, stainless blade, wedding,
12 1/4 in. $40
Spoon-baby, straight handle, 4 1/4 in. $34
Spoon-casserole, pierced stainless bowl,
7 scallops, 9 1/4 in. $40
Spoon-demitasse, 4 in. $18
Spoon-dessert/oval soup, tear-shaped bowl,
7 1/8 in. $42
Spoon-dressing, stainless bowl, tear-shaped
bowl, 10 7/8 in. $40
Spoon-fruit, scalloped bowl, 6 in. $30
Spoon-iced tea, 7 1/2 in. $28
Spoon-salad serving, plastic bowl, clear bowl,
10 3/4 in. $35

Spoon-salad serving, stainless egg bowl,
11 1/8 in. $45
Spoon-soup, round bowl, cream, 6 in. $34
Spoon-soup, round bowl, gumbo, oval bowl,
7 1/8 in. $40
Spoon-sugar, 6 in. $18
Spoon-teaspoon, 6 in. $15
Spoon-utility/serving, stainless bowl, 7
scallops, 9 3/8 in. $40
Tablespoon, (serving spoon), 8 1/4 in. $50
Tablespoon, (serving spoon), pierced,
8 1/4 in. $85

John & Priscilla by Westmorland, 1940

Butter spreader, flat handle, 6 1/8 in. $24
Butter-master, flat handle, 7 3/8 in. $16
Carving set, 2 pieces, small, stainless blade,
steak $80
Cleaver-cheese, stainless blade,
6 1/2 in. $45
Fork, 7 1/4 in. $18
Fork-baby, 4 3/8 in. $30
Fork-carving, small, stainless prongs, steak,
9 in. $40
Fork-cocktail, 5 1/2 in. $24
Fork-cold meat/serving, large, stainless tines,
10 1/2 in. $40
Fork-cold meat/serving, small, solid, four tines,
7 3/4 in. $65
Fork-fish, stainless tines, hollow handle,
individual, 7 3/4 in. $45
Fork-ice cream, 5 3/4 in. $30
Fork-salad serving, stainless prongs,
11 in. $45
Fork-salad, individual, 6 5/8 in. $28
Knife-carving, small, stainless blade, steak,
10 1/4 in. $40
Knife-cheese, stainless blade, 7 in. $45
Knife-fish, stainless blade, individual,
8 1/8 in. $50
Knife-fruit, stainless blade, individual,
7 in. $45
Knife-modern, hollow handle, 9 in. $28
Knife-new french, hollow handle,
9 in. $28

Knife-steak, individual, 8 3/8 in. $45
Ladle-gravy, hollow handle, stainless bowl,
   8 1/8 in. $40
Ladle-gravy, solid, 6 in. $54
Ladle-punch, stainless bowl,
   12 5/8 in. $60
Ladle-soup, stainless bowl, 10 3/4 in. $55
Salad set, 2 pieces, plastic bowl,
   11 in. $70
Scoop-ice cream, stainless bowl,
   8 1/8 in. $40
Scoop-ice, silver plate bowl, 8 1/2 in. $50
Server/knife-fish, stainless blade,
   11 1/8 in. $45
Server-cranberry, stainless bowl,
   8 1/4 in. $40
Server-jelly, 6 1/4 in. $34
Server-lasagna, stainless blade,
   9 1/2 in. $45
Server-pasta, stainless bowl,
   10 1/4 in. $45
Server-pie and cake, stainless blade,
   10 1/2 in. $40
Server-pie, stainless blade, 9 7/8 in. $45
Server-tomato, solid, 7 5/8 in. $80
Spoon-baby, straight handle, 4 1/8 in. $30
Spoon-casserole, stainless shell bowl,
   9 7/8 in. $40
Spoon-casserole, smooth bowl, solid,
   9 in. $110
Spoon-demitasse, 4 3/8 in. $20
Spoon-dessert/oval soup, 7 1/4 in. $34
Spoon-dressing, stainless bowl,
   10 7/8 in. $45
Spoon-fruit, 6 in. $30
Spoon-iced tea, 7 3/4 in. $28
Spoon-pierced rice, stainless bowl,
   9 3/8 in. $40
Spoon-salad serving, stainless bowl,
   11 in. $45
Spoon-soup, round bowl, cream,
   6 1/8 in. $30
Spoon-soup, round bowl, gumbo,
   6 7/8 in. $40
Spoon-sugar, 5 7/8 in. $15
Spoon-teaspoon, 6 in. $16
Spoon-utility/serving, stainless bowl,
   9 1/4 in. $40
Tablespoon, (serving spoon), 8 5/8 in. $75
Tablespoon, (serving spoon), pierced,
   8 1/2 in. $80
Tongs-sugar, 4 3/8 in. $56

Lady Hilton by Westmorland, 1940

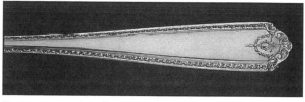

Butter spreader, flat handle, 5 5/8 in. $25
Butter spreader, hollow handle, stainless
   paddle, 6 1/8 in. $25
Butter-master, flat handle, 6 7/8 in. $20
Carving set, 2 pieces, small, stainless blade,
   steak $80
Cleaver-cheese, stainless blade, 6 5/8 in. $45
Fork, 7 1/4 in. $20
Fork, 7 3/4 in. $56
Fork-baby, 4 3/8 in. $25
Fork-carving, small, stainless prongs, steak,
   9 1/8 in. $40
Fork-cocktail, 5 1/2 in. $22
Fork-cold meat/serving, large, stainless tines,
   10 3/4 in. $40
Fork-cold meat/serving, small, solid,
   7 5/8 in. $65
Fork-fish, stainless tines, hollow handle,
   individual, 7 3/4 in. $45
Fork-salad serving, stainless prongs,
   11 in. $40
Fork-salad, individual, 6 1/8 in. $32
Knife-carving, small, stainless blade, steak,
   10 1/4 in. $40
Knife-cheese, stainless blade, 7 1/8 in. $40
Knife-fruit, stainless blade, individual,
   6 7/8 in. $40
Knife-modern, hollow handle, 9 1/8 in. $22
Knife-new french, hollow handle, 4 1/4 in.
   handle, 10 in. $40
Knife-new french, hollow handle,
   8 3/4 in. $20
Knife-steak, individual, beveled blade,
   9 in. $40
Ladle-gravy, hollow handle, stainless bowl,
   7 3/4 in. $40
Ladle-gravy, solid, 6 1/2 in. $60
Ladle-punch, stainless bowl,
   12 1/2 in. $60
Ladle-soup, stainless bowl, 10 1/2 in. $50
Napkin clip, (made for sugar) $22
Napkin clip, (made for teaspoons), ... $22
Napkin clip, 2 in. $28
Plane-cheese, stainless plane, 9 in. $45
Server/knife-fish, stainless blade, 11 1/4 in. . . . $40

Server-cheese, silver plate blade, 6 1/4 in. . . . $60
Server-cranberry, stainless bowl, 8 3/8 in.. . . . . $40
Server-lasagna, stainless blade,
    9 1/2 in.. . . . . $45
Server-pasta, stainless bowl, 10 1/4 in.. . . . . . $40
Server-pie and cake, stainless blade,
    10 7/8 in.. . . . . $42
Server-pie, stainless blade, 9 7/8 in. $45
Server-tomato, solid, 7 5/8 in. $70
Slicer-cake, stainless blade, wedding,
    12 3/8 in.. . . . . $40
Spoon-baby, straight handle, 4 1/8 in.. . . . . . . $25
Spoon-casserole, pierced stainless bowl,
    9 1/4 in.. . . . . $40
Spoon-casserole, stainless shell bowl,
    9 7/8 in.. . . . . $40
Spoon-casserole, smooth bowl, solid,
    8 3/4 in.. . . . . $90
Spoon-demitasse, 4 1/4 in. $20
Spoon-dessert/oval soup, 7 1/4 in. $34
Spoon-dressing, stainless bowl,
    10 7/8 in.. . . . . $40
Spoon-fruit, 5 7/8 in. $30
Spoon-iced tea, 7 7/8 in. $26
Spoon-rice, stainless bowl, 9 1/4 in. $40
Spoon-salad serving, plastic bowl,
    10 7/8 in.. . . . . $35
Spoon-salad serving, stainless bowl,
    11 1/8 in.. . . . . $40
Spoon-soup, round bowl, cream, 6 in.. . . . . . . $26
Spoon-soup, round bowl, gumbo,
    6 7/8 in.. . . . . $34
Spoon-sugar, 6 in.. . . . . $15
Spoon-teaspoon, 6 in.. . . . . $16
Tablespoon, (serving spoon), 8 3/8 in.. . . . . . . $50
Tablespoon, (serving spoon), pierced,
    8 1/8 in.. . . . . $80
Tongs-sugar, 4 3/8 in. $60

Milburn Rose by Westmorland, 1940

Baby set, 2 pieces $60
Butter spreader, flat handle, 5 7/8 in.. . . . . $25
Butter spreader, hollow handle, stainless
    paddle, 6 1/4 in.. . . . . $28
Butter-master, flat handle, 7 1/8 in. $30
Cleaver-cheese, stainless blade, 6 7/8 in.. . . . $45
Fork, 7 1/8 in.. . . . . $24
Fork-baby, 4 3/8 in. $30

Fork-carving, small, stainless prongs, steak,
    9 in. $40
Fork-cocktail, 5 1/2 in. $28
Fork-cold meat/serving, large, stainless tines,
    10 3/4 in. $40
Fork-cold meat/serving, medium, solid,
    8 in. $80
Fork-fish, stainless tines, hollow handle,
    individual, 7 3/4 in.. $45
Fork-salad serving, plastic prongs, clear
    bowl, 10 7/8 in.. . . . . $42
Fork-salad serving, stainless prongs,
    11 in. $40
Fork-salad, individual, 6 3/8 in. $42
Knife-bar, hollow handle, 9 in. $45
Knife-carving, small, stainless blade, steak,
    10 1/4 in. $40
Knife-cheese, stainless blade, 7 1/8 in. $40
Knife-fish, stainless blade, individual,
    8 1/8 in. $45
Knife-fruit, stainless blade, individual, 7 in. . . . $40
Knife-modern, hollow handle, 9 in.. . . . . $30
Knife-new french, hollow handle, 9 3/4 in. $50
Knife-new french, hollow handle, 9 in. $30
Knife-steak, individual, 8 1/4 in. $45
Ladle-gravy, solid, 6 in.. . . . . $70
Ladle-punch, stainless bowl, 12 5/8 in. $60
Opener-letter, stainless blade, 7 3/4 in. $40
Pick-butter, 1 tine, 6 in.. . . . . $45
Salad set, 2 pieces, clear plastic bowl $84
Scoop-ice, silver plate bowl $50
Server/knife-fish, stainless blade, design,
    11 1/8 in. $40
Server-cranberry, stainless bowl, 8 3/8 in.. . . . $45
Server-lasagna, stainless blade, 9 1/2 in. $40
Server-pasta, stainless bowl, 10 1/4 in. $45
Server-pie, stainless blade, 9 7/8 in. $45
Server-tomato, solid, 7 1/2 in. $90
Slicer-cake, stainless blade, wedding,
    12 1/8 in. $40
Spoon-casserole, smooth, solid,
    8 3/4 in. $110
Spoon-demitasse, 4 1/8 in. $18
Spoon-dressing, stainless bowl, 11 in.. . . . . . . $40
Spoon-fruit, 5 7/8 in.. $30
Spoon-iced tea, 7 3/4 in. $30
Spoon-pierced rice, stainless bowl,
    9 1/4 in. $45
Spoon-salad serving, stainless bowl,
    11 1/8 in. $40
Spoon-sugar, 6 in. $24
Spoon-teaspoon, 6 in. $16
Spoon-utility/serving, stainless bowl, 7
    scallops, 9 3/8 in.. . . . . $40
Tablespoon, (serving spoon), 8 1/4 in.. . . . . . . $60
Tablespoon, (serving spoon), pierced,
    8 1/4 in. $90

Whiting Manufacturing

WHITING MANUFACTURING CO.

Whiting Manufacturing Co. began in North Attleboro, Massachusetts, in 1866. After a fire destroyed the plant, operations were moved to New York City in 1875. Gorham bought the company in 1924, and in 1926 moved the operations to Providence, Rhode Island.

Adam by Whiting, 1907

Butter spreader, flat handle, 5 3/4 in......... $28
Fork, 7 1/8 in............................ $36
Fork, 7 7/8 in............................ $50
Spoon-demitasse, 4 1/4 in. $22
Spoon-soup, round bowl, bouillon,
    5 1/8 in.............................. $30

Alhambra by Whiting, 1880

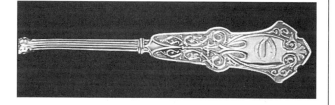

Butter-master, flat handle, twisted,
    7 5/8 in. $40
Spoon-dessert/oval soup, 7 in.............. $60

Antique Lily—Engraved by Whiting, 1882

Fork-youth, 6 3/8 in..................... $50
Ladle-gravy, solid, 6 1/4 in.............. $120
Spoon-demitasse, 4 1/2 in. $24
Spoon-demitasse, 4 in. $24
Spoon-dessert/oval soup, 6 7/8 in......... $60
Spoon-teaspoon, (5 o'clock),
    5 5/8 in. $25
Spoon-teaspoon, 5 7/8 in. $26
Tablespoon, (serving spoon), 8 1/8 in....... $76
Tongs-sugar, 4 3/8 in..................... $70

Arabesque by Whiting, 1875

Spoon-teaspoon, (5 o'clock), 5 3/8 in. $30
Spoon-teaspoon, 5 7/8 in. $40

Twenty-five pieces Whiting Antique Engraved: 6 table forks, 6 dessert forks, 5 dessert spoons, 6 teaspoons, and 2 tablespoons; c.1880-1900. Monogram "M." Some bowl dings. $500

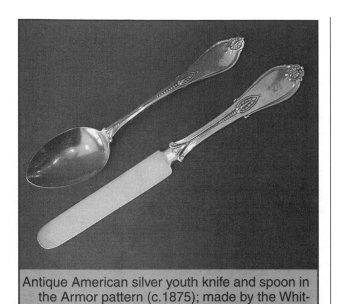

Antique American silver youth knife and spoon in the Armor pattern (c.1875); made by the Whiting Mfg. Co. of New York, New York. Engraved "Augusta" and with monogram "S." Knife 7 1/4 in., spoon 5 7/8 in. $40/pair

Bead by Whiting, 1880

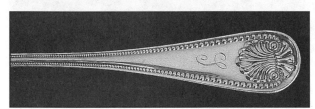

Fork-chipped beef, medium, flared tines,
  6 5/8 in. $85
Fork-cocktail, 5 5/8 in. $26
Fork-cold meat/serving, small, solid,
  7 in. $80
Fork-pickle/olive, short handle,
  6 3/8 in. $34
Fork-pie, 3 tines, 5 1/2 in. $55
Fork-ramekin, 3 3/8 in. handle, 5 in. $45
Fork-ramekin, 4 in. handle, 5 1/2 in. $45
Fork-youth, 5 7/8 in.. $50
Ladle-cream, solid, 5 1/4 in. $46
Ladle-relish, 5 in.. . . . . $53
Salad set, 2 pieces, solid, 8 5/8 in. $220
Spoon-bonbon, 4 3/8 in. $38
Spoon-casserole, smooth bowl, solid,
  7 1/8 in. $100
Spoon-casserole, smooth bowl, solid,
  8 1/4 in. $100
Spoon-demitasse, 4 in. $28
Spoon-dessert/oval soup,
  6 1/2 in. $46
Spoon-fruit, 5 1/8 in. $44

Spoon-fruit, gold wash, 5 1/8 in.. . . . . $44
Spoon-ice cream, 4 5/8 in. $50
Spoon-olive, long handle, 9 1/4 in. $160
Spoon-relish, gold wash, 6 1/2 in. $40
Spoon-sugar shell, 3 5/8 in. long handle,
  5 5/8 in. $48
Spoon-teaspoon, (5 o'clock),
  5 1/8 in. $20
Tablespoon, (serving spoon), 8 in. $80
Tongs-sugar, 3 7/8 in.. . . . . $65

Berry by Whiting, 1880

(multiple motifs)

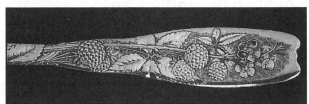

Spoon-demitasse, 3 7/8 in. $30

Eleven Whiting Colonial Engraved gumbo soup spoons. A hand-engraved pattern was expensive to produce and not made in large quantities. 7 1/8 in., fine condition, monogrammed "S." $325/set

Duke of York by Whiting, 1900

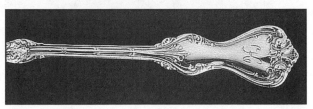

Fork, 7 3/4 in.. . . . . $60
Fork, 7 in.. . . . . $40
Knife-blunt, hollow handle 8 3/4 in. $70

Spoon-demitasse, 4 in. $24
Spoon-dessert/oval soup, 6
   7/8 in. $50
Spoon-fruit, 5 3/8 in. $60
Spoon-soup, round bowl, cream,
   5 7/8 in. $50
Spoon-soup, round bowl, gumbo,
   6 3/4 in. $70
Spoon-sugar, 5 7/8 in. $50
Spoon-teaspoon, 5 7/8 in. $25
Tablespoon, (serving spoon),
   8 1/4 in. $80
Tongs-sugar, 4 in. $70

Egyptian by Whiting, 1875

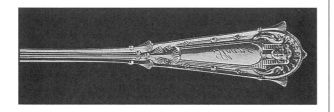

Heraldic by Whiting, 1880

(multiple motifs)

Fork, 7 in. $60

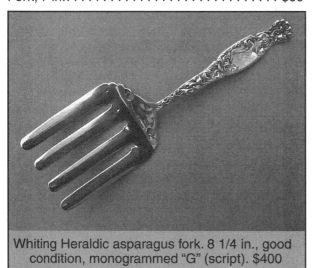

Whiting Heraldic asparagus fork. 8 1/4 in., good condition, monogrammed "G" (script). $400

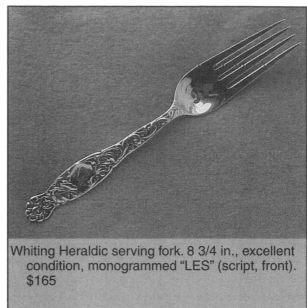

Whiting Heraldic serving fork. 8 3/4 in., excellent condition, monogrammed "LES" (script, front). $165

Hyperion by Whiting, 1888

Butter-master, flat handle, 7 in. $60
Fork, 7 5/8 in. $90
Fork, 7 in. $77
Spoon-dessert/oval soup, 6 7/8 in. $80
Spoon-teaspoon, 5 7/8 in. $40
Tablespoon, (serving spoon), 8 1/4 in. $130

Imperial Queen by Whiting, 1893

Fork, 7 in. $60
Fork, no design, 7 1/2 in. $100
Fork-berry, individual, 4 1/2 in. $70
Fork-chipped beef, small, 5 7/8 in. $110
Fork-olive, long handle, 9 in. $200
Fork-youth, 6 in. $70
Ladle-bouillon, 8 3/4 in. $500
Ladle-gravy, solid, 7 in. $200
Spoon-demitasse, 4 in. $40

Spoon-soup, round bowl, bouillon, 5 in.. . . . . . . $60
Spoon-teaspoon, (5 o'clock), 5 3/8 in.. . . . . . . $30
Spoon-teaspoon, 6 in.. . . . . $42
Tablespoon, (serving spoon), 8 1/2 in.. . . . . . . $100
Tongs-sugar, 3 7/8 in. $100
Tongs-sugar, 5 in. $100

Japanese by Whiting, 1874

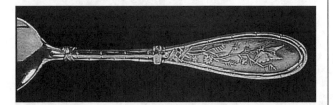

King Albert by Whiting, 1919

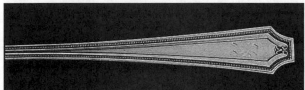

Butter spreader, flat handle, 5 1/2 in.. . . . . $15
Carving set, 2 pieces, small, stainless blade,
   steak $100
Carving set, 3 pieces, small, stainless blade,
   steak $160
Fork, 7 1/4 in.. . . . . $28
Fork, 7 7/8 in.. . . . . $60
Fork-cocktail, 5 3/8 in.. . . . . $26
Fork-cold meat/serving, small, solid,
   7 1/4 in.. . . . . $70
Fork-lemon, 4 3/4 in. $28
Fork-olive, 2 beveled tines, 6 in. $45
Fork-pie, 3 tines not beveled,
   6 1/8 in. $45
Fork-salad, individual, 6 3/8 in. $35
Knife-carving, small, stainless blade, steak,
   9 1/2 in.. . . . . $54
Knife-carving, small, stainless blade, steak,
   9 3/4 in.. . . . . $54
Knife-new french, hollow handle, stainless
   blade, 9 5/8 in.. . . . . $43
Knife-old french, hollow handle, silver plate
   blade, 8 5/8 in.. . . . . $33
Knife-old french, hollow handle, silver plate
   blade, 9 5/8 in.. . . . . $43
Knife-old french, hollow handle, stainless
   blade, 8 5/8 in.. . . . . $33
Knife-old french, hollow handle, stainless
   blade, 9 1/8 in.. . . . . $33

Knife-old french, hollow handle, stainless
   blade, 9 5/8 in.. . . . . $43
Ladle-cream, solid, 5 1/2 in.. . . . . $45
Ladle-mayonnaise, 5 in.. . . . . $42
Server-cheese, silver plate blade,
   6 1/2 in. $50
Server-jelly, 6 5/8 in.. . . . . $25
Spoon-bonbon, 4 3/8 in.. . . . . $40
Spoon-fruit, 5 7/8 in.. . . . . $34
Spoon-relish, 6 in. $36
Spoon-soup, round bowl, bouillon,
   5 1/8 in. $20
Spoon-sugar, 6 1/8 in.. . . . . $30
Spoon-teaspoon, 5 7/8 in. $14
Tablespoon, (serving spoon), 8 3/8 in.. . . . . . . $60
Tongs-sugar, 3 1/2 in.. . . . . $40

King Edward by Whiting, 1901

Fish-fork/salad, solid, individual, large, 1 of
   4 tines beveled, 6 1/4 in. $60
Fork, 7 3/4 in.. . . . . $80
Knife-new french, hollow handle,
   9 1/4 in. $60
Server-pie and cake, stainless blade,
   10 1/8 in. $60
Spoon-dessert/oval soup, 7 1/8 in.. . . . . $65
Spoon-fruit, gold wash, 5 1/2 in.. . . . . $50
Spoon-soup, round bowl, bouillon,
   5 1/8 in. $50
Spoon-soup, round bowl, cream, 6 in.. . . . . $65
Spoon-teaspoon, 6 in. $30
Tablespoon, (serving spoon), 8 1/2 in.. . . . . . . $100

Lady Baltimore by Whiting, 1910

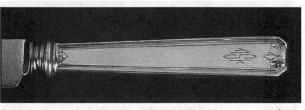

Butter spreader, flat handle, 5 1/2 in.. . . . . $16
Butter-master, flat handle, 6 3/8 in. $30
Carving set, 2 pieces, small, stainless blade,
   steak $110

Lady Baltimore by Whiting, 1910

Fish-fork/salad, solid, individual, large, 2 of
    4 tines beveled, 6 5/8 in. $55
Fork, 6 3/4 in.. . . . . $36
Fork-cocktail, 5 1/2 in. $24
Fork-pickle/olive, short handle, 6 in. $30
Fork-salad, individual, 1 of 4 tines beveled,
    5 1/2 in. $34
Fork-youth, 6 1/4 in.. . . . . $38
Knife-new french, hollow handle,
    8 7/8 in. $33
Knife-new french, hollow handle,
    9 1/2 in. $45
Knife-old french, hollow handle,
    8 3/4 in. $33
Knife-old french, hollow handle,
    9 1/2 in. $45
Ladle-cream, solid, 5 7/8 in. $40
Ladle-gravy, solid, 6 1/4 in. $70
Server-cheese, silver plate blade,
    6 1/8 in. $56
Server-pie, silver plate blade,
    9 1/2 in. $60
Spoon-baby, straight handle,
    4 1/2 in. $36
Spoon-casserole, pierced bowl, solid,
    7 1/2 in. $80
Spoon-casserole, smooth bowl, solid,
    7 1/2 in. $80
Spoon-demitasse, 4 in. $18
Spoon-dessert/oval soup, 7 in. $40
Spoon-fruit, 5 3/8 in. $28
Spoon-iced tea, 7 1/2 in. $34
Spoon-soup, round bowl, bouillon,
    5 in. $30
Spoon-soup, round bowl, gumbo,
    6 7/8 in. $40
Spoon-sugar, 5 7/8 in. $36
Spoon-teaspoon, (5 o'clock),
    5 1/2 in. $18
Tongs-sugar, 3 7/8 in. $60

Lily by Whiting, 1902

Butter spreader, flat handle, 6 3/8 in.. . . . . . . $80
Fork, 6 3/4 in.. . . . . $100
Server-pie, silver plate blade,
    9 7/8 in. $140

Spoon-demitasse, 4 in. $50
Spoon-teaspoon, (5 o'clock), 5 3/8 in. $34
Spoon-teaspoon, 5 7/8 in. $45
Tongs-sugar, 4 in.. . . . . $150

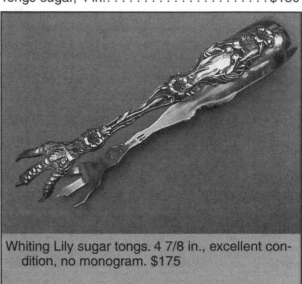

Whiting Lily sugar tongs. 4 7/8 in., excellent condition, no monogram. $175

Lily of the Valley by Whiting, 1885

Fork, blunt end, 7 1/2 in. $260
Fork-cocktail, 5 3/4 in. $80
Fork-salad, individual, pointed end,
    6 1/8 in. $250
Knife-blunt, hollow handle, bolster, silver
    plate blade, 9 1/2 in.. . . . . $360
Ladle-gravy, solid, 6 1/2 in.. . . . . $500
Spoon-bonbon, pierced bowl,
    4 1/2 in. $180
Spoon-casserole, shell bowl, solid, gold wash,
    8 1/2 in. $600
Spoon-demitasse, 4 3/8 in. $60
Spoon-demitasse, gold wash,
    4 3/8 in. $60
Spoon-dessert/oval soup, 7 in.. . . . . $200
Spoon-soup, round bowl, cream,
    6 in. $150
Spoon-soup, round bowl, gumbo,
    6 7/8 in. $200
Spoon-teaspoon, (5 o'clock), 5 3/8 in. $40
Spoon-teaspoon, 5 7/8 in. $45
Tongs-sugar, 4 5/8 in.. . . . . $200

Louis XV by Whiting, 1891

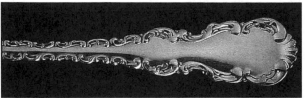

Fork, 6 7/8 in.	$38
Fork, 7 1/2 in.	$60
Fork-cold meat/serving, small, solid, 6 1/2 in.	$80
Fork-dessert, 6 1/8 in.	$90
Fork-pickle/olive, long handle, 9 1/8 in.	$100
Fork-salad serving, solid, 8 7/8 in.	$150
Fork-youth, 5 1/2 in.	$46
Fork-youth, 6 1/8 in.	$46
Knife-sharpener, steel, large, roast, 13 1/2 in.	$80
Ladle-cream, solid, 5 3/4 in.	$50
Ladle-oyster, solid, 10 3/4 in.	$350
Spoon-casserole, smooth bowl, solid, 7 3/4 in.	$100
Spoon-demitasse, 4 in.	$26
Spoon-demitasse, gold wash, 4 in.	$26
Spoon-fruit, 5 3/4 in.	$44
Spoon-fruit, 5 3/8 in.	$44
Spoon-fruit, gold wash, 5 3/8 in.	$44
Spoon-place/oval soup, 6 3/4 in.	$46
Spoon-place/oval soup, 6 3/4 no stamp	$46
Spoon-salad serving, solid, gold wash, 9 1/8 in.	$150
Spoon-soup/oval, old style, 1 5/8 in. bowl, 6 in.	$44
Spoon-soup, round bowl, cream, 6 3/4 in.	$46
Spoon-teaspoon, (5 o'clock), 5 1/4 in.	$18

Spoon-teaspoon, 5 7/8 in.	$24
Tablespoon, (serving spoon), 8 1/4 in.	$60

Madam Jumel by Whiting, 1908

Butter spreader, flat 3 1/2 in. handle, 5 5/8 in.	$25
Butter-master, flat handle, 6 1/4 in.	$38
Butter-master, flat handle, no crimp, 7 1/4 in.	$38
Fork, 6 7/8 in.	$30
Fork-baby, 4 3/4 in.	$48
Fork-cocktail, 5 1/2 in.	$20
Fork-cold meat/serving, small, solid, 6 1/2 in.	$80
Fork-fish, solid, individual, 1 of 4 tines beveled, 6 1/8 in.	$58
Fork-ice cream, 5 in.	$50
Fork-lemon, 6 in.	$35
Fork-pickle/olive, short handle, 2 beveled tines, 6 in.	$32
Fork-pie, 1 of 3 tines beveled, 6 1/8 in.	$45
Fork-salad, 3 tines, 2 of 3 tines beveled, 6 1/8 in.	$55
Knife-blunt, hollow handle, bolster, silver plate blade, 8 7/8 in.	$40
Knife-blunt, hollow handle, bolster, silver plate blade, 9 5/8 in.	$54
Knife-modern, hollow handle, stainless blade, 8 1/2 in.	$40

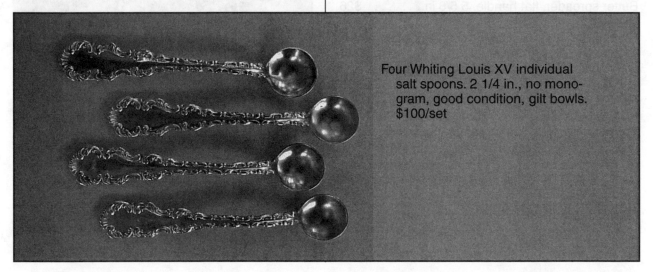

Four Whiting Louis XV individual salt spoons. 2 1/4 in., no monogram, good condition, gilt bowls. $100/set

Knife-new french, hollow handle, bolster,
stainless blade, 8 7/8 in. $40
Knife-old french, hollow handle, bolster,
silver plate blade, 8 3/4 in. $40
Ladle-cream, solld, 5 1/2 in. $50
Ladle-mayonnaise, 5 1/4 in. $53
Pick-butter, 2 flared tines, 6 in. $55
Server-jelly, 6 1/4 in. $34
Server-pie, silver plate blade, 10 in. $70
Spoon-5 o'clock/youth, 3 1/2 in. handle,
5 1/4 in. $14
Spoon-dessert/oval soup, 7 in. $58
Spoon-fruit, rim bowl, 5 7/8 in. $36
Spoon-ice cream, 6 1/8 in. $50
Spoon-iced tea, 7 3/8 in. $50
Spoon-olive, short, pierced bowl,
6 in. $70
Spoon-sherbet, large, 5 1/8 in. $50
Spoon-soup, round bowl, bouillon,
5 in. $30
Spoon-sugar, 5 7/8 in. $40
Spoon-teaspoon, (5 o'clock), 3 5/8 in. handle,
5 1/2 in. $13
Spoon-teaspoon, no rim bowl, 5 7/8 in. $17
Tablespoon, (serving spoon), 8 1/8 in. $75
Tablespoon, (serving spoon), piercccd,
8 1/8 in. $110
Tongs-sugar, 4 1/8 in. $45

Madam Morris by Whiting, 1909

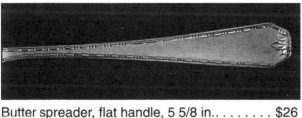

Butter spreader, flat handle, 5 5/8 in. $26
Butter spreader, flat handle, 5 in. $26
Carving set, 2 pieces, large, stainless blade,
roast, ... $140
Carving set, 2 pieces, small, stainless blade,
steak $120
Fork, 6 7/8 in. $35
Fork, 7 5/8 in. $55
Fork-carving, small, stainless prongs, steak,
8 3/8 in. $60
Fork-chipped beef, small, 4 tines, not beveled,
5 5/8 in. $66
Fork-cocktail, 5 1/2 in. $30
Fork-cold meat/serving, small, solid,
7 1/2 in. $80
Fork-fish, solid, individual, 6 1/2 in. $70

Fork-ice cream, 5 1/8 in. $50
Fork-lemon, 5 7/8 in. $30
Fork-pastry, 5 5/8 in. $47
Fork-pickle/olive, short handle,
6 1/8 in. $30
Fork-salad, individual, 6 1/8 in. $44
Knife-blunt, hollow handle 8 3/4 in. $35
Ladle-cream, solid, 5 3/8 in. $47
Ladle-gravy, solid, 7 3/8 in. $85
Server-cheese, silver plate blade,
6 1/8 in. $70
Server-jelly, 6 1/4 in. $32
Spoon-bonbon, 4 1/2 in. $38
Spoon-casserole, smooth bowl, solid,
9 in. $100
Spoon-demitasse, 4 in. $24
Spoon-dessert/oval soup, 7 in. $40
Spoon-fruit, 5 1/4 in. $40
Spoon-salad serving, solid, 9 3/8 in. $100
Spoon-soup, round bowl, bouillon,
5 in. $38
Spoon-soup, round bowl, gumbo,
6 7/8 in. $45
Spoon-sugar, 6 1/4 in. $40
Spoon-teaspoon, (5 o'clock), 5 1/4 in. $22
Spoon-teaspoon, 5 7/8 in. $24
Tablespoon, (serving spoon),
8 1/8 in. $70
Tablespoon, (serving spoon), pierced,
8 1/8 in. $80
Tongs-sugar, 4 in. $60

Thirty-six pieces Whiting Madam Morris (1910): 6 each tablespoons, dessert spoons, teaspoons, dinner forks, luncheon forks, and dinner knives. Three letter monograms include "EPV," "EME," "MRS," and "DES." $625

Mandarin by Whiting, 1918

Fork, 7 1/8 in.............................. $58
Fork, 7 7/8 in.............................. $70
Fork-salad, individual, 6 1/8 in. $60
Knife-new french, hollow handle
    8 3/4 in............................... $45
Knife-old french, hollow handle 9 1/2 in. $50
Spoon-dessert/oval soup, 7 1/4 in. $48
Spoon-soup, round bowl, bouillon, 5 in....... $50
Spoon-soup, round bowl, gumbo, 7 in. $55
Spoon-teaspoon, 5 3/4 in.................. $30
Tablespoon, (serving spoon), 8 1/4 in........ $95

Old King by Whiting, 1890

Fork, 7 in.................................. $50
Knife-blunt, hollow handle, 8 7/8 in.......... $70
Spoon-teaspoon, 5 7/8 in.................. $40
Tablespoon, (serving spoon), 8 5/8 in........ $90

Pompadour by Whiting, 1898

Fork, 6 7/8 in.............................. $60
Fork, 7 3/4 in.............................. $70
Fork-cocktail, 5 5/8 in. $34
Fork-cold meat/serving, small, solid,
    7 1/2 in............................... $130
Fork-fish, solid, individual, 6 1/2 in. $60
Fork-youth, 5 1/2 in........................ $50
Spoon-dessert/oval soup, 6 5/8 in. $60
Spoon-soup, round bowl, bouillon,
    5 1/8 in............................... $50

Spoon-soup, round bowl, gumbo,
    6 7/8 in............................... $70
Spoon-teaspoon, (5 o'clock), 5 1/4 in........ $26
Spoon-teaspoon, 5 3/4 in. $30
Tablespoon, (serving spoon), 8 in........... $90
Tongs-sugar, 4 in.......................... $80

Radiant by Whiting, 1895

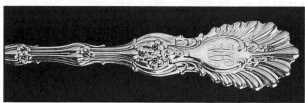

Fork-salad, individual, 1 of four tines beveled,
    6 in.................................. $80
Spoon-demitasse, 3 7/8 in. $32
Spoon-dessert/oval soup, 6 7/8 in.......... $80
Spoon-soup, round bowl, gumbo,
    6 7/8 in............................... $75
Spoon-teaspoon, 5 3/4 in. $40
Tongs-sugar, 3 in.......................... $90

Stratford by Whiting, 1910

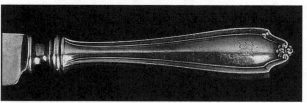

Butter spreader, flat handle, 5 7/8 in......... $23
Fork, 6 7/8 in.............................. $40
Fork, 7 1/2 in. $48
Fork-chipped beef, 6 in. $53
Fork-cocktail, 5 5/8 in. $24
Fork-cold meat/serving, small, solid,
    6 3/8 in............................... $70
Fork-cold meat/serving, small, solid,
    7 5/8 in............................... $70
Fork-salad, individual, 6 1/4 in. $34
Knife-baby, 5 1/4 in. $34
Knife-blunt, hollow handle 9 5/8 in. $40
Server-pie, silver plate blade, 10 3/8 in....... $55
Spoon-dessert/oval soup, 7 1/8 in.......... $40
Spoon-fruit, 5 7/8 in....................... $33
Spoon-ice cream, 5 1/4 in................. $33
Spoon-iced tea, 7 1/2 in. $30
Spoon-olive, short, pierced bowl,
    5 3/4 in............................... $65
Spoon-salt, individual, 2 1/2 in. $14

Stratford by Whiting, 1910

Spoon-soup, round bowl, bouillon, 5 in.. . . . . . $30
Spoon-soup, round bowl, gumbo,
    6 7/8 in. $40
Spoon-sugar, 5 7/8 in. $33
Spoon-teaspoon, 5 7/8 in. $23
Tablespoon, (serving spoon),
    8 3/8 in. $50
Tongs-sugar, 4 in. $50

Violet by Whiting, 1905

Fork, 6 3/4 in. $60
Knife-blunt, hollow handle 9 in. $110
Spoon-demitasse, gold wash, 4 in. $40
Spoon-soup, round bowl, gumbo,
    6 7/8 in. $100
Spoon-teaspoon, 5 7/8 in. $36

WOOD & HUGHES

Gadroon by Wood & Hughes, 1860

Fork, 8 in.. . . . . $60

Louis XV by Wood & Hughes, 1880

Fork, 7 1/2 in.. . . . . $60

Fork-cocktail, 5 1/2 in. $34
Spoon-dessert/oval soup,
   7 1/8 in. $50
Spoon-fruit, 5 3/8 in.. . . . . $40
Spoon-teaspoon, 5 7/8 in. $24
Tablespoon, (serving spoon),
   8 1/8 in. $85

Wood & Hughes Byzantine serving fork, engraved above tines, 10 1/4 in. long, excellent condition, no monogram. $400

Antique American silver butter knife in the Fiddle pattern; made by Wood & Hughes of New York, New York, and retailed by James Gould of Baltimore, Maryland, c.1845-1850. Monogram "JCO," 7 7/8 in., 1.2 troy oz. $70

Other American Makers

Bailey & Co.

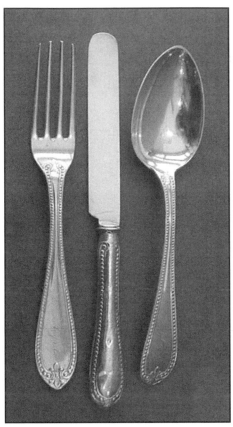

Antique American silver youth knife, fork, and spoon in the Oval Bead pattern; marked by Bailey & Co. of Philadelphia, Pennsylvania, c.1850-1870. Engraved "Augusta." Knife 7 in.; fork 6 1/8 in.; spoon 6 1/4 in. Hollow knife handle dinged..................................$70

Blackinton

Blackinton medicine spoon. Excellent condition, no monogram, 6 3/8 in. long................$125

Charles Brewer & Co.

Antique American silver sauce ladle in the Fiddle pattern; marked [C.B.&Co] between eagle and star trademarks probably for Charles Brewer & Co. of Middletown, Connecticut, c.1835-1860. Monogram "DBD," 6 1/8 in., 1 3/4 in. across bow, 0.6 troy oz $55

Henry S. Brown

Antique American silver sauce ladle in the Fiddle pattern with lobed bowl; made by Henry S. Brown of Utica, New York, and retailed by W. N. Tuttle, c.1852-1867. Monogram "HDA," 6 1/4 in., 1 3/4 in. across bowl, 0.6 troy oz. $60

Robert Brown

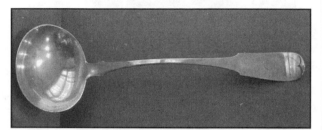

Antique American silver soup ladle in the Fiddle pattern; marked by Robert Brown of Baltimore, Maryland, c.1845-1860. Monogram "JG," 12 1/2 in., 3 7/8 in. across bowl, 5.8 troy oz. $300

Robert Campbell

Antique American silver soup ladle in the Fiddle pattern; marked [R.C] and [10.15] for Robert Campbell of Baltimore, Maryland, c.1835. Monogram "ESS," 13 1/4 in., 4 in. across bowl, 4.9 troy oz. $450

Albert Coles

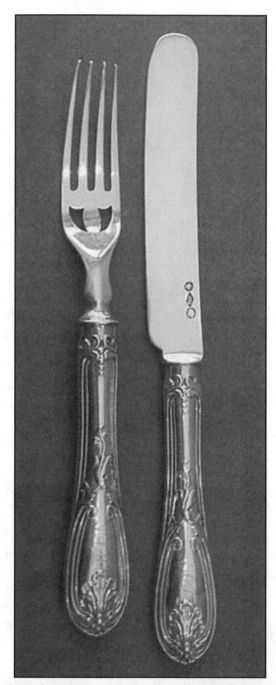

Antique American silver youth knife and fork in an unidentified leaf and scroll pattern; made by Albert Coles & Co. of New York, NY, c.1850-1870. Monogram "SAD." Knife 7 1/8 in., fork 6 1/4 in.; both with hollow handles $65

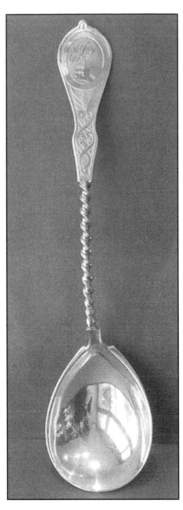

Antique American silver soup ladle in the Engraved Medallion pattern (c.1862) with twisted stem; made by Albert Coles of New York, New York. Monogram removed, 12 1/4 in., 3 in. across bowl, 4.1 troy oz $500

Duhme Co.

Antique American silver butter knife in the Double Swell Fiddle pattern with half-twisted blade; marked by the Duhme Co. of Cincinnati, Ohio, c.1850-1875. Monogram "MBM," 7 3/8 in., 1.0 troy oz. $100

Four Duhme & Co. dessert spoons, four broad back Fiddle pattern spoons, 8 1/4 in. long, with a short front midrib decoration. An example of

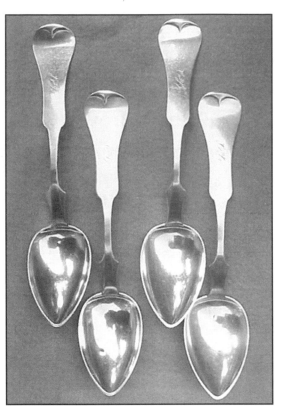

mid-19th Ohio flatware. Some minor bowl dents, but fine overall condition and unusually heavy weight for coin silver. ....4 for $140

Thomas Fletcher

Antique American silver butter knife in the Fiddle pattern marked by Thomas Fletcher of Philadelphia, Pennsylvania, c.1925-1950. Monogram "CV," 7 3/4 in., 1.6 troy oz. Some surface wear..................................$110

William Gale & Son

Samuel Lewis of Washington. D.C., c.1844-1860. Monogram "MET," 13 in., 4 1/8 in. across bowl, 6.8 troy oz. $350

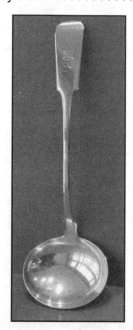

Antique American silver butter knife in the Italian pattern (1860) made by William Gale & Son of New York, New York. Monogram "A.E.F.," Marked "925 STERLING," 7 1/8 in., 1.1 troy oz. $35

Antique American silver soup ladle in the Fiddle pattern; made by Philo B. Gilbert and retailed by Henry Salisbury & Co., both New York, New York c.1840-1860. Monogram "EGC," 11 1/2 in., 3 1/2 in. across bowl, 4.7 troy oz. $250

Philo B. Gilbert

Antique American silver soup ladle in the double struck Fiddle Thread pattern; made by Philo B. Gilbert of New York, New York, and retailed by

Antique American silver soup ladle in the Oval Thread pattern with quatrefoil bowl; struck with the trademarks used by Philo B. Gilbert of New York, New York. Monogram "EAJ," 12 in., 3 3/4 in. across bowl, 5.5 troy oz. $225

Edward & David Kinsey

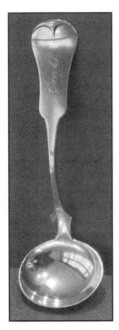

Antique American silver sauce ladle in the Double Swell Fiddle made by Edward & David Kinsey of Cincinnati, Ohio, working 1844-1861. Engraved script "Crooks," 6 in., 1 7/8 in. across bowl, 0.8 troy oz. $85

Lincoln & Reed

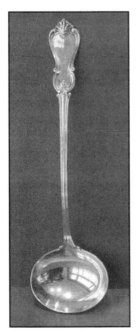

Antique American silver soup ladle in the Prince Albert pattern marked by Lincoln & Reed of Boston, Massachusetts, working 1838-1848. Mono-

gram "L," 13 in., 3 3/4 in. across bowl, 6.5 troy oz. $300

Joseph Lownes

Antique American silver soup ladle in the Fiddle pattern; marked by Joseph Lownes of Philadelphia, Pennsylvania, c.1800-1820. Fancy foliate monogram "APB" above later monograms "CS" and "FR," 13 3/4 in., 4 1/2 in. across bowl, 7.6 troy oz., 1/4 in. crack in bowl. $350

Edward Mead

Antique American silver butter knife in the Double Swell Fiddle pattern marked by Edward Mead & Co. of St. Louis, Missouri, c.1850-1865. Monogram "GLF," 7 7/8 in., 1.3 troy oz. $100

Ludwig/Aug. E. Meyer

Antique American silver table forks in the Fiddle pattern marked by either Ludwig or Aug. E. Meyer of St. Charles, Missouri, c.1850-1870. Engraved "Overall," 7 3/4 in., 7.2 troy oz. Tines with usual wear, one fork with knife cuts on tines....................................$600

Henry Oakes

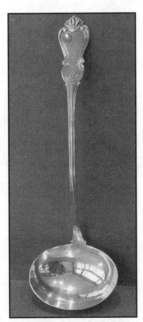

Antique American silver sauce ladle in the Fiddle pattern marked by Henry Oakes of Hartford, Connecticut, working 1842-1847. Monogram "LCB," 6 in., 1 1/8 in. across bowl, 0.9 troy oz. $70

John Owen Jr.

Antique American silver soup ladle in the Fiddle pattern; marked by John Owen Jr. of Philadelphia, Pennsylvania, c.1820-1840. Original monogram erased, later "EHC," 12 3/4 in., 4 1/4 in. across bowl, 5.4 troy oz. $225

Oliver D. Seymour

Antique American silver sauce ladle in the Fiddle pattern marked by Oliver D. Seymour of Hartford, Connecticut, c.1840-1860. Monogram "MK," 6 in., 1 1/8 in. across bowl, 0.7 troy oz. $50

Arthur Stone

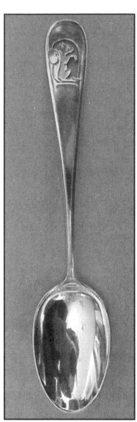

Arthur Stone cut-out squirrel youth spoon. Whimsical piece from the dean of American Arts & Crafts silversmiths, 6 in.; fine condition; engraved "ANN / 1923" (reverse); craftsman: George Erickson. $225

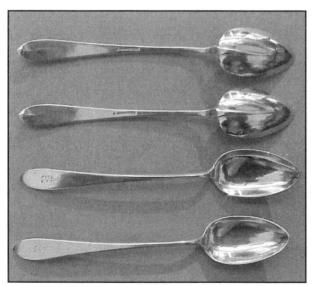

Eight handwrought coffee spoons pointed end "rat tail" five-o-clock style by Arthur Stone. Fine condition, engraved "P." $200/set

Abijah B. Warden

Antique American silver soup ladle in the double struck Fiddle Thread pattern with unusual foliate and scroll drop; marked by Abijah B. Warden of Philadelphia, Pennsylvania, working 1842-1856. Monogram "JWS," 12 5/8 in., 4 1/8 in. across bowl, 6.1 troy oz. Surface lightly scratched by fine steel wool. $350

Wendt

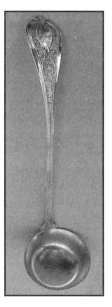

Wendt Florentine ladle. No pouring spout. Length: 11 1/4 in., diameter of bowl 3 in.; monogrammed "JMR" (script, front); minor dent in bowl but otherwise fine condition. $325

Robert & William Wilson

Antique American silver soup ladle in the Fiddle pattern made by Robert & William Wilson of Philadelphia, Pennsylvania, c.1840-1860. Engraved "E.J.-E.B," 13 1/8 in., 4 1/8 in. across bowl, 5.8 troy oz. $280

Others

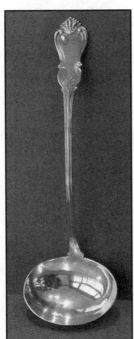

Antique American silver oyster ladle in the Prince Albert pattern sold by John & William Moir of New York, New York, working 1844-1870.

Engraved "Barkley" (defaced), 10 5/8 in., 3 1/3 in. across bowl, 2.9 troy oz. $200

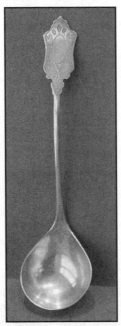

Antique American silver punch ladle with plain narrow shaft terminating in short flat cartouche shaped handle with engraved decoration; unmarked c.1850-1875. Monogram "ELW," 9 3/8 in., 2 3/8 in. across bowl, 2 troy oz. $85

Antique American silver gravy ladle in the Fiddle pattern; sold by Samuel Lewis of Washington, D.C., c.1845-1870. Monogram "JEW," 7 3/8 in., 2 3/8 in. across bowl, 1.8 troy oz. $100

Antique American silver sauce ladle in the Fiddle pattern sold by Henry Sargeant of Springfield, Massachusetts, c.1840-1860. Monogram "FS," 6 1/8 in., 1 7/8 in. across bowl, 0.9 troy oz. $50

Antique American silver butter knife in an unknown bead and foliate scroll pattern; possibly from Boston, Massachusetts, c.1850-1870. Monogram "EPK," 6 1/2 in., 0.9 troy oz. $35

English/Continental/Asian/Other

Austria

Twenty-one pieces Austrian flatware: 7 each luncheon knives, luncheon forks, and teaspoons; sold by "MOE" of Vienna, c.1925-1960. Monogram "AH." $250

China

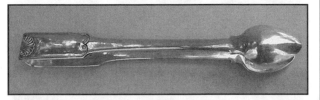

China trade Fiddle shell and thread serving tongs, Kheechong, Canton province c. 1825, 8 1/4 in.; fully marked; no monogram. $500

England

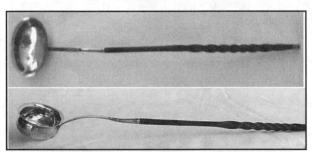

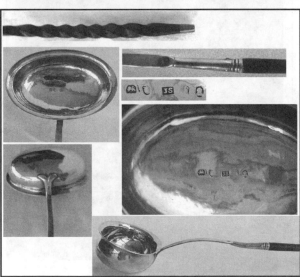

GEORGE III STERLING SILVER TODDY LADLE J SNATT 1798

George III sterling silver and twisted whalebone toddy ladle made by Josiah Snatt, London, 1798. Measures 15 in. long. Bowl is 3 1/4 in. wide. Oval shaped bowl, very good patina. Hallmarked in the center: lion, leopard head, JS (maker), somewhat worn date mark, and monarch's head. Handle is also silver with forked connection to back of bowl. Curves gently and changes from flat to round, where it joins the whalebone section of the handle, which ends in a sterling silver cap. $600

GEORGE III SMALL STERLING SILVER TODDY LADLE 1797

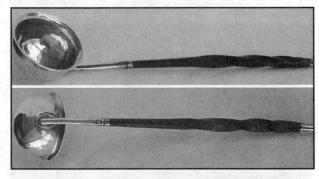

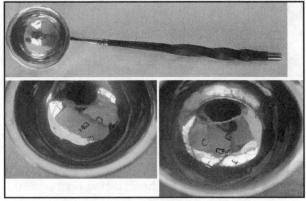

Small sterling silver and twisted whalebone toddy ladle, made in 1797 by Edward Mayfield, London. Measures 6 5/8 in. long. Round bowl with hallmarks in a circle around the maker's mark (EM). Lion, leopard head crowned, date letter B. Twisted whalebone handle. Small restoration where the handle and bowl meet at the back $400

PAIR GEORGE III 1792 STERLING SILVER SAUCE LADLES

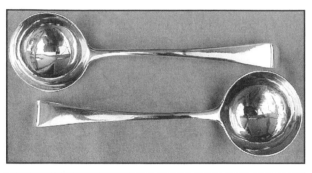

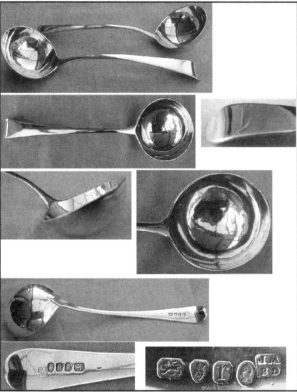

Pair George III sterling silver sauce ladles, London 1792, maker George Smith & William Fearn. Length 7 in., weight 3 oz. Round deep bowls for ladling gravy or sauce. Classic handles, widening at the ends. Excellent condition. Marked with makers marks GS over WF, lion, leopard, date letter r and monarch's head facing right . . .$500

VICTORIAN SILVER GILT FRUIT SERVING SET

Five-piece Victorian sterling silver and gilt fruit serving set, made London, 1886 by John Aldwinckle and Thomas Slater. Spoons 8 1/4 in. long. 365 g. With original fitted case, silk-lined with gilt lettering under a crown: Mappin & Webb, Silversmiths to the Queen, London & Sheffield. Set consists of 4 serving spoons and a sugar sifter. The handles are chased with masks, rams, etc. Urn-form terminals. Hallmarks: JA TS in a 4-lobed hallmark. Leopard head, lion passant, date letter L and monarch's head. Very good condition $900

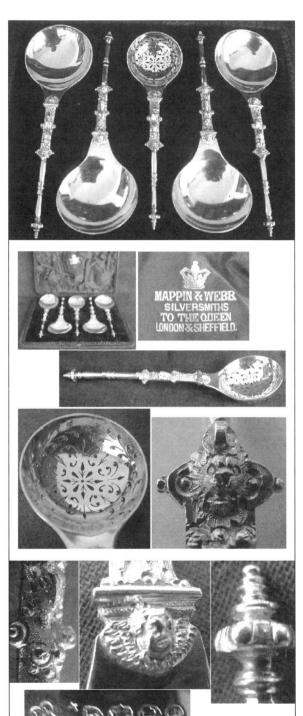

GEORGE III STERLING SILVER MARROW SCOOP 1769

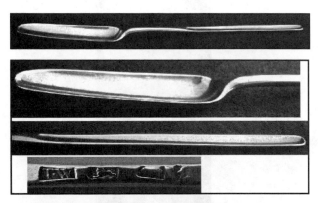

A George III sterling silver marrow scoop, made in 1769 by Thomas Wallis I or Thomas Wynne, London. 9 1/4 in. long. Weighs 2 oz. $400

OLD ENGLISH PATTERN PIECES

Courtesy Sotheby's, New York

Old English pattern dinner service: 36 each dinner knives and dinner forks, 24 each luncheon knives, luncheon forks, and dessert spoons, 12 each fish knives, fish forks, dessert knives, dessert forks, tablespoons, and teaspoons, four sauce ladles, pair of salad servers, pair of fish servers, one gravy spoon and four-piece carving set; in fitted oak cabinet with five drawers and double doors, Francis Higgins, London, England, 1936, 229 pieces. $20,700

France

LOUIS XIII RICHELIEU PIECES

Louis XIII Richelieu pattern dinner service: 12 each dinner knives, dinner forks, luncheon knives, luncheon forks, tablespoons, dessert spoons, lobster forks, teaspoons, fish knives, fish forks, demitasse spoons, three butter knives, two serving forks, and one each soup ladle, sauce ladle, slice, cake knife, and cheese knife; monogrammed, with rattail bowls, trifid ends and cannon-handled knives with stainless steel blades, Puiforcat, Paris, France, 20th century, in three fitted trays stamped with maker's name, 144 pieces. $28,750

Courtesy Sotheby's, New York

EARLY FRENCH SILVER & GILT SPOON

Silver and silver-gilt spoon. Made in France pre-revolution (1789-90) but imported to London 1894. Measures: 6 3/4 in. long; weighs 2 oz. Gilded bowl. Handle consists of pierced cartouche join, followed by pierced and twisted neck and finally a large figural group, beginning with a shell and pair of dolphins on either side of a base on which stands a heroic figure of a woman with flowing robes, holding one child while another child clings to her skirts. Fine detail, casting, patina. Marks: The front of the bowl has French hallmarks. A crowned elaborate letter signifies the charge; a complex cartouche is the maker's mark. According to *Antique Silver*, Ian Pickford, page 25, these are pre-revolutionary marks, i.e., pre-1789-'90. The back of the bowl has the English marks as follows: BM; lion passant; date letter t (1894); an F in an oval; leopard's head (London). Condition: very good. $150

SILVER PIERCED REPOUSSÉ SUGAR SIFTER

Pierced, repoussé silver sugar sifter, possibly French, 19th century. Measures 7 1/2 in. long; bowl is 3 1/4 in. across and it weighs 3 oz. Round bowl with crimped rims. Lobed end of the handle with a central mask and radiating openwork scrolls. The bowl consists of a pierced floral center, radiating openwork patterns with interlocking borders. A ring of masks alternates with scrolling openwork foliage. The masks are classical Greek in style. There are two hallmarks on the rim of the bowl near the neck: one is indistinct and the other is 800 for the silver standard. Very good condition with minor wear $350

Germany

Twenty pieces German flatware: 11 dinner knives and 9 dinner forks sold by L. Posen, c.1910-1940. Monogram "D." $400

Eighteen pieces Vereinigte Silberwaren-Fabriken flatware: 6 tablespoons, 6 table forks, and 6 table knives; c.1895-1915. No monogram. $900

Holland

DUTCH LONDON STERLING SILVER NUT/ BONBON SPOON

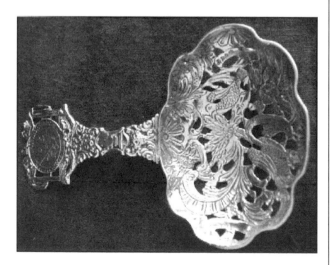

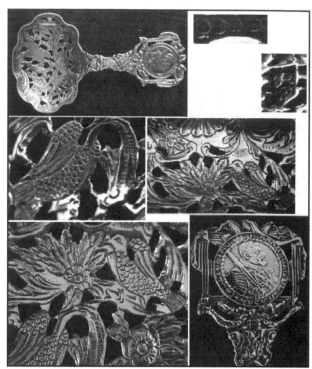

19th century pierced silver bonbon or nut serving spoon made in Holland and imported to England in 1891. Measures 5 7/8 in. long and 3 in. across bowl. Foliate scrolling handle widens towards the end to form a square container for an old silver coin, set in the center. The bowl has ruffled, lobed sides. It consists of pierced openwork and engraved birds, leaves, and flowers. 930 is embossed and there is a line of hallmarks with maker LL, date mark Q, import mark, London mark, and lion passant. Other hallmarks, presumably Dutch, are to be found on the handle. Excellent condition $250

SET STERLING SILVER SPOONS

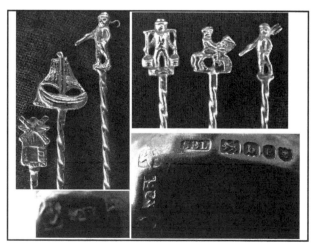

Set of 6 sterling silver demitasse or teaspoons, each with a figural end. Made in Holland and imported to England in 1903. Each is 3 5/8 in. long. Twisted handles end in shallow-bowled spoons. The end of each handle is in the form of a different Dutch symbol: windmill, lady riding sidesaddle on a horse, farm boy in britches carrying a large pitchfork, milkman with two pails of milk, yacht, and lad carrying a folded umbrella. Each piece is double hallmarked on the back. The Dutch hallmarks cross the English. The latter include maker: SBL, lion passant, date letter h, import letter in a circle F, leopard head. A Dutch hallmark is also to be found on the front bowl of each spoon. Very good condition. $100/set

EARLY DUTCH SILVER MANGO FORK

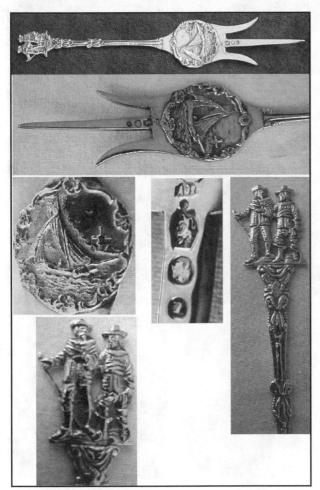

Classic Dutch silver mango fork. Measures 7 3/8 in. long. Three splayed tines spread out after a round repoussé scene featuring a yacht sailing on the seas, a windmill in the background, the scene surrounded by a wreath of flowers. The fluted handle has a ribbon in its center and ends with two Dutch burghers in 17th century attire. The central tine of the fork has a number of hallmarks: a date letter N; a head in profile signifying that tax was paid; a lion in a hexagon for the standard of the silver (835); and a maker's mark. Very good condition. $100

STERLING SILVER OPENWORK TOMATO LIFTER

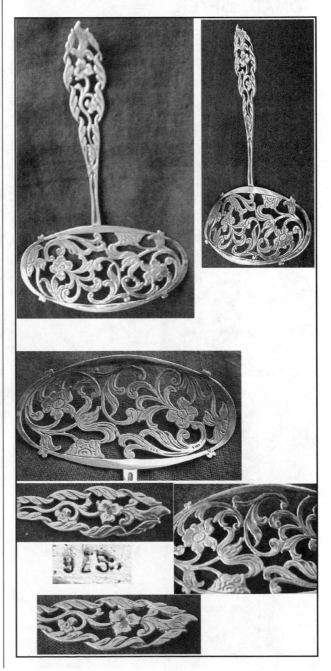

Pierced openwork sterling silver lifter for tomatoes or crudités. Made in Holland. Late 19th century or early 20th century. Measures 5 5/8 in. long; bowl is 3 1/2 in. long and weighs just under 2 oz. Large oval curved lifter made of openwork sterling silver in the form of scrolling ferns, leaves, and flowers. The handle is bordered by scrolling ferns that echo the bowl, surrounding delicate flowers. Back is engraved 925 for sterling silver standard. Condition is excellent $200

STERLING SILVER OPENWORK TOMATO LIFTER

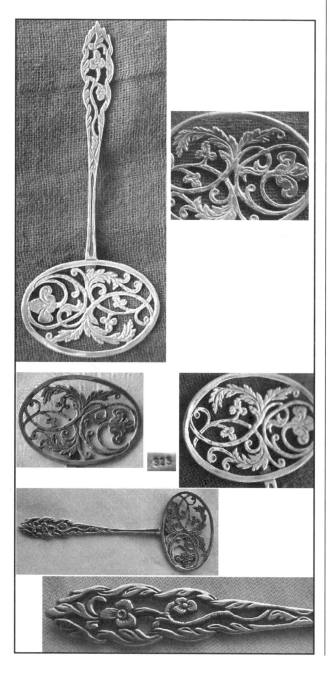

Pierced openwork sterling silver lifter for crudités or tomatoes. Made in Holland. Late 19th century or early 20th century. Measures 4 in. long and bowl is 1 3/4 in. across. Large oval curved lifter made of openwork sterling silver in the form of scrolling ferns and leaves. The handle is bordered by scrolling ferns that echo the bowl, surrounding delicate flowers. Back is engraved 925 for sterling silver standard. Condition is excellent $100

DUTCH STERLING SILVER REPOUSSE CADDY SPOON

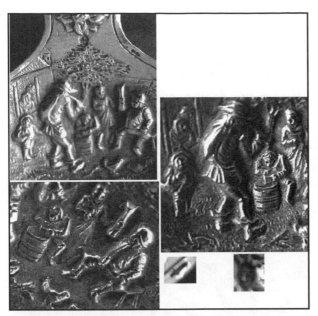

19th century Dutch sterling silver caddy spoon. Measures 2 3/8 in. long and bowl is 1 3/4 in. across. Repoussé work depicting hunter and his dog standing above a stylized flower. The bowl depicts a typical Dutch tavern scene of revelers, chickens in the foreground, children, women, and fat-bellied men. All hand-hammered. Marks: Roman sword on the right-hand rim; circular hallmark with CS on either side of a flower or key. Condition: very good. $100

aside from wear to one tine, engraved with crest of a lion atop a gryphon $125

Mexico

HECTOR AGUILAR

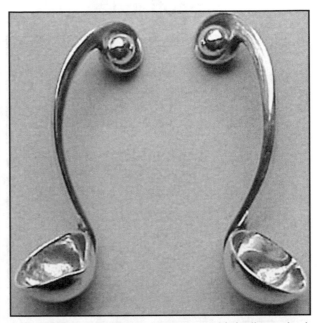

Pair of Hector Aguilar salt spoons with ball terminal and single pouring spouts. They look like miniature bouillon ladles. Just shy of 2 in. long, good condition, no monogram. $75/pair

Ireland

Antique Irish dinner fork (detail only). Upturned Fiddle pattern with square shoulders and short front midrib decoration, Dublin 1836/7, maker PW (P. Weeks?), length 8 in., fine condition

Norway

Norwegian art deco enamel tea caddy spoon. Silver gilt with inlaid black and raised blue enamel. 4 1/8 in.; good condition; marked "925S" with maker's mark of two V's superimposed upon each other at 180 degrees. $150

Scotland

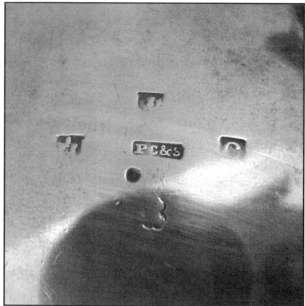

Antique Scottish master salt (two views). Edinburgh, 1808, maker P. Cunningham & Son. Oval with gadroon edge and four applied shell feet. Good condition, 3 1/4 in. by 2 1/2 in. by 2 in. $375

South Africa

SOUTH AFRICAN STERLING SILVER SPOON

Unusual sterling silver spoon made in South Africa. Has sculpted openwork model of The Castle (by Jan Van Riebeeck in Cape Town). Measures 5 3/4 in. long. Generous, wide bowl, sturdy handle, unadorned. The end consists of a sculpted model depicting the entrance to The Castle, built by Van Riebeeck in 1652. The back is hallmarked as follows: CM; S925; STG; springbok head; F. The condition is excellent $100

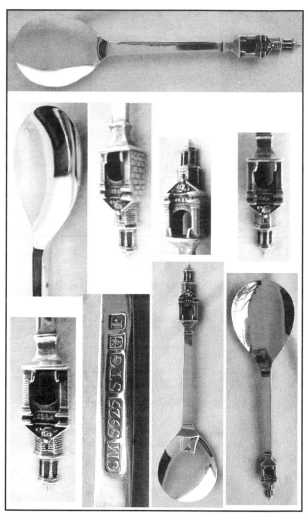

Unknown

Shell pattern, 4 dinner forks. Just under 7 5/8 in. long, with some slight wear at the top of the shell, not monogrammed, and the tines have no wear $160/set

Glossary

Production Terms

Chasing: Decorating in high or low relief, achieved by the use of tools that push the surface of the metal into patterns. In chasing, no metal is removed.

Engraving: The process of cutting shallow lines into metal, reproducing artwork that has been drawn on a metal article. Unlike machine engraving, hand engraving removes metal when cutting. Bright cutting is another form of engraving with a flat, angled cut.

Hallmark: The official mark of a company or assay office, or "hall" in England, stamped on articles of gold or silver to indicate their purity. In North America the hallmark is the word "sterling" accompanied by the name or mark of a manufacturer.

Repoussé: A process used to roughly emboss a metal object from the back or inside with larger imprints than those used in chasing.

Sterling Silver: An alloy of fine silver (92.5%) and copper (7.5%). Fine silver (99.99% pure) is generally too soft when producing large functional objects. U.S. law states that all objects marked "sterling," "925," or "925/1000" must contain no less than 92.5% fine silver.

Troy Weight: The unit of weight employed by silversmiths. One pound avoirdupois = 14.58 troy ounces; 1 ounce avoirdupois = .91 troy ounces.

Vermeil: Silver that has been gilded.

Serving Pieces

Bonbon or nut spoon—used to serve nuts, candies, and certain hors d'oeuvres.

Cheese serving knife—used to cut and serve pies, cakes, aspics, and frozen desserts.

Cocktail/oyster fork—used for seafood or fruit cocktails, lobster, and crab legs.

Coffee or cocktail spoon—often used for after-dinner coffee.

Cold meat or buffet fork—used to serve platter salads, cold meats, and food served on toast.

Cream or sauce ladle—used to ladle gravy, other liquids, dressings, stews, and cream sauces.

Cream soup spoon—used for soups served in dishes or bowls, and also for the serving of sauces.

Gravy ladle—used to serve sauces, gravies, or dressings.

Iced beverage spoon—a tall spoon used for iced coffee or tea, fruit drinks, milkshakes, parfaits, and floats, and as a highball mixer.

Jelly server—used to serve cream cheese, preserves, jams, marmalades, and relishes.

Lemon fork—used to serve lemon slices.

Luncheon fork—used for lunch and informal meals, at other times for souffles, salads, meats, vegetables, desserts, and the fish course in formal meals.

Luncheon knife—used for lunch and informal meals, and at other times as a salad knife or for meats and vegetables.

Olive or pickle fork—used to serve olives and pickles.

Pierced table or serving spoon—used to serve vegetables and fruits.

Relish or jam spoon—used for relishes, jams, jellies, and preserves.

Roast carving fork—used to support roasts and poultry while carving.

Roast carving knife—used to carve roasts, poultry, and ham.

Salad or serving spoon—used to serve fruits, berries, desserts, salads, and vegetables; handy as a spare serving spoon.

Slicer—a sharp, slim and long tool used to thin-slice meats.

Small teaspoon—used for fruit cocktails and sherbets, and as a sugar spoon.

Spreaders or individual butter knives—used for butter or on a sandwich tray with cheeses, relishes, jams or jellies, and hors d'oeuvres.

Steak carving knife—used to carve steaks and small roasts, poultry, etc.

Sugar spoon—used for the sugar bowl or small bowls of sauce, dressings, or mayonnaise.

Sugar tongs—used in a sugar cube container or candy dish.

Table or serving spoon—used to serve salads, vegetables, and fruits.

Tomato or flat server—used to serve platter salads, cucumbers, eggs, and tomatoes.

Bibliography

A Sterling Past, The Silversmiths of Canada, An Exhibition of Antique Canadian Silver From the Henry Birks Collection, Province of British Columbia. Softbound.

Banister, Judith, Collecting Antique Silver, New York: Galahad Books, 1972. Hardbound.

Belden, Louise Conway, Marks of American Silversmiths in the Ineson-Bissell Collection, University Press of Virginia/UMI, 1980, 2000. Hardbound, 505 pages.

Caldicott, J.W., The Values of Old English Silver and Sheffield Plate, 1906. 300 pages, folio with 87 full-page plates.

Culme, John and John Strang, Antique Silver and Silver Collecting, London: Hamlyn, 1973, 96 pages with index.

Delieb, Eric, Investing in Silver, London: Transworld, 1967. 158 pages.

Dolan, Maryanne, American Sterling Silver Flatware, 1830s to 1990s, Books Americana, 1993, 221 pages. Softbound.

Dragowick, Marilyn E. (edited by), Metalwares Price Guide (Antique Trader Books), Dubuque, Iowa: Antique Trader Publications, 1995. Softbound.

Ensko, Stephen G.C., American Silversmiths and Their Marks II, New York: Ensko, 1937. Hardbound, 82 pages.

Feild, Rachael, MacDonald Guide to Buying Antique Silver and Sheffield Plate, London: MacDonald Orbis, 1988. 1st Edition. Hardbound.

Fennimore, Donald L., Antique Hunter's Guide to American Silver and Pewter (Antique Hunter's Guides Series), New York: Black Dog & Leventhal Publishers, Inc., 2000. Softbound.

Forrest, Tim, Bulfinch Anatomy of Antique China & Silver, Boston: Little, Brown & Co., 1998.

Gilchrist, Brenda (editor), Silver, Smithsonian Institution, 1981.

Harris, Ian, The Price Guide to Antique Silver, 1969/70, 1969. 532 pages.

Hayward, Helena, The Connoisseur's Handbook of Antique Collecting. A Dictionary of Furniture, Silver, Ceramics, Glass, Fine Art, etc., London: The Connoisseur, 1970.

Holland, Margaret, Old Country Silver. An Account of English Provincial Silver with Sections on Ireland, Scotland and Wales, Newton Abbot: David & Charles, 1971.

Hughes, G. Bernard, Small Antique Silverware, New York: Bramhall House, 1957. 224 pages.

Hyde, Bryden B., Bermuda's Antique Furniture and Silver, Bermuda National Trust, 1971.

MacDonald-Taylor, Margaret, A Dictionary of Marks. Ceramics, Metalwork, Furniture. The Identification Handbook for Antique Collectors, London: The Connoisseur, 1970. Hardbound.

Oman, C.C., English Domestic Silver, London: A & C Black, 1934. 232 pages.

Painter, Kenneth S., A Roman Silver Treasure from Canterbury, extracted from The Journal of the British Archaeological Association, Vol. 28, 1965.

Pearsall, Ronald, A Connoisseur's Guide to Antique Silverware (Connoisseur's Guides Series), 1997. Hardbound.

Pickford, Ian, Starting to Collect Series: Antique Silver, Antique Collectors Club. 192 pages, full color.

—, Antique Silver, Wappingers Falls, N.Y.: Antique Collectors' Club, 1997. Hardbound.

—, Silver Flatware English, Irish and Scottish 1660-1980, Woodbridge, England: Antique Collectors' Club, 1995.

Rabinovitch, Seymour Benton, Antique Silver Servers for the Table, Joslin Hall Rare Books, 1991. Hardbound.

Rainwater, Dorothy T. and H. Ivan, *American Silver*, Schiffer, 1988. Cloth. Revised Edition.

Ramsey, L.G.G., *Antique English Silver and Plate*, London: The Connoisseur, 1962. 1st Edition.

Schwartz, Marvin D., *Collectors' Guide to Antique American Silver: History, Style and Identification*, New York: Bonanza Books, 1982. Hardbound.

—, *Collectors' Guide to Antique American Silver*, London: Robert Hale & Company, 1976.

—, *Collectors' Guide to Antique American Silver*, New York: Doubleday & Company, 1975. Hardbound.

Stow, Millicent, *American Silver*, New York: Gramercy Pub. Co., 1950.

Virginia Museum, Richmond, *Church Silver of Colonial Virginia*, Richmond, Virginia: Virginia Museum, 1970. Softbound.

Waldron, Peter, *The Price Guide to Antique Silver*, Second Edition, Wappingers Falls, N.Y.: Antique Collectors' Club, 2001. Hardbound.

—, *The Price Guide to Antique Silver*, England Antique Collectors Club, 1982.

Index

Hallmark Silver

International Silver

Jenkins & Jenkins

Kirk Stieff Silver

Richard Dimes Co.

Royal Crest Silver

Schofield Co.

State House Silver

Tiffany & Co.

Towle

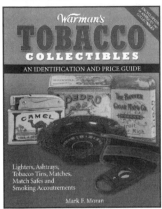

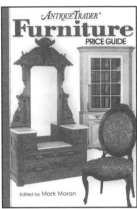
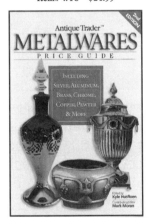
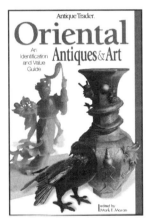
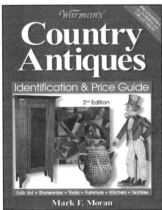

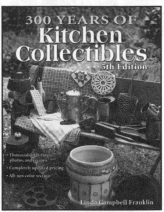

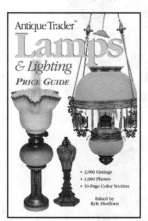